3-99

Financial Services Marketing

For Caryl

and

For Gerardine, Róisín, Cara,
Marianne, Jonathan

Financial Services Marketing

An International Guide to Principles and Practice

Christine T. Ennew and Nigel Waite

AMSTERDAM • BOSTON • HEIDELBERG • LONDON • NEW YORK • OXFORD
PARIS • SAN DIEGO • SAN FRANCISCO • SINGAPORE • SYDNEY • TOKYO

Butterworth-Heinemann is an imprint of Elsevier

Butterworth-Heinemann is an imprint of Elsevier
Linacre House, Jordan Hill, Oxford OX2 8DP, UK
30 Corporate Drive, Suite 400, Burlington, MA 01803, USA

First edition 2007
Reprinted 2007

Notice
No responsibility is assumed by the publisher for any injury and/or damage to persons
or property as a matter of products liability, negligence or otherwise, or from any use
or operation of any methods, products, instructions or ideas contained in the material
herein. Because of rapid advances in the medical sciences, in particular, independent
verification of diagnoses and drug dosages should be made

British Library Cataloguing in Publication Data
A catalogue record for this book is available from the British Library

Library of Congress Cataloging-in-Publication Data
A catalog record for this book is available from the Library of Congress

ISBN: 978-0-7506-6997-9

For information on all Butterworth-Heinemann publications
visit our website at books.elsevier.com

Printed and bound in *Great Britain*

07 08 09 10   10 9 8 7 6 5 4 3 2

Working together to grow
libraries in developing countries

www.elsevier.com | www.bookaid.org | www.sabre.org

ELSEVIER   BOOK AID
              International   Sabre Foundation

Contents

Foreword

By Ron Sandler

There is an urgent need to upgrade standards of financial literacy. This was one of the principal messages arising from the Savings Review that I led recently on behalf of the UK Government. Finding ways to deliver effective financial education represents one of the most important challenges that we face if consumers are ever to become empowered to make informed financial decisions about their future. It is equally important that those involved in developing and marketing financial products and services are properly alert to the interests of their customers. This textbook represents an important step in seeking to align the interests of the financial services consumer, be that a private individual or a business customer, with those of the financial services provider.

The financial services industry across the globe has a pivotal role to play in facilitating economic development, eradicating the joint scourges of poverty and exploitation, and safeguarding the well-being of all of human kind. These aspirations will only be realized if products and services are designed such that they meet the genuine needs of customers. Amongst other things, this calls for product design that emphasizes simplicity and ease of understanding; communication that is concise and clear; and the provision of advice and information by knowledgeable and confident staff. All of these features must be bound together by a coherent marketing strategy.

This book has been conceived and written to improve the quality of financial services marketing. It is intended to have equal value as a core text in a university setting, and as a training resource in the world of the practitioner. I sincerely hope you gain personally from studying it and, as a result, are able to contribute further to the development of a financial services sector that functions well and efficiently, with all the wider societal benefits that this brings.

Ron Sandler is chairman of **pfeg**, a charity created to deliver personal finance education in schools. In 2001/02, at the request of the Chancellor, he led an independent review of the long-term savings industry in the UK. In his business career, he has been Chief Executive of Lloyd's of London and Chief Operating Officer of NatWest Group.

Preface

A formal approach to the marketing of financial services is a relatively recent phenomenon, even within the developed nations of the world. The marketing of packaged goods, such as confectionery, food, soft drinks and toiletries, has been subject to an enormous investment in classical marketing skills and capabilities since the early part of the twentieth century. A continuity of investment in marketing has enabled brands such as Coca Cola, Wrigleys, Gillette, Campbells and Cadbury to become, and remain, leading brands in their respective sectors from the 1920s and onwards into the twenty-first century. Competitive pressures have played a major role in sharpening the marketing appetites of the packaged goods sector. Additionally, the relative simplicity of the products and the transparency associated with them have also been catalysts for the development of marketing edge. Cost proximity and the need for economies of scale have added further impetus to the development of the marketing skills of this product area.

The financial services sector, on the other hand, has not been subjected to the same market pressures in order to survive and prosper. Until comparatively recently, the financial services industry in many countries has operated within a comparatively benign market environment and, in some instances, has been substantially state managed and controlled. In contrast to the packaged goods arena, rivalry amongst financial services providers has tended to be more collegiate than competitive. Diversity of supply and relatively low individual company market shares have been particular features of many sectors of financial services. For example, in spite of the received wisdom of mergers and acquisitions, there were 613 companies authorized to carry on general insurance business in the United Kingdom in 2004, compared with 627 some 11 years earlier.

Financial services products, in general, are far more complex than their packaged goods counterparts. It is fair to say that consumers evidence low levels of knowledge and self-confidence when it comes to comparing and contrasting the range of products on offer. The issues associated with product transparency serve to further weaken consumer power, resulting in a less vigorous form of competition. The drive for economies of scale has been far less of a feature of financial services, and this too has lessened the need to be at the leading edge of marketing.

Two further factors of note that have played a part in lessening the need for state-of-the-art marketing are the influence of government, and consumers' attitudes towards financial products. In many respects, governments have played a crucial role in the development of new products and the associated promotion of those products. This is in marked contrast to the packaged goods industry. The introduction of personal pensions and tax-advantaged savings schemes has presented the industry with major new business opportunities. It is salutary to note how, in the case of personal pensions in the UK, this government-initiated product resulted in wholesale abuse and long-term damage to the reputation of the industry. Arguably, this arose because the industry was far too sales-orientated and insufficiently customer-orientated. It certainly shows up the marketing shortcomings of the sector. Similarly, the government-induced withdrawal of products and the lessening in tax favourability have acted as highly potent sales promotions.

Turning to consumer attitudes, it is in the nature of financial services products that consumers do not gain explicit enjoyment from their consumption. On the contrary, a great many financial services products involve a reduction in current consumption pleasure, because money is diverted from such consumption as a contingency for some future event. You might even say that financial products are not only boring but also lessen the pleasure to be had from consuming other products that do offer explicit enjoyment. The absence of consumption-associated pleasure and the general level of consumer disinterest have therefore served to reduce the importance of marketing within the financial services industry.

All too often one senses that, at least for some financial services organizations, marketing is a term that applies to a department that produces promotional material. As will be seen in this book, marketing is (or should be) a broad cultural and philosophical approach to overall organizational behaviour, and not some narrow field of functional competence. This book sets out to present financial services marketing as an overarching set of processes that aim to achieve a balance between the key components of the wider environment.

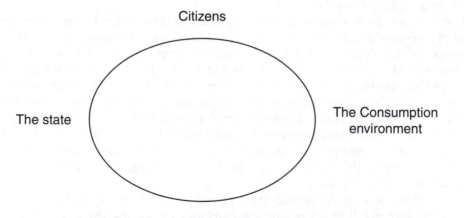

For this reason, this book comprises three core parts. Part I is devoted to the strategy and planning elements associated with marketing. Here, we examine the complex inter-relationships that exist between the financial services industry, the state and the citizen. A theme that runs throughout this entire text is that a positive-sum game should be at play in which all three parties are mutually advantaged through their interactions. Across the globe, we see evidence of financial services industries that appear to be engaged in a perpetual struggle for the trust of consumers and confidence of government and regulators. The present authors argue in favour of a marketing approach that is consumer-centric and founded upon core values of value for money, integrity, trust, security and transparency. In our view, the adoption of such values is axiomatic of good marketing practice and a prerequisite for the development of successful financial services industries throughout the world.

Additionally, Part I describes the participants that comprise the financial services marketplace. This provides the context necessary for a full understanding of how the marketplace operates in servicing the needs of customers. Included in this part are details of the product ranges that comprise the financial services domain. All too often, both students and those employed in financial services display a lack of breadth concerning financial services products and providers; this book aims to provide the necessary knowledge.

Importantly, Part I provides concrete approaches to the processes associated with developing marketing strategies and plans. These approaches will not only equip students with a solid grounding in the disciplines associated with strategy, but also be of real practical value to those actively engaged in working within financial services organizations.

Part II focuses upon the principles and practices that are associated with becoming a customer of a financial services provider. Traditionally, this has been the primary focus of general marketing textbooks; indeed, it is a key element of this present one. However, it is grounded in good practices that are in evidence both in the financial services domain as well as in other commercial marketplaces. Of particular note are the vignettes that have been sourced from organizations throughout the world.

Part III is dedicated to the principles and practices that concern the development of customer relationships over time. This is of particular importance in the context of financial services. The incidence of short-term organizational gain, to the long-term detriment of the consumer, has been far too prevalent in the past. Insufficient attention has been given to how to manage existing customer relationships in favour of new customer acquisition, and this book hopes to help redress the balance. Again, examples of good practice from a range of countries are given to make the concepts and principles more concrete.

In conclusion, this is a book that will help both the student and the practitioner to develop a firm grounding in the fundamentals of financial services strategy, customer acquisition and customer development. It draws upon both relevant conceptual and theoretical models as well as relevant practical applications. Every effort has been taken to adopt a style of English that will make this text accessible to the widest possible audience. Of course, there is a role for special marketing-related terms; however, these are used within a written context that seeks to be straightforward and free of 'corporate speak'.

Many people have helped with the development of this book, and we are grateful for their contributions. In addition to the various organizations that have provided information and insights into their marketing practices, we also wish to thank Anna Fabrizio and her colleagues at Elsevier, who provided support and enthusiasm through the process, and, last but not least, Miranda Hancock and Gerardine McCullough, who both deserve our gratitude for sterling work in the preparation of the manuscript. Thank you!

Christine Ennew
Nigel Waite

Acknowledgements

The help of the following people in the preparation of this manuscript, and in particular in the provision of vignettes, is gratefully acknowledged:

Will Adler	Munich Reinsurance
Ahmed Al Safadi	Syria
Lisa Axel	American Express
Martin Bellingham	The Children's Mutual
Stuart Bernau	Nationwide Building Society
Graham Berville	Police Mutual
Ned Cazalet	Cazalet Consulting
Vladimir Chludil	Kooperativa
Adrian Coles	Building Societies Association
Leonora Corden	Royal Mail
Stephen Diacon	Nottingham University Business School
Pierre Deride	Inter Mutuelles
Jim Devlin	Nottingham University Business School
Jason Gaunt	Cheshire Building Society
Thomas Gilliam	Mutual of America
Theodore Herman	Mutual of America
David Hicks	Mulberry Consulting
Paul Italiano	HBF Australia
Rob Jackson	Yorkshire Building Society
Deepak Jobanputra	Swiss Reinsurance
Yalman Khan	Response Tek
Sue Knight	Nationwide Building Society
David Knights	Keele University
Faye Lageu	International Cooperative and Mutual Insurers Federation
Eric Leenders	British Bankers Association
Tan Kin Lian	NTUC Singapore
Philip Middleton	Ernst & Young
Alicja Mroczek	Poland
Martin Oliver	Kwik-Fit Financial Services
Shilpa Pandya	Vimo Sewa
John Reeve	Family Investments
Richard Sharp	Response Tek
Harvey Sigelbaum	Multiplan New York
Nigel Stammers	HBOS
Ken Starkey	Nottingham University Business School
Shaun Tarbuck	Association of Mutual Insurers

Robert Tayler	Cooperative Insurance Society
Suzanne Tesselaar	TCI Communications
Allison Thompson	Northern Rock
Justin Urquhart Stuart	Seven Investment Management
Wendy van den Hende	pfeg
Jill Waters	National Savings and Investments
Heidi Winklhofer	Nottingham University Business School
Kjell Wiren	Folksam
Bob Wright	Northern Rock
Lukasz Zaremba	Poland

Part I

Context and Strategy

The role, contribution and context of financial services

Learning objectives

By the end of this chapter you will be able to:
- understand the economic and social significance of the financial services sector
- recognize the diverse ways in which financial services can impact on key aspects of everyday life.

1.1 Introduction

Product and market context exert a significant influence on the nature and practice of marketing. Marketing activities that are effective for fast-moving consumer goods may be wholly inappropriate when marketing fine art. What works in Canada may be ineffective in China. Accordingly, an appreciation of context is essential in order to understand the practice of marketing. Nowhere is this more evident than in the financial services sector. Social, political, economic and institutional factors create a complex context in which financial services organizations (FSOs) and their customers interact, and, of course, these in turn may vary considerably across countries. All too often, discussions of marketing practice fail to recognize the importance of explaining and understanding these contextual influences. The purpose of this current chapter is to provide an overview of the context in which financial services are marketed and to explain the economic significance of the sector. Further detail on the nature of the sector itself is provided in Chapter 2.

The following sections outline aspects of social and economic activity where the financial services sector has a key role to play and where its activities have significant implications for economic and social well-being. We begin with a discussion of the potential contribution of the sector to economic development in general. The subsequent sections go on to explore the role of the financial services sector in welfare provision, in income smoothing and in the management of risk. We then explore the significance of financial exclusion and its potential impact on the welfare of the poorer groups in society, before reviewing distinctive features of the financial services industry – namely the coexistence of mutual and joint stock companies. Finally, there is an overview of the issues relating to the regulation of financial services.

1.2   Economic development

Although economic and political theorists sometimes have very different opinions on the nature and value of economic development, there is a widely accepted view that controlled, managed economic development is, on the whole, a desirable means of furthering the well-being of humankind. Moreover, economic development that combines the positive aspects of the market economy (particularly innovation and resource efficiency), with the collectivist instincts and community focus of state legislatures is, arguably, most likely to serve the common good.

Economic development is being pursued by governments throughout the world, with varying degrees of success. Access to investment capital facilitates economic development, and a vibrant banking sector has a pivotal role to play in this regard. The liberalization of financial services in the former Communist countries of Eastern Europe has enabled inward investment to occur that has allowed many of them to be successful in joining the European Union. Similarly, many of the rapidly developing economies of Asia are focusing attention on liberalization of their financial sectors as an aid to economic growth and development.

As well as the provision of investment capital through competitive banking systems, the development of stock markets has provided a further means for the raising of capital. In turn, this has broadened the classes of assets that are available in which financial organizations and individuals can invest.

In addition to its significance at the macro-level in facilitating the process of economic development, the financial services sector also plays an important role in delivering social well-being through its impact on the provision of welfare, as the next section explains.

1.3   Government welfare context

The welfare of humankind, at least for the vast majority of the world's inhabitants, is significantly influenced by financial well-being. At a macro-level, nation states, organizations and individuals all require access to the financial resources necessary to safeguard their rights of self-determination. Ever since the time of Bretton Woods, at which the International Monetary Fund was established, countries that have sought support from global financial institutions have had to cede an element of, at least, economic autonomy to such institutions. Similarly, companies that fail to safeguard their solvency and capital adequacy find themselves subjected to the constraints imposed by the financial institutions from which they seek assistance.

However, it is at the level of the individual citizen that we see the relationship between financial assets and autonomy most acutely. As individuals progress through the various stages of life, the balance between income/financial assets and expenditure will vary. In childhood we require money to fund education and health requirements in addition to the expenses necessary to support everyday life. At the other end of the lifetime continuum, in old age we require relatively high levels of healthcare provision in addition to the money needed to support the necessities of life. Both of these extremes of the human lifecycle are typically associated with the individual not being engaged in paid employment – at least, not in the developed countries of the world.

Throughout history, the family has acted as a mechanism for addressing the challenges posed by income and expenditure discontinuities. A feature of the developed countries of the world is that the family has become of lesser importance regarding this role. Family size, structures and role definitions have undergone rapid change since the Second World War in countries such as Italy, the Netherlands and the USA. Indeed Italy now has the lowest birth rate in the European Union, with around 1.3 children born per female. The diminution in the relative importance of the family as a self-sustaining welfare system has evolved in parallel with the expansion of welfare systems organized, provided and funded by the state in much of the developed world. Quite how causality and correlation are at play in this development is a source of much deliberation and debate. What is not open to debate is that the role of the state, in matters concerning welfare, advanced significantly during the course of the twentieth century in countries such as the United Kingdom and USA. Individual needs such as income during periods of unemployment or retirement, healthcare and education, were progressively transferred from the private and voluntary domains to the public sector.

Thus, across the world governments have, to a greater or lesser extent, assumed a significant role in safeguarding the welfare needs of their citizens. During the period of Communist rule in Eastern European countries, the state was all-pervasive with regard to the provision of welfare services. While the transition process undoubtedly reduced the role of the state, it certainly did not eliminate its responsibility for aspects of individual welfare. However, in many developing countries the state remains more at the periphery of welfare provision, primarily as a consequence of limited resources. In such places, the family – and especially the extended family unit – continues to perform the primary welfare role for its members. It is interesting to note that the respective contributions made by state and citizen are not static but dynamic. For example, although the public sector continues to play a significant role, recent years have seen a notable reduction in state welfare provision in many developed economies and a tendency to redistribute responsibility back to the private sector. This has significant implications for the financial services sector, and particularly for products designed to provide benefits such as income protection or payment for medical expenses.

A range of factors has exerted influence in the relationship between public and private sectors in terms of welfare provision, but one of particular note is what might be termed consumerism. This is allied to the growth of consumer cultures throughout the world, which has been driven by a growth in real earnings, increased competition, product innovation, greater sophistication in marketing practice, and changes in culture and value systems.

The practical consequence of the growth of consumer cultures is that citizens have become increasingly accustomed to receiving choice, quality, convenience and value from their experiences as consumers in the marketplace. Thus, consumer expectations have been fuelled predominantly by private-sector suppliers of consumer goods and services. For the state, this has posed two particular problems. First, citizens are increasingly coming to expect the same standards of consumption experiences from state-provided services as they obtain from the private sector. It is proving to be increasingly costly and difficult for state bureaucracies to live up to such expectations. There is the ever-present concern of two-tier delivery of welfare services such as education and healthcare. It is acknowledged that great disparities exist in respect of the differentials between state- and privately-funded provision. For example, the health services provided by, say, France and Germany through their socially-funded systems are the envy of many other parts of the world. Nevertheless, those with money can, as a rule, enjoy the freedom to source a much wider array of health and education facilities than those without. Secondly, the state has to struggle to maintain standards of living that are increasingly defined by a culture of consumption. This places growing strain on the ability of governments to use their social welfare budgets to fund appropriate lifestyles for claimants such as those of retirement age. In recognition of this difficulty, the Thatcher government of 1980s Britain severed the link between increases in the basic retirement pension and the index of average earnings. Instead, it reviewed pension increases in line with the (lower) index of retail prices. This in turn forced many individuals to reconsider the effectiveness of their pension provision, and was one of a number of developments that stimulated the growth of the private pensions industry.

In summary, then, welfare provision underpins the economic well-being of society. Its provision is increasingly based around a complementary mix of public- and private-sector activity. Private-sector welfare provision is predominantly dependent on the financial services sector, and thus the efficiency and effectiveness of this sector has important implications for the economic and social health of an individual country. This is a theme to which we will refer at various points. For the moment, it is perhaps most pertinent to note that one essential element of welfare provision is the concept of income smoothing, and the role of the financial services sector in this process is explored more fully in the next section.

1.4 Lifetime income smoothing

Both the state and the financial services industry work in a complementary manner to facilitate the smoothing of income flows throughout an individual's lifetime. Typically, during childhood individuals are acquiring the knowledge and skills upon which their future employment will be based. This is a period in life which is all about cost in the absence of any income. Although the family is the principal source of money during childhood and adolescence, the state plays a significant role in financing the costs associated with this life-stage. The intergenerational transfer of funds from adulthood (as parents) to one's children forms part of the income smoothing process.

Towards the later stages of life, people (at least in the developed nations of the world) cease participating in the labour force. As with childhood, this is a period characterized by considerable cost and no income from employment. This concept of retirement is a generalization that is becoming challenged to an increasing extent in countries from the USA to Australia. The stereotypical model of retirement holds that money is transferred to the pensioner in one of two principal ways. First, there is a generational transfer of funds via the taxation system (this refers to taxation in the round, and includes all government-related levies such as National Insurance in the UK) whereby today's workers pay taxes that, in part, contribute to the pensions of those in retirement. Secondly, and to an increasing extent, income in retirement is funded out of the money that individuals have saved during the course of their working life in the form of a pension. Importantly, employer-sponsored occupational pension schemes have made a growing contribution to individual's pension entitlements during the course of the second half of the twentieth century. In simple terms, a funded pension scheme involves the transfer of income from an individual's years in paid employment to the post-employment years. Thus it is a form of income smoothing that comprises elements of state- and privately-organized money management.

In many parts of the world life is more challenging, and old age can be simply a continuation of the toil of an individual's earlier working life. Again, in many developing countries the family is often the only significant vehicle for supporting the elderly.

The need to provide an appropriate level of income in retirement is rising up the agendas of virtually every country. A number of factors have contributed to this phenomenon, the most significant of which are demographic. In essence, the proportion of the world's population that is older than 65 years is growing. The principal drivers of this ageing effect are the extension in life expectancy and lower birth rates. In the UK, for example, the birth rate has fallen more or less continuously since the mid-1960s, as can be seen in Table 1.1.

The reduction in birth rate appears to be a consistent feature of most countries as they become more economically developed. This is a consequence of a range of social, economic and cultural factors, and the changing nature of lifestyle choices that are in evidence. In contrast, many (but not all) developing economies have much higher birth rates and relatively young populations, although, as levels of

Table 1.1 UK total fertility rates, 1960–2005

Fertility rate	(%)
1960–1965	2.8
1995–2000	1.7
2000–2005	1.6

Source: Willetts (2003), p 50.

development increase, the number of children per family does tend to fall. An exception is China which, despite its relatively early stage in the development process, has a relatively low birth rate, largely as a consequence of deliberate policies to control the size of the population.

A major consequence of the ageing effect in developed economies is that the dependency ratio is growing in countries across the globe. This refers to the ratio of dependants (i.e. individuals who have ceased work) to people in the labour force. With more retired people and fewer workers, the flow of funds from those in employment that is needed to support those in retirement is increasingly under pressure. This issue is set to grow in importance, as currently available projections indicate a continuing trend in the proportion of the population that is elderly.

Another challenge to income smoothing in developed countries is that people's working lives have shortened in recent times. Figures released by the National Audit Office (NAO) in the UK in September 2004 illustrate vividly the growing trend in labour force inactivity in the years before the age of 65, especially among men. Whereas more than 70 per cent of men in the age group 60–64 years were in employment in 1974, that figure has now dropped to just 40 per cent. Thus, not only is the dependency ratio increasing, but the proportion of an individual's lifetime spent in employment is also reducing. Altman (www.rosaltmann.com) indicates that within a comparatively short timescale this has fallen from 67 per cent of an individual's life being spent in employment to 55 per cent. Arguably, Altman's analysis is unduly conservative, as it assumes that individuals retire at the age of 65. On the basis of the NAO data, the average male productivity quotient has fallen to the order of 47 per cent.

A range of possible solutions is in prospect to address what has been called the retirement savings gap. However, these boil down to some basic options, namely that people will have to work for an additional number of years or save more money, or, more likely, a combination of the two. In any event, the government and private sector have to work together to address this particular feature of income smoothing.

Having talked about smoothing income flows during childhood and retirement, what about the in-between period when people are in employment? This represents a period of challenge and opportunity for the financial services industry. Notwithstanding societal and cultural variations, consumer needs vary substantially during the early, middle and late career periods of working life.

Indebtedness has assumed an increasing significance for people in the early stages of their working lives, and this seems likely to become ever more acute. The growth of the credit-card culture has served to increase young people's indebtedness across countries. The problem is being further exacerbated by the rising incidence of student debt. In the UK, it is estimated that the typical graduate begins working life with debts in the order of £12 000. Figure 1.1 illustrates the typical profile of financial assets during an individual's period in employment.

Figure 1.1 illustrates a typical asset profile, and shows how substantial net assets only really begin to accumulate relatively late in an individual's working life. The financial services industry has an increasing role to play in providing the wide range of products and services that are necessary to smooth income and expenditure flows throughout that working life.

Alongside the important issues that arise in relation to the variability of assets, income and expenditure over a lifetime, consumers also face a variety of

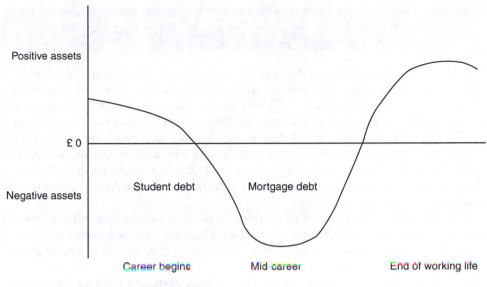

Figure 1.1 Marketing as a facilitator of balance.

short-term risks. The ability to protect or insure against the adverse consequences of those risks has important implications for social and economic well-being. Section 1.5 explores the role of the financial services sector in managing risk.

1.5   The management of risk

An important aspect of how financial services organizations further the cause of economic development is through the provision of the means to manage risk. In simple terms, this is the role played by insurance. General insurance (e.g. insuring risks to property and possessions), health insurance and life assurance are effective means of enabling individuals and organizations alike to take on risks associated with economic advancement. For example, a bank will be unwilling to lend money to a businessman who wants to invest in additional manufacturing capacity without some form of security. A common type of security is some form of life insurance that will enable the bank loan to be repaid in the event of the death of the borrower.

In many developing parts of the world we are seeing the development of what is called *micro-insurance*. Typically, this refers to general insurance cover of a very basic level that can provide security from the risks that apply to relatively low-cost yet high-impact assets. For example, micro-insurance is enabling home-workers in India to afford to insure productive assets such as sewing machines, as shown in Case study 1.1. To the Westerner this may not seem a big deal, but an entire family's livelihood may depend upon this fairly basic piece of equipment. A common cause of poverty among the rural poor of countries such as Cambodia is the forced sale of land to pay for unexpected medical expenses. Again, low-cost forms of health insurance can make a huge contribution to human well-being.

The Self-Employed Women's Association (SEWA) in India is a trade union with 700 000 members – all poor working women in the informal economy – in seven Indian states. SEWA started in 1972 in Gujarat, the western part of India, as a union seeking to unite urban and rural women informal workers on the issue of 'full employment', which SEWA defines as work, income, food and social security. The second objective of SEWA is to make its members self-reliant, both individually and collectively, not only economically but also in decision-making. It has also promoted similar movements in countries like South Africa, Yemen and Turkey.

SEWA's experience of years of working at the grass-roots level with women in the informal economy has shown that social needs, such as health, childcare, education and housing, are all linked to economic capabilities of the women workers. They need economic security – a continuous flow of employment through which they can earn enough in terms of cash and kind to meet their needs. They also need social security to combat the chronic risks faced by them and their families. Social security has four main components – healthcare, childcare, shelter and insurance. The insurance programme of SEWA is called Vimo SEWA (*Vimo* is a local word for insurance).

In 1992 SEWA started its insurance scheme, which provides insurance for natural and accidental death, hospitalization expenses and asset insurance to SEWA members. The primary policyholder will always be the SEWA member. A husband cannot enrol in the programme unless his spouse is an enrolled SEWA member. Children can also be enrolled by paying additional premiums. Women must be 18–58 years of age to enrol for annual membership. Life insurance coverage terminates at the age of 70 years.

Vimo SEWA offers two types of payment schemes to its insurance members. Members can either pay their premium annually or through a fixed deposit with the SEWA Bank. Under the fixed deposit option, members deposit a lump sum in a fixed deposit at the SEWA Bank and the interest accrued on this deposit goes towards the annual premium. Thus, a woman gets continuous insurance coverage and obtains much-needed, long-term social protection.

As SEWA works with poor, self-employed, informal-sector women workers who don't have any income security or work security, they live on a daily basis. It is very difficult to explain the risk-sharing and risk-pooling aspects of insurance to individuals and convince them of the benefits. Furthermore, regular contact with ever-growing numbers of the women poses a big challenge, spread out as they are over a geographically dispersed area.

Vimo SEWA has developed a cadre of local village-level community leaders for the marketing and education for its insurance programme. In fact, they are the real workforce of SEWA insurance and also the real hand-holders of insured members. They organize village or area meetings to explain the importance of insurance in poor, vulnerable women's lives and also how the schemes work. Moreover, when required, they also help the members in collecting required

> **Case study 1.1   Insurance to improve the lives of poor women in India—cont'd**
>
> documentation for submitting claims. Currently VIMO SEWA has around 100 such leaders, who are called 'spearhead aagewans' (leaders in our language).
>
> After 15 years of experience in insurance, SEWA wants to form its own women-owned and managed life-insurance co-operative. To achieve this, SEWA is trying to step towards viability through growing the scale of the business and cost control. According to the projections made with the help of a Canadian actuary, viability can be achieved by the year 2010.
>
> *Source: Shilpa Pandya, Self-Employed Women's Association.*

Finally, it is worth pointing out that governments make extensive use of financial services instruments as a means of managing public finances. Virtually all countries use government bonds as a means of raising money. In the UK, National Savings & Investments is a government-owned organization that promotes a wide range of retail financial services products that play a role in the government's fiscal strategy.

1.6   Financial exclusion

A key tenet of the United Nations is that the citizens of the world be relieved of the scourge of poverty. Indeed, the relief of poverty has been of fundamental concern to communities for centuries. In Britain, the nineteenth century saw a rapid acceleration of poverty up the agenda of all political parties. It was also a period of rapid development of charitable and philanthropic endeavours to address the poverty so graphically commented upon by Marx and Engels and depicted in the works of Dickens. While Europe may have emerged from the worst of the poverty associated with industrialization in the nineteenth century, the problem persists throughout the globe and remains a daunting challenge to national and international policy-makers.

As will be discussed in Chapter 2, easing poverty depends not just on the creation of an income stream, but also on the creation of assets. Exploring the development of the financial services sector in the UK during the nineteenth century provides an illustration of the positive impacts associated with the provision of these services. Nineteenth-century Britain was witness to the development and growth of building societies and friendly societies. The former aimed at helping ordinary people to build and own their own homes, whilst the latter were often initially formed to ensure that working people could afford a dignified burial. In York in 1902, Joseph Rowntree commenced his pioneering work to help improve the quality of life of the slum dwellers of that city. The Joseph Rowntree Foundation was founded in 1904, and in 2004, its centenary year, poverty remained a fundamental aspect of its activities.

In spite of the economic progress seen in countries such as the USA and Great Britain, these societies remain highly polarized in terms of the gap between rich and poor. This issue continues to exercise governments mindful that increasing affluence has not eradicated poverty. Indeed, in 1997 the incoming Labour government of Tony Blair set out to eliminate child poverty in Britain within a 20-year timeframe. Darton *et al.* (2003) illustrate graphically that the poorest groups in society have missed out on the economic growth of the 1980s and 1990s. Their analysis points to a near-doubling of the number of people in relative poverty in Britain in the 20 years from 1981, to 13–14 million people by 2001.

Britain is not alone in displaying a significant degree of relative poverty, although it is towards the upper end of the range in OECD countries. OECD figures suggest that poverty in member countries ranges from 10 per cent in Sweden to almost 24 per cent in the USA (Foster, 2000). Geography is a significant factor in poverty, with wide variations in evidence both within and between countries. For example, GDP per head of population in the town of Acortes in Portugal is less than 25 per cent of that for Brussels.

In the context of financial services, there are real concerns regarding the incidence of financial exclusion. By financial exclusion, we mean the lack of access to and usage of mainstream financial services products and services in an appropriate form (Panigyrakis *et al.*, 2003). No textbook on financial services marketing would be complete without paying due regard to this phenomenon. As commented upon already, financial services perform a key enabling role in advancing economic development and well-being.

There is a real danger of financial services being increasingly the prerogative of the relatively affluent sections of world societies. In part, this is a consequence of the rising costs of serving customers. Take the UK as an example. Throughout the twentieth century, working-class communities in Britain were able to gain access to a range of saving, investment and insurance products through what were termed the Home Service distribution arms of mainstream providers such as Prudential Plc, the Co-operative Insurance Society and Liverpool Victoria Friendly Society. Home Service was based upon having agents who called at the homes of customers to collect payments, often cash, and to provide information and advice. As Knights *et al.* (2004: 14) point out, Home Service continued to thrive:

> until Financial Services Authority regulations combined with intensified competition in the sector in the 1990s and began to threaten the viability of its expensive, labour-intensive door-to-door operations. By late 2003, all Home Service insurance companies had abandoned new industrial branch business.

In addition to the withdrawal of Home Service insurance facilities, poor neighbourhoods and rural communities in the UK have seen a reduction in the availability of bank branches. Put bluntly, the pressure to deliver maximum growth in shareholder value has rendered it uneconomic for mainstream banks to serve an increasing number of people. In particular, recent research has shown that the number of bank branches in the UK fell by some 32 per cent between 1989 and 2003, down from 12 775 to 8681. The highest rate of closure occurred in areas described as 'multicultural metropolitan'. These are characterized by high unemployment and having a higher than average proportion of people identifying themselves as black, Indian, Pakistani or Bangladeshi (Leyshon *et al.*, 2006).

Thus, a number of contemporary insurance and banking practices are excluding many thousands of citizens from essential financial services. The Office of Fair Trading has observed (OFT, 1999) that:

> Such people are being left behind in an expanding market where choice is between a range of complex and highly regulated products primarily aimed at well-off and low risk consumers.

This results in financially excluded individuals falling prey to non-mainstream organizations that exploit the vulnerability of such consumers. This is particularly in evidence with regard to credit and loans, where Knights *et al.* (2003) refer to APRs being charged in a range of 116.5–276.4 per cent. Credit unions offer a viable alternative to many such consumers. Unfortunately, all too often they have neither the resources required to provide the necessary infrastructure nor sufficient promotional muscle. Ideally, financial services should be viewed as providing an inclusive means for improving the financial well-being of all. That is not to say that companies should be expected to become unreasonably philanthropic to the detriment of key stakeholders – indeed, it is perfectly legitimate for a provider to operate on a niche or 'preferred lives' basis. However, the means exist to adopt an inclusive approach to financial services that obviates the need for exploitation of the vulnerable. Policy-makers and regulators must focus on the need for inclusiveness and avoidance of exploitation within their goals for the development of the financial services industry.

1.7   Mutual and proprietary supply

Financial services organizations present themselves in two forms as far as ownership is concerned: mutual and proprietary. In simple terms, proprietary companies are owned by shareholders while mutual suppliers are owned by their customers. However, this is indeed an oversimplification and, in the UK, a review of the governance of mutual insurance companies carried out by Paul Myners (2004) found the precise definition of mutuality a rather more complex issue.

A substantive body of literature exists which sets out to compare the operations of, and outcomes associated with, proprietary and mutual forms of supply. A particular area of focus has been the relative expenses and payouts associated with life insurance firms. Of particular note are the studies carried out by Armitage and Kirk (1994), Draper and McKenzie (1996), Genetay (1999), Hardwick and Letza (2000) and Ward (2002). These and other studies concern the merits and demerits of mutual and proprietary forms. Underlying many of these studies is the presumption that the form of ownership is independently implicated in corporate performance. This is based upon a view that there is an inherent conflict of interest between the interests of shareholders and those of consumers. Therefore, mutuals may be at liberty to concentrate more effectively on meeting the needs of consumers.

Supporters of the mutual form point to the tangible performance benefits of mutuality as well as its philosophical advantages. Fundamental to the former is the argument that the absence of the need to pay a dividend results in tangible benefits to customers. Analysis by the Building Societies Association (2001) in the UK indicates that building societies (mutuals) display lower operating cost ratios, lower rates of interest charged to borrowers and higher rates of interest paid to depositors than do the so-called mortgage banks that had previously operated under the mutual form. Analysis performed by the International Co-operative and Mutual Insurers Federation (ICMIF) compares and contrasts the performance of mutual with proprietary organizations. The analysis is based upon a sample of 105 insurance companies operating in 11 European countries (ICMIF, 2003). The sample includes both life and general insurance companies, and is based upon performance data covering the period from 1995 to 2001. The measures of performance assessed by the study include:

- growth in new premium income
- expense ratios
- claims ratios
- investment returns
- solvency.

The report's authors conclude that mutuals outperform their proprietary counterparts on almost all measures of performance studied. In addition to the tangible performance advantages claimed for mutual providers there is the philosophical advantage. The argument centres on the claimed absence of conflict between the interests of customers and shareholders. Mutuals claim that their single-minded focus on the consumer is embedded in their culture, and this results in a range of corporate behaviours that engender consumer trust.

Supporters of the proprietary form point to the powerful influence of shareholders, especially institutional shareholders with their substantial voting power, in exerting pressure on boards of directors to perform. The argument runs that the members of mutual organizations lack the power required to bring due influence to bear on boards of directors, and that this results in the potential for underperformance and, possibly, the abuse of power. At worst, the CEO could run the firm like some form of personal fiefdom. Indeed, critics of mutuality will often cite the difficulties of Edinburgh-based Equitable Life as an example of how the governance shortcomings of mutuals can have a devastating impact upon consumer interests.

There is also a view that proprietaries enjoy high levels of consumer trust. Research conducted by the Citigate Group shows that mutuals featured only twice in the top-20 trusted investment brands; Standard Life at number 11 and Royal London at number 20. Interestingly, the brands positioned as numbers 1, 2 and 4 (Halifax, Norwich Union and Scottish Widows) were all mutuals until comparatively recently. Critics of this piece of research argue that it confuses familiarity with trust. Undoubtedly, there is reason to believe that consumers do tend to view being a well-known household name as implying trustworthiness. Research carried out by the Financial Services Consumer Panel in the UK appears to bear out the point that consumers use brand presence as a proxy for trustworthiness. Thus, because proprietaries are large organizations with substantial marketing communications budgets, they appear to enjoy a greater degree of consumer trust than do mutuals which, because of their size, are unable to invest in brand-building to the same degree. There is no doubt that branding is becoming increasingly important in financial services, and the creation of global power brands is likely only to be achieved by major proprietary concerns. The recent attempt by Aviva to spend £17bn acquiring Prudential is clear evidence of intent to create a major global insurance brand. Attractive synergies are to be seen between the two, and Prudential's strength in Asia and the USA would complement Aviva's position in Europe.

In Britain, steps have been taken to address the concerns regarding the governance of mutuals as a result of the Myners' review. For example, the Association of Mutual Insurers was created in 2004, and one of its first tasks was to draft a code of conduct for the governance of its members. This code takes as its core the rules for governance set down by the FSA, which are proprietary-focused, with its explicit references to shareholders and shareholder interests. It adds additional requirements aimed at safeguarding the interests of both members (with ownership and voting rights) and policyholders (who do not enjoy membership rights).

Arguably, there is a role for both proprietary and mutual providers of financial services; both forms provide for the diversity necessary to solve the requirements of the marketplace as it continually evolves. The evidence does seem to support the view that demutualization has not necessarily been in the long-term interests of consumers as a totality. There have been short-term gains to directors in the form of share options, and windfall payouts to those with membership rights. In practical terms, typical forms of mutual providers that are encountered are as follows:

- credit unions
- building societies
- mutual insurers
- co-operative insurers
- friendly societies.

Case study 1.2 provides an overview of how one mutual provider of financial services operates. Both mutual and proprietary forms of financial services supply are to be found in most parts of the world; however, there has been a trend of mutuals converting to proprietary status, most notably in the English-speaking countries of North America, Australia and UK in recent years. Table 1.2 shows the composition of the US insurance market in terms of ownership form.

Table 1.2 Life insurers doing business in the United States*

In business at year's end	2002	2003
Stock	1,060	1019
Mutual	99	92
Other	12	12
Total	1171	1123

*Source: American Council of Life Insurers.

Case study 1.2   Police Mutual Assurance Society Limited (Police Mutual)

Police Mutual provides financial services to the police family. Originally that meant just serving officers, but as the police service has changed so has Police Mutual, and today membership of the Society is open to serving and retired police officers and police staff and their families (which includes partners, children, parents, and brothers and sisters). In essence, it operates as an affinity group-based organization and is a compelling example of how cost-effective and efficient such a model can be. In spite of what would appear to be its somewhat limited market potential, Police Mutual has 176 000 members and manages funds of the order of £1.2 billion.

Police Mutual uses a form of governance that is based upon the delegate method, and has a President, Vice President and Chairman as well as an 80-strong delegate body drawn from the police service. The Society displays an array of significant relative competitive advantages that arise from its affinity-based model. Of particular note is the strength of real democratic involvement in the policy-making of the Society through its delegate conference, as well as the involvement in more operational decision-making through the role played by the Committee of Management. These structures, and their associated processes, facilitate the development of extremely close bonds and relationships between the Society and those it seeks to serve.

The strength of relationships between the Society and its membership is instrumental in supporting its core means of distribution. Its range of savings, investments, pensions, mortgages and insurance services are distributed largely on a direct-offer basis (the launch of an advice service aimed at retiring officers is the only variant from this model), and distribution is via a number of channels, such as direct mail, on-line, phone-based and through a business development team, but also, uniquely, via a network of volunteers known as Authorized Officers (AOs). There are over a thousand AOs, the vast majority of whom are serving police officers, and they perform largely a communication role in displaying and distributing promotional material and directing people to Police Mutual's head office if they have any queries. This role is unpaid and, as a consequence, Police Mutual has extremely low business acquisition costs. Its cost–ratio benefits are reduced further by receiving the majority of its premium contributions by payroll deduction.

The Society has an extremely good record with regard to persistency. In the last FSA survey, the industry 3-year average persistency level for regular premium endowment plans was 84.9 per cent for direct-offer business; Police Mutual achieved persistency of 90.5 per cent. Industry average figures for other distribution methods are even lower, at 81.2 per cent for Independent Financial Advisers and 75.3 per cent in respect of company representatives.

A particular feature of Friendly Societies is their ability to 'go beyond contract'. What this means is that their philosophy and style of mutuality permits them to provide benefits to members under certain circumstances that do not strictly accord with the terms and conditions of any specific policy contract.

> **Case study 1.2   Police Mutual Assurance Society Limited (Police Mutual)—cont'd**
>
> A case in point concerns when the 'Troubles' of Northern Ireland caused police casualties that affected morbidity and mortality experience. It was put to the delegates that this ought to result in members of the Police Service of Northern Ireland (formerly known as Royal Ulster Constabulary) having their premiums rated to reflect the higher risk. In the event, the Society decided to maintain a policy of treating them in the same way as all other members.
>
> It is also important for Police Mutual to be able to react to the needs of the police market, and, perhaps uniquely, it considers wider issues within the police family and provides help and assistance where it thinks it will make a positive difference, even if there isn't necessarily a direct link to current products. Affordable Housing is one such example. The cost of housing in the south-east of England has been a cause for concern for many years. Police Mutual used their financial expertise to develop a solution to this problem, which affects many police officers and staff. Funding was secured from business partners and the scheme helped over 300 people to purchase their homes.
>
> Police Mutual is flexible and innovative, and introduced a stakeholder pension in April 2001 and a Child Trust Fund in April 2005 – both very soon after legislation allowed this. Over the past few years Police Mutual has expanded its own product offerings as well as those offered by business partners, and these relationships have enabled Police Mutual to provide members of the police family with access to exclusive, competitive products.
>
> Police Mutual shows the capability of the friendly society model to provide low-cost, high-value financial services within a highly participative and democratic regime of governance.

1.8   Regulation of financial services

The need to safeguard the interests of key stakeholders in the financial services domain has been an important force driving new approaches to regulation around the world. Governments, trading blocs and various inter-governmental and non-governmental organizations have been pursuing economic growth and trade liberalization for at least the past two decades. There has been a desire to encourage the efficient operation of the financial services marketplace through the removal of traditional sector boundaries and the encouragement of competition. In the UK, the mid-1980s was a watershed in the restructuring of the financial services marketplace and the approach to regulation.

Before this point in time there were quite clear lines of demarcation between the range of products and services that were supplied by banks, insurance companies and building societies. New legislation resulted in the removal of the previous sector boundaries. In this new unbounded marketplace, banks were free to operate insurance companies and insurance companies could apply for banking licences.

During the second half of the 1980s, the government of Margaret Thatcher initiated an ongoing programme of legislation aimed both at the liberalization and regulation of the financial services marketplace. The Financial Services Act 1986 was aimed at defining and regulating investment business, as well as promoting competition in the marketplace for savings. The focus of the FSA 1986 was the conduct of investment business and the accompanying provision of advice. As such, it excluded products such as mortgages, credit card loans, general insurance and short-term deposits, which were subject to separate legislation. In May 1997 the then Chancellor of the Exchequer, Gordon Brown, announced his decision to merge banking supervision and investment services regulation into the Securities and Investment Board (SIB). Later that same year, the SIB was renamed the Financial Services Authority (FSA). In December 2001 the Financial Services and Markets Act was implemented, whereby the FSA became the UK's highest single financial services regulator. As well as being responsible for the regulation of banks and securities, it also assumed responsibility for the following organizations:

- Building Societies Commission
- Friendly Societies Commission
- Investment Management Regulatory Organization
- Personal Investment Authority
- Register of Friendly Societies
- Securities and Futures Authority.

The scope of the FSA was widened further with responsibility for the regulation of mortgages in 2004 and general insurance in 2005. The FSA is an independent non-governmental body which operates as a company limited by guarantee and is financed by the financial services industry. The FSA has a Board which is appointed by Her Majesty's Treasury, and the FSA is accountable to Treasury Ministers and, through them, to Parliament. The Financial Services and Markets Act lays down four statutory objectives for the FSA, namely:

1. Market confidence – maintaining confidence in the financial system
2. Public awareness – promoting public understanding of the financial system
3. Consumer protection – securing the appropriate degree of protection for consumers
4. Reduction of financial crime – reducing the extent to which it is possible for a business to be used for a purpose connected with financial crime.

The FSA seeks to achieve its objectives by way of a vast array of rules and directives, the contravention of which can result in a range of penalties. It is of the essence that all those involved in financial services provision have a sound grasp of the rules that apply to their particular product sector and functional discipline. The rulebook of the FSA spans an enormous gamut from issues of strategic, overarching significance, such as solvency margins, to matters of fine detail, such as the nature and wording of individual advertisements.

An area of particular significance in a marketing context concerns the development of regulations regarding the distribution and sale of financial services and the integral issue of financial advice. The 1986 Act led to the introduction of what might be termed the doctrine of polarization. In practice, this meant that financial advice, and any resulting sale, must be provided by one of two variants of advisers. Thus, the concepts of Independent Financial Advisers (IFAs) and Tied Agents (TAs) was initiated. IFAs were to act as *de facto* agents of the consumer, and were bound to give 'best advice' in response to the consumers' financial needs from all possible sources of supply in the marketplace. At the other 'pole of advice' were the TAs, who could give advice and sell products purely from one company. TAs were of two primary forms, namely Company Representatives (CRs) and Appointed Representatives (ARs). The CRs worked directly for the financial services company upon whose products they gave advice and sold products. This could be either as a salaried employee or as an adviser paid on a commission-only basis. Appointed representatives, on the other hand, were staff under the control of a separate company that had a distribution agreement with a given life insurance company. For example, The Cheshire Building Society is an AR of Norwich Union, which means that the financial advisers employed by the Cheshire can only give advice on the products supplied by Norwich Union.

Through polarization, it was intended that the consumer interest would be best served in that consumers would have absolute certainty whether they were receiving completely independent advice or advice on the product of just one company. Prior to this time there was a plethora of *ad hoc* distribution arrangements, and consumers were often unclear regarding the degree of independence that was attached to the advice they received. In practice, the introduction of polarization resulted in a somewhat unedifying scramble for distribution as life companies vied with each other to attract AR and CR arrangements. In the short term, it did nothing to reduce the costs associated with advising on and selling investment products. Moreover, the need for each company with a TA form of distribution to have a full product range available for its agents to advise on and sell did nothing to improve the efficiency of the industry. Arguably, the reverse happened as companies filled out their product ranges with products, some of which were sold in extremely low volumes and offered relatively poor value for money. Standards of financial advice were also slow to respond to the spirit of regulation. Indeed, the mis-selling of personal pensions was at its height between 1987 and 1991, resulting in the so-called 'pension mis-selling scandal' which to date has cost the industry in the order of £15bn in compensation and allied administration costs. Other examples of consumer detriment have arisen since the 1986 Act, including the mis-selling of mortgage endowments and a number of investment schemes.

In 2005, following a lengthy period of consultation, the polarization rules were revised to permit a form of multi-tied distribution. To quote the FSA (www.fsa.gov.uk):

> from 2005, tied advisers selling any type of investment (not just stakeholder schemes) will be able to offer the products of more than one provider if they are tied to a company which has adopted the products of other providers in its range.

A critical step forward in improving the consumer interest was the introduction of new rules regarding the training and competence of advisers in the early 1990s. This acted as a watershed for the industry by introducing more exacting standards of knowledge that financial advisers and their managers could demonstrate. It also resulted in a significant increase in the costs of employing an adviser. As a consequence, there was a dramatic fall in the number of people involved in advising and selling life and pension products between 1991 and 1996. Some estimates have suggested that this number collapsed from the order of 220 000 to about 50 000 during the 5-year period. This has had the effect of forcing incompetent and unproductive advisers out of the industry, and has thus raised the standard of professionalism of the typical financial adviser.

The preceding commentary and views of just one narrow aspect of financial services regulation are intended to demonstrate the paramount importance that the authors attach to students and practitioners having a sound appreciation of the regulations that apply in their respective countries and industry sectors. Some examples of how the regulation of insurance business is approached in a number of other countries are given in Box 1.1.

Box 1.1   International approaches to insurance regulation

USA: In the USA, each individual state has its own regulator. Their titles vary, depending on the state, and include commissioner, superintendent or director. In some states, governors appoint the commissioner; in others, the general public elects commissioners. The commissioners from the various states together form the National Association (NAIC) to promote uniformity in regulation. Other officials with some oversight functions include the representatives of guaranty funds and certain federal government agencies.

Australia: In Australia, the APRA, or Australian Prudential Regulatory Authority, is the integrated prudential regulator of the Australian financial services industry. It was set up in 1988, and oversees banks, credit unions, building societies, general insurance and reinsurance companies, life insurance companies, friendly societies and most members of the superannuation industry. The APRA is funded primarily by the industries it supervises.

Singapore: In Singapore, the Insurance Supervision Department is the primary regulator of the Monetary Authority of Singapore (MAS). The Insurance Supervision Department (ISD) administers the Insurance Act, its main objective being the protection of policyholders' interests. ISD adopts a risk-focused approach in the prudential and market conduct supervision of insurance companies. ISD carries out its responsibilities by way of both off-site surveillance and on-site examination, and works with foreign supervisors as part of a holistic supervisory approach. In its standards development role, ISD works closely with industry associations to promote the adoption of best practices by the industry.

South Africa: The Financial Services Board (FSB) was established as a statutory body by the Financial Services Board Act (No. 97 of 1990) and is financed by the financial services industry itself, with no contribution from government. It supervises the control over the activities of non-banking financial services and acts in an advisory capacity to the Minister of Finance.

> **Box 1.1   International approaches to insurance regulation—cont'd**
>
> **India:** In 1999, the Insurance Regulatory and Development Authority (IRDA) was set up to regulate, promote and ensure orderly growth of the insurance business and reinsurance business.
>
> *Source: Faye Lageu, Vice President, Intelligence Unit ICMIF.*

1.9   Summary and conclusions

The financial services industry has a vital role to play in safeguarding the prospects for economic development across the globe. At the micro-level, financial services underpin the overall well-being of individuals. The challenge is for standards of marketing within the financial services domain to reflect the necessary degree of market and consumer orientation. An appreciation of the potential offered by financial services marketing requires it to be placed within the context of government-sponsored welfare systems on a country-by-country basis. The state and private sectors of financial services have to work in a complementary manner if aggregate stakeholder interests are to be optimized. Finally, financial services ought to be provided for the benefit of all, not just the affluent few.

Review questions

1. Identify and critically evaluate the respective roles of the state and private sectors in the provision of healthcare, education and welfare in your country. To what extent do you consider that the two sectors complement or compete with each other?
2. What forms of mutual financial services provision take place in your country? Compare and contrast the ways in which mutuals and proprietary providers serve the needs of your country's citizens.
3. Which body (or bodies) is responsible for the regulation of financial services in your country? What are its principal goals, and to what extent do you think it is successful in achieving them?
4. How are the provision of financial advice and sale of financial services products regulated in your country? To what extent do you think those regulations safeguard the interests of private consumers and business customers?
5. Some people would argue that the resources devoted to corporate social responsibility (CSR) represent theft from the shareholder. How do you feel that CSR impacts upon the interests of various stakeholder groups?

The financial services marketplace: structures, products and participants

Learning objectives

By the end of this chapter you will be able to:
- identify the different types of organizations engaged in the provision of financial services
- understand the range and diversity of financial services and how they relate to customer needs
- comprehend the complexity of the industry.

2.1 Introduction

All too often difficulties are encountered associated with the overall use of the term financial services. A large proportion of the general public – including many consumers – has a limited appreciation of the geography of the financial services landscape. This is partly because of the complexity of the industry and partly because, for many people, financial services are intrinsically uninteresting. Poor knowledge and understanding of the sector as a whole and of the product sectors it comprises also applies to those employed in the area. Research conducted by Alferoff *et al.* (2005) revealed that the knowledge base of the typical financial services employee was limited to his or her narrow field of task expertise:

Many front-line and back office staff did not understand some or all of the range of investment products. They were in fact little more knowledgeable than non-financial services respondents and even less knowledgeable than those from the Chamber of Commerce or MBA students (other groups comprising the sample frame of the study).

Equally, there are people within practitioner communities who display only a partial knowledge of the big picture beyond their functional area.

This chapter aims to provide an overview of the financial services sector from two perspectives. First, it will set out to describe the geography of supply. The early sections will seek to identify the major groupings of organizations that make up the significant forms of product/service supply. Secondly, the chapter will seek to provide a solid grounding in the products that comprise financial services. It does not set out to discuss every possible product type and variant that may be encountered in all parts of the world; rather, it seeks to identify the major product variants that are commonly encountered. Prior to exploring the marketplace in detail, the chapter begins by providing some historical context for the industry.

2.2 Some historical perspectives

Whilst various forms of financial services provision can be traced back many centuries, the development of commercial organizations of substance and scale coincided with the expansion of international trade as the eighteenth century progressed. Indeed, economic development is inextricably linked to the development of allied financial instruments. Banks grew in response to the need for services such as loans, safe deposit and financing of consignments of exported and imported goods. Commercial banking in the UK originated in London, based largely upon the growth of goldsmith bankers in the mid-seventeenth century. A century later, the number of provincial banks was still in single figures. However, by 1784 the number had grown to 119 and by 1810 had expanded to some 650 (information provided courtesy of the Royal Bank of Scotland). Banking grew similarly apace in Scotland in response to rapidly expanding trade, and similar trends were in evidence throughout Europe. Interestingly, the great majority of these banks were based upon just one branch; the consolidation process had yet to commence. The proliferation of banking firms resulted in the need for the creation of a clearing house in London for the settlement of inter-bank payments.

Numerous sources across the globe attest to the link between economic development and the expansion of a financial services sector. The changing needs of commerce required banking to adapt. Trinidad is cited as an example of the need for greater flexibility going back to the latter part of the nineteenth century (Paria Publishing Co. Ltd, 2000):

In that time of economic growth the Colonial Bank's old way of doing business in the West Indies was challenged by the West Indian Royal Commission for their excessively restrictive lending policies. The commission was told by several peasant witnesses, black people and 'cocoa pa-ols' of the necessity for loans to expand their small operations.

In Iran, banking in its modern form also began to emerge in the mid-nineteenth century. It was not until 1925 that the first bank was established with Iranian capital in the form of the Bank Pahlavi Qoshun. In Ethiopia, the Bank of Abyssinia was inaugurated in 1906 and was given a 50-year concession period. In short, throughout the world there are well-documented examples of the development of commercial banking from the nineteenth century onwards.

As with banking, insurance too can be traced back to seventeenth-century London. The Great Fire of London in 1666 must have acted as a major catalyst for the provision of a suitable form of insurance for perils of this nature. *The History of Insurance* (Jenkins and Yoneyama, 2000) observes that some of the earliest companies identified include the Sun Fire Office, Royal Exchange Assurance and Hand in Hand. In its commentary on the historical development of insurance, the Insurance Bureau of Canada (www.ibc.ca/gii_history) observes that:

> The history of insurance is the story of Western society's development. As agriculture gave way to industrial growth it became clear that expansion depended on capital money that would be risked for the profit it offered. For those risk-takers, insurance provided a guarantee that all would not be lost through error, bad judgement or bad luck.

It was during the sixteenth century that the forerunners of Lloyd's of London met in Lloyd's coffee house and devised the means by which risk could be mitigated. Again, the need to protect the risks associated with international trade was the primary catalyst for this development. The eighteenth century saw the development of general insurance in what is now the USA. Indeed, Benjamin Franklin, one of the signatories to the US Declaration of Independence in 1776, was also the founder of the Philadelphia Contributorship for the Insurance of Houses from Loss by Fire in 1752. The closing years of the eighteenth century saw the birth in England of a type of insurance company called a friendly society. Friendly societies grew apace during the nineteenth century; many of them began as burial societies and, as the name implies, set out to provide the funds for a respectable burial for their members. By 1910, almost 7 million British citizens were policyholders in friendly societies.

In common with friendly societies, the later part of the eighteenth century saw the initiation of building societies in Britain. The first known society began in 1775. It was known as Richard Ketley's Building Society, and its members met at the Gold Cross Inn in Birmingham. By 1860 there were in excess of 750 societies in London alone, and a further 2000 outside of the capital (Building Societies Association, 2001). Building societies arose and prospered from the desire of ordinary women and men to finance the purchase of their own homes. The twentieth century saw building societies go through a process of consolidation into fewer but larger organizations. Subsequently, during the course of the final decade of the twentieth century, a number of societies (notably the larger ones) converted to become shareholder-owned proprietary companies. Thus, names such as the Halifax, Abbey National, Alliance and Leicester, Northern Rock, Woolwich, Cheltenham and Gloucester, and Bradford and Bingley are no longer building societies but operate as quoted banking companies on the London Stock Exchange or have been taken over by other banking organizations. The Building Societies Association identifies that, as at 2002, its members numbered some 65 societies with combined assets of over £170bn.

In an era of suspicion and mistrust of the financial services industry, it is easy to lose sight of the fact that the product and services it provides make a major contribution to the well-being of citizens across the globe. Economic development and prosperity cannot flourish in the absence of a suitable infrastructure of financial services provision. Indeed, it is interesting to note the desire of the Syrian government to promote economic development by breaking the monopoly of its state bank in 2003 with the award of licences to three privately owned banks, namely the Banque de Syrie et d'Outre Mer, The International Bank for Trade and Finance and the BEMO-Saudi-Fransi bank. This is a measured and creative means of introducing competition in a sector characterized by state control. It is expected that this process will be replicated elsewhere in the world as currently underdeveloped countries seek to embrace economic progress.

2.3   The geography of supply

The structure of financial services marketplaces around the world varies according to local environmental characteristics. Factors such as the stage of economic development, government policy on competition, and regulation all exert an influence on local market structures. Physical geography, logistics and infrastructural features such as telecommunications also have a part to play in determining the local evolution of financial services, as do social, religious and cultural factors.

A feature of the recent financial services landscape has been the breaking down of boundaries between historical lines of demarcation of supply. Deregulation of markets, such as that which occurred in the UK in the mid-1980s, has blurred the lines that hitherto separated the domains of banking, insurance and mortgage lending. The Financial Services Act 1986 had two primary purposes: first, it set out to define and regulate investment business; and secondly, it sought to promote a greater degree of competition in the market for savings products. The practical consequence of this and other related legislation, such as the Building Societies Act 1986, was to create what might be termed 'unbounded' financial services markets. No longer would the current account be the sole domain of the traditional high-street banks, or mortgages for residential property be limited to building societies, or life assurance and pensions be supplied solely by insurance companies. Instead of product supply silos we have witnessed the metamorphosis of banks, building societies and insurance companies into financial services organizations spanning the range of core money management, loan, pension and investment products. Worldwide, the most obvious manifestation of this process has been the emergence of *bancassurance* (or allfinanz), a distribution system which involves partnerships between banks and insurers to make insurance products available via bank networks.

The idea of retailers selling insurance has not been a significant feature in other countries. For example, in the US, regulation is such that it is not allowed. In France, it is argued that such an approach would not sit well culturally. To the best of the authors' knowledge, banks are really the only alternative channel for the rest of the world. Bancassurance has had major take-up in most European countries. In Canada, however, by law, any bank selling insurance in its branch is still required to have a separate sales counter.

However, in spite of the breaking down of legal lines of product demarcation, banks, building societies and insurance companies have retained a degree of core competence that reflects their historical strengths. Thus, breadth and depth is still vested in the product set of the company's heritage. For example, whilst Barclays provides a vast array of retail financial services, it retains a wealth of expertise in core banking skills which the banking arm of, say, an insurance company would not typically possess. Barclays can offer a far wider range of business-related banking services than can, for example, Standard Life Bank. Moreover, in spite of remote forms of banking (such as the telephone and Internet), bank branches remain an important part of the banking proposition that non-branch based organizations cannot fulfil.

In a similar way, insurance companies retain a degree of capability that the insurance arm of, say, a building society is unlikely to possess. For example, flexibility has become a growing requirement for the pensions industry, and features such as pension drawdown and Self-Invested Pensions Plans are a common need of Independent Financial Advisers (IFAs). Companies such as Legal and General and Friends Provident have such facilities as part of their core product set. On the other hand, the Nationwide Building Society has a more basic approach to pensions (industry jargon often refers to 'vanilla' or 'plain vanilla') and does not currently provide that degree of sophistication within its range of pension products. Equally, the Nationwide offers much wider range of deposit-based savings options than does, say, Skandia Life.

In simple terms, the geography of product providers is based upon the core elements outlined in Table 2.1.

As already discussed, the marketplace is far more complex than it has been historically, with large, diversified financial services groups spanning many of the above core product domains. Nonetheless, many companies can be found that are specialists with a narrow product focus. Sometimes these are specialist arms of larger organizations – such as the Zurich Financial Services subsidiary Navigators and General, which specializes in insuring small boats. Equally, there are independent companies that retain a discrete niche focus – such as Cattles Plc, which specializes in providing unsecured loans to the near prime market.

Table 2.1 The geography of supply

Type of activity	Specific forms
Banking	Retail banks/Commercial banks
Savings and Loans	Building Societies (UK)
	Credit Unions
	National Savings
Insurance	Life Insurers
	General Insurers
	Friendly Societies (UK)
	Health Insurers
	Lloyd's syndicates
Investment companies	Mutual fund/Unit Trust Companies
	Investment Trusts
	Pensions providers

A further feature of the geography of supply is the evolution of what are often termed 'new entrants', although they are no longer quite so new. This term refers to providers with no historical pedigree as suppliers of financial services. For these companies, the move into financial services is part of an overarching strategy of brand stretch as a means of diversification. Examples of such 'new entrants' in the UK include Virgin, Marks and Spencer, and leading supermarkets Asda, Tesco and Sainsbury.

The 'new entrants' tend to be based upon fairly simple products that are, typically, bought rather than sold. Examples include general insurance products, such as motor, travel and home contents insurance, which are commonly found in display racks at the checkouts in supermarkets. There is a feeling that there are limits to the extent to which the core brand can extend into financial services (Devlin, 2003), and that consumers form a view on the saliency of certain brands and supplier types. Thus, for example, consumers might feel comfortable with purchasing a basic general insurance product from a supermarket, but may have reservations about purchasing a more complex, specialist financial service (such as a pension) from such a non-specialist provider. Consumer perceptions of an organization's core competences have important implications for the marketing strategies of those involved with the supply of financial services.

A further complication concerns the issue of distribution. Whilst many services are provided to consumers on what might be termed a direct basis, third-party distribution arrangements are often an important feature of financial services. In the UK, for example, the Financial Services Act 1986 led to the creation of IFAs and Appointed Representatives (ARs). IFAs and ARs are deemed to represent either end of a polarized form of financial advice. At one end of the pole is the IFA, who acts as the agent of the consumer and must give product recommendations that represent best advice from sources of supply. At the other end is the AR, who must give best advice based upon the products of just one provider company. The AR may be a member of a distribution network owned by the product provider, such as Nationwide Life (part of the Nationwide Building Society); alternatively, the AR could be a third-party organization that has an agreement to advise solely on the investment products of a separate insurance company. An example of this latter arrangement is to be found in Barclays, which is an AR of Legal and General. Thus, no understanding of the geography of supply would be complete without taking due account of organizations involved in product distribution.

2.4　An outline of product variants

The purpose of this section is to provide a solid grounding of the key product variants that comprise the domain of retail financial services. Readers wishing to learn about aspects of the wholesale market are referred to Pilbeam (2005).

It is arguable whether this issue should be addressed from the perspective of specific products, or the needs such products seek to satisfy. The adoption of a pure product focus is problematic on both philosophical and practical grounds. From a philosophical viewpoint, it places undue focus upon the products provided rather than the needs of consumers. In so doing, it offends the sensibilities of those who place consumer needs, as opposed to products supplied, as the fulcrum of a marketing orientation. For such individuals, any intimation of 'product orientation' is to be avoided wherever possible. At the practical level, it is just not feasible to identify every possible product variant from around the globe in a text of this nature. Therefore, a pragmatic approach has been adopted whereby significant mainstream consumer needs are presented together with typical product solutions that are widely encountered. This approach is summarized in Table 2.2.

The needs and product solutions given in Table 2.2 are representative of those that are typically encountered throughout the world. It does not set out to be exhaustive, but gives a sound overview of generally expressed needs and the means of addressing them. The following sections of this chapter set out to tie together consumer needs with product solutions and the means of supply in order to enable the reader to develop some sense of the real world of financial services.

2.5 Banking and money transmission

Until the latter part of the twentieth century, the provision of current account services was the sole prerogative of the high-street clearing banks. The current account represents the primary means by which salaried employees receive payroll credits from their employers and manage payments and cash withdrawals. The extent of current account penetration in a given country typically reflects the proportion of the population paid by salary. Thus, in the UK some 95 per cent of the population have bank accounts, while in India the proportion is probably around 15 per cent and in South Africa it is estimated to be between 30 per cent and 40 per cent ((http://in.rediff.com and www.euromonitor.com, both accessed January 2005).

In addition to the traditional high-street banks, building societies in the UK also often provide current accounts. Indeed, those building societies that demutualized, such as Alliance and Leicester, the Halifax and Bradford and Bingley, became known collectively as mortgage banks. This term reflects the relative importance still attached to the provision of residential mortgages, and their orientation towards the retail sector. As yet, the mortgage banks have not made any material impact upon the business and corporate banking arena. As previously observed, there is a saliency issue in that businesses do not yet view mortgage banks as being credible suppliers of business banking services. Competitive pressure has been responsible for a great deal more price-competition for personal current accounts. The payment of interest on current account balances was almost unheard of in the UK until the second half of the 1980s. It could be argued that the rate of interest paid on the typical current account is so derisory that many consumers benefit from such payment to only a limited degree.

Current account supply has broadened ever further in recent years as a consequence of factors such as technological development and the arrival of the so-called 'new entrants'. Initially, telephone banking, pioneered in the UK by First Direct, facilitated lower-cost current account provision and the payment of interest on current account positive balances. Costs have been lowered further still by the advent

Table 2.2 Customer needs and product solutions

Consumer need	Product solution
A secure depository for readily accessible cash	Current accounts
A means of managing receipts of funds and payment of expenses (money transmission)	Current accounts
A secure depository for cash that pays interest	Current accounts
	Deposit accounts
	Credit Union deposits
A simple means of accumulating a fund of cash on which interest is paid	Deposit Accounts
	High-Interest Current Accounts
Tax-advantaged cash savings for the medium term	Cash ISA[5] (Individual Savings Account)
A means of accumulating a lump sum in the medium to long term	Regular Saving endowments
	Regular saving mutual funds, such as OEICS[6] and Unit Trusts
A means of investing a lump sum for long-term growth	Mutual Accumulation funds
	Investment Bonds
	Investment Trusts
	Corporate Bonds
	Government bonds
A means of investing a lump sum to generate income	Mutual Income Funds
	Income Bonds
	Corporate Bonds
	Annuities
A means of saving for retirement	Occupational Pension Schemes
	Personal Pensions
	401k Savings Schemes[7]
	Central Provident Fund[8]
A means of deriving income from a Pension Fund	Annuities
	Income drawdown[9]
A means of financing current consumption from future earnings or income	Credit cards
	Unsecured loans
	Secured loans
A means of financing home purchase	Residential mortgages
A means of releasing liquid funds from one's residential property	Equity release schemes
A means of protecting outstanding loans	Payment protection insurance
	Mortgage indemnity guarantees
A means of protecting tangible assets from fire, theft, accidental damage and perils of nature	General insurance
A means of protecting people and organizations from claims for pecuniary loss arising from negligence, oversight or non-performance of duties	Liability insurance
A means of protecting human assets from risks associated with death, illness and medical conditions	Life Assurance
	Critical illness insurance
	Health insurance
	Permanent Health insurance

Box 2.1   Price competition among Internet banking providers in the UK

When Sainsbury's bank launched its current account in 1992, it offered an interest rate of 6 per cent on positive current account balances. This sparked something of a current account interest rate war, with Tesco offering 6.5 per cent when it subsequently launched its high-interest rate current account, only to be topped by the Prudential offshoot, Egg, when it launched in 1995. At the time of writing, Egg is the highest-paying current account provider, paying a gross rate of 5.50 per cent. However, Egg is solely an Internet bank, and consumers must judge the extent to which this offsets the disadvantages of not having access to a branch network.

---

of Internet banking. This new technology has enabled new entrants to offer so-called high-interest current accounts, as illustrated in Box 2.1.

Technology and changing consumer tastes have also facilitated greater diversity regarding money transmission and payments. The usage of cheques has declined significantly in recent years owing to factors such as the growing use of debit and credit cards. According to the British Bankers Association, the number of cheques handled by the clearing system has fallen from a peak of 4.472bn in 1990 to 2.454bn by 2004. Cheque usage fell by 39 per cent between 1994 and 2004, and is predicted to fall a further 44 per cent by 2014. This has made it easier for new entrants and virtual banks to compete in the market for current accounts.

The introduction of interest-bearing current accounts has served to drive margin out of these aspects of banking. It could be argued that it has also acted as a catalyst for suppliers to become increasingly stealthy in terms of how they levy charges. UK banks and others have come in for growing criticism regarding what are often considered to be opaque charging practices. Charges for services such as unauthorized overdrafts and the presentation of cheques on accounts with insufficient funds have added to a popularly held sense of mistrust in the banks. The counter-argument is that financial institutions have to find a means of covering the costs of providing current accounts, given that they are now interest-bearing. Admittedly, providers of current accounts do advise their customers of their menu of charges from time to time – indeed, they are obliged to do so by law. However, the overall approach to charging acts to favour the financially astute and well-off, whilst penalizing those who are less affluent and less financially aware.

The current account has increasingly become a 'loss-leader' – that is, it is seen as acting as a gateway for the sale of other products that offer meaningful margin potential. Indeed, it has been suggested that the majority of current accounts held by the typical clearing bank are loss-making. This has resulted in the need to cross-sell other products and services via what are termed customer relationship management (or marketing) programmes (CRM for short). This particular marketing phenomenon will be addressed in full in Part III of this book.

2.6   Lending and credit

The provision of loans is one of the oldest financial services, dating back thousands of years. In a sense, it performs a key role as a facilitator of income smoothing by enabling consumers to enjoy current consumption from future earnings. Such a process seems entirely defensible under circumstances where there is an expectation of future income surpluses to fund prior income deficits. Equally, it makes eminent sense in respect of purchases of a magnitude well beyond current income, such as residential property mortgages. The difficulties arise when there is a mismatch between current consumption expectations and future income surpluses. In short, the affordability of credit has become a major concern through the world. For example, in May 2004 the *Straits Times* in Singapore ran a series of features highlighting the problems of over-indebtedness, especially with regard to young people.

In addition to affordability, there is a somewhat philosophical concern regarding the relationship between the timescale of the consumption experience and the repayment of any accompanying form of loan or credit. The traditional view was that short-term loans and credit should apply to short-term forms of consumption. Examples of this are, say, loans of up to 12 months' duration to pay for a holiday, or short-term credit to fund clothing purchases. The corollary to these are long-term loans, such as 25-year mortgages to fund home purchase. In between lie intermediate loans for purchases of cars and consumer durables such as furniture. Traditional practice has been for consistency between the purpose of loan (in terms of timescale of the consumption experience) and the duration of the repayment period. In recent years there has been a weakening in this relationship, principally by individuals obtaining long-term loans for short-term consumption. Indeed, the Halifax was criticized on the BBC Radio 4 programme *Moneybox* (29 January 2005) for a direct mail exercise that offered a mortgage repayment holiday of up to six months to allow customers to enjoy additional current consumption. Critics of the promotion were concerned at the lack of transparency regarding the long-term impact upon interest payments. In effect, there were concerns that short-term consumption pleasure would be at the expense of long-term interest repayments.

Consumers face an enormous array of loan and credit arrangements. In simple terms, a loan represents the granting of a specific sum of money to an individual or organization for them to spend personally in respect of some specific, previously agreed item. Credit, on the other hand, refers to a means of financing an item or items of expenditure whereby the funds are transferred to the product provider directly by the source of credit. In this way, the consumer receiving the goods or services financed by the credit undertakes to reimburse the credit provider for the principal sum plus any interest that may be due.

The principal types of loans encountered are shown in Table 2.3.

A mortgage may appear to be a straightforward product, simple in design and pricing structure. In practice, the range of mortgages available has become increasingly complex. In February 2005, the Portman, based in Bournemouth in the UK, had some eleven separate mortgage products in its home-loan range, as shown in Table 2.4.

Table 2.3 Types of loan

Loan type	Key characteristics
Unsecured loan	Relatively high interest rates to compensate lender for lack of security.
Secured loan	Usually secured on the borrower's residential property equity via a second (or subsequent) charge, these are known as second mortgages. Relatively low interest rates charged owing to the presence of the security.
Mortgages	A loan made for the purpose of purchasing one's home. Typically a long-term loan which is at a relatively low rate of interest and is secured upon the property. In the UK most mortgages are variable, whereby the rate of interest charged fluctuates as base rates vary. Many other countries favour the certainty of fixed-rate mortgages.
Re-mortgage	This too applies to situations in which a homeowner wishes to replace an existing mortgage with one from another lender. This normally occurs because the borrower can obtain a home loan at a lower rate from an alternative lender.
Equity release schemes	These are loans that are secured upon residential property for older people. There are two principal variants one by which the lender secures an interest in the property and the other which does not.

Consumers are therefore presented with an array of mortgage offers with different terms and conditions and different prices, and Table 2.4 demonstrates the complexity associated with what might be expected to be a relatively straightforward product. It must be said that the degree of complexity grows when other mortgage variants are added to the array of possibilities, such as endowment, interest-only and deferred-interest mortgages.

Business loans are also to be found in both secured and unsecured forms. In contrast to personal loans, business secured loans will consider a much wider range of assets as potential sources of security.

Principal forms of personal unsecured credit are as follows:

- credit cards
- storecards
- unsecured loans
- credit vouchers and cheques
- pawn-broking
- home credit
- overdrafts.

The scale of the growth in credit has been dramatic in the UK during this decade, so far. Total net outstanding lending to individuals broke through the £1 trillion barrier in 2005 and, as can be seen from Table 2.5, has continued to grow.

Secured/unsecured credit provision has grown dramatically in the UK since 1994, and reached outstanding balances of £1 trillion in 2003. The scale of outstanding loans was equivalent to £17 000 of debt for every man, woman and child. Put another way, this level of debt exceeds the whole external debt of Africa and South America combined. The growth of indebtedness is to be found in many countries, as

Table 2.4 Portman Building Society mortgage products, 2005

Product	Initial interest rate (%)	Changing to for rest of term (%)	Overall cost rate (%)	Further terms and conditions
2-year fixed	2.35%	6.74%	6.3%	£500 acceptance fee
2-year fixed	4.48%	6.74%	6.7%	£399 acceptance fee
2-year fixed cashback	4.85%	6.74%	6.7%	£250 cash back for valuations up to £500,000
3-year fixed	4.79%	6.74%	6.7%	£499 acceptance fee
3-year fixed cash back	4.95%	6.74%	6.6%	No acceptance fee, free valuation and £250 cash back for valuations up to £500,000
5-year fixed	4.89%	6.74%	6.6%	No acceptance fee, free valuation and £250 cash back for valuations up to £500,000
5-year fixed cash back	4.99%	6.74%	6.35%	No acceptance fee, free valuation and £250 cash back for valuations up to £500,000
2-year discount	4.48%	6.74%	6.7%	£399 acceptance fee
2-year discount cash back	4.85%	6.74%	6.7%	No acceptance fee, free valuation and £250 cash back for valuations up to £500,000
Flexible tracker	4.99%	5.50%	5.7%	£399 acceptance fee, interest calculated monthly with daily adjustment, no early repayment charge.
2-year base-rate tracker	4.69%	5.50%	5.7%	£399 acceptance fee, Early repayment charge of 4% of balance on which interest is charged until 31.03.2007

The published terms and conditions specified that:

ALL PRODUCTS (EXCEPT CASH BACK AND EASY REMORTGAGE) AVAIL-
ABLE UP TO 95 per cent WITH A HIGHER LENDING CHARGE PAYABLE
OVER 90 per cent.

Table 2.5 Net lending to individuals

	£ millions			% changes on year; seasonally adjusted		
	Secured	Unsecured	Total	Secured	Unsecured	Total
2002 Jan	595,856	142,070	737,927	10.2	14.5	11.0
2003 Jan	682,417	157,778	840,195	13.6	15.0	13.9
2004 Jan	782,665	167,627	950,292	15.0	13.8	14.8
2005 Jan	882,812	183,946	1,066,758	12.5	14.2	12.8
Apr	902,964	186,858	1,089,822	11.3	13.5	11.7
Jul	924,633	189,367	1,114,001	10.4	12.0	10.7
Oct	947,797	191,112	1,138,909	10.1	10.7	10.2
2006 Jan	974,582	193,183	1,167,765	10.6	8.7	10.3

Source: Bank of England.

the consumer culture extends its spread. Figures from the Bank of England suggest that the ratio of household debt to household income in 2003 was around 200 per cent for the Netherlands; around 140 per cent for the UK, the USA and Australia; around 120 per cent for Japan; and fractionally above 100 per cent for Germany.

2.7   Saving and investing

2.7.1   Background

Saving and investing represents the reciprocal of lending and credit. Whereas the latter concerns the allocation of elements of future income in order to finance current consumption, the former concerns sacrificing present consumption in order to provide for some future consumption event or requirement. It is interesting to note that disagreements exist between various groups of practitioners regarding the exact definition of these terms. One group, typically those in the life-assurance sector, regards *saving* as referring to a process whereby sums of money are contributed to some form of saving scheme on a regular basis in order to accumulate a large capital sum at a future point in time. This process of accumulation could see the contributions credited to any of the array of asset classes that are available. The asset classes could include cash-based deposit accounts, such as bank or building society accounts, or pure equity-based vehicles, such as a mutual-fund saving product. In other words, it is the *process* of making a regular contribution that is deemed to be saving rather than the characteristics of the asset class into which the contributions are made. This group of practitioners regards *investment* as the process by which lump sums, which have already been accumulated, are deployed to achieve one of two goals: generation of income or further capital growth. Again, the nature of the underlying asset class is not the issue, as it could be anything from cash to equities.

By contrast, there is another group, typically found in the banking community, that uses *saving* not as a verb but rather to describe a certain class of asset – namely, those that are cash-based. *Investment*, on the other hand, concerns the accumulation and deployment of funds into non-cash asset classes such as bonds, equities and property.

Throughout this book, the term 'savings' will be used to describe a process associated with the accumulating of a larger fund through regular contributions, while the term 'investment' will be used to describe the process of managing a lump sum for the purpose of income or further capital growth.

Numerous studies have pointed to the benefits that accrue to individuals from having recourse to some form of financial assets, however modest. In the USA, Page-Adams and Sherraden (1996) reviewed the finding of 25 studies that addressed the personal and social effects of asset-holding, including: personal well-being, economic security, civic behaviour and community involvement, women's status, and the well-being of children. The studies that were analysed indicate the positive effects that assets have on life satisfaction, reduced rates of depression and alcohol misuse. It was noted that assets appear to be associated with an individual's sense of self-direction and being orientated towards the future. In discussing the beneficial impact of the Central Provident Fund in Singapore, Waite (2001) noted that there is a positive association between assets and higher levels of social status for women in particular.

Of particular note is the evidence that points to the beneficial effects of asset-holding on children, especially with regard to children from low-income families. The USA introduced the Assets for Independence Act in 1998, which has served as a catalyst for the majority of states to introduce asset-accumulation programmes. The Act was an attempt to address poverty by building wealth among the poorer sections of society rather than just by redistributing income.

The notion that the encouragement of personal financial assets, albeit of quite modest proportions, represents a social policy goal has resonated with governments across the globe. In Singapore, the government has introduced an analogue to America's IDA called the Children's Development Co-Savings Scheme. Introduced in April 2001, this new approach to saving comprises two elements: the Baby Bonus and the Children's Development Account (CDA), known as 'tier one' and 'tier two' respectively. Under the provisions of the Baby Bonus scheme, parents receive a cash payment of $500S for their second child and $1000S for their third. Every year for the next five years, the parents will receive an additional $500S and $1000S respectively for the second and third children. Thus, there will be payments totalling $3000S and $6000S for the second and third children of the family respectively. In commenting on this scheme, Sherraden observes:

> In domestic policy, it {Singapore} is probably the most innovative nation on the planet ... the baby Bonus and CDA policy is a bold and positive step forwards.

Also in Asia, the Taiwanese government introduced the Family Development Account in June 2000. The FDA is a matched savings scheme aimed at low-income families, and forms part of the government's strategy to relieve poverty.

Research in the UK by Brynner and Despotidou (2000) has corroborated evidence from the USA regarding the impact of financial assets on life outcomes. Their study has played a role in the decision by the British government of Tony Blair to introduce the Child Trust Fund and saving gateway. The Child Trust Fund is a scheme whereby children born after September 2002 are eligible to receive a lump sum from the government – £500 for those from less affluent families, or £250 for those from more affluent families. The scheme went live with effect from April 2005, and Case study 2.1 outlines the responses of one provider, Family Investments.

Thus there is a growing realization of the benefits to be gained from encouraging the saving habit. The remainder of this section provides some perspectives on the nature of the savings and investment markets and producers.

Case study 2.1   Family Investments and the Child Trust Fund – an example of private-sector support for public policy

The Child Trust Fund (CTF) represents the UK government's most radical initiative to date in the area of asset-based welfare. The principal aim of the CTF is to provide every child in the country with a nest egg of savings when they reach adulthood at age 18. All children born on or after 1 September 2002 and whose parents or guardians are in receipt of child benefit are included in the CTF scheme.

Case study 2.1   Family Investments and the Child Trust Fund – an example of private-sector support for public policy—cont'd

The mechanics of the CTF are as follows; when a parent registers for child benefit, he or she also receives a CTF voucher worth £250, an Inland Revenue booklet explaining the CTF scheme, and a list of companies which are involved in its provision. The parent then contacts a CTF provider to set up a CTF account for the child and sends the voucher to the provider, who then claims the money from the Inland Revenue to invest in the particular CTF account. Once this has been done, voluntary savings of up to £1200 per annum can be added to the account by parents, grandparents or indeed anyone involved in the financial welfare of the child. The government automatically sets up CTF accounts for children whose parents do not do so. The money placed into a CTF account accumulates free of income and capital gains tax, and may be invested into various asset classes, including equities, bonds and cash.

A key feature of the scheme is that money deposited in a CTF account is owned by the child and will be locked in the account until he or she reaches 18. Only in extreme cases involving the death or terminal illness of the child can the money be accessed before the age of 18.

According to Family Investments:

> As the leading provider of long-term tax exempt savings for children, Family Investments sees the CTF as an exciting addition to our product range.

Our analysis of the market is that, as with anything new, it will take time for the public to get used to the CTF, especially because of its universal nature, which means that over half the parents involved will be new to long-term savings in any form, let alone saving specifically for children. On the other hand, with an official launch date of 6 April 2005 but eligibility backdated to 1 September 2002, some 1.6 million vouchers have been issued in the first quarter of 2005, giving a massive kick-start to the CTF scheme.

Despite the best endeavours of the Revenue, which has issued a comprehensive brochure explaining the CTF, many parents remain confused by the choices available to them. Our approach has been to keep our proposition as simple as possible. This we have done by solely promoting the CTF stakeholder account, which we believe over 18 years carries the best balance of risk and return on the money invested.

Secondly, we have used our existing expertise in the children's savings market to put our proposals to parents at the right time using our established marketing style involving the Mr Men characters, with which many parents are familiar.

Thirdly, we have partnered with a number of well-known and trusted brands whose endorsement will provide confidence to people entering the savings

Continued

> **Case study 2.1   Family Investments and the Child Trust Fund – an example of private-sector support for public policy—cont'd**
>
> market for the first time. Our present partnerships include Barclays, Sainsbury's Bank and the Post Office, and altogether Family's CTF has exposure through more than 18 000 high-street outlets, making it easily the most widely available CTF.
>
> Finally, we have devised a number of ways to encourage voluntary savings which we believe are simple to understand and use. We see this as a vital part of the overall scheme because unless as a provider we are able to help more people to save, the scheme will have limited meaning.
>
> Our long-term aim is to make the Family CTF as recognizable, as available and as easy to use as, say, Heinz Baked Beans. These are early days, but the signs are encouraging.
>
> *Source: John Reeve, Chief Executive, Family Investments.*

2.7.2   Saving

Deposit accounts

The accumulation of a larger sum from small contributions can be accomplished in a wide variety of ways. The simplest vehicle for savings is some form of cash-based deposit account, such as those offered by a wide range of providers in countries across the world – including post offices, banks, building societies, credit unions and some of the newer entrants, such as retailers like Sainsbury in the UK. It is worth pointing out that product innovation has somewhat blurred the boundaries between current and deposit accounts in recent years. Indeed, many high-interest current accounts offer significantly higher rates of interest to depositors than those offered by traditional deposit accounts.

The typical deposit account might be considered to be a somewhat passive approach to saving in that additional contributions tend to be made on a largely *ad hoc* basis. Whilst the facility exists for arrangements such as direct debits to be used to make regular contributions into a deposit account, this is not the norm. Cash deposits act as a default option for individuals who either do not want a more disciplined approach to saving or feel ill-equipped to pursue a more sophisticated approach to saving for the future.

Pensions

Saving cash sums in a deposit account on an *ad hoc* basis represents the simplest form of saving, whereas pensions represent arguably the most complex form of saving. Indeed, a pension is nothing more than a form of saving for a future event. The event in question is the time at which an individual ceases full-time employment.

It is normal for there to be some form of incentive from the government to engage in this form of saving. The rationale is simple: the greater the extent to which individuals provide for their own retirement needs, the less will be the burden placed on state finances and the taxpayer.

It is customary to conceptualize pensions as being either personal or occupational. Whereas the former is a scheme which is entered into on behalf of the individual, typically by that individual, the latter is a group scheme run on behalf of an employer.

Occupational pension schemes (OPSs) are principally of two types: defined benefit (also known as final salary) and defined contribution (also known as money purchase). Defined benefit schemes enable employees to accumulate a pension entitlement that is based upon a proportion of their salary in the 12 months leading up to their date of retirement, hence the term 'final salary'. In the typical scheme, each year of pensionable service will entitle employees to a pension equivalent to one-sixtieth of their final salary. Such a scheme would be termed a 'sixtieth' scheme. Less generous employers may offer an 'eightieth' scheme, whereas more generous firms may offer a 'fortieth' scheme. There are usually rules that limit the maximum number of pensionable years too; in the case of the UK, this is a pension equivalent to two-thirds of the employees' final salary. For example, individuals working for a company with a sixtieth scheme would have to work for the firm for 40 years to be in receipt of the maximum pension of two-thirds of their final salary.

A crucial feature of the defined benefits scheme is that the risk for meeting future pension liabilities rests with the employer. The drop in share prices between 2000 and 2003 has resulted in many OPSs experiencing severe funding difficulties. For this reason, there has been a marked shift away from defined benefit and towards defined contribution schemes. The latter variant has much in common with personal pensions in that contributions from the employee and employer are credited to the employee's individual pension account. Upon retirement, the employee will receive a pension which is based upon the value of his or her personal fund as at the date of retirement. Thus, the fund will reflect the value of contributions made and the performance of the assets into which the contributions have been allocated. Accordingly, the risk is shifted from the employer to the employee. This benefits the employer by introducing control and certainty, as its pension liabilities are discharged fully on the basis of any contributions that it makes on behalf of its staff. In a typical OPS employees contribute in the order of 5 per cent of their wages to the pension scheme, whereas the employer might contribute of the order of 7.5 per cent – the actual amount varies considerably from employer to employer.

An associated form of further pension saving within OPSs are AVCs – Additional Voluntary Contributions. These may be linked to the company's pension scheme (known as in-house AVCs) or be a stand-alone arrangement contributed to an independent insurance company (so-called Free-Standing AVCs, or FSAVCs). In-house AVCs usually offer low costs in a limited range of funds, and are relatively inflexible. The FSAVC usually offers access to a wider range of funds and gives a greater degree of individual control; however, these benefits come at the cost of higher charges.

Personal pensions operate in a similar way to defined contribution OPS schemes. Individuals select a pension provider and then make contributions to a fund of their choice made available by that provider. At the date of retirement the fund so accumulated is used to purchase an annuity, and this becomes the source of income in retirement. Thus individuals will not be certain of the value of their ultimate pension until they reach retirement, as it will be a function of investment performance and prevailing annuity rates. This is a simplification of the variants to be found in the field of pensions. No reference has been made to features such as income drawdown and withdrawal of tax-free lump sums. Details vary enormously from country to country, depending upon local tax regimes and prevailing legislation and rules. However, it does capture the essence of the major forms of this vital form of saving.

Savings endowments

A savings endowment is a form of regular saving that in the UK is offered by companies authorized to offer life assurance contracts. Indeed, a defining characteristic of the savings endowment is that lump sum is payable to the beneficiary in the event of the death of the customer before the targeted maturity date of the contract. Most countries have an endowment type of product, although often described under another name. In Germany, in particular, mortgages and life plans are very heavily based upon endowment-type vehicles.

Sales of this type of savings scheme have fallen dramatically during the past 10 years in the UK. A major reason for this decline has been the sharp reduction in commission-paid direct sales forces, for which this type of product played a core role. At the same time, there was a growing view that the high front-end loaded charging structure made the product poor value for money. This charging structure meant that initial payments into the scheme were used to cover the costs of providing the scheme – including commissions to salespeople. As a consequence, it was common for the break-even point between contributions made and value of fund not to be reached until the policy was at least 7 years old. Prior to this point, savers would have done better had the money simply been saved in a deposit account, although they would have benefited from the lump-sum death payment in the event that they died before the break-even point was reached. Indeed, the product has experienced high rates of early surrender, which usually results in customers receiving less back than they paid in because of the high up-front costs – much of which arose from the commissions that were paid to salespeople.

A variant on the savings endowment is the *mortgage endowment*, a product which has been widely sold in the UK. This has a structure which is virtually identical to the savings endowment. However, as the name implies, this form of saving performs the dual roles of building up a fund, the value of which is intended to be equivalent to the mortgage sum provided by the mortgage lender, and acting as a means of repaying the mortgage in full should the customer die prior to the contractual maturity date of the loan. In common with the savings endowment, sales of mortgage endowments have fallen dramatically during the past 10 years. The rationale of this reduction in sales relates to high charges (again to pay for commission) and a sharp worsening in investment returns, as shown in Case study 2.2.

Collective savings variants

Individuals can save on a regular or periodic basis by making contributions to some form of a collective savings scheme. Examples of this include:

Case study 2.2   The performance of mortgage endowments in the UK

Mortgage endowments are designed to build a fund, typically over a 25-year term, that will match the debt at maturity and thereby ensure the mortgage is fully discharged. For the duration of the term the borrower typically merely pays interest on the loan outstanding to the lender of the mortgage funds. The achievement of the target fund value is based upon assumptions regarding contributions from the customer, fund performance, and associated charges. As might be imagined, fund performance represents the major imponderable. In the UK, the FSA lays down standards for projected future fund growth. For life products, such as savings and mortgage endowments, provider companies may use annual investment growth rates in the range of 5–8 per cent. However, between January 2000 and January 2005 the FTSE 100 (the index of the leading 100 UK companies ranked by market capitalization) fell by approximately 29 per cent. Set against this fall, a mortgage endowment may well have been assumed to achieve fund growth of the order of 35 per cent during the same 5-year period. This leaves a performance gap of some 64 per cent. The effect of this performance gap has been to reduce projected maturity values to an extent that many savers are likely to experience a shortfall in fund value and have insufficient funds to repay their mortgage debt. Many thousands of consumers have been notified by their endowment providers that they face the probability of a deficit in fund value at maturity. The shortfall can be made up by increasing the amount saved into the endowment policy, or by the customer finding an alternative source of funds at maturity.

There have been many cases of mortgage endowments having been sold to people in inappropriate circumstances. This had led to what has been termed the 'endowment mis-selling scandal'. The consumers' organization *Which?* has been especially vocal on this matter, and has set up a website that consumers can use to register their concerns and seek guidance regarding how to investigate claims for compensation. Well over half a million hits have been registered by the website, an indication of the extent of consumer concern.

Mortgage endowments performed well in the past, especially when they attracted tax concessions, resulting in customers experiencing windfalls when funds actually performed better than their assumed growth rates. However, they are now considered too much of a risk for the typical consumer who is risk-averse and is unwilling to engage in what might be considered a gamble.

- unit trusts (mutual funds)
- investment trusts
- open-ended investment schemes (OEICS).

In a number of countries there may be preferential tax allowances that governments provide in order to incentivize the savings habit. In the UK, the ISA (Individual Savings Account) is just such an arrangement.

These types of savings schemes are largely based upon contributions being made into stock that is traded on the world's stock markets. As such, savers make their contributions on the basis that share prices can fall as well as rise, and thus the schemes carry a degree of risk. For this reason they are not generally suitable for savers who are either highly risk averse or are saving on a fairly short-term timescale. By contributing on a regular monthly basis, savers can mitigate fluctuations in share prices. When share prices fall, a given contribution level buys more units in a fund then when share prices rise. This process is called pound-cost-averaging.

2.7.3   Investing

The present authors consider 'investing' to more properly refer to the process of how to deploy a lump sum for the purposes of capital growth or income generation. By convention, the typical investment vehicles and their underlying assets are specified in Table 2.6.

No discussion of investment would be complete without reference to investment in property. In many countries, residential property equity represents a substantial proportion of domestic assets. In short, residential property equity represents the most significant form of personal financial assets in the UK. This has been a key driver of contemporary saving behaviour, as the evidence shows that individuals are choosing to invest in property in preference to other forms of investment and saving such as pensions and the stock market.

Table 2.6 Investment vehicles and asset classes

Investment vehicle	Underlying asset classes
Deposit account	Cash deposits that pay interest
Direct share holding	Shares from which income is derived in the form of the dividend and rising share values provide for capital growth
Unit trust/mutual fund	A collective investment medium whereby risk is spread through the investment of the lump sum in the shares of a range of stock markets and companies; Assets may also comprise property and cash
Investment trust	Another form of collective investment whereby the bundle of assets are used to create a closed company
Insurance bond	Typically a form of packaged investment comprising equities, usually presented as income bonds or equity growth bonds
Corporate bond	This is a loan that the bond holder makes to the bond issuer; interest is paid periodically at a given rate, known as the coupon; the principal is repaid at a specified time
Government bond	This is a loans made to the government (and sometimes to municipalities) like corporate bonds, interest and principal are paid/repaid according to agreed rates and time
Premium bond	An open-ended non-interest-bearing loan to the government where cash prizes are paid in lieu of interest.

Table 2.7 International life insurance market 1998

	Premium (US$m)	World market share	Premium per capita US$
North America	368032	29.1	1224
Latin America	10693	0.9	21
Europe	402348	31.8	361
Asia	439020	34.7	24
Africa	21668	1.7	27
Oceania	22396	1.8	842
Total	1264156	100	145

2.8 Life insurance

The term *life insurance* is somewhat ambiguous in that it is often used to denote the range of product groups that are supplied by the life insurance industry. As such, it comprises life and health protection and savings products, pensions and collective investment schemes. Table 2.7 shows the international life insurance market (1998) from data supplied by Swiss Reinsurance to the American Council of Life Insurers.

Table 2.7 shows graphically how the global insurance market is dominated by the continents of North America, Asia and Europe. Within those continents, a few countries are of particular significance. According to data supplied by SIGMA, Swiss Re (UK), the top five markets by premium income in 2003 were the USA, Japan, the UK, France and Germany (see Table 2.8).

It is customary for the life insurance market to be segmented according to whether products are provided on an individual or a group basis. Quite simply, the former related to policies priced, provided and paid for at the individual consumer level. The latter refers to pooled arrangements – typically schemes that are provided to an employer and which provide a given level of cover to all members of staff, such as a death-in-service benefit of, say, three-and-a-half times salary.

The major categories of protection products are as follows:

1. Life insurance
   - whole of life
   - level term
   - decreasing term

Table 2.8 Leading life insurance markets

Country	$USbn
USA	480919
Japan	381842
UK	154842
France	105436
Germany	76738

2. Health insurance
   - critical illness
   - sickness and disability (in the UK this is usually referred to as permanent health insurance, or PHI)
   - private medical health insurance (this is usually treated as a form of general insurance)
   - long-term care.

2.8.1   Life insurance

As the name indicates, a *whole-of-life* policy provides for the payment of an agreed sum-assured upon death on an open-ended basis. On the other hand, a *term life* policy provides for the payment of a given sum-assured upon the death of the life-assured within a specified number of years – for example, within a 10-year period in the case of a 10-year term policy. Compared with whole-of-life, term insurance is normally considerably cheaper, and thus provides relatively high levels of cover for comparatively low premiums.

A variant of term insurance is *decreasing term insurance*. This provides for a sum-assured to be paid upon death that gradually reduces as the term progresses. Most commonly, it is used as a form of mortgage protection where the customer is gradually paying off the debt through what is called a capital repayment mortgage.

2.8.2   Health insurance

Critical illness insurance was first devised in South Africa in the 1970s, and pays out an agreed sum-assured upon the diagnosis of a life-endangering illness such as cancer or coronary heart disease. It can be bought as a stand-alone policy or as an added feature to, say, a term insurance policy, as a means of guarding against a range of risks.

Permanent health insurance (PHI) is a form of policy that provides for the replacement of lost income should the policyholder be unable to work as a result of an acute illness or chronic disability. This is particularly important for individuals who are self-employed or do not enjoy generous sickness benefits from their employers. In recent years it has been suggested that the policy has been abused by people who use it as a means of facilitating early retirement.

Private health insurance provides the policyholder with cover in respect of medical costs. The insurer either reimburses the policyholder for costs incurred, or makes direct payment to the medical services provider up to an agreed limit. The nature and extent of private health insurance is closely linked to the state-provided health services of any given country. For example, the scope of private health insurance in the UK is comparatively limited, given the role played by the National Health Service (NHS). In the USA, on the other hand, there is an enormous private medical health insurance sector whereby more than half of all healthcare funding is provided by the private insurance sector, compared with just 15 per cent in the UK. France sits somewhere between the two, with about 28 per cent of healthcare being funded by the private insurance sector.

Long-term care insurance is a form of insurance that pays toward the costs associated with long-term nursing care for the elderly. As with private medical insurance, the extent of demand for this type of insurance is heavily dependent upon the scope and extent of provision made by individual countries' welfare systems. Even within the UK, long-term care costs are state financed in Scotland and Wales but not in England.

2.8.3   Annuities

An annuity is the means by which a lump sum, typically a maturing pension fund, is converted into regular income. Once entered into, it pays a regular monthly income until death. This is an open-ended arrangement which involves the pooling of thousands of customers' funds to arrive at a given level of income. Therefore, consumers (annuitants) bear the risk of losing the bulk of their pension fund if they die soon after retiring as their surplus fund then remains part of the general pool. As might be imagined, this is becoming an increasingly contentious matter as people choose to avoid taking such a risk with their long-term savings.

The level of annuity payable is determined by actuarial calculations, and is a function of variables such as the age at which the annuity commences, gender and health status. Additionally, there are variations such as whether the annuity is level, escalating or indexed.

2.9   General insurance

In simple terms, whereas life insurance provides benefits in the event of human death or illness during a prolonged contract period (possibly for the whole of an individual's life), general insurance provides for the payment of benefits in respect of risks to tangible and intangible non-human assets. The typical range of general insurance risks is as follows:

- motor vehicles
- property
- personal possessions
- liability
- financial loss
- creditor
- marine, aviation and transport
- accident and health.

General insurance is normally based upon annual contracts, whereby the premium is paid in respect of a 12-month period of cover. Thus the cover expires at the end of 12 months, and in order to maintain cover the customer must then either renew the policy for the next 12-month period or seek cover from another supplier.

General insurance tends to be more price-led than life insurance, and is a fiercely competitive marketplace. In the UK it remains a highly diverse sector; there were some 613 companies authorized to transact general insurance in 2004. In Australia, with a population less than one-third of that of the UK, there were some 112 general insurers as at June 2005, according to the Australian regulator APRA.

Motor vehicle insurance has become fiercely competitive, and the introduction of the telephone and Internet as means of transacting business has served to heighten the intensity of competition in this price-driven market.

Box 2.2 outlines one form of insurance that is less well known but is of considerable importance – namely reinsurance. This is relevant to all forms of insurance, both life and general.

Box 2.2 Reinsurance – what is it and how does it work?

Introduction

In simple terms, reinsurance is insurance for the insurance providers. The obvious question is, why should an insurer, whose business is to underwrite risk, wish to insure some of the risks that it has accepted?

When it is pricing the risks that it insures, the insurer will rely on historic claims data and trends in the claims data to derive its best estimate of the future claims experience. It will rely on its underwriters to ensure that the premiums charged for insurance are in line with the risks presented. However, even if the pricing and underwriting processes are properly carried out, this will not guarantee that a portfolio of insurance business will be profitable.

By its very nature, insurance business is unpredictable, and random variations from the pricing basis in either the number of claims or the average claim size (or both) can have a very significant effect on the profitability of the portfolio. Reinsurance can protect an insurer's portfolio from these sources of variability, and hence provide a more stable claims experience.

How does reinsurance work?

A portfolio of insurance business is made up of many policies covering broadly similar risks (in terms of the events covered). If the insured event occurs, the insurer is liable to make a payment to the policyholder and reinsurance does not affect this liability. Reinsurance works by reimbursing part of each claim to the insurer under a reinsurance arrangement (often referred to as a reinsurance treaty). The agreement will specify:

- the group of policies to which the treaty applies
- the rights and obligations of each party under the treaty
- what proportion of each claim is payable by the reinsurer
- how the reinsurance premium is calculated.

Where a treaty is in place and a policy falls within the group of policies covered by the treaty, then the insurer must reinsure the business and the reinsurer is obliged to accept the business.

	Box 2.2 Reinsurance – what is it and how does it work?—cont'd

What types of treaty are there?

Treaties are either proportional or non-proportional.

Under a *proportional treaty*, any claim is shared in the same proportions between insurer and reinsurer. This is often referred to as *quota share reinsurance*. This will damp down (but not eliminate) the effect of the claims frequency being higher than expected, or the average claim amount being higher than expected.

There are three situations where quota share reinsurance is common:

1. Where the insurer is expanding into a new business line and has little or no practical experience of the line. The reinsurer often has knowledge, pricing data and expertise, and can provide technical help to the insurer as well as helping to limit the insurer's risk exposure.

2. Where the insurer wishes to write greater volumes of business to reduce claims volatility and to increase the portfolio of business across which it spreads its fixed costs. However, it may have capital constraints (in the form of solvency requirements imposed by the regulator). By reinsuring part of the risk, the insurer is able to reduce the capital it needs to hold to cover the same volumes of business and hence can write higher volumes of business.

3. Where the reinsurer has a lower cost of capital. This may be because it has surplus capital and is willing to accept a lower return than the insurer, or because it has a regulatory advantage in terms of the amount of capital it needs to hold to cover the same amount of risk as an insurer. The latter often happens, as reinsurers have much larger risk pools than the insurers and hence lower claims volatility. Regulators therefore require reinsurers to hold lower margins against an adverse claims experience than their insurer counterparts.

If the insurer's claims frequency is as predicted, the claims experience can still be poor if the average claim amount is higher than expected. This can arise either because all claims are higher than expected by roughly the same amount, or because there is a disproportionate number of large claims. Non-proportional reinsurance provides effective protection against the effect of a disproportionate number of large claims.

Under a *non-proportional treaty*, the reinsurer reimburses the amount of any claim in excess of a limit defined in the treaty. This limit is known as the insurer's retention, and is usually the same for all policies covered under the treaty. As such the proportion of the total claim that is covered by the reinsurer will vary from claim to claim, and hence the name 'non-proportional'. Non-proportional treaties are often referred to as *surplus* or *excess-of-loss* treaties.

There is often a limit on the amount that the reinsurer will reimburse. Once this limit is reached the insurer may meet the rest of the claim, or there may be additional layers of reinsurance with other reinsurers.

Continued

> **Box 2.2   Reinsurance – what is it and how does it work?—cont'd**
>
> A different type of non-proportional treaty can protect the insurer from the effect of catastrophes. A catastrophe is defined as a single event giving rise to a large number of claims (for example, 9/11 in 2001, the European floods in 2002, Hurricane Katrina in 2005). Under a catastrophe excess-of-loss treaty, the reinsurer will reimburse the insurer once claims arising from a catastrophe reach a certain level (the retention level). Again, there is usually a limit on the amount that the reinsurer will reimburse. Once this limit is reached the insurer may meet the rest of the claims, or there may be additional layers of reinsurance with other reinsurers.
>
> *The reinsurance market*
>
> The global reinsurance market writes in excess of £100 billion in premiums. This covers both life and non-life reinsurance business. The top five global players are Munich Re, Swiss Re, Lloyd's, Hannover Re and Allianz Re. In the UK, the top five non-life reinsurers are Munich Re, Swiss Re, Faraday, Transatlantic and XL Re.
>
> The top five life insurers are Munich Re, Swiss Re, GE Insurance Solutions, XL Re and Revios. The purchase of GE Insurance solutions by Swiss Re, effective in 2006, brings Hannover Re into the top five.
>
> *Source: Will Adler, Head of Marketing, Munich Reinsurance.*

2.10   Summary and conclusions

This chapter has outlined the diverse range of organizations involved in the provision of financial services and provided an introduction to different types of products that these organizations offer. As such, it provides the background against which the marketing of financial services takes place. Financial services are provided by many different organizations, and traditionally, specific organizations such as banks specialized in the provision of specific services (i.e. banking services). Increasingly, across the world, these institutional boundaries have begun to break down, and while organizations continue to be defined by their type (bank, insurance company) they increasingly offer a much broader range of financial services.

The products described as 'financial services' are many and varied, and while this chapter has only provided a brief introduction to how these products work, it should be apparent that they are designed to meet a range of very different financial needs and that many are highly complex. It is perhaps unsurprising, then, that many actual and prospective customers find such products difficult to understand. As will be explained further in Chapter 3, the complexity of the product creates important marketing challenges.

Review questions

1. What is meant by the term gateway product, and to what extent do you believe that the current account performs such a role in your marketplace?
2. In what ways has the business-customer sector benefited from new forms of competitor in the fields of banking and insurance?
3. How has technological innovation impacted upon product supply and services delivery in your country?
4. What incentives does your government give to encourage its citizens to save for their future?

Introduction to financial services marketing

Learning objectives

By the end of this chapter you will be able to:
- identify how and why services in general and financial services in particular are different from goods
- understand the implications of these differences for marketing practice
- understand the way in which services can be classified and the position of different types of financial services within this classification.

3.1 Introduction

Marketing is an approach to business which focuses on improving business performance by satisfying customer needs. As such, it is naturally externally focused. However, marketing cannot just focus on consumers; good marketers must also be aware of and understand the activities of their competitors. To deliver what the customer wants and do so more effectively than the competition also requires an understanding of what the organization itself is good at; the resources and capabilities it possesses and the way in which they can be deployed to satisfy customers. While, in very general terms, marketing processes and activities (such as environmental analysis, strategy and planning, advertising, branding, product development, channel management, etc.) are relevant to all organizations, we should still note that services in general and financial services in particular are rather different from many other physical goods. As a consequence, the focus of attention in the marketing process will be different, as will the implementation of marketing activities. The kind of advertising that works for Coca Cola is probably not right for

Aetna, and the selling strategy used for Ford cars would not work for a Citibank Unit Trust.

The purpose of this chapter is to outline how both services and financial services differ from physical goods, and to explore the implications of these differences for the process of marketing. The chapter begins by defining financial services; it then examines, from a marketing perspective, the differences between goods and services. Building on this discussion, the next section explains the distinctive characteristics of financial services and their marketing implications. As part of the discussion, a number of generic principles are identified which can be used to guide financial services marketing. The chapter concludes with an examination of service typologies, and considers their relevance to financial services.

3.2   Defining financial services

As discussed in Chapter 2, financial services are concerned with individuals, organizations and their finances – that is to say, they are services which are directed specifically at people's intangible assets (i.e. their money/wealth). The term is often used broadly to cover a whole range of banking services, insurance (both life and general), stock trading, asset management, credit cards, foreign exchange, trade finance, venture capital and so on.

These different services are designed to meet a range of different needs, and take many different forms. They usually require a formal (contractual) relationship between provider and consumers, and they typically require a degree of customization (quite limited in the case of a basic bank account, but quite extensive in the case of venture capital).

The marketing issues that arise with such a variety of products are considerable:

- Some financial services may be very short term (e.g. buying and selling stocks), while others are very long term (mortgages, pensions)
- Products vary in terms of complexity; a basic savings account for a personal consumer may appear to be a relatively simple product, whereas the structuring of finance for a leveraged buy-out may be highly complex
- Customers will vary in terms of both their needs and their levels of understanding – corporate customers may have considerable expertise and knowledge in relation to the types of financial services they wish to purchase, while many personal customers may find even the simplest products confusing.

With so much variety and so many different types of financial service, it may appear to be difficult to make general statements about marketing financial services. Indeed, not all marketing challenges are relevant to all types of financial services, and not all solutions will work in every situation. The art of marketing is to be able to understand the challenges that financial services present and to identify creative and sensible approaches which fit to the circumstances of a particular organization, a particular service and a particular customer.

3.3   The differences between goods and services

Financial services are, first and foremost, services, and thus are different from physical goods. Like many things, services are often easy to identify but difficult to define. In one of the earliest marketing discussion of services, Rathmell (1966) makes a simple and rather memorable distinction between goods and services. He suggests that we should recognize that 'a good' is a noun while 'service' is a verb – goods are things while services are acts.

However, perhaps the easiest definition to remember is that proposed by Gummesson (1987):

> Services are something that can be bought and sold but which you cannot drop on your foot.

Fundamentally, services are processes or experiences – you cannot own a bank account, a holiday or a trip to the theatre in the same way as you can own a car, a computer or a bag of groceries (see, for example, Bateson, 1977; Shostack, 1982; Parasuraman *et al.*, 1985; Bowen and Schneider, 1977). Of course, we can all talk about services in a possessive sense (my bank account, my holiday, or my theatre ticket), but we do not actually possess the services concerned; the bank account represents our right to have various financial transactions undertaken on our behalf by the account provider, while the holiday ticket gives us the right to experience some mixture of transportation, accommodation and leisure activities. Thus, despite these apparent signs of ownership, financial services themselves are not possessions in any conventional sense (according to some writers, this absence of ownership rights with respect to a service is one of the key factors which distinguishes physical goods from services). The bank account details and the holiday ticket are, in effect, merely 'certificates of entitlement' to a particular experience or process.

It is equally possible to argue that most physical goods are simply there to provide a service, and that the entertainment provided by a TV or the cleansing provided by washing powder is as much of a process as is using a bank account or going to the theatre. This argument in itself is something that few would disagree with. However, it does not automatically discount the case for treating goods and services as being distinct. Although we can recognize the service element in many (if not all) physical goods, the ownership distinction remains and the process or experience element is much greater in the case of services.

It is the fact that services are predominantly experiences that leads to their most commonly identified characteristic – services are *intangible*. That is to say, they lack physical form and cannot be seen or touched or displayed in advance of purchase. As a consequence, customers only become aware of the true nature of the service once they have made a decision to purchase. Indeed, the service does not exist until a customer wishes to consume a service experience, and this is the next characteristic of services – *inseparability*. Services are produced and consumed simultaneously, and often (but not always) in the presence of the consumer. One particular consequence of this characteristic is that services are *perishable* – they cannot be inventoried. The fact that customers' service needs are different and that service consumption involves interaction between customers and producers also tends to lead to a much greater potential for variability in quality (*heterogeneity*) than is the case with physical goods.

This approach to categorizing the distinctive characteristics of services is sometimes referred to by the acronym IHIP (Intangibility, Heterogeneity, Inseparability, Perishability). Although widely used in services marketing, it has attracted criticism in recent years. For example, Lovelock and Gummesson (2004) argue that the framework has serious weaknesses. Intangibility, they argue, is ambiguous. Many services involve significant tangible elements and significant tangible outcomes. Heterogeneity (variability) is seen to be less effective at distinguishing goods from services because variability persists in many physical goods and is being reduced in many services as a consequence of greater standardization in systems and processes. Inseparability, though important, is not thought to be able to differentiate goods from services, as an increasing number of services can be produced remotely and thus are in fact separable. Similarly, it is argued that some services are not perishable and some goods are. Thus, Lovelock and Gummesson suggest that the IHIP simply does not adequately distinguish between goods and services. They argue instead for a focus on ownership (or lack of it) and the idea that services involve different forms of rental (rental of physical goods, of place and space, of expertise, of facilities or of networks). Vargo and Lusch (2004) are similarly critical, and also highlight the inability of IHIP to distinguish between goods and services.

While recognizing that the IHIP framework is open to criticism, it is probably the dominant paradigm in services marketing and, provided that it is used sensibly, it remains a useful framework for understanding the differences between goods and services. Each of the IHIP characteristics will be explored in greater detail in the following sections in relation to financial services, but at this point it is important to emphasize that it could be misleading simply to view services and physical goods as complete opposites. While seeking to maintain a distinction between the two types of product, many services marketers recognize the existence of a goods–services continuum with highly intangible services (such as financial advice, education or consultancy services) at one extreme and highly tangible goods (such as coffee, sports shoes or kitchen utensils) at the other extreme. Then, towards the centre of this continuum there are many goods which are similar to services (such as cars) and many services which are similar to goods (such as fast food). Grönroos (1978), however, is rather critical of this notion because it has the potential to distract from the idea that fundamental differences do exist between goods and services. He suggests maintaining a much sharper distinction to enable academics and practitioners to recognize the need for rather different marketing approaches. As Box 3.1 shows, this idea has been recognized for almost as long as we have acknowledged the existence of services marketing.

3.4 The distinctive characteristics of financial services

The discussion above briefly outlined some of the areas in which services are different from physical goods and introduced some of the basic features of financial services. This section explores the characteristics of services in more depth and considers

Box 3.1   G Lynn Shostack - 'Breaking free from product marketing'

Lynn Shostack's paper in the *Journal of Marketing* in 1977 is one of the formative articles in the development of services marketing. Shostack starts by noting the problems experienced by practising marketers who have switched from product to services marketing. Academic marketing appeared to have no readily available frameworks which could guide marketing practice in these environments. Shostack's response is to emphasize the importance of intangibility, not just as a modifier but as a fundamental characteristic of services – she notes that no amount of physical evidence (however provided) can make something as fundamentally intangible as entertainment or advice into something tangible. A service is an experience rather than a possession.

Of course, physical goods do provide a service, but the distinction between the two is illustrated with the example of cars and airlines. Both provide a transport service, but the former is fundamentally tangible but with an intangible dimension, while the latter is intangible but with tangible dimensions. The car provides transport but is also something that the customer can own; the airline also provides transport but without any ownership element.

Thus, Shostack argues that we should view goods and services as existing on a continuum from intangible dominant to tangible dominant. She supports this framework with a molecular model of products which comprises a core or nucleus and several external layers. The nucleus represents the core benefits provided to the consumer, while the layers deal with the way in which the product is made available to the consumer – including price, distribution and market positioning via marketing communications. The nucleus for air travel is predominantly intangible, while that for the car is predominantly tangible.

Finally, Shostack considers the marketing implications of her analysis. She suggests that the abstract nature of services requires the marketing processes to emphasize concrete, non-abstract images or representations of the service to provide consumers with a tangible representation of the service which will make sense to them. By contrast, because consumers can see, picture and feel physical goods, such tangible images are far less important and marketing programmes can therefore concentrate much more on abstract ideas and images to attract consumers' attention.

Source: Shostack, G. L. *(1977).* Breaking free from product marketing.
Journal of Marketing, 47, 73–80

specifically their implications in the context of financial services. In what follows, intangibility is considered as the dominant service characteristic; intangibility then leads to inseparability and this in turns results in perishability and variability (heterogeneity). Finally, three further characteristics are introduced which relate specifically to financial services – fiduciary responsibility, duration of consumption and contingent consumption – and their marketing implications are discussed.

3.4.1   Intangibility

Since services are processes or experiences, intangibility is generally cited as the key feature that distinguishes services from goods. In practice, this means that services are impalpable – they lack a substantive physical form and so cannot be seen, touched, displayed, felt or tried in advance of purchase. A customer may purchase a particular service, such as a savings account, but typically has nothing physical to display as a result of the purchase. In some cases, services may also be characterized by what Bateson (1977) and others have described as 'mental intangibility' – i.e. they are complex and difficult to understand.

From the customer perspective, these characteristics have important implications. Physical intangibility (impalpability) and mental intangibility (complexity) mean that services are characterized by a predominance of experience and credence qualities, phrases used to describe attributes which can either only be evaluated once they have been experienced or even when experienced cannot be evaluated. Physical goods, by contrast, are characterized by a predominance of search qualities, which are attributes that can be evaluated in advance of purchase. Thus, the potential purchaser of a car may take a test drive, the buyer of a TV can examine the quality of the picture, and a clothes shopper can check fit and style before buying.

In comparison, the service offered by a financial adviser can only really be evaluated once the advice has been experienced, leaving customers with the problem that they do not really know what they're going to get when they make the purchase decision. Even more difficult from the consumers' perspective is not being able to evaluate the quality of the service. The technical complexity of many services may hinder consumer evaluation of what has been received; a lack of specialist knowledge means that many consumers cannot evaluate the quality of the financial advice they have received, and only the most fanatical investment enthusiast would really be able to determine whether a fund manager has made the best investment decisions in a particular market.

Of course, it is possible to argue that, ultimately, a consumer can evaluate financial advisers or investment managers based on the performance of a portfolio or a particular product. However, inadequacies in either service may take time to come to light, and even when a particular outcome occurs – for example, the value of a portfolio of assets falls – how certain can the consumer be that this failure was due to poor advice or to unforseeable market problems? In contrast, with relatively complex products such as a PDA or a TV there are visible manifestations of the quality of the product (information stored and retrieved by the PDA, pictures displayed on the TV screen), giving the consumer something tangible to evaluate and potentially a clearer idea of the relationship between cause and effect – a poor-quality picture is most likely to represent a problem with the performance of the TV set.

Overall, the predominance of experience and credence qualities means that financial services consumers are much less sure of what they are likely to receive and, consequently, rather more likely to experience a significant degree of perceived risk when making a purchase decision. Thus, financial services marketing must pay particular attention to ways in which the buying process can be facilitated. The following issues may be particularly important:

1. Providing physical evidence or some physical representation of the product. Physical evidence *per se* may take the form of items directly associated with

a service (e.g. the policy documentation that accompanies an insurance policy) or the environment in which the service is delivered (e.g. the rather grand premises in prime locations occupied by banks). An alternative or even a complement to actual physical evidence is to create a tangible image such as *'Citibank – where money lives'*, or to offer physical gifts to prospective consumers.

2. Placing particular emphasis on the benefits of the service – customers do not want a mortgage as such, but they do want to own a house; they do not want a savings account, but they do want to be able to pay for their child's education. Thus, for example, the Malaysian bank, Maybank, promotes its Platinum Visa card with an illustration of a Korean vase bought using the card. Similarly, in Hong Kong, HSBC promotes its PowerVantage banking service as *'Helping you build better returns on your life ... on your money ... on your time ... on your opportunities'*.

3. Reducing perceived risk and making consumers feel less uncertain about the outcome of their purchase, perhaps by encouraging other customers to act as advocates for the service, by seeking appropriate endorsements or even by offering service guarantees. For example, the State Bank of India Mutual Fund reassures prospective customers by drawing attention to its links with the State Bank of India – *'India's premier and largest bank'*. In the US, US Bank promotes itself with the slogan *'Other Banks Promise Great Service, US Bank Guarantees It'*.

4. Building trust and confidence to reassure consumers that what they receive will be of the appropriate quality. Many financial services organizations make particular efforts to emphasize their longevity – the fact that they have been in business for, in some cases, hundreds of years serves as a mechanism for signalling their reliability and trustworthiness. In the US, Bank of America's private banking arm emphasizes its longevity as a means of building confidence – *'For more than 150 years, The Private Bank has been the advisor of choice for the affluent'*. Others, such as HSBC and Axa Insurance, emphasize their worldwide coverage and the size of the organization in order to reassure customers that their money and business will be safe and secure.

3.4.2   Inseparability

The nature of services as a process or experience means that services are inseparable – they are produced and consumed simultaneously. As Zeithaml and Bitner (2003: 20) put it:

> Whereas most goods are produced first, then sold and consumed, most services are sold first and then produced and consumed simultaneously.

A service can only be provided if there is a customer willing to purchase and experience it. Thus, for example, financial advice *per se* can only be provided once a specific request has been made; until that request is made, the advice does not exist – there is only the potential for that advice embodied in the mind of the adviser. The provision of a service will typically also require the involvement of the consumer to a greater degree than would be the case with physical goods. As few services are totally standardized, the minimum input from the consumer would be information on needs and wants. For example, an investment adviser would, as a minimum, need to know an individual's attitude to risk, and whether that individual wants to invest for capital growth or income, before advice could be given. In many instances, the input from the customer will need to be more extensive. Because the customer actively engages and interacts with the provider, services are often described as interactive processes. While this interaction has traditionally been face-to-face, developments in telephone and information technology mean that an increasing amount of customer provider interaction is taking place remotely.

As a consequence of the interactive nature of services, the way in which the service is performed may be as significant to customers as the actual service itself. A financial services provider's staff may be of particular importance in this process. As the group with whom the customer has greatest involvement, the staff can and do play a decisive role in customer evaluations of the service experience.

From a marketing perspective, then, inseparability presents some interesting challenges. Given the interactive and inseparable nature of service provision, the following issues will be of particular significance:

1. Ensuring that the processes of service delivery are clearly specified and customer orientated – in effect, the service should be designed to suit the customer rather than to suit the organization. For example, many banks might find it preferable to have product specialists – i.e. staff who focus attention only on specific products – but a customer with multiple services from a particular company will much prefer to deal with a single individual. Westpac Banking Corporation in New Zealand stresses to its business customers that it offers 'One number for all your banking needs'. United Overseas Bank of Malaysia promotes its 'Privilege' banking service, emphasizing that 'you need to only deal with one person'.
2. Ensuring that all staff involved in service provision appreciate the importance of a customer-orientated approach and are empowered to be responsive and flexible in customer interactions. Pacific Crest Savings Bank in the US reassures its customers that 'Premier customer service is delivered by a staff empowered to make decisions. The Pacific Crest service guarantees ensure that customers receive the high level of service they are promised.'
3. Identifying methods of facilitating customer involvement in a way which will enhance the quality of the service provided. This may be as simple as making clear exactly what information is required from the customer, or may extend to outlining and explaining the responsibilities of the customer. Most financial services providers have terms of use which outline customer responsibilities, although often these are presented in the style of legal documents, which may limit the extent to which customers really understand their responsibilities.

3.4.3   Perishability

The fact that services are produced and consumed simultaneously also means that they are perishable. Services can only be produced when consumers wish to buy them, and when there is little or no demand the service producers cannot 'manufacture' surplus services for sale when demand is high. Thus services are perishable and cannot be inventoried. If an investment adviser's time is not taken up on one particular day, it cannot be saved to provide extra capacity the next day. If the counter staff in a bank have a quiet period with no customers, they cannot 'save' that time to use when queues build up.

This characteristic of perishability presents marketing with the task of managing demand and supply in order to make best use of available capacity. Issues that require particular consideration include:

1. Assessing whether there are identifiable peaks and troughs in consumer demand for a particular financial service. Bank branches, for example, may be particularly busy during lunch breaks, while tax advisers may experience a peak in the demand for their services as the end of a tax year approaches.
2. Offering mechanisms for reducing demand at peak times and increasing it at off peak times. Tax advisers, for example, might consider offering discounted fees for customers who use their services well in advance of tax deadlines.
3. Assessing whether there is the opportunity to adjust capacity such that variability in demand can be accommodated (either through changing work patterns or some degree of mechanization). Many banks employ part-time staff to boost capacity during periods of heavy customer demand, and ATMs provide many standard banking services quickly as an alternative to queuing for face-to-face service.

3.4.4 Heterogeneity

The inseparability of production and consumption leads to a fourth distinctive characteristic of services: variability or heterogeneity.

Service variability can be interpreted in two ways. The first interpretation is that services are not standardized – different customers will want and will experience a different service. This source of variability essentially arises from the fact that customers are different and have different needs. To varying degrees, services will be tailored to those needs, whether in very simple terms (such as the amount a consumer chooses to invest in a savings plan) or in very complex ways (such as the advice provided by accountants, consultants and bankers to a firm undertaking a major acquisition).

The second interpretation of variability is that the service experienced may vary from customer to customer (even given essentially similar needs), or may vary from time to time for a particular customer. In effect, this type of variability arises not because of changing customer needs; it is primarily a consequence of the nature of an interaction between customer and service provider, but may be influenced by events outside the control of the service provider.

The first source of variability is easily understandable as a response to differences in customer needs. The obvious implications for marketing are as follows:

1. Service processes need to be flexible enough to adapt to different needs, and the more varied are customer needs and the higher customer expectations, the greater the need for flexibility. Thus, for example, business banking for small and medium-sized enterprises will need to accommodate the needs of the long-established small, local shop and of the fast-growing biotechnology company which

primarily sells in international markets. Equally, brokers may need to be able to adapt their service to the person who buys and sells stock infrequently on a small scale and the enthusiast who tracks the market and trades frequently and/or in volume.

2. It is becoming increasingly important that staff are empowered to respond to different needs and situations, so that processes can be adapted as and when necessary. Typically, this implies decentralizing service systems and delegating authority such that non-contentious modifications to a service can be dealt with by customer-contact staff. Thus, for example, a bank may delegate a range of lending powers to account managers such that every requested change in the normal terms of a loan to a small business does not always require head office approval.

The second form of variability provides more problems as it represents fluctuations in the level of quality that the consumer receives, rather than variations in the type of service. Essentially, this form of heterogeneity arises as a consequence of inseparability and the importance of personal interaction, but may also be influenced by external events. Customers are different and so are service providers; customer contact staff are people rather than machines, and will experience the same range of moods and emotions as everyone else. Differences arise between individuals (from one employee to another) and within individuals (from one day to another). The service provided by an account manager who is feeling happy, relaxed and positive at the start of a new week will almost certainly be better than that provided by the same account manager at the end of a long day, suffering from a headache and feeling undervalued.

From the consumer side, quality variability within and between service experiences may also arise if customers are not able to articulate their needs clearly. The greater the willingness of customers to supply appropriate information about their needs and circumstances, the more likely it is that they will receive the quality service they expect. Customers who are able to explain clearly their risk preferences, the purpose of their investment and the characteristics of the rest of their portfolio are likely to get better advice than customers who simply request advice on an investment that will give a 'decent return'.

In addition to the impact of personal factors on quality, it is important also to recognize that there are many factors which are outside the control of a service provider but which may have a significant effect on the overall service experience and the quality of the service product. The performance of an investment fund, for example, may be influenced by broad macro-economic forces which fund managers cannot change. The major fall in stock markets during the early 2000s had a significant negative impact on the performance of many personal pensions and equity-based investment products, but was outside the immediate control of the institutions which supplied these products (although many UK-based financial services providers were criticized following these events for having raised customer expectations by assuming continued rapid growth in stock markets).

Thus, both personal interactions and uncontrollable external factors can result is consumers feeling that they have experienced considerable variability in the service and in some case, an unsatisfactory experience. To address this aspect of variability, service marketers may need to pay particular attention to the following issues:

1. Motivating and rewarding staff for the provision of good service and encouraging consistency in approach. Internal marketing campaigns to emphasize the

importance of good customer service may be one aspect of this – equally important may be the way in which staff are treated and rewarded. A reward mechanism based simply on the number of calls taken by a customer service agent for a telephone banking service may create an incentive for the service agent to close calls as quickly as possible (to maximize throughput) rather than properly addressing the customer's needs (which would take longer and mean a lower call throughput).

2. Identifying ways of trying to persuade customers to articulate their needs as clearly as possible, whether by identifying scripts for use by the service provider or through marketing communications which specifically ask customers to share information. The growth in on-line provision of services and on-line quotations has helped this process by structuring and clarifying the types of information that customers need to provide – at least for some of the more straightforward financial services such as insurance quotations and standard loans.

3. If a service is relatively simple from the consumer perspective, considering mechanization to limit quality variability. ATMs and self-service banking over the Internet are one example of this process of mechanization. Automated telephone banking is another.

4. Considering carefully how a service is presented to customers; being explicit about the factors which can affect the performance of a product. Most equity-based products do highlight to customers that the value of investments can go down as well as up, but often such warnings are presented in small print and it is debatable whether customers read or understand these warnings. It is common to see companies relying on past performance figures as a way of signalling the quality of their product, despite the fact that these are largely unreliable as indicators of future performance. Furthermore, research has suggested that the way in which such past performance information is presented may have a significant impact on risk perceptions and consumer choice (Diacon, 2006).

3.4.5 Fiduciary responsibility

Fiduciary responsibility refers to the implicit responsibility which financial services providers have in relation to the management of funds and the financial advice they supply to their customers. Although any business has a responsibility to its consumers in terms of the quality, reliability and safety of the products it supplies, this responsibility is perhaps much greater in the case of a financial service provider. There are probably two explanations for this.

First, many consumers find financial services difficult to comprehend. Understanding financial services requires a degree of numeracy, conceptual thinking and interest. Many consumers are either unable or unwilling to try to understand financial services. For example, a recent study undertaken on behalf of the FSA in the UK (Atkinson *et al.*, 2006) reported that, in total, 20 per cent of respondents did not understand the relationship between inflation and interest rates, with the lack of understanding being much greater among younger and lower-income consumers. Some customers rely on a professional – whether a bank, an investment company, an insurer or a financial adviser – to provide them with appropriate financial services; others rely upon the advice they receive from members of their reference group, such as family members, friends and work colleagues.

Secondly, the 'raw materials' used to produce many financial products are consumers' funds; thus, in producing and selling a loan product, the bank has a responsibility to the person taking out a loan but at the same time also has a responsibility to the individuals whose deposits have made that loan possible. Similarly, insurance is based on pooling risk across policyholders. When taking risks (selling insurance) and paying against claims, an insurer has a responsibility to both the individual concerned and to all other policyholders.

Thus, rather than just having to consider responsibility to the purchaser, many financial services organizations must also be aware of their responsibility to their suppliers – indeed, it is conceivable that the needs of suppliers may take precedence over the demands of a customer. For example, because of its responsibilities to its existing car-insurance customers, an insurer may feel that it cannot respond to a demand from a customer considered to be high risk. Similarly, a bank may decide not to offer credit to a borrower if it is concerned that the granting of a loan simply allows that borrower to build up an even greater volume of debt. Indeed, a failure fully to appreciate this responsibility has led to heavy criticism of credit card companies in the UK for providing credit cards to individuals who have little prospect of repaying their debt.

From a marketing perspective, this presents the rather unusual problem of customers wishing to purchase a particular product (e.g. a loan, insurance, credit card, etc.) and the organization turning them away and refusing to supply that product because they are considered too risky.

To recognize the issue of fiduciary responsibility, it is important to consider the following issues:

1. The process of segmentation, targeting and positioning should be assessed to ensure that products are not targeted at customers who are unlikely to be eligible. Careful market targeting can help prospective customers to judge whether the product is appropriate for them. If market segmentation is clear, this can be a relatively straightforward process – for example, the motor insurer 'Sheilas' Wheels' makes it very clear that it is an insurance company targeting female drivers (see Figure 3.1). If segmentation is more complex, then targeting the right group can be more challenging.
2. Staff involved in selling financial services to customers must be clearly aware of their responsibilities not to sell products that are inappropriate to the customer's needs. Probably one of the most damaging experiences for the financial services sector in the UK was the extensive mis-selling of personal pensions to people who could not afford them or did not need them. When the scandal came to light, it cost the industry billions of pounds in compensation and probably more in loss of reputation.

3.4.6   Contingent consumption

It is in the nature of many financial services products that money spent on them does not yield a direct consumption benefit. In some cases it may create consumption opportunities in the future; in other cases it may never result in tangible consumption for the individual who made the purchase. Saving money from current income reduces present consumption by the same amount, and for many

Figure 3.1 Car insurer 'Sheilas' Wheels' makes the nature of its target market very clear.

people present consumption is far more enjoyable than saving. For some individuals, the level of contributions required to build up a reasonable pension fund at retirement requires just too much foregone pleasurable consumption to provide the necessary motivation.

In the case of general insurance, most customers would not wish to consume many aspects of the service – they would hope never to have to make a claim against a given policy. Similarly, in the case of life insurance, consumers will never be the recipient of the financial benefits of the contract, given that their payment will only occur upon their death. Of course, in both cases consumers buy more than just the ability to make a claim against the insured event; they buy peace of mind and protection. However, these latter two benefits are particularly intangible, and consumers may still be left questioning the benefits that they receive compared to the prices they pay.

Such contingent consumption presents major challenges to marketing executives as they seek to market an intangible product that reduces current consumption of consumer goods and services for benefits that may never be experienced. To address the issue of contingent consumption, the following may be helpful:

1. The benefits associated with the product must be clearly communicated and in as tangible a form as possible. Marketing strategies for long-term savings plans (including pensions) might seek to demonstrate the significant benefits and pleasure associated with future consumption while also demonstrating that losses in current consumption are minimal. Similarly, insurance providers seek to convince

policyholders that they receive the benefit of peace-of-mind from having been prudent enough to safeguard the financial well-being of their dependents or their assets.
2. Issues relating to product design which might increase the attractiveness of products designed for the longer term should be considered. For example, some flexibility in payments, the ability temporarily to suspend payments or even the ability to make short-term withdrawals may help to reduce consumers' concerns about their ability to save on a regular basis.

3.4.7   Duration of consumption

The majority of financial services are (or have the potential to be) long term, either because they entail a continuing relationship with a customer (current accounts, mortgages, credit cards) or because there is a time lag before the benefits are realized (long-term savings and investments). In almost all cases this relationship is contractual, which provides the organization with information about customers and can create the opportunity to build bonds with them that will discourage switching between providers. The long-term relationship between customer and provider creates considerable potential for cross-selling, reinforced by the amount of information that providers have about their customers. However, for such a relationship to be beneficial and for cross-selling opportunities to work, the organization has to work at the relationship – simply ignoring customers for several years and then expecting them to make further purchases is unlikely to be effective.

From a marketing perspective, this suggests that the following areas will require particular attention:

1. Manage relationships carefully. If the product is long term, then regular contact between organization and customer can help to maintain a positive relationship. If the product is one that is continuous (e.g. a mortgage), regular communication is probably an integral feature of the product but should still be managed carefully to ensure that forms of customer contact are appropriate. In both cases there may be opportunities for cross-selling, but bombarding customers with lots of different products may be far less effective than carefully targeting a smaller number of offers.
2. Be prepared to reward loyalty, where appropriate. Valued customers that the organization wishes to retain should be treated as such.
3. Respect customer privacy and ensure that data that are collected relating to customers are managed appropriately.

3.5   The marketing challenge

In the discussion above, we have identified a range of marketing challenges which confront services marketers. Perhaps one of the most commonly recurring themes in this discussion has been the importance of people and the ways in which the service delivery process is managed. In contrast with a discussion of physical goods, we have placed much less emphasis on the conventional forms of marketing which involve communications (in their broadest sense) from the organization to the customer. That is not to imply that the more traditional forms of marketing are not relevant; they most certainly are, but there are other dimensions of marketing that are equally important to services marketing. These are neatly summed up by Philip Kotler in his services marketing triangle, shown in Figure 3.2 (Kotler, 1994). Service marketing requires external marketing (from the organization to the customer) to present the nature and attributes of the service offer. It also requires internal marketing to ensure that staff have the motivation and information to deliver the service offered. Of course, interactive marketing between customer and employee also takes place during every service interaction; in many respects, any service organization employees who come into contact with a customer will find themselves in a marketing role. The intrinsic quality of the core service is important, but so is the way in which a service is delivered, and the nature of the service interaction may have a significant impact on the customer's evaluation of the overall experience.

3.6   Classifying services

From the discussion so far, it should be clear that there are a number of important differences between physical goods and services. However, as was emphasized earlier, these differences appear to exist not so much as absolute differences but

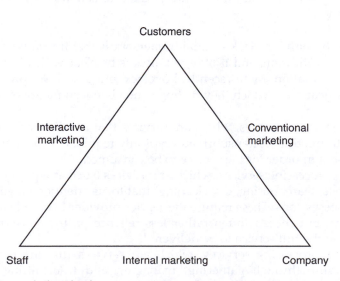

Figure 3.2 Services marketing triangle.

rather as points on a continuum. Even in that part of the continuum which we would classify as services, there is considerable variety among different types of services. In so far as we have argued that many marketing activities are context-specific, it would be misleading not to discuss some aspects of these variations. After all, services with different sets of characteristics will present different types of marketing problems.

Recognizing this issue has encouraged many service marketers to search for systematic approaches to classification in order to provide further guidance on the conduct of marketing. Indeed, this process dates back to the early days of services marketing. The resulting classification schemes are many and varied, and make distinctions such as:

- professional services versus other services
- individual customers versus organizational customers
- people-based versus equipment-based services
- high or low customer-contact services
- public sector or private sector/profit v. non-profit.

Probably one of the most comprehensive attempts to categorize and classify services was provided by Lovelock (1983). He produced five different classification schemes:

1. The nature of the service act (whether it involves tangible or intangible actions) and the recipient of the service (people versus things)
2. The nature of the relationship with the service provider (formal or informal) and whether the service is delivered continuously or on discrete basis
3. The degree of standardization or customization in the core service and the extent to which staff exercise personal judgement in service delivery
4. The capacity to meet demand (with/without difficulty) and the degree to which demand fluctuates
5. The number of outlets and the nature of the interaction between customer and service provider.

The difficulty with Lovelock's initial framework is that it results in five different systems for classification, and it may not always be clear which is the best to use for any given situation. More recently, Lovelock and Yip (1996) produced a much simpler classification in which they distinguished between the following:

1. People processing services, which are services that are directed towards people (e.g. healthcare, fitness, transport) and typically require the consumer to be physically present in order for the service to be consumed.
2. Possession processing services, which are services (such as equipment repair and maintenance, warehousing, dry cleaning) that focus attention on adding value to people's possessions. These require the service provider to be able to access those possessions, but there is often rather less reliance on the consumers' physical presence for the full service to be delivered.
3. Information processing services, which are services that are concerned with creating value through gathering, managing and transmitting information. Obvious examples include the media industry, telecommunications, consulting and

most financial services. Although inseparability may be important in some applications (e.g. consultancy, financial services), there is much greater potential for remote delivery because there is a reduced dependence on physical interactions.

Financial services are essentially directed towards individuals' assets, and so in that sense they may be partly possession processing services; some financial services may also be directed to people (tax advice, financial advice). Most financial services have the potential to be considered as information-based in the sense that they can effectively be represented as information and delivered remotely. For example, an individual can withdraw money from a bank account in Germany using an ATM in Australia because information can be conveyed to the Australian bank that there are sufficient funds available to allow the cash withdrawal to be made via the Australian bank's system, which is then credited with the appropriate sum by the German bank. As we shall see in Chapter 6, the idea that many financial services are essentially information processing services can have important implications for the ways in which services businesses internationalize.

3.7 Summary and conclusions

Any product, whether it is a physical good, a service or some combination of the two, exists to provide some mix of functional and psychological benefits to consumers. Through providing benefits to consumers and delivering long-term satisfaction, such products should enable organizations to achieve their stated goals. In that sense, services and physical goods have much in common. They also display some very important differences, and those differences have significant marketing implications. Services are processes, deeds or acts – they are not something that the consumer possesses, rather they are something that the consumer experiences. In essence, services are intangible – they lack any physical form. As a consequence they are also inseparable, being produced and consumed simultaneously, with the customer involved in the production or delivery of the service. Inseparability in turn leads to perishability and quality variability.

As a consequence of these characteristics, services marketing must pay particular attention to tangibilizing the services and reducing consumer perceived risk. Furthermore, the process of service delivery also attracts marketing attention because the involvement of the consumer in the process suggests that the nature of delivery may have a significant impact on consumer evaluation of the service. Finally, within that process the 'people' element may be of considerable significance, because it is typically the service provider's staff with whom the customer interacts. The rather different elements of marketing in a service business are neatly summed up by Philip Kotler, who stresses a need for not only external marketing but also internal marketing and interactive marketing.

Inevitably, not all services are the same, and the degrees of intangibility, inseparability, perishability and heterogeneity will vary considerably. In fact, most service marketers would probably recognize goods and services as existing along a continuum rather than as polar extremes. Many attempts have been made to classify services according to the characteristics they possess and their marketing implications.

While such schemes are necessarily crude, they do provide useful insights into both current marketing challenges and areas for new service development.

Review questions

1. Choose a financial services provider and look at examples of how it markets its services. How does this provider seek to address the issues of intangibility, inseparability, perishability and heterogeneity?
2. What are the differences between external marketing, internal marketing and interactive marketing?
3. Look at the way in which three insurance companies market life insurance products. How effective are these insurers in conveying the benefits of risk reduction and peace of mind?
4. Look at the way in which three pension providers market personal pensions. How effectively do these marketing campaigns deal with the fact that pensions are long-term products characterized by considerable potential uncertainty?

4

Analysing the marketing environment

	Learning objectives

By the end of this chapter you will be able to:
- understand the key elements of the marketing environment and evaluate their impact on financial services providers
- analyse key elements in the macro, market and internal environments
- understand the process of SWOT analysis and its role in making sense of information about the marketing environment.

4.1 Introduction

In Chapter 3, marketing was described as being concerned with satisfying customer needs, trying to do so more effectively than the competition, and making appropriate use of the organization's own resources and capabilities in this process. Accordingly, one of the first stages in any marketing process is to understand the environment in which an organization operates. Indeed, the concept of being 'market orientated', originally championed by Kohli and Jaworski (1990) and Narver and Slater (1990), has at its heart the ideas of gathering, sharing and responding to information relating to both customers and competitors. Like many other organizations, providers of financial services operate in a rapidly changing environment. Globalization and developments in information and communications technology (ICT) combined with changes in customer needs and government policies create increasing degrees of complexity and uncertainty. Marketing forces organizations to look outside and to develop an awareness and understanding of the environment in which they operate. An organization that understands and responds to its operating environment should be able to deliver superior performance through its ability to satisfy customers more effectively than the competition and to anticipate changes and developments in its key markets. However, an analysis of the external environment must be accompanied by a good understanding of the internal environment to enable an organization to deploy its resources and capabilities most effectively in meeting the challenges posed by the changing marketplace.

Historically, the financial services sector had always been thought of as very stable. Heavily regulated, the marketplace did change, but slowly and predictably; competition was limited and the types of financial services required by, and offered to, customers were relatively simple. In such an environment marketing was largely a tactical activity, concerned with determining how best to advertise and sell the existing set of services. Indeed, in many cases financial services organizations had Advertising and Sales Departments rather than Marketing Departments. As the pace of change accelerated and uncertainty increased, the marketing function had to take a more active role in understanding the changing environment and identifying implications for the products and services offered by its particular organization.

This chapter will introduce the key elements of environmental analysis that are relevant to financial services providers. The term 'marketing environment' is used to describe the range of external and internal factors that affect the way in which an organization interacts with its markets. As such it is very broad, and any analysis of the environment will generate a large volume of information. Thus, effective environmental analysis must be able to distinguish the more important factors from the less important ones. That is to say, analysing the environment involves first of all identifying and understanding what is happening, and then assessing which developments are most important to the organization concerned.

The chapter will begin by defining the elements that comprise the marketing environment. Subsequent sections will review the process of analysing the external environment (both at a macro- and a market level) and then explore the analysis of the internal environment, focusing particularly on resources and capabilities. Finally, the nature of SWOT analysis will be explained as a method for summarizing information about the marketing environment and identifying options for future strategy. By its very nature, the process of analysing the environment and attempting to anticipate how a market will develop in the future is not a one-off but, rather, a continuous process. The nature of the operating environment and the ways in which it changes is one of the main sources of uncertainty confronting marketing planners. Environmental analysis cannot remove this uncertainty, but it can help to reduce it.

4.2 The marketing environment

There are several components in the overall marketing environment. At the simplest level, we can distinguish between the internal environment (conditions within the organization) and the external environment (conditions outside the organization).

The external environment can then be divided into the macro-environment and the market environment. The macro-environment is concerned with broad general trends in the economy and society that can affect all organizations, whatever their line of business. The market environment describes those factors that are specific to the particular market in which the organization operates. The external environment may create opportunities for the organization to exploit, or may pose threats to current or planned activities. An outline of the key elements of the marketing environment is presented in Figure 4.1.

Marketing as a strategic activity is concerned with managing the relationship between the organization and its environment. This may mean adjusting and adapting the organization's marketing activities to respond to external changes in the environment. It may also mean trying to change the environment to make it better suited to what the organization wishes to do. That is to say, the environment should not be viewed simply as a constraint; rather, it should be viewed as something which can, if necessary, be influenced and changed by an organization. Lobbying for changes to the regulatory framework is one very obvious example of an attempt to change the external environment. Equally, mergers and acquisitions serve as a means of altering patterns of competition and changing the resources and capabilities available to a particular organization. Some forms of marketing communications may be employed to influence customer needs and expectations, while branding decisions and distribution strategies can sometimes be used to build barriers to market entry by potential competitors. The extent to which aspects of the environment can be managed varies. Typically, macro-environmental factors are seen as being least controllable, while market environmental factors are most controllable.

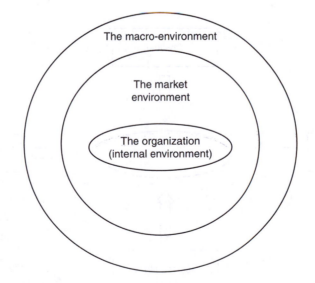

Figure 4.1 The marketing environment.

4.3 The macro-environment

The macro-environment is concerned with broad general trends within the economy and society. The macro-environment is typically of much greater relevance when considering the development of broad strategies, while the market environment is much more important when considering the development of specific business/product strategies. Traditionally, the analysis of the macro-environment was referred to as PEST or STEP analysis, where:

- PEST = Political, Economic, Social, Technological
- STEP = Social, Technological, Economic, Political.

More recently, these acronyms have been extended to include, for example:

- STEEP = Social, Technological, Economic, Environmental, Political
- SLEPT = Social, Legal, Economic, Political, Technological
- PESTLE = Political, Economic, Social, Technological, Legal, Environmental.

These different acronyms simply serve as an easy way of remembering which factors to cover. What is most important is that any analysis of the macro-environment is comprehensive and includes all the factors likely to affect an organization. The following discussion is structured around the PEST framework, for simplicity. This framework is shown in Figure 4.2 and discussed in more detail below.

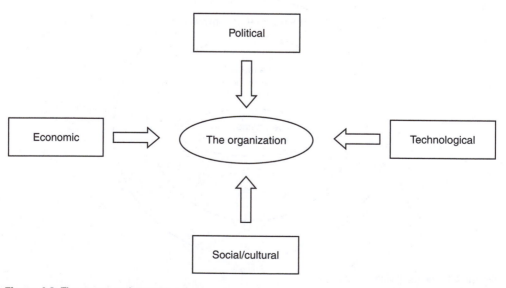

Figure 4.2 The macro-environment.

4.3.1   The political environment

The term 'political environment' is used to cover a range of issues, including party politics, the political character of the government itself, and also the legal and regulatory system. The financial services sector is, perhaps, one of the more politically sensitive sectors of any economy because of its role in the economic development and economic well-being of a country (explained in Chapter 1). The risks, complexities and importance associated with financial services also mean that it is one of the most heavily regulated sectors of an economy.

The political character of a government, and the potential for change, can have important implications for business both nationally and internationally. Some political parties may be more favourable to the business community than others, and this attitude is often reflected in legislation and regulation. The importance of government macro-economic policies is mentioned later, but there is a wide range of government activities that affect the financial sector, including sector-specific policy formulation, legislation, decisions on government spending, and partial privatization. For example, the policy of privatizing a range of previously state-owned industries in the UK during the 1980s is widely credited with having changed public attitudes to share ownership and created demand for small-scale share-dealing services.

Two aspects of the political environment, defined in its broadest sense, are of particular relevance to financial services – namely, industry regulation and consumer protection. Regulation generally refers to a set of rules and legal requirements that guide the operation of the industry and the conduct of firms within the industry. As such, it is specific to financial services. *Financial regulation* is typically concerned with licensing providers, guiding the conduct of business, enforcing relevant laws, protecting customers, and preventing fraud and misconduct. *Consumer protection* refers to a regulatory system which focuses specifically on the rights and interests of consumers in their interactions with businesses and other entities. Typically, consumer protection legislation applies across all sectors of the economy and, consequently, there will be some overlap between industry-specific regulation and economy-wide consumer protection systems.

Some aspects of financial services regulation were discussed in Chapter 1. In the UK, for example, the Financial Services Authority is the highest single financial services regulator with responsibility for building market confidence and public awareness, providing consumer protection and reducing financial crime across the sector. Its rule books and directives provide detailed guidance on all aspects of the conduct of business, and including product design and marketing. It is responsible for the regulation of deposit-taking, mortgage lending, insurance, investments and financial advice. However, Britain is also a member of the European Union, and financial services providers must also be aware of, and understand, the regulations relating to the single European market in financial services.

In contrast, in the US the responsibility for regulation is effectively split between the Securities and Exchange Commission (SEC), which regulates all aspects of the securities industry, and both the Federal Reserve System (FRS) and the Federal Deposit Insurance Commission (FDIC), which regulate most of the banking sector. (The term 'security' is usually used to refer to any readily transferable investment and includes company stocks and shares, corporate bonds, government (sovereign) bonds, mutual funds and a range of other financial instruments. Typically, such products are represented by some form of certificate.) The SEC has as its mission 'to protect investors, maintain fair, orderly, and efficient markets, and facilitate capital formation' (SEC, undated). It places particular emphasis on informed decision-making, and requires all public companies to disclosure any meaningful information so that that all investors have access to the same pool of knowledge on which to base purchase decisions. The Federal Reserve is the central bank of the US and has, as one of its responsibilities, the supervision and regulation of the banking and financial system. It has particular responsibility for domestic banks that choose to become members of the Federal Reserve, and for foreign banks. The FDIC is the primary regulator of banks that are chartered by individual states but which choose not to be members of the Federal Reserve. Its primary function is to promote public confidence in the financial system of the USA, and one of its best-known policy instruments is deposit insurance (to a maximum of ($100 000). A similar split arrangement operates in Australia, where the Australian Prudential Regulation Authority (APRA) is responsible for the supervision of banks, insurers, credit unions, building societies, friendly societies and superannuation funds. The APRA seeks to establish and enforce appropriate standards to create an efficient, stable and competitive financial system and, as with the FSA, relies on an approach which is essentially self-regulation – i.e. senior management in regulated institutions is responsible for compliance with APRA requirements. The Australian Securities and Investments Commission (ASIC) is responsible for regulating financial markets, securities, futures and corporations in order to protect customers, investors and creditors.

Regulations relating to consumer protection cover a wide range of topics, including (but not necessarily limited to), information provision (particularly advertising), product liability, privacy rights, unfair business practices, fraud, misrepresentation, and other forms of interaction between businesses and consumers. Regulations for consumer protection vary considerably across countries. In the UK, national priorities regarding consumer protection are set by the Office of Fair Trading (OFT) and enforced locally by Trading Standards offices throughout the country. The OFT is also responsible for regulating one major area of financial services that is not covered by the FSA – namely consumer credit. All businesses offering credit or lending to customers have to be licensed by the OFT and are required to make certain specified types of information available to consumers to aid with decision-making and to clarify their roles and responsibilities. Similar systems operate in many other countries. For example, in the US, the Federal Trade commission and the US Department of Justice have responsibility for enforcing federal legislation, and there are parallel organizations at state level. In Australia, the Trade Practices Act 1974 and related consumer protection legislation is enforced by the Australian Competition and Consumer Commission (ACCC), and its work is supplemented by equivalent state level agencies. In Singapore, the Consumer Protection (Fair Trading) Act of 2004 is a major component of the consumer protection regime. Its aim was to create a much fairer trading environment by identifying a series of unfair trading practices where consumers would have recourse to the law.

With growing economic integration, the analysis of the political environment must also consider the role of supra-national organizations such as ASEAN (the Association of South East Asian Nations), APEC (the Asia Pacific Economic Community), NAFTA (the North American Free Trade Area) and the EU (European Union). As Case study 6.2 in Chapter 6 outlines, the EU has been active in trying to create a single market for financial services in Europe with a view to increasing competition in enhancing consumer choice. Similarly, the moves by ASEAN and the General Agreement on Trade in Service (GATS) to liberalize the financial sectors of South East Asian economies is often cited as one of the factors that contributed to the need for much greater consolidation in the domestic banking and insurance sectors. Specifically in the banking sector, the Basel Committee on Banking Supervision, which comprises central bankers from thirteen countries, has developed international standards for measuring the adequacy of a bank's capital with a view to creating greater consistency in the management of risk across banking systems. The resulting standards, enshrined in the Basel II Accord, can have important implications for lending decisions.

Of course, when thinking about the political and legal environment we should also recognize other more general provisions that might affect the operation of financial services organizations, including health and safety legislation and employment legislation. Not all aspects of work-related legislation and regulation will directly affect marketing, but good environmental analysis will at least allow awareness of their existence and their potential impact.

4.3.2   The economic environment

The economic environment covers all aspects of economic behaviour at an aggregate level, and includes consideration of factors such as growth in income, interest rates, inflation, unemployment, investment and exchange rates. Government economic policy (both actual and intended) is typically a central component of the macro-environment because of its impact on economic performance. The nature of consumer demand for financial services will inevitably be affected by economic performance; higher levels of economic growth will result in higher levels of demand for existing financial services, as well as creating demand for new ones. The growth in equity investments by private consumers and the increased demand for mutual funds is one aspect of this change in patterns of demand. In addition to the level of income and rate of growth, the proportion of income that is saved is likely to be another key consideration. For example, the US is currently reporting a national savings rate of less than 14 per cent, with household savings at less than 1 per cent of income. In contrast, national savings rates are estimated at around 20 per cent in Europe, 25 per cent in Japan and close to 50 per cent in China (www.businessweek.com/magazine, accessed 27 February 2006). As well as affecting overall economic performance, the savings rate provides an indicator of the potential size of the market for savings and investment products.

Equally important macro-economic influences will be interest rates and inflation. High real interest rates (based on the difference between inflation and nominal interest rates) may encourage savings; low real interest rates will tend to encourage borrowing. Equally, the current low interest rate and low inflation environment in the UK and the US constrains the extent to which cost increases can be passed on to consumers in the form of higher prices.

Often it is not sufficient to consider individual economic variables by themselves, as the interaction between variables can be important. It would be easy to assume that a fall in interest rates will increase demand for mortgages, but if those low interest rates are accompanied by either rising unemployment or falling average incomes then the expected change in demand may not materialize. Conversely, just because aggregate income rises we cannot assume that aggregate savings will also rise, because the savings decision will also be affected by other factors – including prevailing interest rates and taxation.

4.3.3   The social environment

The social environment is extremely broad and covers all relevant aspects of a society, including demographics, culture, values, attitudes, lifestyles, etc. The following discussion will highlight those aspects that may be of particular significance in relation to the financial services sector.

Demographics

The demographic environment encompasses all factors relating to the size, structure and distribution of the population. The potential market for any product is affected not only by the number of individuals within the population but also by the age structure and regional distribution of that population. Although world population is growing, the pace of change in many Western economies is slow, and in some cases virtually zero. Population changes depend on both birth and death rates, and while death rates have been falling worldwide, the fall in birth rates in many economies has largely counteracted this effect. For example, the birth rate (number of births per 1000 people) in the UK was estimated at 7.80 for 2005; for Hong Kong SAR the figure was 7.26 and for the United States, 14.14 (*CIA World Fact Book*, accessed on-line at www.cia.gov/cia/publications, March 2006). Countries with low birth rates typically have ageing populations – a feature that may have important implications for pension products, health insurance and long-term care insurance. In contrast, other countries are experiencing rapid growth in population, largely as a consequence of high birth rates and falling death rates. For example, Oman has a birth rate of 36.73, Pakistan has a birth rate of 30.42 and Paraguay has a birth rate of 29.43. Even allowing for falling death rates, such countries will have a very young population and potentially a very different profile of demand for financial services.

There are several other aspects of population structure that might be relevant to financial services. The regional distribution of the population, and particularly the balance between urban and rural areas, may be important – particularly so in relation to retail banking and the distribution of branches. Household structure is also relevant; in many Western economies such as the UK there has been a tendency towards a declining household size and an increase in the number of single-person households as individuals leave home but delay marriage. This trend will have implications for mortgage products and life insurance products – single mortgage-holders may feel less need for life insurance cover if they have no dependants to worry about. Of course, the decline of the extended family in many parts of the world also creates greater demand for products that provide financial support in retirement, including pensions, care insurance and equity release products.

Culture

Understanding consumer needs is central to any marketing activity, and those needs will often be heavily influenced by cultural factors. Culture is a complex idea, and is difficult to define. As a general rule, it can be thought of as a term that defines 'how we do things here' – it relates to how people behave, what they believe, what they value, their customs and traditions, and what is considered acceptable and unacceptable. Any type of marketing must recognize the significance of culture, and financial services are no exception. In principle, the biggest challenge that culture presents is in relation to international markets, where an ability to understand the prevailing culture and adjust and adapt to it are essential. However, an understanding of culture and cultural changes is also relevant in domestic markets. The nature of marketing communications, the use of colour and particular symbols can all touch on cultural sensitivities. Some countries may have a relatively homogeneous culture, while others can be very diverse. In the US, for example, marketers must be sensitive to the different heritage and cultures of the Hispanic, African and white communities. In the UK there is also considerable diversity, with significant proportions of the population being of south Asian or Caribbean heritage. Different cultural backgrounds may be reflected in different response to marketing communications, different decision-making processes and different product preferences. One of the strongest elements of culture is religion, and this provides a very clear example of the way in which culture can affect marketing. Paying or receiving interest (*riba*) is against the teaching of Islam, and is thus *haram* (unlawful). Islam forbids all forms of economic activity that are morally or socially injurious. *Riba* is harmful because it is seen as wealth generated purely by the ownership of money rather than by genuine economic activity. The prohibition of interest in Islamic law (*Shari'ah*) presents a major challenge for traditional banks, whose business revolves around interest margins, but equally presents a major opportunity for the growing number of specialist Islamic banks. Further detail about Islamic financial services is provided in Chapter 10.

Other social influences

A range of other issues relating to social structures and social values may also be important for financial services providers, including changing patterns of work, changing social structures and changing values. These factors may affect the ways in which people may wish to access financial services – for example, people who are working longer hours may place greater importance on being able to access their bank accounts through ATMs, telephone banking and Internet banking. Social influences may also affect the types of financial services demanded. Thus, for example, with an increasing value being placed on education, prospective parents may seek financial services that allow them to save for their children's education. With more people travelling internationally, demand for internationally recognized debit and credit cards will continue to increase. Where consumers are concerned about environmental or ethical issues, there may be a demand for financial services that are provided in a way that is consistent with these values. This trend has been touched on in reference to the earlier discussion on Islamic finance, but its impact may be broader still if consumers seek to invest in stocks or mutual funds which have a 'green' (environmentally friendly) dimension.

4.3.4   The technological environment

Technology essentially refers to our level of knowledge about 'how things are done'. That is to say, understanding this aspect of the marketing environment is much more than simply being familiar with the latest hi-tech innovations. Technology affects not only the type of products available, but also the ways in which people organize their lives and the ways in which goods and services can be marketed. In the financial services sector, the single most important aspect of technology has been ICT – information and communications technology. ICT has had a dramatic impact on the delivery of financial services, the types of financial services that can be offered and the ways in which those services are marketed.

Financial services may now be delivered via ATMs, by telephone and via the Internet (by either PC or Wap phone). ATMs were first introduced in the US in the 1970s, and at that stage their main function was to dispense cash. As technology developed and consumer acceptance of ATMs increased, machines were developed with a much wider range of functions which allow individuals to undertake an extensive range of banking activities. Customers of many banks, including ABN-AMRO, Standard Chartered and HSBC, can undertake most standard banking transactions 24 hours per day, including withdrawal, deposit, balance updates, balance transfers, and bill payment and passbook updates. The ICICI Bank in India is one of a growing number of banks with an even wider range of services offered via their ATMs, including top-ups to pre-paid mobile phones, charity donations, calling cards, mutual fund transactions and even donations for blessings at selected temples. The development of ATMs has certainly provided much greater flexibility for consumers in terms of their access to bank services; it has also served as an additional marketing tool, as banks use the ATM transaction to promote other services.

The telephone has a long history of use in the purchase and management of financial services, supporting interpersonal interactions and paper-based transactions (for example, customers telephoning to obtain an insurance quotation). Phone banking was probably the next major initiative in service delivery, with the first systems appearing in the mid-1980s. Most financial services providers now offer or are developing phone banking systems using a mixture of automated voice recognition outside of reasonable working hours, and personal contact during reasonable working hours. In the UK, First Direct was launched in 1989 as the country's first purely phone bank, and rapidly became one of its most successful. In another innovation, First Direct launched text-messaging banking and is currently the UK's largest provider of this service.

A growing number of financial services are now available on-line. The development of the worldwide web provided a major impetus for the development of computer-based banking. Until this point in time, and with a few notable exceptions, computer-based banking was largely restricted to corporate markets. In the mid-1990s the early adopters launched their Internet-banking services in the

US, Europe, Japan, Australia and New Zealand. Regions such as South East Asia, South Asia, the Middle East and South America rapidly followed. Yet, for retail customers, Internet banking has not replaced the traditional branch – it has become essentially an alternative, complementary channel of distribution, and the number of purely Internet banks remains limited. The Internet has also proved effective for dealing in a range of other financial services, including simple insurance, loans, mortgages, share trading and mutual fund trading. However, research on customer attitudes does tend to suggest that more retail customers feel comfortable when using the Internet for relatively simple products and many are much less comfortable with the idea of using it for more complex products (Black *et al.*, 2001).

Clearly, these technology-enabled distribution channels offer many benefits to certain customer segments. They also offer significant cost benefits to organizations, with the cost of Internet-based transactions being estimated at 10 per cent of the cost of phone transactions and 1 per cent of the cost of in-branch transactions. However, Internet-based distribution may also pose a marketing problem if fewer customers visit the branch and there is, therefore, less of an opportunity actively to sell to those customers. A growing challenge for many banks concerns the management of large branch networks at a time when more and more of their customers are looking to alternative forms of delivery.

The impact of ICT developments is probably most visible in relation to external developments in delivery channels. However, the internal marketing implications of ICT are considerable. Rapid developments in processing power (based on both hardware and software improvements) allow financial services organizations to collect and process huge volumes of customer information. Marketing databases can be developed based on the information provided by customers in, say, an application for a credit card or a mortgage. These data can then be used to understand existing customers more thoroughly, and also to identify the types of consumers most likely to buy certain products. The nature and importance of customer relationship management and the significance of effective use of customer information is discussed in greater detail in Part III of this book.

4.4   The market environment

The market environment focuses on the immediate features of the market in which the firm operates. Understanding this aspect of environment is of particular importance, as the market environment will have a very immediate impact on an organization's activity. There are many different approaches that might be used to understand what is happening in the market environment. One of the most widely employed is the idea of analysing the five forces that determine market/industry profitability – an approach that was developed in the 1980s by Michael Porter. This is shown in Figure 4.3.

An effective marketing strategy will need understanding of how these forces work together and what they mean for the organization. If a particular market environment is favourable or attractive, then an organization should find it easier to compete effectively. A market is considered favourable or attractive if the forces

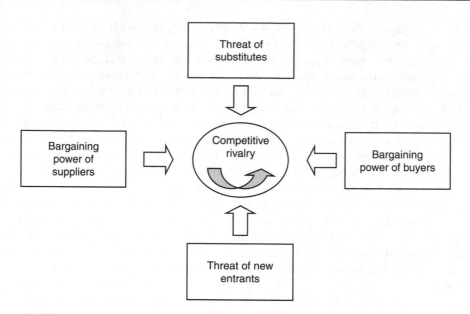

Figure 4.3 Five-force analysis (source: Porter, 1980).

working against an organization are relatively weak. Where the forces are strong they impose constraints upon what an organization can do, and marketing strategies will need to consider how best to neutralize and respond to the problems that the organization faces. Thus, for example, customers may be in a strong position (high bargaining power) because it is relatively easy to switch between different providers. In this situation, a bank may consider focusing attention on marketing strategies that build a strong relationship with customers (perhaps via cross-selling a range of products), making them more likely to remain with the bank. If successful, this strategy will make the market more attractive and thus enhance the bank's competitive position.

Porter argues that market or industry attractiveness and profitability depends (as economic theory would suggest) on the structure of the industry, and specifically on five key features:

1. *The bargaining power of suppliers.* Powerful suppliers can force up the prices paid by an organization for its inputs, and thus reduce profitability. Suppliers in financial services include the suppliers of essential business goods and services (computing equipment, training, etc.), and to the extent that these suppliers are in a strong position they can affect the prices paid for relevant goods and thus affect costs. It could also be argued that, in some instances, the term 'suppliers' could also include customers. Customers making deposits with financial institutions are effectively acting as suppliers of certain essential raw materials, and again, if these suppliers are in a relatively strong position they can impact on the cost of providing certain related financial services.
2. *The bargaining power of consumers.* Powerful consumers can insist on lower prices and/or more favourable terms, which may impact negatively on profitability.

Clearly, the bargaining power of buyers in financial services varies considerably. In personal markets it seems that the bargaining power of individual consumers is relatively weak, although consumer pressure groups may partly counterbalance this – particularly through their evaluations of the performance of financial institutions. In corporate markets the situation may be rather different, with relatively large businesses being in a rather more powerful position.

3. *Threat of entry*. A profitable industry will generally attract new entrants; if it appears relatively attractive for new organizations to enter a market, profitability will tend to be eroded. While there are certainly barriers to entry to the financial marketplace, not least of which are the many regulatory requirements, the financial sector does attract a variety of new entrants. In some cases, these are new entrants from other sectors of the domestic economy. A growing number of retailers offer consumer credit and store cards to fund consumer purchases. In the US, General Motors offers credit cards, while in the UK, supermarkets such as Tesco and Sainsbury offer a wide range of financial services alongside their traditional grocery products. Richard Branson's Virgin Group, originally in the music business, now offers a range of financial services ranging from credit cards to personal pensions. In many cases these new entrants may still rely on traditional financial services providers, which are then offered to consumers using the new entrant's own brand. Even though they may depend upon existing suppliers of financial services, they still constitute a significant new source of competition. The threat of new entry is not restricted to firms in other sectors of the economy; there is increasingly a very real threat from new entrants from overseas, as is discussed in greater detail in Chapter 6.

4. *Competition from substitutes*. The existence of products which are close substitutes enhances customer choice and provides an alternative way of meeting a particular need. Thus, in markets where there are close substitutes, the buying power of consumers is effectively enhanced because they have a much greater degree of choice. The extent to which there are real substitutes for financial services is perhaps limited, although in certain sections of the market, such as investment services, gold, jewellery, antiques and other collectibles may be regarded as substitutes for investments in mutual funds, equities and other forms of saving. It is interesting to note the extent to which increasing numbers of people view investment in property as a substitute for traditional investment in pensions as a vehicle to provide income and capital in old age. This, in part, has fuelled a rapid increase in what is termed the 'buy-to-let' market.

5. *Rivalry between firms*. Clearly, the greater the degree of competition, the more likely it is that the industry will be less profitable and therefore less attractive. While there are few close substitutes for financial services (as indicated above), there is considerable competition within the industry. Most countries have seen some degree of consolidation in their financial services sector and, while this has reduced the number of competitors, the remaining players are often strengthened, resulting in increased competition. Moreover, as financial markets have liberalized and the barriers between institutional types have been reduced, competition has also increased. Insurers no longer compete just with other insurers – they also compete with banks, savings institutions and investment companies. The development of bancassurance (a term used to describe a system in which banks broaden their product offerings to include a more extensive range of insurance,

savings and investment products which would have traditionally been offered by more specialized companies) in many financial sectors worldwide is just one example of this type of development. Equally, in the banking sector, current accounts and housing finance may be offered by companies that traditionally specialized in insurance. In Malaysia, for example, the insurer AIA now offers housing finance in direct competition with traditional suppliers. In the UK, the insurer Prudential launched the on-line bank Egg, which offers a range of traditional banking products with very competitive terms and conditions.

These five forces determine the attractiveness of the industry through their impact on either costs incurred or prices received, or both. The development of an effective marketing strategy will depend upon a thorough examination of the market in order to enable the organization to identify strategic approaches to counterbalance the effects of these five forces.

4.5   The internal environment

Clearly, the internal environment is the area in which the firm can exercise greatest control. Understanding the internal environment requires analysis of an organization's resources and capabilities in order to understand how these might be used to create a competitive edge in the delivery of financial services to the organization's target market.

4.5.1   Resources

The term *resources* is used to describe any inputs which are used by an organization in order to produce its outputs. Resources are normally categorized as either tangible or intangible. Tangible resources include the following:

1. Human resources, including issues such as the number and type of staff, and their particular skills and qualities (attributes such as flexibility, adaptability, commitment, etc., may be of particular significance in many organizations). The UK bank First Direct might point to its staff – their customer orientation, expertise and skill – as being a key tangible resource.
2. Financial resources, including a variety of factors such as cash holdings, levels of debt and equity, access to funds for future development, and relationships with key financial stakeholders (for example, bankers and shareholders). Leading international banks such as HSBC and Citibank may see their financial strength as a significant resource.
3. Physical/operational resources, encompassing premises, equipment, internal systems (e.g. IT systems) and operating procedures. CapitalOne, the credit card company, might point to its systems for rapid development and product customization as being a key resource for the company. For a domestic bank the branch network may be a key resource, particularly when competing against new international entrants.

Intangible resources typically do not have any physical form, and some may not have any obvious monetary value, but for many organizations they can be one of the key resources that help to create competitive advantage. Examples of intangible resources might include specialist knowledge or experience, brand names and brand equity, and the internal culture within an organization. American Express might cite the strength of its brand as a significant intangible resource; investment companies might focus on the skills and knowledge of their fund managers in delivering superior returns to customers. Corporate culture, which is typically defined as the prevailing value system within an organization, is widely recognized as an important intangible resource. This value system may be one that has arisen through time, or it may be one that is actively created and managed by senior staff. A corporate culture associated with rapid innovation and risk-taking will have different marketing implications to a culture orientated towards high quality and an exclusive image, and this in turn will differ from an organization with a low-risk culture looking to follow the market with a standard product.

Some commentators also make a distinction between internal resources, which actually belong within the organization, and external resources, which are outside the organization but still under its control (such as formal or informal networks, personal contacts, locations, surroundings, etc.). Some financial services providers might look to their relationships with networks of financial advisers as an important external resource.

4.5.2   Competences/capabilities

The words 'competence' and 'capability' are often used interchangeably, although some would suggest that they have slightly different meanings. For our purposes, we will use the two words interchangeably. They refer to certain skills or attributes that are necessary in order to be able to operate within a particular industry. Competences or capabilities would be present amongst most organizations in an industry – without those competences, the organization would not be able to operate. Operating in the banking industry requires competences in relation to deposit-taking, lending, service provision, financial management, treasury, etc. Equally, insurers require competences in relation to premium collection and management, underwriting, customer service and claims management. Key to an analysis of competences is the ability to identify those in which an organization is noticeably more effective than its competitors. These core competencies or distinctive capabilities provide a basis for delivering superior customer value, and thus creating competitive advantage. A core competence will typically arise from a combination of resources and competences which are of value in relation to a particular market. In the US, Wachovia Bank's competence in credit, derived from both people and systems, has enabled it to report much lower write-off rates compared to the industry average, resulting in a significant positive impact on return on equity (Coyne et al., 1997).

The distinguishing features of core competences are that they are only possessed by the successful organizations in an industry, they are important in fulfilling customer needs and they are difficult to copy. Core competences provide an organization with a genuine competitive edge in the marketplace. When properly exploited, core competences are the basis for delivering superior customer value (Prahalad and Hamel, 1990).

4.5.3   Auditing the internal environment

Analysis of the internal environment requires a careful evaluation or audit of the organization's resources and capabilities. This is more than just assessing the quantity or a resource or capability – it is also about assessing quality. A good audit might consider the following:

- Specificity – are the resources/capabilities unique to a particular type of industry or are they generic? Resources/capabilities that are unique and important to a specific industry are often more likely to provide bases for developing a core competence.
- Substitutability – can this resource/capability be replaced with another? Substitutability may allow for greater flexibility in the process of delivering value for customers.
- Mobility – could this resource/capability be easily transferred to a competitor? (For example, staff may be an important resource, but are potentially quite mobile.) Where resources are mobile, there is a need to think careful about how to protect them and retain their value within an organization.
- Contribution – what is the importance of a particular resource/capability in terms of adding value to the overall offer? Resources/capabilities with a key role to play in value added may require more protection and investment than resources that are not strategically significant.

An internal analysis may also focus on internal structures (for example, how does marketing relate to other activities?), recruitment and reward systems for staff, the effectiveness of internal communication and the degree of centralization. Although these may not be directly related to marketing, they can have important implications for what marketing does. Thus, for example, a bank that rewards a group of staff based on the number of credit cards it sells or the number of new accounts it opens may create an incentive for those staff to deal with every customer as quickly as possible and pressure them into buying. This may yield short-term benefits, but the danger is that in the longer term the customers recruited in this way will be less satisfied and perhaps less profitable.

4.6   Evaluating developments in the marketing environment

The kind of analysis described in the previous sections will generate a large amount of data. The process of SWOT (Strengths, Weaknesses, Opportunities, Threats) analysis is one of the simplest techniques for summarizing information about the marketing environment and guiding the direction of strategy. The information collected in the environmental analysis can be classified as either external (i.e. it relates to the outside environment) or internal (i.e. it relates to the organization itself). External information may present the organization with an opportunity, or it may create a threat. Equally, internal information may describe either a strength or a weakness. Any evidence produced by the environmental analysis will therefore belong to one of these groups:

- *Strength.* Any particular resource or competence that will help the organization to achieve its objectives is classified as a strength. This may relate to experience in specific types of markets – for example, HSBC may point to its accumulated knowledge of Asian markets. Specific skills or abilities may also constitute a strength, as will resources such as a strong brand image, or an extensive branch or ATM network.
- *Weakness.* A weakness describes any aspect of the organization that may hinder the achievement of specific objectives. Weaknesses are often the opposite of strengths, so, for example, a small branch network, poor internal information systems or an unfavourable brand image may all constitute weaknesses.
- *Opportunity.* Any feature of the external environment that is advantageous to the organization, given its objectives, is classed as an opportunity. Credit card issuers may see the growing demand for foreign travel as an opportunity to increase the sale of credit cards. Insurers looking at the Chinese market might see the current low take-up of life insurance as an opportunity.
- *Threat.* A threat is any environmental development that will create problems for an organization in achieving its specific objectives. Opportunities for one organization may be a threat for others. The efforts of the EU to create a single market in financial services might be classed as a threat by some providers because of its potential to increase competition.

Once information has been classified in this way, it can be presented as a matrix of strengths, weaknesses, opportunities and threats. For SWOT analysis to be of value it is important to ensure that strengths and weaknesses are internal factors specific to the organization, and that opportunities and threats are factors which are present in the external environment and are independent of the organization. A common mistake in SWOT analysis is to confuse opportunities and threats with strategies and tactics. For example, the ability to contact customers via direct mail is not an opportunity, it is a marketing tactic. The relevant opportunity would be the existence of a segment in the market that would respond favourably to promotion via direct mail.

Given the volume of information, a SWOT analysis should concentrate only on the most important strengths, weaknesses, opportunities and threats. Whether something is important depends upon how likely it is to happen and how significant its effect would be. Thus, for example, a provider of housing finance may consider a major economic downturn to be something that would have a big impact on new and existing business, but if the likelihood of this happening is low, then this factor should not be seen as a serious threat. In the example in Figure 4.4, the information in each cell is ranked to account for these factors.

Having formulated this matrix, it then becomes feasible to make use of SWOT analysis in guiding strategy formulation. The two major strategic options are:

1. *Matching*, which entails finding (where possible) a match between the strengths of the organization and the opportunities presented by the market. Strengths that do not match any available opportunity are of limited use, while opportunities that do not have any matching strengths are of little immediate value from a strategic perspective. Thus, for example, the bank in Figure 4.4 may consider a strategy of using its captive account base to pursue a strategy of cross-selling

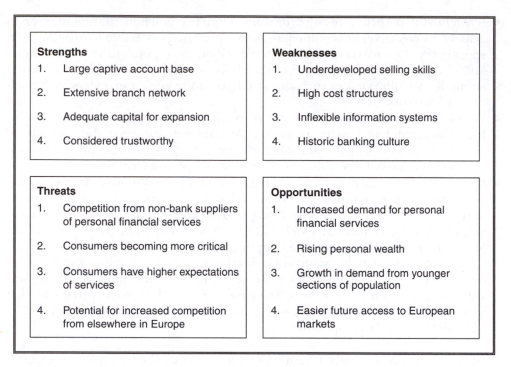

Strengths	Weaknesses
1. Large captive account base	1. Underdeveloped selling skills
2. Extensive branch network	2. High cost structures
3. Adequate capital for expansion	3. Inflexible information systems
4. Considered trustworthy	4. Historic banking culture

Threats	Opportunities
1. Competition from non-bank suppliers of personal financial services	1. Increased demand for personal financial services
2. Consumers becoming more critical	2. Rising personal wealth
3. Consumers have higher expectations of services	3. Growth in demand from younger sections of population
4. Potential for increased competition from elsewhere in Europe	4. Easier future access to European markets

Figure 4.4 SWOT Analysis for a UK clearing bank in relation to the market for personal financial services (adapted from Ennew, 1993).

other financial products through direct mail campaigns that emphasize the bank's trustworthy image.

2. *Conversion*, which requires the development of strategies that will convert weaknesses into strengths in order to take advantage of some particular opportunity, or converting threats into opportunities which can then be matched by existing strengths.

Case study 4.1 shows how the Czech insurer Kooperativa was able to build on key strengths, relating to staff skills, expertise and willingness to learn, to exploit the opportunities created by liberalization and the low penetration of insurance products.

Case study 4.1   Kooperativa Insurance Company Ltd

Kooperativa pojistovna a.s. (Kooperativa Insurance Company Ltd.) is one of the largest and fastest-growing insurance companies in post-Communist Eastern Europe. In just 15 years it has grown from scratch to become the Czech Republic's second largest insurance company, with a record-breaking US$1.1bn of written premiums in 2005.

Case study 4.1   Kooperativa Insurance Company Ltd—cont'd

The following factors have been of significance in enabling Kooperativa to achieve its success:

- the formation of a group of competent and well-skilled staff from the insurance business who were willing to take the risks associated with leaving the former monopolist company to set up the new venture
- support from shareholders, chief of which was Wiener Staedtische Allgemeinge Versicherung
- a favourable backdrop whereby the Czech insurance market was open to new kinds of insurance
- the extensive use of reinsurance to hedge risk
- a willingness to gain know-how from foreign shareholders and reinsurers.

Kooperativa strengthened its position as second in the market, and by the end of 2005 its market share had increased to 22.9 per cent; non-life insurance accounted for 28.9 per cent of the market. Life assurance written premiums had grown by 25 per cent to a total of CZK 6 billion. It has more than two million clients – indeed, Kooperativa insures every fifth Czech citizen. The financial results are also positive; for example, in 2004 Kooperativa achieved a gross profit of CZK 765 million (US$30m) and in 2005 it was CZK 1300 million (US$52m) – a year on year increase in profit before tax of 11.9 per cent and 70 per cent respectively.

Today, Kooperativa offers a complete insurance service for all kinds of clients – business as well as individuals. Its product range comprises general insurance and life assurance, including insurance for liability risks. From the beginning, Kooperativa positioned itself in the market with an individual approach to the client – a new phenomenon in the Czech insurance market. For the country's budding new entrepreneurs, it has helped to identify the risks that most endanger their economic prospects in both their personal and business affairs. It offers modern contracts drafted in order to inconvenience them as little as possible. Being simple and quick to complete, they save time and provide a wide range of insurance coverage according to customers' wishes, needs and financial possibilities – from its very start the company has always provided insurance to fit closely both their product and service needs.

Another reason for Kooperativa's success is the quality of its claims adjustment. This includes the ability to report losses by telephone, the use of up-to-date methods of communication, and technologies such as digitalization and the Internet.

In 2004, the company acquired four smaller insurance businesses and established the development of a strategic co-operation with the Ceska Sporitelna Financial Group (one of the biggest Czech banks). These events represented the company's response to changes in its business environment – including: the Czech Republic's entry into the European Union, new competition, and the continuing adaptation of the Czech market to the up-to-date insurance trends found in more commercially advanced countries. This has enabled Kooperativa to respond to the

Continued

Case study 4.1   Kooperativa Insurance Company Ltd—cont'd

challenges posed by bancassurance and other financial new product developments in an effort to provide for all clients' financial needs at a single sales point.

Kooperativa's trade representatives are gradually becoming true financial
advisers, able both to satisfy all clients' insurance needs and to act as brokers for
other financial services – whether obtaining a credit card or a mortgage, or execut-
ing contracts on building savings or supplementary annuity insurance. They are
also able to broker consumer loans for clients, or to assist them in opening a
bank account.

Recently, the company has reaffirmed that the core of its corporate strategy
for the next few years will be based upon:

- developing Kooperativa as a large, modern insurance company transacting all
  types of life assurance and non-life insurance based on the needs of the clients
- continuously improving the quality and comprehensiveness of the services
  offered, to transact business swiftly, and to take a flexible and personal
  approach to the clients
- guaranteeing the clients a considerable level of security based on high registered capital and a high-quality reinsurance programme.

Kooperativa endeavours to be not only an insurer but also a reliable partner,
providing advice and support under all circumstances.

Again, a key strategic objective of the company is to strengthen its position in
the domestic insurance market and increase its market share.

Source: Vladimir Chludil, Kooperativa.

SWOT analysis is probably one of the most widely used tools in marketing and
strategic planning, and is simply a method of structuring information of both a qualitative and a quantitative nature. Its advantages arise from the fact that it is easy to
use, does not require formal training and therefore is accessible to all levels of management across a broad field. This simple technique provides a method of organizing information and identifying possible problems and future strategic directions.

4.7   Summary and conclusions

The environment within which organizations operate is becoming increasingly complex and turbulent and, as a consequence, increasingly uncertain. Understanding the
nature of this environment and its implications for the organizations is a key element in any marketing strategy. The environment must be analysed at a number of
different levels, from broad, macro-factors to market-specific and finally organization-
specific factors. However, although these elements of the environment constrain the

activities of the organization, it is increasingly important to recognize that the organization itself, through its marketing activities, can influence the environment to produce conditions which are more favourable to the success of its strategies.

Review questions

1. Why is it important to understand the external environment? What role does marketing play?
2. Choose a financial services provider. What are the opportunities and threats that the macro-environment creates?
3. Choose a market that you know well (e.g. current accounts, mutual funds, credit cards, housing finance) and analyse the five forces. What are the opportunities and threats?
4. Prepare a SWOT analysis in relation to an organisation in the market that you analysed in Question 3. What are the market-level opportunities and threats and macro-level opportunities and threats that you think may be relevant? Include them in the analysis.
5. In what ways do factors in the physical environment, such as climate-related issues, impact upon financial services?

5

Strategic development and marketing planning

Learning objectives

By the end of this chapter you will be able to:
- explain the importance of planning marketing activities
- understand the value of taking a strategic approach to marketing
- outline stages in the process of planning marketing
- understand some of the tools and techniques that are used in developing marketing strategies.

5.1 Introduction

Planning is an essential element of marketing. Planning will help to ensure that an organization's marketing activities are consistent with its objectives, with the capabilities of the organization and with the needs of the marketplace. Planning provides a systematic analysis of what marketing activities are being undertaken, why and how. Effective planning must establish targets, identify how and when those targets are to be achieved, and establish who will take responsibility for the relevant marketing tasks. By stating objectives, procedures, processes and personnel requirements prior to undertaking marketing activities, the plan also provides a framework for the monitoring and control of marketing.

Planning has always been an important activity, and in the current environment it is particularly important. Chapter 4 discussed some of the changes that have occurred in the marketing environment. Change is increasingly common, it happens quickly and it can often be complex. For example, the European Union's Financial Services Action Plan, when launched in 1998, proposed a series of policy initiatives to establish a single market in wholesale financial services, to make retail markets open and to strengthen the rules on prudential supervision. In so doing, it heralded a period of significant change for the financial services sector. Planning encourages the organization to think about the future and to adopt a strategic focus, which means that the organization should be much better placed to respond to a rapidly changing environment.

The sort of changes described in the previous chapter have created significant competitive threats for established financial services organizations. At the same time, many of these changes have also created new opportunities. Faced with this environment, it would be unwise to adopt an unplanned approach to marketing. It would be equally unwise to rely on a simple tactical approach, supplying the same products to the same markets. When faced with a complex, changing and uncertain environment, it becomes increasingly important for organizations to adopt a strategic approach to their markets. Such an approach will encourage careful consideration of products offered and markets served, and should provide an organization with the means to allocate its resources effectively and efficiently in the pursuit of specified objectives.

This chapter deals with both strategy and planning in relation to marketing. It will begin by defining strategic marketing, and will then examine the structure of a marketing plan and briefly review stages in the planning process. The later sections will examine strategy development and explore the different tools that can be used to guide strategic thinking. The focus throughout will be on the strategic aspects of marketing planning, including strategies for growth, sources of competitive advantage and methods for planning the product portfolio.

5.2   Strategic marketing

It is generally thought that organizations in the financial services sector have been slow to adopt a strategic approach to their marketing activities. For a long time, the marketing of financial services was largely concerned with how best to advertise and sell an existing set of products in a given market; indeed, many people think that this is what marketing is all about. However, there is more to marketing. A strategic approach to marketing in the financial services sector needs to concern itself with understanding consumers and deciding how best to respond to their needs. It must also focus attention on the competition and try to identify how to outperform key competitors.

The adoption and implementation of a strategic approach to marketing should impact positively on organizational performance. An understanding of customer and competitors will enable an organization to deliver superior customer value to the market. In turn, superior customer value will facilitate both customer acquisition and customer retention. Successfully growing new business and keeping existing customers will have a positive impact on organizational performance, and particularly on profit and cash flow. However, for life and pensions business there is the added consideration of the need for capital to support the new business strain that accompanies growth. This serves to strengthen further the need for effective long-term marketing planning. The concept of the service–profit chain which is discussed in more detail in Part III of this book, stresses the importance of retention in improving performance on the grounds that it costs less to retain a customer than it does to acquire one. More generally, Doyle (2000) argues that investment in strategic marketing in order to increase revenues is a far more effective way of improving shareholder value than trying to reduce costs. The degree to which costs can be reduced is limited and, while cost control will be important, the best opportunities for enhancing financial performance arise from growing the volume and/or the value of sales. Strategic marketing is essential to revenue growth because it focuses the organization on customers, competitors and the challenges of a constantly changing marketplace. Central to Doyle's view is the argument that marketing expenditure should be viewed as an investment (rather than an annual cost) and its impact monitored over a longer time period. Investment in activities such as brand-building, establishing new distribution networks or moving into new markets are all long-term activities. Their initial impact on sales may actually be quite limited; their longer-term impact could be quite considerable.

Thus, a strategic approach to marketing has at its heart organizational performance and the idea that performance can be enhanced if the organization is market orientated , if it understands the changing market environment and can respond in ways which result in the delivery of a level of value to customers that is superior to that offered by competitors. In that sense, we can think about strategic marketing as being a broad, generic approach to marketing. The specific form that strategic marketing takes will vary across organizations and markets, and will be represented by the organization's marketing strategy.

Within any financial services provider, strategies develop at several levels. A corporate strategy is concerned with the overall development of the business and will include specific strategies for different areas (e.g. an IT strategy, a human resource strategy, a marketing strategy). The marketing strategy focuses specifically on the organization's activities in relation to its markets.

Like any strategy, marketing strategy is concerned with being both efficient and effective. Efficiency is about doing a particular activity well. An efficient phone banking operation will be one that is highly cost-effective and reliable. In contrast, effectiveness is concerned with doing the right thing. Thus, an effective phone banking operation is one that offers the right services to the target consumers – the services that consumers need and want. To be effective, a financial services provider must have the right sort of services and be offering them to the right market. This in turn means that an understanding of the environment is essential, because it is only by understanding the market, and how it might change, that an organization can be confident that it is doing the right thing. When the Indian banking sector liberalized in the mid-1990s, the success of one of the early entrants, HDFC Bank, was largely due to its awareness of changing customer expectations and the identification of a significant group of mid-market customers who were prepared to pay for better service (Saxena, 2006).

A good marketing strategy will:

- identify specific objectives that the organization wishes to achieve
- commit resources (money, time, people) to help achieve these objectives
- involve a thorough evaluation of the marketing environment

- aim to match environmental opportunities and organizational capabilities
- focus on the delivery of superior value.

Delivering superior value to customers lies at the heart of strategic marketing and the development of a competitive marketing strategy. The notion of 'superior value' highlights the importance of outperforming the competition. Indeed, when talking more broadly about competitive strategy, Porter (2002) notes that:

> Competitive strategy is about being different. It means deliberately choosing a different set of activities to deliver a unique mix of value.

Clearly, delivering superior value starts with the organization itself and the activities in which it is able to excel. What is delivered must then be superior to the competition and relevant to customers. Superior value may arise from reducing costs to the customer or from increasing benefits, and those benefits may be functional or emotional. The emotional benefits associated with leading brands (e.g. reduced risk, increased confidence) may be a particularly important element of value in some areas of financial services.

5.3   Developing a strategic marketing plan

A marketing strategy is essentially a statement of how an organization plans to compete for business in its particular market, and most marketing strategies will be presented in the form of an overall marketing plan. Philip Kotler (1994) defined strategic planning as:

> the managerial process of developing and maintaining a viable fit between the organization's objectives and resources and its changing market opportunities. The aim of strategic planning is to shape and reshape the company's business and products so that they combine to produce satisfactory profits and growth.

Every organization has its own approach to preparing marketing plans, and there is no single correct approach. However, a good plan does have a number of important features. It should:

- have a logical structure
- contain explicit marketing objectives which link to corporate objectives
- analyse the environment (both internal and external) and the current position of the organization
- based on this analysis, identify which combinations of products and markets the organization will serve and how it will compete (segmentation, targeting and positioning)
- contain specific decisions relating to key marketing variables such as product, price, promotion and place (the marketing mix)
- conclude with an outline of the appropriate methods for implementing the identified strategy, including issues relating to budget, accountability and evaluation.

Although the plan needs to provide clear guidelines as to how marketing activities are to be managed, it should have some flexibility to allow the organization to adapt and respond to unexpected changes.

As we have said, there is no single format for a plan, but one possible approach is outlined in Figure 5.1. This presents the key elements of a marketing plan and also highlights the importance of feedback, which may lead to adjustments to the plan once it has been put into operation.

5.3.1   Company mission and objectives

The mission statement essentially requires that the organization defines the area of business in which it operates, and defines it in way that will give focus and direction. In effect, the purpose of the mission statement is to outline the goals of the organization and identify, in broad terms, the ways in which the organization will achieve those goals. For example, the mission of the Indian based Bank of Baroda is:

> To be a top ranking National Bank of international standard committed to augmenting stakeholders' value through concern, care and competence.

The nature of the corporate mission depends on a variety of factors. Corporate history will often influence the markets and customer groups served – for example, Credit Agricole's rural and mutual tradition influences the way in which it approaches its market. Although it is in no way restricted to serving the agricultural community,

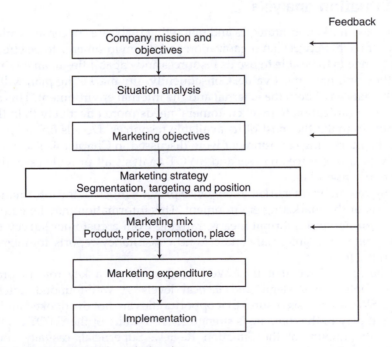

Figure 5.1 An illustrative strategic marketing plan.

Credit Agricole's heritage means that the bank places particular importance on involvement in the local community, being close to the customer, and the bank prides itself on having the largest high-street branch network. Similarly, culture in its broadest sense will also be an important influence – perhaps most notably with Islamic banks, as is apparent in the mission statement of Malaysian-based Bank Islam:

> To seek to operate as a commercial bank functioning on the basis of Islamic principles, providing banking facilities and services to Muslims and the whole population of this country, with viability and capability to sustain itself and grow in the process.

Typically, a corporate mission will be defined in terms of the types of customers (e.g. Muslims and the whole population), the needs being satisfied (banking facilities) and the technology used (Islamic principles). This way of defining the mission is helpful from a marketing perspective, because it forces managers to think about customers and their needs. Indeed, ideally the mission statement would avoid mentioning a product. For example, an insurance company should perhaps think of its mission as being 'meeting consumer needs for risk reduction and financial security', rather than simply 'insurance'. By focusing specifically on needs and not on the product, the mission statement can help to guide the future development of the organization. It can also help the organization avoid 'marketing myopia' – a problem that arises when organizations focus too much attention on their products and not enough on their customers' needs.

5.3.2　Situation analysis

In many senses, marketing strategies and marketing plans are concerned with obtaining a 'fit' or 'match' between an organization and its environment. To be effective, an organization needs to be able to use its resources and capabilities in an environment in which they will have most value. Consequently, any marketing plan will require a thorough analysis of both the external and the internal environment. This analysis will help the organization to meet customers' needs more effectively than the competition, and to make the most of its available resources. Details on the process of analysing the marketing environment were discussed in Chapter 4. The results of a PEST analysis, a five-force analysis and SWOT analysis all provide essential input to a good marketing plan.

Marketing research and market intelligence provide much of the information used in an analysis of the marketing environment. This information may be gathered by a variety of formal and informal means, ranging from a customer survey through commercial databases, informal contacts and consultancy reports to, increasingly, material on the Internet.

It must be appreciated that the SWOT analysis plays a key role in producing guidance at both the strategic and tactical levels. A well-founded, intelligently approached SWOT analysis ensures that opportunities are not overlooked and choices are made that play to the company's strengths. The quality of the SWOT analysis is a function of the quality of the Situation Review. Superficial, casually conducted Situation Reviews result in anodyne, somewhat pointless, SWOTs. A degree of detail is required that is commensurate to the market or product area in question.

It is important to grasp the point that when we refer to a strength, we should seek to identify aspects of the organization's assets, capabilities and competencies that represent *a relative competitive strength*. It is not sufficient simply to identify those aspects of the company's operation that it considers it is good at. The search for competitive advantage calls for the matching of external opportunities with a company's relative strengths. Similarly, the identification of weaknesses should search for areas of *relative competitive weakness*. Such features render the company particularly vulnerable to external threats, and need to be addressed with far more vigour than those areas in which the company performs no worse than the rest of the industry.

Therefore, SWOTs will often benefit from the degree of focus that can often only be achieved at the product group level. In the case of a life insurance company, this might involve separate plans for protection, pension and investment product groups. Each plan will have to be consistent with the bigger picture, and it is the job of senior marketing management to ensure that effective co-ordination occurs.

5.3.3   Marketing objectives

Once the nature of the marketing environment has been fully analysed and a suitable SWOT conducted, it is then possible to specify appropriate marketing objectives. These marketing objectives are not ends in themselves; they are intermediate outcomes which will lead to the organization achieving its corporate objectives. Thus, when specifying marketing objectives, it is essential to ensure that they are derived from and will contribute to corporate objectives. For example, if corporate objectives emphasize expansion, then marketing objectives may be specified in terms of growing market share or sales volume or sales value.

Marketing objectives should be clear, measurable, realistic and time-limited. A particular problem in specifying objectives is the potential confusion between intended goals and the means by which those goals should be attained. The former represent objectives, whereas the latter concerns processes. Sometimes, what are specified as objectives in a marketing planning document are in fact simply a representation of planned activities. Some examples of marketing objectives may serve to illustrate the point:

- *Example 1: To achieve a 12.5 per cent increase in volume sales of new personal pensions during the budget year.* This example represents a sound objective, as it specifies a measurable outcome (i.e. 12.5 per cent growth in sales), qualifies that it concerns personal pension sales volumes and specifies a timescale for achievement.
- *Example 2: To increase pension sales by year end.* This example is still an objective, albeit one that is poorly drafted. It gives no target level for the increase to be achieved, nor does it qualify whether it concerns case volumes or premium value. Finally, it does not specify whether it concerns all sources of pension growth, or whether it relates to growth from new sales as opposed to securing growth from existing pension customers.
- *Example 3: To promote personal pensions through the branch network.* This is simply not an objective – at least not at the level of a marketing plan. Instead, it represents but one of a range of actions that, in combination, should achieve a given objective.
- *Example 4: To re-price the personal pension product to improve competitive rating.* This is an example of a *process* element; not of a valid objective.

To qualify as a valid marketing objective, the following minimum conditions must be satisfied:

1. The desired outcome must be specified – for example, growth in sales, growth in market share, level of consumer awareness, level of customer satisfaction
2. The outcome must be sufficiently well-qualified to eliminate ambiguity and facilitate precise measurement – for example, growth in number of policies sold to new customers, growth in market share by new business premiums
3. A specific quantum of outcome must be proposed – for example, a 7.5 per cent growth in new business sales volumes
4. The timescale for achievement of outcome must be specified – for example, by the end of the second quarter.

Without well-defined objectives, it is impossible to evaluate outcomes properly.

5.3.4 Marketing strategy

Once the environment has been analysed and the objectives set, the market plan must move on to consider the choice of marketing strategy. Of course, the overall corporate strategy will affect the choice of marketing strategy, but the marketing strategy focuses specifically on the choice of markets and how the organization plans to compete and create value in those markets.

The main component of a marketing strategy is often described as the STP (Segmentation, Targeting and Positioning) process:

1. *Segmentation* involves identifying the different groups (segments) of consumers that exist in the market, and understanding their wants and needs
2. *Targeting* involves evaluating the attractiveness of different segments, choosing which ones to target with the organization's products and services
3. *Positioning* involves identifying the organization's competitive advantage, the way in which it can create value for customers, and how this offer should be presented to customers.

Case study 5.1   Parish National Bank (PNB), New Orleans – segmentation, targeting and positioning in strategic marketing

The financial services sector in the US has experienced a period of deregulation, technological innovation and changing patterns of competition. The Financial Modernization Act of 1999 repealed many of the restrictions that had previously restricted competition in US banking. Barriers to operating across sectors were lifted, and at the same time restrictions on interstate and international banking were disappearing. Regulatory changes, combined with changing market conditions, resulted in increased competition and a trend towards greater consolidation. Small local and regional banks were increasingly becoming 'endangered species'.

> **Case study 5.1   Parish National Bank (PNB), New Orleans – segmentation, targeting and positioning in strategic marketing—cont'd**
>
> Parish National Bank (PNB) is a small commercial bank operating in four parishes of New Orleans. Faced with this changing environment, the bank needed to develop an appropriate response. Some smaller banks had responded by aggressively looking to grow in consumer markets and thus position themselves as acquisition targets; others sought to identify particular niches where they could continue to compete effectively. PNB choose the latter course of action. Among the different market segments available, the bank identified local small businesses and small business employees as an attractive market segment. To deliver value to customers in this segment, PNB positioned itself as 'high tech and high touch', and aimed to provide customers with good banking relationships, innovative services and appropriate use of web-based technologies to support delivery.
>
> *Source: Henson and Wilson (2002).*

The process of segmentation, targeting and positioning is discussed in more detail in Chapter 8. Case study 5.1 outlines the efforts of a small US bank to build a successful marketing strategy through careful segmentation, targeting and positioning.

5.3.5   Market-specific strategy

A market-specific strategy outlines specific decisions about how to market particular products and services to particular groups of consumers. This stage will include an indication of the necessary level of marketing expenditure, as well as details on the product itself and how it will be promoted, priced and distributed (the marketing mix). These decisions must be guided by the choice of market position. Thus, for example, if an organization has chosen to position itself as serving wealthy consumers with a high-value, personalized product, then the market-specific strategy will need to look for an appropriate (relatively high) price, decide on which product features to customize, and choose ways of promoting and distributing the product that will appeal to the chosen consumer groups. These decisions are discussed in more detail in Part II of this book.

5.3.6   Implementation

Implementation is concerned with how the marketing plan is put into practice. It must consider budgets, accountability and evaluation. Timescales should be identified, and some consideration may also be given to contingency planning. However well thought-out the marketing plan may be, the market is always changing and, consequently, certain planned activities may turn out to be inappropriate or ineffective. It is important to be aware of these and be in a position to respond – i.e. to modify the strategy as new information becomes available.

Effective financial control is essential for the credibility of a marketing plan – indeed, it is vital for the credibility of a marketing function as a whole. Budgets need to be produced on an accurate and defensible basis. They require a sufficient level of detail to facilitate effective control and the pursuit of efficiency gains. Lack of attention to detail can be a particular problem. For example, it may be relatively easy to identify the total cost of a direct-mail campaign, but if cost per individual contacted and cost per sale are ignored, resources may be badly allocated. For example, one direct-marketing team in the banking sector established a total budget for a campaign which resulted in them planning to spend more in terms of cost per sale than the total margin of the product being promoted.

The plan should make it clear where responsibility and accountability lie for the different activities within the plan. Ownership should be clarified and unambiguous and sole ownership for a particular task should always be sought. It is common to encounter a plethora of shared accountabilities, which results in an unclear sense of ownership. Indeed, well-defined accountability is a necessary prerequisite of an appropriate appraisal system and performance review.

One increasingly important dimension of implementation is internal marketing. Internal marketing deals with the way in which an organization manages the relationship between itself and its employees at all levels. It plays an important role in creating and maintaining a market-orientated corporate culture. The process of internal marketing is seen as particularly important in the financial services sector, not least because of the importance of people in the marketing process. Internal marketing helps to ensure that staff understand the product itself and believe in what the organization is trying to do. If an organization's own employees are not market orientated, if they do not support the overall corporate and marketing strategies, then the chances of successful plan implementation are minimal.

5.4   Tools for strategy development

Later chapters will consider many elements of the marketing plan in more detail. The remainder of this chapter will introduce some of the techniques that organizations can use in order to help develop marketing strategies within the context of the development of the marketing plan. These tools help managers to think about what may be the best strategy to pursue. They can provide useful insights and recommendations. However, good marketing managers will use these tools carefully – they will not provide definite answers and they will not tell you exactly what your organization should do. What they can do is to help you think about the marketing challenges being faced and about how the organization might respond to these challenges.

We begin by looking at options for growth, and then consider tools that might be used when choosing the product portfolio (the mix of products and services to be offered to different target markets). Thereafter, the discussion will examine the issue of competitive advantage.

5.4.1   Growth strategies

An organization that is looking at how best to grow and expand can think about this problem by considering whether to look at new products or new markets. The available choices are represented in Ansoff's Product/Market matrix. This suggests four possible options, which are outlined in Figure 5.2 – market penetration, market development, product development and diversification.

Market penetration

Market penetration means trying to sell more of the existing product in the existing market. To do this, an organization may try to persuade existing users to use more, or non-users to use, or to attract consumers from competitors. There are many examples of marketing tactics that would support a market penetration strategy. Promotional offers such as 'Air Miles' are designed to encourage existing customers to make greater use of their credit cards. In Malaysia, Public Bank's offer of a free mobile phone to new and existing customers for its ACE account (subject to a minimum balance) is another attempt at market penetration by encouraging new purchases from existing and new customers. Usually, a market penetration strategy is more appropriate when the market still has room to expand. In a mature market (where most of the likely buyers have already bought the product), market penetration is more difficult because the organization will need to attract customers directly from competitors, and this is often more difficult than trying to attract new customers to the market. In the UK, the market for current accounts is largely saturated. One or two of the newer entrants, such as the Internet bank, Smile, have tried to follow a market penetration strategy by encouraging customers of other banks to switch their accounts, but most providers appear to be focusing their efforts on retaining customers and exploiting opportunities to cross-sell.

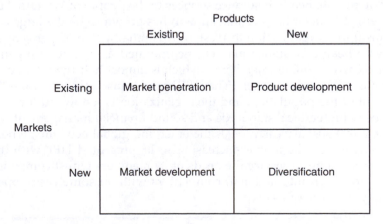

Figure 5.2 Ansoff's Product/Market matrix.

Market development

Market development involves the organization trying to identify new markets for its existing products. Most commonly, this strategy is associated with expansion into new markets geographically. For example, when American International Group (AIG) became the first foreign insurer to obtain a licence to operate in China, it was engaging in market development via geographical expansion. In the US, Morgan Stanley was originally established as an investment bank. The Glass-Steagall Act prevented an expansion into other domestic markets, and so Morgan Stanley grew primarily by overseas expansion. However, deregulation has mean that movement into new market segments is also an important approach to market development. For example, following its conversion from building society to bank, the UK-based Alliance and Leicester pursued a market development strategy by expanding its banking services into corporate markets.

Product development

Growth through product development means developing related products and modifying existing products to appeal to current markets. The diversity of new mortgage products that have become available in the UK market provides an example of modifying existing products to make them more attractive to current markets. The history of American Express is dominated by a series of examples of product development. Initially, the company focused on money orders, travellers' cheques and foreign exchange. In 1958, American Express issued its first charge card. Subsequently the company also launched credit cards, targeting both new customers and existing charge-card customers. A strategy of this nature relies on good service design, packaging and promotion, and often on company reputation to attract consumers to the new product. Case study 5.2 demonstrates the use of product development as a strategy by HBF Health Fund Inc. in Australia.

Case study 5.2   HBF Health Fund Inc.

The Hospital Benefits Fund of Western Australia Inc. was incorporated in 1941 to provide private health insurance services to the people of Western Australia. Since then, HBF (as it has become known) has grown to be the largest private health insurance organization in Western Australia, with a 65 per cent share of the private health insurance market. Incorporated as a mutual organization, HBF has nearly a million members – which is almost half the total population of the state of Western Australia. The HBF brand is instantly recognized by over 99 per cent of the population, and the organization is renowned for its service to members, high ethical standards and sound financial management.

In the late 1980s and early 1990s the emerging global economy, where competitive advantages lie in ever-increasing scale, presented HBF with the challenge of continuing to service the needs of its members whilst competing with national (and even international) competitors with, in some cases, operations many times the size of its own.

Case study 5.2   HBF Health Fund Inc.—cont'd

Without a member-base or any brand awareness in other parts of Australia, it was soon realized that attempting to replicate the scale-based strategies of the major competitors by expanding HBF's operations nationally would expose the organization to an unacceptably high level of risk whilst simultaneously diverting attention away from servicing the needs of its members, all of whom lived in WA. Rather, a decision was taken to expand the organization's operations to cover complementary services for members, focusing on the key strategic advantages available to HBF, particularly the relationship it had with its members.

The first products identified were domestic general insurance products for home, contents and motor vehicle. However, the general insurance market in WA was already mature and dominated by a small number of well-established players. Also, with a history deeply rooted in private health insurance, the HBF brand had become synonymous with this in WA. Stretching the brand to cover domestic insurance products was therefore a significant challenge.

The approach taken by HBF was to differentiate its general insurance products from those already in the market by emphasizing the attributes that had developed around the HBF brand as a provider of private health insurance. HBF focused on its organizational strengths of service to members, mutuality and high ethical standards. Whilst the established players in the domestic insurance market clearly held a competitive advantage in the 'manufacture' of general insurance products, they were unable to match the depth of the relationship HBF had with its members.

Although growth in the general insurance portfolio was slow initially, HBF members who purchased domestic insurance products from the organization soon discovered that the qualities attributed to the health insurance service were also present in the general insurance service.

Despite slow growth initially, HBF was able to persevere with its product development initiative because, as a mutual organization, it is accountable to its members (customers) and not the capital market. Where the traditional capital markets would have demanded a financial return from the investment in a new line of business, HBF was able to take into account the strategic value being generated, represented by a growing acceptance of the new line of business by members.

By 2005, HBF's general insurance business had gained a 12 per cent share of the market in Western Australia. It is generating annual returns on capital of approximately 25 per cent and is growing policy numbers by 15 per cent per annum. The investment in the general insurance business has produced an average annual return of over 20 per cent after tax.

HBF followed a similar strategy with the launch of a Retirement and Investment Advisory business in 2003. After only two years of operation, HBF Financial Services reached an operating break-even. It is projected to generate positive cash flows by the end of 2006.

Continued

> **Case study 5.2   HBF Health Fund Inc.—cont'd**
>
> As in the launch of general insurance 15 years ago, HBF emphasized the orga-
> nization's strengths, applying them in an industry that had experienced a series
> of scandals arising from inappropriate behaviour by existing players. Despite a
> complete lack of scale in the financial advisory industry, HBF has been success-
> ful in capturing a segment of the market that is seeking the trust and security
> offered by a reputable organization.
>
> *Source: Paul Italiano, HBF.*

Diversification

Diversification tends to be a more risky strategy, as it involves an organization
moving into new products and new markets. Pure diversification may be relatively
unusual in financial services, but the development of bancassurance represents a
form of diversification as established banks move into the provision of insurance-
related products. Similarly, the decisions by traditional banks to offer Islamic banking products can also be seen as a form of diversification.

5.4.2   Selecting the product portfolio

Part of any marketing strategy involves consideration of how to manage a range of
different products. This requires decisions about which products need to be developed, which products need to be maintained and which products should be dropped.
Details of product strategy are discussed in greater depth in Chapter 10, but at
a strategic level there are tools available to help marketing managers to evaluate the
existing range of products and make decisions about what should happen with each
product. Two common approaches which are used to determine product portfolios
are the matrix-based approaches of the Boston Consulting Group (BCG) and the
General Electric (GE) Business Screen, and the concept of a product lifecycle.

Matrix-based approaches

Both the BCG and the GE matrices require a classification of products/business
units according to the attractiveness of a particular market and the strengths of the
company in that market. The BCG matrix bases its classification scheme purely on
market share and market growth, while the GE matrix relies on multivariate measures of market attractiveness and business strengths. In both cases, the appropriate
strategy is determined by the position of a product in the matrix.

A simple example of the BCG matrix is presented in Figure 5.3; the division on the
horizontal axis is usually based on a market share identical to that of the firm's nearest
competitor, while the precise location of the division on the vertical axis will depend
on the rate of growth in the market – with 10 per cent usually seen as a reasonable

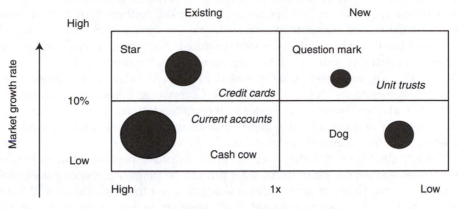

Figure 5.3 The BCG matrix.

cut-off point. Products are positioned in the matrix as circles with a diameter proportional to their sales revenue. The BCG matrix relies on the assumption that a larger market share results in lower costs and thus higher margins.

The appropriate strategy for a particular product will depend upon its position within the matrix. The question mark (or problem child) has a small market share in a high-growth industry. The basic product is popular, but customer support for the specific company versions is limited. If future market growth is anticipated and the products are viable, then the organization should consider increasing marketing expenditure on this product. Otherwise, the possibility of withdrawing the product should be considered.

The star has a high market share in a high-growth industry. By implication, the star has the potential to generate significant earnings currently and in the future. At this stage it may still require substantial marketing expenditures to maintain this position, but can be regarded as a good investment for the future. By contrast, the cash cow has a high market share but in a slower-growing market. The traditional bank current account probably falls into this category. Product development costs for the cash cow are typically low and the marketing campaign is well established, so the cash cow will usually make a reasonable contribution to overall profitability.

Finally, the dog represents a product with a low market share in a low-growth market. As with the cash cow, the product will typically be well established, but it is losing consumer support and may have cost disadvantages. The usual strategy would be to consider withdrawing this product unless cash flow position is strong, in which case the recommended strategy would be to cut back expenditure and maximize net contribution.

The BCG matrix is potentially useful, but its recommendations must be interpreted with care. In particular, it is important to recognize that it focuses only on one aspect of the organization (market share) and one aspect of the market (sales growth). The GE matrix works on similar principles, but concentrates more generally on trying to measure the attractiveness of the market (rather than just measuring market growth) and competitive strength (rather than just market share). This means that the GE matrix gives a broader picture of the strengths and weaknesses of the product portfolio, although it is often more difficult to construct.

Best (2005) suggests using the GE matrix to guide the choice of offensive versus defensive strategies, as shown in Figure 5.4. Comparing market attractiveness and competitive strength results in a series of recommendations about the most appropriate way for the organization to compete in its market. These strategic options are classified as either offensive or defensive.

Offensive strategies include: invest to grow, improve position, and new market entry. These are very similar to Ansoff's growth strategies. *Invest to grow* involves marketing expenditure to grow market share or even to grow the overall market. It is essentially equivalent to a market penetration strategy. *Improve position* involves investing resources to enhance the value offered to consumers relative to the value offered by competitors. Such an approach is analogous to a product development strategy. *New market entry*, as the description suggests, is effectively equivalent to market development and diversification strategies.

Defensive strategies are classified as: protect position, optimize position, monetize, and harvest/divest. A strategy of *protect position* is appropriate where an organization has a currently strong position in an attractive market, and the aim is to discourage new entrants and limit the expansion potential of other competitors. In a market where growth is slowing down, *optimize position* involves focusing attention on maximizing the return on marketing investment. Typically, such an approach would involve trying to focus attention on the profitable customers and controlling marketing expenditure. Trying to persuade less profitable customers to make more use of low-cost channels (such as the phone and Internet) and less use of high-cost channels (such as the branch) is one example of an optimizing strategy.

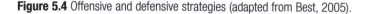

Figure 5.4 Offensive and defensive strategies (adapted from Best, 2005).

Monetize is a more aggressive version of optimize, and focuses on maximizing cash flow without actually preparing to exit from the market. Finally, a *harvest/divest* strategy goes a stage further and involves maximizing cash flow from a product prior to exiting the market. If there is no opportunity to maximize cash flow, then an early market exit would be preferred.

The product lifecycle

The product lifecycle (PLC) is widely used as a tool for market planning, in that it can be employed to guide an organization both in the determination of the appropriate balance of products and in the development of a suitable strategy for the marketing of those products. Its usefulness has been regularly challenged, and clearly there is a risk that the PLC could oversimplify the evolution of a product. While recognizing these limitations, it remains a potentially helpful way of thinking about the strategic management of products.

The product lifecycle, as shown in Figure 5.5, suggests that a given product or service will pass through four basic stages: introduction, growth, maturity and, eventually, decline. The role of marketing is generally considered to be one of prolonging the growth and maturity phases, often using strategies of product modification or product improvement, which are frequently regarded as less risky than developing completely new products.

Assessing the existing product range according to lifecycle position can give some indication of the balance of the existing product portfolio. Furthermore, according to stage in the lifecycle, the organization can obtain some guidance as to the appropriate marketing strategy.

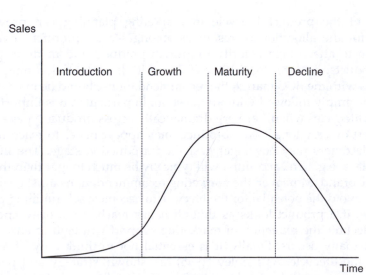

Figure 5.5 The product lifecycle.

Detailed stages of the lifecycle are as follows:

1. *Introduction*. A period of slow growth and possibly negative profit, as efforts are being made to obtain widespread acceptance for the service. Cash flows are typically negative and the priority is to raise awareness and appreciation of the product, with the result that the marketing mix will place a high degree of emphasis on promotion. Mobile banking is one example of a service in the introductory stages of its lifecycle.
2. *Growth*. Sales volumes increase steadily, and the product begins to make a significant contribution to profitability. Increases in sales can be maintained by improvements in features, targeting more segments, or increased price competitiveness. It is at this stage that the new service will begin to attract significant competition. Growth services currently include telephone banking, and the more sophisticated types of ATM. Unit trusts and other related types of investment product have probably also reached the growth stage of the product lifecycle.
3. *Maturity*. Sales growth is relatively slow, and the marketing campaign and product are well established. Competition is probably at its most intense at this stage, and it may be necessary to consider modification to the service and the addition of new features to prevent future decline. Many bank current accounts are products that can be seen as having reached maturity, and in many cases are being modified in attempts to prolong their lifecycle.
4. *Decline*. Sales begin to drop away noticeably, leaving management with the option of withdrawing the product entirely – or at least withdrawing marketing support. In the financial services sector product withdrawal may be difficult, as some products (such as life insurance) cannot simply be withdrawn because some customers will still be paying premiums. Endowment policies (life insurance based savings) are probably now in the decline phase of a lifecycle.

The use of the product lifecycle in marketing planning can provide some guidelines for the allocation of resources among service products, enabling the organization to attach high priority to growth products and medium priority to mature products, and to consider possible withdrawal of declining products. However, as with the BCG matrix, the recommendations should be interpreted with care and not simply followed without question. In particular, it is important to recognize that lifecycles will differ very dramatically across product types – they may be very short or very long. Some products may appear never to reach the decline phase, while others may never get past the introduction stage. The lifecycle for a product class (e.g. bank accounts) will typically be much longer than the lifecycle for a specific brand. Moreover, the marketing recommendations must be interpreted with care to avoid the potential for the lifecycle to become a self-fulfilling prophecy – for example, if a product looks as though it has reached maturity and possibly started to decline, the reduction of marketing support will tend to ensure that the predicted actually occurs. Finally, it is essential not to think only of a product's position in the lifecycle. As Hooley (1995) has shown, strategy and performance may be driven as much by market position (specifically, market share) as by lifecycle stage.

5.4.3   Competitive advantage

Identifying the organization's competitive advantage is an essential part of any marketing strategy. Michael Porter suggests that to compete effectively, an organization must focus either on low costs or on differentiation. A low-cost strategy relies on a relatively standardized product, and the organization offers value through low costs and thus low prices. The differentiation-based approach means that the organization offers a product that is distinctive and offers value to the customers because of the range of features it possesses. For differentiation to be successful, the higher price received by the organization must outweigh the costs of supplying the differentiated product. At the same time, the customer must feel that it is worth paying extra for the distinctive image of the product and the additional features offered.

Using these two routes to competitive advantage and considering the nature of the target market, Porter identifies three broad strategic options:

1. *Cost leadership*. A cost leadership strategy involves trying to be the lowest-cost producer, usually by concentrating on providing relatively standardized products. Low costs allow the organization to attract customers by offering lower prices. Such a strategy typically requires up-to-date and highly efficient service delivery systems. It can be argued that cost leadership was a traditional strategy in many areas of financial services. However, many organizations are finding it increasingly difficult to gain a significant cost advantage over their competitors, and are instead tending to focus more attention on differentiation.
2. *Differentiation leadership*. A differentiation-based strategy means trying to offer something that is seen as unique and distinct. A perceived uniqueness and the associated customer loyalty protect the firm from its competitors, the threat of entry and substitute products. HSBC, Citibank and American Express may all attempt to claim a perceived uniqueness based on their global presence and experience. However, research in the financial services sector suggests that this goal may be difficult to attain for many providers. Devlin and Ennew (1997) have highlighted the difficulties that UK providers of financial services experience in trying to create a clear competitive advantage based on either price or differentiation in a mass market, and also the greater opportunities associated with either focus or niche-based strategies.
3. *Focus/nicheing*. This strategy uses either costs or differentiation, but concentrates on specific segments of the market – market niches. The aim is to identify parts of the market with distinctive needs which are not adequately supplied by larger organizations. Differentiation focus is the most common form of focus strategy, and implies producing highly customized products for very specific consumer groups. For example, in Malaysia, Scotia Bank pursues a focus strategy in relation to a range of products. One such product is its housing loan. Like most other providers, Scotia Bank offers discount rates, but what makes it special is the way in which the bank tries to build relationships with its customers and tailor products to their particular circumstances. Profits arise not from housing loans as such, but from the other products that Scotia Bank can sell to these customers. Another example of a differentiation-based focus strategy is the UK's Ecology Building Society, which specializes in lending that supports sustainable housing, sustainable communities and sustainable enterprises.

Porter's analysis stresses the importance of avoiding a situation where the organization is 'stuck in the middle' – i.e. trying to be all things to all consumers. The firm trying to perform well on costs *and* on differentiation is likely to lose out to firms concentrating on one strategy *or* the other. However, this concept of 'stuck in the middle' has been criticized for its ambiguity, and in any consideration of Porter's framework it is essential to be aware of the importance of value. Value is a based on the relationship between the costs to the consumer and the benefits. Superior value can be created by either adding benefits or reducing costs. Porter's cost- and differentiation-based approaches to building competitive advantage can most sensibly be thought of as approaches to delivering value that concentrate on either reducing costs relative to a given range of benefits (cost leadership) or improving benefits relative to a given cost (differentiation).

5.5 Summary and conclusions

The market for financial services has become increasingly competitive in recent years. Regulatory changes (current and future), developments in information technology, globalization, and fluctuations in economic performance have resulted in an increasingly competitive market environment. In such an environment, success requires a planned and strategic approach to marketing. Developing a plan to guide marketing is of considerable value, because it encourages careful thought and analysis.

The organization must have a clear mission and objectives, it must understand its operating environment and it must be clear about the products and markets it serves. In making choices about products and markets, it is essential that the organization tries to develop a match between its own particular strengths and the needs of the different segments of the market.

There are many different tools available to help an organization develop its marketing plan and its marketing strategy. These tools provide a way of analysing information about the organization and what it is doing. They also provide recommendations about strategic choices which, when combined with the marketing manager's knowledge and understanding of the environment, can be a useful aid for strategy development.

Review questions

1. Why is it important to plan marketing activity?
2. What is your organization's corporate mission, and how might this help guide the future development of marketing activity?
3. What are the essential elements of a marketing plan?
4. What are the differences between market development and product development? Find examples of both from the financial services sector.
5. What is the difference between cost leadership and differentiation leadership? Using Michael Porter's generic strategies, how can organizations try to create a competitive advantage? Identify examples of organizations that you think are using these approaches.

Internationalization strategies for financial services

By the end of this chapter you will be able to:
- identify key drivers of internationalization in the financial services sector
- understand the factors influencing the choice of internationalization strategy
- identify the marketing implications associated with internationalization.

6.1   Introduction

Internationalization is a broad term. It goes beyond the basic notions of trade and exporting to encompass all aspects of business activity that extend beyond national borders. Exporting is often thought of as simply the first stage in this process, which can extend to the establishment of a fully-fledged business presence in an overseas market. Most discussions of service marketing, including those relating to financial services, tend to focus on marketing in a domestic context. Equally, most textbooks on international strategy and marketing tend to focus predominantly on the activities and issues associated with companies providing physical goods. Yet services account for an increasingly large share of world trade, and there is a long tradition of international activity within the financial services sector. World Trade Organization figures suggest, that in 2003, services accounted for some 20 per cent of world trade by value, having grown some 13 per cent on the previous year (World Trade Organization, 2004). The US-based Citibank has been operating in France since 1906, Argentina since 1914 and Brazil since 1915. The UK bank, Barclays, formed its international division in 1925 through the merger of the Colonial Bank, the Anglo-Egyptian Bank and the National Bank of South Africa. In the insurance sector, Prudential established its first overseas agencies for the sale of general insurance products in the 1920s and for the sale of life products in the 1930s. Yet, despite this long tradition of international activity, most discussions of financial services marketing pay relatively little attention to the activities of firms in overseas markets.

The purpose of this chapter is to provide an overview of the issues relating to the internationalization of financial services, and their marketing implications. The next section explores the relationship between the characteristics of financial services for the process of internationalization. Thereafter, a brief review of the drivers of internationalization in financial services is presented. The chapter then proceeds to outline internationalization strategies and their relevance to financial services. Finally, there is a brief discussion of the marketing challenges associated with international environments.

6.2   Internationalization and the characteristics of financial services

The distinctive characteristics of financial services and their marketing implications were discussed in Chapter 3. These characteristics also have implications for internationalization. The intangibility of financial services means that actually there is nothing physical to move from producer to consumer. In principle this intangibility may make it relatively easy to export some financial services, particularly in corporate markets. For example, if the investment bank UBS handles an equity trade in New York for a client in Japan, it is effectively exporting its services – nothing physical is being transported, but a service is provided remotely. In retail markets, exporting is often more difficult: consumer reactions to intangibility often make it difficult to supply financial services without a physical presence in the domestic market. Inseparability implies a need to focus particular attention on how to manage interactions with customers in different locations, while heterogeneity reminds us of the additional challenges associated with providing a consistent service across different countries. Of course, concerns about fiduciary responsibility mean that financial services providers also face the challenge of operating in potentially diverse regulatory environments if and when they internationalize.

In terms of service classifications, financial services are typically heavily information-based services, and in principle are easily digitized. It is this feature that makes export relatively straightforward in theory. However, the complexity of many financial services suggests that significant interpersonal interaction is often required in their delivery. This has important implications. First, there is often strong pressure for a financial services organization to have a physical presence in the market in which it is delivering its services. Many buyers (particularly those in retail markets) feel the need to be able to access their service provider and are reassured by a physical presence (even if they may deal with a provider remotely), and regulators commonly require such a presence. Thus, in comparison with suppliers of manufactured goods, financial services providers will often be less reliant on exports and much more likely to internationalize by establishing overseas operations. This in turn raises important issues in relation to the nature and management of service delivery.

One of the major challenges that organizations face when operating internationally relates to cultural differences, and the greater the difference in cultures, the greater the challenges. Cultural differences impact on financial services internationalization in two ways. First, there are issues related to familiarity and use of financial products. In many Islamic countries, the prohibition on interest means that credit-card holders will seek to pay off accounts at the end of each month rather than accumulating interest charges. Variable-rate mortgages are widespread in the UK, whereas many countries in continental Europe have a longstanding tradition of fixed-rate mortgages. Secondly, culture can impact significantly on interactions where the two parties have different heritages. Cultural differences can affect the development of long-term relationships, where the creation of trust plays a central role – for example, the rather direct negotiating styles of the British and Americans may appear quite threatening and even rude in Japan, thus inhibiting the development of mutual trust. In addition, cultural differences are often a source of misunderstanding in communications, with all sorts of negative consequences for service provision. For example, Egg, the UK-based Internet bank, invested £280m expanding in France but withdrew after 2 years; a poorly thought through and culturally insensitive advertising campaign was one of a number of factors that contributed to the failure of this venture. In contrast, UK banks relying on offshore outsourcing to deliver customer service to domestic customers from bases in India have invested considerably in ensuring that local staff are familiar with key aspects of British culture.

Given the significance of cultural differences, it is perhaps not too surprising to observe that many examples of the internationalization process in financial services started with moves into environments that are in some respects culturally similar. It is no accident, for example, that many Spanish banks have tended to concentrate their international activity in South America, or that many UK financial services providers initially established overseas operations in countries which were then colonies and in which there were substantial anglophile market segments. 'Cultural proximity' is a useful piece of shorthand to describe this phenomenon.

Although the nature of financial services presents important challenges to the internationalization process, it is apparent that there are clear attractions to international operations and these are encouraging many financial services to expand beyond their domestic market. The next section explores the conditions that influence financial services providers to operate globally.

6.3   The drivers of internationalization

When considering the drivers to internationalization, it is useful to distinguish between firm-specific and macro-environmental factors. Firm-specific factors are those factors that create incentives for individual firms to move into international markets.

Macro-environmental factors are those features of the overall environment that create conditions which favour internationalization for all firms. Naturally, the two are related and interdependent.

6.4   Firm-specific drivers of internationalization

At the level of the individual firm, the motives for expanding beyond the domestic market by a given provider may be divided into 'push' and 'pull' factors. Push factors are essentially domestic market conditions that will tend to encourage a firm to look outside its national markets, while pull factors are features of non-domestic markets that encourage a firm to consider expanding operations overseas.

Push factors focus essentially on conditions in the domestic market that may in some way inhibit a firm from achieving its strategic goals. The simplest example of a push factor might be slow growth, high costs or high levels of competition in the domestic market. Cost considerations, for example, have been a major driver of the decision of many financial services providers to establish call-centres in countries such as India. Another push factor might well be domestic regulation. For example, in the US the Glass-Steagall Act of 1933 which, until its repeal in 1999, prevented banks from engaging in both commercial and investment banking has been identified as one factor that encouraged US banks to expand overseas where they could engage in activities which were not permitted domestically. In Spain, domestic competition and pressures on profit margins were identified as one reason why a number of banks looked to expand into international markets.

More commonly, overseas expansion is thought to be influenced by pull factors which make overseas markets attractive as places to do business. Probably the commonest pull factor is the size and growth of markets in other countries. The liberalization of the economies of India and China has contributed to rapid growth in both countries, and this, combined with their size, has made these markets highly attractive and has encouraged a large number of financial services providers to seek to establish a presence in these countries. ING, for example, has acquired a 20 per cent stake in Vysya Bank in India, while Chase Capital has taken a 15 per cent stake in HDFC Bank. Banks currently operating in China include Citibank, HSBC, Standard Chartered, BNP Paribas, Dresdener Bank and the Industrial Bank of Korea. Both markets are also attractive to insurers because of the combination of growing incomes and the relatively low levels of expenditure on insurance products. Cardone-Riportella and Cazorla-Papis (2001) note that the low level of competition, the low level of banking services and increasing deregulation in many Latin-American countries has made them attractive target markets for Spanish banks looking to move overseas. International markets may also be attractive because they provide an opportunity to leverage a particular competitive strength or because they provide a means of adding value to the company's service. For example, many financial services providers moved overseas to follow their international customers and thus be in a position to offer an integrated service to those customers.

While the factors that affect individual firms and create incentives for expansion overseas are clearly important and need to be fully understood, there are also broader, macro-level factors which mean that some industries or some sectors may be more suited to globalization than others. These factors are discussed in the next section.

6.5   Macro level drivers of internationalization

At the macro-level, there is a series of developments in the business environment which make internationalization an increasingly attractive activity. The different forms that such internationalization can take are discussed in greater detail in the next section, where specific distinctions are drawn between global, international and transnational strategies.

Yip (1992) originally identified five drivers of globalization, namely market, cost, technology, government and competition. Lovelock and Yip (1996) subsequently explored the applicability of these factors in the service sector. The rest of this section explores the drivers for globalization in financial services, based on Yip's framework.

Market drivers

This category refers to those features of the marketplace that encourage globalization. The following are of particular significance are:

1. *Common customer needs*. In markets where customer needs are essentially the same across the world, globalization is thought to be an attractive strategy because a business can offer a relatively standardized product across a series of markets. In the global securities business the needs and expectation of investment houses are generally very similar across countries, and consequently the securities houses that serve those customers are increasingly operating in a global market.
2. *Global customers*. If customers themselves operate globally, then again there is an incentive for the companies that supply them to operate on a similar scale. One of the important drivers in the internationalization of banking has been the internationalization of the businesses that those banks serve. Equally, in the personal market, a company such as American Express needs to operate globally because the customers it serves are effectively global, not just in terms of where they live but also in the extent to which they travel.
3. *Global distribution channels*. If channels of distribution are themselves global, then it is much easier for companies that sell through those channels to operate globally. Although we tend to think of financial services as being characterized by relatively short distribution channels, it is important to remember that financial services are typically information-intensive and that developments in electronic distribution systems have, in some senses, created global distribution systems. Networks such as Cirrus, for example, which allow customers to withdraw funds

from ATMs worldwide, provide a means by which banks can make some aspects of their service available to customers globally.

4. *Transferable marketing.* If marketing campaigns developed in one country are easily transferred to other countries, then global operations are much easier to implement. Marketing activities which are specific to a particular environment and not easily transferred increase the costs associated with operating overseas. Indeed, many companies operating or looking to operate globally pay particular attention to ensuring that their campaigns are designed to be transferable. The HSBC brand-building exercise which demonstrates an understanding of cultural differences worldwide, supported by the claim to be 'The World's Local Bank', is a case in point. Although the bank aims to localize its services to individual countries, it gains significant economies from a globally transferable marketing campaign and a global brand.

Cost drivers

Cost drivers are concerned with the extent to which expansion globally can enable a firm to reduce its costs. Most commonly, cost drivers are associated with economies of scale – the cost savings that are associated with expanding the scale of operations. Such cost savings are often thought to be relatively unimportant in the service sector, including financial services. However, cost savings may arise in other ways, most obviously through access to lower-cost resources. In financial services the developments in IT have facilitated the separation of front- and back-office processing, and consequently one form of expansion overseas has been in the form of outsourcing business processes to lower-cost countries. This has more recently been augmented by the outsourcing of certain front-office functions, including outbound telemarketing and customer service. In the UK, a range of financial services providers (including Lloyds TSB, Barclays, Zurich Financial Services, Prudential and Capital One) have all outsourced a range of activities to India to benefit from lower costs in that market.

Technology drivers

Technology drivers are in many respects closely related to cost drivers – at least in a financial services context. Developments in information and communications technology have supported internationalization by facilitating global distribution and supporting outsourcing for a range of business processes.

Government drivers

Government drivers to globalization refer to any aspects of government or public policy that make it easy (or difficult) for foreign firms to operate in a domestic market. Most commonly, government drivers are the presence or absence of restrictions on market entry, or the presence of regulatory systems which restrict what foreign entrants may do. Case study 6.1 outlines the consequences of China's entry into the World Trade Organization for potential entrants to the banking and insurance sectors.

> ### Case study 6.1   China and the WTO
>
> The World Trade Organization produced the following statement in response to the conclusions of negotiations on China's accession.
>
> *Banking*
> Upon accession, foreign financial institutions will be permitted to provide services in China without client restrictions for foreign currency business. For local currency business, within two years of accession, foreign financial institutions will be permitted to provide services to Chinese enterprises. Within five years of accession, foreign financial institutions will be permitted to provide services to all Chinese clients.
>
> *Insurance*
> Foreign non-life insurers will be permitted to establish as a branch or as a joint venture with 51 per cent foreign ownership. Within two years of China's accession, foreign non-life insurers will be permitted to establish as a wholly-owned subsidiary. Upon accession, foreign life insurers will be permitted 50 per cent foreign ownership in a joint venture with the partner of their choice. For large-scale commercial risks, reinsurance and international marine, aviation and transport insurance and reinsurance, upon accession, joint ventures with foreign equity of no more than 50 per cent will be permitted; within three years of China's accession, foreign equity share shall be increased to 51 per cent; within five years of China's accession, wholly foreign-owned subsidiaries will be permitted.
>
> *Source: WTO (2001).*

Competition drivers

Competition drivers relate to a range of factors associated with the nature and level of competition in different markets. A move into an international market might be prompted by the entry of a competitor into the home market. Equally, the entry of a competitor into a new market might create an incentive for a company to follow suit in order to maintain some degree of competitive parity.

6.5.1   The extent of internationalization in the financial services sector

Clearly, there are many examples of financial services providers operating internationally and in many sectors of the industry, the macro-environment favours international operations. In particular, financial services targeted towards large corporates lend themselves to international operations because of the similarity in customer needs and the fact that many customers themselves are global. In contrast, personal financial advice is more suited to domestic provision because needs do vary, distribution is essentially personal and regulations are very different.

Retail banking is predominantly domestic, but there is a growing number of banks (e.g. HSBC, Citibank, Standard Chartered) offering their services in a range of markets worldwide; some of the target market may be expatriate staff, but the rest will be domestic nationals and the service provided is usually broadly similar to that offered in other countries. Many insurers are following a similar strategy and establishing networks of operations worldwide. Case study 6.2 outlines the experience of the European Union (EU) in trying to encourage greater international activity in financial services among member countries.

Case study 6.2   Internationalizing financial services in the European Union

In 1985 the European Commission published a White Paper, 'Completing the Internal Market', which proposed a series of measures to create a single internal market among the countries of the then European Community. This was codified in the Single Europe Act of 1986, the first major amendment to the Treaty of Rome (which had initially established the European Union in 1957). This Act required that the measures outlined in the 1985 White Paper should be implemented by the end of 1992, and included provision for mutual recognition of national product standards and a range of other measures to eliminate barriers to trade within the Union. The Single European Market formally came into being in 1993, underpinned by the 'four freedoms' – free movement of goods, services, labour and capital.

In the case of financial services, the single European market aimed to eliminate restrictions on cross-border activity, thus encouraging greater competition, greater efficiency, lower prices and better service for customers. Given the high level of regulation in financial services and considerable differences in industry tradition, the single market relied on the principle of mutual recognition – if a financial services provider was licensed to operate in its home market, then it was effectively free to provide services to consumers throughout the European Union.

Although formal legal restrictions on cross-border activity in financial services have been largely removed as a consequence of the Single European Act, progress towards a genuine single market in retail financial services has been slow. Genuine cross-border trade in financial services failed to grow substantially, and most providers serving non-domestic markets did so by establishing a physical rather than an export presence, with that physical presence typically being via mergers and acquisition rather than greenfield developments. In principal, there is no reason why many retail financial services need to be provided locally; in practice, most are. Take the case of a mortgage; while it is technically possible for a resident of Germany to obtain a mortgage for a house in Germany from a Spanish bank, in practice many customers are nervous of non-domestic providers with no physical presence in the market. Equally, banks may be concerned about lending into a different legal environment where it may prove costly to recover the security (i.e. the house) in the event of default. Differences in tax treatment and consumer protection legislation between countries may also

Case study 6.2 Internationalizing financial services in the European Union—cont'd

serve as a disincentive to the purchase of savings and investment products across borders. In business markets, progress has been rather faster and the degree of integration is much greater, although considerable effort has been required to address areas such as capital adequacy requirements and accounting standards.

Recognizing some of the particular difficulties with financial services, the European Commission developed a Financial Services Action Plan (FSAP) in 1998 which focused on eliminating barriers to cross-border trade. The Action Plan concentrated on developing a genuine single market for wholesale financial services, creating open and secure retail markets, ensuring the continued stability of EU financial markets and eliminating tax obstacles to financial market integration. Considerable progress was made in relation to the wholesale markets; progress with retail markets was slow and the scale of cross-border activity remained low.

Subsequently, in December 2005, the Commission published a White Paper, 'Financial Services Policy 2005–2010', to outline its policies for the rest of the decade. The White Paper focused its attention on ensuring that existing policy changes were implemented and consolidated, improving regulation, enhancing supervisory convergence, increasing competition between service providers and expanding the EU's influence in global financial services.

Source: European Commission (2006), The Internal Market, available at http://europa.eu.int/comm/internal_market/index_en.htm (accessed 4 March 2006).

As well as there being variety in the extent to which financial services providers operate globally, there are variations in the approaches that they adopt. The next section explores in some detail the different ways in which organizations may choose to operate in non-domestic markets.

6.6 Globalization strategies

Thus far, the words internationalization and globalization have, to some extent, been used interchangeably. However, researchers in international business would distinguish between the two and see them as potentially quite different approaches to operating outside of domestic borders. In particular, Ghoshal and Bartlett (1998) suggested that the right approach to internationalization would depend on the extent to which there were:

- pressures to integrate activities across markets – i.e. pressures to exploit economies of scale and offer a relatively standardized product which leverages around particular assets or competences

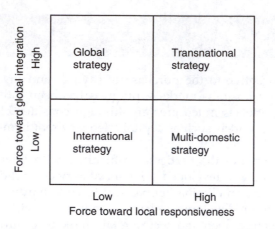

Figure 6.1 Different forms of internationalization (adapted from Ghoshal and Bartlett, 1998).

- pressures to be locally responsive, adjusting and adapting a service offer to local (country-specific or regional) needs.

This led to the identification of four basic options for internationalization, as outlined in Figure 6.1.

6.6.1   International strategies

An international strategy is, in many senses, a weak or unstable position. Such a strategy involves doing broadly the same thing in a series of different markets, but without any attempt to integrate to get costs down or to tailor the service to the specific market. While pressures for integration or responsiveness may not be strong, firms following an international strategy will always be vulnerable to competitors who are able to integrate and outperform them in terms of costs or competitors who are able to customize and outperform them in terms of benefits offered to the consumer. Historically, this is probably the strategy that many financial services organizations operated in the early stages of internationalization. HSBC, for example, traditionally operated across a range of markets, offering relatively standard banking services but under a different brand and name in each country. In the UK, HSBC traded as the Midland Bank, in Australia as the Hong Kong Bank of Australia, in the Middle East as the British Bank of the Middle East and in the USA as the Marine Midland Bank. In 1998, the bank announced a move to create a unified brand for all its operations worldwide in order to be able to integrate marketing activities, improve marketing effectiveness and increase shareholder value. In effect, HSBC was moving away from an international strategy and towards a global strategy by more fully integrating its marketing activities worldwide.

6.6.2 Global strategies

A global strategy essentially focuses on integrating business activities across markets in order to ensure greater efficiency in operations; differences between markets tend to be discounted and the pressure to be locally responsive is considered to be weak. Rather than focusing on possible differences in customer needs, a global strategy focuses on similarities and sees different international markets as being essentially homogenous. Typically, such a strategy is associated with manufacturers of highly standardized physical goods and emphasizes economies of scale in production and marketing. Matsushita is the example cited by Ghoshal and Bartlett (1998), with 90 per cent of its production concentrated in highly efficient plants in Japan and yet 40 per cent of its revenue coming from sales overseas.

In many senses, it is difficult for any financial services provider to be truly global because regulatory regimes vary across countries and limit the extent of true standardization. However, in retail markets, banks such as HSBC and Citibank are arguably following something close to a global strategy, with recognized global brands and strong presence worldwide. The same may be said of American Express, Visa and Mastercard. In corporate markets, Bank of Tokyo Mitsubishi, with its diversified global network and ability to provide a full range of services to customers worldwide, is probably also following something close to a global strategy.

6.6.3 Multi-domestic strategies

A multi-domestic strategy arises when the pressures for integration are low and the pressures for local responsiveness are high. Such a strategy is characterized by operations across multiple markets, but with a high degree of decentralization to ensure that services are tailored to the needs of those local markets. Any pressures on costs which might encourage integration are outweighed by the importance of local responsiveness; if a head office exists, its control is relatively weak and the organization is perhaps best thought of as a federation of semi-autonomous companies. Multi-domestic strategies are probably most closely associated with manufacturers of products that are in some way culturally sensitive (such as food and personal care) and where adaptation is essential. Multi-domestic strategies are relatively unusual, but in the financial services sector such an approach would apply to relatively information-intensive and people-focused services such as financial advice, where local responsiveness is essential. For example, De Vere and Partners – one of the largest chains of independent financial advisers – operates in 30 different countries worldwide. Differences in regulation and differences among consumers mean that scope for integration is limited, and that advice must be tailored to customer and country context.

6.6.4 Transnational strategies

According to Ghoshal and Bartlett, transnational strategies are a relatively recent phenomenon and have emerged in markets where there are significant pressures to keep costs low through global integration, and also a need for a high degree of local responsiveness. This approach requires a high degree of global co-ordination and careful management of operations to fully exploit opportunities for increased efficiency, while retaining the flexibility to tailor the service to a given market. In principle, a transnational strategy creates a strong competitive position, being more locally responsive than a global strategy and of a lower cost than a multi-domestic strategy. There are probably relatively few examples of genuinely transnational strategies in services, not least because of the difficulty of delivering both integration and responsiveness. In the service sector more generally, MacDonald's is sometimes cited as an example of a service-based company moving towards a transnational strategy. It uses supply-chain management systems and global branding to ensure a high degree of integration whilst, within this framework, adjusting the products offered in each country to accommodate the tastes and expectations of domestic consumers. In financial services, given that IT enables a greater degree of remote delivery and facilitates the separation of front- and back-office activities, there may be the potential for some of the providers who are moving towards global strategies to become increasingly transnational.

6.7   Strategy selection and implementation

From the discussion of different strategic approaches to international markets in the previous section, it is apparent that the choice of strategy is likely to depend on the type of service and the nature of the business environment. For example, services that require a high degree of interpersonal interaction (what Lovelock and Yip (1996) would describe as people-processing services) will probably be most suited to a multi-domestic strategy, particularly if cultural or regulatory differences between markets are significant. In contrast, services that have limited requirements for interpersonal interaction (information- or possession-processing services) will be more suited to global or transnational strategies. The choice between the two will then be driven by the extent to which customer needs differ, and the ability of the organization to deliver a differentiated service.

In addition to thinking about the right strategic approach to adopt for international operations, there are three other important decisions that require consideration: which markets to enter, how to enter those markets, and how to market services within those markets.

6.7.1   Which markets to enter

In very simple terms, the choice of markets to enter is based on identifying those that offer the best long-term returns. Superficially this may sound like a straightforward decision; in reality, it is potentially very complex. The factors discussed in Chapter 5 as being the basis for an evaluation of target market attractiveness domestically will all be relevant to the choice of target market internationally. Cultural proximity is frequently a major factor in determining international developments, at least during the early stages of a strategy for overseas expansion.

However, broader macro-influences must also be considered and factored into the market selection decision. Factors such as size of population, levels of income and rate of growth will have important implications for the attractiveness of a market. One of the reasons why both India and China are attractive to many financial services organizations is that they are large markets and, although income levels are relatively low, economic growth rates are high, suggesting considerable long-term potential. Economic variables are imperative in determining the attractiveness of a market, but it is equally important to consider the feasibility of operating in a particular market. Infrastructure is one important consideration, encompassing the quality and capacity of communications networks, access to essential supporting services (e.g. market research) and the ability to access suitable premises. Given the importance of people in a service business the availability of appropriate quality staff must be considered, and this may be of particular significance in cases where there is a significant cultural difference between home and target market (a high psychic distance). In financial services, understanding the nature of domestic market regulation and its implications for the conduct of business is essential. Finally, of course, it is important to remember that some international markets may be strategically significant and that, irrespective of the other factors, firms need to have a presence in those markets. For banks operating internationally, a presence in the key markets of London, Tokyo and New York will probably be essential quite simply because customers and competitors expect to see them there.

6.7.2   Method of market entry

Methods of market entry are normally divided into three categories: export, contractual and investment. In very simple terms we can think about these forms of market entry as being distinctive in terms of cost and control, with exporting at one extreme seen as offering low cost but low control, and investment being high cost but high control. The choice of entry mode can then be thought of in terms of the extent to which the firm needs to control the marketing and delivery of its products and services to customers, and the extent to which it wishes to control costs. Exporting is often presented as being the first stage in internationalization, because it involves a relatively low resource commitment. As firms build up experience they are thought to move on to more complex and high commitment method of market entry, such as a contractual arrangement or direct investment in overseas markets. In practice, of course, the choices are rarely that straightforward, and the nature of financial services does tend to constrain the choice of mode of market entry. A helpful overview that highlights some of the complexities associated with internationalization and methods of market entry is provided by Whitelock (2002).

The methods of market entry are described below:

1. *Export*. Exporting involves supplying goods from the home country to customers located in international markets. Provider and customer essentially remain at arm's length. Different regulatory systems and customer preferences for a physical presence make this form of market entry difficult for providers of financial services, although deregulation within the European Union has sought to encourage increased trade in financial services through a system of mutual recognition.

Moreover, it has been suggested that high levels of information intensity in some financial services, combined with the ability to digitize, have increased the potential for service exports (McLaughlin and Fitzsimmons, 1996). Certainly the global securities business, which relies heavily on digitized information relies on growing volumes of export-style activities with, for example, an investment house in New York dealing with a securities house in Hong Kong who will then provide a service remotely, based around information.

2. *Contractual*: A contractual entry mode involves some form of partnership arrangement with a domestic provider which typically does not involve any shared ownership. Contractual entry modes are rather more costly than exporting, but also provide rather more control. The most immediately recognizable forms of contractual entry are franchising and licensing. Both these arrangements grant an overseas firm the right to use some of the knowledge and expertise associated with the firm wishing to internationalize, and, because they draw on local managerial expertise, can be of particular value when there is a need to be sensitive to and adapt to local culture. Licensing arrangements are common in the physical goods sector – a variety of different types of soft drinks and food stuffs available worldwide are manufactured 'under licence', i.e. using licensed recipes, manufacturing processes etc. Franchising extends the licensing concept to cover not just the product but also a broader business format. Service businesses such as Hertz, Hilton Hotels and MacDonald's rely heavily on franchising as a method of market entry, but it is relatively less popular in the financial services sector for internationalization, although it is used in domestic markets for activities such as financial advice and broking.

3. *Investment*: Investment-based entry describes any type of operation in which a control is established over physical assets in an international market. It is the highest-cost mode of entry and requires considerable commitment, but it also offers the highest level of control over the conduct of business. Investment-based entry may involve wholly new developments (sometimes referred to as greenfield developments) or some form of joint venture, strategic alliance or merger/acquisition. Greenfield developments are costly, but allow the organization to do exactly what it wants. Citibank's entry to the Japanese market in the 1980s was managed as a wholly new development. Joint ventures and strategic alliances are less flexible, because they entail working with local partners, but they do ensure access to organizations with local knowledge (which can be very important in some markets). In many countries, government regulations require that foreign entrants operate in a joint venture (see Case study 6.1 regarding China), so new market entrants may simply not have a choice. Mergers and acquisitions can be attractive as routes to market, because they provide speedy access to an existing customer base and save the new entrant the difficulty of building up the business from nothing. The acquisition of the British-based Abbey plc by the Spanish Banco Santander is a good example of such an approach. However, there are clear challenges associated with integrating the staff and systems of two or more businesses, and this can make mergers and acquisitions difficult to manage. In general, investment entry modes have been widely used in financial services; there are numerous examples of joint ventures where required by regulations and market conditions, but many of the larger international financial services organizations have reached their position through

a series of mergers and acquisitions. For example, Deutsche Bank became a global bank through the acquisition of Banca d'America e d'Italia in 1986 (Italy), Morgan Grenfell in 1989 (UK), Bankers Trust in 1999 (USA), Scudder Investments in 2002 (USA), Rued Blass & Cie in 2003 (Switzerland) and United Financial Group in 2006 (Russia).

The choice of method of market entry is subject to a variety of influences, including the nature of the service, the internal resources and capabilities of the firm, the regulatory environment and the host-country environment. This means that it can be difficult to generalize about the best mode of market entry for any given service, but investment modes do appear to be the preferred route to market for most financial services providers – reflecting, perhaps, the importance of a physical presence in the market, regulatory considerations, the value of local knowledge and the need for control over the service itself and the way in which it is delivered.

6.7.3   How to market in international markets

Once a method of market entry has been selected and implemented, the issue of marketing needs to be addressed. Discussions of international marketing have traditionally revolved around the debate between standardization and customization – should an organization operate with the same marketing strategies and tactics across all markets, or should strategy and tactics be tailored to the local market? In basic terms, this can be thought of as directly analogous to the choice between a global strategy (low levels of local responsiveness) and a multi-domestic strategy (high levels of local responsiveness). Although this debate has attracted much attention in academic literature and international marketing textbooks, most academics and practitioners would recognize that some degree of customization is unavoidable and that sensible approaches to international markets will involve standardizing where possible (the brand, advertising messages, logos, use of colour, methods of distribution) and being prepared to customize where necessary (product features, creative presentations, use of language, price). The leading global financial services providers such as Standard Chartered Bank, American Express, HSBC and Citibank all provide examples of how this is done. Some marketing activities are adapted to the specific context, but there remains considerable standardization in terms of the marketing communications, thus ensuring that the brand is recognizable worldwide.

6.8   Summary and conclusions

This chapter has introduced some of the major issues relating to internationalization in the financial services sector. Although it is commonly assumed that financial services are very much domestic markets because of regulatory frameworks and consumer expectations regarding a physical presence, many aspects of the industry are highly international. A variety of factors may encourage internationalization. At a micro-level, we can distinguish those factors which 'push' an organization overseas and those which 'pull'. At a macro-level, variations in the environment can make international operations more or less attractive.

A series of broad strategic approaches to international activity can be identified based on the degree to which there is pressure for integration to exploit economies of scale and the degree to which there is a need for local responsiveness. As well as establishing a broad strategic approach to operating internationally, organizations must also give careful consideration to the choice of markets in which to operate, the method of market entry, and the right approach to marketing its services once established.

Review questions

1. Why are banks more international than financial advisers? Why are corporate financial services more international than retail financial services?
2. What are the benefits to HSBC of the development of a global brand?
3. Compare and contrast exporting and investment modes of market entry for financial services. Why have investment modes of entry been more widespread?

Understanding the financial services consumer

Learning objectives

By the end of this chapter you will be able to:

- understand the factors that influence consumer decision-making in financial services
- recognize the ways in which financial services providers can influence the buying process
- recognize the differences between final consumers and business consumers in relation to financial services.

7.1   Introduction

Understanding consumers is central to effective marketing, and yet our understanding of how consumers buy financial services is rather limited. For many personal consumers, financial services are not seen as particularly interesting or exciting purchases; they are seen as complicated, and often it is difficult for consumers to identify differences between a bank account from, say, HSBC and one from Standard Chartered, or between an insurance policy from Aetna and one from AIA. Consumers find it difficult to evaluate their purchase in advance, and consequently experience high levels of perceived risk. Furthermore, as explained in Chapter 3, financial services are often seen as uninteresting and consumption is contingent – that is, the services in themselves do not generate a current consumption benefit; indeed, they can serve to reduce current consumption pleasure. In some cases financial services may create consumption opportunities in the future; in other cases they may never result in tangible consumption for the individual who made the purchase (e.g. life insurance). Many consumers regard them as 'distress purchases' – things that they have to buy but don't want to – and often have little incentive to learn more about such products. Thus, many personal consumers are often rather uninterested and relatively passive consumers.

The same may not be true of business customers, many of whom will have detailed knowledge of financial services and their companies' financial needs. Their purchases of financial services will be seen as important factors contributing to the performance of the business, and consequently they are likely to be much more active and better informed during the buying process. Of course this is something of a generalization, care must be taken not to stereotype consumers too much. However, the comparison helps to show that trying to understand financial services buying behaviour can be very complicated.

This chapter, which is substantially based on Ennew and McKechnie (1992), aims to provide an explanation of how consumers make decisions when buying financial services. The main focus will be on personal consumers, but, where appropriate, the experiences of personal consumers will be contrasted with the experiences of business customers. The chapter begins with a discussion of consumer decision-making based on established information-processing models of consumer choice.

7.2   Consumer choice and financial services

It is important to bear in mind that the term 'customer' is multifaceted, whereby a number of roles combine together to result ultimately in consumption. For example, there is the role of *initiating* the desire to satisfy a given need; this may be followed-up by the role of the *influencer* and lead on to the *decider*, *purchaser* and *user*. In the consumer domain all five roles are frequently performed by the same person, especially with regard to what are termed routine purchases. However, in the B2B domain they are very often carried out by separate individuals or, possibly, groups of individuals. We call this a decision-making unit (dmu), and it has significant implications for the organization of marketing activities. It calls for detailed knowledge of the dmu at the level of the individual business entity, and this is a major challenge when marketing financial services to corporate clients.

There are many different frameworks for understanding consumer behaviour. Indeed, there is a growing interest in researching consumers from interpretivist perspectives to understand the meaning, nature and significance of consumption of certain types of goods and services to individuals. However, the majority of research on financial services consumers has relied on traditional cognitive-based approaches to understanding consumer behaviour. These approaches to understanding consumers are based on the notion that consumer choice is the result of some form of systematic processing and evaluation of information. The consumer is seen as a problem-solver who moves sequentially through a series of stages in a decision-making process prior to making a purchase. One of the best examples of

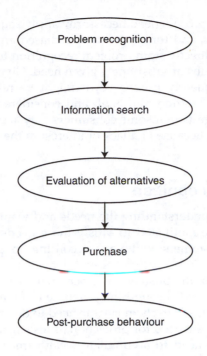

Figure 7.1 The Engel–Kollat–Blackwell model.

this approach for final consumers is probably the Engel–Kollat–Blackwell model (Engel *et al.*, 1991), which is outlined in very simplified form in Figure 7.1.

In essence, the decision process begins when the buyer recognizes a 'problem' (that is, a difference between a desired and an actual state) and is motivated to act. Need recognition may be stimulated by either external factors (e.g. advertising, promotion, awareness of the consumption of others) or internal factors (e.g. hunger, thirst, need for security). To solve the problem, the buyer engages in a search for relevant information (either from memory or external sources, or from both). Based on that information, the consumer evaluates the alternative options that are available and makes a purchase decision based on which option best meets the initial need. Finally, once the purchase has been made, there will be further evaluation and responses including, typically, evaluations of satisfaction, willingness to recommend and willingness to repurchase.

Treating consumer choice as a problem-solving process may have a certain intuitive appeal, but it also has a number of weaknesses. In particular, such an approach assumes a high degree of rationality in purchase decisions; it assumes that decision-making is very logical and linear, and it assumes a degree of consistency in behaviour. It is important to recognize these limitations and to be aware that consumer choice in financial services is potentially a very complex process. However, the simple framework outlined in Figure 7.1 is helpful as a way of structuring the discussion of consumer choice in financial services. In particular, it is useful as means of understanding some of the different ways in which marketing can and does influence the choice process. It should be appreciated that not all five steps in the

Engel–Kollat–Blackwell process need necessarily apply sequentially to all purchase occasions. In some cases, and for frequently purchased and simple products, consumers might proceed directly from problem recognition to purchase because they are familiar with the means of satisfying a given need. Given that financial services are complex and infrequently purchased, it might be reasonable to expect that the choice process may be more thorough and considered, although, in practice, anecdotal evidence suggests that some consumers may actually make quite impulsive purchases, not least because of a lack of interest in the product.

7.2.1   Problem recognition

This is concerned with understanding the needs and wants of consumers and the extent to which they are motivated to satisfy those needs and wants. Needs and wants for personal customers will vary according to personal circumstances, whereas the needs of business customers will depend upon the stage of development and the situation of the business. For personal customers there is a range of 'needs' that may be satisfied through the purchase of financial services, including the need to make payments (e.g. cheques), the need to defer payments (loans, mortgages, credit cards, etc.), the need for protection (house insurance, health insurance, life insurance, etc.), the need to accumulate wealth (managed funds, stocks, life insurance based savings, etc.) and the need for information and advice (tax/financial planning, etc.). For many personal consumers, 'needs' of this nature are intrinsically uninteresting; there is often also a preference to ignore certain 'needs' which may be associated with unpleasant events such as burglary, illness or death. Because financial services are often products which consumers would prefer not to think about, there is a danger that they will not recognize a need for a financial service. The relatively low take-up of products such as critical illness insurance (which pays out on the diagnosis of a life-threatening condition) may in part be due to consumers' reluctance to consider the possibility that this will happen to them. Equally, the complexity of many financial services and the lack of transparency in marketing may mean that customers are unable to recognize the ways in which those services might meet their needs.

As a consequence of the lack of intrinsic appeal and the complexity of the range of financial services available, it is often argued that consumers do not actively recognize that they have 'needs' for various financial products; rather, they remain essentially passive participants in a decision process until the point of sale (Knights et al., 1994). At this point, the marketing process then starts to focus on the identification and activation (some would even suggest creation) of those needs. This raises a number of issues. Clearly, marketing is much more difficult in those instances in which customers are largely uninterested and unaware of the benefits of the product. It becomes impractical to rely to any degree on consumer 'pull', and instead many organizations will place considerable emphasis on 'sales push' – i.e. actively pushing products to consumers and persuading them of the benefits of purchase. This comparatively greater reliance on sales push is reflected in the widespread use of personal selling, particularly for the more complex products. A reliance on sales push does create potential problems – a situation in which customers have limited knowledge and interest combined with an industry which has to rely heavily on active selling creates considerable potential for mis-selling (i.e. selling products that are clearly inappropriate for the person concerned).

The difficulties that consumers experience in relation to problem recognition are often compounded by a lack of transparency in marketing. A common source of complaint in many parts of the world is that key aspects of product design and pricing are not clearly displayed and explained. *Transparency* is the word applied to this form of openness.

In recent years there have been great strides forward in a range of countries as regulators seek to make products more transparent. However, it is particularly difficult to achieve the desired degree of transparency in an area which is often characterized by variable and uncertain outcomes, product complexity and relatively poorly informed consumers. Chapter 12 explains the complexity that applies to financial services, and the range of different pricing concepts with which consumers need to be familiar in order to make well-judged choices.

In addition to whatever written rules apply to standards of transparency, it is important that marketing managers embrace the spirit of transparency. This will be in the long-term interests of providers, as such an approach will result in much better-managed consumer expectations and enable customers to recognize their needs and identify suitable products more clearly.

For corporate customers the range of basic needs is likely to be similar, although many of the products used to satisfy those needs may be more complex, particularly when the customer represents a large business organization. In addition, business customers, particularly those from larger organizations, will have a much better understanding and awareness of their own needs, suggesting that marketing may need to be less concerned with helping consumers to understand what their needs are and more concerned with deciding how best to meet those needs.

7.2.2   Information search

Information search describes the process by which consumers gather relevant information either from their own memories of from external sources – whether marketing communications, from other consumers or from independent third parties. To the extent that the nature of financial service induces consumer passivity, the degree of information search is likely to be limited. Even when consumers are willing to be more active in the purchase process, information-gathering presents problems. A significant element of information-gathering typically relates to search qualities, but intangibility and inseparability mean that financial services are low in search qualities while high in experience and credence qualities (Zeithaml, 1981). Unless consumers can draw on their own prior experience of the product (and this is likely to be rare, since most financial services are long term, continuous or both) there will be a tendency to rely heavily on the experience of others in the form of word-of-mouth recommendations, and on the credibility of the organization as a whole.

Even allowing for the difficulties that consumers face in gathering information, there are further problems in relation to the validity and accessibility of information. First, many financial services are long term in nature; consequently, even when consumers gain vicarious experience from word-of-mouth recommendations, that experience may be at best very partial since the full benefits of a product (a 10-year savings plan for example) may not have been realized. Secondly, since many products are effectively customized to individuals (reflecting health status, age, martial status, etc.), drawing on the experience of others can be misleading if personal circumstances differ. Thirdly, the complexity of many financial services means that many consumers may collect information but not actually interpret it, or may interpret it incorrectly. The difficulties associated with information search may be compounded by lack of transparency, as discussed above. In the UK, the financial services sector has been criticized for lack of transparency in the representation of so-called guaranteed equity bonds (GEB). Caine (2005) observes that over 200 bonds of this type were launched in 2005. Caine is particularly critical of the way in which the guarantee of the return of the initial investment does not always make clear the opportunity cost of loss of interest that investors should consider. She also argues that insufficient profile is given to the fact that explicit reference to the respective role and contribution of dividends as well as pure share price growth is absent.

While information search is clearly problematic, it is important to recognize that there has been a notable increase in consumer understanding and knowledge of financial services and considerable expansion in the various sources of independent information. Most daily papers have sections devoted to personal finance, and there is a growing number of specialist magazines to provide information and advice to customers – including *Smart Investor* (Australia), *Outlook Money* (India), *Investors' Chronicle* (UK) and *Money* (US). In addition, organizations such as *Which?* in the UK and the Consumers' Union in the US provide regular advice and product comparisons. In addition, most leading web portals provide a growing amount of financial information. For example, in the UK, Motley Fool (www.fool.com) provides advice about investment and other financial services, Money Expert (www.moneyexpert.com) provides product comparisons, and uSwitch (www.uswitch.com) provides product comparisons and advice on switching. Thus, personal consumers are generally thought to be better informed now than was the case in the past. However, the simple availability of information does not necessarily mean that it can always be used to good effect.

It is probably easier for corporate customers, who have more experience of using financial services and are better able to evaluate competitor offerings. In addition, the key decision-makers are likely to have more specialist knowledge, and so information search should be more straightforward, even if the original needs are rather more complex.

7.2.3   Evaluation of alternatives

If there are difficulties for consumers with respect to the gathering of information, these difficulties are magnified when the consumer attempts to evaluate alternative services. Like many services, financial services are processes rather than physical objects; the predominance of experience qualities makes pre-purchase evaluation difficult and, where credence qualities are significant, post-purchase evaluation may also be problematic. Typically, alternatives are evaluated in relation to dimensions specified in the initial problem-recognition stage; if consumers are in some senses inert or inactive in relation to problem recognition, then the criteria being used for evaluation are likely to be poorly defined. However, even accepting that consumers can make evaluations, the process of so doing will be complicated by a number of features of financial services. There is a variety of different products that may satisfy a particular need; for example, the consumer who wishes to accumulate wealth may consider a range of products – national savings certificates, guaranteed equity bonds, unit trusts and simple equity investments. The risk–return characteristics of these services vary considerably, as do the prices, and there is rarely any easy way to make direct comparisons across different service types. These problems have been exacerbated by the lack of transparency in the pricing and promotion of many financial services (Diacon and Ennew, 1996). Although recent regulatory changes regarding commission disclosure have partly remedied this situation, comparisons across service types remains difficult.

The presence of credence qualities in many financial services also makes evaluation complex. Products that need a significant element of advice, or which require 'managing' over the course of their life, may be difficult to evaluate even after purchase. In particular, the performance of many long-term investment products is determined partly by the skill of the relevant fund managers, but partly by economic factors which are beyond the control of the supplier. Thus, consumers expose themselves to certain risks (both actual and perceived) in purchasing these products, but will subsequently experience difficulty in determining whether poor performance was due to company-specific factors or external contingencies. A consequence of this situation is a tendency for customers to evaluate service providers (rather than the services themselves) and to rely heavily on trust and confidence as attributes of those providers. Indeed, trust is a concept that lies at the heart of the relationship between a financial services supplier and its customers. The fund of trust that a financial services brand can instil in the public represents a major asset, as observed by HSBC's Group CEO Stephen Green (in Ennew and Sekhon, 2003):

> If customers have faith in the HSBC brand, they will give us a trusted role in their lives and help us build our business.

Those involved in marketing financial services must place priority on engendering the trust of consumers, and avoiding policies and practices that serve to undermine trust.

7.2.4   Purchase

Purchase is normally expected to follow logically as the result of the evaluation of alternatives, unless any unexpected problems materialize. However, earlier discussions have suggested that, for many financial services customers, needs are only created or activated at the point of purchase. Accordingly, the actual process of purchase will often be the result of an active selling effort by a supplier. Customer interaction with sales staff is then likely to be of particular significance in the purchase process. Even with developments in relation to the Internet and in ATMs and telephone sales, the significance of face-to-face interaction is likely to continue in the medium term. However, while sympathetic, unpressured selling may be highly effective, the complexity and riskiness of financial services, combined with their common status as 'avoidance' products, means that many customers may be vulnerable to 'hard' or 'over' selling. There can be little doubt that this has been the case in the past in some parts of the market (Ennew and Sekhon, 2003), and that it has resulted in a significant loss of consumer confidence in those parts of the industry where confidence is so important.

Furthermore, the purchase process is influenced by the inseparability of production and consumption in financial services. The frontline service employees play an important 'boundary spanning role' in the production of services, as do the consumers themselves in their capacity as 'partial employees' (Bowen and Schneider, 1988). Therefore, an important influence on the purchase process will be the interaction between buyer and supplier. Since services depend upon input from both service employees and consumers for their production, the quality of the service output very much depends on the nature of the personal interactions of these parties.

Fiduciary responsibility is often highlighted as an important characteristic which distinguishes financial services from other services and goods; one dimension of fiduciary responsibility is that suppliers need to exercise discretion with respect to the sale of certain products. For example, it would be inappropriate for a bank to lend money to a business that has few prospects for survival and success. However, until a consumer has signalled the intent to purchase it may not be possible to identify whether or not it is appropriate to provide that product to that customer. Thus, the consumer effectively faces the added problem that even if a conscious decision to purchase has been taken, the financial institution concerned may be unwilling to provide the product.

7.2.5   Post-purchase behaviour

The post-purchase evaluation of financial services is difficult, for the reasons mentioned earlier. Indeed, it is often suggested that evaluation may place rather more emphasis on functional aspects of the service (how things are done) than on technical aspects (what is done) because the latter are more difficult to evaluate (Zeithaml, 1981). The difficulties of post-purchase evaluation would tend to suggest that the risk of cognitive dissonance among consumers is high, and that this may subsequently reduce brand loyalty. Evidence for this is ambiguous; for continuous products such as bank accounts, a high level of cognitive dissonance might be reflected in high levels of switching. In practice, the number of consumers changing bank, although increasing (Burton, 1994; Ennew and Binks, 1996b), is still low. This may reflect a low level of dissonance; alternatively, given switching costs, consumers may be willing to tolerate high levels of dissonance before being motivated to act. In the case of savings and investment products the levels of switching are higher, and the relatively low proportion of retained customers may reflect the high level of dissonance experienced.

However, where a high degree of trust is established between buyer and seller, there can be considerable benefits for both parties. The establishment of trust can bring about a degree of inertia in buyer–seller relationships. Since an irreversible amount of time and effort is required by an individual in order to acquire the necessary experience and information on which to assess an institution's reliability, it is usually the case that, once satisfied, a consumer is more likely to remain with that institution than to incur the costs of searching for and vetting alternative suppliers. This does create a potential problem for marketing, in that organizations may fall into the trap of assuming that, once acquired, customers will remain with the organization, resulting in insufficient attention to customer retention and an overemphasis on customer acquisition.

The Engel–Kollat–Blackwell model assumes a highly rational approach to decision-making whereby individuals seek to optimize their well-defined preferences, and mitigate the associated risks through the acquisition of knowledge. Such a rational approach is more likely to be a feature of the B2B environment, where purchasing takes place in order to satisfy the financial goals of a company. However, this model of economic rationality may not hold true to such an extent in the consumer domain. Factors such as relative financial illiteracy and the often-observed low level of interest in and engagement with financial services products can result in consumer behaviour that seems far less economically rational. Behavioural finance and economic finance are fields of knowledge that seek to explain why it is that human beings individually and collectively approach decision-making in what seems to be an irrational and illogical manner. This gathering body of knowledge is based upon combining relevant concepts from the disciplines of psychology and economics. Readers interested in learning more about this field are referred to the work of people such as Daniel Kahneman at Princeton University.

7.2.6   Summary

From the discussion above, it should be clear that there are good conceptual reasons for expecting consumers to encounter difficulties with respect to the choice of financial services. The severity of these problems will vary across market segments. For example, the problem of complexity may be rather less important for a corporate buyer evaluating different leasing companies than for an individual evaluating pension providers. Furthermore, corporate buyers may well be expected to express needs more actively and accurately than personal customers. Nevertheless, within the personal market there are clearly some subgroups of customers who are more actively aware of their needs than are others. Allowing for this variation in the degree and type of difficulties consumers may experience, there is a number of themes that seem to be of particular relevance to the choice process. These include the importance of trust and confidence in the supplier, the concern about customer passivity, the relative importance of functional aspects of the service product, and the importance of interaction and contact with people.

7.3   Consumer buying behaviour in financial services

The previous section has highlighted some of the difficulties that customers encounter in the purchase of financial services. In this section we examine briefly some of the existing empirical research relating to buying behaviour, and consider the extent to which it corroborates the issues discussed in the previous section. The results of a variety of studies of buying behaviour for both personal and corporate financial services are summarized in Tables 7.1 and 7.2. Most of the work to date has emphasized specific aspects of buying behaviour, such as factors affecting the choice of bank, usage of financial services and customer loyalty, rather than attempting to

Table 7.1 Personal financial services buying behaviour

Author(s)	Field of study	Geographic area	Key finding(s)
Laroche et al. (1986)	Factors influencing choice of bank	Canada	Importance of location convenience, speed of service, competence and friendliness of bank personnel
Jain et al. (1987)	Customer loyalty in retail banking	USA	Customer loyalty is a useful construct; bank non-loyal segment swayed by economic rationale, whereas greater emphasis placed on human aspects of banking by bank loyal segment
Joy et al. (1991)	Link between ethnicity and use of financial services	Canada	Ethnicity should be considered as a construct having strong potential impact on consumption
Leonard and Spencer (1991)	Importance of bank image as a competitive strategy for increasing customer traffic flow	USA	Preference for banks amongst students as providers of financial services; greater confidence in large to medium-sized banks; importance of courtesy of personnel, competitive deposit rates, loan availability
Lewis (1991)	International comparison of bank customers' expectations and perceptions of service quality	UK/USA	Very high expectations of service quality and high perceptions of service received, yet gaps did exist
Ennew (1992)	Consumer attitudes to independent advice	UK	More importance may be attached to image and reputation of an independent financial adviser than their status
Chan (1993)	Banking services for young intellectuals	Hong Kong	Financial sophistication of youth market
Boyd et al. (1994)	Consumer choice criteria in financial institution selection	USA	Reputation and interest rates (loans/savings) more important than friendliness of employees, modern facilities, drive-in service
Harrison (1994)	Segmentation of market for retail financial services	UK	Distinct segments identified based on financial maturity (based on likely range of product holdings) and perceived knowledge of financial services
Burton (1996)	Ethnicity and financial behaviour	UK	Evidence of considerable variety in the take-up of pensions according to ethnic origin; suggests that financial services providers have not yet accommodated the needs/ expectations of distinct ethnic groups

Reference	Title	Country	Findings
Goode et al. (1996)	Satisfaction with ATMs	UK	Levels satisfaction and overall usage of services influenced by customer expectations and by perceived risk
Kennington et al. (1996)	Study of banking habits and bank choice in a transitional economy	Poland	Consumers in a transitional economy select banks using the same criteria as consumers in other countries, although pricing concerns do appear to be particularly significant
Levesque and McDougall (1996)	Determinants of satisfaction in retail banking	Canada	Satisfaction influenced by service quality, service features, service problems and service quality; these variables also affect intentions to switch bank
Veloutsou et al. (2004)	Determinants of bank loyalty	Greece	Examines role of satisfaction, perceived quality and image as drivers of bank brand loyalty
Verma et al. (2004)	Understanding customer choices in E-Financial Services	US	Suggests customer swilling to pay more for an online service that gives offline value and online benefit
Pont and McQuilken (2005)	Customer satisfaction and loyalty across two divergent bank segments	Australia	Investigated retirees and university students; no significant difference in satisfaction levels between segments, but a significant difference on three behavioural intentions dimensions – loyalty, pay more and customer relations

Table 7.2 Corporate financial services buying behaviour

Author(s)	Field of study	Geographic area	Key finding(s)
Turnbull (1982a)	Purchase of international financial services by large/medium-sized UK companies with European subsidiaries	UK	Greater effort required to understand the nature of customer needs and bank/customer relationships through detailed application of the Interaction theory
Turnbull (1982b)	Role of branch bank manager in bank services marketing	UK	Lack of customer orientation amongst bank branch managers
Turnbull (1982c)	Use of foreign banks by UK companies	UK	High concentration of decision-making and extent of split banking; crucial importance of development and maintenance of a company-bank relationship
Turnbull (1983)	Relationship between banks' corporate customers and their sources of financial services	UK	Small/medium-sized companies do not always consider major UK banks as an appropriate source for all financial services
Turnbull and Gibbs (1989)	Relationship between large companies and its lead and closest substitute bank	South Africa	Predominant bank selection criteria: importance of quality of service, quality of staff and price of services; split banking common
Chan and Ma (1990)	Corporate customer buying behaviour for banking services.	Hong Kong	Great importance attached to banks understanding their clients' attitudes in order to serve them better
File and Prince (1991)	Purchase dynamics of SME market and financial services	USA	Existence of three distinctive sociographic segments adopting innovations in bank services: return seekers, relevance seekers and relationship seekers
Edwards and Turnbull (1994)	Current and future use of foreign banks by UK middle corporate market	UK	Very conservative approach to domestic banking, with foreign banks used as secondary banks
Zineldin (1995)	Bank–company interactions	Sweden	Smaller companies tend to have stable relationships with a single bank, but larger organizations operate with a variety of banking relationships; there is evidence of low levels of satisfaction among smaller companies

Ennew and Binks (1996a)	Impact of service quality on customer retention	UK	Both product characteristics and service quality affect potential for small businesses to switch bank
Ennew and Binks (1996b)	Customer involvement in banking relationships	UK	Greater degrees of customer involvement in a banking relationship result in improved service quality
Turnbull and Moustakatos (1995)	Empirical research using a sample of investment banks and their large corporate customers.	UK	Suggests likely polarization in industry structures. Major players will be full service investment banks with a worldwide capability accompanied by specialist niche players on a geographical or product basis
Mols et al. (1997)	European corporate customers' choice of domestic cash management banks	Europe	Differentiation between the service offering as perceived by managers towards individual and business customers; evidence of superior service experience of individual rather than business customers
Athanassopoulos and Labroukos (1999)	The nature relationships between corporate companies and financial institutions	Greece	Evidence that profitable firms resist cross-selling; need for relationship marketing to expand scope; product-bundling not sufficient to ensure lasting relationships
Lam and Burton (2005)	Bank selection and share of the wallet among SMEs: apparent differences between HK and Australia	HK/Australia	Firms in both countries view a bank's willingness to accommodate their banking and credit needs as being important. Hong Kong firms appear to give this factor higher priority, while Australian firms appear to place higher emphasis on long-term relationships.

examine the buying process as a whole. This largely reflects the difficulties associated with testing decision-process models in their entirety.

Empirical studies relating to the personal market highlight the importance of factors such as confidence, trust and customer loyalty. Some of the common choice criteria in bank selection include dependability and size of the institution, location, convenience and ease of transactions, professionalism of bank personnel, and availability of loans. It would appear, therefore, that the personal consumer is more interested in the functional quality dimension of financial services (i.e. how the service is delivered) than in the technical quality dimension (i.e. what is actually received as the outcome of the production process) (see Grönroos, 1984). This is hardly surprising, given the difficulties consumers have in evaluating services.

In contrast, work relating to corporate customers places much greater emphasis on the importance of interaction and understanding. This is consistent with the notion that issues such as passivity, complexity and problems of comparison are perhaps less important to corporate decision-makers, but that the intangibility and the lack of search qualities means that personal relationships, trust, confidence and reliability continue to be important influences within the purchase process.

7.4   Industry responses

The first part of this chapter highlighted some of the problems which confront consumers when choosing financial services. These difficulties are due partly to the generic characteristics of services, partly to the unique features of financial services and partly to the practices employed within the industry itself. Given the existence of these problems, effective marketing must concern itself with reducing or minimizing the difficulties that consumers face in the purchase process. In order to examine the current evidence on industry responses, this section considers the nature of strategies and tactics employed in relation to selected characteristics of financial services – intangibility, inseparability/perishability, heterogeneity, fiduciary responsibility and the long-term nature and uncertainty of many of the products. However, it should be noted that many of these responses can address more than one service characteristic.

7.4.1   Intangibility

Intangibility is probably the dominant characteristic of any service, and there is a variety of strategies that can be used to mitigate its effects. The simplest approach is to find some means of tangibilizing the service. The provision of some physical evidence (whether essential or peripheral) is probably the most common approach to dealing with intangibility (Shostack, 1982). Examples of peripheral physical evidence might include wallets with insurance policies, cheque-book covers, and even promotional free gifts. Essential physical evidence is typically associated with branch networks or head offices, with the appearance and layout being used to give a tangible representation of the organization. Often, physical evidence of this nature is supported by the use of a tangible image or name. Thus, for example, the

'Leeds Permanent' and the 'Northern Rock' are both organizational names that try to link to an image of stability and security. Equally, a tangible image or association such as the Black Horse (Lloyds) or Direct Line's red telephone on wheels can serve a similar purpose. Using physical evidence or imagery to tangibilize a financial service is a key element of most marketing strategies. Nevertheless, there are pitfalls associated with this approach, particularly with respect to the development of a tangible image. The image developed necessarily creates expectations in the consumers' mind and if the organization cannot match those expectations then customer satisfaction may decrease.

Tangibilizing a service addresses the problem of lack of physical form, but is less effective in relation to product complexity and lack of consumer interest (a form of mental intangibility). Two key strategies are important in this respect. First, to address the complexity issue there is a need to focus on reducing perceived risk through building trust and confidence; if consumers cannot fully understand the nature of the service, then they must be able to trust a supplier and feel confident that their finances are being safely managed. Attempts to build such trust and confidence often rely on the longevity of the organizations. For example, The Royal Bank of Scotland claims in its literature that:

You can also be sure that your money is in safe hands. We have been around for more than 260 years, which gives us a wealth of banking experience.

Similarly, MAA claims in its advertising that it is:

a tried and trusted insurance company with over 30 years' experience in protecting the savings of Malaysian families and investors.

Equally important is the use of third-party endorsements to indicate quality and reliability. Thus Arab Malaysian Unit Trusts Bhd emphasizes endorsements from Standard and Poor's Micropal for several of its funds, while China Construction Bank draws attention to its status as 'Bank of the Year' in The Banker Awards.

The lack of consumer interest in many financial services and the fact that consumption is essentially contingent can often be addressed by focusing on the benefits gained from the purchase of the product. Thus, promotional material for personal loans tends to emphasize the purchases which can be made as a result of the loan (whether cars, hi-fi equipment, holidays or houses). Similarly, marketing for life insurance and other related protection products will emphasize the benefit of security for the policyholder's dependents. Because financial services are generally products that consumers would prefer to avoid and because they have no obvious value in themselves, marketing must put extra effort into emphasizing the benefits that these services provide.

7.4.2 Inseparability/perishability

The fact that they are typically produced and consumed simultaneously means that financial services are perishable and, most significantly for this discussion, that customers have considerable difficulties with respect to pre-purchase evaluation. Although an *ex ante* evaluation of a particular product may be difficult, consumers can evaluate the organization and can draw on the experience of others. Accordingly, a common theme in the marketing of financial services is to emphasize the performance and quality of the organization and its people in order that there will be a halo effect from organization to product. Such approaches are often reinforced by active attempts to secure word-of-mouth recommendations. American Express, for example, actively encourages existing customers to recommend new customers, and rewards those customers who do introduce new members.

Furthermore, given the importance of the interaction between customers and employees and the potential role of employees in inspiring trust and confidence, many organizations are increasingly looking at human resource policies, training and internal marketing as means of building more effective relationships with customers in order to encourage retention and re-purchase. These relationships are seen as being of considerable significance in reducing the levels of both perceived risk pre-purchase and dissonance post-purchase. First Direct, for example, when recruiting staff for the launch of its telephone banking service, placed much greater emphasis on the interpersonal skills of customer contact staff than it did on their detailed knowledge of banking practice.

7.4.3   Heterogeneity

A logical consequence of inseparability and the important role played by people is that the quality of service delivery has the potential to be highly variable. Clearly, the potential for such variability will hinder the process of evaluation by consumers. Mechanization of service delivery through ATMs, automated phone-based systems and Internet-based systems, for example, or even through the use of expert systems, has the potential to reduce quality variability, although this option may not be available for all services. Where delivery cannot be mechanized, then financial institutions must emphasize internal marketing and training to ensure higher levels of consistency in service delivery.

7.4.4   Fiduciary responsibility

The concept of fiduciary responsibility concerns itself with the implicit and explicit responsibilities of financial institutions with respect to the products they sell. The impact of fiduciary responsibility is arguably at its greatest at the purchase stage, when a consumer may find that, despite an active marketing campaign which has stimulated a decision to purchase, the institution indicates that it is unable to provide the product. For example, a common complaint from both personal customers and smaller businesses is that banks will actively promote the fact that they offer a variety of loans, but will then turn down applications from some customers. Similar issues arise in relation to insurance, where many companies are increasingly looking to sell only to good risks. In part this may simply reflect the overall importance of profit and an unwillingness to supply loans or insurance when the risk is too high (Knights *et al.*, 1994). However, we should perhaps note that such decisions may also reflect an element of fiduciary responsibility in the sense that financial services suppliers are obliged to recognize that many of their 'raw materials' are actually funds provided by other customers. An extension of the idea of responsibility in relation to the management of funds is evidenced in the case of the Co-operative Bank. The bank's positioning and promotional campaign revolves around its ethical stance and its commitment to the responsible sourcing and distribution of funds.

The selling process itself is also an area of concern because of the substantial information asymmetries which exist between supplier and customer. To address these problems is difficult. The simplest route is perhaps to emphasize honesty and prudence as themes in promotional campaigns. Consider, for example, the HSBC campaign which claims:

> We believe that the way forward is to offer a range of financial services honestly, simply and with integrity. That is how we have accumulated 23 million customers in 81 countries and territories.

Furthermore, there are difficulties for financial service organizations in that fiduciary responsibility means that they may be promoting products to those individuals who are unlikely to be able to purchase because they are considered to be poor risk. While clearly this is something that many suppliers seek to avoid, in practice the identification of exactly who is an appropriate customer is difficult and, even with sophisticated marketing information systems, this process will be less than perfect.

Finally, with respect to fiduciary responsibility, there is the issue of the purchase (sales) process itself. Given the information asymmetries that exist between supplier and customer, many customers are vulnerable to high-pressure selling and bad advice. Indeed, this is probably the issue that has done most to undermine the image of the financial services sector in recent years. Nevertheless, there are ways in which these issues can be tackled both internally and externally. One approach which a number of organizations have adopted is to reconsider their reward systems with a view to eliminating or at least reducing the reliance on commission-based selling. In a number of cases the nature of the reward structure (e.g. 'our salesmen aren't paid just on commission') is used as a component of advertising in order to reassure consumers of the high standards of the supplying organization.

7.4.5 The long-term nature and uncertainty of products

Many financial services are either consumed continuously (current accounts, credit cards) and therefore require a long-term relationship, or only yield benefits in the longer term, and the precise nature of these benefits may be uncertain. As indicated earlier, these features of financial services will tend to increase the perceived risk associated with the purchase and decrease consumers' ability to evaluate the service both *ex ante* and *ex post*. To address this problem, there is again a tendency to rely heavily on marketing activities that emphasize the longevity of the supplier, trust, confidence and reliability. A good illustration of this approach is the TV advertising used by Clerical Medical, which emphasizes the origins of the company during the early part of the nineteenth century and its success at serving particular customer groups since that time. More recently, Royal Insurance has used a campaign that focuses on the relationship between a particular financial adviser and a client; the advert depicts the two individuals growing older together and seeks to highlight the company's ability to provide a continuous relationship that meets the individual's changing financial needs.

7.5   Summary and conclusions

Although there has been a variety of empirical research examining customer choice, understanding of the buying process for financial services is still limited. However, what is apparent both conceptually and from existing empirical evidence is that certain characteristics of financial services present a number of problems for consumers when they make choices. Financial services are low in search qualities and high in experience and credence qualities. Information is difficult to collect and interpret, and there is a tendency to rely heavily on the experience of others rather than on supplier-provided information. Evaluation is even more complex, partly because of the lack of search qualities but also because of the complexity of many of the products and the reluctance of many suppliers to facilitate comparisons across products. Consumer needs often do not become apparent until the actual point of sale, and the problems of information search and evaluation mean that buyers are always likely to be vulnerable to the 'hard' sell. Having bought a particular financial service, a customer may still find evaluation difficult, and many buyers experience high levels of cognitive dissonance post-purchase.

There is a variety of strategies and tactics that marketers can use to address these problematic aspects of consumer choice; they include tangibilizing the service, emphasizing particular dimensions of image, and investing in staff training and internal marketing. However, there are also many aspects of the marketing of financial services that have tended to reinforce some of the problems experienced by consumers. In particular, pricing and product benefits are often not clearly presented, and the historic reliance on commission-based selling has resulted in a number of well-publicized and damaging cases of over-selling of certain products. Some of these problems are being rectified by a combination of company-specific actions and industry-wide regulation. However, from a marketing perspective it is crucial that financial services organizations recognize that they operate in a high-contact business where the nature of buyer–seller interactions and the establishment of long-term relationships based on confidence and trust have real implications for the successful retention of customers and recruitment of prospects.

Review questions

1. What are the main differences in buyer behaviour between retail and business consumers, regarding financial services?
2. How might consumers collect information to help them choose between financial services? How can marketing help this process?
3. Why is it important to tangibilize a financial service?
4. How can financial services organizations build trust and confidence?

8

Segmentation targeting and positioning

☐ Learning objectives

By the end of this chapter you will be able to:
- explain the different approaches to segmenting a market
- understand the issues involved in selecting a target market
- understand the role of positioning in communicating the value proposition.

8.1 Introduction

The process of segmentation, targeting and positioning is central to effective strategic marketing. Segmentation is concerned with the process of identifying different groups of customers who are similar in ways that are relevant to marketing. In order to segment a market, it is important to understand who customers are, why they behave in particular ways and how they may be grouped together. Targeting decisions can then be made based on the range of identified segments. In order to choose the most appropriate target markets, it is necessary to understand what different segments want and the extent to which the organization can supply those wants. Finally, having identified target markets, the organization must then consider how to position itself in those markets. Positioning refers to the way in which an organization tries to communicate its value proposition to its target market in order to convince customers that it has a distinct offer. In effect, positioning is about the way in which the organization tries to build and communicate its competitive advantage.

This chapter will review segmentation, targeting and positioning. It will begin by explaining the benefits of market segmentation and targeting for both providers and customers. The requirements for successful segmentation will be examined in general terms, and approaches to segmenting final consumer and corporate markets will then be explored in more detail. The chapter continues with a discussion of different approaches to market targeting, and the final sections will explain the key elements of positioning and repositioning.

8.2   The benefits of segmentation and targeting

Segmentation is essentially a process whereby a provider of goods or services chooses to group prospective customers together on the basis of a set of common characteristics that have significant implications for its marketing activity. Common characteristics that might be used to segment a market include variables such as age, income, personality and lifestyle. On the basis of those common characteristics, segments are expected to respond differently to marketing activities – they may want different features, be more or less price-sensitive, respond to particular types of marketing communications, or use different channels. Targeting is then concerned with the identification of an appropriate set of segments which the organization will seek to serve. Implicit in any decision to undertake segmentation and targeting is the realization that no single organization is capable of being all things to all men. It is inevitable that certain products will have particular appeal to certain kinds of individuals. At one extreme, each individual customer could be presented as a segment of one because each individual has different needs. In such a case, the marketing mix is bespoke to match the characteristics and needs of a single person or organization. This practice is perhaps more common than might at first be imagined. In retail markets, financial advisers provide a service encounter that is unique to the individual client – as do private bankers. In corporate markets, a customized approach is essential when dealing with large corporate clients. At the other extreme, the whole population could be treated as if it were a single homogenous segment. Traditionally, banks have treated the personal banking market as homogenous and provided a single standard current account to all customers. Increasingly, however, there is recognition that customers do have differing banking needs and that there is the potential to develop specific products for specific segments. Thus, for example, Barclays now offers over ten different current accounts in the UK market, targeted to a variety of segments – including children, students, people with very high incomes and people with very low incomes.

Segmentation and targeting is a means by which a number of important benefits are secured for both providers and consumers of products and services. In summary, the benefits of segmentation and targeting are as follows:

1. *It facilitates efficient resource utilization.* Indiscriminate use of the marketing mix is a wasteful use of precious resources. By identifying and targeting discrete segments of consumers (retail or corporate), a company is able to limit the scope of individual components of the mix and thus reduce costs. To take a simple example, an advertising programme involving the use of the press media will be less expensive if it involves the use of magazines that are read by a discrete target segment of consumers rather than the entire population. Similarly, products designed to meet the particular needs of a given segment will not need features

they do not require. Thus, segmentation results in greater resource efficiency, which benefits consumers through better value, shareholders through reduced waste and lower costs, and the environment through resource efficiency.

2. *It allows effective targeting of new customers.* The logical next step from segmenting a market is the selection of segments to target for marketing activities. Nowadays, it is unusual for a company to have a completely indiscriminate approach to targeting new customers. As the costs of customer acquisition have increased and companies become increasingly focused upon customer profitability, they have to be selective in respect of which kinds of people or organization they want to be their customers. It must be appreciated that different customers display different characteristics and behaviours that impact upon customer value. For example, in the UK, SAGA targets people aged over 50 for its range of leisure and financial services. SAGA is able to price its motor insurance premiums very keenly, as the over-50s represent a low-risk group in terms of propensity to incur motor claims. Thus, SAGA can be very price-competitive and deliver superior value to this group of consumers in a way that would not be possible if the company was trying to serve a mass market.

3. *It facilitates competitive advantage.* The more specific an organization's approach to segmenting the market, the easier it is to establish and maintain competitive advantage. This arises by virtue of the fact that competitive advantage is a relative concept that involves differentiating an organization from its rivals in the eyes of its customers. Self-evidently, the more indiscriminate the approach to targeting, the wider the array of competitors against whom an organization will have to seek to differentiate itself. In the case of SAGA, it is required to maintain a competitive advantage over those other organizations that also seek to target the over-50s – such as RIAS. This presents SAGA with a smaller set of key rivals than if it were to target the entire adult population. In turn, this makes it easier to achieve and maintain differentiation.

4. *It directs the marketing mix.* Best practice dictates that each target segment chosen by an organization should be subject to a specific and relevant marketing campaign. In this way, marketing is managed to achieve the best fit with each target segment. Consider the case of the NFU Mutual Insurance Company. Originally aimed at providing for the insurance needs of Britain's farmers, it has repositioned itself to address the insurance and investment needs of the following segments:

- farmers
- people who live in rural communities
- people who live in non-metropolitan towns and have an affinity for the countryside.

The mix for the farming segment includes insurance products that are specific to farmers, such as crop and livestock insurance. In terms of promotion, it advertises extensively in the farming press. As far as rural dwellers are concerned, it uses radio and television selectively to target those who live in predominantly rural parts of the country. Its product range is geared towards rural dwellers with a special interest in country pursuits such as horse-riding.

Some financial service providers are affinity-based, and this allows for particularly close targeting of the marketing mix. The Police Mutual Assurance Society (PMAS), based in Lichfield, Staffordshire, has a mix that makes full use of its affinity relationship with the UK's police service. For example, it makes use of locally-based police officers as part of its distribution processes. So-called 'Authorized Officers' act as a conduit for communication between serving police officers and civilian staff, and PMAS. Authorized Officers have introducer status, and this enables PMAS to enjoy exceptionally low new business acquisition costs. PMAS's low-cost provision is further enhanced by the way in which it arranges for deduction of premiums through the police payroll system. The promotional element of the mix makes full use of specialist forms of communication, such as police magazines and publications. The Bournemouth-based Teachers Provident Society enjoys a similar affinity relationship with Britain's largest teaching union, as does Maif with respect to teachers in France. Their marketing mixes take advantage of the close relationships they enjoy with their respective affinity groups in order to achieve a bespoke approach.

5. *It enhances customer satisfaction*. Segmentation and targeting is an effective means of enhancing customer satisfaction through the ways in which the mix should achieve a close match with customer needs and wants. Clearly, the more precisely a product and its features reflect the characteristics of a given group of individuals, the greater the degree of satisfaction they should experience from its consumption. The corollary to this is that the absence of well-managed segmentation results in a generalized approach to the market. This results in customers feeling that a number of product features are irrelevant to them, and that communications messages are ill-judged and lacking real relevance to their personal circumstances and preferences. As a consequence, such consumers will always be vulnerable to competitors with a more focused approach to segmentation that enables them to deliver greater customer satisfaction.

Alongside these benefits, there are also costs associated with segmentation. Identifying, measuring and maintaining a system of segmented markets is a cost in itself. Additionally, costs are incurred through the development of different products and different marketing campaigns for these different segments. Any exercise in market segmentation must be aware of these costs, and look to implement market segmentation only where the benefits outweigh the costs.

8.3   Successful segmentation

There is no best way to segment a market. On the contrary, as will become clear in subsequent sections, there is a variety of approaches that can be used with varying degrees of complexity and sophistication. Ultimately, a commercial judgement must be made to ensure the best fit between the incremental costs that segmentation entails and the incremental value that can be realized. For an organization to get an approach to segmentation that is 'right' for it depends on a good understanding of the market, the right skills and knowledge, and careful evaluation of the different options. In terms of skills and knowledge, the following areas are of particular importance:

1. *A sense of touch for the market*. Managers seeking to segment a market have to display a sound understanding of the marketplace in which they operate.

This understanding should be based upon the ability to integrate all relevant sources of knowledge to form a cohesive, whole picture of the market. Not only does this involve hard, objective facts such as market values, number of customers, frequency of purchase, competitors and their respective market share, but it also involves more subjective and qualitative-based inputs. Such inputs include an understanding of consumer choice and an awareness of the strategies of competitors. A sense of touch for the market provides the marketing manager with the capacity to identify opportunities for differentiation and competitive advantage.

2. *Analytical skills and resources.* Access to appropriate data and the ability to manipulate and interpret it is vital. The more varied the data about a market, the greater the number of options for segmentation. Markets vary considerably with regard not only to the variety of data sources that are available but also in respect to recency, frequency, consistency and accuracy of data. The ability to source and analyse relevant data is a competence that is not always in evidence. Therefore, there has to be a commitment to developing this competence if it is not already present.

3. *Commercial judgement.* A wide range of 'common characteristics' can be used in market segmentation. These vary from basic demographic criteria, such as age and gender, through to subtle and complex criteria based upon personality traits. It must be appreciated that choice of target segments is a crucial part of marketing strategy and a key facilitator of competitive advantage. A fine judgement has to be made regarding the impact that a chosen approach to segmentation is likely to have on the commercial outcome. This entails careful consideration of costs and benefits for any given method of segmentation.

4. *Creative insight.* To be successful, segmentation calls for a combination of elements of marketing as both art and science. Science is required in terms of the gathering of factual information, its analysis, and the use of various modelling and simulation processes. Ultimately, a judgement has to be made regarding which approach is most likely to facilitate effective differentiation and competitive advantage. This requires a high degree of creative insight if a segment is to be identified that can be successfully penetrated. It also requires creative intuition regarding how to translate the company's aspirations to penetrate a given segment into a concrete marketing mix that appeals to the segment. It is understood that the Co-operative Bank chose the ethical consumer segment more on the basis of creative insight than conventional factual analysis.

Thus, good segmentation combines elements of science and art, elements of the quantifiably objective and qualitatively judgemental.

In terms of evaluating different options for segmentation, there are several factors that require consideration. Organization-specific criteria relating to fit with current activity and ability to serve will clearly be important. Equally, it is helpful to evaluate proposed methods of segmentation in terms of their performance in a number of key areas. One common approach is to focus attention on the following criteria:

1. *Measurability.* This is concerned with the extent to which the preferences, size and purchasing power of different segments can be measured. Certain segmentation

variables are difficult to measure, making segment size and purchasing power difficult to identify. An investment company may identify small investors who are risk averse as an attractive market segment, but may find it difficult to find out exactly how many people fall into this category because of the difficulties of measuring risk aversion. In contrast, the segment of women aged over 60 will be much easier to measure.

2. *Profitability*. This is the degree to which segments are large and/or profitable enough. A segment should be the largest possible homogenous group worth going after with a tailored marketing programme. Medical students are one very distinctive and homogenous segment of the market, but it would probably not be viable for a bank to develop a distinct current account just for this particular group.

3. *Accessibility*. This refers to the degree to which the segments can be effectively reached and served. A bank that wishes to target individuals in social class AB will usually be able to gather enough information about the television programmes that such individuals watch and the newspapers that they read, and this should make such a segment relatively accessible. In contrast, a bank that has identified the existence of a segment of internationally orientated companies that it wishes to target with a range of export financing products may find it more difficult to identify which firms are in that segment and communicate with them.

4. *Relevance*. This is the degree to which the common characteristics used to group customers are relevant to customer decisions. A segmentation system which groups individuals in terms of lifestyle and establishes that the type of credit card carried (standard, gold, platinum) depends on an individual's aspirations and self-concept uses a personality-based characteristic to explain preference. This type of characteristic is likely to be a more relevant predictor of consumer decisions on which card to carry than, say, a characteristic such as age or income.

From the discussions so far, it is clear that there is a variety of approaches used to segment markets. What they all have in common is the search for a set of common characteristics – i.e. characteristics that all customers in a group share and which are in some way associated with the way in which those consumers respond to marketing activities. A very simple example of a common characteristic would be age or income; a more complex example might be personality. The next sections explore the common characteristics that are used in segmenting customer and business markets.

8.4 Approaches to segmenting consumer markets

Earlier in this chapter, segmentation was described as grouping consumers around a common characteristic that is of relevance to marketing. The choice of *common characteristics* is crucial in determining a successful outcome when segmenting a marketplace, since this effectively defines target markets and thus impacts on what the organization will be expected to deliver to that market. The types of common characteristics than can be used to segment consumer markets can be divided into two broad categories, which give rise to customer- orientated segmentation and product-based segmentation.

8.4.1   Customer characteristics: customer-orientated segmentation

This category comprises characteristics that define who the customers are, where they live, the kind of people they are, the kind of lifestyle they lead and the views they hold. Thus, it is entirely consumer-centric as an approach to segmentation. In specific terms, the sort of characteristics used in segmentation can be broken down as follows.

1. Demographic:
   - age
   - gender
   - family relationships
   - ethnic group
   - religious affiliations
   - life stage
   - educational attainment
2. Socio-economic:
   - income
   - financial assets
   - social class
   - occupational status
3. Geographic:
   - country of domicile
   - region or locality
   - metropolitan
   - urban v. rural
4. Psychographic:
   - attitudes
   - lifestyle choices
   - beliefs
   - motives
   - personality type.

One increasingly common approach to consumer-orientated segmentation is based around geo-demographics – a combination of demographics, socio-economic and geographical information. The underlying principle of geo-demographics is the belief that households within a particular neighbourhood exhibit similar purchasing behaviour, and have similar attitudes, expectations and needs. Neighbourhoods can therefore be classified according to the characteristics of the individuals who live there and can then be grouped together, even though they are widely separated. Geo-demographics is thus able to target customers in particular areas who exhibit similar behaviour patterns.

A number of commercial systems for this type of segmentation are available. In the UK, leading products include MOSAIC (Experian) and ACORN (CACI), both of

Table 8.1 Distribution of UK households by financial ACORN and financial mosaic classification

Financial mosaic	%	Acorn	%
Adventurous spenders	14.5	Wealthy investors	28.7
Burdened borrowers	6.6	Prospering families	11.3
Capital accumulators	6.3	Traditional money	13.4
Discerning investors	5.1	Young urbanites	12.9
Equity-holding elders	4.2	Middle-aged comfort	11.7
Farm-owners and traders	6.5	Contented pensioners	5.1
Good paying realists	19.5	Settling down	4.1
Hardened cash payers	18.7	Moderate living	6.7
Indebted strugglers	4.7	Meagre means	2.1
Just about surviving	13.9	Inner city existence	2.2
		Impoverished pensioners	1.4
		Unclassified	0.4

Source: WARC (2003) and Financial Acorn – http://www.caci.co.uk/pdfs/facornprofiler1.pdf (accessed 21st March 2005).

whom offer generalized classification and financial services-specific classifications. The latter are shown in Table 8.1. These systems are typically constructed on the basis of census data, which are then updated by each organization on a regular basis and may also be supplemented with additional information such as consumer surveys. Classification occurs at the postcode level. Thus, users are able to categorize individual postcodes (usually groups of around fifteen households) into one of the segments shown below (or into sub-segments) and then profile those segments on a range of consumer and purchase characteristics.

Elsewhere in the world, Experian provides generic geo-demographic systems in a range of countries including the US, Australia, Hong Kong, Japan and Spain. Experian also offers a similar system (SUPERMAP) in China, and a worldwide product, Global MOSAIC. Acxicom provides geo-demographics in Japan with its Chomonicx system, and SIG offers its CAMEO system in Mexico.

It must be appreciated that choice of characteristic to use in segmentation is a contextual matter dependent upon the considerations given at the start of this section. Trade-offs often have to be made, especially with regard to practical issues concerning implementation. Demographic variables are usually the most simple to use, as they readily lend themselves to requirements of accessibility and measurability, although they are often weak in relation to relevance as demographics alone rarely explain why an individual makes a particular purchase. From the point of view of promotional aspects of the mix, media typically provide data on readership, listenership and viewership that is based upon demographic variables.

Life stage is an approach to segmentation that is of particular relevance in the context of financial services. This is because of the long-term nature of many of the products encountered and the duration over which utility is experienced. The basic principle upon which the life-stage approach is based is that people progress through varying stages in their lives, each of which is associated with different product needs. Figure 8.1 shows schematically a set of typical life stages and the associated product needs that are indicated.

Looking at Figure 8.1, the role performed by the current account as a gateway product can be fully appreciated. It also demonstrates the ways in which financial

Lifestage

Single in Fulltime Education	→	Single working	→	Married	→	Young Married with Children	→	Married Middle-Aged with Children	→	Married Middle-Aged Empty Nester	→	Married Active Retired	→	Independent Single Retired	→	Dependent Single Retired

Product Needs

Single in Fulltime Education	Single working	Married	Young Married with Children	Married Middle-Aged with Children	Married Middle-Aged Empty Nester	Married Active Retired	Independent Single Retired	Dependent Single Retired
Current A/c	Current A/c	Current A/c	Current A/c	Current A/c	Current A/c	Current A/c	Current A/c	Current A/c
Deposit A/c	Credit Card	Credit Card	Credit Card	Credit Card	Credit Card	Credit Card	Credit Card	Credit Card
	Travel Ins	Travel Ins	Travel Ins	Travel Ins	Travel Ins	Content Ins	Content Ins	Content Ins
	Loans	Loans	Loans	Loans	Loans	Building Ins	Building Ins	Building Ins
	Motor Ins	Mortgage	Mortgage	Mortgage	Mortgage	Motor Ins	Motor Ins	
	Deposit A/c	Life Ins	Life Ins	Life Ins	Life Ins	Deposit A/c	Deposit A/c	Deposit A/c
		Content Ins	Content Ins	Content Ins	Content Ins			Investments
		Building Ins	Building Ins	Building Ins	Building Ins	Investment	Investment	Power of attorney
		Motor Ins	Motor Ins	Motor Ins	Motor Ins	Travel Ins	Travel Ins	Long-term care
		Deposit A/c	Deposit A/c	Deposit A/c	Deposit A/c	Annuities	Annuities	
			Pension	Pension	Pension			
					Investments			

Figure 8.1 Typical life stages and associated financial-product needs.

complexity develops as individuals progress from adolescence through to being middle-aged with children. It is interesting to note how the balance between assets and liabilities alters at different life stages. By the time an individual has graduated, he or she can be expected to be in debt to the order of £12 000 in the UK. This indebtedness continues to grow as credit card and unsecured loan debts accumulate. A major step increase in indebtedness occurs when the individual takes out a mortgage to fund home-purchase. Gradually net indebtedness reduces until a point – typically at an age of between 50 and 60 – where the individual becomes a net asset holder. This is precisely why the over-50s are the primary target for investment product marketing activity. Alternative forms of life stage can be designed to reflect different lifestyles, such as people who remain single, those who marry but have no children, those who get divorced and so on.

Psychographic variables may offer the greatest potential for differentiation and creativity in executional terms. However, there are particular challenges in terms of determining: measurability, profitability and accessibility. Since the early 1990s, the Co-operative Bank has targeted that segment of the population which has a particular preference for socially responsible banking practices. Thus the bank has set out to position itself as *the ethical bank*. It is an interesting example of a bank using what is essentially a psychographic variable as the basis of its segmentation strategy.

8.4.2 Customer needs and behaviours: product-orientated segmentation

This approach comprises variables that define the nature of the utility that consumers seek to gain from the consumption of a product or service. It also incorporates the nature of the consumer's interaction with the product. Thus it is more of a product-centred approach to segmentation than its customer-orientated counterpart. In specific terms, it can be broken down as follows.

Core financial needs	Banking
Savings	
Investing	
Home ownership	
Retirement planning	
Life assurance	
Health insurance	
Possessions insurance	
Product/service usage	Frequency of purchase
Frequency of service usage	
Quantum of purchase	
Means of accessing service	
Means of purchase	
Timing of purchase	
Timing of accessing service	
Product attributes	Pricing
Value	
Ownership status of provider	
Feature simplicity/complexity	

In practice many financial service providers use multivariable approaches to segmentation, which draw upon characteristics that are both customer- and product-orientated. For example, an investment company might choose to target a segment defined in the following terms:

Women in the age group 35 to 60 who want to invest for retirement and favour an ethical approach to investment.

In such a case, due attention must be paid to matters concerning measurability and so on, to ensure that the segment is executionally and commercially viable.

8.5 Approaches to segmenting business-to-business markets

The benefits that accrue from segmentation apply equally within the context of business-to-business marketing. Indeed, the costs of acquiring a new customer in the organizational business arena are usually considerably greater than in the consumer arena, and so too are the income flows. This makes effective targeting of marketing resources all the more important. As discussed elsewhere, managing B2B and B2C relationships involves points both of comparison and difference. As with the consumer domain, there are various approaches to segmenting the organizational domain; the following characteristics are those most widely used.

Business demographics
Industrial sector   Financial services: banks, general insurance,
                                                                         building societies etc.

    Retailing: food, clothing etc.
    Professional services: management consultancies,
    accountants, legal practices
    Engineering
    Information technology

Organization size   Turnover
    Assets
    Funds under management
    Number of employees
    Fee income

Organizational structure   Centralized
    Branch-based

Ownership   Proprietary
    Mutual
    Core quoted company
    Subsidiary company

Business geography

International   Head office domicile
    countries represented

Single country   National centralized
    Regions

Continued

Business geography—cont'd	
Metropolitan	
Town	
Local/regional	Metropolitan
Town	
Business processes	
Purchasing	Centralized
Devolved	
Decision-making	By tender
By negotiation	
Individual/committee-based	
Choice criteria	Lowest cost
Degree of customization	
Service intensity	
Product/service range	
Performance criteria	
Image and positioning	
R&D and innovation	
Business performance	
Business growth rate	
Return on capital	
Market sector growth rate	
High margin/low margin	
Markets served	
Commercial markets	
Consumer markets	
High net-worth individuals	
Mainstream mass market	
Lower social-economic groups	
Niche markets	
Product specialisms	

As with consumer market segmentation, multivariable segmentation is often encountered in the B2B domain. For example, a general insurance company might choose to target a business segment defined in the following terms:

> businesses in the hotel, catering and leisure sectors with a turnover of less than £25m per annum serving high net-worth individuals and with a particular need for liability insurance.

8.6   Targeting strategies

In addition to choosing the basis upon which to segment a market, choices must be made regarding which segments to target. This is not necessarily a sequential process. Indeed, choice of segmentation criteria and choice of targets (i.e. the targeting strategy) is an interactive and interdependent set of processes which may well require a high degree of iteration before a final strategic position is arrived at. Segments must be evaluated in terms of their attractiveness to the organization, their profit potential, and the organization's ability to deliver the required service. This information can then be taken into consideration when deciding which segments to target. The basic array of targeting strategies is as follows:

- *Undifferentiated* – serves an entire marketplace with a single marketing mix which does not distinguish between sub-segments of the market
- *Differentiated* – an aggregate marketplace, such as banking, is organized into a number of segments, each of which is targeted with a tailored marketing mix
- *Focused* – a choice is made to target a small subset of the segments of a multi-segment marketplace with a single marketing mix that best suits the needs of that segment
- *Customized* – each individual that comprises the target market is the subject of a marketing mix that is tailored in some way to the individual's specific needs.

8.6.1   Undifferentiated targeting

It should not be assumed that an undifferentiated strategy is necessarily an inherently inferior form. An analysis of customer characteristics may simply reveal the absence of a compelling variable upon which segmentation could be based. Equally, it may be the case that the cost of segmenting the market and producing a set of bespoke marketing mixes is not commercially justifiable.

In the recent past, life insurance companies operating in the UK and using an essentially commission-only sales-force adopted a largely undifferentiated strategy. This was sometimes referred to as 'playing the numbers game', whereby the low cost of new customer acquisition and the heavy up-front charges meant that almost any new customer thus acquired was likely to contribute to embedded value profits. A range of developments, such as the regulation-induced increase in new customer acquisition costs, lower product margins and the pressure to improve persistency rates, have all served to make the life insurance industry more discriminating in its approach to gaining new customers, and thus there has been a growing tendency to move away from an undifferentiated approach. Admittedly, the attempts to introduce segmentation have sometimes been somewhat elementary, often based simply upon a minimum income threshold. Most of the life insurance companies that operated an undifferentiated approach are no longer open to new customers.

8.6.2   Differentiated targeting

This arises when a company has been able to identify a commercially valid basis upon which an aggregate market can be broken down into segments. The fast-moving consumer goods sector has probably been the best exemplar of differentiated marketing. Differentiated segmentation is gaining in popularity within the financial services sector. There is a sense in which its development has been held back by a relative lack of suitable marketing orientation within the sector; however, the major clearing banks, such as Barclays, Lloyds TSB and HSBC, are showing a growing usage of differentiated marketing. Typical generic segments that are encountered among mainstream clearing banks include:

Business banking marketplace segments	Business start-ups
Sole traders and partnership	
Small businesses (typically with 5–50 staff)	
Medium business (typically 50–250 staff)	
Large business (typically 250–1000 staff)	
Large Corporate Market (more than 1000 staff)	
Retail banking marketplace segments	Student banking
Ordinary current account customers	
High net-worth customers (e.g. earning more than £50 000 pa)	
Private banking customers (e.g. have investable assets in excess of £500 000)	

The illustrative banking segments shown above reveal a fairly basic approach to segmentation. In the case of B2B banking, segmentation is typically based on business demographics. As far as B2C banking is concerned, it is typically based upon demographic or socio-economic characteristics. To a large extent, this comes down to the practicalities of the typical large clearing bank which, in the UK, might have over 50 000 staff of whom more than 10 000 are based in some 2000 or more branches. Segmentation has to reflect the practicalities of gaining the engagement of a huge and diverse workforce in implementing a segmentation strategy.

8.6.3   Focused segmentation

This approach to segmentation is encountered in circumstances where a company breaks a market down into a set of segments but chooses to target a small subset of available segments or, in some cases, only a single segment. A focused approach may take a number of different forms:

1. *Single segment concentration.* In this approach, the organization concentrates only on a single segment in the market and supplies products tailored specifically to the needs of those customer groups. This approach is often described as niche marketing. It is potentially highly profitable, because the organization focuses all its efforts on a particular segment of the market where it has a strong differential advantage. At the same time there are risks associated with this approach, because if the segment were to disappear or a new competitor enter the market, the organization could be vulnerable to a significant loss of business. The general insurer Hiscox focuses on high net-worth clients, whereas the Ecclesiastical Insurance Company focuses upon providing general insurance to churches and allied organizations. Endsleigh Insurance has carved out a niche for itself by focusing on the student segment.
2. *Selective specialization.* Selective specialization is another type of niche marketing. However, rather than concentrating only on one segment the organization chooses to operate in several (possibly unrelated) segments. This approach to targeting is less focused than single segment specialization, but probably less risky.
3. *Product specialization.* Most markets can be seen as comprising a number of different customer groups and a number of different but related products. The organization

that concentrates on supplying a particular product type to a range of customer groups is pursuing a product specialization strategy. This approach to market targeting may be particularly appropriate to organizations with particular strengths or knowledge in relation to a given technology or product. Thus, Al Baraka Islamic Bank in Bahrain, Bank Islam in Malaysia and the Islamic Bank of Britain can be seen to be pursuing a product specialization strategy by offering Islamic financial services (a particular product type) to a range of different customer groups (segments) which range from retail customers needing very simple banking products through to businesses requiring very complex financing arrangements.

4. *Market specialization*. This approach is the opposite to product specialization. Rather than concentrating on a particular product, the organization chooses to specialize in meeting the needs of a particular customer group. This strategy may be most suitable where knowledge of the customer group's particular needs is a particularly important basis for establishing a competitive advantage. Private banks pursue this type of approach in relation to high net-worth individuals – they seek to provide a range of different financial products to meet the needs of the high net-worth customers.

8.6.4   Customized targeting

This approach represents the ultimate manifestation of the segmentation concept, based as it is upon a separate, tailored marking mix for each customer. Some markets lend themselves more naturally to a customized approach, especially those that are in service sectors involving a high degree of human interface. In the financial services sector, customized targeting is most in evidence as part of a hybrid strategy in which a distinct set of services (such as investment banking) is offered to a particular segment (such as large corporations) and then the service is customized to individuals within that segment.

8.7   Positioning products and organizations

Positioning represents a logical step that follows the processes of segmentation and targeting. Having selected the criteria upon which to segment a market and made the choice of which segments to target, the company must then decide how best to present itself, either corporately or as a specific product brand, to the individuals that comprise the target segments. Positioning is a piece of marketing jargon that concerns the issue of perception. At the core of positioning lies a brand's or company's competitive advantage in terms of how it differentiates itself from the competition and how it delivers value to its customers. Thus, positioning is about how a company or brand wants itself to be perceived in the minds of the individuals who comprise its target segments. The choice of position is based upon the agreed form of differentiation. The objective of positioning is to generate and maintain a clear value proposition to customers, thus creating a distinctive place in the market for the brand or organization. When successful, positioning results in a brand or company being seen as distinctive from its competitors.

To be commercially advantageous, positioning should be based upon product and service characteristics that:

- are relevant to the target segment
- achieve differentiation from the competition
- can be communicated clearly to the market
- can be sustained.

Positioning is a truly strategic concept that requires a considerable investment over a prolonged period of time. It is the primary manifestation of competitive advantage, and represents a considerable source of brand and corporate value. To be successful, it requires alignment between how an organization (or brand) wants itself to be perceived and how it is actually perceived by consumers.

The brand characteristics upon which positioning may be built can relate to demonstrable product and service attributes or image-related factors. McDonald's has historically based its positioning on features concerning fun, food and family, which is perceived appropriately through the entirety of the consumer's engagement with the brand. The company employs the tag-line *'mmmm, I'm loving it'*, which conveys the sense of enjoyment. Burger King, on the other hand, has a positioning that is based on more explicit reference to product quality communicated in a more serious manner than McDonald's. L'Oréal is an example of a brand whose position is based more on image than specific product features. Its hair- and skin-care products use the tag-line *'Because I'm worth it'* to convey the notion of products that are about self-indulgence, and they are priced accordingly. Designer-label luxury goods are positioned very much on the basis of an image of exclusivity rather than the tangible features of the products themselves.

Positioning is less well-developed as a concept in the field of financial services than in the field of consumer goods. Given the earlier assertion that it takes time to establish a successful position in the mind of the consumer, it is perhaps rather early days to give a definitive view on financial services positioning. What we can say is that financial services positioning operates to an overwhelming extent at the corporate level as opposed to that of the individual product or brand. In this context, organizations have relied on positioning with respect to product/service attributes or image-related factors in much the same ways as is observed in the tangible goods domain. Morgan Stanley's position is based on product/service attributes and emphasizes *'excellence in financial advice and market execution'*. Similarly, the Standard Bank of South Africa aims to be *'Simpler. Faster. Better'*. Examples of approaches that are more image-based include HSBC, which positions itself as *'the world's local bank'* to create the image of a bank that delivers value on the basis of both local knowledge and global strength. Similarly, in Japan, where banks have traditionally placed most emphasis on serving corporate clients, Shinsei Bank emphasizes its orientation towards satisfying retail customers and building strong relationships.

The Co-operative Bank is an example of an organization that positions itself on the basis of an image-related attribute. When it conducted a review of its competitive position in the early 1990s, it anticipated that its future position would be based upon product or service attributes. Such attributes could have included factors like the number of branch outlets, range of services, quality of service delivery, charges, interest rates, investment returns and so on. This is a fairly predictable approach to branch-based financial services, and it would have been difficult for the Co-operative Bank to differentiate itself from its larger rivals on such a basis. A spark of intuition and judgement resulted in its choice of *the ethical bank* as the basis for its position.

Case study 8.1 shows how Co-operative Bank's allied financial services business CIS has reflected an ethical stance in its approach to investment fund management.

Case study 8.1   Ethical investment policies and the ethically-orientated investor segment – the Co-operative Insurance Society Limited (CIS)

Headquartered in Manchester, England, CIS is the only Co-operative insurer in the UK and is one of the largest providers of personal financial services in the country. A particular point of interest is that the Co-op has developed a strong affinity with that section of the population that displays a strong ethical orientation towards a range of issues. Indeed, the Co-operative Bank has clearly positioned itself as *the ethical bank*. What is interesting is the way in which the Co-op Bank and CIS have adapted their marketing mixes in ways that are consistent with their approach to segmentation and positioning. Here, we consider how the needs of the ethically-orientated segment have been reflected in CIS's approach to investment management.

As a member of the Co-operative movement, CIS shares this ethical underpinning which, when applied to investment, has always been construed as requiring the optimization of financial returns for customers. Recognizing the increasing sophistication of the market, in 1989 CIS introduced a range of unit trusts (mutual funds) to which was added, in 1990, a fund that screens companies on environmental, health and safety criteria. These positive criteria are supplemented by negative criteria relating to animal testing, armaments, oppressive regimes, tobacco and nuclear power. Like other CIS products, units in this fund, now known as the CIS Sustainable Leaders Trust, are sold through the Society's direct sales-force in people's homes. The availability of this product has extended the interest in social investment within the Society's customer base, and the Trust has always been amongst the largest funds of its kind, although it represents less than 1 per cent of CIS's overall assets. The managers of the fund have been able to demonstrate that the adoption of an ethical approach to a fund's structure is financially as well as ethically sound. Indeed, the following data, supplied by S&P Micropal, show how well the Trust has performed compared with industry acknowledged benchmarks

£1000 invested on 31 December 2002 was, on 31 December 2005, worth:

- £1664 if 'invested' in the FTSE All-Share Index
- £1672 on the basis of the Average UK All Companies Fund
- £1733 if used to purchase units in the Trust (assuming the income was reinvested).

Continued

Case study 8.1   Ethical investment policies and the ethically-orientated investor segment – the Co-operative Insurance Society Limited (CIS)—cont'd

There is a continuing market for screened investments, although the potentially greater financial risk must be made clear to customers. Nevertheless, the trend has been towards using enhanced analysis required to integrate social, ethical and environmental (SEE) considerations with the investment mainstream. In 1999 CIS launched a programme known as 'Responsible Shareholding', applying to all equity funds and based on engaging with companies on matters of concern. These matters were identified through a customer consultation exercise, from which an ethical engagement policy was developed which provides the basis for approaching companies. In part, this represents a reaffirmation of the Co-operative movement's democratic roots, but it also acknowledges the fact that SEE issues are increasingly important in establishing a company's social responsibility and future sustainability. This does not relate only to a company's community activities, but also to the way in which it develops its workforce, for instance, and above all how it governs itself in the relationships between management, board, shareholders and other stakeholders. Analysis of corporate governance is an important part of Responsible Shareholding, and CIS undertakes to vote on every motion put to investee company AGMs (whenever possible), supplemented if necessary by attendance to raise questions from the floor. Reporting is seen as an essential component of corporate responsibility, and detailed analysis takes place of disclosure on matters such as executive remuneration and SEE issues, in order to determine how the Society's votes will be exercised. Along with some other UK investors, CIS has been recognized in the press as one of the foremost UK institutions practising Socially Responsible Investment (SRI). It is becoming increasingly accepted that such activities contribute to investment sustainability – UNEP's Asset Management Working Group concluded in 2004 that environmental, social and corporate governance issues affect long-term shareholder value, sometimes profoundly. If this is proved, it will demonstrate that an active response by companies to SEE and governance concerns voiced by customers does enhance the financial returns that they receive.

Source: Robert Taylor, CIS Investment Management (personal communication).

A variant on product/service positioning is positioning that is based upon serving the needs of the distinct target segment – i.e. a focused positioning strategy. By means of such a strategy, the organization is trying to create the perception that it has a unique understanding of the needs of the individuals that compromise its target segment. The implication is that the overall value reposition will be seen to be superior to that of competitors in the eyes of customers. Police Mutual Assurance and Teachers Assurance position themselves as specializing in the needs of employees of the police service and education sector respectively.

Although positioning in the field of financial services is overwhelmingly at the corporate rather than product-brand level, there is a growing incidence of portfolios of organizational brands that reside within an overall corporate structure. Smile.co.uk is positioned as a youthful, approachable high-tech brand within the Co-operative Financial Services umbrella organization that includes the *ethical* Co-operative Bank. HBOS retains the clearly distinctive positioning of organizational brands such as the Bank of Scotland and Halifax. Similarly, Lloyds TSB continues to support the distinctive positioning of the Scottish Widows and Cheltenham and Gloucester brands within its overall brand architecture.

8.7.1   Perceptual mapping

It is important to have some understanding of the type of processes that are used to determine a company's or product's position. One commonly used approach is perceptual mapping, which relies primarily on information about consumer perceptions of both the organization and its competitors. This information may be based upon either quantitative research-based data or more subjective judgements. It is important to remember that it is not simply a product that is being positioned but, rather, the complete product or corporate offer, including product and service features, image, quality and pricing. Perceptual mapping requires that an organization first identifies the main feature of a product category available to consumers. The next step is to establish the relative importance of those features to consumers, and the relative performance of competing offers. Market research is used to arrive at the relative importance of features and competitive ratings. Qualitative research methods, such as the use of focus groups and individual depth interviewing, are useful means of seeking original and insightful new positions.

Through the research and evaluation process, the organization typically tries to identify two major dimensions of itself or its product that could form the basis of competitive advantage. This is partly a matter of judgement, but may also be supported by more detailed statistical analysis of consumer perception. Figure 8.2 presents a hypothetical perceptual map that might apply to the investment fund management sector. It assumes that the chosen discriminators upon which Company A wishes to base its position are *reputation for investment performance* and *concern for the investors' interests*.

Company A has a competitive advantage arising from its position as a company that is seen to deliver competitively superior investment performance and cares about its customers. Its nearest rival is Company F, and it needs to maintain a close watch on F to ensure that Company A continues to maintain a relatively superior position. Company D is clearly competitively disadvantaged on the basis of its investment performance and perceived concern for investors' interests. Company E displays relatively high levels of concern for its investors' interests, but fails to deliver with regard to investment performance. Company B delivers very good investment performance, but comes across as having an uncaring approach to investor interests. Finally, Company C is pretty much stuck in the middle, being just average or both constructs of performance.

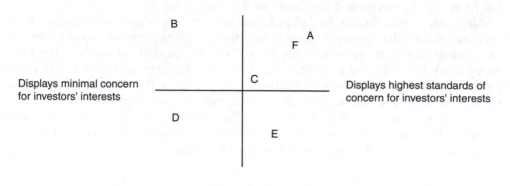

Figure 8.2 Perceptual map for investment fund management companies.

Whatever position is decided upon, it must satisfy some basic tests of its likely effectiveness. Jobber (2004) identifies a set of four such tests, namely:

1. *Clarity* – is the basis of the position clear and straightforward to grasp?
2. *Credibility* – can the position be justified and validated by the evidence available?
3. *Consistency* – is the essence of the position communicated consistent over time in all elements of the marketing mix?
4. *Competitiveness* – does the position result in benefits to the customer that are demonstrably superior to those provided by its competitors?

The crucial test is whether the company (or brand) is perceived to be distinctive. Positioning presents particular challenges to the financial services industry, owing to the intangibility of its products, the absence of patent protection and the ease with which products and services can be copied by competitors. Arguably, positioning is still in its infancy in many areas of financial services around the world. There often seems to be little that discriminates between the mainstream banks and insurance companies, certainly as far as the perceptions of consumers are concerned. In time we can expect to see more distinctiveness, but it will require a degree of sustained consistency that has so often been absent in the past.

8.8 Repositioning

An important aspect of positioning is that it is contextual and impacted upon by forces within the marketplace. By its very nature, it requires customers to draw comparisons between the array of competing offers to which they are exposed. As with any aspect of marketing strategy, positioning needs to be reviewed on an appropriate basis to ensure that it delivers the required differentiation. Over time, market forces may exert pressures that threaten the relevance and value of the position. Consumer preferences and priorities alter, competitors are continually creating change, and new ways of satisfying needs arise from the forces of innovation. Thus, companies must be very vigilant in protecting their competitive advantage.

However, a given position can sometimes be threatened or, indeed, lose credibility and competitive relevance. Examples of problems with longstanding successful positions abound in the consumer goods and retailing areas. In the 1980s, the Guinness brand's position, based as it was on connotations of health-giving properties within a context of traditional beer drinking, was becoming increasingly irrelevant. At about the same time, Toyota came to realize that, no matter how hard it tried, it just could not establish and maintain the Corolla brand's position in the executive car market. The Tesco of the 1980s also found itself a hostage to positioning based upon a product range with limited consumer appeal and a somewhat outmoded estate of outlets.

Guinness, Toyota and Tesco have all had to engage in major repositioning activities which have resulted in new positions that have achieved differentiation and renewed competitive advantages. In the case of Guinness, the brand has been repositioned with new product variants and a somewhat quirky modern style of advertising, initially featuring the cult actor Rutger Hauer. Toyota undertook a far more radical approach to repositioning itself in the executive car market with the Lexus brand. In addition to a new brand, a whole new range of vehicles has emerged and is distributed and serviced through distinctive dealerships. Tesco also embarked upon a vigorous repositioning exercise, beginning in the late 1980s, and this has seen it grow to become Britain's most profitable retailer, accounting for some 15 per cent of all retail spending.

Jobber has identified four basic repositioning strategies, which are outlined in Figure 8.3.

The approach illustrated in Figure 8.3 is helpful in enabling managers to conceptualize the nature of repositioning that they could consider should there be concerns regarding the robustness of their current position. In common with similar such 2×2 matrices, a degree of caution should be exercised because a degree of ambiguity can often be encountered when seeking to apply them in practice. The important learning point is not to get unduly hung up on precise categorization, but rather to use the model to think though the extent to which repositioning should involve the

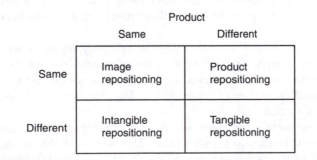

Figure 8.3 Repositioning strategies.

consideration of product/service development, new market development, or a combination of the two. It might also lead to the conclusion that the answer lies in creating new perceptions about the product among existing markets – i.e. image repositioning.

An interesting example of repositioning in the banking sector is afforded by the experience of Mitsubishi UFJ Securities (MUFJ). In October 2005, Mitsubishi Tokyo Financial Group (MTFG) merged with UFJ Holdings to create MUFG, the world's largest bank, with total assets in excess of US$600bn. Historically, the Japanese banking market has been dominated by the needs of the business sector – indeed, according to Standard & Poor's, retail banking represents just about 30 per cent of total Japanese banking profits. This compares with 50 per cent for Barclays and 70 per cent for Bank of America. The proportion of MUFG's business profits that is accounted for by retail banking is of the order of 15 per cent, and the bank's management intends to grow the proportion to 35 per cent during the course of the next few years.

In order to realize this goal, the company has embarked upon a strategy to reposition itself as a consumer-orientated retail banking brand capable of competing on equal terms with banks such as HSBC and Citigroup. This has required changes to the marketing mix, comprising elements such as a wider product range, new branch layouts, new pricing structures, more responsive systems (including 24-hour ATM access) and, crucially, the creation of a new culture. Reorienting staff to relate more appropriately to retail customers has required the company to set up an internal retail academy. Training courses lasting from a single day to over 3 months are evidence of the seriousness that the company attaches to the *people* element of the marketing mix. Independent commentators have made the point that there will also be a requirement to increase staffing levels to deal effectively with the retail market sector. It is to be hoped that the anticipated higher margins will be sufficient to offset the inevitable costs associated with the bank's repositioning strategy.

8.9   Summary and conclusions

Segmentation, targeting and positioning are at the heart of the development of any marketing strategy. To compete effectively, an organization must first identify different groups of consumers or business customers within the market place. These groups need to be different from each other, but customers within each group must be relatively similar in terms of their needs and wants – i.e. the common characteristic.

Few organizations have the resources to serve every segment within the market, and therefore companies must select a series of market segments to target. These target markets must be chosen according to the nature of customers' wants and the organization's ability to supply those needs. The decision must also take levels of competition into account.

Once target markets have been identified, the organization must pay careful attention to how it wishes to present itself. This means that the organization must have a clear idea of its source of competitive advantage, and be able to communicate it effectively to target consumers.

Review questions

1. What are the criteria for effective segmentation?
2. What variables do you think are most suitable for segmenting the market for credit cards?
3. What are the advantages of a differentiated approach to market targeting?
4. When will focused market targeting be most appropriate?
5. What factors should be taken into account when trying to develop a competitive position?

Part II

Customer acquisition

9

Customer acquisition strategies and the marketing mix

Learning objectives

By the end of this chapter you will be able to:

- understand the relationship between marketing strategy and the marketing mix
- appreciate the differences and relationship between annual marketing planning and the strategic marketing plan
- explain the nature of the marketing mix as it applies to financial services
- understand the challenges associated with developing a financial services marketing mix.

9.1 Introduction

Discussions of marketing have traditionally focused attention on how to attract new customers – a process typically described as customer acquisition. Increasingly it is recognized that the retention of existing customers may be every bit as important as the acquisition of new ones. The elements of marketing used for acquisition and retention are in many respects very similar, but the ways in which they are used can be quite different. In Part II of this text we focus upon aspects of marketing management which are particularly concerned with the acquisition of new customers. Specifically, we focus on the well-established concept of the marketing mix which is introduced in this chapter and subsequently explored in more detail.

The marketing mix is a term used to describe the marketing tools that a manager controls. Managers must make decisions about these different tools in order to create a clear competitive position in the market for the organization's products and services that is consistent with the nature of the overall marketing strategy. The tools that make up the marketing mix are often referred to as the '4-Ps' – product, price, promotion and place – although in services marketing this is often extended to 7-Ps by adding people, process and physical evidence. It is through the marketing mix that strategy takes practical effect. In other words, the marketing mix is the practical expression of the marketing strategy. Consumers have little or no knowledge of, or interest in, strategy. What concerns them is the utility they experience from the contact they have with the marketing mix.

It is important to recognize that decisions about the marketing mix have both strategic and tactical dimensions. The strategic dimension of the marketing mix is primarily concerned with decisions about the relative importance of the different elements of the marketing mix. For example, promotion, and particularly television advertising, may play an important role in the marketing mix for many retail financial services, but be almost irrelevant for specialized corporate financial services. Equally, a mass-market financial service such as a standard bank account or mortgage will need a distribution system that makes it easily available to a large proportion of the population, whereas a highly specialized product can rely on a far more selective system of distribution. In contrast, the tactical dimension of the marketing mix is concerned with specific decisions about the individual marketing tools. Thus, for example, once a decision has been taken about the general approach to pricing (e.g. premium pricing), a specific decision is required regarding the actual price to be set.

The purpose of this chapter is to provide an overview of the marketing mix for financial services, paying particular attention to the way in which the marketing mix may be used for customer acquisition. The traditional 4-Ps are discussed more fully in the following chapters. The chapter begins with a brief discussion of short-term, annual marketing planning, to set a context for discussion of the mix elements. This is followed by a discussion of the strategic issues relating to the marketing mix, and the subsequent section provides an overview of the individual mix elements and their relevance in a financial services context. The chapter moves on to explore the challenges associated with using the marketing mix for customer acquisition in financial services.

9.2 Short-term marketing planning

In Chapter 5 we considered strategic marketing planning and recognized that its primary role is to set direction over the medium to long term – typically 3–5 years. It is upon the platform of the strategic marketing plan that major policy decisions are made, such as selecting which segments are to be served and establishing how the organization will differentiate itself in delivering value to customers and thus achieve competitive advantage. To complement the strategic marketing plan, best practice dictates that an organization should have an *annual marketing plan*. If the strategic marketing plan is about the setting of long-term direction and the determination of competitive advantage, the annual marketing plan is about achieving a joined-up and co-ordinated approach to achieving short-term marketing objectives.

In the way that there is no universally agreed process and template for strategic marketing planning, there is no such model for the annual marketing plan. However, it is important that there is consistency between a given organization's strategic and annual marketing plans. Moreover, it is important that organizations that comprise a number of individual strategic business units (SBUs) or business lines adopt a common approach to marketing planning. For example, a broad-based financial services provider such as HSBC might choose, say, to produce an annual marketing plan for its range of mortgage and property finance products. This may be quite separate from, for example, its pension product range. Whilst both of these product groups will be guided by the overall corporate positioning statement of being 'The World's Local Bank', they each nonetheless operate in quite distinct marketplaces. Therefore, each will have quite different requirements in respect of the market-specific objectives that they specify, the elements that need to be considered when analysing the marketing environment, and the characteristics of the segments that they identify and target. For example, the competitor set that applies to pensions products will vary greatly to that of the mortgage area. This is an important point, as there are real dangers of conducting a marketing plan at too aggregate a level. There are no straightforward solutions to this difficulty other than to say that all organizations must approach the issue in a way that best suits their particular circumstances, such as product range, scope and organizational structure.

The conduct of the annual marketing plan comprises two components, namely: the process and the written plan itself. It must be borne in mind that there should not be a strict one-size-fits-all approach to the annual marketing plan; rather, it should be tailored to suit the particular characteristics of any given organization. However, the model shown in Figure 9.1 represents a sound core structure for the ultimate output of the planning process.

The plan should make it clear where responsibility and accountability lies for marketing objectives and the successful completion of marketing-mix activities.

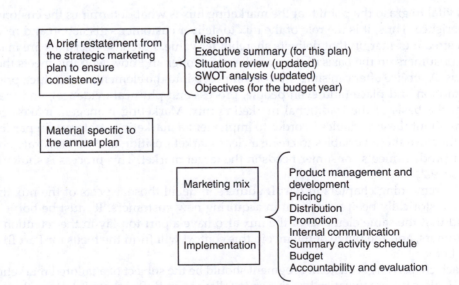

Figure 9.1 The annual marketing plan.

Ownership should be made clear and unambiguous, and sole ownership for delivery should always be sought. It is common to encounter a plethora of shared account-abilities, which results in an unclear sense of ownership. Indeed, well-defined accountability is a necessary prerequisite for an appropriate appraisal system and performance review. This section of the plan can also be used to summarize the array of key performance indicators (KPIs) that arise from the marketing-mix activities.

In the discussion of strategic marketing planning in Chapter 5, explicit reference was made to *internal communication*. The lack of sufficient emphasis upon this issue is a major contributory factor to the failure of marketing plans to achieve their objectives. It is very rare for a marketing objective in the field of financial services to be accomplished without the involvement of people in other functions. In the case of an insurance company there may be a sales-force to consider; a building society must take care to inform branch staff. In all types of financial services companies it is vital that administration staff are made fully aware of marketing activities that will impact upon their work. Similarly, IT and business systems colleagues need to know how plans for new products or new product features should be factored into their own functional plans.

A central component of any annual marketing plan will be decisions about the marketing mix and details about how key marketing variables will be managed and controlled. The remainder of this chapter will explore in more detail the concept of the mix as it applies in financial services.

9.3   The role of the financial services marketing mix

It is vital to grasp the point that the marketing mix is what determines the customer experience. Thus, it is the role of the mix to deliver customer satisfaction and result in a stream of margin that delivers shareholder value. Purchase decisions are made by consumers on the basis of the overall service offer and how well this meets their needs. A service offer can simply be decomposed into the elements of product, price, promotion and place (and even people, process and physical evidence), and these form the basis of the traditional marketing mix. Marketing managers make decisions about these variables in order to implement a marketing strategy – in particular, they use these variables to create a clear market position and demonstrate how their product meets consumer needs in the target market. This process is shown in Figure 9.2.

The remaining chapters in Part II address in detail those aspects of the mix that have historically been prominent in acquiring new customers. It must be borne in mind that the same elements of the mix also have a part to play in the retention of customers, and the range of the mix in this context will form the focus for Part III of this book.

Each chosen target customer segment should be the subject of a tailored marketing mix. Unless the organization has chosen to follow an undifferentiated strategy, the mix must be adjusted to suit the particular characteristics of each individual segment.

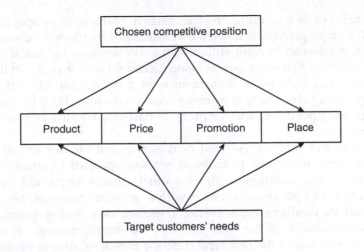

Figure 9.2 Customer needs and the marketing mix.

In addition to segmentation, the strategy will identify the basis of the company's competitive advantage. The chosen form of competitive advantage provides a reference point for the marketing mixes designed for each target segment. Thus, there must be consistency in the design of segment-specific mixes to ensure that the core competitive advantage is in evidence across the range of mixes employed. All elements of the marketing mix must be designed, presented and delivered in ways that are mutually reinforcing and faithfully reflect the company's chosen basis for differentiation.

In practice, there is a range of different marketing tools that marketing managers can use. Thus, when we use the term 'the 4Ps' it is important to remember that each 'P' encompasses a range of different marketing tools. Some examples of these are as follows:

- Product – includes range of products offered, features, brand, quality, packaging, warranties, terms and conditions
- Price – includes listed price, discounts, payment periods, credit terms
- Promotion – includes advertising, personal selling, sales promotion, publicity, public relations
- Place – includes channels of distribution, location, access (opening hours), staffing.

In managing the marketing mix, it is important to remember that each decision about a particular tool will send a message to consumers. A high price, for example, may be interpreted as indicating high quality. A limited number of outlets for a product or service may imply that it is exclusive, as might advertising in expensive magazines with limited circulation. Thus, if the marketing mix is to be used to create the organization's desired competitive position there are two key requirements;

1. *Consistency with position.* The decisions about each mix element must be consistent with the position that has been chosen. Thus, for example, when Maybank

decided to promote a youthful lifestyle image in Malaysia, it supported that decision with a major promotional event that included a live band, promotional offers for mobile phones and a competition with a VW Beetle as the major prize. These were all activities that were seen as being consistent with a youthful image. If the same event had included a performance by a string quartet, and a Volvo as the competition prize, many consumers would have found this inconsistent with the image being portrayed and the promotional event would have been much less successful.

2. *Synergy from mix elements.* As well as ensuring that an element of the mix is consistent with the chosen position, it is also important to ensure that all the mix elements are consistent with each other. This is important because each element of the mix presents customers with a very clear message about the organization and its products and services. There are very real synergies generated when each element of the mix conveys the same message to consumers. Equally, if elements of the mix send different messages, then consumers may be confused. For example, the American Express Platinum charge card is associated with high-income consumers and symbolizes prestige and success. It is the fact that it is exclusive that makes it attractive. A press campaign in mass-market media will be inconsistent with the product and the image it projects. There will be no opportunity for synergy, and the image of the card may be damaged because the real target market will not recognize the appropriateness of the card for them.

Thus, an effective marketing mix must aim for consistency and synergy – consistency with strategic position, and synergy from the individual elements. Individual elements of the mix should not be viewed in isolation; constant cross-referencing is essential to ensure consistency with other elements in the mix.

9.4   The financial services marketing mix: key issues

In Chapter 3, the distinguishing features of financial services were identified and their marketing implications discussed. The main differences between financial services and physical goods were listed as:

- intangibility – financial services have no physical form and are often complex and difficult to understand
- inseparability – financial services are produced and consumed simultaneously, they cannot be stored, and there needs to be significant interaction between customer and supplier
- heterogeneity – the quality of financial services is highly variable because of differences between consumers and a heavy dependence on people to provide the service
- perishability – financial services cannot be inventoried; they have to be produced on demand.

To address intangibility, marketing activities might consider:

- making the service more tangible by providing consumers with some physical evidence (or at least a tangible image)
- building trust and confidence through the people that help deliver the service.

To address inseparability, marketing activities might consider:

- training to ensure that staff are friendly and responsive
- developing processes for service delivery that are customer orientated.

To address heterogeneity, marketing activities might consider:

- standardizing service delivery processes
- managing and training staff to encourage a high and consistent level of quality.

To address perishability, marketing activities might consider:

- automating services features via processes for remote access
- managing demand through careful use of staff rosters or by using special price mechanisms.

Thus, the provision of physical evidence, staff management (people) and the systems for delivering service (process) are all likely to be important elements of marketing decision-making for financial services. As a consequence, Booms and Bitner (1981) proposed that people, processes, and physical evidence should be added to the original 4-Ps framework to create what is termed the extended marketing mix (7-Ps). The remainder of this book will be structured around the traditional marketing mix, but a brief description of the elements of the extended marketing mix is provided below. The decision on whether to adopt the 4-Ps or 7-Ps approach can only be determined in the light of the specific circumstances of an individual company or product group. There is little point in being slavish to the 7-Ps model at the tactical level if the 4-Ps version is perfectly fit-for-purpose. What matters is that the marketing-mix decisions outlined in the plan serve to identify a range of actions under suitable headings that will result in the achievement of the desired outcomes – the objectives.

9.4.1 People

The 'people' factor in the marketing mix emphasizes the important role played by individuals in the provision of financial services. Consumers will frequently find the precise details of a financial service difficult to understand, they often do not see anything tangible for their expenditure, and the benefits from many financial services may only become clear at some time in the future. Furthermore, the provision of information and purchase of a financial service depends on the interaction between the consumer and representatives of the organization. These features of financial services mean that the purchase decision may be heavily influenced by the way in which consumers perceive the staff that they deal with and how they interact. The people who provide a service affect the way in which customers see the product, how it is promoted and how it is delivered.

In particular, the people component of services marketing is most commonly associated with personal selling which relates to both the promotion and distribution (place) elements of the marketing mix. It is also relevant to the product element of the mix, because it can have a significant impact on the quality of service.

9.4.2   Process

Process is concerned with the way in which the service is delivered, including business policies for service provision, procedures, the degree of mechanization etc. There are several reasons why process is important. First, the heterogeneity of services raises the issues of quality management and control. Secondly, inseparability suggests that the process of providing the service may be highly visible to the consumer and will need to be flexible enough to accommodate potential demand variations. Thirdly, the intangibility of services means that the process by which the service is provided will often be an important influence on the consumers' assessment of service quality. Accordingly, the main concern with process is typically in the context of distribution, but it also has relevance to pricing decisions.

In developing distribution systems for financial services, the intangible nature of the product means that there is nothing physical to supply to the consumer; the consumer is paying only for a bundle of benefits and the delivery process will need to emphasize these benefits. Furthermore, the variability of service quality leads to pressure for automation in service delivery wherever possible. For some services (such as money transmission) this is relatively easy, whereas for others (such as financial advice) this is more complex, although recent developments in expert systems are assisting with the automation of some of the more complex services.

Although process is important in relation to distribution, it is also relevant to price through its impact on the monitoring and measurement of production costs. Careful attention to the process of delivering a service can be of value in understanding the nature of costs and thus developing a sensible approach to pricing.

9.4.3   Physical evidence

Physical evidence refers to anything tangible which is associated with a given service – it may be the buildings that an organization occupies, the appearance of staff, or the cheque-book holders or wallets that are provided for documents. The need for physical evidence within the marketing mix arises directly from the typically intangible nature of the service. It is generally recognized that physical evidence can be subdivided into two components:

1. Peripheral evidence, which can be possessed by the consumer but has little independent value (e.g. a document wallet)
2. Essential evidence, which cannot be possessed by the consumer but has independent values (e.g. a bank branch).

The provision of physical evidence is likely to be most obvious in the product and place components of the marketing mix, but it is also relevant to promotion. In the product element of the marketing mix, brand-building is important in the process of tangibilizing a service. Building an image and a brand is seen as increasingly important in the financial services sector, because the brand is a way of reducing risk and emphasizing quality. Increasingly, brands are accompanied by a variety of forms of peripheral evidence (cheque books, plastic cards, document wallets, etc.) to reinforce the brand's message.

The need for physical evidence is also significant in the context of promotion. The particular problem facing suppliers of financial services is that they have no physical product to present to consumers. Thus, from a marketing perspective, promotion must try to develop a message and a form of presentation which makes a service seem more tangible. It is also interesting that the more successful forms of sales promotion have tended to be those offering tangible items as free gifts (calculators, watches, etc.) and competitions rather than simple price promotions.

9.5   Customer acquisition and the financial services marketing mix

Thus far, this chapter has given an overview of the key elements associated with the marketing mix for financial services. This section focuses on the challenges which might confront organizations when trying to manage these elements with a view to the acquisition of new customers. Case study 9.1 provides an example of how HDFC Bank in India has effectively integrated its marketing strategy and marketing mix to promote customer acquisition.

Case study 9.1   Customer acquisition at HDFC Bank

Until the 1990s, the banking sector in India was dominated by two main groups – the public-sector banks and the international banks. The former dealt with the mass market, although the quality of products and services provided was generally considered to be poor. The latter focused on the more wealthy segments and were typically very selective in terms of accepting new customers. Liberalization during the 1990s paved the way for the influx of new private-sector banks, the first of which was HDFC, launched in 1995. The bank's research had identified a significant middle-class market, which expected a high quality of service and was willing to pay for it. These customers were not prepared to tolerate poor service and long queues in the public-sector banks, but equally were less trusting of the international banks and less attractive to those banks because they were outside the very high-income brackets.

As a new entrant, HDFC needed to develop its marketing mix in order to target these customers and persuade them to switch to HDFC. The basic value proposition that underpinned HDFC's approach was that of 'international levels of service at a reasonable price'. Specific marketing mix decisions were as follows.

Continued

| | Case study 9.1   Customer acquisition at HDFC Bank—cont'd |

Product

To meet the needs of the chosen mid-market segment, HDFC offered a comprehensive range of banking services, comparable to the product range of international banks. This was supported by the targeting of specific products to sub-segments based on differences in needs, expectations and behaviours. Staff were recognized as being of considerable importance, particularly those on the frontline, and the bank paid particular attention to recruiting staff with good customer service skills.

Price

HDFC offered its initial bank account with the requirement for a minimum balance of Rs 5000 – significantly below the typical international bank requirement of Rs 10000, and so significantly cheaper, but still higher than the public-sector requirement of Rs 500. This ensured that HDFC had the margin to support the delivery of superior service, while remaining significantly cheaper than the international banks.

Promotions

HDFC supports its product and service offer with the usual range of above and below the line marketing promotion, with direct mail, e-mail and SMS becoming increasingly important. A significant recent innovation has been the use of sophisticated analytical techniques to test and evaluate campaigns. This has enabled HDFC to gain a better understanding of how customers respond to marketing promotions and use this information to develop more effective campaigns in the future. In addition, this analysis has enabled HDFC to target its communications more effectively, thus reducing marketing spend and the costs of acquisition.

Place

HDFC focused attention on the 10 largest cities in India, which account for close to 40 per cent of the population, and concentrated on gaining maximum market share in those areas before expanding to other cities. The decision to operate with a central processing unit allowed the bank to keep the cost of establishing a branch network relatively low, and thus supported more extensive coverage (around 500 branches in around over 200 towns and cities). Alongside its branch network, HDFC also delivered its services via ATMs, phones, the Internet and mobiles to ensure that it met the diverse set of needs of its mid-market customers.

The success of HDFC is evidenced in growth rates of 30 per cent per annum and a string of awards from AsiaMoney, Forbes Global, Euromoney and many others.

Sources: Saxena (2000); Interview with Ajay Kelkar (available at http://www.exchange4media.com/Brandspeak/brandspeak.asp?brand_id=811; HDFC Bank (www.HDFCBank.com).

However, not all financial services providers have been so successful in managing the mix for consumer acquisition. Historically, the financial services sector has received considerable criticism for tending to focus on new customer acquisition to the detriment of existing customers. Indeed, the cynical practice of offering unsustainably attractive benefits to consumers at the time of acquisition, which are subsequently reduced, remains a feature of certain parts of the industry. It is undoubtedly true that companies have the right to use promotional pricing as part of its new customer acquisition activities. Promotional pricing is prevalent in virtually every category of consumer goods and service marketing, so why should financial services be exempt? Promotional pricing does indeed have a perfectly legitimate role to play in financial services. However, it has to be used with care, given the complexity of the products, the timescale over which they operate, and limited consumer understanding. With the one-off purchase of, say, a television or a holiday, consumers understand clearly the net price they have to pay and are in a position to make a well-informed choice. When 'buying' a deposit account from a bank or a building society, consumers may well be in possession of the facts regarding the short-term price promotion but not in a position to judge the long-term competitiveness of the interest rate. In the field of mortgages, an attempt has been made to factor-in the effect of special introductory offers through the introduction of the Annual Equivalent Rate (AER). The key point to grasp is that care must be taken with the use of new-customer price promotions to ensure the appropriate management of expectations.

In addition to concerns about the way in which marketing mix variables are used, we must also recognize that the specific features of the financial services sector may create additional challenges. Chapter 2 devoted considerable attention to the array of products that comprise the domain of retail financial services. In Chapter 10, we present key models and concepts concerning the successful management of products. Meanwhile, it is important to appreciate that the relationship between *product* and *process* is particularly close in the case of financial services. When a person 'buys', say, a current account; that person is seeking to secure access to a range of service benefits on a continuing basis. The availability of Internet banking facilities may be perceived as a *product* feature or a *process* associated with the consuming of the product. However, in the context of customer acquisition – the focus of this part of the book – we should consider *process* in terms of how an individual first becomes a current-account customer of a given provider. It must be borne in mind that the processes associated with customer acquisition comprise things that the organization chooses to require, and certain things that are imposed by external agents such as the regulator. To continue with the example of a current account, many countries have strict rules regarding money laundering. This results in the need to provide original forms of documentary evidence as proof of identify and address. It adds a degree of complexity to the new customer acquisition process and may cause frustration for the customer; however, it cannot be avoided, and this must be explained and managed.

A further aspect of the mix that may be challenging in a financial services context is *place*. In the conventional consumer goods context, *place* is pretty straightforward; it concerns the means by which the consumer gains access to buying the product – i.e. the channel of distribution. This meaning of the term also applies in the case of financial services. For example, IFAs represent the primary means of distribution by which a consumer gains access to the products of Skandia, the Swedish-owned life insurer. However, having become a customer of Skandia, ongoing service contact is likely to be directly with the company via the telephone, for example. Thus *place* is a rather ambiguous concept, since it can refer both to the channel of distribution that a consumer uses to become a customer and to the means by which a customer engages in service interventions with the provider company.

Owing to the economics of new customer acquisition, it is becoming increasingly important for companies to market themselves on the basis that there will be an ongoing customer relationship in which a number of products will be bought by the customer over a prolonged timescale. In other words, the profit is in the lifetime value of a new customer, and not necessarily in the profitability of the first product purchased. Customer profitability is determined to a large extent by a surprisingly small group of variables that apply fairly consistently to most forms of financial services products. Consider the case of, say, a loan that is secured on the value of a consumer's home. This type of loan is sometimes referred to as a second mortgage because, in law, the lender can only gain access to the property's security value once any first mortgage debt has been discharged. The profitability of a new second-mortgage customer is a function of:

- the amount of money loaned
- the term of years over which repayment of the loan takes place
- the likelihood of the customer defaulting on the loan
- the interest margin
- the purchase of other products from the lending company.

Relatively small changes, either positive or adverse, in one or more of these variables can exert significant impact on profitability, especially if all five variables are affected. This model works equally for first mortgages and unsecured loans.

In the life insurance sector, the profitability of a new customer is a function of:

- the value of the sum assured
- the term that the policy remains in force
- the likelihood of a claim being made
- policy margins
- the purchase of other products from the insurance company.

Again, the cumulative impact of positive or adverse variances with respect to these key variables has a compounding effect upon customer profitability. These variables should be factored into the plans that are designed to achieve a targeted level of new customer acquisition. The logic of this thinking indicates a balanced scorecard approach to new customer target-setting. To target crudely on the basis of maximizing new customers or products sold in a given budget year is to play a pure numbers game that invites considerable long-term commercial risks. Case study 9.2 gives some examples to illustrate this point.

> ## Case study 9.2   Centralized mortgage lending – a salutary story

The latter part of the 1980s in the UK witnessed the rapid birth, and almost equally rapid nadir, of what were termed centralized mortgage lenders. Names such as The Mortgage Corporation, National Homeloans and Mortgage Express came from a standing start to take of the order of 25 per cent of new mortgage business by 1990. Their success was based upon a combination of opportune timing and the unresponsive nature of traditional sources of mortgages, most notably the building societies.

In terms of good timing, the centralized lenders were able to take advantage of a period of time during which the cost of funds on the wholesale money market was cheaper than retail-sourced funds. Building society mortgages were largely funded by retail-sourced funds – indeed, there were strict limits on the percentage of their mortgage funds that could be sourced on the wholesale money market. Being centralized lenders, they had no branch infrastructure costs to carry and were able to administer new mortgage applications efficiently from one central administration centre. This gave them additional cost advantages which, together with lower funding costs, gave them a clear pricing advantage over their traditional rivals.

Three other factors worked together with their pricing advantage to give the centralized lenders a tremendously strong competitive edge. First, they were able to process new mortgage applications very fast (often within 24 hours, compared with the 4–6 weeks that was typical for building societies at the time). Speed is of the essence for the typical homebuyer as, once a desirable new home has been found, there can often be a race to cement a deal with the seller of the property. Secondly, the centralized lenders appreciated the importance of intermediaries, such as estate agents, mortgage brokers and insurance company sales agents, in placing new mortgage business. In the late 1980s, in the order of 60 per cent of new mortgages were placed with lenders via intermediaries. This resulted in a very low cost of new business acquisition compared with the branch costs of the traditional lenders. Recognizing the role of intermediaries, the centralized lenders focused their own new customer acquisition activities upon them. Thus, high volumes of new business were generated at low cost, and in a short period of time the newcomers were challenging the supremacy of a well-established incumbent industry. Thirdly, the centralized lenders brought product as well as service innovation to the mortgage business. They were able to use their treasury skills to provide new forms of interest rate management, such as fixed rate and 'cap-and-collar' loans.

They began to use securitization as a means of putting their loan books off balance sheet and thereby enhancing the return-on-capital to their shareholders. They introduced so-called deferred rate mortgages, most notably the 3:2:1 scheme, whereby the interest rate payable in the first year of the mortgage was a full 3 per cent less than the standard variable rate (SVR), reducing to a 2 per cent discount in the second year and 1 per cent in the third year. The '6 per cent' deferred interest arrived at in this way was to be added to the outstanding loan at the end of Year 3, and the new, higher amount would be repaid at the prevailing SVR from Year 4 onwards.

Continued

Case study 9.2   Centralized mortgage lending – a salutary story—cont'd

The meteoric rise of the centralized lenders was also assisted by three factors external to their control. First, the house-purchase market in the UK experienced a sustained boom from 1985 onwards. Secondly, interest rates were falling steadily towards the end of that decade. Thirdly, in 1999 the Thatcher government gave advance warning that it was going to remove a tax-break known as 'multiple MIRAS'. This had the effect of lighting the blue touch paper on a firework – the housing marketing rocketed property values to stratospheric levels.

Just as propitious timing had brought about the dramatic growth of centralized lending, so too did a set of negative economic factors result in its almost equally dramatic demise. During the course of 1990 interest rates began to rise – indeed, in little over a year the base rate doubled from 7.5 per cent to 15 per cent. Unsurprisingly, the housing market went from boom to bust within just a few short months. The centralized lenders' price-edge evaporated, causing already declining sales to fall even faster. The rapid rise in interest rates caused hardship for borrowers, and mortgage payment defaults began to grow. At the same time, falling property prices rapidly eroded the margins of security of the lenders. To make matters even worse, many borrowers on deferred-rate mortgage schemes were among the defaulters. This meant that the interest outstanding grew rapidly and added to the losses that would be incurred as security margins disappeared. It should be borne in mind that the centralized lenders' 'asset' base of mortgages was accumulated when property prices were at or near their historical peak, and that loan-to-value ratios were typically 90 per cent. In other words, the lenders had a margin of security of just 10 per cent, while between 1990 and 1992 the average property value fell by the order of 30 per cent. The outcome was that the new lenders withdrew from the market by ceasing to accept new business in order to limit further potential losses for their shareholders. All operational focus was upon damage limitation by acting quickly to gain access to whatever security remained in the valuations of properties in default. Repossessions rose sharply, and so did the financial losses of the centralized lenders.

Inevitably, it was the more 'successful' companies which had built the largest books of business that suffered most, and the majority of the high-profile lenders went out of business. Some of the smaller ones managed to survive, and have carried on at the margins of the mainstream business.

So what is to be learned from this case study? First, it is probable that undue emphasis was laid upon the key performance indicators of volume and value of new customer business. Insufficient emphasis was placed upon the quality of the new loan books. Secondly, greater caution should have been exercised in assessing the drivers behind the growth of this new market sector. This should have included the use of scenario planning to stress test the probable impact of adverse environmental factors.

Thirdly, more detailed analysis of the drivers of the behaviour of intermediaries and their working practices should have occurred. This would have revealed the impact of inappropriate remuneration systems and the poor-quality customers with whom many of the intermediaries dealt. Fourthly, there should have been greater investment in default mitigation resources and processes, and a greater degree of caution built into provisions made for bad debts. Finally, the business model should have taken a more holistic approach to the assessment of new customer value, as described earlier in this chapter.

Elements of this case study are in evidence in other marketplace settings, such as the personal pension boom of the latter 1980s and early 1990s, and the dot-com boom of the mid-1990s. All rapidly expanding new market phenomena should be subject to a greater degree of scrutiny. Particular attention should be focused upon developing a thorough understanding of:

- the underlying drivers that are fuelling the growth
- the motives and behaviours of customers
- the motives and behaviours of intermediaries and other distributors
- the customer value model.

9.6   Summary and conclusions

The effectiveness of any marketing strategy depends on the development of an effective marketing mix. The marketing mix consists of all the marketing tools that can be used to communicate an organization's service offer to its target markets. To be effective, the elements of the marketing mix must be consistent with the organization's chosen position and with each other. In financial services, the marketing mix must recognize and respond to the distinctive features of service products. In particular, when managing the elements of product, price, promotion and place, marketers in the financial services sector need to pay particular attention to the people delivering the service, the process by which the service is delivered and the physical evidence which represents the service.

Review questions

1. Why is consistency important in the development of an effective marketing mix?
2. What makes the marketing mix for financial services different from the marketing mix for physical goods?
3. What are the major challenges for financial services providers when developing a marketing mix for customer acquisition?
4. Which practices on the part of a financial services provider undermine consumer trust, and which practices and activities can enhance trust?

Product policies

By the end of this chapter you will be able to:
- explain the nature of financial services products
- explain the operation of key Islamic financial services
- outline the issues influencing product policy
- provide an overview of issues relating to the management of existing products
- develop an understanding of the implications of the product lifecycle concept for the marketing mix
- outline the issues associated with the development of new products.

10.1   Introduction

By definition, the product is fundamental to any marketing activity, since it is by consuming the product that a customer experiences enjoyment and utility. Clearly, a product which does not offer what consumers want at a price they are prepared to pay will never succeed. Decisions about the products that an organization offers are both strategic and tactical. The strategic issues associated with the management of the product portfolio were introduced in Chapter 5, and discussed further in relation to segmentation, targeting and positioning in Chapter 8. Alongside these strategic-level decisions about the product, there are also important tactical issues which must be considered. These relate to the development, presentation and management of products which are offered to the marketplace. Thus the product element of the marketing mix deals with issues such as developing an appropriate product range and product line, as well as considering decisions relating to the attributes and features of individual products. In this context, the issue of branding is becoming increasingly important for individual products as well as for the organization as a whole. The product element of the marketing mix also deals with issues relating to new product development. Extending product ranges and product lines, either by new product development or through the modification of existing products, is increasingly important for organizations that wish to remain competitive in a rapidly changing market environment.

This chapter begins by providing an overview of financial services products and how they present particular challenges for marketing. It introduces the main types of Islamic financial services which have recently become more widely available. The next section examines the factors that will influence decisions about the development of the product element of the marketing mix. Here we revisit the product lifecycle concept and consider its uses and limitations in further detail. Subsequent sections deal specifically with aspects of the product range strategy and the process of new product development in the financial services sector.

10.2   The concept of the service product

In the tangible goods domain the notion of what constitutes a product is pretty straightforward, as it comprises palpable physical characteristics. However, the situation is less straightforward when it comes to financial services because product comprises both utility features and service features. The former concerns the primary need for which the product was bought – for example, a personal pension to provide an income in retirement. Amongst the utility features associated with a pension may be a choice of investment funds, the ability to switch between funds, and an option for income drawdown. Services features are somewhat analogous to the process element of the extended marketing mix of the 7-Ps. In the case of a personal pension, it could include ability to access a fund's value and make additional contributions on-line, or perhaps access to information and assistance via a 24/7 call-centre. Sometimes the boundary between the two types of feature can appear to be somewhat blurred.

An additional dimension to appreciate is the role played by service features where third-party intermediaries form part of the distribution processes of a product provider. In these cases, real competitive advantage can be achieved by providing intermediaries with a range of helpful and responsive service features such as the ability to input new cases on-line and the provision of connectivity between the IT systems of the provider and the intermediary.

Thus, when we refer to terms such as product, product management and product development in the context of financial services, we must ensure that both utility and service features are given due consideration.

Products are only purchased because they provide these benefits to the consumer. Therefore, in order to understand products and how they should be managed, it is important to understand what those benefits are and how they are provided. Understanding the nature of the service product requires an understanding of both the needs of customers and the organization's ability to meet those needs.

10.2.1   What customers want

The majority of organizations offer a range of products to a variety of customer groups in order to meet a variety of customer needs. In financial services, the prime customer groups are personal, institutional and corporate. In personal markets, financial institutions will often separate high net-worth individuals (HNWI) from other customer groups. In the corporate markets, banks will typically separate large corporates from small and medium-sized enterprises. These customer groups have a wide variety of financial needs. The diversity of customer needs outlined in Chapter 2 can be classified under six main headings:

1. The need to move money and make payments (e.g. current accounts, ATMs debit cards)
2. The need to earn a return on money (e.g. savings accounts, unit trusts, bonds)
3. The need to defer payment or advance consumption (e.g. loans, credit cards, mortgages)
4. The need to manage risk (e.g. life insurance, general insurance)
5. The need for information (e.g. share price information services, product information)
6. The need for advice or expertise (e.g. tax planning, investment planning, advice on IPOs, advice on mergers and acquisitions).

Box 10.1 outlines the key features of a common but often misunderstood financial product, namely bonds, which are used to satisfy buyer needs to earn a return on money and issuer needs to advance consumption.

Box 10.1   What is a bond?

A bond, very simply, is a loan that the bondholder makes to the bond issuer. Governments, corporations and sometimes municipalities issue bonds when they need capital. If you buy a government bond you are lending the government money, and the same with a company. Just like any other loan, a bond pays interest periodically at a given rate; this is known as a coupon, and it repays the principal at a stated time. The risk to the bondholder is that the bond issuer may default in the interest payments or the actual repayment of the loan.

Bond characteristics

A bond can be traded in the secondary open market after it is issued, and its market price is dependent on a range of variables, including interest rates, supply and demand and maturity – although, in theory, a bond's price is supposed to equal the present value of all future cashflows, including the final redemption.

Bonds are normally issued with face (nominal or par) value of £100, which can be simply understood as the amount returned to the investor upon redemption. A bond's price is normally quoted in pence or cents, depending on which country and currency the bond is issued in. For example, if a bond is quoted at 99p, the price is £99 for every £100 of the face value of the bond. If that same bond is quoted at 101p, the price is £101 for every £100 of the face value. In the first instance, the quoted or market price of the bond is said to be at a 'discount' to (i.e. lower than) the nominal price (of £100), and money can be made (a 'capital gain') on redemption. In the second instance, the bond is said to be trading at a 'premium' (where the quoted price is higher than the nominal price). In this case, money would be lost (a 'capital loss') on redemption. If the bond is at its face value of £100 (meaning the quoted price is 100p), it is then described as trading at 'par'.

Continued

Box 10.1   What is a bond?—cont'd

Another important character of a bond is its yield. At the most basic level, this can be understood to be the return an investor can expect from such an instrument. The 'nominal yield' is the amount of income the bond generates per year as a percentage of its nominal value. Thus the nominal yield (calculated by dividing annual income by nominal value) on a £100 bond which pays 5 per cent interest a year is $(5/100) \times 100 = 5$ per cent. This yield can normally be found in the description of the security – for example, 'Treasury 4.25% 2016', where the nominal yield in 4.25 per cent. Whereas this yield might be useful for someone who buys a bond at issue or 'at par', it cannot be used when a bond is bought at a premium or discount to nominal value. Here, it is appropriate to use the 'current yield', which is calculated by dividing the annual income by the current market price of the bond. If the above-£100 bond which pays 5 per cent coupon is trading at £95, then the yield is $(5/95) \times 100 = 5.26$ per cent. The limitation of the current yield is that it only provides a snapshot based on the market price today, and takes no account of a capital loss or gain made if the bond is held until maturity. The widely used 'gross redemption yield' solves this problem and provides a standard with which individuals can compare many varying bonds of different coupons and maturities, and discover whether they are at a discount or premium. The aim of the redemption yield is to show the total return of the bond while taking into account the interest/coupon that will be paid (before tax), the number of years left until the bond matures, and the capital loss or gain involved if the bond is bought at the current market price and held it until it is redeemed. An important thing to note when using gross redemption yield (or yield to maturity, as it is otherwise known) is that the return is calculated based on the assumption that the investor reinvests the coupons received at the same yield as that at time of purchase of the bond.

The bond price always moves in the opposite direction to its yield, so that if interest rates rise, bond prices will fall and yields rise – and *vice versa*. This relationship between interest rates and price is not a perfect linear relationship, but a slightly curved one. An imaginary line is then drawn at a tangent to this curve and the resulting estimate of change in price for a given change in yield is known as 'modified duration'. The idea behind duration is pretty simple – for example, if a bond has a duration of 3 years, then the price of that bond will rise by 3 per cent for each 1 per cent fall in interest rates or decline by 3 per cent for each 1 per cent increase in interest rates. Such a bond is less risky than one that has a 10-year duration. That bond is going to decline in value by 10 per cent for every 1 per cent rise in interest rates.

There is also another relationship specific to bonds, that between the yield and time left till maturity, arising from the fact that changes in interest rates affect all bonds differently. The longer a bond has until redemption, the greater the risk that interest and inflation rates will fluctuate or rise higher, prompting the investor to expect a higher yield for taking on the extra risk. A line that plots the yields of bonds at a given point in time with differing maturities is known as a 'yield curve'. This curve generally rises from lower yields on shorter-term bonds to higher yields on longer term bonds. The shape of the yield curve is closely scrutinized because it helps to give an idea of future interest rate change and

Box 10.1   What is a bond?—cont'd

economic activity. There are three main types of yield curve shapes: normal, inverted and flat (or humped). A normal yield curve (Figure 10.1) is one in which longer-term bonds have a higher yield compared to shorter-term bonds due to the risks associated with time.

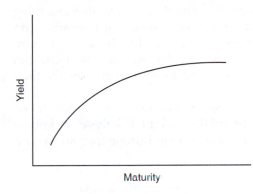

An inverted-yield curve is one in which the shorter-term yields are higher than the longer-term yields, which can be a sign of impending recession. This has recently been the case with the US yield curve, where the 2-year Treasury bond is yielding more than the 10-year Treasury bond. A flat (or humped) yield curve is one in which the shorter- and longer-term yields are very close to each other, which is also a predictor of an economic transition. The slope of the yield curve is also seen as important: the greater the slope, the greater the gap between short- and long-term rates.

Figure 10.1 The yield curve
Source: Investopedia.com.

Credit quality and rating

When evaluating a fixed-income security the credit quality is an important consideration, as the bond may not reach maturity for a number of years and during which time an investor needs to be secure in the knowledge that the bond issuer will pay interest payments on schedule and return the nominal value on redeeming said bond. There are many different types of bonds issued by various differing entities, and a credit rating provides a standard way of evaluating the credit-worthiness and financial soundness of issuers. There are rating agencies (such as Standard & Poor's, Moody's and Fitch) that assign ratings to many bonds when they are issued and monitor developments during the bonds' lifetime, measuring the willingness and ability of the issuer to make interest and principal payments when due. The highest rating (i.e. the bond least likely to default on payment, also known as 'default risk') is AAA for S&P and Aaa for Moody's. It then proceeds down the rating scale – AA+, AA, AA−, A+, A, A−, BBB+, BBB, BBB−, BB+, BB, BB− and so on. Any rating equal to or above BBB- is known as 'investment grade', and represents those entities with low probability of default. Ratings equal to or lower than BB+ are known as 'high-yield bonds' or 'junk bonds'.

Types of bonds

There is a broad range of types of bonds, which can be described in the following categories:

- Bonds issued by governments or sovereign entities, which go by various titles – UK, Gilts; USA, Treasuries; Germany, Bunds; Japan, JGBs; France, OATs.

Continued

Box 10.1   What is a bond?—cont'd

These securities are thought to pose the least risk to investors, as governments are generally thought of as trustworthy issuers who will provide interest payments annually and return the nominal value at redemption. There are, however, many more bonds issued from smaller emerging market countries, some of which are far riskier, including Columbia and Ukraine. There is also a class of 'quasi' government bonds issued by non-governmental organizations such as the World Bank and the European Investment Bank, which are often compared to sovereign debt for their similar characteristics.

- Index-linked bonds. A number of governments also issue index-linked bonds, which are linked to the rate of inflation. In the US, these are known as TIPS (Treasury Inflation Protected Securities); in Europe they are known as Linkers.
- Local government bonds. These have virtually disappeared in the UK, but are more common elsewhere – especially in the US and Canada.
- Floating rate notes. These are bonds that can be issued by governments or companies without a fixed coupon – i.e. the interest payments are not a fixed amount but usually quoted as some percentage over the rate of LIBOR (London Interbank Offer Rate).
- Corporate bonds. These are bonds issued by corporations to finance their spending or investment, and currently account for more than 50 per cent of the UK fixed interest market. It is here in particular that the credit rating of the issuer becomes important. They are divided into two main rating categories – investment grade and high-yield bonds – with the rating for each bond depending on the financial conditions, management, economic and debt characteristics of the company. High-yield bonds represent higher default risk, and were established to provide bonds for more speculative and higher-risk companies. They often trade at either a substantial discount or higher coupon, to reflect the additional risk being taken by the investor.
- Securitized bonds or asset-backed securities. In this area, cash flows from various types of loans and payments (mortgages or credit-card payments, for example, and also recording revenues like the famous 'Bowie' bond) are bundled together and resold to investors as securities.

Bonds, although not traded or listed on a Regulated Investment Exchange, which is the common place for equities, are dealt through dealers who are regulated by the FSA. The fixed interest market is much larger than the equity markets in most countries; in the UK it is approximately 4.5 times larger. Bonds form a key part of professional portfolio construction, providing income, diversification, protection against economic slowdown when other investments can be affected, and (for index-linked bonds) protection against inflation. The asset class, unlike many equity markets, is still growing with increased popularity from companies of all sizes.

Source: Justin Urquhart-Stewart, Marketing Director,
Seven Investment Management.

Organizations in the financial services sector concentrate on the development of products and services which meet these particular needs. However, to be successful it is not enough just to have products that meet these very basic needs. Organizations must also seek to understand customers' wants and preferences, and identify ways in which they can make the product particularly attractive and convince the customer to purchase. In order to understand how organizations can make their products attractive to customers, we must understand the nature of the product itself.

10.2.2   What organizations can provide

Organizations provide products to meet customer needs. One common way of thinking about products is to see them as a series of layers surrounding the central core:

1. *The core*. The core product represents the basic need that is being provided – in the case of a bank current account, the core product is money transmission. At the core-product level, all organizations in the market are basically the same – all current accounts offer money transmission, all credit cards offer the opportunity to delay payment, and all unit trusts provide an investment opportunity.
2. *The tangible product*. The next layer of the product is usually described as the tangible product, and at this level the organization will make the product identifiable by adding certain features, facilities, brand name, etc. The products of different organizations will be slightly differentiated although, from the consumers' perspective, all the features offered in this layer are what they would expect as a minimum before purchasing. This suggests that it would be difficult really to differentiate products at this level.
3. *The augmented product*. The third layer, which is described as the augmented product, is usually used to refer to those features which organizations add to make their products distinct from the competition, such as the special customer service offered to holders of platinum credit cards. It is at this level that an organization hopes to gain a competitive edge by offering attractive features that competing products do not offer. Of course, as explained in Chapter 3, this is difficult because of the ease with which the features of financial services can be copied.
4. *The potential product*. The final layer of the product is described as the potential product. This refers to features that are either very new or not yet available, but which can potentially be added to a product to make it very distinct.

An illustration of these different layers is shown in Figure 10.2. In Figure 10.2, the financial service being illustrated is a unit trust. The core element of a unit trust is that it provides customers with a way of investing existing wealth and generating a return in the future. The tangible elements would include an association with a specific supplier (branding), a choice of investment realization method (income v. capital growth), projected returns, accessibility, etc. The augmented element would then incorporate additional features which go beyond those that would be expected by the consumer. In the case of a unit trust, this might include the option to invest only in environmentally responsible companies. Finally, the potential product might include a facility that allows consumers to buy and sell over the Internet.

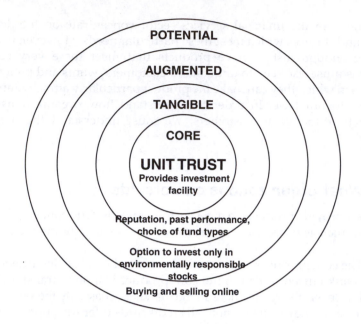

Figure 10.2 The service product.

Based on this way of thinking about products, marketing managers must:

- understand the core benefit that their product offers, and the needs of customers
- identify the tangible elements that consumers would expect the product to offer
- identify augmented product features that would provide the basis for differentiating the product
- monitor developments that could provide the basis for potential future features.

In performing these tasks, it is important to be aware of the distinctive features of services (discussed in Chapter 3). In particular, there is a clear need to create some tangible representation of the product for consumers, and also to address the issues that arise in relation to the variability in quality.

10.3   Islamic financial instruments

In Chapter 2, the range of conventional financial services was discussed in some detail. Such products are widely available across many different markets worldwide, and have been so for some time. In addition, over the past 30 years a new range of financial services has emerged that is structured around Islamic principles. Islamic financial services in themselves are not new, but their widespread development owes much to the pioneering work of the Central Bank of Malaysia, Bank Negara (Hume, 2004). The core product for an Islamic financial service is the same as the core product for a conventional financial service. Murabaha and a mortgage will both fulfil the consumer's need to purchase an asset and pay for it in the future, but operate in rather different ways. In particular, since paying or receiving interest is against the teaching of Islam and is thus *haram* (unlawful), financial institutions use alternative, non-interest based approaches to providing Islamic financial services (see, for example, Mills, 1999). The following are examples of some of the main approaches to the provision of Islamic financial services:

1. *Murabaha*. This is an alternative to conventional loans, and is sometimes referred to as cost plus financing. Under *Murabaha*, the bank purchases the goods which the customer requires from a third party. The bank then sells the goods to the customer for a pre-agreed (higher) price with deferred payments. Customers wishing to deposit money with a bank may make deposits into a Murabaha fund, and then will share in the returns from such transactions. In Malaysia, Bay Bithamin Ajil (BBA) is the most common form of Murabaha, with payments being made in instalments sometime after the delivery of the specified goods. Arab Malaysian Bank's al-taslif Visa card is a product based on BBA financing, while Bank Muamalat offers both house purchase and fixed asset purchase on BBA principles. In the UK, the Islamic Bank of Britain provides unsecured personal lending based on Murabaha, while Al Baraka Islamic Bank in Bahrain provides financing for commercial clients to purchase finished goods, raw materials, machines or equipment on the same basis.

2. *Musharakah*. This is a form of equity funding (partnership finance) in which both a business and a bank invest in a particular venture. The profits are be shared between both parties, and both parties bear any losses. This is probably the purest form of Islamic financing, with return being uncertain and both parties sharing the profit and the loss. Jordan Islamic Bank offers Musharakah-based financing to commercial clients, as does Emirates Islamic Bank.

3. *Mudarabah*. This is a contract between provider of capital and an entrepreneur. The provider (referred to as the *rabb al-mal*, or the sleeping partner) entrusts money to the entrepreneur (referred to as the *mudarib*, or the working partner) in connection with an agreed project. When the project is complete, the *mudarib* returns the principal and a pre-agreed share of the profit to the *rabb al-mal*. Any losses are borne by the *rabb al-mal*. The operation of Mudarabah with the bank as the provider of capital is a basis for making loans. Where the depositor is the provider of capital and the bank is the entrepreneur, then Mudarabah serves as a basis for taking deposits – as, for example, with Arab Malaysian Finance's GIA Quantum deposit service or Affin Bank's Tiny Tycoon Savings account.

4. *Al-Ijara*. This is a form of leasing finance. The bank will purchase the asset required by the customer and then lease the asset to that customer at a pre-arranged rate, with the asset to be used productively and in ways that do not conflict with Shari'ah law. Emirates Islamic Bank is one of many banks that provides leasing for equipment, vehicles, etc. on the principles of Al-Ijara.

5. *Qard Hasan*. This is a beneficial (interest-free) loan in which the borrower is obliged to repay the principal to the lender, but any additional payment is entirely optional. Qard Hasan loans are offered by most Islamic banks, although are often restricted to particularly needy customers. Qard Hasan loans are usually funded through some bank capital, and also through *zakat* donations.

6. *Amanah and Al Wadi'ah.* These approaches are both concerned with guaranteeing and securing a sum of money. In practical terms, products based around Amanah (in trust) and Al Wadi'ah (safe-keeping) are similar. They all guarantee the return of the principal (whether an individual takes a loan or makes a deposit), but there is no additional payment. Affin Bank bases its current account on Al Wadi'ah, while HSBC bases its Mastercard on Amanah.

7. *Al Kafalah.* These are effectively documentary credits, but with a non-interest-based commission. Most commercial banks will offer these letters of credit for a variety of business activities.

8. *Takaful.* This is a form of Islamic insurance based on the Koranic principle of *Ta'awon,* or mutual assistance. It provides mutual protection of assets and property, and offers joint risk-sharing in the event of a loss by one of its members. In Takaful, the equivalent of insurance premiums (donations) are divided between two funds. A small part of the donation is paid to the mutual fund, and this fund is used to make payouts should the insured event happen. The larger part of the donation is paid into an investment fund, and the surpluses from the investment fund are subsequently equitably distributed between the participants and the insurer according to the principles of al-mudarabah. The size of individual donations is dependent upon both risk factors (such as health and lifestyle) and the desired compensation (amount payable on death).

It should be clear that these financial instruments can meet the same set of financial needs as conventional products. What makes these financial instruments distinct is the avoidance of interest payment and a reliance on an approach which is much closer to equity-based finance, such that both parties effectively share the risk element. For many Muslim customers this approach to providing financial services is very attractive, because it is consistent with religious beliefs. Increasingly, products provided on Islamic principles are also proving attractive to non-Muslim customers. In Malaysia, for example, it is estimated that as much as 70 per cent of Islamic finance is actually supplied to non-Muslims (Hume, 2004). At the same time, some customers are concerned about the apparent risk associated with many Islamic financial services. While these risks are very small in practice, their existence does mean that the marketing of Islamic financial services must emphasize safety and security and try to reduce consumers' perceptions of risk – particularly if the bank or insurance company wishes to extend its target market beyond Muslim customers.

10.4   Influences on product management

Financial services organizations will look to develop services that meet some or all of the financial needs of some or all customer groups. Some organizations will concentrate on serving a subset of customers (described in Chapter 8 as market specialization). Some organizations will focus on a subset of needs (described in Chapter 8 as product specialization). A small number of organizations – typically the major banks – will attempt to serve the majority of customer groups and meet the majority of customer needs.

Table 10.1 Product lines at Southern Bank Berhad

Savings	Investment	Current account	Home loans	Credit cards
Regular Savings Account	Regular FD	Regular Current Account	SUMO 1	Gold Mastercard
Teen-in-Charge	Golden Time Deposit		Home Sweet Home	Mastercard Classic
Maxplus Savings	Maxplus Fixed Deposit			Eco Gold Mastercard
Maxplus Two-in-One				Eco Mastercard Classic
				Espre Gold Mastercard
				Espre Mastercard Classic
				Jordan Gold Mastercard
				Honda Gold Mastercard
				Gold Visa
				Visa Classic

To meet the selected needs of selected customers requires a range of differing products. A simple example of the product range that might be offered to personal customers is presented in Table 10.1, for the Southern Bank Berhad in Malaysia.

The *width of the range* refers to the number of different broad product types or lines (savings, investment, credit card). Each type or line will consist of a number of related products, and the number of such products determines the *length of the line*. In the case of Southern Bank Berhad, the credit card line consists of ten different variants, while the savings line consists of only four different individual products.

A key aspect of product management is to make decisions about the development of this range to ensure that the organization maintains and improves its competitive position. As explained in the introduction to this chapter, this involves both strategic and tactical decisions and covers a broad range of activities. For the purpose of this discussion, product management will be discussed under two broad headings:

1. *Management of existing product lines*. This includes product design (features, quality, brand, points of differentiation, etc.), product modification (checking product performance and making adjustments to product design where necessary) and product line management (addition of new variants of existing products).
2. *Product range management*. This focuses on the overall choices regarding the range of products to offer. Of particular importance in this area are the introduction of new products and the removal of older, poorer-performing products.

While each of these aspects of product management will be considered separately later in this chapter, it should be recognized that they are necessarily interdependent; product attribute decisions have implications for the product range, and decisions relating to the product range will also have implications for aspects of the new product development process, managing products over their lifecycle, and product elimination.

Chapter 5 introduced the concept of the product lifecycle (PLC). The PLC has many detractors, whose issues with the concept are threefold. First, there are those who argue that the progress of a product through the stages from growth to decline and extinction has more to do with poor quality marketing of the product than with any immutable law concerning its natural life. This flawed marketing approach is often in evidence in companies that have direct sales-force distribution. A new product is launched and, if successful, the product manager responsible is promoted and the product loses its champion. Additionally, with perhaps an annual rate of sales-force turnover of 40 per cent, within a couple of years most of those present at the initial product launch have left the company. Meanwhile, another new product has been launched to a largely new sales-force, and the previous 'new product' loses a major part of its distribution capability. Unsurprisingly, the previous 'new product' goes into rapid decline.

The second group of critics is often to be found in the packaged goods domain. These people simply see no reason why, so long as there is a need for the product and it is properly marketed, it should not achieve growth on an indefinite basis. Mars has always been of the view that the PLC does not apply to its brands. Having been launched in the UK in the early 1930s, the Mars Bar continues to flourish as a brand over 70 years later. Mars ensures that successive generations of brand managers conform to what might be termed a policy of 'brand husbandry' to ensure that the legacy of the brand is maintained to ensure its continuing success.

The third issue cited by detractors from the PLC concept is that, with an established product, it is very difficult to determine at precisely what stage in the lifecycle the product has reached. For example, if a product's sales level is at roughly the halfway point in the growth phase, how can you tell whether it is about to enter its maturity phase or has several years of continued growth ahead of it?

While noting these criticisms, the PLC has its uses, when handled with due caution, as a conceptual device to determine how to structure and make adjustments to the marketing mix in support of a product. For example, the pre-launch mix will place a great deal of emphasis upon gaining distribution and staff training. During the launch phase, there will be heavy use of the promotional elements of the mix to achieve awareness and encourage a desire to find out more about the product. In the tangible goods field, this is a phase when there may be a lot of money spent on sampling and special price promotions to encourage trial purchase. As growth continues, there may come a time when additional features could be introduced to the product to refresh it and revitalize interest by distributors and consumers. A prolonged period of flat sales may indicate the need to reposition the product, possibly in conjunction with product performance improvements.

Like any aspect of marketing, the product management process will be influenced by a range of external factors; in particular, it will be important for organizations regularly to monitor customers, competitors and the external and internal environments to identify new ways of meeting consumer needs. Equally, of course, product management must be based on a clear understanding of the organization's strengths and weaknesses. Each factor is considered here in turn.

1. *Customers*. Consumer needs, wants and expectations are a major influence on product management. In personal markets, factors such as customers' tastes and preferences, lifestyles, patterns of demographic change and income levels will be of particular importance. For corporate customers, marketing managers must focus on the objectives and strategies of customers and on understanding the

environment in which customers' businesses operate in order to identify likely financial needs. Understanding consumers, particularly retail consumers, can be very difficult. Financial services are often complex and seen as uninteresting, and are therefore difficult to research. One important factor to take into consideration is the idea of trying to understand consumers' changing lifestyles and the implications that these will have for customer financial needs. For example, an awareness of the increasing time pressure on many consumers and the increased desire for flexibility should lead banks consistently to look for ways of delivering service in a more flexible and convenient fashion (24-hour ATMs, WAP phones, Internet, etc.).

2. *Competitors.* The regular monitoring of competitors is an important source of information for product managers, for several reasons. First, changes in a competitor's product range and product features will indicate a possible change in the pattern of competition. Secondly, because it is relatively easy to copy financial services, monitoring what competitors are doing can be an important source of new product ideas.

3. *External environment.* The importance of the external environment and its influence on marketing strategy was discussed at length in Chapter 4. Marketing managers must be aware of general trends in the environment so that they can identify new threats and opportunities. For example, China's accession to the WTO created a major opportunity for non-domestic financial services providers to access a market with one of the highest savings rates in the world. Similarly, the development of WAP technology provided an opportunity for the development of a new method of distribution. In contrast, the progress of the EU policy to create a single European market in financial services might be regarded as a significant threat by many domestic providers.

4. *Internal factors.* As explained in Chapter 5, understanding internal factors is important because it defines what is possible. To make good product decisions, managers must have a clear understanding of the resources available to the organization and its particular strengths and weaknesses in order to understand how best to respond to a particular opportunity or threat. Thus, for example, Prudential's strengths and track record in life insurance and investment management give the company a strength that it has been able to match to emerging market opportunities in countries such as Vietnam, Thailand, Indonesia and the Philippines.

This analysis of self, customers, competitors and the external environment is a continual process. Marketing managers must keep abreast of these factors and consider how best to respond to key changes. It is not operationally or financially feasible for an organization to react to every change in the marketing environment; at the same time, no organization can afford to miss key opportunities that may be presented by legislative, social or economic change.

10.5   Managing existing product lines

The management of existing product lines covers two broad areas: the first deals with decisions about the features to attach to a particular product; the second deals with product line management and, in particular, issues relating to product modification and line length modification.

10.5.1   Product attributes

One of the most basic sets of decisions relates to the choice of product attributes (features, brand name, quality, etc.). These attributes are used to create a tangible or augmented product, as described earlier in this chapter. Thus, the generic service product (life insurance, for example) has to be developed into some tangible or augmented form (General China's GC Living Assurance Plan, for example) through the addition of various features such as cover for total and permanent disability, premium waivers in the event of disability and so on.

The features that are offered as part of a particular service product are one means of differentiating the service. Thus, for example, the main distinction between NatWest Current and NatWest Current Plus is that the former pays no interest on cash balances but has a slightly cheaper overdraft rate and therefore is suited to consumers who hold small amounts of surplus cash and overdraw regularly. By contrast, the Current Plus account pays interest but charges a higher overdraft rate, and therefore is more suited to those customers who have larger cash balances and do not overdraw.

However, the actual range of distinct features which can be attached to a particular financial service is limited and may not provide a long-term basis for differentiation, since such features are easily copied. Offering interest payments on chequeing accounts will be an extra attraction for customers, but is one that can easily be copied by competitors. It therefore becomes very difficult to differentiate in terms of product attributes. Thus, any attempt to differentiate a product at the expected or augmented level must look beyond simple product features and consider instead issues such as quality, branding and organizational image.

Quality is regarded as an increasingly important product feature, and refers to the ability of a product to perform its intended task. As explained in Chapter 15, quality in the service sector in general, and in financial services in particular, can be a rather more complex concept. Some researchers (Grönroos, 1984) suggest that customers should assess service quality based on both technical and functional quality:

- technical (or outcome) quality is concerned with how the product performs (e.g. does a capital growth investment trust provide an acceptable rate of capital growth?)
- functional or (process) quality is concerned with the way in which the service is delivered, and might include factors such as the way staff behave towards customers, and the speed of response to questions.

Often, the way the service is delivered (process) can be every bit as important as the technical quality of the product itself.

Branding is well developed in the marketing of products, and is now increasingly important in financial services. Branding has particular value because it provides a means of creating a clear identity in a competitive marketplace. It is important to recognize that branding is more that just creating a memorable name. Effective branding aims to create a relationship between the product and the customer; when that relationship exists, the brand provides a means of communicating information about quality, differentiating the product from the competition and encouraging customer loyalty. For many financial services providers, it is the perceived strength of their brand that provides a justification for the move into bancassurance. Thus, the strength of the Banco Santander brand in Spain provides a basis for customers to choose insurance-related products from the bank as opposed to dealing with a specialist insurance provider.

In the financial services sector, it is arguably the customer's image of the organization that is the most important type of branding available. Most financial products are identified primarily by the supplier's name, and where individual product brands are created (such as Citibank EZ Checking and Citibank Everything Counts), these are typically a combination of both company name and product name. The company name is seen as being of particular importance in branding because of relatively high levels of recognition in the marketplace and the potential to exploit the overall corporate reputation. Despite the undoubted importance of brand in financial services, research in the UK suggests that financial services brands are relatively weak, lack relevance to customers and fail to build a strong emotional bond with target markets (Devlin and Azhar, 2004). This research highlights the importance of thinking carefully about the best way to connect with customers and differentiate a brand from the competition. Making a connection with customers relies on emotional appeal as well as appeal based on the functional values of products, and most financial services organizations have not adequately developed such appeal (Dall'Olmo Riley and de Chernatony, 2000; O'Lauglin *et al.*, 2004). Traditionally, financial services organizations have relied very heavily on functional values such as size and longevity. While these are clearly important in building trust and confidence, they are probably not enough to create a real connection with consumers. Indeed, Devlin and Azhar (2004) suggest that the relative success of non-traditional entrants into financial services is that their brands are much better developed, much more clearly differentiated and much more able to connect with customers. For example, the Virgin group has seen significant success in the financial services sector, building on its brand image of unconventional customer champion.

10.5.2   Product modification/product development

Once a product is established, there are two broad areas that require attention: product modification and product development. Product modification is concerned with changing the attributes of a product to make it more attractive to the marketplace. Product development involves creating a new variant of an existing product, and is typically associated with either product-line stretching or product proliferation.

Product modification in financial services aims to improve the performance of an existing product. This may mean making the service easier to use (fixed annual repayments on existing mortgages, for example), improving the quality of the service (personal account managers for corporate clients) or improving the delivery system (redesigning an on-line banking site to make it more useable). With increases in competition and with high consumer expectations, product modification is important for organizations seeking to maintain and expand the customer base.

Obviously, if a product is at the mature or decline stage in its lifecycle then additional expenditure on that product may be risky. At the same time, trying to develop completely new products is also risky, so an approach that concentrates on modifying existing products can be very attractive.

Product-line stretching or product proliferation involves adding new services to an existing service line, and has traditionally accounted for much of the new product development activity in financial institutions. One widespread example of this form of activity is the development of premium bank accounts providing customers with a range of additional services. For example, in addition to its Regular Savings Account, HDFC Bank in India offers a Payroll Account, a Classic Salary Account, a Regular Salary Account and a Premium Salary Account, each of which offers a slightly different set of features and attributes. The rationale for stretching a product line is to further differentiate existing products in order to appeal to more specific segments of the market. Since line stretching is a form of new product development in a market with which the organization is familiar, the risks tend to be relatively low.

There are dangers with line stretching. In particular, it is possible to identify a large number of segments among the consumers of financial services and develop variants of existing products to meet the needs of these segments. However, if these segments are not large enough or distinct enough to be viable, then the effect of line stretching may be to increase costs but not increase revenue. The organization will have too many different variants of a product, the product line will be long and difficult to manage, and this can cause confusion amongst consumers who almost face too much choice. Accordingly, product line management must be aware of the need to consider withdrawing existing products as well as introducing new ones. This is a particular problem in many areas of financial services owing to the extended lives of many products (see, for example, Harness and Marr, 200). For example, a company might launch a new mortgage product (let's call it the maxi-mortgage) and then, some time later, launch another new mortgage (the mega-mortgage). Unlike the tangible goods marketplace, the company cannot simply cease manufacture, run down stocks and remove the maxi-mortgage from its product range. Instead, it has to maintain the product for those customers who have already bought it and may well wish to continue using it for, say, the next 25 years. Such a product is known as a *legacy product*, and the world's established financial services companies are frequently burdened with the costs of running a plethora of legacy systems. This is why new entrants to financial services can often be highly cost-effective compared with their established rivals: they don't have to carry the legacy system cost burden. The implication of this is that new product development and launch needs to be based upon significant new products that can be expected to have a prolonged life for the provider. It is also important to design products and contracts in such a way as to facilitate migration of current products to newer variants in order to mitigate the legacy cost problem.

10.6   New product development

Developing new products is an important aspect of product management because it ensures that the range is up to date, innovative, and meets changing consumer needs. The term New Product Development (NPD) covers a range of types of innovation; some new products are genuinely new, but others are actually developments of existing product. It should be borne in mind that innovation can be in areas concerning service features as well as utility features. In this section we will consider two specific types of new product development:

1. *Major innovations*, which are products that are new to the organization and new to the market. As such, while they offer great potential in terms of returns they are also more risky since they will typically require a much higher level of investment and the use of different and new technologies. They may also involve the organization moving into areas in which it is comparatively inexperienced. Such major innovations are rare in financial services. Critical illness insurance, launched in the 1980s, was one such product, as were equity release and the launch of the Virgin One offset account in the 1990s, both having spawned a range of variants. Box 10.2 outlines some of the key features of one of these innovations, namely equity release.

Box 10.2   Equity release as a financial planning option for the elderly

Equity release is a sector of the UK financial environment that is growing rapidly. For many years it has been common for homeowners to extend their mortgage commitments in order to release equity from their property. Historically, the funds released in this way were typically used to fund home improvements such as building extensions or loft conversions. More recently, household equity has been released to fund a much wider array of purposes, including the purchase of second homes, cars and even aspects of current consumption. However, the focus here is on older homeowners who do not intend to draw down equity with intent to repay during their lifetime, but instead trade off the value of their housing asset which would otherwise have been inherited through their estate. This affords them the ability to enjoy the spending power locked in their home in the shorter term.

Market drivers

In common with many European countries, in the UK there are increasing concerns about the adequacy of retirement income provision. Two distinct types of generic customer have emerged: the 'needy', who have a specific and urgent need for funds not available from elsewhere for property maintenance, medical care or other pressing requirements; and 'lifestyle' customers, who wish to use releases to improve or maintain their standard of living.

The new generation of retirees are increasingly seeing their home as an investment that they have worked many years to acquire, and feel it is their right to draw on its value as an asset rather than pass it on as an inheritance. These factors combine to create a favourable environment for the development of equity release.

Market development

The total amount released has grown from £33m in 1995 to £1.5bn in 2005, and is forecast to grow to £5bn by 2010 (Northern Rock Plc forecast, December 2005).

Continued

Box 10.2   Equity release as a financial planning option for the elderly—cont'd

There are two main product types that dominate the market as methods of releasing equity:

1. Lifetime mortgages – interest is allowed to roll-up during the term of the loan and the total accumulated debt is repaid when the borrower dies, moves into long-term care or sells the property. The transfer of risk and the long-term nature of the fixed rate funding mean that interest rates are slightly higher than for conventional fixed-rate mortgages. For example, in December 2005 a fixed-for-life rate for a typical lifetime mortgage had an interest rate of 5.89 per cent, compared with 5.19 per cent for a 15-year fixed rate for conventional house purchase purposes.
2. Reversions – the reversion provider purchases either all or a share of the property, so technically the transaction is not a mortgage but a sale. The seller enjoys the same right of continuing occupation as with a mortgage, but does not pay rent. Consequently, the purchase price paid by the provider is discounted from the market value; the discounted value is actuarially calculated to reflect the life expectancy of the seller.

Lifetime mortgage selling standards have been regulated by the Financial Services Authority since October 2004. Similar regulation will apply to reversions from 2006/2007. When both types of product are regulated, reversions are expected to represent 10–15 per cent of the market – significantly more than recently.

Competition

The structure of the market for lifetime mortgages reflects its lack of maturity, with three dominant lenders, Mortgage Express, Northern Rock and Norwich Union, each holding approximately 25 per cent market share, the remainder being split between a number of other lenders. A greater degree of competition is anticipated as some of the major mortgage brands enter the market. There is also an increasing amount of innovation in product development taking place, with Northern Rock being particularly active.

The reversion market is far more fragmented, with business spread across a number of smaller providers. The absence of any major brands seems to have inhibited this market; however, the entry of Norwich Union into this sector in 2005 is likely to give it new stimulus.

Similar equity release products to those outlined above have been available in the USA for a number of years (known as 'reverse mortgages'), and during 2004/2005 Australia, New Zealand and Sweden also saw the emergence of similar products.

Source: Bob Wright, Assistant Director,
Northern Rock Plc.

It is interesting to note that governments have often been the source of major new product developments for the industry. For example, in the UK the Thatcher government of the 1980s was largely responsible for the huge growth of the personal pension market. Similarly, that same government also devised the Personal Equity Plan (PEP) and the Tax Exempt Savings Account (Tessa). Not to be outdone, the government of Tony Blair has thus far introduced the Stakeholder Pension, the Individual Savings Account (ISA) and the Child Trust Fund. The so-called Sandler suite of stakeholder products represents a major initiative on the part of the Blair government to provide a set of easy-to-understand products that represent good value for money for unsophisticated consumers.

Britain is not alone in this, as governments around the world play a major role in product development. The Polish government has introduced the IKE personal pension account. The IKE is one of the forms of the Polish government's third level of pensions, and can be in a form of a life insurance policy or different kinds of bank investments or investment funds. There are tax allowances – for example, no capital gains tax is payable when consumers receive their accumulated fund on retirement, but if they want to withdraw money beforehand then they pay the tax. The Ghanaian government has brought out a students' savings account, while in Libya the government has been responsible for the introduction of new tax-advantaged loans for home purchase.

As well as being responsible for the introduction of new products, governments also influence product policy in other ways. For example, the stakeholder products mentioned above place price caps on the charges that may be levied on the products that comprise the range. Similarly, regulations have had a major impact, notably at the service feature level, by introducing rules such as hard disclosure of charges and commissions, and rules regarding fact-finding.

Arguably, it is in the area of service features that innovation has had the most noticeable effect upon the customer experience. For example, innovation in telephone and Internet banking, ATMs and call-centres have probably affected customers more profoundly and directly than utility feature innovation in recent years.

2. *New service lines.* These are products that are new to the organization but not new to the market. Sometimes they are referred to as 'me too' products, and this aspect of product development has been more in evidence than wholly original product development during the past. Since there are competing products already established in the market the potential returns may be lower, but at the same time the organization is moving into an area with which it is considerably more familiar, in terms of either the technology or the markets. It is probably one of the most common forms of NPD in the financial services sector, particularly so as regulatory changes have reduced some of the restrictions on what organizations can do. For example, a number of competitors have copied the offset account that was originally devised by Virgin. Indeed, it is impossible to recollect a single new product that has not been taken up by any number of rival companies. The same goes for product features and fund variants. No sooner was the first ethical fund launched in the late 1980s than a range of analogues gradually entered the market.

The factors that influence the success of new-product development programmes in financial services have attracted considerable research interest. Athanassopoulos and Johne (2004) highlight the importance of customer involvement at an early stage, and the significance of communications with key or lead customers. The importance of leadership, teamwork and empowerment were highlighted in a study of consumer banking in the UK by Johne and Harborne (2003). In the case of Thailand, Rajatanavin and Speece (2004) have highlighted the important role played by sales staff as a conduit for customer information, and also the importance of cross-functional teamwork.

Whether considering genuine innovations or the addition of new service lines, there are many benefits from operating a structured process to consider which developments are most suitable. The basic components of a new-product development process are outlined in Figure 10.3.

1. *New-product development strategy.* A clear strategy is important to ensure that all those involved understand the importance of NPD and what the organization wishes to achieve. For example, it is essential that all those involved should understand whether the process of NPD is to be orientated towards taking advantage of new market segments, seen as crucial to the continued competitiveness of the organization, required to maintain profitability, or designed to reduce excess capacity or even out fluctuating demands. The ideas that should be considered are likely to vary according to the purpose of the NPD programme.
2. *Idea generation.* Ideas may be generated from both inside and outside an organization. Ideas may be generated internally from specialize NPD teams, from employee feedback or suggestions. Externally, ideas may be generated based on customer feedback, market research, specialist new product development agencies or by copying competitors. One common failing in idea generation is a tendency to

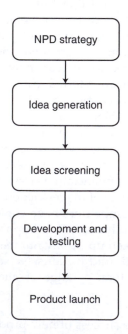

Figure 10.3 The new-product development process.

focus on what is possible rather than what the market wants – this has been particularly apparent with new technology-based products, where too much attention has been paid to what the technology can do and not enough to what consumers want.

3. *Idea screening*. The variety of ideas produced at the idea-generation stage must be screened to check that they are suitable. This usually means deciding, in advance, a set of criteria to be used when ideas are evaluated. The sort of criteria used can vary, but questions asked are likely to include the following:
   - Does the idea fit with the organization's strategy?
   - Does the idea fit with the organization's capabilities?
   - Does the idea appeal to the right market segments?
   - Is the idea viable in terms of cost and profit?

   Often the screening process passes through several stages; initially all ideas are screened, using simple criteria to eliminate any obviously unattractive suggestions. The remaining ideas are then screened much more thoroughly, involving a more detailed examination of their operational and financial viability, and often some product-specific market research.

4. *Development and testing*. Ideas that have survived the screening process are then worked up into specific service concepts – that is to say, the basic idea for the new product must be translated into a specific set of features and attributes which the product will display. At this stage it is common to test this newly defined product and to identify consumer and market reactions in order to make any necessary modifications to the product before it is launched. The problem with test-marketing in the financial service sector is that it gives competitors advance warning of an organization's latest ideas and thus offers competitors the opportunity to imitate. As a consequence, test-marketing of financial services is comparatively unusual. Many organizations argue that the actual costs of developing new products are often low, but the losses from giving advance warning to competitors may be quite high.

5. *Product launch*. The product launch is the final stage and the true test of any newly developed product; it is the point at which the organization makes a full-scale business commitment to the product. At this stage, the major decisions are essentially of an operational nature – decisions regarding the timing of the launch, the geographical location of the launch and the specific marketing tactics to be used in support of that launch.

Effective new product development is clearly important to the maintenance of a competitive position. Consequently, the process of developing new products has been extensively researched and a number of important practices that contribute to success have been identified:

1. Maintain regular contacts with the external environment to identify changes in market characteristics and customer requirement
2. Encourage a corporate culture which is receptive to innovative ideas
3. Operate a flexible approach to management to stimulate and encourage the NPD process
4. Identify key individuals with specific responsibility for the NPD process

5. Encourage a supportive environment
6. Ensure support and commitment from head office/senior managers
7. Ensure effective communications both internally and externally
8. Choose a product that fits well with the company
9. Develop strengths in selling
11. Offer product quality
12. Use market knowledge and customer understanding.

These practices cannot guarantee success, but it is clear that an open, supportive and flexible approach to NPD, supported by good marketing at product launch, can contribute significantly to the success of NPD activities.

10.7 Summary and conclusions

The key to successful product management is the development and maintenance of an appropriate product range. This requires that a financial service be developed with a set of features which correspond to consumer requirements, and that this range is constantly monitored so that existing services can be modified and new services can be developed. The process of new product development in the financial services sector has tended to concentrate on the redesign of existing products within an organization's portfolio, and the development of products which are new to the organization though not necessarily new to the sector. The perennial problem that faces the provider of financial service products is the ease with which such products may be copied and the consequent importance of ensuring rapid market penetration in the desired segment when new products are launched.

Review questions

1. Choose a product with which you are familiar. What are the different layers in that product? Choose what you think is the main point of differentiation between this product and other competing products.
2. Why is line stretching an important part of product management? What are the risks associated with this approach to product management?
3. What are the key stages in the NPD process? Why is it useful to have an organized process for developing new products?
4. What are the main types of Islamic financial services? What do you see as the main challenges when marketing financial services?

11

Promotion

☐ **Learning objectives**

By the end of this chapter you will be able to:
- explain the basic principles of communication for marketing
- examine the process of planning a promotional campaign
- provide an overview of the strengths and weaknesses of different approaches to promotion for financial services.

11.1   Introduction

The term 'promotion' refers to the range of methods used by an organization to communicate with actual and potential customers (e.g. advertising, publicity/public relations, personal selling and sales promotion) in order to evoke an attitudinal position and an appropriate behavioural response. In service businesses in particular, internal communication and promotion is also important in helping to build a market orientation. Thus, promotion (or marketing communications) increasingly focuses attention on employees as well as customers. Marketing communications play a key role in the process of building a brand and giving value to that brand, both by creating awareness and also by building favourable images/associations in the minds of customers. Building a clear brand image or brand association in the minds of consumers (and employees) depends on a high degree of co-ordination across promotional activities. The message presented by TV advertising needs to be consistent with what press advertising says, with what sponsorship implies and with the message communicated by sales staff. As with the marketing mix overall, if marketing communications are consistent and integrated, the impact of the overall campaign will be that much greater (synergy). Indeed, the concept of integration has attracted so much attention in recent years that practitioners increasingly refer to 'integrated marketing communications' (IMC) rather than just 'marketing communications'.

Promoting financial services is very similar to promoting physical products in many respects. However, financial services organizations do face some significant challenges. As explained in Chapter 3, they have no physical product to present to consumers, and consequently a major requirement of promotion is to develop a message and a form of presentation which allows the organization to present a product that is essentially intangible in a tangible form. Furthermore, financial services can be difficult to differentiate, and this can make it difficult for an organization to develop a clear message about the superiority of its own products. Finally, consumers tend to be relatively uninterested in financial services, and this suggests that there may be a greater need to attract attention; thus, developing creative approaches to communication may be particularly important for financial services organizations.

This chapter addresses the issues surrounding the development of an effective promotional strategy in financial services. The following sections provide an overview of the communications process in financial services and examine the development of promotion campaigns. The relative merits of different forms of promotion are then discussed, followed by a summary and conclusions.

11.2   Principles of communication

From a marketing perspective, the term 'communications' refers quite simply to the way in which organizations are able to send messages to target markets. The communications process is most commonly thought to be concerned with telling consumers about the features, benefits and availability of a particular product and attempting to persuade them to make a purchase. Increasingly, however, it is being recognized that communication has a rather broader role to play. In addition to stimulating consumer interest in a product, the communications process is also concerned with the way in which an organization projects itself and the image and identity it seeks to create with various interest groups and stakeholders.

The communications process is outlined in Figure 11.1. The main components of this process are:

1. *Source* (or sender). The source is whoever sends the message. Usually this is the organization or its representatives. However, if publicity or public relations is the chosen form of communication, then the source may be presented as a quasi-independent body giving 'objective' support to the particular product or service.
2. *Coded message*. The idea that the organization wishes to convey through the communications process must then be coded, either verbally or in symbols, in a form that is understandable to the target audience. For example, Phillips Securities wishes to emphasize the safety aspect of their Asset Savings Plan, and to do so they rely on the words '*As Safe As Possible*' (virtually the same letters as the product name) and the image of a man with three inflatable life belts.
3. *Medium*. The medium describes the particular channel through which the message is transmitted, and may be either personal (sales staff) or non-personal

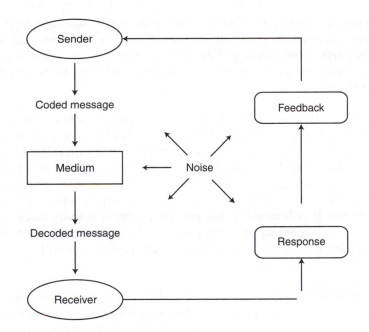

Figure 11.1 The communications process.

(advertising, publicity or sales promotion). The selection of an appropriate medium is crucial to ensure that the message reaches the target audience. Financial services targeted to a mass market will often rely on media such as TV, radio and general newspapers, whereas those services targeted at niche markets are likely to focus on more specialist media (e.g. *Investors' Chronicle, Mortgage Magazine*).

4. *Decoded message.* As the message is transmitted, the receiver interprets and assigns some meanings to the words and symbols that comprise that message. The sender hopes to encode the message in a way that results in the consumer interpreting the message in the way that was intended. This can be a particularly difficult task, since it relies on the sender being able to understand how consumers are likely to see the world.

5. *Receiver.* The receiver represents the target audience for the communications process. This may be a specific market segment, or the general public as a whole, or even the company's employees.

6. *Response.* Response describes the way in which the receiver reacts to the message, based on his or her interpretation of it. Typically, this refers to the sort of attitudes which the target audience forms in relation to the product.

7. *Feedback.* Some of the receiver's responses will feed back to the sender. Feedback may be in the form of enquiries or purchase if the message has been successful, but could equally be in the form of complaints if the message has been a failure or has been offensive.

8. *Noise.* Noise refers to any unplanned interference with the communications process which distorts the message. The presence of noise in any communications process is unavoidable. There will be few messages that are not distorted in some

way; the target audience may receive only part of the message being communicated, may interpret it in accordance with their own preconceptions and may recall only parts of the message. Effective communications will aim to minimize distortions by keeping messages brief, distinctive, relevant to the target audience and unambiguous.

Communication is essential in any marketing strategy to ensure that consumers are aware of what the organization offers (features, benefits, etc.) and how that offer is positioned in the marketplace. However, any form of communication can be misinterpreted or distorted. Thus, an effective communications strategy requires careful thought and planning to ensure that the organization has a clear and coherent message to present. This message must be clear, simple, honest and believable. Finally, of course, it is important that any promotional activity does not promise something that the organization cannot deliver. Apart from any legal implications that this might have from the point of view of advertising standards, etc., promising what cannot be supplied will lead to consumer dissatisfaction with the purchase and the potential loss of future consumers.

Although it is usual to think of communications as being concerned with particular products or services, a growing number of financial services organizations rely on communication and promotional activities to build a positive image and reputation for the organization itself. In effect, financial services organizations are placing greater emphasis on corporate branding, and marketing communications are becoming an important tool for building the corporate brand.

11.3   Planning a promotional campaign

The previous section highlighted the importance of a well-managed and planned promotional campaign to ensure that the communications process is effective. Careful planning is also important to ensure that the different methods of marketing communications are sending consistent messages, and that marketing communications are consistent with other elements of the marketing mix. The simplest way to think about the planning of a promotional campaign is to think of it as a series of stages, as shown in Figure 11.2 and described below.

11.3.1   Objectives

Defining objectives is important so that all involved in a promotional campaign know what they are trying to achieve. Often objectives are specified in terms of an increase in sales, but other objectives may concern themselves with raising awareness, creating a particular image, evening out patterns of demand, etc. In general, there are two broad types of objective that may underpin any promotional campaign:

1. Influence demand. Promotions may be directed explicitly towards influencing the level of demand for a service or range of services. Normally, this would imply

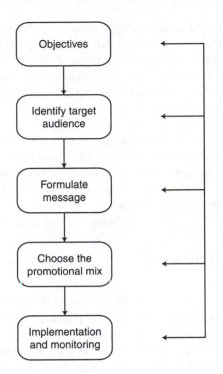

Figure 11.2 Planning a promotional campaign.

increasing the level of demand through attracting new customers away from competitors, increasing usage by existing customers, and encouraging non-users of the product to use.

2. Corporate image. Many promotional campaigns are directed towards creating and maintaining a particular corporate image. Such campaigns are particularly noticeable in the financial services sector because the characteristics of financial services (as discussed in Chapter 3) mean that organizations must pay particular attention to their brand and reputation.

As far as possible, objectives should be quantified. The guidelines given in Chapter 5 regarding the criteria for a suitably robust marketing objective are equally relevant for promotional objectives. This may simply mean specifying a target for increased sales volume or value. Alternatively, in the case of image-based objectives, targets may be set based on levels of awareness of the organization or on attitudes towards the organization.

11.3.2   Target audience

The next stage in promotional planning requires the identification of which groups are to be the target of the promotional activity – that is, which groups are to receive the message. At one level, this may simply involve defining the target market for a specific service or specifying 'the general public' (if the promotion is concerned with corporate image). However, it is also important to recognize that there will be differences between consumers in terms of their knowledge and awareness of an organization's image and range of services. In particular, researchers have suggested that consumers pass through four different stages when considering a purchase. This is known as the AIDA model, because consumers are expected to moved from Awareness to Interest, to Desire and finally to Action. Defining the target audience should consider which stage in the AIDA sequence consumers have reached. A promotional message and medium which is concerned with creating awareness of (or interest in) a product is likely to differ from one that is trying to create a desire to purchase or stimulate an actual purchase.

11.3.3   Formulate message

Having identified the target audience, the next stage is to establish what form the message will take. Any message can be divided into two key components – the message content and the message form. The message content relates to the basic ideas and information that the sender wishes to convey to the receiver. It should make clear why the product is different, what benefits it offers and why the consumer should buy this product rather than one of the available alternatives. Once the basic content of the message has been established, the next stage is to consider the form this message should take. It is at this point that the creative input from outside organizations such as advertising agencies becomes important. This process involves finding the most appropriate combination of verbal, audio and visual signals that will present the content of the message in a form which is most suitable for the target audience. This means that great care must be taken with the process of encoding, to avoid possible misunderstandings. At the same time, the information must be presented in a form that will attract attention and maintain sufficient interest in an advertisement or a leaflet to enable the potential consumer to absorb the information being conveyed. Sometimes this may involve using humorous sketches or indirect comparisons with competitors, or it may simply focus on the product or the organization itself. For example, in the UK, Sainsbury's Bank uses a character, 'Little Bill', to promote its car insurance, playing on the fact that 'Bill' might refer to both a person and also the cost of the car insurance (see Figure 11.3). Financial services organizations often make heavy use of their staff in the creative element of advertising to emphasize the personal touch. Thus, for example, Halifax Bank uses a staff member, Howard Brown, to promote a range of financial services.

Accuracy and honesty in the design and presentation of a message is essential in any form of advertising, and arguably particularly so in financial services because consumers find the products complex and difficult to understand. Most countries have policies in place to protect consumers from the potentially detrimental effects of misleading advertising. Nevertheless, the accuracy and honesty of advertising continues to be a cause for concern. For example, a recent study of financial services advertising in the UK by business and financial advisers, Grant Thornton,

Figure 11.3 Sainsbury's 'Little Bill' promotion.

suggested that over three-quarters of financial services adverts were misleading and do not conform to guidelines laid down by the Financial Services Authority (Grant Thornton, 2006). Particular problem areas were misleading price comparisons, headline rates for products which in practice were not available to customers, excessive use of jargon, claims that could not be justified, and a failure to include warnings about risk.

11.3.4   Budget

A budget must be established for the promotional exercise as a whole, and, at a later stage, for the individual components of the promotional mix. There are no hard and fast rules for determining the size of the promotional budget and, even within the same broad market, organizations will vary enormously in terms of promotional expenditure. There are a number of different approaches to the formulation of promotional budgets, including:

1. *The affordable method.* This simply suggests that the organization's expenditure on promotion is determined according to what the overall corporate budget indicates is available. The organization basically spends what it thinks it can afford.
2. *Sales revenue method.* This approach sets the promotional budget as some percentage of sales revenue. By implication, this means that sales 'lead' promotion rather than promotion 'leading' sales – which is what might be desired. That is to say, the size of the promotional budget will be dependent on past sales rather than desired future sales.
3. *The incremental method.* The budget is set as an increment on the previous year's expenditure. This is widely used, particularly by smaller firms. However, it offers no real link between the market and promotional expenditure, and does not allow promotional or marketing objectives to guide the level of expenditure.
4. *The competitive parity approach.* This approach focuses on the importance of promotion as a competitive tool, and entails setting budgets to match those of competitors.
5. *The objective/task method.* This is probably the most logical approach to the establishment of promotional budgets, but perhaps also the most difficult to implement because of the complexity of many of the calculations. As a consequence, it is not used widely. It relies on specific quantified objectives, and then requires that a precise cost is calculated based on the activities required to achieve these objectives. The budget is then based on these costs, so that marketing managers have a precise budget which should allow them to achieve their stated objectives.

A growing number of researchers argue that the marketing budget in general and a promotional budget in particular should be seen not as an annual cost but rather as an investment (see for example, Doyle, 2000). This approach argues that many marketing activities, and particularly advertising, have a cumulative effect and pay a key role in building the brand. If the effects of promotional expenditure have an impact over a number of years, then it would be misleading to focus on costs on an annual basis.

11.3.5   Choosing the promotional mix

Having determined the appropriate level of promotional expenditure, this must be allocated between the various promotional tools available to the organization – namely, advertising, publicity, sales promotions and personal selling. This mix will vary across organizations, products and markets. While it is difficult to generalize, retail markets will often make more use of mass-communication methods such as advertising, sales promotion and public relations/publicity, while personal selling will be more important to corporate customers. In financial services, as explained in Chapter 12, personal selling is relatively widespread in retail markets for more complex financial services. However, mass forms of communication remain popular for the less complex products, such as credit cards, current accounts and savings accounts.

There is a high degree of substitutability between promotional tools, so organizations must consider the strengths and weaknesses of different methods of communication and choose the combination that is most appropriate to the particular product and market. The individual components of the promotional mix will be examined in more detail in the next section.

11.3.6   Implementation and monitoring

As with any plan, the final stage concerns the process of implementation and monitoring. Implementation concerns itself with the allocation of tasks and the specification of timescale. Monitoring focuses on the regular evaluation of the progress of the promotional campaign and the identification of any areas where changes may be necessary. The problem that faces many organizations is the difficulty of measuring the effectiveness of promotional activities. There is a number of approaches that might be used to assess the effectiveness of promotional campaigns:

1. *Pre-testing*. Pre-testing involves demonstrating the promotional campaign to selected consumers. Based on their response, the organization attempts to predict the likely effectiveness of a campaign and eliminate weak spots. However, pre-testing does not guarantee effectiveness, and many successful advertisements have failed pre-tests.
2. Ex post *commercial market research*. Commercial market research once a campaign has started is widely used to determine levels of recall and comprehension. Recall and comprehension surveys can indicate whether the basic message has been conveyed to the target audience, but are less suitable for assessing how effective a campaign has been in terms of encouraging purchase. Simply because people say that they have recalled an advertisement or are aware of or interested in a product does not mean they intend to buy it.
3. *Statistical analysis*. Statistical analysis is often used to assess the impact of advertising on the level of sales. Basically, this involves a comparison of sales before the campaign with sales after the campaign. The findings of such studies can often show a change in sales after the campaign, but it is difficult to demonstrate that the campaign actually caused the change to occur.

Thus, evaluating campaigns can be difficult and, ideally, organizations would use several different sources of information and undertake detailed research with consumers. In practice, the costs of different types of research often lead to a reliance on general, commercial studies and an acceptance of some loss of detail and relevance in the evaluation.

11.4   Forms of promotion

As the previous section has indicated, there is a range of different promotional tools available to suppliers of financial services. This section discusses some of the more important methods of promotion in greater detail, and highlights their strengths and weaknesses. In blending together the different promotional tools, it is essential to focus on the issue of integration – namely, ensuring that the message contained in each form of promotion is consistent and integrated with other promotional messages. HSBC Bank provides a good example of this approach. The colour combination of red, white and black is consistent across all communication channels, as is the use of the strap line *'The World's Local Bank'*. The 'Cultural Collisions' series of TV adverts draws attention to HSBC's worldwide strength and local knowledge – a message that is replicated in print media, posters, point-of-sale material, air-bridge advertising and, of course, on the HSBC website.

11.4.1   Advertising

Advertising is a form of mass communication which is paid for and involves the non-personal presentation of goods/ideas. As such, it covers television, radio, Internet and press advertising, along with other approaches such as direct-mail and direct-response advertising. Advertising is usually classified as being of two types:

1. *Above-the-line advertising* refers to all forms of advertising where a fee is payable to an advertising agency, and includes press, TV, radio, Internet, cinema and poster advertising. The major advantage of above-the-line advertising is that it enables an organization to reach a large and diverse audience at a low cost per person. A further strength is that the sponsor (i.e. the organization) retains a good degree of control over the message content, its presentation and timing. A potential disadvantage is that advertising messages are highly standardized, and as such advertising can be an inflexible promotional tool. It may also be wasteful, because it reaches a large number of individuals who are not potential consumers.
2. *Below-the-line advertising* describes forms of advertising for which no commission fee is payable to an advertising agency, and includes direct-mail and direct-response advertising, exhibitions and point-of-sale material. In comparison with the types of media advertising described above, these methods tend to be much more focused; they reach a smaller number of people at a higher cost per person, but this is often counterbalanced by the higher degree of accuracy associated with such methods. Case study 11.1 explains how ING Direct used direct mail to target new products to its existing customer base.

Case study 11.1   A direct-mail campaign at ING Direct

Since bursting onto the scene in 2003, ING Direct has used its high-interest, hassle-free savings product to win the hearts and wallets of UK consumers. Demand has remained strong, and the company has become the world's leading direct savings bank in a short space of time. However, a proportion of ING Direct's customer base was flagged as 'do not mail'. This was preventing the company from giving their customers the opportunity to hear about (and take advantage of) promotions and offers that might potentially be of interest. ING Direct is not alone in encountering problems with the 'opt-out' option. Many financial services companies believe that customers fail fully to understand the implications of ticking the box marked 'do not wish to receive further marketing communications'.

At present, ING Direct offers only one product to the UK marketplace. Although the company's customers are exceptionally loyal, with 98 per cent happy to recommend ING Direct (TNS surveyed 1934 customers in September 2004), any future product launches could be hindered by the number of opted-out customers. The aim of this test campaign was therefore clear-cut: to open the door (and the letterboxes) to the potential of cross-selling across ING Direct's existing customer base. To re-engage with these customers, the company needed to communicate directly and present a simple yet compelling reason for them to re-think their decision not to receive marketing communications.

'After talking to our Royal Mail Key Account Manager, we discovered that a financial services company in a similar situation had used a mailing to achieve the success we were looking for,' explains Sarah Barnes, Direct Marketing Manager at ING Direct. 'So direct marketing, with its ability to reach and influence named individuals while minimizing cost, was the logical medium for us.'

The campaign objectives were as follows:

- to invite customers to opt back in to receiving marketing material
- to explain how they are currently missing out on future product and service news, as well as other offers and promotions that could be of interest
- to target a random 10 000 customers from the ING Direct database
- to encourage the target audience to complete and return a postal response or call the ING Direct call-centre
- to measure the campaign against three key criteria – response rate (%), cost per customer, and number of complaints received.

The company chose to mail a straightforward A4 folded letter, with a perforated reply slip, in a C5 branded envelope that promised 'no catches with ING Direct'. The letter outlined the key benefits that customers would enjoy once they had decided to opt back in. These focused on being kept up-to-date with future ING Direct products, services and promotions. To illustrate the point, the letter spelled out that the customer may have already missed out on the chance

Continued

Case study 11.1 A direct-mail campaign at ING Direct—cont'd

to celebrate the company's first birthday on board the Orient Express. The letter also reassured customers that there were no hidden catches – ING Direct never passes personal information to other companies, so customers would never receive unwanted communications from elsewhere.

'Royal Mail worked very hard to help us with the campaign', says Sarah Barnes. 'As well as suggesting the mailing in the first place, they advised us on including a Business Response envelope to ensure maximum response, something we had not initially intended. We decided to use Mailsort 2, and are delighted with the results. The power of Royal Mail is clearly demonstrated by the fact that every single response was received by post – there was no telephone response whatsoever.'

ING Direct mailed 10 000 letters at a cost of some £9000. The campaign achieved an excellent response rate, which means that the company can now communicate its offers and promotions and cross-sell future products and services with more of their customers.

Source: Leonora Corden, Head of Market Development, Royal Mail.

Advertising is one of the most widely used promotional tools in retail financial services because of its ability to reach large numbers of customers cost-effectively. However, the features of financial services do present some difficulties when developing advertising. As mentioned earlier, financial services are intangible, so there is little to show in an advert. Furthermore, customers often require large amounts of information in order to make purchase decisions, but many forms of above-the-line advertising are not very effective at making this information available. Press advertising can provide more information than TV, radio, cinema and poster advertising, but the quantity of information is still limited. The Internet can provide rather more information to consumers once they have clicked on a particular advert.

However, to date, Internet advertising has not proved to be very effective for financial services. In particular, although many organizations have invested in banner advertising, consumer click-through rates have been disappointing, suggesting that this may not be a very effective advertising medium. In contrast, the organization's own website may offer much greater potential for communicating with customers. However, websites provide a very passive form of communication, since they rely on the customer choosing to visit the site rather than allowing the organization actively to communicate with its customers.

Because customers will often need a lot of information in order to make a decision, above-the-line advertising is often thought to be more suited to the process of raising awareness and generating interest, while other promotional tools are used to encourage desire and action (remember the AIDA model discussed in the previous section). For example, many unit trust companies will operate campaigns to raise customer awareness of their fund performance and encourage interest. These adverts provide minimal information – rather, their aim is to encourage a sufficient level of interest that the consumers will think about approaching the company for a prospectus, or alternatively will respond positively if a prospectus is mailed to them.

Above-the-line advertising can also be particularly effective in building organizational reputation and image, because this type of communication does not require detailed information but rather focuses on a broad general message. An example of this latter type of advertising would be Great Eastern's *'Great Trust Great Confidence'* campaign, which involved minimal information – just a logo and a message. Equally, HSBC's campaign which illustrates the bank's local knowledge is run worldwide and plays a major role in building the HSBC brand.

The particular advantage of both direct-mail and direct-response advertising is that they can potentially provide customers with a lot of the detail necessary to make a final purchase decision. Indeed, direct mail which is accurately targeted to the right customer group can be very effective at generating new business, as well as cross-selling to existing customers. Accordingly, these methods of advertising are likely to be more effective in encouraging the final stage in the AIDA model – namely, the purchase (action). In addition, direct mail has the advantage that it is invisible to competitors. However, the ability to use direct mail effectively does depend on the organization having a good, accurate and up-to-date customer database, and this can present a problem for many financial services organizations.

Advertising of financial services is carefully regulated in many countries because of its potential to mislead. The combination of product complexity and limited consumer interest means that some forms of creative presentation can give the wrong impression. Interest rates are a particular area of concern, because many consumers do not fully understand different forms of presentation (such as APR and AER) and their relationship with headline rates (Buch *et al.*, 2002). The presentation of investment performance is another area of concern. Many advertisements rely heavily on figures about past performance to demonstrate the quality of their products, and then accompany such adverts with a disclaimer in small print to indicate that past performance is no guide to what will happen in the future. In addition, the actual formats used to present investment performance figures may result in the same real performance being interpreted differently according to style of presentation, as is shown in Box 11.1.

> ### Box 11.1   Consumer reactions to the presentation of past performance information
>
> Existing research suggests that past performance of market-based financial services (e.g. equity-based funds, bond funds, etc.) is of little use to investors as it does not serve to predict future performance, but it remains widely used by providers and customers alike. Financial services regulators have long been concerned about the ways in which companies selling market-based financial services can present information on past performance selectively in order to create a more favourable (and perhaps unrealistic) view among customers of the quality of the products they offer. Past performance is often presented in a graphical format.

Continued

> ### Box 11.1   Consumer reactions to the presentation of past performance information—cont'd
>
> This piece of research used actual past performance charts in a controlled experiment to assess the impact on customers of different forms of presentations and the use of data over different timescales. The experiment used a choice of fixed interest v. equity investment fund, with past performance presented as an annual percentage yield either on investment or on the changing absolute value of the fund. The results suggested that timescale had no effect on investor preferences, but presentation format did. In particular, when performance was charted using annual percentage yields, respondents were less likely to choose an equity-based fund. Of those respondents who had selected a FTSE-based tracker fund when shown information based on fund values, around half changed their choice when shown the same information using annual percentage yield figures. Furthermore, the use of annual percentage yield figures as a measure of past performance was also found to increase risk perceptions.
>
> *Source: Diacon (2006).*

Thus, advertising can take many forms, and the type of advertising used by a financial services organization will be influenced by the stated objectives and the nature of the target audience. Whatever type of advertising is used, particular attention must be paid to trying to make the service more tangible, reducing customers' perceived risk, being transparent, and trying to build trust and confidence.

11.4.2   Personal selling

Personal selling is discussed in more detail in Chapter 13. Personal selling has a dual role to play in the marketing of financial services. It is a channel of distribution and also a method of communication. Personal selling is probably most common in corporate markets, but is also widely used in personal markets in relation to some of the more complex financial services.

One of the major benefits of personal selling as a form of communication is that it allows immediate feedback from the consumer to the organization (or its representative). Other forms of communication are basically one-way, but personal selling is two-way. The customer can raise queries with the salesperson, and those queries or concerns can be dealt with immediately. This means that the information communicated can be very accurately tailored to the needs of particular individuals. Furthermore, because personal selling allows queries and responses, it is often thought to be very effective towards the end of the AIDA process – in encouraging action (purchase).

Thus, although personal selling can be a valuable and effective form of promotion, it is also very expensive. It therefore tends to be used more heavily for relatively high-value products and when customers are close to making a purchase. As well as being expensive, it is also a form of promotion that can be difficult to manage.

11.4.3   Publicity/public relations

Publicity is normally defined as being any form of non-paid, non-personal communication and, like advertising, it involves dealing with a mass audience. For this discussion, we broaden the concept of publicity to include an additional element, namely public relations. Public relations is paid for, whereas publicity is assumed to be 'free'. However, it is included under this heading because it is concerned more generally with building and maintaining an understanding between the organization and the general public.

Publicity offers a number of benefits to the organization. It has no major time costs, it provides access to a large audience, and the message is considered to have a high degree of credibility. The information is seen as coming from an independent or quasi-independent source rather than from the organization itself. However, it is also one of the more difficult forms of promotion to implement and control, since the final presentation and timing of information about the organization will usually be edited by the media, such as television, newspapers and online news providers.

Traditionally, publicity and public relations were seen as being centred on producing regular, informative press releases and building up good contacts with journalists. As a consequence, their importance has often been underestimated. However, with increasing pressure on advertising space and costs, the importance of publicity seems likely to increase. Two areas merit particular attention – the creation of a corporate image, and sponsorship.

Corporate image

The importance of corporate image and organizational branding has been mentioned earlier in this chapter. The development of a suitable corporate image is an aspect of public relations which is of particular importance to financial services organizations, because the reputation or image of the company has a major impact on consumer choice. Indeed, corporate image is often seen as one of the most important forms of branding that is available to a financial services organization. Each December, the magazine *PR Week* publishes a report on corporate reputation based upon the extent and nature of public relations coverage that businesses receive in the UK. Similar reports are to be found in many other parts of the world; however, it is unusual for financial services companies to feature in the upper echelons of such surveys. In the Australian 2005 report, the top three places went to Toyota, Microsoft and Sony respectively. Writing in the *Wall Street Journal* Online on 6 December 2005, Ronald Alsop reported that the top five companies, based upon public perception of their reputations, were Johnson & Johnson, Coca Cola, Google, UPS and 3M.

The factors that contribute to the creation of a favourable image are many and varied. A clear corporate identity is important, to make the organization instantly recognizable. An organization's corporate identity can be represented by a variety of visual symbols associated with promotional material, the branch network, and staff appearance. Other forms of communication can be used to help create an image and personality. Internal marketing can be used to encourage staff to commit to the corporate identity and believe in the image that the organization wishes to create.

Sponsorship

One increasingly important aspect of public relations and the creation of a desirable corporate image has been the growth in sponsorship. The extent to which this method of communication is used varies considerably across organizations, but with increased competition for advertising slots on television and rising media costs in general, sponsorship is seen as an important and effective way of projecting the image of the organization.

Particular features of the usefulness of sponsorship include the ability of the sponsoring brand to be associated with the characteristics of the sponsored activity (the so-called presenter effect), and the facility to be used for corporate hospitality. The latter feature is why sponsorship is often favoured by financial services companies involved in B2B marketing. Financial services organizations are involved in sponsorship of a variety of events, including sports events (e.g. football), entertainment (e.g. music concerts) and cultural events (e.g. art exhibitions). This type of sponsorship can be very effective at getting the organizations noticed by retail customers. For corporate customers, the sponsorship of local business seminars is also a widely used technique. The advantage of sponsorship, apart from its cost-effectiveness, tends to be that it is viewed less cynically by the consumer than are more traditional forms of advertising.

11.4.4   Sales promotions

Sales promotions in financial services are usually described as being demand–pull methods of promotion. Demand–pull promotions are specifically concerned with providing consumers with a direct incentive to try and buy a product. The use of sales promotions as part of a marketing campaign has increased considerably in recent years, as is evidenced by the rapid growth in the volume of business conducted by specialist sales promotion agencies.

There is a variety of techniques available, although the most popular are probably as follows:

1. *Benefits tied to product use*. This is one of the most popular forms of promotion used in financial services and in many other sectors. If the consumer uses/buys a particular product or service, he or she receives a free or discounted gift. Barclays has offered new personal pension customers the equivalent of three months' free contributions as a promotional tool to encourage new customer acquisition. The promotion was supported by in-branch promotional material and reinforced by branch staff in their interactions with customers. Loyalty schemes, which provide rewards such as Air Miles based on the level of spend on a credit or charge card, are widely used in financial services, and are another example of promotion

based on product-use benefits. These schemes are discussed in more detail in Part III of this book.

2. *Reduced price.* This constitutes the most direct method of sales promotion, in that it simply involves offering the product to the consumer at a reduced price. It is similar to couponing (see below), but is available to anyone rather than being restricted to those consumers with a coupon. For example, Citibank offered a 1-year fee waiver as a promotional device when they launched their Citibank Blue Credit Card.

3. *Competitions.* Competitions are a popular and easy-to-manage form of promotion. Consumers of the product are offered the opportunity to enter a competition to win attractive prizes. Citibank's *'99 Wishes'* campaign was a competition which allowed card-holders to send their top 9 wishes from a list of 99, and if their list matched the popular list for that day then the customer's number-1 wish was fulfilled. As only Citibank customers were able to enter, this can be seen as the kind of competition that would encourage new customers to Citibank as well as generating publicity. Similarly, Standard Chartered offered prize-draw entry to anyone who signed up for the Standard Chartered Motorists' Club Visa.

4. *Couponing.* Money-off coupons are probably the technique that is most commonly associated with sales promotions. It is less common in financial services, although a number of companies will offer particular discounts through direct mailing to certain target customers, and this can have a similar effect in that it should encourage purchase. A related concept is that of the introductory offer, and a growing number of financial services providers are offering either initial discounts on credit products or introductory interest premia on savings products.

Sales promotions can be very effective towards the final stage of the AIDA process, as they are designed to encourage the consumer actually to make the purchase.

11.5   Summary and conclusions

Promotional strategy deals with all aspects of communication between an organization and its customers, its employees and other interested parties. Four main promotional tools are available to an organization – advertising, publicity, sales promotion and personal selling. The balance between these tools will vary according to the nature of the overall marketing strategy, the characteristics of the product, the resources of the organization and the nature of the target market. Whatever promotional mix is chosen, the effectiveness of the communications process depends on the development of a clear and unambiguous message that is presented to the right target audience, at the right time and through the most appropriate medium.

Promotion has always been important in financial services, but if anything its importance is increasing. The market for financial services is going through a period of rapid change, and levels of competition are increasing. Deregulation, increased consumer sophistication and technological developments have encouraged a rapid growth in marketing, and particularly in promotional activity. Financial services institutions now spend significant amounts on communicating a variety of product and brand messages to a range of target audiences. With promotion attracting a significant level of marketing expenditure, it is important that promotional activity is careful planned and implemented and that it is consistent with the rest of the organization's marketing activities.

Review questions

1. Think of an advertising campaign that an organization has used. What were the different stages in the communications process? Explain these, using this campaign as an example.
2. What do you understand by the term AIDA? How can this framework be used to help choose the best method of promotion for a particular financial service?
3. What are the differences between above- and below-the-line advertising? Which do you think would be most effective for the marketing of a unit trust?
4. What are the strengths and weaknesses of the four main promotional tools?

12

Pricing

Learning objectives

By the end of this chapter you will be able to:
- explain the role of pricing in the financial services marketing mix
- understand the complexities associated with pricing in financial services
- understand the different approaches and methods of setting price.

12.1   Introduction

Of all of the component elements of the marketing mix, pricing is often the most problematic for marketing executives to manage. Unlike all other constituent parts of the mix, pricing is concerned with the determination of revenue and plays a crucial role in the derivation of product margins and profit. In many financial services organizations, price is the one element of the mix that is not under the control of the marketing function. Indeed, it is commonplace for the marketing team to have little influence in the setting of prices, but for them to be passive recipients of prices set in other parts of the organization. In the case of an insurance company, prices are often prescribed by one of the actuarial functions. In banks, prices are often set by the finance or treasury division, whilst in building societies it is often the prerogative of the finance team. Thus, pricing is often the source of much internal organizational politicking and must therefore be handled with care to ensure that all relevant parties participate in the process in a suitably joined-up fashion.

This chapter provides an overview of pricing in relation to financial services. It begins with a brief discussion of the role and characteristics of pricing and then moves on to explore in more detail some of the challenges associated with pricing in financial services. Subsequent sections consider approaches to price-setting, the issues associated with price discrimination, the process of price determination and the nature of overall pricing strategy.

12.2   The role and characteristics of price

Price has been defined as the value of a good or service for both the buyer and seller in a market exchange. For our purposes price is expressed as a monetary value, and as such is the metric by which the financial performance of an organization is evaluated. Thus price is a measure of value for both buyers and sellers, or, rather, customers and providers. From the customers' point of view, price performs a number of functions:

1. It is used as a yardstick to compare competing options
2. It is the means by which value is assessed
3. It may be used as an indicator of product or service quality
4. It represents the cost of the good or service
5. It can influence the frequency of purchase or quantum of an individual purchase.

As far as providers are concerned, price is important for the following reasons:

1. It is a crucial determinant of margin and profit
2. It influences the level of demand for its products and services
3. It plays a key role in affecting relative competitive position
4. It can be adjusted quickly, under certain conditions, to enable the provider to achieve short-term volume or margin priorities
5. It can be varied at different stages in the product lifecycle in conjunction with other elements of the marketing mix.

In the conventional tangible-goods marketing texts, it is customary to observe that price can be changed quickly in response to events in the marketplace or opportunistic situations. However, for some products the changing of price can be extremely time-consuming and costly. For example, in the life assurance arena the implementation of a price change can be a complex matter requiring major resource inputs from actuarial and systems departments. Depending upon the prevailing systems architecture, a price change can require as much resource as and involve a lead-time comparable to that of the launch of a new product. However, there are other products that are highly flexible and responsive to urgent deadlines, such as certain interest-rate driven products.

12.3   The challenges of pricing financial services

For the marketers of packaged goods, pricing is a relatively straightforward matter whereby the cost to the customer is simply the price he or she pays. It is similarly straightforward as far as the customer is concerned. The emergence of profit is similarly simple to grasp; it is the purchase price minus all direct and indirect costs. However, pricing is far more complex for financial services; indeed, the terminology associated with pricing is itself a complex and diverse issue. For example, consider the following products and the ways in which price is expressed:

Product	Terms associated with price
Whole-of-life assurance policy Bid : offer spread Initial charge Annual management charge Policy fee Early surrender penalty Market value adjustment Cost of advice Reduction in yield	Premium
Mortgage Interest rate Average equivalent rate (AER) Early redemption penalty	Arrangement fee
Unsecured loan Annual percentage rate (apr)	Interest rate
Current account Charges – overdraft arrangement fee Charges – unauthorized overdraft fee Charges – additional statements Charges – cheque representation fee	Overdraft rate
Personal pension Initial charges Bid : offer spread Charges Policy fee Annual management charge Cost of advice Reduction in yield	Contribution
Credit Card Annual percentage rate (APR) Average equivalent rate (AER) Late payment charge Interest charge	Annual fee
General insurance Excess charge	Premium

From this set of examples, it can readily be appreciated that customers are faced with the need to develop a familiarity with a wide range of terms used for expressing price. Additionally, the overall cost to the customer is often arrived at through the accumulation of several differently expressed charges. In the case of a number of products, there is the added confusion that arises from the fact that the notional amount of money paid into certain products represents an investment by the customer from which certain charges will be deducted. Thus, the *contributions* paid into a pension, the *premiums* paid into an endowment savings plan and the *investment* made in a mutual fund all represent sums of money that are being invested on behalf of the customer. They do not strictly represent *price*, where price means the sacrifice made by the customer. In these cases, *price* is represented by the various charges that are deducted by the product provider. However, in the case of general insurance products such as home contents and motor insurance, the premium does actually represent the price to the customer. In such cases there is no investment content incorporated into the premiums, and thus no return of funds at the expiry of the contract period. Indeed, there may well be additional charges levied on the customer, such as the payment of an *excess charge* should a claim arise.

Term assurance is similar to general insurance in that there is no investment content incorporated into the premiums paid by the customer. Thus the premium is used in its entirety to provide for the costs of providing the given level of life protection cover.

The difficulties which consumers face in fully appreciating the price they pay for certain financial services products are compounded further by a combination of complexity and the accumulation of charges. We have already observed how complexity arises from the range of terminology that applies to financial services pricing, and from the added confusion surrounding the treatment of the sums of money that the consumer invests in one form or another. A further issue that must be appreciated is the way in which charges accumulate during the period of the life of the product. Consider the case of a personal pension, shown in Box 12.1.

Attempts are made to present the cumulative impact of charges during the lifetime of an investment policy. One method is called the *reduction in yield* (RIY). RIY operates by showing the impact of charges in terms of how it reduces average

---

Box 12.1   Personal pension – indicative cumulative effect of charges

Let us assume that a consumer undertakes to contribute £300 per month to a personal pension (PP) and does so during a 30-year period. Let us also assume that the PP comprises the following charging structure:

Initial charge	5 per cent is deducted from each contribution made
Policy fee	A fee of £2 per month is deducted
Annual management charge	An AMC of 1 per cent of the consumer's fund value is deducted per annum

Thus, during the course of the 30-year term the consumer will have incurred the following charges:

Initial charges (£300 × 5 per cent × 12 × 30)	£5400
Policy fees (£2 × 12 × 30)	£720
AMC (assumes average annual growth of 7.5 per cent)	£32 730
Total costs	*£38 850*

Thus, during the course of the 30 years that the personal pension has been in force, the consumer will have paid £38 850 in total charges.

annual returns on the consumer's investment. For example, if the cumulative impact of charges on a personal pension have a RIY of 2.8 per cent, it means that instead of a consumer receiving annual growth of, say, 7.5 per cent from his or her contributions, the consumer receives an actual return of 4.7 per cent. Looked at another way, the effect of the 2.8 per cent RIY is to reduce the return on investment by 37 per cent ($2.8 \div 7.5 \times 100$).

The complexity and confusion already discussed contributes to a relative lack of transparency regarding costs and pricing. Llewellyn and Drake (1995) suggested that, when considering the pricing of financial services, it might be helpful to distinguish between two main forms of pricing, namely explicit or overt pricing and implicit or covert pricing.

12.3.1   Explicit or overt pricing

This approach makes the price paid for the service very clear. Consumers are presented with clear and precise figures about what they will pay for this service. When a bank charges for an ATM withdrawal or a credit card company charges an annual fee, this is an example of explicit pricing. This approach has the advantage of being very clear to both consumer and to supplier. The supplier is likely to be better able to predict likely revenue, and the consumer is much more obviously aware of what the service costs. Furthermore, an explicit price allows the organization to signal costs of different services and use price as a way of influencing consumer behaviour. For example, if branch-based transactions were priced relatively high (because of their high costs) and ATM transactions were priced relatively low (because of their lower costs), the organization could use pricing to try to encourage consumers to move from branch-based transactions in favour of ATMs. However, to operate a good and efficient system of overt pricing does require a thorough understanding of the cost base and principles of cost allocation. As explained earlier, this can be a difficult area for financial services organizations.

12.3.2   Implicit or covert pricing

This is a system of pricing in which the actual price to the consumer is unclear and appears not to be paid by consumers. The bank that offers free banking but pays no interest on credit balances is pursuing an implicit pricing policy. Consumers may not be aware of it, but they are effectively paying a price based on the size of any outstanding credit balances. Similarly, an organization providing a regular savings product may not explicitly charge for its services, but will take a share of the initial payments in order to cover costs and contribute to profit.

Implicit pricing has the advantage of being very simple for both the organization and the customer, and it is relatively low cost to administer because it does not necessarily require the same sort of detailed understanding of costs. However, there are significant disadvantages to this approach. First, both the price paid by the customer and the revenue paid by the bank will vary according to the interest rate or the amount that consumers wish to save/invest. Secondly, there is no incentive for consumers to move to lower-cost services because all services offered appear to be free of charge. Thirdly, implicit pricing creates potential for cross-subsidization. Thus, for example, the customer with significant positive credit balances will pay a much higher price for a given service than will the customer with a minimal credit balance. In effect, the customer with a large credit balance subsidizes the service provided to the customer with a small credit balance.

12.4   Methods for determining price

A number of elements of economic theory are helpful in enabling us to understand how price levels are arrived at. The demand curve is useful as an aid to understanding the relationship between price and demand. As we see in Figure 12.1, in simple terms, the lower the price of the given product the greater the level of demand for that product.

In Figure 12.1, as price increases from £P1 to £P2, demand falls from Q1 volume to Q2 volume. From the supply side, the higher the price, the greater will be the volume of output that manufacturers and product providers are willing to supply. However, this is an oversimplification, since it assumes economic rationality on the part of consumers and an ability clearly to identify best value. It also implies that high price is a proxy for high margin from the supplier's point of view. Indeed, the basic economic theory of price implies the characteristics associated with perfect competition. Fundamental to the notion of perfect competition is consumer sovereignty, whereby the consumer is both highly knowledgeable about all aspects of the product in question and has full and unhindered access to all forms of information regarding the entire universe of suppliers. In practice such conditions seldom apply in the field of financial services, and the term *information asymmetry* is commonly used to describe the balance between consumer and provider knowledge.

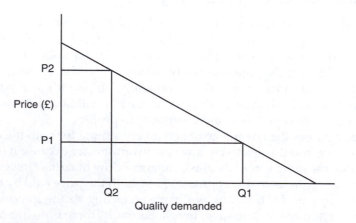

Figure 12.1 The demand curve.

Nevertheless, under certain circumstances there is little doubt that demand is stimulated by price reductions, and that price increases can be used to lessen demand. For example, in September 2005 Fidelity announced that it would be increasing the charges that apply to new investments in its Special Situations fund as part of a process of reducing the overall scale of the fund.

Shapiro and Jackson (1978) propose three core approaches to the determination of price:

1. Cost-based
2. Competitive
3. Market-orientated.

12.4.1   The cost-based approach

In simple terms, the cost-based approach to pricing operates by identifying the costs associated with a given product and then adding on a profit margin to arrive at a price. In practice, there are two main variants of the cost-based approach to pricing: full-cost pricing and marginal-cost pricing. Whereas full-cost pricing takes account of all components of cost (overhead as well as direct or variable costs), marginal-cost pricing relates just to the direct costs associated with the manufacture of the good or service. Two examples will help to illustrate these alternative approaches.

Example: Full-cost pricing

Fixed overhead costs	£100 000
Variable (direct) costs per unit	£25
Forecast sales	5000 units
Profit margin mark-up	20%
Total costs	£100 000 + (5000 × £25) = £225 000
Full cost per unit	£225 000 ÷ 5000 = £45
Mark-up (20%)	£9
Price	£54

The advantage of full-cost pricing is that it should ensure that profit is achieved and that all costs have been covered. However, it suffers from the potentially major disadvantage that it can result in an uncompetitively high price. Such a situation can arise from two perspectives. First, the adoption of a cautious approach to forecast sales will limit the extent to which fixed costs can be attributed to units of output. In the above example, if we had forecast sales volume of 20000 units instead of 5000 we would have arrived at a materially different set of costs and price, as can be seen below:

Fixed overhead costs	£100 000
Variable (direct) costs per unit	£25
Forecast sales	20000 units
Profit margin mark-up	20%
Total costs	£100 000 + (20 000 × £25) = £600 000
Full cost per unit	£30

| Mark-up (20%) | £6 |
| Price | £36 |

The difference in the two examples is explained by the reduction in overhead cost per unit from £20 to £5. Had the provider been more bullish about sales, it would have opted for a higher sales forecast and thus set a price some 36 per cent lower than the price based upon the cautious forecast of 5000 units. The second weakness is that we do not know the price level that applies to the nearest competitor. If we assume a competing product is priced at £45, it seems reasonable to assume that a £54 price tag will be unattractive. If such a scenario were to result in actual sales of 3000 units instead of the 5000 forecast, the price would have to be reviewed again as follows:

Fixed overhead costs	£100 000
Variable (direct) costs per unit	£25
Forecast sales	3000 units
Profit margin mark-up	20%
Total costs	£100 000 + (3000 × £25) = £175 000
Full cost per unit	£58.33
Mark-up (20%)	£11.67
Price	£70

Thus, this example shows the creation of a self-fulfilling prophecy whereby price is based upon conservative forecasts that do not fully reflect what the competition is charging. It results in a price that is uncompetitive, sales are below expectation, and this in turn results in a further price increase and commensurately lower sales.

Example: Marginal cost pricing

The marginal cost-based price is arrived at by adding a profit margin onto the direct, variable costs of manufacture. Taking the earlier example:

Direct cost per unit	£25
Mark-up (20%)	£5
Price	£30

Marginal costing results in a much lower price than the full-cost approach because no account is taken of overhead cost attribution. It is sometimes used in highly competitive situations on the basis that so long as the price at least covers direct costs, it is making a contribution to the fixed-cost overhead. However, in practice it means that the price is set at an unrealistically low level and other products will, in effect, be subsidizing the direct cost-based product. It is an economic fact of life that overhead has to be paid for somehow, and there has to be a compelling commercial reason to use marginal cost as a basis for pricing decisions.

Branch-based organizations often have difficulty in arriving at an accurate apportionment of fixed costs to individual products. Banks typically have very wide, diverse product ranges, and identifying how much of branch costs should be allocated to individual products is fraught with difficulties. Nevertheless, some arbitrary cost allocation bases can be used to ensure that an appropriate contribution be made to overhead costs.

12.4.2   The competitive approach

Rather than set price on the basis of cost, with the disadvantages that have been identified, price can also be based upon competitors' price levels. Two variants are commonly encountered: going-rate pricing and competitive bidding.

Going-rate pricing implies that there is little heterogeneity between competing products, and that providers are in effect price-takers rather than price-setters. The idea of going-rate pricing seems at odds with strategies based upon product and service differentiation. Indeed, it suggests a largely commoditized marketplace with little scope for premium pricing. However, it is undoubtedly true that what we might term benchmark pricing applies in many commercial areas. There has to be a very good reason for a price premium being charged in the real estate market, for example, where a 1.5 per cent fee is a common benchmark. Sometimes governments and regulators can establish going-rate pricing, such as the 1.5 per cent charge cap on the Child Trust Fund and stakeholder pension in the UK.

The second basic approach to competition-based pricing is competitive tendering. In this case, prospective suppliers are invited to submit their most competitive bid to the prospective customer. Such an approach to pricing is rarely encountered in the domestic marketplace, and is more a feature of the business-to-business environment.

As can be readily appreciated, such a method is fraught with the twin dangers of bidding too high a price and failing to get the business or bidding too low, and damaging margins. Success in an area that involves competitive tendering requires great expertise in understanding both your own organization's cost base and the cost bases of your competitors. It can be remarkably difficult to achieve differentiation and premium pricing in marketplaces that are characterized by competitive tendering. Once successful with a bid, the service or product provider can render themselves vulnerable to the customer, who can assume a great degree of power.

12.4.3   The market-orientated approach

The limitations associated with cost- and competition-based pricing have resulted in the development of marketing-orientated pricing. Marketing-orientated pricing sets out to reflect a broad range of variables in the determination of price. Significantly, it recognizes that price has a strong strategic dimension in being closely implicated in issues such as positioning and competitive advantage. David Jobber (2004) identifies an array of ten components of a marketing-orientated approach to pricing as follows:

1. Marketing strategy
2. Price–quality relationships
3. Product line pricing
4. Negotiating margins
5. Political factors
6. Costs
7. Effect on distributors and retailers
8. Competition
9. Explicability
10. Value to customer.

Marketing strategy

Pricing presents valuable opportunities for a company to craft extremely subtle approaches to the implementation of its marketing strategy. This is in part made possible by the multi-variable nature of financial services pricing. Consider the example of level term assurance (LTA). This is one of the simplest types of life assurance, and its price (premium) varies from customer to customer depending upon the following customer attributes:

- amount of sum-assured
- duration of term
- age
- gender
- smoker/non-smoker
- health status
- occupation
- leisure pursuits.

The maximum number of permutations, and hence individual prices, that arise from the above variables will run into thousands. An insurer has to make choices regarding where it wants to position itself with regard to its competitors for those thousands of individual prices. Amongst the choices to be made are which competitors to benchmark against. This is far from straightforward, as different groups of competitors are to be found in different parts of the market for LTA. The answer lies in adopting a pricing policy that is designed to complement the marketing strategy with regard to target segments, and positioning. Let us consider two hypothetical providers of LTA and the ways in which they can use pricing that are consistent with their respective strategies.

Example: Hallmark Insurance

Hallmark Insurance is an insurance company that is based in the eastern seaboard of the USA. It specializes in providing LTA on high sums assured for terms of up to ten years. A particular field of expertise is the use of Hallmark's LTA as a loan protection policy for SME company directors who are taking out high-value loans for purposes such as corporate buy-outs and acquisitions. As such, they target corporate financiers and investment banks to promote their products and services. Hallmark has designed a pricing strategy to enable it to be competitive in the following areas:

- sums assured from $1m to $20m
- terms of 5 to 10 years' duration
- individuals aged 35–55.

Figure 12.2 shows where Hallmark has set its pricing in terms of quartile ranking on the key variables indicated above. By the term 'quartile' we mean 25 per cent – thus the first quartile means the top 25 per cent of companies ranked on the basis of price competitiveness.

Sums Assured – 5–10 years, Age Range 35–55 years

	$1m–5m	$5m–10m	$10m–15m	$15m–20m
Q1			Hallmark	Hallmark
Q2		Hallmark		
Q3	Hallmark			
Q4				
No of Competitors	200	50	25	10

Figure 12.2 Hallmark's LTA price positioning in preferred sectors.

It can be seen that Hallmark has set its stall out to be highly competitive, the more so as its sums assured increase. Note how the number of competitors falls as sums assured increase, thus making positioning all the more important.

Example: Everyman Insurance – a subsidiary of Everyman Bank

Everyman Insurance is based in Melbourne in Australia, and is the bancassurance arm of one of Australia's leading high-street banks. An important part of its strategy is that it seeks to support the bank's small-business operation, which has the goal of trebling the size of its loan book during the next five years. The small-business banking operation enjoys close relationships with its customers, who show a high degree of loyalty to the bank. Part of the Everyman Bank strategy is that its small-business owners go on to become owners and directors of much bigger businesses in due course.

Everyman Insurance has designed a primary strategy to enable it to be competitive as part of an overall Everyman loan and insurance package to its small-business customers. Thus it seeks to be especially competitive in the following areas:

- sums assured from $50 000 Au to $250 000 Au
- terms of 5 to 10 years' duration
- individuals aged 30–40 years.

Figure 12.3 shows where Everyman Insurance has positioned its prices in quartile ranking terms according to its preferred business profile.

Figure 12.3 shows Everyman Insurance structuring its price positioning to become increasingly competitive as the sums assured increase to its optimum position. At these levels of sums assured, the number of competitors remains almost static. Everyman's price positioning in non-target areas of sums assured, term and age are typically pitched at the mid-point of the third quartile. This enables them to achieve good margins on business they do not seek to chase.

These two hypothetical examples should give a clear indication of how pricing can be organized to fit the overall marketing strategy. In a study of the UK term assurance market conducted on a private basis by one of the authors in the late 1990s, it was noteworthy how random price-positioning appeared to be. Of some

	$25–50,000	$50–100,000	$100–200,000	$200–250,000	$250–400,000
Q1			Everyman	Everyman	
Q2		Everyman			Everyman
Q3	Everyman				
Q4					
No of Competitors	75	75	75	75	70

Figure 12.3 Everyman Insurance's LTA price positioning in preferred sectors.

20 insurance companies studied, only 1 demonstrated the kind of logical coherent approach illustrated in Figures 12.2 and 12.3. Thus, pricing should be used in a thoughtful and commercially astute manner in a way that is consistent with the company's approach to market segmentation.

Price–quality relationships

Consumers form a judgement about the relationship between price and quality. It is understood that a high-quality, personalized service will incur higher costs to the provider than will an undifferentiated basic form of commoditized service.

Product line pricing

Product line pricing refers to the need for integrity between all of the products that comprise an overall product range. Thus an investment management company will be expected to charge more for a personalized portfolio management service than it does for managing a packaged portfolio of investments.

Negotiating margins

Negotiating margins apply in circumstances where customers expect to be able to haggle over prices. Thus, an extra margin is included in the basic list price to allow for negotiation. The inclusion of negotiating margins is a particular feature of B2B marketing, where sellers are faced with professional buyers. Such buyers are skilled at conducting negotiations and usually have personal objectives to achieve, which include successful negotiation of procurement activities.

Costs

Clearly, costs have to be taken into account when setting price if the company is to avoid making a loss. Financial services present particular problems in respect of the allocation of variable as well as overhead costs to individual products. This problem is further exacerbated in circumstances where the marketing team is on the periphery of the pricing process. In such circumstances, marketing staff can miss out on the opportunity to develop a keener sense of commercial judgement. Organizations that view pricing as a responsibility of the marketing team can be expected to benefit from marketing executives who have a solid grasp of costs and of how profit emerges.

Effect on distributors and retailers

Distribution channels can have a profound effect upon pricing, since they require a level of remuneration that motivates them to work in a vigorous and committed manner on behalf of the product provider. This argument applies to both direct and indirect distribution channels. Some forms of distribution become too costly for product providers to be able to satisfy the remuneration needs of the distributors and their own profit requirements. It is common for, say, banks and insurance companies to decide not to market certain products, such as stakeholder pensions, insurance ISAs and the Child Trust Fund, because their cost bases do not leave enough margin for their distributors to earn what they consider to be an appropriate level of remuneration.

A common dilemma for product providers is that distributors seek to maximize their remuneration from their distribution activities, yet want to be able to offer a competitive price to their end customers. We see this in the grocery domain, where supermarkets seek to negotiate good margins for distributing products yet want to offer consumers the lowest possible prices. This has tipped the balance of power very much in favour of the supermarkets and resulted in a weak position for producers. Thus brokers might also expect to receive high levels of commission for distributing, say, motor insurance, but want to offer low premiums to their customers. This particular dynamic has been a major catalyst for the development of remote, IT-based distribution methods in a number of areas such as motor insurance.

It is fair to say that the ability to make sound judgement calls in respect of setting a price that optimizes distribution margin and customer attraction is a crucial marketing competence. The preferred approach is to argue that lower customer prices will result in such a high volume of demand that distributors will ultimately earn more cash, albeit at a lower margin per unit, than they would from selling a lower volume at a higher margin. Such an approach assumes elements of a perfect market and price-elasticity-of-demand that are not necessarily in evidence universally in the financial services sector.

Competition

In some respects, the pricing of financial services has been less influenced by competition than have many other product categories. Until comparatively recently, life, pension and investment products were priced more to secure distributor support than to ensure competitive value for money. Importantly, the complexity and lack of transparency of financial services pricing act as inhibitors to highly competitive pricing. Fortunately, a combination of regulatory, legislative, technological and competitive development are acting to achieve a significant increase in the role played by competition in the pricing of financial services.

Competition exerts its most powerful effect in circumstances characterized by product simplicity, consumer knowledge and confidence, low perceived risk from buying largely on the basis of lowest cost option, limited product differentiation, simplicity of purchase process, ease of switching, and a wide number of competing providers. Thus, it can be appreciated that motor insurance is influenced by competition to a far greater degree than is the provision of banking services to small companies or critical illness insurance.

Explicability

By explicability, we mean the ability to explain and justify why a product is significantly more (or indeed less) expensive than competing offerings. Products that are materially cheaper than the norm may attract consumer suspicion in product areas that are typified by relative consumer ignorance and the risks associated with making a poor choice. A corollary to this is that, under conditions of consumer ignorance and perceived riskiness, a price higher than the norm may be seen to imply quality and instil consumer confidence. This is somewhat akin to the so-called 'Giffen effect', from the eponymous Victorian economist Sir Robert Giffen. According to the Giffen effect, under certain circumstances demand increases as prices rise. This may in part explain the attractiveness of certain exclusive or designer-label goods.

Explicability is more difficult to achieve the closer market conditions approximate to perfect competition. The implication for marketers is that those seeking to achieve a premium price position must invest in an appropriate level of product/service differentiation that can justify the price premium. It is interesting to note that a number of high-street banks, such as Barclays and Lloyds TSB, have attempted to market higher net-worth current account banking services at a premium price in recent years. The impression conveyed is that neither has been particularly successful, as consumers fail to place sufficient value on the premium price they are charged.

Value to customer

The ultimate test of a price must be the extent to which customers feel they are receiving fair value and will maintain a mutuality advantageous relationship with the provider. As discussed earlier, customer value (from the provider's perspective) is a function of a remarkably discrete set of variables such as, in the case of a loan:

- value of sum borrowed
- duration of loan
- incidence of default
- cross-sale/purchase of other products.
- interest margin

Thus, the retention of customers based upon their perceptions of the value-for-money they enjoy is assuming ever greater importance in companies' marketing strategies.

12.5   Price differentiation and discrimination

In many marketplaces there are rules and regulations concerning price discrimination. Discrimination refers to a product or service being offered to a buyer at a lower price than applies to other buyers. Implicit in price discrimination is the notion that the buyer presented with the higher price is being treated unfairly. Resale price maintenance was once a common feature of the consumer goods marketplace in the UK. However, such a rigid approach to pricing has become increasingly out of step with the contemporary competitive environment. In practice, there is a growing recognition that the charging of differential pricing is a legitimate, and indeed desirable, feature of a consumer-orientated marketplace. As a component of the marketing mix, price can be adjusted to suit a range of buying situations. Such variations in price may be a reflection of genuine lower costs that apply to differing buying scenarios. In the consumer goods domain, for example, buying soft drinks in bulk quantities involves genuine cost savings to the distribution channel that can be reflected in a lower cost per unit to the end consumer. Similarly, bulk discounts are a defensible aspect of the pricing structure that applies to the distribution channels associated with the soft drinks market. A retailer committing to buy a million cases of Pepsi Cola should expect to receive a better price than one buying just a dozen cases at periodic intervals.

Equally, it seems perfectly reasonable for a railway company to stimulate higher levels of off-peak usage of its trains by charging a lower price than applies during the rush-hour period. In this way differential pricing serves the interests of not only the supplier and customer but also the wider community, by using resources in a more efficient manner. In turn, this makes a contribution to the goal of sustainability – an issue that is assuming ever growing importance in a wide variety of contexts.

Thus, deliberately disadvantaging one group of customers through price discrimination represents a highly undesirable practice. Price differentiation, on the other hand, has a number of positive features that serve the interests of a wide range of stakeholders. Differential pricing can be based upon a number of factors, reflecting both genuine commercial considerations on the part of providers and also customer characteristics, including:

- lower costs associated with bulk purchase
- costs that vary according to different factors, such as geographical variation in labour costs and rents
- costs that vary according to buyer characteristics – for example, people with a poor credit history indicate a greater propensity to default on loans and therefore may pay a higher rate of interest
- utilization of off-peak capacity
- demographic factors – age, employment status, gender.

Arguably, price differentiation is particularly well-advanced in the field of financial services. The most graphic example is life assurance, where prices vary according to age, sex, occupation and health status. Price differentiation in this case is based upon genuine cost-related factors, concerning mortality, that vary with age and so on.

Differential costs associated with different types of customer have acted as the basis for what are termed *preferred lives* insurance companies. This is a form of niche marketing where the company targets a specific segment based upon clearly defined cost advantages that are in evidence. For example, SAGA Financial Services offers relatively low premiums on motor insurance because it only sells to the over 50s – an age cohort that has relatively low claims experience. By excluding younger drivers from its book of business, SAGA is reducing the costs associated with their higher incidence of claims.

The preferred lives approach can be applied in a number of situations where clear customer characteristics have a direct and material bearing upon customer value.

In health insurance, for example, a company might choose to target just those individuals who have favourable health status. It should be borne in mind that there some marked differences around the world with regard to the acceptability of pre-ferred lives insurance. For some people and political organizations preferred lives insurance is seen as an oxymoron, in that insurance should be about the use of pool-ing in order to best serve the overall public good. This philosophical principle underpins the approach of the French health mutuals, whose premiums do not dis-criminate on the basis of age. In South Africa there is hostility to the concept, because consumers do not like to divulge the kind of information that would be needed to adopt a preferred lives approach on a mass-market basis. Preferred lives insurance is at its most advanced in the US insurance market.

12.6   Price determination

Some form of process is required for an organization to arrive at the finally agreed selling price. Earlier in this chapter we considered the three main bases upon which price can be developed – namely cost-based, competitive and market-orientated.

Step 1   Decide upon pricing objectives

Step 2   Assess influence of 10 pricing factors

Step 3   Propose indicative pricing approach

Step 4   Model price/demand relationships

Step 5   Assess impact on pricing objectives

Step 6   Assess responses expected from competitors and distributors

Step 7   Consult relevant internal departments and gain agreement to price

Step 8   Set up implementation project

Step 9   Launch price

Figure 12.4 Price determination process.

However, whichever basis is used, a number of steps need to be considered when setting price. The nature of these steps will vary according to whether the cost-based, competitive or market-orientated approach is used. Here we will consider a process that might be applied when setting price in accordance with the marketing approach; Figure 12.4 indicates the steps involved, and these are discussed below.

12.6.1   Step 1: Decide upon pricing objectives

At the outset, there needs to be clarity regarding the financial and non-financial objectives that are being sought. Typical financial objectives might include:

- sales value
- margin
- profit
- return-on-capital.

Non-financial objectives may comprise one or more of the following:

- sales volume
- market share
- market position
- customer value.

12.6.2   Step 2: Assess influence of 10 pricing factors

Having formed a view on the desired pricing objectives, it is important that an assessment be carried out of how the following 10 factors might be expected to exert an influence on the final price:

1. Marketing strategy
2. Price–quality relationships
3. Product line pricing
4. Negotiating margins
5. Political factors
6. Costs
7. Effect on distributors
8. Competition
9. Explicability
10. Value to customer.

12.6.3   Step 3: Propose indicative pricing approach

Armed with a clear set of price objectives and an assessment of relevant influences, an indicative price can be proposed. This stage in the process can be relatively complex in the case of insurance-related business, where there is a huge array of individual premiums to be calculated. In such a case, it is recommended that a number of specific headline premiums be proposed that are indicative of key market positioning. For other sectors of financial services – mortgages, for example – it can be far more straightforward, as it may simply be a case of proposing a single rate of interest.

This is also the stage where factors such as special promotional pricing are considered. For example, it is commonplace for companies seeking new depositors to offer a bonus rate of interest for, say, the first 6 months.

Other aspects of price that might also be addressed at this stage are:

- status requirements – for example, no claims bonuses on motor insurance, income, occupation, previous financial history, track record
- volume-related factors – for example, lower rates of interest charged for high-value loans
- allied charges – for example, penalty fees on overdue payments, unauthorized overdraft charges
- customer contributions – for example, the level of excess payments on general insurance contracts, and early settlement penalties on, say, fixed-rate mortgage loans.

12.6.4   Step 4: Model price/demand relationships

It is advisable to model how price elasticity of demand might operate, given the proposed price. This can be used to make various trade-offs, such as whether a lower price could result in significantly enhanced results in terms of market share or sales volumes. Such outcomes will need to be judged in the light of their impact upon the break-even point and emergence of profit. For a life assurance policy, this could have a material impact upon new business strain and hence capital requirements.

12.6.5   Step 5: Assess impact on pricing objectives

The modelling carried out in step 4 is a key input to assessing the likely impact of the indicative price on the achievement of the desired pricing objectives. An unfavourable outlook may result in the need to make changes to the pricing objectives or indicative pricing approach. It is advisable to ensure that relevant parties are aligned at this stage, before committing further resources to the overall process.

12.6.6   Step 6: Assess responses expected from competitors and distributors

To some extent, certain aspects of this stage will have already been incorporated into steps 3, 4 and 5. However, this is the point at which a more explicit assessment needs to be made. Scenario planning may be a useful approach to adopt as a means of considering the range of distributor and competitor options.

12.6.7 Step 7: Consult relevant internal departments and gain agreement

It is expected that an appropriate level of consultation and collaboration will already have taken place. Many companies have formal pricing and credit committees whose endorsement is required before the price can be finally agreed.

12.6.8 Step 8: Set up implementation project

There is a wide range of complexity when setting prices in financial services, and in some cases extensive project management will be required. It is especially important that pricing events involving a significant amount of IT resources are planned well in advance – probably well before step 1 of this process. Systems resources are usually key elements on the critical path, and the availability of relevant personnel has to be scheduled at an early stage if target launch dates are to be met. Staff from other functions may have an equally significant role to play – pricing actuaries, for example – and so the expectation of their availability has to be suitably planned for. Due regard must be paid to gaining the timely involvement of appropriate administration staff. It is by no means uncommon for them to be treated as somewhat of an afterthought in such activities; such oversights must be avoided. Other requirements that need to be factored into the implementation plan include price lists, documentation and rate books, computerized illustration systems, trade communication, customer communication and staff training.

Finally, price changes on existing products need to take account of cut-off dates regarding pipeline business.

12.7 Pricing strategy and promotional pricing

It is axiomatic of all components of the marketing mix that they interact in a complementary and consistent manner to support the chosen product or corporate position. Thus, a premium-quality service can be expected to yield distinctive value-added features to its customers, and should be promoted in a manner that is in keeping with its high-quality market position and attract a price that reflects its superior characteristics. Pricing must therefore be consistent with a product or corporate position, as well as achieving its financial objectives. Indeed, the two are closely inter-related. In this way, strategies in respect of the use of price must align with the wider marketing strategy. However, any such adjustments must be made by paying due regard to overall product positioning and not be used superficially in response to possible tactical pressures. At the very outset of a new product's life it can be helpful to consider the options shown in Figure 12.5 with regard to pricing strategies.

Consideration of the four options presented in Figure 12.5 needs to pay due regard to product characteristics, such as the degree and value of any competitive advantages it enjoys, as well as market characteristics, such as the likely timescale over which demand may be expected to materialize. It also depends upon the expectations of the company with regard to return-on-investment.

		Promotion	
		High	Low
Price	High	Rapid skimming	Slow skimming
	Low	Rapid penetration	Slow penetration

Figure 12.5 New product: pricing strategies.

An aspect of pricing strategy that is often a source of contention concerns the relationship between prices charged to new, as opposed to existing, customers. In effect, this is a further variant of the price differentiation discussed earlier in this chapter. This practice is especially common in the field of savings, loans and credit, and poses real dilemmas. Take the case of savings deposit accounts. It is commonplace for deposit-takers to offer higher rates of interest to new depositors than those that apply to existing depositors.

Arguably, the premium rates frequently offered to new depositors are unsustainably high and imply a degree of cross-subsidy on the part of current depositors (sometimes referred to as the 'book'), or that, in due course, the rate offered to the new depositors will be reduced to a substantially lower rate of interest. In effect, the advantageous price offered to new customers is an example of promotional pricing and is a variant of the rapid penetration strategy shown in Figure 12.5. A similar approach can often be observed when new credit-card customers are offered, say, a zero rate of interest for the first 6 months. In the mortgage market, it is commonplace for new mortgage borrowers to be offered lower repayment interest rates for a period of time.

In the early part of this decade, the Nationwide Building Society adopted what it considered to be the highly ethical stance of having no differential pricing between new and existing borrowers and depositors (see Case study 12.1). As a result, its deposit products tend not to appear in any of the best-deal tables promoted in the consumer financial press. This has had a detrimental impact upon Nationwide's market share. However, when presented as a weighted rate to savers over a longer timeframe – say 3–5 years – Nationwide compares favourably with its peers. Thus the company has adopted what it considers to be a responsible and morally correct pricing strategy, and hopes that consumers will recognize this and take a long-term view of interest rates.

Case study 12.1   Nationwide Building Society's pricing philosophy

Far from being a building society purely focused on mortgages and savings, Nationwide competes effectively across all aspects of the financial services market, including current accounts, credit cards and personal loans.

Nationwide's approach to its customers is based firmly on the fundamental beliefs it holds as a mutual organization. It delivers best value to its membership by providing financial services products with competitive interest rates

Case study 12.1   Nationwide Building Society's pricing philosophy—cont'd

and lower fees and charges, and this is all underpinned by a policy of fairness, honesty and transparency. It has also successfully campaigned on the issues of greater transparency for credit cards, personal loans and cash-machine charges, as well as calling on the Treasury to review stamp duty.

Nationwide's approach to mortgage pricing is based on the belief that existing borrowers should not have to pay higher interest rates to subsidize the lower rates offered to new customers – as is common amongst many of its competitors. This fair and transparent approach means that new and existing customers have access to the same great-value products, which are generally at market-leading rates. They also have the reassurance of knowing that any fees and charges are kept to a minimum and, where they are necessary, these are competitive, fair, and disclosed upfront.

Savings rates offered by Nationwide are subject to a similar philosophy, and are underpinned by the same brand beliefs of honesty, transparency and fairness. The Society is committed to offering competitive savings rates that represent long-term value. Nationwide, unlike many of its competitors in the savings arena, does not offer 'flash-in-the-pan' introductory bonuses or place unreasonably restrictive caveats on its products. All of Nationwide's customers have access to a wide choice of fixed- and variable-rate savings products, and these are available across a choice of branch, postal and Internet channels. All are simple to understand and use.

Nationwide has recently launched several products across the savings and insurance fields aimed at the 'silver generation'; these demonstrate its commitment to delivering good value and are designed to meet the needs of the older age group.

It has also begun campaigning on the issue of children's savings, and in December 2005 issued its Children's Savings report. The report carries with it an action plan which Nationwide believes will help to change attitudes to saving and the way people manage their finances. It calls upon the government to do more to encourage people to save, and to promote the benefits of starting from a young age.

Investment products are also offered through its wholly-owned subsidiary, Nationwide Investment Group. The products have no initial charges and a low annual management charge – both of which set them apart in the marketplace. NIG aims to offer customers competitive annual management charges across the range of products, and strives to ensure that its pricing is both fair and unique in the marketplace.

Some might think that having a policy of not offering introductory bonuses or overly-inflated headline rates would stop Nationwide from appearing at the top of many best-buy tables. While it is acknowledged that many other players manipulate their accounts and rates to ensure that they appear in best-buy tables on a regular basis, this doesn't show the bigger picture to the consumer. Will the once attractive rate simply slide away to obscurity and be managed down? How will the customer service and experience stack up? Recently, the compilers of

Continued

> **Case study 12.1   Nationwide Building Society's pricing philosophy—cont'd**
>
> these tables have started applying a different (and some might say fairer) approach, and in doing so seem to be making some progress towards quietly illustrating that taking a snapshot of just one feature of a product isn't always a good guide to the longer term. Hopefully, in the future more tables will start to reflect products that offer a good, consistent rate over a period of time – and when that happens, Nationwide will appear even more frequently.
>
> *Source: Stuart Bernau, Commercial & Communications Director,*
> *Nationwide Building Society.*

In practice, many consumers choose not to take a long-term view and are attracted by headline rates offered to them as new customers. Once the promotional pricing period is over, buyer inertia sets in and the customer reverts to a lower rate (having become part of 'the book'). Alternatively, some consumers become serial new customer deal-chasers (sometimes referred to pejoratively as 'rate tarts'). These customers take advantage of special offers on credit cards and deposit accounts, in particular, to gain maximum advantage.

It is interesting to observe the ways in which financial services companies are emulating the promotional pricing approaches encountered in the packaged-goods and high-street retail domains. In December 2005, HSBC used heavyweight promotional displays to communicate a range of price-based promotions with the banner headline: *'Up to Half Price Sale and other Great Offers'*. The body copy of the promotional leaflet presented the special price promotions as a 'sale' that started on 28 December 2005 and ended on 31 January 2006. It included a special promotion on mortgages that offered:

Up to 50 per cent off, We've reduced our six-month fixed rate mortgage by a massive 50 per cent – down from 5.30 per cent to 2.69 per cent for borrowings up to £100 000. Taking up this offer is quick and easy, but hurry – it's only available while stocks last.

In a somewhat similar vein, Scottish Widows had an in-store promotion in Lloyds TSB branches promoting:

Save 50 per cent on initial charges for lump sum ISA Investments. From 1 February 2006 to 30 April 2006, Scottish Widows is offering a 50 per cent discount on the initial charge for lump sum ISA investments.

Not to be outdone, Sainsbury's had an in-store display showing a special promotion on loans with the headline of:

Loan sale. Best ever instore rate. 6.1 per cent APR (typical). Ends 31 March. There's never been a better time to borrow money. That's because the

Sainsbury's bank loan sale is on now, offering you our best ever instore rate at just 6.1 per cent APR typical. But hurry, this offer ends 31 March.

And so we see the financial services sector endeavouring to mimic the promotional approaches more typical of the mainstream consumer goods and retail markets. Senior management of banks have often commented that they consider themselves to be in the retail market and have recruited staff from the traditional retail sector. Perhaps the above examples are evidence of those new recruits seeking to transfer their skills from one domain to another. The extent to which such approaches work in the financial services sector remains to be seen.

12.8   Summary and conclusions

This chapter has highlighted the importance of pricing in the marketing process. Pricing is the only element of the marketing mix that contributes to revenue rather than cost, so its importance must not be underestimated. For any organization, the pricing decision is influenced by a range of internal and external factors. Financial services organizations do face some additional challenges when dealing with pricing decisions because of the greater complexity of costing, the need to deal with risk, the problems of variability, and the difficulties that consumers have in understanding price.

Review questions

1. What role does pricing pay in the marketing mix?
2. What are the particular difficulties that marketing managers face when trying to set prices for financial services?
3. Explain the difference between implicit and explicit pricing. What are the advantages of explicit pricing?
4. Which type of pricing strategy do you consider most appropriate for banking services?
5. To what extent do you believe that the price promotion techniques of the fast-moving consumer goods and retail sector transfer to the world of the high-street bank and supermarket?

13

Distribution channels: routes-to-market

Learning objectives

By then end of this chapter you will be able to:
- understand the distinctive nature of distribution in financial services
- explain the different forms of distribution used by financial services providers
- evaluate the strengths and weaknesses of different distribution channels.

13.1 Introduction

In any marketing mix, the place component (distribution) is concerned with making sure that a product reaches the target market at a convenient time and place. In relation to physical goods, distribution decisions are concerned with both channel management and logistics. Channel management refers to all those activities involved in managing relationships between the producer and the various organizations that distribute the product (e.g. wholesalers and retailers). Logistics is concerned with the physical movement of products from the place where they were made to the place where they will be purchased. Within the consumer goods domain, retailing represents the dominant channel through which goods are purchased. This channel may operate on a direct basis by which products are shipped direct from manufacturer to consumer. Supermarkets represent the best example of the direct distribution channel for consumer goods. Alternatively, goods can be moved from site of manufacture to the site of purchase on an indirect basis. Indirect distribution channels may involve some combination of agents, brokers and wholesalers interposed between producer and retailer. The logistical dimensions of tangible-goods distribution is often referred to as supply chain management. Success in the field of tangible-goods distribution requires expertise in both the strategy and management of sales channels, and in supply chain management.

Of course, with financial services there is no physical product, so the logistics element of distribution is of little relevance. Instead, distribution in financial services marketing is concerned with how the service is delivered to the consumer, making sure that it is available in a location and at a time that is convenient for the customer. In Chapters 3 and 8 we saw the ways in which financial services products differ from tangible goods, and those differences have important implications when developing channel strategies and deciding upon routes-to-market. For example, by virtue of their intangibility, financial services do not involve the logistical aspects of supply chain management. Similarly, the characteristic of perishability obviates the need for warehousing and inventory management and control. Other important features of financial services, such as duration of consumption, uncertainty of outcome, contingent consumption, lack of transparency, consumer financial illiteracy and fiduciary responsibility, all have important implications for the distribution of financial services.

This chapter provides an overview of the nature and management of distribution for financial services. The chapter begins by exploring the distinguishing features of distribution, then moves on to examine in detail the different channels that may be used to deliver financial services to the target market and discusses their advantages and disadvantages.

13.2   Distribution: distinguishing features

As far as financial services are concerned, distribution fulfils the following roles:

1. The provision of appropriate advice and guidance regarding the suitability of specific products
2. The provision of choice and a range of product solutions to customer needs
3. The means for purchasing a product
4. The means for establishing a client relationship
5. Product sales functions
6. The provision of information concerning relevant aspects of financial services
7. Access to the administration systems and processes required for the ongoing usage (consumption) of the product or service
8. The means for managing a customer relationship over time
9. The cross-selling of additional products to existing customers.

During the course of this current chapter we will largely focus upon the ways in which distribution addresses roles 1–6 listed above. In Part III, we will devote specific attention to items 7, 8 and 9.

As a component of the marketing mix, distribution has a number of distinctive features that distinguish it from the other elements of the mix; these are discussed below.

13.2.1   Cost

The costs associated with distribution may well dwarf the combined costs of all of the other components of the mix. For example, the real-estate costs of a branch-based retail bank could well be in excess of a billion pounds sterling. Similarly, the staffing costs associated with a substantial branch network will run into several hundred million pounds. For a life assurance company, the costs associated with developing and maintaining a direct sales-force of scale will incur an annual operating cost well in excess of a hundred million pounds.

The use of the Internet may appear to offer dramatic cost savings to a potential new entrant to the banking or insurance sector. However, these savings may well be nullified by the heavy costs associated with marketing communications and promotion aimed at generating awareness and demand, and establishing trust and credibility. Clearly, the costs associated with channel strategy have major implications for pricing and profitability.

13.2.2   Timescale

The development of certain channels can take a considerable period of time to come to fruition. Obvious examples of this are the timescales associated with the creation of a branch infrastructure or of a direct sales-force of scale. Similarly, once entered into, the timescales associated with certain third-party distribution arrangements can place limitations on strategic options over a protracted period of time.

13.2.3   New business strain and capital requirements

The costs associated with the distribution and set-up of a range of investment-related products can impose significant pressure upon capital. Take the case of personal pensions. A new personal pension policy may well not achieve its break-even point until the policy has been in force for many years. Until break-even point is achieved, each policy sold will represent a deficit in cash flow terms to the product provider. This deficit is referred to as *new business strain*, and an appropriate amount of capital is required to finance the strain until a surplus begins to be generated.

Thus, product features and the costs associated with certain channels of distribution will have major implications for capital. This, in turn, will influence the structure of the product range, the source of product supply and the method of distribution. For example, in 1999 Barclays took the decision to cease being the sole supplier of its life assurance and pensions products and entered into an agreement with Legal and General for the manufacture of such products. Whilst Barclays would of course forego the underwriting profits arising from these products in the long term, the change would reduce the need for capital to fund the associated new business strain. Thus, Barclays could enhance its internal return-on-capital or divert the capital thereby saved into other potentially more attractive aspects of its business – such as, say, business banking.

13.2.4 Contractual arrangements

The involvement of third parties in the distribution of an organization's products may require a commitment to a contract term lasting a number of years. Whilst this can facilitate a degree of certainty and assist in long-term planning, it does involve a degree of inflexibility during the term of the contract.

13.2.5 Loss of control

Product providers who distribute their products through third parties, such as insurance brokers, finance brokers and appointed representatives, risk being unable to exert the required degree of control regarding consistency amongst all distribution channel members. This may result in damage to the product provider's reputation should a material degree of customer dissatisfaction arise. Additionally, it may add to costs if sub-standard documentation occurs, and can weaken the quality of an overall book of business if a broker introduces relatively poor-value customers to the provider.

As an aside, the UK pensions mis-selling scandal saw product providers having to accept full responsibility for compensation in cases where policies had been mis-sold through sales agents directly in their employ. However, consumers who had been mis-sold by IFAs had to seek redress from the IFAs concerned. In such cases, product providers could not be deemed to be in a position to have controlled the selling practices of IFAs.

13.2.6 Interdependencies with other mix elements

The choice of which routes-to-market to employ has potentially far-reaching implications for all other elements of the marketing mix. These implications arise in the form of capability, resources and costs and, amongst other factors, timing and responsiveness.

For example, a general insurance company planning to adopt a purely Internet-based method of distribution might, at least in theory, have the opportunity for a highly competitive pricing structure. However, such a strategy means that the organization restricts its potential market solely to individuals that have ready access to the Internet and are willing to transact their insurance requirements in this way. It also results in the need to have well-developed skills and competencies with regard to the use of the promotional mix. Esure is a good example of a new general insurance brand that has adopted this approach to the distribution of its products. The company is having to invest heavily in a range of high-profile forms of marketing communications in order to create awareness and stimulate purchase. This has included a major television campaign featuring movie director Michael Winner, together with poster advertising in places such as the London Underground system and press advertising.

The case of telesales as a channel of distribution places heavy demands upon the *people* and *process* elements of the mix. It may also be co-ordinated with a major investment in the use of direct mail as a means of both stimulating inbound enquiries for quotations as well as fulfilling post-quotation requirements. This calls for significant expertise in the use of direct mail and, possibly, direct-response advertising in the press.

13.2.7   Product interface

There is an extremely close relationship between product characteristics and route-to-market. It is in the very nature of certain products that they lend themselves to certain types of channel or, indeed, rule out other options. Pensions are a classic case of the need for a channel strategy that involves face-to-face interaction between customer and seller/adviser (not necessarily product provider). For a number of reasons, consumers appear, for the most part, to be unwilling to buy a personal pension on a remote basis via the Internet, direct response or, indeed, telesales. Issues concerning trust, uncertainty of outcome, timescale for delivery of outcome, and consumer financial illiteracy mean that the consumer feels a strong need to be advised by a suitably qualified individual in a face-to-face setting. This seems to be an obvious example of risk-reducing behaviour on the part of consumers. As yet, no pension product producer has built a book of business of any scale by relying solely on remote channels of distribution. On the other hand, motor insurance distributed via remote channels has been an enormous success. Again, this is very much a function of factors such as the greater degree of familiarity that consumers have with motor insurance and the low level of perceived risk that they associate with this type of product.

13.3   Distribution methods and models

13.3.1   Direct versus indirect distribution

Having discussed the role and characteristics of distribution, it is appropriate to crystallize the array of options available in the twenty-first century environment. It is customary to make reference to the basic paradigm of direct versus indirect channels of distribution in texts of this nature – indeed, these alternative modes of distribution have already been referred to. The concept of direct/indirect distribution is pretty straightforward and unambiguous within the context of tangible-goods markets. However, it is somewhat less straightforward as a means of addressing the major approaches for the distribution of financial services. Indeed, the use of the term *direct* in the context of financial services is liable to give rise to confusion, owing to the ambiguity with which it is used.

In purist terms, direct distribution concerns the provision of a good or service from manufacturer/provider to customer in the absence of an intermediary that is under separate ownership, management and control. Therefore, it is channel ownership rather than the structure of the distribution channel that determines whether distribution is direct or indirect. In the case of a direct route-to-market, all of the steps involved in acquiring a customer and selling a product are owned by the product provider. Indirect distribution, on the other hand, involves the use of agents of one form or another that are owned by a third-party organization. As can be imagined, direct distribution facilitates a far greater degree of control over the customer experience than does indirect distribution. However, that degree of control may be bought at the price of a lower level of sales than might occur if some form of indirect distribution is employed. A range of factors must be considered when addressing the issue of direct versus indirect distribution, and these are summarized below.

Direct distribution

The advantages and disadvantages of direct distribution are as follows.

Potential advantages:
- Control of brand values
- Control of customer experience
- Control of corporate reputation
- The maintenance of competitive advantage from unique products and features
- Control of regulatory obligations
- Freedom of action
- Strategic flexibility
- Clarity and consistency of internal communication.

Potential disadvantages:
- Direct distribution limits distribution coverage
- It restricts sales volumes
- It limits market share
- Requires considerable amount of capital.

Indirect distribution

In many ways the potential advantages and disadvantages of indirect distribution are the obverse of those given above. However, it is helpful to see them presented as a discrete list.

Potential advantages:
- The provider can focus on core competencies, of which distribution may not be one
- The ability to focus on product quality and costs
- The avoidance of set-up costs associated with new forms of distribution
- Allows for rapid penetration of markets, nationally and internationally
- Access to higher sales volumes may result in lower aggregate costs that could feed into enhanced price competitiveness
- The added cachet of having products distributed by high-profile intermediaries with strong brand reputations
- Flexibility to experiment with new sales channels within limited cost parameters
- It may limit access to marketplace by competitors
- It can enable provider and major distributors to test a working partnership that could ultimately result in a merger
- Can reduce need for capital.

Potential disadvantages:
- Lengthy and variable communication arrangements can slow down reactions to tactical events

Table 13.1 UK sources of general insurance premiums, 2003

	Personal lines	Commercial lines	Marine & aviation	Total
National brokers	10	54	88	31
Chain brokers and telebrokers	5	5	–	5
Other independent intermediaries	16	24	4	19
Direct	32	7	6	21
Company staff	3	1	–	2
Company agents	5	5	2	5
Other	28	3	–	16

Source: ABI Statistical Bulletin.

- Loss of control over brand values, customer experience and reputation
- Regulatory risks
- Long-term distribution contracts can limit strategic options
- Indirect distribution can result in undue reliance on dominant distributors.

Elements of direct and indirect distribution models are to be encountered in most areas of financial services. However, some areas display a greater tendency towards one than others. For example, retail banking remains overwhelmingly direct. Life Assurance has become increasingly indirect in the UK – indeed, in the 12 months to 31 December 2003 some 66 per cent of new individual life and pensions business was accounted for by IFAs. If we add to this the business introduced by tied agents, the proportion is of the order of 80 per cent. It is important to note that certain product categories within an aggregate financial services sector display a marked bias towards either direct or indirect distribution. Table 13.1 shows the ways in which this bias is displayed in the general insurance sector.

13.3.2 Whether products are bought or sold

Before presenting an overview of currently available distribution methods, it is important to grasp the thorny issue of whether financial products are bought or sold. This issue is of fundamental significance to the marketing of financial services, and was initially discussed in Chapter 7.

Although the needs expressed for the range of financial services are easily understood and readily appreciated, the motivation on the part of consumers to engage in proactive product search and buying behaviour is more muted. We can all grasp the benefits of enhanced income in retirement from buying a pension, or the security a family gains when the breadwinner buys a critical illness insurance policy. However, the level of expressed demand and proactive purchasing behaviour is of a relatively low order. A range of factors is implicated in this reluctance, not least of which is affordability. Additionally, there is the opportunity cost to current consumption of other more pleasure-inducing goods and services. Undoubtedly there are circumstances in which the consumer does actively seek to buy; this is most apparent with mortgages and motor insurance. In the latter example, there can be simply a legal obligation for motor vehicle owners to ensure they have at least third-party insurance cover.

Whilst it is certainly the case that some products are predominantly *bought* whilst others fall more generally into the category of being *sold*, it is far from a product-specific issue. Rather, it is a complex and multi-faceted matter which involves the interplay of product, customer and situational considerations. An individual might proactively *buy* into, say, a mutual fund on one occasion; equally, he or she might well decide to make an unplanned purchase on another occasion as a result of proactive sales activity on the part of a product provider or intermediary.

A financial services sector based purely upon products distributed to proactive buyers would be of a materially smaller scale than one that engages in proactive selling. It is in the interests of all parties (consumers, providers, intermediaries, regulators and governments) that proactive sales activity is fully appropriate to the customer's circumstances. In other words, great care must be taken to ensure that the rights of all parties are respected. It is similarly important that all parties are aware of their responsibilities, and act in ways that are commensurate with those responsibilities.

Although the role played by intermediaries is notable within the context of life and general insurance, indirect channels play an important role in other areas, including:

- mortgages
- credit cards
- secured loans
- unsecured loans
- health insurance
- creditor protection insurance
- hire purchase
- share dealing.

13.4   Distribution channels

There is a diversity of channels used in the distribution of financial services. These include the following:

- Specialist financial services branch outlets, such as banks, building society branch offices, credit union offices
- Non-financial services retailers, such as supermarkets, electrical goods, motor dealers, clothes shops, department stores
- Quasi-financial services outlets, such as post offices, real estate agents
- Face-to-face sales channels, such as financial advisers, direct sales-forces, credit brokers, insurance agents
- Bancassurance
- Telephone selling via both outbound and inbound call-centres

- The Internet
- Direct mail
- Direct-response advertising, including newspapers and magazines, commercial radio and television
- Affinity groups, such as employers, trades unions, football clubs, universities.

The above methods of distribution are described below.

13.4.1   Specialist financial services branch outlets

The branch outlet has until recently been the dominant means of gaining access to the mainstream products associated with banking and mortgages. In this context, the branch has performed the dual roles of acting as a retail outlet in which buying and selling activities could take place as well as providing a range of processing functions to facilitate the ongoing administration of products. The importance of the branch network in retail banking is evidenced by the fact that there are very few banks worldwide which operate without a branch network. For example, HDFC Bank in India draws attention to the rapid development of its branch network as a key factor behind its successful market-penetration strategy. However, with the development of bancassurance, bank branches have become orientated more towards being product sales outlets and less involved in administrative functions. This transition from the branch as essentially a customer services outlet to being a customer sales outlet has not been without its difficulties. For established branch networks, the culture of the branch has had to undergo a major transformation as staff have had to adapt to a new sales-orientated role – a process which many traditional bank staff find challenging (Sturdy and Morgan, 1993).

The branch itself is a complex environment. It is an area where consumers make routine transactions, staff may try to make sales and a range of back office tasks have to be accomplished. Traditional branch designs placed very heavy emphasis on back-office processing, and the traditional bank branch provided a relatively unwelcoming environment. Recent developments in branch design have placed much greater emphasis on ensuring a customer-friendly environment and increasing the amount of space available for customers. Thus, banks rely on open-plan layouts and decoration which is themed according to the bank's corporate identity. For example, Standard Chartered's new 'Financial Spas' dedicate the majority of floor space to customers, the branch is softly lit and it has reading materials, comfortable seats, computer terminals and television screens.

Many banks have also introduced 'zoning'. This means that the floor area is divided up so that there are distinct areas for particular types of banking transaction. Thus, for example, a bank may decided to have a separate 'self-service' area for basic money transmission, balance enquiries, etc., often relying only on ATMS. A different area of the branch will then be dedicated to standard products such as account opening, credit-card applications and basic loans. Finally, a third area may be set aside for customers looking for more complex products requiring detailed discussions with a member of the branch staff.

Many banks are also looking to expand the range of services available via the branch in order to make more efficient use of their network. Again, a prime example is

Standard Chartered's Financial Spa, which is presented as a one-stop financial management centre or 'financial supermarket'.

The advantages and disadvantages associated with specialist financial services branch outlets as a means of acquiring customers are summarized below:

Advantages associated with specialist financial branch outlets as a means of new customer acquisition are that they:

- represent physical evidence of intangible services
- provide reassurance and represent solidity of the provider
- give confidence to customers that they can gain access to services features and help
- achieve reinforced awareness of brand
- provide access to face-to-face service and advice
- allow complex transactions to be easily conducted
- facilitate easy deposit and withdrawal of cash and cheques
- are particularly effective as a means of selling complicated products
- are highly effective as a means of achieving so called 'cross-selling', i.e. selling additional products to existing customers.

Disadvantages associated with branch outlets are that:

- rural and poor communities are often poorly served
- limited opening hours restrict access to services
- branch geography is based on historical usage patterns
- they have high costs
- pressure on staff to achieve cross-sale targets can cause customer dissatisfaction.

13.4.2 Non-financial services retailers (NFSRs)

A wide range of retail outlets has some involvement in the distribution of financial services as an adjunct to their core business. Some of these outlets are involved in the direct distribution of their own manufactured products, whereas others act as agents for third-party product providers. Additionally, some retailers are hybrids in that they distribute their own products (direct) as well as products manufactured by other providers on an agency basis. A characteristic of most forms of NFSRs is that financial services are not their core business. Table 13.2 provides some examples of typical NFSRs' variants.

In the UK, supermarkets such as Tesco and Sainsbury have established their own banking subsidiaries and have acted as catalysts for greater competition in the market for current and deposit accounts. Other forms of retailer have provided various forms of finance, such as hire purchase, for many years – indeed, for many it represents a significant source of margin. However, being a non-core part of the mainstream business places certain limitations on the scope of financial services that can be distributed in this way. For example, services tend to be a single product provided by a single provider, such as car finance distributed via an automobile dealership. In this case, motor vehicle finance is viewed by the consumer as a credible adjunct to the dealer's own business of automobile sales. The resonance between a car dealership and automobile finance is reasonably viewed as being salient,

Table 13.2 Typical NFSRs' variants

Retail outlet	Typical financial services distributed
Supermarkets	Current banking accounts, general insurance: motor, health, holiday, unsecured loans, credit cards
Motor dealers	Car loans, creditor protection insurance
Home improvement companies	Finance, creditor protection insurance
Electrical goods retailers	Hire purchase, extended warranties, creditor protection insurance
Department stores and clothes-retailing chains	Own-label credit cards
Furniture outlets	Hire purchase, creditor protection insurance

or representing a good fit. However, the relationship between a car dealership and other forms of financial services may not be viewed as having the same degree of saliency. For example, if the car dealership was considering selling, say, mutual funds, consumers might be expected to be somewhat resistant because the product (mutual funds) is not readily associated with the provider (car dealer).

The issue of brand saliency plays a role in the case of supermarkets. They have made material progress in distributing relatively straightforward products, such as motor and holiday insurance, but have yet to register a significant breakthrough as a vehicle for distributing products such as pensions and investments. It is interesting to speculate on why major retailer branches have stretched into simple financial services products but not, as yet, into the more challenging areas of financial services. The answer to this issue may have less to do with brand saliency than with the issue of whether products are bought or sold. Arguably, brands such as Virgin, Tesco and Sainsbury can stretch successfully into product areas characterized by the *bought* mode of acquisition, but do not yet have the capability to operate effectively in the *sold* mode.

There is evidence from research by Devlin (2003) that consumers are willing to place their trust in brands that are primarily not financial services-orientated as a source of financial products. This suggests that, at least in the UK, non-traditional financial services brands could leverage their brand associations into the financial services arena. However, the extent to which brand saliency or selling capability lies at the heart of the current limitations on the penetration of major retailing and consumer brands into complex financial services product areas is as yet unclear.

Advantages of NFSRs as a means of new customer acquisition are that:
- well-respected consumer brands can create high levels of trust and imply value and dependability
- the physical branch presence facilitates low-cost promotional displays
- the branch facilitates access to help and assistance
- face-to-face help can be provided at relatively low marginal cost
- in their role as intermediaries, they can provide access to high volumes of new customers
- they are well-suited to the distribution of complementary products (e.g. car finance via car dealers
- they can be a relatively low cost means of distribution.

Disadvantages of NFSRs are that:

- they may not be seen as credible providers of financial advice
- they may not be seen as credible providers of complex products such as pensions, mortgages and investment funds
- loss of control over quality of business is introduced
- there is loss of control over the quality of the customer experience
- there are the potentially high costs of commission paid to introducers
- over-dependence on high-volume producing agents can make a supplier vulnerable.

13.4.3   Quasi-financial services outlets (QFSOs)

This term refers to channels that, whilst not being traditional financial services outlets, have a strong affinity with them. The best examples of QFSOs are post offices and real-estate agents. Throughout the world, post offices are often the channel through which state social security payments are made, and this positions them as having a money transmission role. As well as making cash payments of state benefits, post offices are typically used for providing access to state-owned savings institutions such as National Savings & Investments in the UK. Thus, they may well be limited in their ability to distribute products supplied by the private sector. However, in an era of deregulation of financial markets worldwide, this may become less of a hurdle in the future. Japan is considering privatizing its postal system, and this could well create new opportunities for the private sector to gain access to the post-office channel.

We consider real-estate agents as QFSOs rather than NFSRs because of the complex nature of real-estate finance. The financing of a real-estate purchase involves, potentially, the interplay of a range of complex financial products, including: mortgages, endowment insurance schemes, life protection policies, pensions and critical illness insurance. Thus, the real-estate channel has the potential to be a highly profitable method of customer acquisition, given the bundle of products that can be packaged together. Indeed, this was an important part of the rationale of major banks and insurance companies acquiring real-estate chains in the late 1980s and early 1990s. Many of those acquisitions foundered as the new owners failed properly to value the chains they acquired and recognize the competencies needed to run businesses that were outside their previous experience. Unfortunately, it also coincided with a dramatic recession in the UK housing market.

Advantages of QFSOs as a means of new customer acquisition are that:

- a highly localized branch network of post offices provides ready access to all consumers
- post offices are seen as trustworthy and secure
- post offices handle cash sums and have the systems capability for a range of money transmission options
- post offices often have extended opening hours compared with banks
- post offices can play a vital role in facilitating financial inclusion
- real-estate agents can provide access to high-value sales opportunities
- branch outlets are conducive to face-to-face advice and assistance.

Disadvantages of QRSOs are that:

- although well-suited to simple products, QFSOs may be less suited to the distribution of complex products where advice may be required
- there is often a lack of privacy which consumers find inhibits the nature of their transactions
- there is often limited space for effective point-of-sale promotion
- queues are often a feature of post offices, and this inhibits their usefulness as distribution outlets
- real-estate agents often suffer from a poor reputational image which may undermine consumer trust
- real-estate firms are often led by strong local characters with a highly independent approach
- there is the potential for loss of control re. compliance with regulations and customer experience.

13.4.4   Face-to-face sales channels

Direct sales-forces have been the backbone of the life assurance industry throughout the world for decades. However, their role, culture and style of working have changed radically as more and more markets are adopting strict standards of regulation. For example, during the 1980s it was estimated that in excess of 200 000 people in the UK were registered with the then regulator of life assurance direct sales-forces (LAUTRO; the Life Assurance and Unit Trust Regulatory Organization). By the turn of the last millennium, this number had reduced dramatically to fewer than 20 000.

Historically, a key driver of the direct sales-force model was the notion that life assurance, investment and pension products had, fundamentally, to be sold rather than be bought. Although there is undoubtedly a given level of business that is *bought*, the adherents to the *sold* model argue that it is in the nature of life, pension and investment products that a significant element of demand is latent rather then expressed. The primary role of the direct sales-force is to turn latent demand into real new business through its capability to prospect for new customers. Thus, the capacity of a direct sales-force to work as a powerful means of prospecting has been seen as key to its success. Often referred to as 'a numbers game', the traditional prospecting direct sales-force was underpinned by a funnel model shown in Figure 13.1.

It has not been uncommon for the ratio of suspects to prospects to customers to be of the order of 100 : 10 : 1 – i.e. it takes 100 suspects to produce 10 prospects leading to just 1 customer. Hence, direct selling has sometimes been seen as essentially a numbers game. The more skilful the individual salesman, the narrower the angle of the sales funnel. Until the rigours of financial regulation and control began to take effect, the direct sales-force was driven to increase its headcount year-on-year since, so the theory went, the bigger the sales-force, the greater the sales volumes. Unsurprisingly, direct sales-forces can often display extremely high staff turnover rates. Indeed, in the UK in the late 1980s it was often in excess of 40 per cent per annum. Thus, a company with a direct sales-force of 3000 advisers would have to

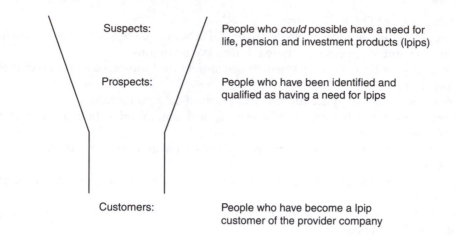

Figure 13.1 The prospecting funnel.

recruit 1200 new salesmen per annum (assuming a 40 per cent turnover rate) just to stand still. As can be imagined, the recruitment of 100 new salesmen each and every month is a challenging task. For this reason, sales managers would spend a disproportionate amount of time sourcing new recruits relative to the time spent training and developing their existing salesmen and women.

Such a model is clearly highly inefficient, and has resulted in unsustainably high distribution costs. It is a model which is predicated by the notion that life, pension and investment products are fundamentally sold rather than bought, and results in the costs associated with overall prospecting activities being borne by the customer who actually buys. Thus, in the example of the prospecting funnel given earlier, the costs associated with the 99 people who do not buy are loaded onto the single person who does. This had resulted in distribution-related costs that have been criticized for delivering poor customer value.

The means by which direct sales-forces are remunerated has been the subject of much controversy and debate. In essence there are two basic approaches, namely commission, or salary plus bonus. However, a number of variations based upon these two basic approaches are to be found. In the commission-based approach, the salesperson receives payment purely on the basis of sales made. Thus, an individual who works diligently but fails to make a sale will receive no income. This may well seem to benefit the provider company, since it results in the avoidance of certain overhead costs associated with the sales-force. Critics of this method of remuneration argue that it places undue pressure upon the salesperson to make a sale, which in turn results in coercive sales practices to the detriment of the consumer interest (Diacon and Ennew, 1996).

Adherents of the salary-based model argue that this method of remuneration is more consistent with present-day employment philosophies by recognizing the professionalism of the salesperson. Importantly, it is argued that a salaried approach reduces the pressure on the salesperson to make a sale, and that this in turn results in better quality of business and greater levels of customer satisfaction. However, the costs associated with time spent prospecting still have to be paid for, and these costs are loaded onto the customer who buys in much the same way as in the commission-based approach. Arguably, the costs are even higher in the salaried model than in the commission-based model since it results in a higher level of fixed cost to the provider.

The discussion regarding remuneration so far assumes that the advisory function provided by the salesperson is available free of charge to prospective customers. A contrary point of view is that financial advice should be seen to be a professional service in much the same way as the advice given by a lawyer or an accountant. Accordingly, the argument runs that prospective customers should be offered the opportunity to pay a fee for advice, whether or not they subsequently make a purchase. Ultimately, it is presumed that the distribution costs loaded into product charges will fall as actual purchasers are relieved of the cost burden associated with prospecting activities. This may well sound good in theory, but in practice the vast majority of domestic consumers and business customers are, as yet, unwilling to pay up-front fees for advice. This seems odd, given that consumers seem increasingly willing to pay arrangement fees (frequently of the order of £600) for a wide range of mortgages. Clearly this is a complex matter concerning human attitudes, perceptions and behaviours.

In 2005, changes to the sales polarization rules in the UK resulted in IFAs having to offer their customers the opportunity to choose to pay either an up-front fee for advice or receive 'free advice' on the understanding that it will be paid for in the commission that the product provider pays to the IFA.

There are instances where salespeople are paid purely on the basis of a flat-rate salary with no sales-value or volume-related bonus. The advantages claimed for this approach are that it frees the salesperson from any pressure to sell and results in good-quality sales and high levels of customer satisfaction. However, the prevailing corporate orthodoxy maintains that some degree of incentive is necessary to encourage high performance, and thus remuneration based upon sales results remains the norm.

Since the early 1990s there has been a sharp reduction in the proportion of direct salespeople who are remunerated purely by commission, and a commensurate increase in the proportion who are salary-based. This has forced the companies concerned to become far more professional in their approach and achieve significant improvements in the productivity levels that are achieved by the sales-force. This latter point is of great importance, as the average number of sales of the typical direct sales-force in the early 1990s was in the order of one sale per person per week. In practice, a small cadre of highly productive salespeople were achieving well in excess of one sale per week, and a disproportionately large group of individuals were woefully unproductive – the so-called 'tail' of the sales-force.

It is worth commenting a little upon the cultural differences that apply to commission and salaried direct sales-forces, since they have far-reaching implications. Commission-based sales organizations revere high-performing individuals and have been accused of almost encouraging the cult of the sales prima donna. Such organizations position the role of the salesperson as a self-employed business person who enjoys considerable freedom to act. In extreme cases, salespeople enjoy the freedom to organize their work very much as an independent contractor.

The value of what are termed 'renewal commissions' can be commuted to achieve a capital value that high-performing advisers can realize in much the same way as small entrepreneurs can sell their business and realize a capital gain. Notwithstanding the rigours of regulation, self-employed commission-based sales advisers set their own target regarding sales performance at a level that satisfies their personal lifestyle aspirations. They are often disdainful of their sales managers, who they consider to be their inferiors in the highly-charged field of life assurance sales.

The culture of the salary-based direct sales-force represents a far more controlled business environment. As an employee, the individual salesperson is expected to conform to the values, style and processes of the employer company in much the same way as other employee, such as those working in administration or IT. A more traditional approach to the managerial hierarchy is in evidence, whereby top-performing advisers are not encouraged to feel that they have a direct line to the Chief Executive. Importantly, strict standards are laid down for the achievement of input-orientated performance, such as the number of appointments carried out per day or per week.

It is appropriate to make some additional comments regarding independent financial advisers. This form of face-to-face distribution has become the dominant form of distribution for a number of products in the UK. In principle, the IFA is viewed as the agent of the consumer. This contrasts with Appointed and Company Representatives (ACRs), who are deemed to be the agents of the provider company. As a result, IFAs are viewed as having a particular duty of care to provide the best-possible outcome for the client's needs from the full spectrum of product providers in the marketplace. Box study 13.1 provides an overview of the IFA sector in the UK.

Box 13.1   IFAs in the UK

IFAs are organized in a number of ways, from large national sales-forces down to one-man bands. According to information supplied by Matrix-Data Ltd, the IFA domain was structured as follows as at mid-2004:

IFA type	Total no. of firms
Nationals	109
Big IFAs	235
Regionals	560
Small IFAs	11 207
Total	12 111

The trade association representing IFAs is AIFA, and it estimates that in the order of 25 000–30 000 individual financial advisers are employed by the 12 111 firms shown above. New rules regarding the provision of financial advice were introduced in June 2005, related to a regulatory initiative termed *de-polarization*. The practical effect has been to replace the clear demarcation between fully independent and tied advice with the addition of multi-tied agents

> **Box 13.1 IFAs in the UK—cont'd**
>
> (referred to earlier in this chapter). The early indications are that IFAs are, by and large, choosing to remain fully independent. However, under the new rules IFAs have to allow the customer the opportunity to pay a fee for advice as an alternative to product-loaded commissions. A firm choosing not to offer the advice fee option will no longer be able to call itself an IFA; instead, it is deemed to be a 'Whole of Market Financial Adviser' (WMFA) It seems likely that these developments will serve to create an even greater degree of consumer confusion, given the following array of types of adviser.
>
> 1. IFAs:
>   - must give the most suitable advice from all the products in the marketplace
>   - must offer the customer the option to pay a fee for advice instead of a product-loaded commission.
> 2. WMFAs:
>   - must give the most suitable advice from all the products in the marketplace
>   - advice is funded purely by product-loaded commission.
> 3. Multi-tied agents:
>   - must give the most suitable advice from the products provided by their panel of supplier companies
>   - advice costs are funded by commission.
> 4. Company representatives:
>   - are contracted directly to a single supplier company, as either a salaried employee or a self-employed adviser
>   - must give the most suitable advice from the product range of their supplier company
>   - advice costs are levied on the customer in the form of a product-loaded commission.
> 5. Appointed representatives:
>   - work on behalf of a third-party intermediary distributor and not directly for the product provider
>   - may be remunerated by a commission or salary
>   - must give the most suitable advice from the product range of the supplier company
>   - advice costs are levied on the customer in form of product-loaded commission.

13.4.5 Bancassurance

As the name implies, this is a form of distribution that has its origins in France. In simple terms, it concerns the provision of life, pension and investment products by a banking organization. Indeed, in many parts of continental Europe bancassurance has become the dominant distribution channel for products of this nature – in countries such as France and Spain, bancassurance may account for 60–80 per cent of insurance sales. Bancassurance expanded rapidly in the UK between 1986 and 1992, in the immediate post-deregulation period. At that time, many industry pundits were predicting that bancassurance might capture of the order of 40 per cent of the market by the second half of the 1990s. In the event, bancassurance peaked at about 15 per cent of the UK life assurance market and has remained at about that level. Bancassurance has also become an important channel for distribution in Latin America, Singapore (where it may account for as much as 24 per cent of new life insurance sales), Australia, Malaysia, India and China. Bancassurance emerged in India at the end of the 1990s, when the life insurance sector was privatized. New insurance entrants into both India and China are using bancassurance models to compete against established insurance companies with their own extensive branch networks. Both countries are expected to display significant growth in bancassurance-based distribution over the next 10 years, partly because of the impact of foreign entrants to the domestic market and partly through the growing use of this channel by domestic insurers.

The real power of the bancassurance model derives from its ability to:
- achieve low customer acquisition costs
- maximize cross-selling opportunities
- utilize relevant customer data.

Bancassurance comprises elements of both the *bought* and *sold* aspects of customer acquisition addressed earlier. We might term these the *passive* and *active* models of bancassurance.

The passive model of bancassurance is as follows
- Step 1: A current-account customer decides to solve a financial problem by visiting the bank branch. Most typically, this will concern the need for a mortgage or loan of some kind.
- Step 2: The customer's primary need (e.g. for a mortgage) is resolved by the relevant member of the branch's staff.
- Step 3: In the example of a mortgage, some form of loan-related insurance will be required to provide security to the bank in the event of the death of the borrower before the loan is repaid. Depending upon the prevailing regulatory rules, the loan-protection may need to be transacted by a properly authorized financial adviser.
- Step 4: The financial adviser conducts a fact-find and completes the purchase of the insurance policy. In this way, the bank has gained a customer for its insurance business.

It can be readily appreciated that this passive model operates reactively to instigation by the client. Two notable consequences arise from this model. First, the mix of life, pension and investment products displays a marked bias in favour of loan-protection insurance policies. Secondly, it fails to engage that proportion of the total current account customer base which does not proactively use the branch to engage in suitable problem-solving behaviour.

These consequences were overlooked by the bullish commentators of the early 1990s, and hence their projections were completely unrealistic. Indeed, the over-reliance of bancassurance on the residential mortgage market was a critical weakness in the product sales mix, and explains why its market share fell as the housing market experienced a sharp period of decline between 1991 and 1995.

The limitations of the passive model of bancassurance gives rise to the *active* model. In this model, the bancassurer recognizes the need to achieve the dual goals of optimizing sales opportunities presented by the current-account customer base as a whole and achieving a well-balanced product sales mix.

The bancassurance model can only begin to achieve its full potential when it adopts the active model. However, this requires a different approach to the passive model, as the organization seeks to make the transition from a customer-pull method of distribution (the *bought* approach) more towards a supplier-push method (the *sold* approach). In the mid-1990s, Barclays recognized the need to adopt a more active approach to its bancassurance business. This change of approach required a well-coordinated programme of change management involving a range of initiatives such as:

- strengthening the systems, procedures and resources needed to ensure high standards of compliance with advice-related regulations
- adjusting the remuneration system to lessen reliance of advisers on the passive model
- improving the competitiveness of the product range to ensure good value for customers and give confidence to advisers
- strengthening the effectiveness of in-branch promotional activities of non-loan related products
- communicating proactively with potential customers who do not tend to visit branches
- strengthening sales management supervision to raise the work rate of the sales-force
- increasing the training given to sales advisers and the managers to build upon their skill base
- achieving higher levels of communication between the branch staff and their management and the bancassurance organization
- making better use of data held on existing bancassurance customers.

A key issue to grasp when adopting the active model of bancassurance is the relationship between the insurance and branch banking operations. Although a wide range of organizational structures is encountered, there is usually some form of structural boundary that separates the two entities of insurance and branch banking. A typical model is one in which cashiers and other branch-based customer service staff perform the role of introducer of prospective customers to the sales advisers of the bancassurance operation. Therefore, it is of paramount importance that excellent working relationships are fostered between the two. Indeed, it is the norm that branch staff have a balanced scorecard of objectives to achieve, and the bancassurance advisers should work closely with them to achieve the valuable synergies that exist. This requires a high degree of mutual understanding and respect. Organizations that fail to recognize the importance of managing the introducer–adviser interface are unlikely to succeed in achieving their aspirations for bancassurance.

When it operates effectively, bancassurance can be a highly successful means of acquiring new customers for the life, pension and investments organization of a banking institution. A typical bancassurance adviser can be expected to achieve sales productivity levels greatly in excess of the prospecting sales-forces of the stand-alone life assurance company.

Advantages of bancassurance as a means for new customer acquisition are that it:
- provides access to high volumes of good quality potential customers
- has high levels of adviser sales productivity
- has potentially lower acquisition costs than prospecting sales-forces
- is backed by the reputation of the core bank brand
- permits face-to-face advice in the branch, the home or office
- can use current account data and transactions as triggers for sales opportunities
- has potential for developing a bundled pricing approach involving bank and life, pension and investment products
- has ongoing administration synergies.

Disadvantages of bancassurance are that:
- a poor banking reputation can limit customers' willingness to buy its life, pension and investment products
- a bank brand may not convey sufficient saliency regarding certain products – i.e. may lack a degree of credibility
- overzealous telephone prospecting harms the core banking relationships
- overzealous prospecting in branch harms the core banking relationship
- face-to-face advice can be expensive for low-margin products
- the passive model fails to achieve the expected success.

13.4.6   Telephone-based distribution

The telephone has become a powerful means for the achievement of a range of purposes in the field of retail financial services. At its simplest, it can act as a cost-effective means of prospecting for potential new customers by seeking to secure sales leads. At its most complex, it can provide a fully-functional banking service. In between these two extremes sits the use of the telephone as a highly successful means of product distribution, especially for general insurance products.

During this current section we will focus primarily upon the role of the telephone as a channel of distribution in the context of new business acquisition. The role played by the telephone in managing ongoing customer relationships will be addressed in Part III of this text.

It was during the 1980s that the telephone began to assume major significance as a distribution channel in financial services; prior to that it had been employed typically as a promotional tool associated with canvassing for leads for sales people. However, as the 1980s progressed, advances in telecommunications capability and data processing facilitated a far more integrated approach to the use of the telephone as a distribution channel. Throughout the world, these advances have seen the development of a teleworking industry on an enormous scale. By 1998 the European Commission guesstimated that somewhere in the region of 1.1 million to 4 million people were employed in teleworking in the EU. The top European countries identified for teleworking were Denmark (9.7 per cent of the workforce) and the

Netherlands (9.1 per cent). Since that time telemarketing has become far more global, with major telephone call-centres established in India and other parts of Asia. Indeed, Indian-based telephone call-centres have formed the core of the fast-evolving offshore outsourcing of financial services.

Two terms that are commonly encountered in the context of telemarketing are *outbound* and *inbound*. By *outbound*, we mean that the call centre proactively seeks to make contact with people by initiating the telephone contact. This could take a variety of forms, such as cold calling from telephone lists or in response to an initial contact prompted by, say, a direct mail shot. Inbound calls, as the name implies, relate to when the call-centre responds reactively to a call initiated by the consumer. The consumer may well be calling in response to some forms of stimulus from the provider company, such as a television or magazine advertisement.

The economics of *outbound* calling have presented major difficulties. This arises from practical problems such as low daytime response rates and the relatively high incidence of engaged lines. Again, technology has helped, with the advent of the predictive dialler that automatically dials a list of numbers and presents a call to an agent only when the phone has been answered by the consumer. Even so, *outbound* calling tends to be more limited than *inbound* calling.

As a distribution channel, the telephone has been especially successful with relatively simple products such as motor insurance using the *inbound* approach. Originating in 1985, Direct Line has grown to become a major player in the direct insurance market. Direct Line has evolved its strategy in response to the growth of Internet usage, and began to distribute its products on-line in 1999.

Telephone-based distribution permits real-time person-to-person interaction without the need for expensive branch networks or direct sales-forces. However, there are limitations on the nature of business that consumers are willing to transact on this remote basis, and it remains firmly based upon relatively simple, low-risk transactions. However, there is growing use of this form of distribution for a range of investment products and services on a purely outbound basis, such as broking services and investing in wine, commodities, and the other non-mainstream asset classes. Case study 13.1 shows how telephone-based distribution channels have been used to good effect by a new entrant to the financial services sector, Kwik-Fit Insurance Services.

Case study 13.1   Kwik-Fit insurance services

Since opening its first Kwik-Fit Centre in Edinburgh back in 1971, the company has grown to become one of the world's largest independent automotive repair specialists and has established its credentials as a leading brand in the field of motoring. During 1994, Kwik-Fit came to the realization that technology in terms of advanced telephony and database management techniques provided an opportunity to address both of the strategic imperatives of defending the customer franchise and creating cross-selling possibilities. Thus, the idea of Kwik-Fit Financial Services (KFFS) was born. KFFS signalled a major form of

Continued

Case study 13.1   Kwik-Fit insurance services—cont'd

diversification for Kwik-Fit. Motor insurance was the obvious first product for KFFS, and so it set up a panel of motor insurance providers and commenced its telemarketing operations in 1995.

To begin with, KFFS created an inbound model using significant above-the-line advertising and promotion to create consumer demand-pull. It did not take KFFS long to realize that this model presented logistical and commercial challenges. First, it is difficult to plan the resources needed to handle demand-pull telemarketing when using in-house facilities, and KFFS did not wish to outsource these functions. Secondly, the cost per sale did not make economic sense. Kwik-Fit responded quickly to this experience and created a wholly new model. This involved the creation of four separate groupings of telephone call agents, namely Research, Sales, Customer Service and Claims.

The research team role contacts customers who have used a Kwik-Fit Service Centre during the previous two days. Following an assessment of satisfaction, customers are asked whether they would like to receive a quotation for motor insurance, and a positive response to this line of questioning results in a lead. The motor insurance lead and relevant customer data are transferred electronically to the sales team, which makes outbound sales calls.

This new model has proved to be a great success solving the problems of resourcing and cost encountered in the earlier phase. Initially, the research team contacted some 5000 customers each day; more recently, the company has adopted a more precisely targeted approach by only telephoning those customers to whom it believes it can offer a competitive deal. By using this research encounter to obtain leads, Kwik-Fit has driven down the cost of customer acquisition dramatically. At the same time, it can manage sales call resourcing much more efficiently through the adoption of an outbound approach. This business model is an example of a service organization leveraging a real source of competitive advantage to achieve what in Ansoff's terms is a strategy of product development. An unexpected spin-off from this research–lead–outbound call process was a material level of inbound requests for quotations as a consequence of word-of-mouth advocacy by 'delighted' customers.

So successful has this new business acquisition model become that the company has ceased all forms of demand-pull advertising and promotion. Its sole form of publicity is advertising in Yellow Pages. As at the end of 2005, some 75 per cent of KFFS' new customers were sourced from the Kwik-Fit Service Centres, an additional 15 per cent originated via the directories, and the remaining 10 per cent via the Internet.

The third call agent grouping concerns customer service, and has the role of dealing with inbound customer service requirements such as a change of address or including an additional driver on the policy. Customer service call agents also have objectives – to generate leads to cross-sell other products which have now been added to the KFFS portfolio, including breakdown insurance, home contents and buildings insurance. In addition to general insurance products, the company also sells life assurance as an Appointed Representative

Case study 13.1   Kwik-Fit insurance services—cont'd

of Legal & General. A further broadening of the product range concerns an arrangement the company has developed with Scottish Power to sell gas and electricity on its behalf. Again, calls are monitored frequently to ensure the quality of the call-agent–customer dialogue. The fourth team is responsible for the initial handling of claims in response to inbound customer contact. However, the actual claims management process is handed-off to the individual insurance companies.

KFFS has faced ever more intense competition from a widening variety of sources, including supermarkets and on-line brands such as Esure and the HBOS subsidiary Sheilas' Wheels. It might be imagined that Direct Line poses the single most important threat. However, Direct Line does not have KFFS' competitive advantage of low-cost acquisition via the nationwide Kwik-Fit Service Centre network. Direct Line would appear to be pursuing a somewhat selective customer recruitment policy, given that it underwrites its own policies. KFFS, on the other hand has an altogether more inclusive approach based upon its strategy of acting as an intermediary to a range of underwriting companies.

Now in its eleventh year of operation, it is estimated that KFFS has built an in-force book of more than 500 000 policies, and for the last financial year it posted an operating profit of £6.8m. Its operation has grown to comprise some 800 employees, and it is considering further product range extensions. The company is believed to have the largest insurance outbound telephone marketing operation based in the UK. Moreover, KFFS has been rated as one of the UK's best 100 companies to work for some four years in a row.

Source: Martin Oliver, Chief Executive, Kwik-Fit Financial Services.

Advantages of telephone-based distribution channels as a means for new customer acquisition are that it:

- avoids the high cost of a branch infrastructure
- is very flexible and can offer 24/7 access
- allows real time person-to-person interaction
- lends itself to third-party administration (TPA) and outsourcing as a means of further reducing costs
- complements direct-mail and other forms of direct-response promotions
- makes good use of existing customer relationship and databases as part of a cross-selling strategy.

Disadvantages of telephone-based distribution channels are that:

- it is not as effective as face-to-face for certain products and services
- automated call-handling systems can cause customer dissatisfaction
- unsolicited outbound sales calls can cause customer dissatisfaction and weaken a customer's relationship with the brand.

13.4.7　Internet-based distribution

The rapid development of the Internet from the mid-1990s onwards has had far-reaching implications for financial services. In common with telephone-based developments, the Internet has resulted in new sales as well as administration solutions to customer needs. However, a great deal of hype surrounded the development of the Internet around the time of the millennium. In the way that the potential of bancassurance was over-inflated during the early 1990s, so too was the near-term impact of the Internet some 10 years later. Indeed, some of the more extreme forecasters were predicting that the Internet (clicks) would make branches (bricks) redundant within a 5-year period. Both sets of prognoses were flawed because they were based upon an inadequate appreciation of how consumers and organizations interact. With regard to the Internet, there was a failure to appreciate the subtle range of variations in distribution preferences that arise from the interplay of customer need, product and segment. The comparisons between the Internet and the development of telephony are marked. Both offer lower-cost alternatives to traditional branch-based or direct sales-force-based methods of distribution. However, neither are as yet viable alternatives to those situations in which customers require real-time face-to-face or branch-based service. Small businesses rely upon the branch to transact much of their cash- and cheque-based business. There are real concerns regarding security and fraud. Additionally, complex products such as mortgages and pensions have yet to become mainstream products sold over the Internet.

The Internet has brought consumer benefits in the form of greater access to financial services with the introduction of Internet banking, Internet trading and greater choice of 24/7 services. It has also resulted in the introduction of products that offer better value for money in areas such as loans and deposit-taking. However, this has been complementary rather than a substitute for more traditional forms of financial services distribution and administration.

The Internet has obvious advantages in countries that are characterized by a geographically dispersed population and where branch networks are patchy. There is a growing body of evidence that consumers are using the Internet in growing numbers as a means of conducting information-gathering, and are then buying either face-to-face or via the telephone. Such behaviour emphasizes the importance to the marketer of attractive, interesting and easy to navigate websites. There is also growing evidence of the competitive superiority of a combined 'bricks and clicks' approach to distribution, as opposed to a pure 'clicks' approach, for general financial services providers such as banks and building societies. A purely clicks-based approach is achieving success at the margins and within specific narrow product categories (the Internet bank Egg, for example, and the general insurer Esure). It can be expected that the relative importance of a clicks-based approach to product purchase will grow over time as a consequence of greater consumer confidence in transacting business in this way.

At the strategic level, the Internet would appear to have presented two basic options to providers. First, it has been used by some simply as another means of accessing their products and services, in much the same way as the telephone was adopted as a complementary means of distribution. Citibank, the Industrial and Commercial Bank of China and the ICICI Bank in India are all good examples of this approach. Secondly, it has been used to allow financial services suppliers to set up completely new organizations with a discrete brand identity that is purely Internet-based. The Co-operative bank did this when it set up Smile.com, as did Abbey with its Cahoot Internet bank. Whichever strategy is pursued, there can no doubt that the Internet is able to achieve dramatic cost savings, especially with regard to routine administration functions such as making payments and funds transfers.

An issue that has to be confronted concerns the capabilities required and the costs associated with generating customer demand for a pure Internet-based brand. As already established, financial services are not routine purchases in the vast majority of cases, but are infrequent, high-involvement purchases. The implication of this is that a provider has to ensure its brand has a consistently high level of awareness and attraction to coincide with the infrequent purchases of a sufficient number of people. This indicates a substantial and sustained investment in above-the-line advertising and complementary promotion through, say, direct mail. Some new entrants with a purely Internet-based approach have discovered that the heavy costs of achieving and maintaining brand awareness have cancelled out the lower administrative costs the Internet offers.

A final point of note is that a material element of cost-saving that accrues from the use of the Internet arises from the transfer of work (sometimes the complete purchase) from the provider's administration staff and onto the customer. The complete purchasing scenario applies to motor and home contents insurance, for example. It indicates the importance of clarity, ease of use and the clear flagging of how to get help if problems arise at any stage during the purchasing process. By no means do all websites conform to a best practice model, and it is not uncommon for an Internet purchase to take far longer to complete than one transacted via the telephone. Marketers must ensure that all new Internet-based services are subject to extensive piloting to ensure that what looks good in theory works in practice for the benefit of the customer.

Advantages of the Internet as a channel for new customer acquisition are that it:
- provides customer access anywhere, anytime
- enables providers to gain universal distribution
- complements other channels
- permits cost-effective proactive communication with existing customers
- has low administration costs
- can be a low-cost purchase channel
- encourages diversity and choice through easy entry by new providers
- allows consumers to transact business in a completely impersonal and remote manner
- results in lower prices
- can allow new products and services to be piloted at low cost, and thus encourages innovation
- allows providers to react quickly to changes in the marketplace
- enables customer research to be conducted easily and cheaply
- can enable providers to bespoke customer services and move towards more finely-tuned segmentation
- can facilitate development of close relationships through customized communication
- lessens demands placed on branch networks and face-to-face sellers and advisers.

Disadvantages of the Internet are that:

- it disenfranchises people who do not have access to the Internet, and thus exacerbates financial exclusion
- concerns regarding security and fraud inhibit consumer purchasing via the Internet
- difficult-to-use sites cause consumer dissatisfaction
- it is not well-suited to complex products and customer encounters requiring person-to-person conversational interaction
- it requires a well-known existing brand or high-cost marketing communication programme for new customer acquisition and product purchase.

13.4.8 Direct mail

In contrast with the recency of the development of the Internet, direct mail is one of the longest-established forms of distribution. According to its UK trade association, the Direct Marketing Association (DMA), it is growing at an annual rate of 9 per cent and accounts for some £13.6bn of marketing budgets. Thus it has not suffered any decline in the face of the rapid growth of telemarketing and the Internet.

Clearly, direct mail performs a number of roles, from simple awareness-raising and information-giving through sales-lead generation and onto the actual closing of a sale. The use of direct mail by the financial services sector has grown on a world-wide basis. In certain respects, this medium has a particularly important role to play within the context of financial services. For example, product complexity coupled with regulatory requirements lends itself to the need for hard-copy communication in many cases.

Advances in the use of databases and the technology associated with direct mail have facilitated a high degree of personalization. In conjunction with these developments, companies are able to use direct-response mail with respect to both their existing customers and prospective customers with a greater degree of accuracy and efficiency than ever before.

Direct mail is a highly controllable means of distribution that lends itself to rigorous analysis of key performance indicators (KPIs) such as cost per individual mailer, conversion-to-sale rate and cost per sale. Although direct mail is frequently referred to somewhat pejoratively as junk mail, with high wastage rates, it can nonetheless be a highly cost-effective means of obtaining sales. Indeed, a number of organizations use it as the primary method for new business acquisition. The successful use of direct mail hinges upon quite a small array of KPIs, namely:

- Accuracy of lists used
- Creative appeal and impact of the individual mailing piece
- Speed and follow-up to responses
- Quality of response follow-up.

There is a rapid rate of decay, from the time at which the recipient of the mailshot posts her or his response, in the recipient's motivation to engage in any subsequent follow-up activity on the part of the originator of the mailshot. This is especially important where a two-stage mailing process is being used, whereby the first mailshot is aimed at stimulating an enquiry and the follow-up mailshot seeks to complete the actual purchase. This rapid decay rate also applies where the initial direct-mail communication is intended to generate a sales lead which is to be followed-up on a person-to-person basis by either a direct salesperson or a telephone sales agent. As a rule of thumb, direct-mail responses should be followed up by the product-provider within 48 hours of the receipt of the response. It is essential that the user of direct mail has the necessary resources, infrastructure, systems and processes to ensure rapid follow-up to prospective customer response. The longer the delay in the follow-up contact, the lower the ultimate sales conversion rate and the greater the cost per sale.

Advantages of direct mail as a channel of new customer acquisition are that it:
- can communicate a great deal of detail
- can communicate detailed regulatory warnings and requirements
- can be retained for future reference
- is a means of providing physical evidence of an intangible product
- allows volumes to be controlled to match resources for follow-up
- allows messages to be highly personalized
- lends itself to a multi-segment marketing strategy
- allows costs and efficiency to be finely monitored
- can complement other channels, such as telesales, direct sales
- can take advantage of opportunities presented by the behavioural cues of existing customers
- permits low-cost entry into a market
- allows for experimentation at low cost.

Disadvantages of direct mail are that:
- it is a common source of consumer irritation and dissatisfaction
- it can place heavy demands upon the literacy skills of recipients
- regulatory requirements can result in a large amount of copy and information that diverts prospects from core sales messages
- low response rates can make it uneconomic
- there is no opportunity to discuss problems and concerns
- it often suffers from a poor image, which can undermine trust in a brand.

13.4.9   Other distribution channels

Direct-response advertising using methods other than direct mail include direct-response radio, television, press, magazine and poster advertising. These forms of direct response are less controllable and less easily targeted than direct mail, but offer their own discrete creative advantages. For example, direct-response television advertising using daytime schedules has become commonplace for organizations targeting the retired sector of society. Equity release schemes and simple forms of life insurance plans are of particular note in this regard. Direct-response press advertising is used extensively by organizations marketing secured loans (sometimes called second mortgages). The preferred media are those aimed at the mass-market, such as *The Sun, The Star* and *The Daily Mirror* in the UK. At the other end of the societal continuum we see investment products such as investment trusts, mutual funds (unit trusts and OEICS) and bonds distributed on a direct-response basis using titles such as *The Daily Telegraph* and the *The Sunday Times*.

A final form of distribution is the use of affinity groups such as trades unions and sports clubs. These often provide a means of access to people, using methods such as telesales, direct mail and direct sales. As such, they are not so much a distribution channel as a means of generating sales leads; therefore, they should be more correctly viewed as forming part of the promotional mix.

13.4.10 Multi-channel distribution

During the course of this chapter we have sought to provide a pragmatic insight into the real world of financial services distribution. Although the major methods of distribution have been discussed as individual channels, it is important to appreciate that, to an increasing extent, companies are simultaneously employing a range of channels. Thus, multi-channel distribution strategies are now the norm for most mainstream, mass-market financial services organizations. For the typical clearing bank, such a multi-channel approach will comprise:

- the branch network
- a direct sales-force
- direct mail
- the Internet
- telemarketing
- direct-response advertising.

A typical mass-market life assurance company will employ a multi-channel distribution strategy comprising:

- direct channels – direct sales-force, telemarketing, direct mail, direct-response advertising and Internet sales
- indirect channels – IFAs and tied agents.

13.5 Summary and conclusions

This chapter has argued that distribution channels play a central role in the marketing of financial services because they provide the opportunity for a purchase or sale to be made. Financial services organizations often employ a multi-channel strategy, using a number of different distribution channels to reach different target markets. These channels may be the organization's own direct channels or they may involve the use of intermediaries (indirect distribution). The range of possible distribution channels available is determined partly by technology and partly by regulation. Cost, customer and competitor influences will determine which channels are actually chosen.

Of the different distribution channels available, the branch network is still the most important for traditional current and savings accounts, while personal selling is probably the most common method of distribution for pensions and investments. However, new electronic-based channels are developing rapidly, and are likely to increase in importance over the next 5 years. Already, ATMs, telephone and web-based distribution systems are well established. Web-based distribution is expected to experience the greatest growth, with the most important developments being concerned first with the method of access, and secondly with what can be done via the web. In terms of method of access, it is anticipated that there will be a much greater variety of ways of accessing the web, with interactive digital TV being one of the most significant. In addition, as bandwidths increase and infrastructure improves, there will be the potential for customers to engage in face-to-face interactions with sales staff via the Internet. Such a development will have major implications for the distribution of financial services, because it will mean that traditional face-to-face selling falls in cost and becomes much more convenient to customers. Furthermore, for many customers, the prospect of dealing with someone face-to-face may reduce some of the resistance to using on-line distribution.

Review questions

1. What is the difference between direct and indirect distribution? Provide one example of each form of distribution channel for a financial services organization.
2. Which channels of distribution does your organization use? Which are direct and which are indirect? Which is the dominant channel, and why?
3. What are the factors that influence the choice of distribution channels for a bank and for a life insurance company?
4. What are the advantages and disadvantages of distributing financial services through a branch network?
5. What are the advantages and disadvantages of distributing financial services using the worldwide web? Why might some customers be unwilling to use the worldwide web to manage their financial affairs?

Customer Development

Customer relationship management strategies

☐ **Learning objectives**

By the end of this chapter you will be able to:
- understand the growing importance of relationship marketing and customer retention in financial services
- understand the interactions between customer acquisition, customer retention and marketing activities
- understand the nature and significance of the concept of customer lifetime value
- be aware of contextual influences on the management of customer relationships.

14.1 Introduction

Until comparatively recently, there has been a presumption that marketing is principally concerned with the processes surrounding the creation of customers for a commercial organization. Thus, decisions concerning the use of the marketing mix were largely geared to this end. In part, this perhaps explains why marketing and sales are often viewed as being one and the same thing. It is undoubtedly true that customer acquisition has historically been the dominant purpose of marketing in the field of financial services. However, from the late 1980s onwards marketing skills and resources have been used increasingly in the context of the existing customer base – that is to say, organizations have increasingly focused attention on marketing their services to their existing customers, encouraging them either to purchase more of the same product or to purchase different products from the organization's product range. This process is described in a number of different ways. Some will simply use the generic term 'relationship marketing'; others will refer to customer retention or customer base marketing. Increasingly, the term CRM – customer relationship marketing (or management as some prefer to call it) is used to describe this form of marketing. Whatever term is used, the important thing to remember is that we are dealing with that branch of marketing which concerns the contribution of marketing inputs once the customer acquisition phase has ended. During the course of the third and final part of this book we will focus upon marketing as it concerns the retention, management and development of existing customers. Thus, this section completes the triangle of strategy and planning, customer acquisition and customer management that forms the basis of this book.

This chapter provides an overview of some of the key issues associated with the management of customer relationships. Subsequent chapters will deal with issues relating to service quality, value, customer satisfaction, service recovery and the management of the marketing mix for customer retention. The chapter begins by exploring the factors that have encouraged a greater focus on the management of relationships with existing customers. The subsequent sections consider issues relating to the acquisition and retention of customers who will be both loyal and profitable. Thereafter, the concept of the relationship chain is introduced and the issues surrounding the management of customers at different relationship stages are introduced. The penultimate section deals with the specific issues that arise when managing customer relationships through an intermediary, and when managing relationships in an international context. Finally, the chapter discusses issues relating to customer lifetime value and customer data. Throughout this chapter, the terms CRM, relationship marketing and customer base marketing will be treated as broadly equivalent and used interchangeably.

14.2   Drivers of change

It is often suggested that the nature of financial services means that providers have always had relationships with their customers and that marketing is inherently relational (Stewart, 1998). While there is much truth in this view, it is also the case that financial services providers have traditionally not managed these relationships well in a mass-market context. This is clearly changing. A range of environmental factors has contributed to the growing concern about customer retention and development of customer-base (or relationship) marketing in financial services, including:

- rising costs of customer acquisition
- increasing focus upon customer value
- competition
- consumerist pressures
- regulation and legislation
- technological innovation
- development of relationship marketing in other sectors.

It is instructive to have some appreciation of how the above factors have influenced the growth of relationship marketing in financial services.

1. *Rising costs of customer acquisition*. As the penetration rate of the marketplace or market segment rises (i.e. the proportion of the total market that is already purchasing a product or service), the marginal costs of acquiring the custom of as yet unpenetrated customers increases. Since the 1980s the penetration rates in most product categories in developed economies have steadily grown, and this has added to marginal acquisition costs. At the same time, the value of customers at the margins of a segment can be expected to be of lesser value than those already served. Rising costs of customer acquisition have affected some areas more than others, especially with regard to regulation-induced cost increases.
2. *Increasing focus on customer value*. The economics of marginal customer acquisition referred to above have acted as a catalyst for an increased focus upon customer profitability as opposed to product profitability. That is not to say that the management of product margin is not important; clearly, such an assertion would be foolish. Both measures of value have a role to play in determining commercial performance. However, it is in the nature of financial services products, notably the characteristics associated with longevity and timescale, that individual product margins are of lesser significance than long-term individual customer value. It makes more sense to appraise the value of a business by reference to its aggregate customer worth, rather than simply the sum total of its in-force product margins.
3. *Competition*. The retail financial services sector is a dynamic and diverse arena with relatively few barriers to new entrants. Innovation in fields such as third-party administration (TPA), web-based distribution, call-centre functionality, and access to capital enable new entrants to participate in what are already highly penetrated market sectors. Additionally, the previous factors make it relatively easy for existing financial services organizations to diversify into new areas, as has happened with, for example, insurance companies setting up banks (Standard Life's Standard Life Bank, and Prudential's creation of Egg). The continual development of the competitive environment in market sectors that are already highly penetrated means that one company's newly acquired customer is increasingly likely to be the lapsed customer of a rival organization. Under such circumstances, the retention of existing valuable customers becomes even more important.
4. *Consumerist pressures*. Organizations representing the consumer interest, such as *Which?* and the National Consumer Council in the UK, the Consumers Union in the US and the Consumers Federation of Australia, have long campaigned to improve the ways in which the financial services industry serves the interests of consumers. Their campaigns have addressed a range of issues, including product charges, the use made of orphan funds, mortgage endowments, and overarching matters of how boards of directors are accountable for serving customer interests. Indeed, *Which?* claims to have received in the order of a million hits on its website, set up to put pressure on the industry to resolve consumer concerns regarding the selling of mortgage endowments. As a result, companies have become more sensitive to accusations that they attract new customers with attractive propositions, only to be subjected to detriment once they have become customers. This has provided further impetus to the need to develop more effective and sophisticated marketing policies and practices with regard to existing customers.

5. *Regulation and legislation*. The range of regulatory and legislative developments that have occurred since the mid-1980s has had far-reaching implications for the industry. That they have added to operating costs cannot be denied, and a new industry based upon compliance has *de facto* emerged. There is an aspiration that, in the long run, such costs will be compensated for by the avoidance of costly mis-selling compensation and more persistent (and hence profitable) product sales. Meanwhile, the costs of new customer acquisition have been impacted upon by the costs associated with sales adviser training, competence and supervision, along with an enormous array of other provisions included in the rule books of regulators around the world.

In addition to their impact upon costs, developments in this area have also impacted upon pricing and charging policies and mechanisms. This issue is becoming increasingly important, especially in areas such as life assurance and pensions. Until comparatively recently, the prevalence of high, up-front product charges meant that regular premium/contribution-based products could be profitable to the provider after they had been in force for quite short periods of time. The imposition of cancellation charges and penalties of one form or another meant that high initial costs associated with sales remuneration, underwriting and policy issue could be met and still yield a profit. Pricing policies of this type are becoming increasingly unacceptable and subject to government and regulatory scrutiny. Indeed, it has been estimated that the typical stakeholder pension with its maximum charge of 1.5 per cent of the fund's value takes at least eight to nine years before starting to achieve break-even for the provider. Under such circumstances, it is even more important that care is taken to recruit customers who have a high propensity to remain loyal to their provider.

6. *Technological innovation*. Innovations in telecommunications, database management and the worldwide web have had a dramatic impact upon customer management. The careful and detailed capture of appropriate data during the customer acquisition process provides an organization with the ability to manage the relationship to far greater effect than was hitherto possible. It is fair to say that technological innovation has been a major facilitator of customer base marketing.

7. *Development of relationship marketing in other commercial sectors*. Arguably, the B2B sector pioneered the concept and practice of relationship marketing because of the importance of forging genuine buyer–seller partnerships. The information asymmetry that is said to characterize retail financial services is far less in evidence in the B2B context. This is because buyers are often professional procurement executives and are considerably more empowered than the typical financial services domestic consumer. Indeed, the B2B business areas of major banks have themselves long practised effective relationship marketing processes in the handling of major corporate-client relationships.

CRM, which is essentially technology-enabled relationship marketing, has increasingly become a vital element of the marketing approach of many consumer goods markets and the retail sector. The rapid expansion of customer affinity schemes by supermarkets such as Tesco's Clubcard perhaps provide the best example of this form of marketing in practice. The extensive use of relationship marketing across the B2B, fast moving consumer goods (fmcg) and retail sectors has added further impetus to its adoption by financial services organizations.

As a consequence of these pressures, financial services providers across the world are now focusing much more actively on the development and management of relationships with their customers. In B2B markets, much of this continues to be conducted at a personal level. Increasingly, in B2C markets, technology (in the form of CRM systems) is supporting the creation of more personalized relationships with customers. Case study 14.1 provides an example of the relationship marketing approach adopted by Rabobank in the Netherlands.

Case study 14.1   Rabobank – building on domestic and business banking relationships in the Dutch market

Rabobank is an AAA rated co-operative bank with 5 million retail customers and a very strong local presence evidenced by approximately 1500 branches. In 1995 Rabobank was the first to introduce Internet banking, and today holds the largest number of Internet bank accounts in Europe. The Dutch banking market has learned that customers are usually unwilling to change from a trusted brand to a new bank, and this places certain limitations on the strategic choices that are available to banking institutions. In practice, this means that a large number of financial institutions opt for a customer penetration strategy, thus devoting resources to their existing customer base. A combination of this strategy of penetration, and what Treacy and Wiersema (1996) call customer intimacy, has proven to be a very successful aspect of the strategy of Rabobank, one of the top three banks in the Netherlands.

Rabobank has concentrated on being physically close to customers through both the Internet and a physical branch network. Cross-selling of mortgage and savings products to current-account customers has allowed Rabobank to become a market leader in retail banking. Similarly, the removal of restrictions on bancassurance in 1990 provided further opportunity for Rabobank to expand the range of services offered to its established customers.

Rabobank's success is not limited to personal markets. Management built on the bank's traditional strengths in agricultural markets and expanded into the non-agricultural small and medium-sized enterprise market. Rabobank now has 21 per cent of the small business market in the Netherlands, and is making solid progress with cross-selling and up-selling to their existing customers. To support the range of services offered to medium and larger companies, Rabobank has built an international network of branch offices, strategic alliances and acquisitions to ensure that the bank can offer a comprehensive service to customers operating internationally.

Source: Suzanne Tesselaar, TCI Communications, The Netherlands.

14.3   Customer persistency – acquiring the right customers

A feature of a great many businesses is that they simultaneously both acquire new customers for their organizations whilst losing a number of existing customers. Such a process of acquisition and attrition can result in a business working incredibly hard to stand still as far as its numbers of customers are concerned. This has been referred to as the *bucket theory of marketing*, a term attributed to James L, Schorr, a former Executive Vice President of Holiday Inn.

It is axiomatic of any organization that it seeks to achieve growth in the number of new customers it acquires and a reduction in the number of customer defections, and thereby to achieve net growth in the total customer base. Unfortunately, the prevalence of the bucket theory can make it a slow and expensive process. Indeed, it is by no means uncommon for a company to appear to be standing still as the number of new customers acquired merely matches the number of those lost.

Faced with this problem, there is an understandable response whereby a company devises a detailed, and costly, customer retention programme. However, such programmes can be misplaced if they result in the retention of relatively poor-value (and possibly negative-value) customers in the process. Some customers have a greater propensity to maintain a relationship with a product provider than others. From the provider's point of view, it is desirable to try to identify customer characteristics that are associated with a high likelihood of lapsing. The need to do this applies to organizational as well as domestic customers, because differential lapse rates apply to customers in both the B2B and B2C domains.

Identifying those characteristics of a customer that are associated with a relatively high propensity to lapse – or to persist, for that matter – is an important marketing activity. It requires the determination of which aspects of customers themselves, as well as of the marketing mix, are causally related to relative persistency. This is by no means an easy and quick procedure to accomplish. Rather, it calls for thoughtful and detailed analysis of possible causal factors over a protracted period of time. Thus, it could take years rather than weeks or months to yield truly valuable insights. In the long run it can have a profoundly beneficial impact upon the bottom line by increasing average customer value and reducing wasteful marketing and administration spend. A decision to conduct a customer persistency measurement programme requires the capture of data that would play a part in influencing persistency. Such data have to be captured during the customer acquisition process and be supported by the development of appropriate systems for analysis and reporting. The characteristics associated with persistency, both causal and correlated variables, differ according to marketplace, customer segment, purchasing situation and so on; there is no one-size-fits-all solution. However, likely candidates for consideration as possible persistency factors are as follows.

1. Customer characteristics:
   - age
   - income level
   - occupation
   - previous history in consuming a given product type

2. Acquisition process characteristics:
   - strength of real need by customer
   - whether product was bought or sold (degree of customer proactivity in acquisition process)
   - distribution channel used
   - individual, distributor or salesperson
   - date of acquisition
3. Other marketing mix characteristics:
   - usage of a sales promotion
   - source of sales leads
   - special price offers
   - product feature variants.

The above list is purely indicative of possible factors; each company must resolve to determine what is appropriate given its particular circumstances. Ultimately, such analysis should inform marketing planning and result in focusing customer acquisition activities upon relatively persistent customers. Thus, the key to effective customer retention is the acquisition of customers who can be presumed to be persistent in the first place.

14.4   Retaining the right customers

The reasons why customers cease their relationships with product providers are of four basic types, namely:

1. *Customer self-induced* – the original need no long exists. For example, a mortgage loan has been repaid early and therefore the loan protection policy is no longer required. Another example could be that the customer wants immediate access to cash, and so surrenders an insurance endowment policy.
2. *Customer environment-induced* – for example, the customer has become unemployed and is unable to maintain the premium/contribution, interest payments.
3. *Provider self-induced* – for example, poor service (service failure) has caused a level of dissatisfaction that leads the customer to sever the relationship. Alternatively, pricing changes may have caused the customer to seek a different supplier.
4. *Provider environment-induced* – for example, an increase in prevailing base interest rates may result in some customers lapsing; a fall in stock markets may cause customers to cash in equity-based investments. It might also be the case that an appealing competitor offer has induced a desire to switch provider.

The implications of the above are that providers must identify those factors on which they can exert some influence whilst developing contingency plans for those outside of their control. Ideally, customer self-induced defections are best mitigated by careful selection of customers during the initial acquisition process. Where they do arise, it is probably best to deal with their request to 'leave' as efficiently, swiftly and at as little cost as possible.

Provider self-induced customer lapsing is a particular cause for concern from a marketing perspective, since it is associated with a failure to deliver the right service experience. Research to date has suggested that switching/exit is a process rather than a response to specific individual events (Stewart, 1998). Triggers for exit are usually charges, facilities, information and service encounters, and usually there is an accumulation of negative experience prior to exit. The fact that exit appears to be a cumulative process would suggest that opportunities do exist for relationships to be rebuilt (and the ability to respond effectively to complaints is often one very important part of such a process, as will be discussed in Chapter 15), although the extent to which financial services providers have been able to capitalize on these is more debatable. One major challenge associated with customers who are lost through provider self-induced lapsing is the potential for negative word of mouth.

Customer environment-induced cases also need to be managed with care. Difficulties associated with the loss of a job may be insurmountable, and should be dealt with in a suitably sensitive yet efficient manner. However, unemployment tends to be a temporary matter, and measures such as contributions holidays or policy loans may enable the customer to maintain the product until he or she is in employment again. Careful analysis of key customer variables, such as income level, occupation, duration of customer relationship, and other products held, is essential in enabling a sound judgement to be made. It makes no sense to allow a customer–product relationship to lapse automatically when a request is received from a customer. Administrative staff must be trained to appreciate the important role they can play in retaining valid customer–product relationships. This calls for the development of suitable management information systems to match product lapse cues with relevant customer data. Such cues might include a missed monthly payment or, say, a request for a valuation or early surrender value, as well as written requests to cancel.

In addition to the availability of appropriate management information, a range of suitable options needs to be easily available to enable the customer to maintain the relationship with the provider, such as those already mentioned. It is important that a company has a clear strategy in respect of customer retention and a set of policies that give guidance to the relevant administration staff. Where customer administration is outsourced to a third-party administrator (TPA) partner, it is important that due regard be paid to issues concerning customer retention. In such situations, care must be taken to ensure that the staff of the TPA have the necessary mandates to engage in purposeful customer retention activities.

The development of effective customer retention practices raises the need for the careful identification of the reasons that induced the prospective lapse. Vital information can be accessed to enable the most appropriate course of action to be followed. Such an approach can be especially useful when employed in conjunction with inbound telephone-based lapse enquiries. It is rather more difficult, and potentially more costly, when used in conjunction with lapse-related enquiries that arrive via the postal system. Internet-based customer-contact processes offer a potentially powerful means of defending against customer defections. Routines can be devised that are able to determine the cause of the prospective lapse with a high degree of reliability. Having identified the underlying cause, customers can be presented with a range of options aimed at helping to solve their problem without recourse to actual product lapsing. This can be a highly cost-effective means of retaining customers by helping them through what might be a temporary period of difficulty.

Customer defections brought about through the actions of competitors present particular challenges for financial services companies. This is likely to be encountered more in some areas than others. For example, credit cards have become a fiercely competitive arena where customer acquisition is commonly based upon transferring a consumer's outstanding balance to the new provider at a highly attractive rate.

In writing about customer retention, Payne (2000), drawing on the work of Reichheld and Sasser (1990), demonstrates graphically just how sensitive profit is to relatively small shifts in customer retention levels, as can be seen in Figure 14.1. Box 14.1 draws attention to research findings which have examined the diversity of financial and non-financial benefits of relationship marketing and customer retention.

The argument that it is much cheaper to retain existing customers than to attract new ones (sometimes referred to as the *economics of customer retention*) is a powerful driver of increased interest in the management of customer relationships. However, it is important to note that this does not imply that all retained customers are profitable, or that all customers should be retained. As explained later in this chapter, the lifetime value of customers varies. In research outside of financial services, Reinartz and Kumar (2002) identified a class of customers who they described as

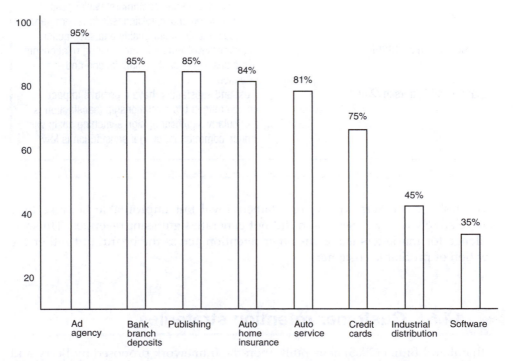

Figure 14.1 NPV profit impact of a 5 per cent points increase in customer retention (based on Reichheld, 1994).

Box 14.1   Relationships and customer retention – research findings

Empirical evidence on the economic benefits of customer retention in financial services is limited. However, measuring the direct financial benefits of loyalty is challenging and, as a consequence, much of the published work focuses attention on addressing the factors that contribute to relationship quality, to loyalty/retention and to satisfaction. Selected findings include:

Crosby and Stephens (1987)	Positive impact of relationships on customer satisfaction and retention
Storbacka (1994)	Positive impact of loyalty on profitability
Council on Financial Competition (1995)	Increasing retention by 5 per cent adds 3 years to the average customer lifetime and account usage increases with length of relationship (in Murphy, 1997)
Ennew and Binks (1996)	Nature of the customer's relationship and service quality have a positive impact on loyalty; distinguish between customers who are genuinely loyal and those who are only partly loyal (considered switching but did not)
Zeithaml et al. (1996)	Highlight the importance of service quality as a determinant of intention to remain loyal
Paulin et al. (1997)	Positive relationship between perceived strength of a relationship and customers' willingness to continue to purchase, willingness to recommend and judgements about quality and satisfaction
Ennew and Binks (1999)	Customer involvement in the banking relationship has a positive impact on satisfaction and retention
Sharma and Patterson (2001)	Trust and satisfaction have a positive impact on commitment to a relationship (satisfaction is particularly significant); high switching costs will induce commitment even if satisfaction is low

'barnacles' – customers who were retained/loyal but unprofitable because they were relatively costly to serve and did not generate significant revenues. Thus the challenge for marketers is not customer retention across the board, but rather the retention of profitable customers.

14.5   Customer retention strategies

Zeithaml and Bitner (2003) have built upon the framework proposed by Berry and Parasuraman (1991) to develop a useful model for the development of a customer retention strategy. Zeithaml and Bitner's model posits that excellent service quality and value must provide the basis for an effective retention strategy. They proceed to identify a sequence of four bonds (financial, social, customization and structural) which, when operationalized by means of the marketing mix, should result in a high probability of retaining valuable customers. These are summarized as follows.

14.5.1   Level 1: Financial bonds – volume and frequency rewards, bundling and cross-selling, stable pricing

At Level 1, the intention is to tie the customer in to the provider through the provision of a range of financial incentives. In this way, the provider is reflecting its perceived worth of the customer relationship by increasing the economic value that the customer gains. A straightforward example of this is to be found in the frequent-flyer programmes operated by airlines such as Singapore Airlines. In the financial services area, companies such as Fidelity offer discounts on initial charges to existing customers when they make subsequent purchases of a mutual fund. General insurance companies will offer discounts to customers who have, say, a home contents policy when they buy a buildings insurance policy too. Credit-card companies frequently offer special deals on a range of other services, such as air travel, hotel accommodation and car hire. Mastercard provides air miles to its customers as a means of encouraging retention. Stable pricing refers to a provider shielding its customers from general price increases as a means of lessening the impact of customer defections.

Financial bonds are relatively easy to implement and straightforward to communicate. For these reasons they are easily copied by competitors, and therefore have limitations as a means of achieving long-term differentiation.

14.5.2   Level 2: Social bonds – continuous relationships, personal relationships, social bonds among customers

The types of actions proposed in Level 2 represent an attempt by the provider to recognize the individuality of the customer. It is based upon interactions that build upon the financial incentives provided by Level 1 to create a sense of affiliation with the provider. A classic example of this is to be found in the life assurance sector, where advisers endeavour to meet clients on a fairly regular basis to review their circumstances and needs. Well-established financial advisers frequently report that in the order of two-thirds of their new product sales in a given year are derived from existing customers. In addition, a further one-fifth of their sales arise from referrals that they receive from their existing customers. Thus, sales to wholly new customers account for less than one-fifth of the total new product sales of advisers who have invested in developing successful long-term customer relationships.

The development of social bonds is a particular feature of the B2B area of financial services. A range of forms of hospitality is frequently encountered, including the use of sponsorship of sporting and cultural events. Such sponsorship activity can be a highly effective means of building bonds not only between the provider and its client, but also amongst the actual client community itself. It is much more difficult for a competitor to replicate the social bonds that a rival provider may have formed with its customers.

14.5.3 Level 3: Customization bonds – customer intimacy, mass customization, anticipation/innovation

Level 3 strategies involve the two-way flow of information between provider and customer, with the aim of creating a marketing mix that is tailored to the particular needs of the customer. Although elements of this process of customizing are in evidence in Levels 1 and 2, in Level 3 the boundaries are pushed out as detailed knowledge of individual customer requirements are translated into customer-specific mix components such as product and service features. Zeithaml and Bitner cite the example of the Zurich Group seeking to build relationships with its customers through the provision of solutions that are customized to the needs of individual customers.

Historically, the costs associated with the development of Level 3 strategies meant that they were a particular feature of the B2B environment. However, advances in customer database technology have allowed the concept of mass customization (i.e. marketing to a segment of one) to become a cost-effective reality within the B2C arena. The Internet has been instrumental in further advancing customization bonds, by acting as a highly efficient means of communicating with customers.

14.5.4 Level 4: Structural bonds – shared processes and equipment, joint investments, integrated information systems

The creation of structural bonds between provider and customer represents the greatest challenge to competitive activity and, in conjunction with activities carried out under Levels 1, 2 and 3, can achieve long-term differentiation and competitive advantage. Examples of this can be seen in the way that IT suppliers integrate their systems with a range of financial services companies. Level 4 strategies afford the potential for significant synergies to occur as each partner contributes its expertise to create unrivalled value. From a customer perspective, there is the risk that such an integrated relationship may in the long term be detrimental. Safeguards should therefore be considered to ensure that customers can mitigate any potential long-term disadvantage. Ultimately, a commercial judgement must be made about the costs, risk and benefits of forming structural bonds with a supplier. Indeed, this type of risk can work both ways, in that a powerful customer may be able to exert a high degree of power over the product-service provider in contract negotiations over the long term.

14.6 The customer relationship chain

So far in this chapter, emphasis has been placed upon the inter-relationships between getting and keeping customers. It has been established that getting the right customers in the first place is instrumental in keeping them. Thus, it is helpful to conceptualize the process associated with customer acquisition and management as forming component elements of an overarching process that we call the *customer relationship chain*, shown diagrammatically in Figure 14.2 and explained below.

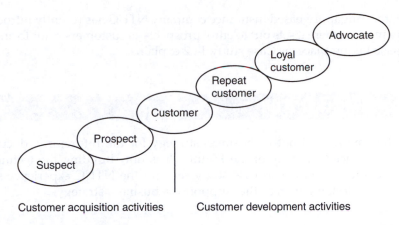

Figure 14.2 The customer relationship chain.

The customer relationship chain is applicable in both the B2C and B2B domains. Indeed, in the latter case the financial consequences of the loss of a valuable customer will be far more significant than in the former.

14.6.1   Suspect

A suspect is an individual who has been identified as being a member of one of the company's target market segments. The company will use its marketing mix to try to attract a suspect's attention and interest in order to engage them in some form of dialogue.

14.6.2   Prospect

Once a dialogue has been established, the suspect becomes a prospect. There is a wide range of behaviours associated with this link in the chain. For example, a television advertisement aimed at suspects could invite contact via a freephone telephone number to find out more about the provider company or a given product. Alternatively, a mailshot aimed at suspects could invite a response to request a personal financial review.

14.6.3   Customer

Becoming a customer is the obvious outcome of effective prospecting activity. It may be that the prospect has agreed to buy, say, an insurance policy, or, as can also be the case, has registered to become a customer without having actually made a product purchase. This frequently happens in the case of stock-broking firms.

However, the Singapore-based insurance company NTUC has recently introduced a marketing model where it sets out to enrol prospects as customers prior to any product purchase taking place, as Case study 14.2 explains.

Case study 14.2   NTUC Singapore

NTUC Income has set out its business strategy for the future, in a document called 'Insurance Company of the Future'. It is now building the technology to support this strategy. This case study sets out the NTUC experience so far regarding the following areas that support the business strategy:

- Website
- Register the customer first
- Educate the customer
- Simple products
- Pull strategy.

NTUC Income's website was voted the best website in the *Asia Insurance Review* Awards 2005. The website (www.income.coop) has 15 million hits each month. It is easy to use, provides information on NTUC products and practices, and is available in three languages.

The customer-centric strategy is to register a customer first and to sell products later. This was successfully implemented 10 years ago with a travel insurance product. NTUC registers customers first and obtains their particulars. When the customers travel, they call the hotline and activate their travel insurance. They enjoy a lower premium (15 per cent discount) and the convenience of immediate, hassle-free cover.

NTUC handles about 120 000 transactions each year, with a premium income of US$6 million from an active base of about 500 000 customers. It holds an estimated market share of 25 per cent. Lower distribution costs and expense ratios allow NTUC to offer a price advantage of 5.5 per cent. The success of this travel insurance product gave NTUC confidence that the 'register the customer first' strategy could work well for other products. The key elements of this strategy are:

- Register the potential customer first
- Obtain the contact information, e.g. name, date of birth, gender, contact number, e-mail address
- Send brief materials to educate the customer
- Introduce the customer to the website
- Invite the customer to attend educational talks on insurance products
- Leave the customer to contact the call-centre later.

NTUC places particular emphasis on educating the customer about the range of insurance products available in the market. Information is provided

Case study 14.2   NTUC Singapore—cont'd

via the website, e-mail broadcasts, educational talks, and video and voice on digital media.

During the past year, NTUC has held an educational talk each week on products such as medical insurance and investment-linked funds. Typically, about 150 people have attended each talk. Potential customers who attend a talk and decide to purchase within 14 days of it are offered special incentives. About 30 per cent of the customers take up the incentive.

Although it is often said that 'insurance has to be sold', NTUC believes that people are willing to 'buy insurance' if they are offered simple products that they can understand, and enjoy a price advantage. Encouraging potential customers to approach NTUC to buy insurance increases the productivity of sales agents, and supports lower commission rates and thus lower prices for customers.

In essence, ICT and particularly web-based technology, has enabled NTUC to build close relationships with customers without initially actively pushing products to them. By educating customers about financial needs and products, they are encouraged to approach NTUC as they identify a need. This helps to keep costs down, relieves sales pressure on consumers and ultimately results in more satisfied customers and enhanced business performance.

Source: Tan Kin Lian, Chief Executive, NTUC Income.

14.6.4   Repeat customer

A common mistake is the belief that, having bought a product, the customer becomes part of what is sometimes termed the 'warm customer base'. As such, this renders the customer well-disposed towards that provider company. The evidence indicates that an individual who has bought a financial services product has a high probability of buying a further product within 18 months of the initial purchase. If the initial product provider has not secured that subsequent purchase, the relationship weakens and a stronger affiliation is likely to be struck up with the provider of the subsequent purchase. In such a situation, the customer will, in all probability, cease to be a *warm customer*. Indeed, there is evidence to suggest that such customers become no more responsive to the marketing efforts of the initial provider company than completely new suspects.

There have been many cases of financial services companies adopting a complacent attitude towards customers who have a single product with them. Effective marketing should be geared towards ensuring that the new customer buys a second product from them rather than from an alternative provider, otherwise there is a strong likelihood of the chain being broken. A hallmark of effective customer marketing at *the customer* link in the chain is that the provider is proactively trying to secure that subsequent purchase.

14.6.5   Loyal customer

A loyal customer is one that has two or more products with a given provider and, when the need arises, takes the initiative to invite the current provider to offer a solution to that need. Customers may well contact other potential providers too, and may not necessarily buy from the current provider. However, they will have experienced a sufficiently high level of satisfaction and confidence in the current provider to give them the first chance of securing the additional business. Customer-initiated proactive behaviour is what defines the loyal customer.

14.6.6   Advocate

Advocates are customers who express such a high level of trust in their provider that they recommend it to any member of their personal reference group should such a third party raise the fact that they have an appropriate need. Thus, friends, family members, workplace colleagues and social contacts represent opportunities for advocacy to take place. Personal recommendations are considered to represent a particularly important aspect of consumer choice in the field of financial services. Just consider the potential power offered by having, say, 10 per cent of your customers become advocates. A company with a customer base of 2 000 000 people could have 200 000 people recommending that company to their respective reference group contacts.

14.7   Lifetime customer value

The notion of lifetime customer value is central to the concept of retaining and developing customer relationships. It moves the thinking about profitability beyond mere one-off product margins, important though they are, and on to a much broader appreciation of customer value. It is entirely possible that attempts to maximize short-term product margins may not result in optimal long-term profitability. For example, high-quality customers may be deterred from buying an investment fund with a relatively expensive charging structure if they are not convinced of the incremental value that the premium price delivers. Instead, they may choose a less expensive alternative that results in a highly persistent provider relationship. Therefore, it is axiomatic that strategies based upon the existing customer base are firmly grounded in a robust model of lifetime customer value.

In simple terms, lifetime customer value involves making a set of assumptions regarding the following variables:

Revenue variables	Number of products bought
	Value of products bought
	Duration of individual product persistency
Cost variables	Costs of providing customer services
	Other costs (e.g. claims or bad debts)
Referral variables	Number of new customers introduced
	Value of referral business

Knowledge about the likely revenue, cost and referral variables that apply to the array of consumer and organizational customer types will have already been reflected in a company's segmentation strategy. This can be further fine-tuned through the careful analysis of the performance of customer groups over time. The resultant data can be used to inform the development of a lifetime customer value model. An illustrative example of what this might look like is given in Case study 14.3.

A similar approach can be applied to the consumer marketing domain. It is simply a case of identifying the relevant revenue, cost and referral variable data and computing the sum. For both final consumers and business consumers, the development of a suitable model of lifetime customer value is essential for the development of effective customer management strategies.

Case study 14.3   Motim manufacturing revenue scenario

Motim Manufacturing has a relationship with Beta Broking, a general insurance broker that began when Motim sourced a public liability policy via Beta. A year later, Motim decided to source its Director's liability cover from Beta. The following year its all-risks buildings and plant policy came up for renewal, and Beta secured the business in competition with the incumbent provider. This was followed by the provision of motor insurance to its fleet of 15 vehicles. The value of premium income secured by Beta with Motim during a 15-year period was as follows.

Revenue variables (assuming no annual policy increase for illustrative purposes)

	Annual premium (£)	Term	Total premium (£)
Public liability policy	2200	15	33 000
Directors' liability	4750	14	66 500
Buildings and plant	12 250	13	159 250
Motor vehicle cover	7500	12	90 000

The total 'lifetime premium income' was therefore £348 750, and the value of commission income generated at 20 per cent of annual premium was £69 750.

Referral variables

Number of new clients introduced by Motim (one per year)	15
Value of referred business (assuming same profile and product mix as Motim itself)	£2 158 000
Commission earned from referrals	£431 600

Thus, the lifetime value to Beta Broking of its relationship with Motim Manufacturing amounted to commission earnings of some £501 350 over the 15-year period.

This illustration gives some idea of the real value of making that initial sale of a £2200 public liability policy that generated just £440 in commission. It also underlines graphically just how valuable it is to follow through the customer relationship chain to achieve customer advocacy. Indeed, in this example the real value is derived from referrals; during the 15-year period of the example, 88 per cent of the lifetime value accruing to the Motim relationship is accounted for by the resultant referrals.

14.8   Relationship marketing in specific contexts

Arguably, the provision of financial services in B2B contexts has always been characterized by a focus on long-term relationships. In mass B2C markets, the focus on building customer relationships and encouraging customer retention has been more recent. Discussions thus far have highlighted the importance of the careful management of customer relationships from acquisition through to long-term retention, highlighting the importance of understanding and focusing attention on those customers who are likely to be profitable. While these principles have general relevance, their application can vary according to context. This section focuses attention on two specific contexts, namely marketing via intermediaries and marketing internationally.

14.8.1   Relationship marketing and the role of intermediaries

Particular challenges are presented in using relationship marketing or CRM approaches where there is the involvement of third-party intermediaries. Typical examples might include high-street general insurance brokers, independent financial advisers (IFAs) or appointed representatives (ARs).

There are inherent conflicts of interest, with the accompanying potential for mistrust. Much of this surrounds the thorny question of 'who owns the customer?' This often depends upon whether any given request by a customer is likely to result in additional sales revenue/commission or lead to the incurring of some administrative task, and the accompanying costs. The incentive structure (additional sales means revenue, administration implies costs) means there is a risk that intermediaries will display a preference to think that they 'own' the customer when a new sale is in the offing, or a potential policy lapse that could result in commission claw-back. By contrast, such intermediaries may defer customer ownership in favour of the core product provider where a non-income related task is indicated.

It is important to grasp that companies that distribute via brokers may have spent decades building and maintaining a culture in which the intermediary is viewed as *the* primary customer. Indeed, it may seem that the needs of the broker take precedence over those of the end customer. Therefore, there is a strong cultural dimension to the development of a relationship or CRM-based approach, whereby the intermediary sales branches of provider companies have to learn to view brokers and their relationship to customers in a new light, with the needs of the end-consumer taking precedence over those of the broker. This may seem straightforward enough, but for some companies and their broker sales support staff it can represent a radically different way of thinking and behaving.

It could be argued that the provider needs to consider a form of relationship marketing or CRM that treats intermediaries and the ultimate consumer as separate customer groups, each being the subject of a CRM programme geared to their respective needs. However, such an approach calls for protocols that achieve a balance between the interests of all three parties. Formal customer–supplier agreements are sometimes used for this purpose. Such arrangements stipulate the respective rights and responsibilities of product provider and intermediary in respect of the array of interactions that could occur with the customer. It can involve the construction of quite sophisticated models for handling all possible forms of customer contact. Perhaps somewhat paradoxically, it is often the case that smaller broking firms like to be involved more intimately in customer contact than do their much larger rivals. The latter can display a tendency to adopt a somewhat more remote and aloof posture regarding customer contact. Those experienced in the intermediary market will often comment that larger broker firms gear their activities primarily towards income-generating activities, to the detriment of pure customer service.

The situation is seldom different with regard to group business such as occupational pension schemes. There is considerable anecdotal evidence to suggest that large firms specializing in the employee benefits market see their role as being one primarily geared towards selling the scheme to the employer. Therefore, there is frequently an expectation that the job of signing up the individual scheme members falls to the staff of the product provider. Indeed, there are situations in which the intermediary simply 'sells' a shell scheme to an employer and expects employee participation to be managed entirely by the product provider.

In the UK the industry has made some progress in developing common systems trading architecture, but as yet it remains somewhat basic and limited in functionality. Examples of progress to date include a common approach to commission messaging, and a common commission statement has been developed. It is perhaps revealing that the needs of the intermediary appear to have taken priority over those of the consumer. Without a fully developed common trading platform, the potential to develop a truly joined-up approach to CRM programmes that seek to integrate customer–broker–product provider activities will be constrained. A number of attempts have been made to develop open architecture-based systems aimed at enabling intermediaries to link up with provider databases on an individual company basis. Providers that have invested in such technology are beginning to realize material commercial benefits. The corollary is that those who have yet to make such investments are exposing themselves to risks to their future new business prospects. Indeed, this might even present risks to their current business as IFAs migrate to those providers that are more technologically advanced. Such an outcome would present the laggards with further competitive disadvantages. It is understood that Friends Provident is one of the most advanced organizations in this endeavour. However, the general lack of a suitable common trading platform for the whole industry acts as a brake on this development.

In the absence of the desired common platform, intermediaries tend to design their own individual set of protocols that they seek to apply to all of the providers with which they do business. Equally, product providers endeavour to apply their own set of policies and procedures to all of the intermediaries with which they trade. As might be imagined, a degree of negotiation takes place as intermediary and product provider seek to best serve their respective interests.

To conclude, the management of CRM programmes is much more straightforward in those instances in which there is no intermediary involvement in the business acquisition and ongoing customer management processes. Where intermediaries are involved, a customer management model is required that:

- positions the end customer as the ultimate beneficiary of the product/service provided and clearly establishes the primacy of their interests
- has a robust set of protocols that establishes the respective rights and responsibilities of the provider and intermediary; a suitable level of security must be

guaranteed such that there are no compromises either to the data protection rules that apply in any given country or from commercial sensitivities between intermediaries

- clearly identifies the array of possible events in the life of the customer relationship, and specifies the respective roles of provider and intermediary in handling those events
- has a CRM programme geared specifically to address the interests of the intermediary sector, in addition to the CRM programme designed for the end-consumer.

14.8.2   Relationship marketing: some international perspectives

In Chapter 6 we considered some of the ways in which operating across national boundaries impacts upon marketing strategy and planning. Operating internationally can give rise to a range of new opportunities and threats, and will require the development and maintenance of a new set of competences. Similarly, each country will present its own unique set of opportunities and threats to be matched with the appropriate set of strengths and weaknesses. Clearly, this adds a material degree of complexity to strategy development and use of the marketing mix. Doole (1998) has identified three particular features that are associated with the strategies of organizations that have competed successfully in international markets:

1. A clear, competitive focus based upon in-depth knowledge of each respective market, a strong competitive positioning, and a truly international marketing strategy
2. Well-managed organizations characterized by a culture of learning, innovativeness, effective monitoring and control procedures, and high levels of energy and commitment to international markets
3. An effective relationship strategy, based upon strong customer relations, the commitment to quality products and services, and a high degree of commitment to customer services across all international markets.

We observe elements of all three of these features in brands such as Singapore Airlines, Ritz Carlton Hotels and American Express. In the case of financial services, particular consideration has to be given to issues such as regulation and culture, as they can vary widely from country to country and be of profound significance, as Kaspar *et al.* (1999) observe:

Formulations of relationship marketing based on contemporary western interpretations may fail if transplanted to overseas countries, where the cultural and economic environments differ significantly from the country for which a relationship policy was originally formulated.

These differences are less likely to be of material significance in the business-to-business domain. Again, relationship management is a particularly important feature of the B2B market. Technology and process innovation have presented new threats and opportunities to financial services organizations that operate on a global basis. Additionally, deregulation and the opening up of markets to new forms of competition have added to the value attached to effective international CRM strategies for financial services companies involved in the B2B domain. It is instructive to consider the four relationship bonds proposed by Berry and Parasuraman (1991) and discussed by Zeithaml and Bitner (2003), presented earlier in this chapter. These have particular relevance in the B2B, context where financial, social, customization and structural bonds can be developed in a cost-effective and potentially meaningful way. There are particular opportunities for the development of customization and structural bonds, these being less easy and cost-effective to employ in the B2C context.

In both the B2B and B2C contexts, decisions regarding the development and execution of international CRM programmes have to take account of issues such as:

- Segmentation – which groups of customers are in sufficient numbers and of a value that it makes sound economic sense to make them the focus of an international CRM programme (ICRMP)?
- Cultural proximity – do the desired target segments for an ICRMP display sufficient cultural proximity to make the programme a practical proposition?
- Devolution – which aspects of an ICRMP should be determined and managed centrally, and which should be devolved to local management?
- Competition – how can an ICRMP protect valuable customers from the overtures of overseas competitors?
- Rewards – how transferable are individual rewards in influencing behaviours by members of the target segment on an international basis?
- Partnerships – how can reward-scheme supplier relationships be leveraged for mutual benefit, preferably on a global basis?
- IT – how can IT be used to increase the cost-effectiveness of an ICRMP, preferably by achieving interconnectivity between local national customer databases and central management facilities?
- Commercial – does it make strategic and financial sense?

The above set of factors is neither exhaustive nor mutually exclusive but, nonetheless, provides a firm basis for considering the development of an ICRMP. American Express has acquired significant expertise in managing customer loyalty programmes on a global scale. In many respects, this is an understandable response to the phenomenal growth of competition in the credit-card market across the globe. Case study 14.4 shows how Amex uses its international loyalty programme to reinforce the relationship it has with its higher-value customers.

Case study 14.4   The American Express international loyalty programme

American Express is one of the best-known and most respected brand names in the world. In the 1960s and 1970s it enjoyed a dominant role in the global credit-card market. However, from the 1980s onwards it has had to respond to an unprecedented growth in competition in all the territories it serves. In the face of such competition, the company has had to work hard to earn the loyalty

Continued

Case study 14.4   The American Express international loyalty programme—cont'd

of customers and build lasting relationships. American Express has fought back in recent years, and has invested heavily in new products, expanded its rewards and loyalty programmes, and strengthened its servicing capabilities to meet the needs of its customers better. As a result, in 2004 it attracted some 5 million new cards-in-force and achieved record spending of more than $416 billion – a wide lead over its competitors in terms of average spending per card.

In sharp contrast to many of its rivals, American Express has generated most of its growth organically, rather than by mergers and acquisitions. Through this approach, the company has grown its card-in-force base to 65.4 million.

American Express first introduced a customer loyalty programme in its home US market in 1991. During the course of the next few years the model proved its worth and was rolled out to many other markets around the world. By 2006, the international Membership Rewards Programme (MRP) had expanded such that it is now operating in 50 separate countries and encompassing some 13 million card holders. In outline, the scheme is as follows.

- Relatively high-value customers are invited to become members of the programme. Value is based upon characteristics such as annual credit drawn down and number of American Express products held by the customer.
- Successful applicants pay an annual membership fee which varies from country to country, roughly in a range from $15 to $50.
- Once enrolled in the programme, the member earns points on the basis of the monetary value of each transaction registered on their card.
- The points accumulate in the member's personal 'bank account', and they can be redeemed for a wide range of goods and services via the Internet or telephone call-centres located locally.

The local American Express management is responsible for promoting the programme to card holders in their respective countries, for negotiating local partnership arrangements with providers of goods and services listed in their member catalogue and for organizing the fulfilment service.

Overall business management of the programme takes place in London to ensure that it is achieving its goals and that the brand is being managed in a consistent fashion. The central function is also responsible for driving new reward innovations that keep the programme evolving, negotiating supplier relationships with major strategic partners such as major airlines and international hotel groups, and ensuring that the common systems platform and infrastructure provide the necessary functionality and access to the programmes being operated across the territories that comprise the MRP.

Partnerships

Some 1300 partners in total provide the goods and services that MRP members enjoy in exchange for the points they have accumulated. They include brands such

Case study 14.4   The American Express international loyalty programme—cont'd

as Canon, Panasonic, Dunhill, Montblanc and Antler, as well as companies such as Hertz, Eurostar and the De Vere Hotels group. Airlines represent particularly important partners, and American Express has partnership arrangements with almost 30 of them, including Virgin Atlantic, Cathay Pacific and Singapore Airlines.

Through becoming a partner with American Express, a company benefits in a number of ways. First, it receives the value of the goods that the member receives in exchange for his or her points from American Express. Secondly, it provides the partner with access to highly desirable customers – currently some 13 million in the markets covered by the MRP. American Express has coined the term 'double-dipping' to describe the phenomenon by which the member spends money with the partner company over and beyond the value of the points that have been redeemed. For example, a member might redeem sufficient points with, say, Air France to receive a return flight from Paris to Cairo, and might purchase a further three tickets on his own account for the remainder of the family to travel with him.

A third benefit that partners gain is access to data about the spending behaviour of the 13 million MRP members. American Express carries out an enormous amount of data interrogation to generate insights into how its card holders consume goods and services. Such analysis examines not only what is bought, but also through which merchants. Notwithstanding the limitations occasioned by the various pieces of data protection legislation, partners are able to inform their individual marketing strategies and programmes by using the behavioural insights they get from American Express.

Results
Highlights of its corporate financial performance in 2004 are as follows:

- A record net income of $3.4 billion, up 15 per cent on the previous year
- Diluted earnings per share up 17 per cent to $2.68
- Record revenues of $29.1 billion, up 13 per cent
- A return on equity of 22 per cent, compared with 20.6 per cent a year ago.

Currently, the international MRP has 2.2 million enrolees in Europe, 1 million in Latin America and 2.6 million in the Japan/Asia Pacific region. These are in addition to the 8 million-plus enrolees in North America. Recent analysis with airline partners demonstrates that the yield of MRP members to an airline is, on average, in the order of 35–60 per cent higher than that of the airline's average non-MRP customer. In 2004, the MRP received a Freddie Award for the 'Best International Affinity Credit Card Loyalty Programme'. In 2006, it was named the 'Best Credit Card Rewards Programme' by *Business Traveller Magazine* for the seventh consecutive year.

Source: Elisabeth Axel, Senior Vice President American Express.

14.9   Customer data management

It is no coincidence that the increasing importance placed upon marketing to existing customers has occurred in parallel with innovation in the area of customer database management. This is because the ability to collect, store, analyse and act upon meaningful customer data is now firmly established as a critical marketing competency. Technology has facilitated the means by which vast arrays of data can be processed to identify events in the provider–customer relationship that have meaning and implications for both parties.

During the course of the past 10–15 years a new industry has evolved, comprising software and hardware companies, information-based organizations, telecommunications suppliers and a range of consultancies aimed at transforming customer information into a highly commercially valuable resource. It is interesting to contrast the relatively sketchy and incomplete data which often typify new customer acquisition with the richness of data that can typify an organization's existing customers. Thus, existing customers present far more potential for accurate and appropriate data capture and analysis than do prospective customers. The data on consumers that are available when prospecting for new customers is pretty much common to all companies that are competing to acquire their custom. However, information regarding actual customers and their behaviour as customers is unique to the given provider. It is in the uniqueness of this information that a company possesses the means for differentiation and competitive advantage.

Storbacka and Lehtinen (2001) conceptualize the collection and organization of customer data as the creation of 'customer relationship memory'. To quote from the authors themselves, 'This customer relationship memory differs from ordinary databases in that it is the memory of a specific customer relationship'. This emphasizes the uniqueness that can be attributed to customer base marketing and the role played by technology in making it cost-effective to market to a segment of one. Data can be used to create knowledge about a customer that results in unique value being created for that customer; it provides the basis for a long and mutually beneficial relationship. Knowledge implies more than simply the awareness of a fact or piece of data. Rather, it implies an understanding and insightful awareness of the circumstances regarding a given subject – in this case, a customer. The notion of a 'customer memory' referred to by Storbacka and Lehtinen indicates the need for an organization to create customer knowledge through the analysis of appropriate inputs of data and information. The platform for the formation of customer knowledge and hence, if you like, a customer memory, is the customer database.

A basic approach to the component elements of a customer database is that it comprises four core components:

1. Customer fact file
2. Customer product file
3. Customer transaction file
4. Customer insight file.

The relationship between these four files is shown in Figure 14.3.

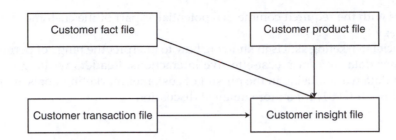

Figure 14.3 Top-level structure of the customer database.

- *The customer fact file* comprises what might be termed the customer's demographic profile, which contains data such as name, postal address, telephone number, e-mail address, gender, age, date of birth, occupation, salary, marital status, number of children, gender and ages of children.
- *The customer product file* comprises data regarding the products held with the provider, and includes information such as product name, optional features selected, value of product holding, funds selected. It also stores data on financial products held with other providers.
- *The customer transaction file* is where data are stored that provide an audit trail of the interactions that take place between the provider and customer. It might include information such as the frequency of using an ATM, the amount of cash withdrawn per transaction, whether an acknowledgement of transaction is requested, the place at which the ATM was used. It also stores written communication between the provider and customer and provides a log of all telephone-based contact, for example.
- *The customer insight file* is where data are recorded that give insights into how the customer views his or her relationship with the provider. For example, information resulting from the customer's involvement in a customer satisfaction survey is stored here. Any complaint-related feedback will also be found in this file. Importantly, it will allow provider staff a place to record their views about customer preferences and dislikes – for example, Singapore Airline's information regarding a frequent flyer's food, drink and reading material may be stored in such a file. A bank might decide to record that a given customer has a preference to deal with a particular call-centre agent when making a query. It can respond by creating a sense of familiarity that customers frequently cite as being important to them.

The customer insight file should benefit from inputs from the other three files. Thus, events in the customer's life act as a trigger for the creation of customer insights and the generation of appropriate actions on the part of the provider to add value to the relationship.

It is important that suitable systems and procedural architecture be devised to allow for the capture of data to populate the four files shown in Figure 14.3. Clearly there are cost implications to consider when developing such a framework for the management of customer information. This underlines the importance of targeting customers with the required commercial potential as part of the customer segmentation strategy.

The crucial marketing skill is in knowing how to interpret the range of permutations of customer data to inform cost-effective interactions. Readers wishing to explore the use of data warehousing in the pursuit of customer marketing goals are referred to Ronald Swift (2001) for a more detailed discussion.

14.10   Summary and conclusions

This chapter outlines the environmental factors that have resulted in the development of customer relationship marketing. In particular, it has demonstrated how the characteristics associated with financial services have a marked resonance with the features associated with CRM. For example, the long-term nature of many financial services products makes them a natural context within which CRM programmes can succeed.

The crucial importance of carefully selecting the *right* customers in the first place is presented as a prerequisite for customer longevity and lifetime value. A range of factors has been discussed that are implicated in customer persistency. Strategies aimed at facilitating customer retention have been explored, notably Zeithaml and Bitner's model concerning the four levels of bonds.

The chapter introduces readers to the customer relationship chain. This model provides a simple yet effective basis for the ways in which the marketing mix can be used to facilitate the progression of both domestic consumers and business customers from suspect to advocate. The value of the customer relationship chain has been augmented with a demonstration of the importance of placing a value on lifetime customer value.

Consideration has been given to the implications of the use of intermediaries when adopting a CRM-based approach, and this led on to some of the particular issues that need to be addressed when considering the use of international CRM programmes. Finally, the significance attached to the role played by data has been discussed. Here, we gained an appreciation of the need for appropriate systems functionality, competence in data analysis and interrogation within any organization seeking to pursue a customer development strategy.

Review questions

1. To what extent is customer development a feature of the financial services sector in your own country?
2. What do you consider to be the relative importance of marketing's role in customer acquisition compared with customer development?
3. What are the respective merits of product profitability and customer lifetime value as measures of new business contribution?
4. In what ways might the design of a customer development marketing mix vary between the B2B and B2C marketplaces?

5. What are the customer environment-induced and provider environment-induced factors that result in customer lapsation in the market for savings deposit accounts?

6. Identify a business customer segment that you think would lend itself to an ICRMP. What practical issues need to be addressed in order to increase the likelihood of success?

Service delivery and service quality

15.1   Introduction

The previous chapter highlighted the importance of developing and managing customer relationships and the growing concern with customer retention. One set of factors that might induce customer switching relate to poor service provision. Central to any approach to build and maintain good customer relationships is the management of service delivery to ensure quality and minimize the risks of service failure. The ability to deliver a high-quality service that meets the needs and expectations of customers is key to building a competitive advantage in the financial services sector. Because it is difficult for financial services providers to gain a sustainable competitive edge just by offering new products or new product features, attention is increasingly being focused on quality – not least because the quality of the service that an organization provides is difficult to copy. Furthermore, research suggests that high levels of quality will lead to higher levels of customer satisfaction, and higher levels of loyalty. The economics of customer retention suggests that retained customers will be important to financial services providers for two reasons. First, retained customers are usually cheaper to serve because the company already knows something about them and their needs, and the level of marketing expenditure required to keep customers is much lower than the cost of acquiring new customers. Secondly, loyal customers can generate more revenue because they tend to be less price-sensitive, they are likely to buy additional products and services, and will engage in positive word-of-mouth. While recognizing that some aspects of this argument may be oversimplified, there are good grounds for believing that loyal customers can generate higher profits. The delivery of a high-quality service is essential to ensuring that customers maintain a productive relationship with a financial services provider, and in that sense, service quality can be expected to have a positive impact on organizational performance. Some research would also suggest that high levels of service quality can contribute to employee satisfaction as well, since staff are typically happier in their work when delivering something that is high quality as opposed to something of low quality.

This chapter provides an overview of service delivery in financial services, and highlights some of the issues associated with managing quality. The chapter begins by introducing the concept of the service profit chain as a way of thinking about the service delivery process and its impact on customers. Thereafter, the discussion focuses more specifically on quality and begins by defining service quality and highlighting its key features. The next sections discuss models of service quality, the service delivery process and the areas where problems may arise with respect to service delivery. The final section in the chapter examines the outcomes of service quality paying particular attention to the issue of service failure and service recovery.

15.2   The service profit chain

The process of delivering service, generating customer loyalty and improving profitability has been conceptualized in the service profit chain (Heskett *et al.*, 1994), which is illustrated in Figure 15.1. This model starts with internal service quality, which refers to the extent to which an organization is able to deliver quality support service to employees to enable them to service customers effectively. Included in the general concept of internal service quality are factors such as job design, working environment, reward systems, training and support systems. Internal service quality will result in higher levels of employee satisfaction, productivity and retention. Employees who are satisfied in their job and well-motivated will deliver a high-quality service to customers. This high quality is the foundation for delivering enhanced service value. Value will, in turn, lead to increased levels of customer satisfaction and retention. Given the economics of

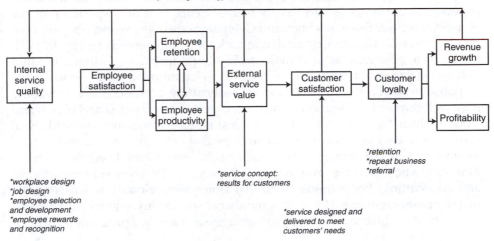

Figure 15.1 The service profit chain (*source:* Heskett *et al.* (1994).

customer retention (see, for example, Heskett *et al.*, 1994), improved revenues and profit are the expected consequences. In essence, the service profit chain highlights the important links between how an organization manages itself internally, the impact of this on the experience of customers and the benefits in terms of organizational performance.

The logic of the service profit chain is very appealing, and the model has been widely adopted by consultants and managers. In particular, it has been used to guide a range of managerial interventions, most notably in relation to internal organization and management, and its usefulness has been demonstrated in a variety of settings (Case study 15.1 demonstrates the application of the service profit chain in the case of Sears). Systematic research to test this model has proved difficult because of the complexities of data collection. One of the first and most comprehensive studies using the service profit chain was undertaken in relation to retail banking in the US. Loveman (1998) used secondary, branch-level data, and found that internal reward systems, the organization's customer focus and the quality of management had a positive impact on employee satisfaction. There was rather limited evidence for a link between employee satisfaction and loyalty. Employee length of service was found to affect customer satisfaction, but the relationship between employee satisfaction and customer satisfaction was weak. Customer satisfaction had a positive impact on loyalty to the bank, and loyalty in turn was found to have an impact on financial performance. Overall, Loveman's evidence provided tentative support for the key relationships that underpin the service profit chain. More recently, however, in a retail setting, Silvestro and Cross (2000) noted that that store profitability tends to be negatively rather than positively correlated with employee satisfaction, although they did find evidence to support the customer dimension of the service profit chain.

The alluring logic that links employee and customer satisfaction to hard-nosed commercial outcomes is particularly well-evidenced by the experience of the American retailer Sears, Roebuck and Company; one of the world's best-known retailing brands, with its origins dating back to the nineteenth century. In 1992, the company experienced a chronic decline in performance, culminating in a loss of $3.9bn on a turnover of $52.3bn. A common and understandable response to such a situation is a radical cost-cutting exercise. Such a response may well buy an organization some time, especially as far as shareholders and stock analysts are concerned. However, cost-based retrenchment is unlikely to result in the kind of competitive advantages that can achieve a sustained turn around and in performance. That said, Sears' new Chief Executive, Arthur Martinez, who joined the company in 1992, carried out a degree of restructuring and cost-cutting. For example, over 100 stores were closed, as was its loss-making Sears catalogue. However, a number of shrewd investments were made, including the realignment of the product range and a major programme of store refurbishment. These and other actions resulted in a marked turn around in performance which saw total shareholder return for 1993 of 56 per cent.

The company was anxious to build upon this initial progress, and the CEO initiated a programme for its long-term revival. Five strategic priorities were identified, including growth in the core retailing business and greater customer focus. An overarching change management group, known as the Phoenix Team, was created, and oversaw the work of a series of task forces. The Phoenix Team became increasingly exercised by the need to devise a model for the business that linked employers, customer and shareholders. Central to the model was a set of three aspirations, namely that Sears should be:

1. For employers – a compelling place to work
2. For customers – a compelling place to shop
3. For shareholders – a compelling place to invest.

The company employed a causal pathway modelling methodology based upon staff and customer surveys linked to financial performance measures. Over time, the company came to appreciate that of the 70 questions comprising the staff survey, 10 had a particularly strong impact on employee behaviour (and consequently upon customer satisfaction). Moreover, they discovered that just two dimensions of employee satisfaction, namely attitude toward the job and toward the company, had a greater impact upon employee loyalty and behaviour toward customers than all the other dimensions put together.

During the course of something like 2 years, Sears revised its methodology and modelling to derive an approach that demonstrated causal relationships between certain key measures of employee attitudes, customer satisfaction and profitability. To have demonstrated such a link is truly impressive and inspirational. Indeed, this also had a material impact upon the Nationwide Building Society's approach to customer and staff satisfaction measurement and the ensuing actions.

Source: Rucci et al. (1998).

What the service profit chain does do is highlight the importance of value (with quality as a key component of value) and the central role of the organization's employees in delivering that value quality. What it doesn't do is provide a detailed insight into that nature of service quality and the ways in which it should be managed. This will be the focus of the rest of this chapter. The concepts of value (as the relationship between quality and costs) and satisfaction will be addressed in more detail in Chapter 16.

15.3 Defining service quality

Quality is much more difficult to define for a service than it is for a physical good. With a physical good, quality can often be measured by specifying certain physical features that the product should possess. For example, the quality of a laser printer can be specified in terms of the number of pages that will be printed each minute and the quality of the printed output. This serves as an objective standard – if the printer reaches this objective standard, then it is considered to be of a particular quality. In financial services it is much more difficult to specify objective standards, because service encounters can vary and the needs of customers can vary.

There is a range of different perspectives on quality. Garvin (1988) suggests that these can be organized under five main headings:

1. *Quality is 'innate excellence'*. This view suggests quite simply that we know excellence from repeated experience of it (either our own or others'). Although it may be one approach that many people would feel comfortable with, from a management perspective it is vague and imprecise.
2. *Quality is product attributes*. This approach assumes that quality is a precise and measurable variable, provided by specified amounts of product attribute (the fuel consumption of a car, its power, its acceleration, etc.). This approach has many attractions because of its specificity and measurability, but fails to take into consideration the needs and preferences of customers.
3. *Quality is user-based*. This approach proposes that definitions of quality are based on the perspective of the customer and the extent to which a product meets those needs.
4. *Quality is supply-based*. This approach has similarities with the product attributes-based approach in that it centres on conformance to internally developed specifications. This is largely an operations-driven approach, which focuses on productivity and cost consideration.
5. *Quality is value-based*. This approach emphasizes the trade-off between performance and price, and is often described as 'affordable excellence'.

When thinking about service quality, the most common view is that service quality is subjective – that is to say, it is based on the customers' perception of how well the service matches their needs and expectations. Service quality is what consumers perceive it to be.

15.4 Models of service quality

While recognizing that the user-based view of service quality means that quality is defined by the customer, any attempt to manage service quality requires an understanding of how customers evaluate the service they receive and which elements are most important. Because we have adopted a subjective view of service quality, the most common way to think about how consumers evaluate a service is the idea that they will have expectations about the sort of service that they will receive. They will then compare the actual service with the expected service. If the actual service meets or exceeds the expected service, then the level of quality will be seen to be relatively high. If the actual service is below what was expected, then consumers will perceive that the quality of service is poor.

While it is widely agreed that service quality will involve a comparison of expectations and actual service performance, there are different views about the aspects of service that are important. In general, there are two main ways of looking at the elements of service quality. In broad terms, attempts to define and understand service quality have developed in two distinct directions – one stream of research originated in Europe (largely Scandinavia), while the other developed in North America. The European stream of research is often described as the Nordic School, and originates in the work of Christian Grönroos (see, for example, Grönroos, 1984, 1988). This approach tends to be more qualitative, and emphasizes the overall image of the organization, the outcome of the service (technical quality) and the way in which it is delivered (functional quality). The North-American stream of research developed from the work of Parasuraman, Zeithaml and Berry (see, for example, Parasuraman *et al.*, 1985, 1988); it explicitly defines service quality as the difference between perceptions and expectations, and measures quality across five main dimensions – Reliability, Assurance, Tangibles. Empathy and Responsiveness (RATER). Specifically, Parasuraman *et al.* proposed a method of measuring service quality using a measurement model called SERVQUAL. This has since been the most widely used approach to the measurement of service quality, and SERVQUAL has been applied to a variety of different services in a variety of different countries. Each of these two approaches will be discussed in more detail below.

15.4.1 The Nordic perspective on service quality

The framework developed by Grönroos is outlined in Figure 15.2. In this framework, it is proposed that customers form expectations and make evaluations of service delivery in relation to both functional and technical quality:

- *Functional quality* is concerned with the way in which the service is delivered, and will cover things such as friendliness, helpfulness, politeness, pleasantness, understanding. etc. It deals mostly with the way in which a service encounter happens. In the case of, say, a financial planner, functional quality would be concerned with the way in which the planner treats customers.
- *Technical quality* is concerned with the quality of the service outcome – that is to say, it is concerned with the extent to which the service is performed correctly

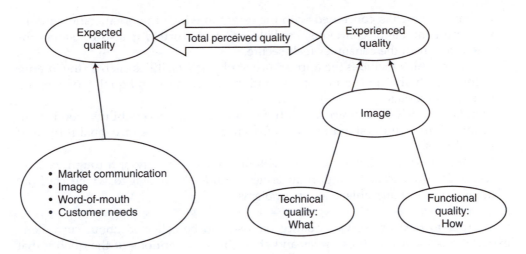

Figure 15.2 The Nordic perspective on service quality (*source:* Grönroos, 1988).

and accurately. In the case of a financial planner, technical quality would be concerned with the quality of the actual advice.

Perceptions of functional and technical quality combine to create an image for the organization, and this drives overall perceptions of quality.

Because overall service quality will be dependent on both functional and technical quality, to deliver a high-quality service will require not just good technical skills but also require good interpersonal skills. In many cases, research in financial services has suggested that functional quality may often be more important than technical quality. It has already been suggested that many personal customers find financial services complex and difficult to understand. In such situations, there will be a tendency for evaluations to be based on the quality of the interaction with the financial services provider rather than the intrinsic quality of the financial service itself.

15.4.2 The North-American perspective on service quality

The North-American perspective on service quality is based on the work of Parasuraman *et al.* (1985, 1988). They explicitly proposed that quality evaluations were based on a comparison of consumer expectations of what they *should* receive with consumer perceptions of what they *did* receive. They proposed that such comparisons would be made in five main areas:

1. *Reliability*, which is concerned with the extent to which customers can depend on the organization to perform the promised service, to do it accurately and to get it right first time.

2. *Assurance*, which is concerned with the extent to which the organization and its staff are competent, courteous, credible and trustworthy. It also considers the extent to which the consumer feels secure.
3. *Tangibles*, which includes the appearance of physical facilities such as the interior of the branch, the appearance of staff and the appearance and quality of communication materials.
4. *Empathy*, which is concerned with factors such as accessibility, good communications, understanding of customer's needs, approachability and friendliness.
5. *Responsiveness*, which is concerned with how the organization, through its staff, responds to customers. Important issues include the extent to which staff are helpful, prompt and able to solve problems.

In order to measure service quality, data should be collected about customers' expectations in each of these areas and about their perceptions of the quality that they receive. Indeed, Parasuraman *et al.* developed a questionnaire – known as SERVQUAL – specifically to collect data on these five aspects of service quality. By looking at the difference between the level of performance and the customers' expectations, an organization can identify the areas on which it should focus its attention. Consider the example in Figure 15.3. The graph plots the value of perceptions minus expectations for each of the five dimensions of service quality. Positive scores indicate that performance is above expectations, and negative scores indicate that performance is below expectations. In the case of this organization, the tangibles dimension is fine, as is empathy – both exceed customer expectations. However, performance with respect to reliability and responsiveness is clearly well below customer expectations. These findings would suggest that, in managing the

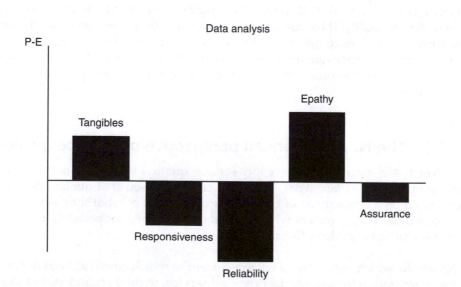

Figure 15.3 Zones of tolerance.

delivery of service quality, attention should be focused on reliability and responsiveness as the areas most in need of improvement.

The SERVQUAL framework has been used extensively in academic and business research, and has also attracted a significant amount of criticism (see, for example, Buttle, 1996). A particular cause for concern has been the idea that service quality is a difference score (i.e. the difference between perceptions and expectation, P – E). Implicit in this approach is the idea that when a score is negative, it indicates poor quality. However, some researchers have suggested that consumers may still perceive a high level of quality despite recording negative difference scores – for example, if expectations are very high and score at 7 while perceptions are positive but score lower at 6. In addition, difference scores do not distinguish between a situation in which P = 7 and E = 6, which indicates very positive evaluations, and one in which P = 2 and E = 1, which indicates very poor evaluations. Both would result in the same quality rating – i.e. 1. Other criticisms have been concerned with the generalizability of the SERVQUAL questions across very diverse services, and the adequacy of the coverage of the core service features. Consequently, many researchers have supplemented SERVQUAL with additional service-specific questions.

In response to criticisms, Parasuraman *et al.* continued to develop SERVQUAL. One important development related to the interpretation of expectations. The initial work on SERVQUAL treated expectations as being ideals – i.e. measures of what consumers think they should get. In recognition of the possibility that such ideal expectations could be unrealistically high, Parasuraman *et al.* (1991) proposed the concept of a 'zone of tolerance'. This approach suggested that consumers might have two types of expectations; ideal (or *should*) expectations and adequate (or *will*) expectations. In effect, it was argued that consumers would distinguish between their ideal standard of service and a realistic standard of service. Whereas the latter concerns the minimal acceptable standard that will provide a solution to their need, the former represents the level of service that they would like to experience. In Berry and Parasuraman's words: 'It is a blend of what the customer believes *can be* and *should be*' (Berry and Parasuraman, 1991).

Between the *desired* and the *adequate* levels of service is the *zone of tolerance*. This represents a range of service performance that the customer will consider satisfactory. Figure 15.4 provides an example of perceptions measured against zones of tolerance.

Consider the following example. A building society customer wishes to deposit some cash in her savings account and expects the entire service encounter, from entering the branch premises to leaving it, to take 4 minutes (the desired service level). However, the customer appreciates that a range of other variables might result in a somewhat longer service encounter. For example, there may be a number of other customers waiting to be served, one of whom may have a particularly large quantity of coins and cash to deposit. The customer may be willing to accept a total service encounter time of 12 minutes, based upon her expectations of likely factors. In this case, the difference between 12 minutes (the adequate service level) and 4 minutes (the desired service level) represents the zone of tolerance. A service encounter that is of a duration within the zone of tolerance will result in a positive assessment of service quality. However, a service encounter that is quicker will result in a highly favourable impression of the quality of service delivered while,

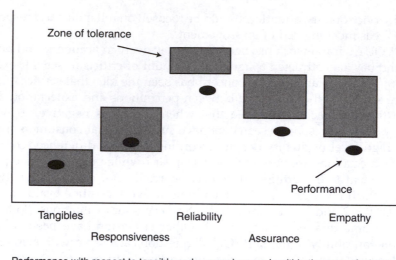

Performance with respect to tangible and responsiveness is within the zone of tolerance.
Performance with respect to reliability, assurance and empathy is a cause for concern
because all lie below the zone of tolerance.

Figure 15.4 Perceptions of service quality and zones of tolerance.

conversely, a service encounter falling below the adequate level will result in a negative assessment.

As can be imagined, the zone of tolerance is a highly flexible concept that varies not only from customer to customer and according to the nature of the given transaction, but may also vary for the same customer depending upon the circumstances surrounding a given transaction. Zones of tolerance vary across individuals because of different personal situations, differences in past experience and different service philosophies. The zone of tolerance also varies across the five key dimensions customers use in evaluating a service – reliability, assurance, tangibles, empathy and responsiveness. Reliability, or keeping the service promise, is thought to have a far narrower zone of tolerance than other aspects of a service. Zones of tolerance may also be affected by service context – for example, when faced with an emergency situation, zones of tolerance may be narrower than in a non-emergency situation. Finally, marketing activities may affect the breadth of the zone of tolerance. Marketing communications place an important role in creating expectations; over-promising in marketing communications can raise the level of 'adequate' expectations, and this reduces the size of the zone of tolerance.

The practical consequences of this model are manifold. For example, the development of customer advocacy is likely to result from customer experiences that are consistently above the upper limit of the zone of tolerance. Companies would do well to develop a firm grasp of the relative importance of zones of tolerance in respect of the more critical encounters of primary target segments. As a rule of thumb, the more crucial a given service feature, the narrower the zone of tolerance and the greater the likelihood of engendering customer negative evaluations of the service. By knowing what the critical service encounters are, a company can take action to ensure high standards of delivery.

In addition to identifying the areas that are important to consumers when evaluating service quality, Parasuraman *et al.* (1985) also developed a model of service delivery to help managers understand how problems might arise in the service delivery process and how service delivery could be managed to ensure high levels of quality. This will be discussed further later in the chapter.

15.4.3   Integrating the Nordic and North-American perspectives

The Nordic and North-American perspectives share many similarities in the way in which they view service quality. In 2002, Brady and Cronin proposed a framework that sought to integrate the key components of the major models of service quality. Drawing particularly upon the work of Grönroos (1984), Rust and Oliver (1994) and Parasuraman *et al.* (1985), they proposed a hierarchical approach to the assessment of service experience by consumers. This is shown diagrammatically in Figure 15.5.

In Figure 15.5, it can be seen that Brady and Cronin propose that there are three primary direct determinants of perceived service quality – interaction quality, the quality of the physical environment, and the quality of the outcome of the service experience. *Interactive quality* is viewed as being a function of how employees' attitudes, behaviours and expertise are perceived to influence the quality of a service interaction. This component of the model illustrates the importance attached to the *people* element of the marketing mix, an issue that will be discussed further in

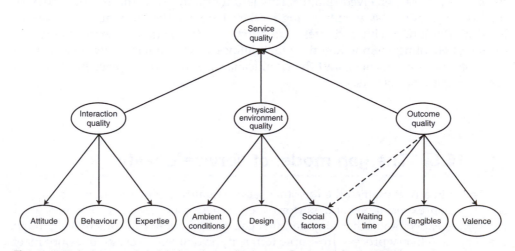

Figure 15.5 An integrated model of service quality (*source:* Brady and Cronin, 2001).

Chapter 17. The role played by the physical *environment quality* is held to be a function of the design and layout of the environment, the nature of the usage level taking place (social factors) and the atmosphere that is perceived (ambient conditions). The ambient conditions are determined by mood-setting devices such as lighting and music. It is interesting that, in Ireland, Permanent TSB bank has music playing in its branches in Dublin. It certainly achieves a form of differentiation when compared to the atmosphere of its rivals in the city.

Finally, *outcome quality* is held to be a function of waiting time, tangibles and value. Waiting time is self-evident, and the above explanation regarding zones of tolerance illustrates how these impact upon customer perception. Tangible evidence closely relates to the *physical evidence* component of the marketing mix.

Valence is a term used by Brady and Cronin to express whether the customer considers the ultimate outcome of the service experience to have been good or bad. This judgement is an overarching evaluation by the customer, irrespective of how he or she evaluates other components of the service encounter. For example, consider the case of a consumer approaching a bank for a home-improvement loan. His perceptions of the interaction quality and physical environment will be of no consequence if his loan application is refused. In other words, the appraisal of whether the core need was satisfied (valence) takes precedence over the other eight elements that influence the consumer's perception of service quality. It should be noted that the reliability, responsiveness and empathy components of the SERVQUAL model have been incorporated into the model as descriptors of the nine sub-dimensions of quality in themselves.

Brady and Cronin have subjected their model to empirical analysis, and the results provide support for its validity. They have succeeded in consolidating a range of service quality conceptualizations into 'a single, comprehensive, multi-dimensional framework with a strong theoretical base'. The authors recognize that the model suggests the need for further investigation, particularly with regard to the issue of valence. They also acknowledge that so far it has only been tested on a narrow range of the services domain, and may thus risk over-generalization. Nevertheless, it provides an extremely useful platform for practitioners as they seek to raise levels of perceived quality. This is important, given the role that service quality appears to play in influencing market share, relative profitability, customer loyalty, premium pricing and rates of re-purchase. Managers can use the model as a means of enabling them to identify what defines service quality, how service quality perceptions are formed, and the significance attached to the place in which the service experience occurs.

15.5   The gap model of service quality

We have already explained the idea that service quality can be based on a comparison between expectations and performance. Where there is a gap between what customers expect and what they get, this gap can be related to four other gaps in the service delivery process. In simple terms, if the delivered service does not meet

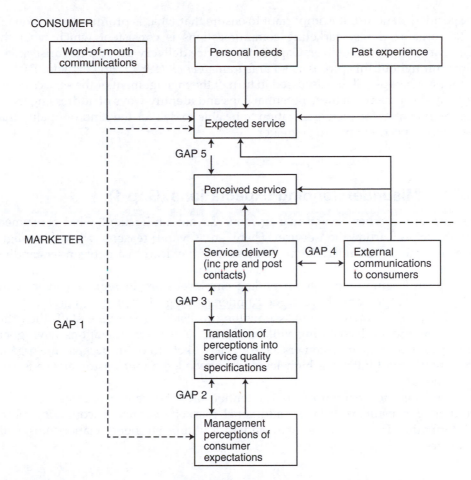

Figure 15.6 The gap model of service delivery (*source:* Parasuraman *et al.*, 1985).

customer expectations (Gap 5), this can be explained by any of four other gaps in the service delivery process:

- Misunderstanding expectations (Gap 1)
- Wrong specifications (Gap 2)
- Failure to deliver (Gap 3)
- Over-promising (Gap 4).

The service delivery process and the gaps are outlined in Figure 15.6.

Delivering a quality service requires a good understanding of what customers expect. Given their knowledge of what customers expect, managers must then set appropriate standards for the service and ensure that staff will deliver a service of the specified standard. It is important to ensure that what is promised to customers by the organization's marketing communications is consistent which what the organization is able to deliver. Gaps in the service delivery process can arise at key points throughout this process, as Parasuraman *et al.* (1985, 1991) explain. Each of the four main gaps will be discussed in turn. If the management of the service delivery process can focus on these potential gaps and identify ways of addressing them, then the potential for the organization to be able to deliver the kind of quality that customers expect will be much greater.

15.5.1   Misunderstanding expectations (Gap 1)

This gap arises when senior management do not understand what consumers actually expect from the service. There are several reasons why this might happen. A failure to undertake market research may lead to a poor understanding of what customers actually want. Equally important as a cause of Gap 1 may be poor upward communication – frontline employees are in regular contact with customers, and probably have a good understanding of their needs and expectations. However, if management is unwilling to listen to frontline staff, then this knowledge and understanding will be wasted. Where organizations have good relationships with their customers, Gap 1 is less likely to occur because the organization will have built up a high level of knowledge about customer needs and expectations.

Clearly, then, to deal with Gap 1, attention must be paid to increasing understanding of consumers through additional market research, encouraging flows of information from frontline staff and to building stronger relationships with customers.

15.5.2   Wrong specifications (Gap 2)

The second gap (Gap 2) arises if service specifications are not consistent with the expected service. This would imply that the company specifies and designs a particular service but the features, etc., are not what customers would expect. There are several reasons why this gap may arise. Some services may be very difficult to standardize; managers may think that customer expectations are unreasonable and cannot be met. In some cases the commitment to service quality may be missing, and consequently there will be a lack of interest in setting sensible services specifications. Closing Gap 2 means ensuring that the service that is specified matches the service that consumers expect. To do this, it is essential to ensure that top management is committed to providing service quality. Once that commitment is present, it is necessary to ensure that customer service expectations are part of the design process – that they are built into service development. Key service features must be identified (what is important to the consumer), and sensible specifications identified based on consumer priorities. Thus, for example, if customers expect quick service when making a loan application, then managers must identify what 'quick' means (is it a response in 1 day, in 1 week?). If customers also expect low interest rates and flexible repayments, then the relative importance of these should be identified and more attention paid to the feature that is most important. Where services can be standardized they should be, as this allows a single set of standards to be used rather than multiple sets.

Senior managers do play a key role with respect to Gap 2. Demonstrating a firm commitment to setting and using customer-defined performance standards can have a major impact on closing service quality Gap 2.

15.5.3   Failure to deliver (Gap 3)

Gap 3 arises when the actual service that is delivered does not match the service that was specified. Even if a sensible, customer-driven specification is in place, there is no guarantee that the service that is delivered to the customer will meet this standard. There are many reasons why Gap 3, failure to deliver, might arise. To deliver to a certain specification requires that appropriate resources (people, systems, and technology) exist and are supported. Broadly speaking, Gap 3 may arise because of problems with human resource policies, customer participation and intermediaries, because of problems with respect to managing supply and demand. If employees are not committed, willing and able to do their job well, then problems will arise with respect to the delivery of the service. If customers do not understand what they are meant to do, then there will be problems with the service that is delivered. If a service provider relies on an intermediary to distribute the service, then there may be difficulties in controlling the quality of what the intermediary does. Finally, if the organization cannot manage supply and demand, then it may be difficult to deliver that appropriate quality when levels of demand are high and staff are under pressure.

Closing Gap 3 requires that considerable attention be paid to staff. To achieve a high level of performance and ensure that high quality service is delivered requires that the organization:

- recruits the right people, with the skills and knowledge to delivery quality service
- ensures that there is a sensible reward system, so that employees received rewards (monetary and non-monetary) for delivering high-quality service.
- ensures that there is a good fit between technology and people – i.e. that people have the right technology for the job
- encourages empowerment and teamwork so that staff can adjust and adapt to differences in customer needs.

Equally importantly, the organization must make sure that customers know what they should be doing and how they should contribute to the delivery process. This requires effective communication regarding, for example, what information they need to provide, what forms they need to complete, etc.

Finally, attempting to synchronize demand and supply will be important to ensure that resources are not overstretched and quality standards can be maintained. Equally important is the need to ensure good co-operative working relationships with intermediaries to ensure that they will be motivated to deliver the standard of service that the organization expects.

15.5.4 Over-promising (Gap 4)

The fourth gap arises when the organization promises a better service than it actually delivers. This raises customer expectations, and when the delivered service then does not match those expectations, quality will be assessed as poor. A failure to deliver what was promised may arise for a number of reasons. The two most important are poor information and pressure to over-promise. Poor information flows between marketing and the rest of the organization may result in marketing having a poor understanding of what the organization will be able to do, and thus the claims that marketing makes will be inaccurate. Equally, there may be a tendency to over-promise in marketing communications, to outperform competitors and to make the organization appear in the most favourable light. Addressing Gap 4 requires that attention be paid to ensuring good, accurate communications between marketing and those involved in the service delivery process. This communication should provide clear and accurate information about what consumers can expect, and the information should then be integrated into all marketing communications to ensure that customers receive a consistent and honest message.

15.6 The outcomes of service quality

As the introduction mentioned, if an organization can deliver a high quality of service, its customers will receive better value and are more likely to be satisfied. In turn, satisfied customers are more likely to be retained and to be loyal. The nature of customer satisfaction and its measurement are discussed in more detail in Chapter 16, as is the nature of value. The remainder of this section focuses on loyalty. The central role of service quality in delivering customer loyalty and advocacy is widely acknowledged. Case study 15.2 explains how Cheshire Building Society gathers data on service quality which it then uses to gain a better understanding of exactly which aspects of their service are the most important in creating loyal customers.

Case study 15.2   Monitoring service quality at Cheshire Building Society

Through the regular gathering of member perceptions at the 'moment of truth', Cheshire Building Society has developed a systematic approach to understanding which members rate them highly, which members will remain loyal and which members are advocates of the organization. The collection of verbatim member comments also allows Cheshire to determine the drivers of loyalty and advocacy.

The key objectives of the programme are:
- to understand the members' perception of the service delivered to them corporately and locally on a monthly basis

- to track re-purchase intention and recommendation levels
- to improve service quality and uplift product purchase
- to provide process owners a monthly feed of information that flags issues and identifies practical ideas to improve service performance
- to benchmark, from a member perspective, performance against best-in-class service providers
- to recognize employees when the member perceives they have consistently delivered excellent service.

Each month 2000 survey questionnaires are mailed to members whose selection is based on a recent transaction (a telephone enquiry, new mortgage, new investment or branch visit). Additionally, a control group of members who have had no contact with the Cheshire in the last 12 months is also sampled. The surveys can also be deployed by telephone or e-mail as different member segments are added to the programme.

The detailed feedback reports provide a complete analysis of the key member experiences, identifying strengths and areas for improvement. Managers review the feedback reports each month, recognizing good performance and focusing attention and investment on correcting weaker areas. The results to date have resulted in:

- improved service delivery to members, across the channels
- development of action plans based on member feedback
- improved understanding of key drivers of what drives loyalty and advocacy
- improved benchmarked performance against best-in-class providers
- improved employee engagement satisfaction through greater recognition of service excellence.

In addition to the monthly survey, the Society utilizes other feedback mechanisms to build a comprehensive understanding of member views. These include:

- *'Have Your Say'* leaflets in branches
- website feedback forms
- member forums.

The complaint-handling process is also used to improve service delivery. Members are asked to rate the quality of the complaints process, irrespective of the outcome of the complaint, with a satisfaction rate in excess of 70 per cent being achieved during 2005.

Our members prioritize our actions and we can now act 'knowingly' rather than 'presumably'. The feedback gathered together with market research, mystery shopping and complaints data gives us an insight to how our members 'feel'. With this knowledge, Cheshire is able to develop new products and to further increase member loyalty and advocacy.

Source: Jason Gaunt, Marketing Director, Cheshire Building Society.

	Retained	Not Retained
Positive attitude	Loyal/Apostle	Mercenary
Negative attitude	Hostage	Defector/Terrorist

Figure 15.7 Attitudinal and behavioural loyalty. (*source:* Heskett *et al.*, 1995).

Loyalty is seen as a particularly significant outcome of service quality because of its impact on profit. However, loyalty is potentially a complex construct – it has both an attitudinal dimension (i.e. what the customer thinks or feels about an organization) and a behavioural dimension (i.e. what the customer does, and whether there is a repurchase). Customers may feel very positively towards an organization and thus be attitudinally loyal, but their situation may mean that no further purchases are made. Conversely, a customer may feel very negatively about an organization (be attitudinally disloyal) but continue to purchase, perhaps because of the lack of alternatives (see, for example, Dick and Basu, 1994). The different configurations of attitudinal and behavioural loyalty are outlined in Figure 15.7.

Customers classified as 'Loyal/Apostle' are those who have positive views about their experiences with the organization and continue to make purchases. 'Mercenaries' may have positive evaluations of an organization but choose not to repurchase for a variety of reasons – consumers buying mutual funds may, for example, choose to spread their business across a number of funds to spread risk, despite having very positive experiences of a given investment company. Other customers may move savings around between different providers in search of the best rates, and not because they have any negative views of the service provided by an individual organization. Customers in the 'Defector/Terrorist' category have a negative evaluation and decide not to repurchase. Such customers have clearly had very poor experience with an organization, and are thus more likely to engage in negative word-of-mouth as a result of their experiences. The final category, 'Hostage', consists of those customers who have negative attitudes to the organization but continue to repurchase because of a lack of alternatives. Such customers appear to be loyal (because they continue to purchase) but are not, and are potentially vulnerable to attractive offers from competitors. For example, many bank current-account customers are thought to fall into this category – they do not have a positive view of the service they receive, but do not switch their bank account because the process is too complex and they perceive few differences between competing banks.

To realize fully the benefits of loyalty depends on having customers who both continue to repurchase and also have positive attitudes. With such customers, there is a variety of potential financial and non-financial outcomes which provide the basis for arguments regarding the 'economics of customer retention':

1. Better knowledge of customer needs – which means that the organization is better able to meet customer needs and at a lower cost (because there is no need to gather new information).

2. Positive word-of-mouth – customers who are attitudinally loyal are likely to say positive things about the organization, and this can be an important (and cost-effective) form of marketing, particularly in financial services.
3. Spreading costs of acquisition – financial services organizations spend a lot of money (marketing expenses) to acquire customers. When a customer is behaviourally loyal, those costs can be spread out over a much longer relationship and over more transactions.
4. Less price-sensitivity – attitudinally loyal customers are thought to be less price-sensitive because they value the relationship with the organization.
5. Cross-selling – attitudinally loyal customers are more likely to purchase additional products from a particular organization.

Overall, then, creating customers who are both attitudinally and behaviourally loyal can mean reduced costs and higher revenues, and thus can have a positive effect on profitability, as argued in the service profit chain framework. Discussions in previous chapters have noted that it may be unwise to assume that all retained customers are profitable. In particular, Reinartz and Kumar (2002) have suggested that some retained customers will be 'barnacles' – retained but unprofitable. This may arise because such customers are more rather than less price-sensitive; they are aware of their potential value to the organization and demand special treatment, making them more rather than less expensive to serve. If such customers do not engage in positive word-of-mouth, then the benefits of retention to the organization may also be curtailed. While it is important to be aware that not all retained customers are profitable, this should not detract from the importance and value of customer loyalty and retention to financial services organizations.

As shown in Chapter 14, there is a developing body of research in financial services that seeks to highlight the beneficial outcomes of service quality. The evidence for service quality having an impact on financial performance is rather limited, although Storbacka (1994) and Loveman (1998) have provided evidence of positive relationships between service quality/customer satisfaction and profitability in banking. Yeung and Ennew (2001) used data from the American Consumer Satisfaction Index (ACSI) to provide evidence that customer satisfaction with financial services providers had a significant positive impact on a variety of measures of financial performance across the period 1994–1999. Other researchers have demonstrated that service quality does have a positive impact on satisfaction (Crosby and Stephens, 1987), retention (Ennew and Binks, 1996), and willingness to recommend and willingness to continue purchasing (Paulin et al., 1997). Thus, while there may be some debate about the precise nature of the outcomes of service quality, there is strong evidence to suggest significant benefits for organizations that focus attention on the delivery of high-quality customer service.

15.7 Service failure and recovery

Of course, we should remember that however much attention is paid to ensuring a high quality of service, there will sometimes be service failures – something will go wrong, a mistake may be made and customers may complain. For example, there may be a genuine mistake, staff may be absent (meaning that a particular customer cannot be dealt with properly), some aspect of technology may fail, etc. A poor service or a service failure will result in customer dissatisfaction and this in turn will prompt a variety of responses, which may include complaining, negative word-of-mouth and decisions not to repurchase. If it is impossible to avoid service failures and dissatisfaction, then it becomes increasingly important for organizations to understand how to minimize their adverse effects. There is a growing body of evidence to suggest that effective service recovery can generate a range of positive customer responses, with complaint handling being seen as a key element in service recovery. Responding effectively to consumer complaints can have a significant impact on satisfaction, repurchase intentions and the spread of word-of-mouth.

In order to be able to deal with service failure, an organization must first be aware that a failure has occurred. This means making it easy for customers to complain. All too often, customers experience a service failure but for some reason – too much effort, or the expectation that nothing will be done – they may choose not to complain to the provider. They simply switch to another provider and/or engage in negative word-of-mouth. The absence of a formal complaint means that the organization has no opportunity to address the individual customer's dissatisfaction and no opportunity to learn from that customer's experience. Thus, it makes sense for an organization to make it easy for customers to complain – perhaps by providing freephone numbers and complaints hotlines, etc. Thus, for example, ICICI Bank in India promotes its 24-hour customer care hotline and promises customers 'We aim to respond to your complaint with efficiency, courtesy and fairness. You can expect a response to your complaint within 2 business days.' Similarly, African Bank Investments in South Africa stresses a commitment to responding to complaints and provides customers with a three-stage process for lodging a complaint. Such guidance and encouragement is increasingly common as organizations recognize the value of responding to and learning from service failures. In addition to making the complaint process transparent and straightforward, organizations may also consider active research to check that the service delivery has gone well; this again provides the consumer with an opportunity to complain if necessary.

If an organization is to learn from service failure, then, in addition to knowing that a failure has occurred, it is important to have a clear understanding of the type of service failure. If the failure arises in relation to the service delivery, then the appropriate focus of attention may be service operations and design. In contrast, if the failure is a consequence of employee behaviour, then the appropriate response may be to reconsider human resource management policies and practices. Service failure can take many forms. Bitner *et al.* (1990) used the critical incident technique to identify and classify three main types of service failure:

1. *Service delivery failure.* Failures in the service delivery system generally fall into three categories. First, the service may simply be unavailable – an ATM or website may not work, or a key member of staff may be unavailable to serve a particular customer. Secondly, unreasonably slow service covers any delivery experience which is unreasonably slow and includes long queues, a website that is slow to respond, and any other delay in providing service to a customer. The third category, other core service failures, is deliberately broad to encompass a range of core failures including, for example, errors in money transmission, errors in claims handling and errors in processing service applications.

2. *Failure to respond to customer needs.* Customers may have a variety of needs and requests in relation to a particular service – whether explicit or implicit. The second category of failure relates to failure to respond to these needs. Implicit needs are not formally articulated by customers, but are nevertheless important. A failure to inform customers about a change in the terms and conditions of a service would constitute a failure to respond to implicit needs. Explicit needs are generally considered to be of four types: special needs, customer preferences, customer errors, and disruptive others. A failure by a financial adviser to select a product that matches an investor's risk preferences would constitute a failure to respond to the special needs of that individual. Similarly, a failure to amend the delivery system at the customer's request, as might occur when a customer requests a different schedule of loan repayments, would be a failure to respond to customer preferences. The third type of explicit request occurs when the customer makes an error and the employee fails to respond appropriately, as could occur with a lost credit or ATM card, or a failure to make a payment on time. Finally, service failures may occur when employees are required to resolve a dispute between customers.
3. *Unprompted and unsolicited employee actions.* Service failures may also occur when employees engage in behaviours that fall outside the normal, expected service delivery system. Included in this category of service failure are behaviours such as poor employee attitudes, rudeness, ignoring customers, discriminatory behaviour, unfairness, and dishonesty.

There is a variety of recommendations about the best way to manage service recovery. For example, Bell and Zemke (1987) suggested a five-stage strategy for dealing with customer complaints:

1. *Apology.* This should preferably be a first-person apology, rather than a corporate apology, and should acknowledge that a failure has occurred.
2. *Prompt response.* Once a failure has been recognized, then a speedy response to attempt to rectify the situation, as far as is possible, is essential.
3. *Empathy.* The process of dealing with the customer's complaint should be characterized by an understanding of the customer's situation.
4. *Symbolic atonement.* The customer should be offered some form of compensation that is appropriate to the nature of the failure (e.g. refunding service charges, small gifts, discounted or free services in the future).
5. *Follow-up.* This involves monitoring customer satisfaction with the recovery process.

Bitner *et al.* (1990) suggested a similar approach, focused on four key elements:

1. Acknowledgement of the problem
2. Explanation of the reason for the failure
3. Apology where appropriate
4. Compensation, such as a free ticket, meal or drink.

In the banking sector, research by Lewis and Spyrakopoulos (2001) has highlighted the importance of ensuring that service recovery results in consumers getting what they originally expected, even if this requires exceptional treatment. Empathy and speed were also identified as important elements in the recovery process. This study suggested that consumers' recovery expectations were generally reasonable, although customers with longstanding relationships with their bank tended to be more demanding when they experienced service failures.

Recent research on service recovery has focused attention on the role of perceived justice in understanding the effectiveness of service recovery strategies (see, for example, Tax *et al.*, 1998). Perceived justice focuses on the extent to which customers perceive the process and outcomes of service recovery to be just. Where levels of perceived justice are high, consumers are more likely to be satisfied. The three dimensions of perceived justice are the fairness of the resolution procedures (procedural justice), the interpersonal communications and behaviours (interactional justice), and the outcomes (distributive justice). These are defined as follows:

- *Procedural justice* relates to factors such as the delay in processing the complaint, process control, accessibility, timing/speed and the flexibility to adapt to the customer's recovery needs.
- *Interactional justice* refers to the manner in which people are treated during the complaint-handling process, including elements such as courtesy and politeness exhibited by personnel, empathy, effort observed in resolving the situation, and the firm's willingness to provide an explanation as to why the failure occurred.
- *Distributive justice* focuses on the perceived fairness of the outcome of the service encounter. In effect, distributive justice is concerned with the level and nature of apologies and compensations.

A growing number of empirical studies have applied perceived justice to examine consumer responses to complaints. Blodgett *et al.* (1997) used retail-based scenarios to demonstrate the importance of interactional justice as an influence on subsequent consumer behaviour. In a cross-sectoral study, Tax *et al.* (1998) presented evidence for the importance of all three dimensions of perceived justice in generating positive evaluations of complaint handling.

One factor that is key to effective service recovery is ensuring that frontline staff are empowered and encouraged to deal with customer complaints and problems as they happen. They should be able to use their judgement and take the initiative in solving customer problems. Indeed, one of the things that distinguishes many of the world's best service providers is the ability of their staff to deal efficiently and effectively with service failure. Like service quality, there are good reasons for investing in service recovery. Successful service recovery can have a positive impact on customer loyalty. In addition, the process of dealing with and resolving customer complaints can provide valuable insights into the nature of the service delivery process and help the organization to identify areas that may require further attention and development.

15.8 Summary and conclusions

This chapter has focused attention on service quality as a central component of service value. It has explained that service quality is increasingly important in financial services, as it provides a source of competitive advantage. It can also contribute to higher levels of profitability because high levels of quality can increase customer satisfaction and loyalty. These benefits mean that organizations must pay considerable attention to managing service delivery and ensuring that customers experience a high-quality service.

In services, quality is based on the customer's perception of what is delivered. In particular, the consumer's assessment of service quality is based on a comparison of the service that was expected with the actual service received. There are different ways of making this comparison; one approach suggests that consumers will consider both functional and technical dimensions of service quality. Another approach suggests that consumers will make comparisons across aspects of service, such as reliability, assurance, tangibles, empathy and responsiveness. Whichever approach is adopted, the assessment of service quality across these dimensions can help managers to identify the areas in which improvements should be made.

To determine how best to manage the delivery of service, it was suggested that we should think about quality as being a gap between customer expectations of a service and the service actually received. This gap could then be related to four problem areas (gaps) – misunderstanding customer expectations, failure to get the right service specifications, failure to deliver to specifications, and over-promising about the quality of the service. To manage the delivery of a high-quality service requires the careful management of people, processes and systems to attempt to ensure that managers understand what customers want, that they specify the right service, that staff are able to deliver to specifications, and that marketing makes accurate promises. This management process should lead to a high level of service quality, although it is probably impossible to guarantee that the organization will always get its service delivery right. Some service failures are bound to occur, and organizations must have a clear strategy for dealing with failures and solving customers' problems.

Review questions

1. Why is service quality so important in financial services?
2. What is the difference between functional and technical quality?
3. What are the differences between Gap 1, Gap 2 and Gap 3 in the gap model of service quality?
4. What are the benefits of customer retention?

Customer satisfaction, customer value and treating customers fairly

Learning objectives

By the end of this chapter you will be able to:
- understand the nature of customer satisfaction and customer value
- identify the issues associated with measuring and monitoring customer satisfaction
- understand the importance of fairness in organizations' interactions with their customers.

16.1 Introduction

One of the fundamental principles of marketing is that an organization can enhance its performance by ensuring that it responds to and satisfies customer needs. This simple idea is at the heart of the service profit chain that was introduced in the previous chapter. In the long run, businesses that fail to deliver customer satisfaction go out of business. Thus, there should be no contradiction between seeking to align the interests of owners and consumers. Problems often seem to occur when attempts are made to satisfy the short-term needs of one group to the detriment of the other. For example, a company might seek to achieve above-trend profit growth by a combination of price increases with cost reductions on the input side (e.g. reducing the number of staff, using less well-trained staff). Product margins might then receive a short-term boost, but competitors and consumers will gradually figure out what is happening and customer defection will occur. On the other hand, a company that is favouring customer preferences for higher quality at lower prices can be expected to achieve short-term growth in market share but will jeopardize the business's long-term viability if profitability is eroded in the process.

Chapter 15 introduced the concept of the service profit chain, and argued that the quality of service delivered to consumers is one of the main determinants of customer satisfaction because of its impact on value. Satisfaction is then expected to result in increased customer loyalty and improved profits and revenues.

Given that the purpose of marketing is getting and keeping customers, it is axiomatic that marketing's success must be judged in terms of how well customer needs and wants are met. It is not sufficient to rely upon levels of sales as a proxy for customer satisfaction. A business may well present a superficial appearance of continuing success based upon performance measures that are essentially financial. Although financial performance measures such as sales value and product margins are clearly important, they are merely financial reflections of consumer behaviour. A bank, for example, may be reporting healthy customer retention rates in a market where there is little competition, even though its customers actively dislike the company. However, the appearance of a competitor that is capable of providing better value for money and higher customer satisfaction could well steal significant share from the incumbent bank.

Therefore, it is vital that organizations develop the means by which they can acquire a well-founded knowledge of how they are viewed by their customers. Indeed, information about customer perceptions can yield valuable insights well in advance of the impact upon levels of sales. This chapter will explore consumer evaluations of a service with particular reference to both satisfaction and value. The chapter will begin by defining satisfaction and value and will then move on to examine specifically how organizations approach satisfaction measurement. The latter part of the chapter then examines issues relating to fairness and the way in which organizations treat their customers.

16.2   Consumer evaluations: value and satisfaction

The successful management of relationships with customers depends on ensuring that consumers have good experiences when they consume a service, that they evaluate that service experience positively and thus have a reason to maintain a relationship with a provider and make future purchases. Chapter 15 focused attention on service delivery, customer evaluations of quality, and service recovery. Consumer evaluations of the quality of service provided are clearly an important aspect of their evaluation of the overall experience of dealing with an organization. More significantly, perhaps, the evaluation of service quality is also an important determinant of value and of satisfaction, and these latter two outcomes are the focus of attention in the following discussions.

However, it is important to note that there is sometimes a degree of interchangeability, if not indeed confusion, regarding terms such as customer satisfaction, product and service quality, and value. All three terms concern the ways in which customers appraise the benefits they receive from engaging in a customer–supplier relationship. Service quality is an evaluation of a particular service offer, judged in relation to customer expectations of the type of service that should be received (i.e. the judgement is made in relation to the consumers' expectations of 'excellence'). *Quality* is generally recognized as an antecedent to customer satisfaction. *Value* is commonly treated as an outcome of service quality, and involves a comparison of the benefits received relative to price or cost. This recognizes the possibility that something which is relatively low quality may still deliver value if the costs of consumption are equally low. *Satisfaction* is also an evaluation of a service experience, and is commonly conceptualized as a comparison of expectations and perceptions. Unlike quality, expectations are based on what customers expect that they will actually get during consumption, thus giving rise to a judgement of the extent to which consumption has provided fulfilment.

16.2.1   Customer value

Zeithaml (1988) observes that the determination of value is not a simple task, in that consumers use the term in a number of different ways about a wide range of attributes and components. She proposes that customers define value in one of four basic ways:

1. *Value is low price*. It is undoubtedly true that in some purchasing situations value is defined primarily in terms that equate to low price, or what we might call cheapness. Customers buying on the basis that value is low price focus upon the essential functional aspects of a given good or service, expect a degree of similarity across different product offers and thus focus attention primarily or even exclusively on low price. It might be argued that in motor insurance this particular approach to value is dominant.
2. *Value is everything I want from a service*. This describes a purchasing scenario in which price plays a far less significant role. Instead, customers attach importance to the extent to which a good or service most closely satisfies their wants as well as their needs. If *value as low price* concerns basic need satisfaction, *value as everything I want* is at the opposite end of the spectrum and concerns the satisfaction of desires. By their very nature, desires are far more complex and multifaceted than needs, and are far more personal and subject to customer idiosyncrasies. Private banking is an example of an aspect of financial services where this concept of value might be most relevant.
3. *Value is the quality I get for the price I pay*. This involves, in a sense, a combination of the previous two approaches to value. It involves customers making a trade-off between the range and quality of benefits they receive and the financial sacrifice they make. For example, when buying household contents insurance the customer might want to ensure they have 'new-for-old' cover, and pay accordingly for it, but be unwilling to pay for comprehensive accidental damage cover for carpets and upholstered furniture.
4. *Value is what I get for what I give*. This assesses value in a particularly quantitative and measurable way. Under such circumstances, customers assess all of the benefits they receive in detail, as well as all of the elements of sacrifice they make. The component of sacrifice comprise time and effort as well as money. For example,

customers might decide that the additional time costs incurred in searching for the single best mortgage deal are sufficiently high that they may actually reduce the value associated with the 'best' product. Such consumers may perceive themselves to have obtained good value by obtaining acceptable product features with little or no search costs and a reasonable price.

Zeithaml (1988) suggests that, looking at these somewhat different perspectives on value, the most appropriate view of value is one which recognizes the trade-off between benefits and costs, defined broadly as follows:

Perceived value is the consumer's overall assessment of the utility of the service based on perceptions of what is received and what is given.

Precise measurement of value is more problematic, and exactly how benefits and costs combine to produce value is unclear (is it simply the difference between benefits and costs, or is it a ratio?). However, what is clear is that value can be increased by either increasing the quality of what is offered or reducing the costs of consumption, or by a combination of the two. In both cases, it is important to recognize that benefits and costs must be thought of in their broadest sense. For example, benefits are not just functional, they are also emotional – a strong brand that inspires trust and confidence in consumers (and thus reduces risk) can be an important benefit in financial services, and may deliver higher value even in the presence of a price that is high relative to the competition. Similarly, on the cost side, we should consider not just price paid but other non-monetary costs of consumption – the increased convenience that telephone banking offers to certain market segments is effectively enhancing value by reducing the non-monetary costs of consumption.

16.2.2   Customer satisfaction

On the face of it, it might seem that customer satisfaction is a pretty straightforward concept that readily lends itself to evaluation. However, upon further consideration it can be appreciated as a complex and multifaceted concept that has attracted enormous attention from both the academic and practitioner communities, not least because it is recognized as being of great significance to the well-being of individuals, firms and the economy as a whole. In its review for The Prime Minister's Office of Public Services Reform, MORI observes that it has been estimated that some 15 000 trade and academic articles were written on the subject in the two decades up to the mid-1990s, offering a variety of different perspectives on the nature and meaning of customer satisfaction. One of the most comprehensive reviews of the nature of customer satisfaction was produced by Oliver (1997), who provided an extended discussion of definitions, theoretical frameworks, and the antecedents and consequences of customer satisfaction.

Satisfaction is generally recognized as a pleasurable outcome, 'a desirable end state of consumption or patronization' (Oliver, 1997, p 10). Precise definitions of satisfaction vary, but common themes emphasize that it is a customer's judgement of the consumption experience formed through some kind of psychological process that involves some form of comparison of what was expected with what was received.

This does not preclude the possibility that interim judgements of satisfaction can be made (i.e. part way through the consumption process), and also allows for the possibility that satisfaction judgements may be made after specific transactions or in relation to an accumulated series of transactions. For example, a customer may form a satisfaction judgement relating to a specific encounter with a financial adviser and a satisfaction judgement relating to the overall relationship with that adviser. Similarly, consumers may form satisfaction judgements about specific attributes of a service (e.g. the responsiveness of staff, the amount of information provided, branch opening hours, etc.) or about the service overall.

The term 'fulfilment' is commonly used in discussions of satisfaction. However, there is a danger in interpreting such a term too narrowly – rather than thinking of satisfaction as simply meeting basic customer requirements, there is an increasing tendency to see satisfaction as being concerned with positive, pleasurable experiences. Some commentators go a stage further and suggest that marketers should go beyond satisfaction and instead focus attention on 'delighting' customers (Berman, 2005). Satisfaction will involve a positive experience and the delivery of a service that matches (or possibly exceeds) customer expectations; delight goes a stage further, delivering beyond expectations and generating a stronger emotional response.

What is evident in most discussions of satisfaction (or even delight) is that consumer judgements are made by comparing the service that is experienced against some pre-existing standard. One of the commonest bases for comparison is that of perceptions against expectations. This is commonly referred to as the Disconfirmation Model of Satisfaction. In simple terms, when perceptions are less than expectations the result is a negative disconfirmation, resulting in a negative evaluation and a lack of satisfaction. Confirmation of expectations or a situation of positive disconfirmation (where performance exceeds expectations) will result in a positive evaluation, usually satisfaction but perhaps also delight. There are clear similarities between this perspective on customer satisfaction and the idea that service quality is derived from the gap between expectations of what should be received and perceptions of what is actually received. The key difference arises in the way in which expectations are specified. In the case of service quality, the starting point for a comparison is some notion of 'ideal' expectations (what I *should* get); in the case of customer satisfaction, the starting point is predicted expectations (what I *will* get). Expectations provide only one comparison standard, although probably the most commonly used. Other comparison standards that may be relevant in satisfaction judgements include customer needs and a sense of what is fair/reasonable (equity theory).

16.3   Managing customer expectations

From the discussion so far, it is evident that quality, value and satisfaction are all influenced by the customer's expectations and perceptions in some form or another. While perceptions are effectively a product of the service encounter and should be managed by careful management of service delivery (as discussed in Chapter 15), expectations (whether ideal or predicted) are formed in advance of experiencing the service. As Berry and Parasuraman (1991) have shown, there is a variety of factors that will affect customer expectations.

The previous experience of the customer will be of importance in determining expectations. Poor service experiences will tend to reduce expectations, while good past experiences may raise them. However, previous experience may not necessarily relate directly to the exact product or service in question, but rather relate to analogous consumption experiences. Even when experiencing a service for the first time, consumers may form expectations based on experiences elsewhere. Customers visiting a financial adviser for the first time may draw on experiences with their bank in forming expectations about the nature of the service they will receive and the nature of interactions with the adviser. It is also the case that customers have become accustomed to higher standards of quality, choice and convenience in certain areas of commerce and these create benchmarks for completely different product and service categories.

Third-party communication also impacts upon the formation of expectations. This may arise from a number of sources, including word-of-mouth information and impressions gleaned from family members, friends, acquaintances and work colleagues. It also includes the views expressed by journalists and media commentators regarding the positive and negative aspects of a product, service or company. Other forms of third-party communication might include evaluations carried out by consumer interest organizations such as *Which?*. In January 2006, for example, *Which?* achieved wide publicity for the research it carried out into home equity release products and the resultant comments on their true costs and pitfalls. This information will inevitably have impacted on the expectations of many customers considering the purchase of such products. Similarly, stockbrokers and analysts produce reports on general industry sectors and the prospects for individual companies that inform the expectations of the investment management community.

Zeithaml and Bitner (2003) draw attention to the idea of explicit and implicit service communication as having a role to play in forming expectations. *Explicit service communication* refers to the formal written and broadcast messages that a company communicates regarding the nature of product and service quality and the performance it provides. The danger here is that a company may make claims about its products or services that it does not deliver in practice. There is a well-developed research-based body of literature that demonstrates the ways in which consumers punish companies that over-promise and under-deliver.

Implicit service communication refers to the range of subtle cues that organizations put out about the nature of what they do and how they do it. Included in this are the physical conditions and state of business premises. For example, an untidy financial adviser's office with poorly produced and displayed promotional material could convey an impression of disorganization and amateurishness that may impact negatively upon customer expectations. Conversely, the elegant marble entrance halls associated with many traditional bank branches may enhance expectations relating to confidence, reliability, trustworthiness, etc.

The values and beliefs system of individual consumers will also have a bearing upon their expectations for a given company. Clearly, these influences are highly variable and subjective. A customer who attaches considerable importance to social responsibility may have particularly high expectations of this aspect of a financial service provider's behaviour. Equally, an individual with a strong belief in personal service will typically have high expectations of the nature of service provided to customers. Other individual-specific factors may also affect expectations.

Expectations may vary according to temporary personal circumstances. For example, a consumer who has lost a credit card may have particularly high expectations about speed of service because of the desire to get the card replaced. A customer experiencing financial difficulties may have high expectations regarding the flexibility of loan repayments.

A financial services provider may believe that it offers a high-quality service to its customers, and one that meets their needs at a competitive price. However, customer evaluations are the ultimate arbiter of quality, value and satisfaction. For this reason, it is vital that organizations have in place a strategy for managing customer expectations and perceptions. Ultimately, perceptions are managed through the process of delivering the service to the customer, as explained in Chapter 15. The management of expectations is equally important. The discussion of the gap model drew attention to Gap 4 – the difference between what an organization promises and what it delivers – and highlighted the importance of having a strategy to manage customer expectations. Such a strategy should comprise the following components:

1. *Objectives*. These define how the organization wants to be perceived by its various primary customer segments. This component is closely allied to the notion of positioning, addressed in Chapter 9. It should not only specify aggregate levels of perception for the customer experience as a whole, but also should break it down according to a set of key performance indicators regarding benefits and sacrifice.
2. *Delivery*. The expectations of customers should be reflected in product design and performance. Equally, they should be factored into the service encounters that customers will experience during the course of their relationship with the provider. Particular attention should be devoted to service encounters that have been described as 'moments of truth'. Importantly, staff must be aware of the required standards and of their personal role in delivering satisfaction on the one hand, or dissatisfaction on the other. Similarly, expectations regarding sacrifice need to be factored into pricing decisions, and systems and process development. In the case of motor insurance, for example, some companies levy an additional charge for taking a car on holiday to another country, whereas others do not. Ensuring that consumers are clear about exactly what they can and cannot expect from their policy, what is included and what incurs an extra charge, will help to minimize any dissatisfaction that might arise as a consequence of perceived poor value.
3. *Recovery*. As explained in Chapter 15, clear policies and procedures are required to ensure effective recovery following a failure to deliver with regard to both benefits and sacrifice. Effective service recovery can result in the creation of customer advocacy if handled well. Indeed, quality failures should be seen as valuable opportunities to demonstrate empathy and responsiveness. All too often, poor recovery policies and procedures (or indeed their complete absence) serve to make a bad situation worse.
4. *Communication*. The provider must ensure that a programme is in place to communicate the actual levels of benefit that it is delivering to its customers. It is not sufficient for a company to assume that customers have noticed that it is achieving a service standard above that which it initially promised. Similarly, customers

may need to be told when a company is holding prices steady for an additional year or giving them preferential treatment regarding the purchase of an additional product.

5. *Measurement*. Processes are necessary that facilitate the tracking of perception over time in order to identify positive or adverse trends. Ideally, the measurement process should incorporate the means to gather perception data from a range of sources, including: formal customer survey, complaints feedback, *ad hoc* customer feedback, feedback from staff, and feedback from external sources such as the media. The latter is important, given the capacity of the media to have a material impact upon corporate reputations. Expectations regarding benefit delivery and sacrifice should be established at the outset. Case study 17.2 (in Chapter 17) provides an example of a company that offers tailored solutions for measuring the experience of customers during their interactions with an organization.

6. *Feedback*. The results of customer value and satisfaction measurement should be fed back into relevant parts of the organization and, as appropriate, communicated to customers. One organization involved in business-to-business supply within the financial services sector undertook a major satisfaction survey. On the majority of key measures of service the company outperformed its three major rivals, and on aggregate it was rated number one for service quality. Unfortunately, a major opportunity was missed by the company's unwillingness to devote sufficient resources to communicating this powerful story to its customers.

16.4   The measurement of satisfaction

Most discussions of satisfaction measurement focus primarily on the measurement of customer satisfaction because of its importance as a performance metric. However, as the service profit chain shows, both employee satisfaction and customer satisfaction may be relevant as performance metrics, and both will be considered in this section.

16.4.1   Customer satisfaction

So far in this chapter we have established that customer satisfaction is a multifaceted concept and far from one-dimensional. As such, individual managers must form a view on the nature of satisfaction for their own organization with regard to factors such as the need being fulfilled, the degree and variety of competition, segment variations, and how the resultant data will be used.

As a rule, customer satisfaction is measured by the use of some form of quantitative survey. Owing to the nature of customer satisfaction and the use that is made of its data, the survey is required to be statistically reliable and robust. For example, its outputs may be used as the basis for major investment in time, money and systems resources in upgrading elements of service delivery. Managers responsible for deciding upon and implementing such investments must only do so on the basis of valid and reliable information. Thus, the sample size and structure of a customer satisfaction survey must be of a scale and scope that engenders the necessary confidence.

The starting point for any customer satisfaction survey must be the identification of relevant, business-orientated objectives that will produce clear, unambiguous results. A useful starting point is deciding which business decisions need to be made and require knowledge regarding customer satisfaction. In common with any data capture and analysis exercise, there is no point in doing it unless it plays a role in influencing a business decision. Thus, customer satisfaction should form an integral part of senior management information flows. In this way it can influence a range of decisions by answering questions such as:

- What do we need to do to improve customer retention?
- What do we need to do to get customers to place more business with us?
- Which competitors pose the greater threat, and what do we need to do to counter those threats?
- What do we need to do to increase market share?
- What opportunities are there to reduce operating costs without harming customer satisfaction?
- What should form the basis of future competitive advantage?

The above six business questions are simply indicative of the range of issues that customer satisfaction information can inform; there are many others besides. Nevertheless, this illustrates the point that such information lies at the very core of the big issues that determines sustainable organizational success. The implications of this are clear: first, the conduct of effective customer satisfaction measurement is non-negotiable; secondly, the highest level of management must actively engage with the results of such surveys and be prepared to act upon them. Common failings are the absence of appropriate customer satisfaction measurement, or the lack of visibility of its findings and ineffective follow-through.

Therefore, the objectives for a customer satisfaction survey (CSS) must be grounded in the nature of the business decisions it will inform. The following list gives an indication of the kind of objectives that might be informed by a CSS:

- What do customers expect from the services we provide?
- To what extent are customers' expectations met by the services they receive from us?
- What level of satisfaction do our customers experience from the individual components that comprise our service?
- Which of our competitors do our customers also use for the provision of services, and what levels of satisfaction do they express for each competitor?
- How do levels of customer satisfaction with our services compare with those of our rivals?
- How do customers rate the value for money they receive from our services compared with our competitors?
- Which elements of our service do we need to improve in order to achieve higher levels of customer satisfaction?
- Which aspects of our services do customers gain little value from and consider to be of little relevance to their experience as customers?

- How does satisfaction vary by customer segment?
- How have customer expectations changed since we last surveyed their perceptions?
- How are customers' perceptions of our service quality trending over time?

The final point is interesting in that it introduces the concept of trends over time. The CSS has a major role to play in the identification of performance-related trends that have important consequences for the organization. For this reason it is important that, at the outset of a CSS programme, a view is taken regarding variables the organization wishes to track over the long term. Thus, such variables will be clearly addressed by the initial study in order to establish benchmarks. Additionally, subsequent surveys should be designed to ensure that wording is entirely consistent, to ensure that any resulting trend data can be relied upon. In a similar vein, it is important that the sample frame used over time is consistent with its predecessors.

Once an organization has some clarity regarding the purpose and objectives it requires from a CSS, it must then consider the process and methodology deemed most appropriate. A basic question concerns whether the survey should be conducted using in-house resources or be subcontracted to experienced agents such as SPSS in the USA or MORI in the UK. Using a specialist agency is usually the best option, owing to the expertise it possesses in questionnaire design, data capture, data analysis, interpretation and presentation. Furthermore, such agencies introduce a necessary degree of independence and detachment. Most such agencies also conduct staff satisfaction surveys (which really should be conducted on an independent basis), and there is a strong logic to combining both forms of survey within the same external agency. A note of caution is warranted. As with the use of all external agencies, the involvement of a specialist CSS supplier should always be subject to the development of a written brief. The writing of such a brief becomes relatively straightforward once there is clarity regarding objectives.

The in-house option may be the viable option where the customer base is relatively small. This might apply in certain parts of the B2B domain, such as where a provider of company pension schemes wishes to assess levels of satisfaction among its large corporate clients. Indeed, in such circumstances it may be desirable to measure satisfaction levels for all customers, given the higher proportion of business accounted for by each corporate client. Although the logistical and analytical aspects of such CSS activities may be of a scale that would allow the survey to be conducted on an in-house basis, the need for independence and impartiality argues in favour of outsourcing to a specialist agency. For those organizations wishing to consider the in-house option, packages are available that can be used in a wide range of circumstances, including high-volume consumer markets. For example, in the USA, AT&T has developed Business Builder as a do-it-yourself package that can be available from under $500.

Whether conducted on an in-house basis or via outsourcing, a written brief is essential. In addition to specifying objectives, it should address issues such as:

- which individual issues it requires data on, such as the specific aspects of service it wishes to investigate (the nine components of service quality proposed by Brady and Cronin (2002) might form the basis for this)

- which categorizations of the customers it wishes to use as a basis for cuts of the data, such as specific; segments; length of customer relationship; whether light, moderate or heavy users of the service; image of certain competitors, etc.
- demographic classification criteria – for example, age, gender, occupation, income, geographical location
- the format of the presentation of results
- the timescale and costs.

Once these issues have been fully resolved, the most appropriate methodology can be considered. Data can be captured in a variety of ways, most commonly by postal questionnaire, telephone interview or, in recent times, via the Internet. Face-to-face interviewing is often encountered with regard to high-value B2B situations which may involve discussions with a number of people comprising the decision-making unit (DMU) and user community. Each of these four principal methods of data capture has its respective advantages and drawbacks, and must be considered in the light of the requirements specified in the brief. For example, the telephone allows the researcher to speak directly with the customer and respond to any issues of ambiguity that might arise. However, it is best limited to calls of no longer than 10 minutes as a rule, and can present some problems regarding the use of certain rating scales. Written surveys administered by the post can permit a greater array of issues to be investigated. It can also allow certain forms of visual stimuli to be used, as well as relatively complex rating scales. However, it can result in low response rates and skewed respondent profiles. The Internet offers much of the functionality of the postal questionnaire but is low-cost and lends itself to speedy, flexible and cost-effective data analysis. User group bias may be an issue, particularly in parts of the world or among segments where usage of the Internet is patchy.

Whichever method of data capture is preferred, it is strongly recommended that an initial pilot study be carried out. The scope of the pilot study should be such that it not only tests the appropriateness of the means of data capture and the nature of the individual questions themselves, but should also test the format of results presentation. Leading on from the final point should be a simulation of the likely outputs. This will enable the organization to judge the extent to which the survey, as proposed, will inform the objectives. As a result of the pilot study, reconsideration may be made of the means of data capture wording of individual questions or, indeed, the number and nature of questions included. In this way, there is a much greater likelihood that the CSS will achieve its objectives.

A high degree of rigour is necessary when carrying out CSS activities, as it is by no means uncommon for research exercises of this nature to be subject to scope creep and redirection of emphasis in the absence of due rigour and control.

As a final point, the results of customer satisfaction surveys should not only be communicated extensively among the organization's own staff; consideration should also be given to communicating the results back to customers. This is especially important in the B2B context, which often involves face-to-face interviews with client staff. In such circumstances there is usually a strong presumption that such individuals will receive feedback on the survey in consideration of the time they have contributed to the actual survey.

A customer group that requires particular consideration in the context of financial services is that of intermediaries and brokers. In many areas of financial services – mortgages and pensions, for example – brokers are of fundamental importance, and the satisfaction they gain from supplier relationships and service must be assessed.

16.4.2   Employee satisfaction

A complementary activity to customer satisfaction measurement is that of the assessment of staff satisfaction. In the same way that the acquisition and retention of customers is important to an organization, so too is the hiring and retention of high-quality staff. Thus, staff satisfaction surveys can yield valuable insights that can assist in the development of staff attraction and retention policies and practices. Given the importance of staff morale and motivation to the provision of good-quality service, it is important that a company possesses a solid knowledge of staff feelings and perceptions.

As with customer surveys, staff surveys should be subject to due rigour with regard to their planning and execution. This means that objectives need to be clearly articulated, data sets specified and classification categories defined. It is particularly important to incorporate questions regarding aspects of customer service into staff surveys. For example, staff should be asked what they believe to be the appropriate expectations of customers with regard to the role that they and their department perform.

A common belief surrounding the use of staff surveys is that senior management will not act upon them. Indeed, far from facilitating better staff morale and motivation, badly executed staff surveys that are poorly communicated can do more harm than good. One company made the results of a staff survey available on its intranet for a period of 1 week and then it was forgotten about. Worryingly, the perception of middle-ranking and junior staff was that senior management appeared to have treated it as a cynical exercise of 'going through the motions'.

Nationwide Building Society represents an example of extremely good practice when it comes to assessing, communicating and acting upon its staff satisfaction survey, as shown in Case study 16.1.

Case study 16.1   Satisfaction surveys at Nationwide Building Society

Nationwide Building Society has been conducting an employee opinion survey called ViewPoint since 1993. The catalyst for its introduction was the merger of Nationwide and Anglia Building Societies – two organizations with different cultures, processes and business systems. A number of years after this merger had taken place, an increasing unease and uncertainty amongst employees about its success was perceived. In addition, the UK PFS business climate was becoming increasingly competitive, with deregulation allowing banks and insurance companies to compete with building societies for mortgage and savings business, leading to further uncertainty.

Case study 16.1   Satisfaction surveys at Nationwide Building Society—cont'd

The objective was (and still is) to give employees a platform from which they can have their say about various aspects of their work, working environment and the manner in which they are led, managed and developed. In summary, where they think Nationwide is doing well and what they believe the Society could do better. Asking for opinions, however, is one thing but it is vital that in addition to listening, companies act (and are seen to be acting) on the issues raised in the survey. Failure to do so will lead to cynicism and apathy towards the surveying process.

Nationwide's ViewPoint survey is conducted annually in April by ORC International, an external consultancy. Using ORCI enables Nationwide to remain impartial and the data confidential. The survey was paper-based until 2004, when it was made available via the Society's intranet with a paper-based option retained. Time is allocated during the working day for completion.

The survey comprises three parts:
1. Employee demographics, including job type, location, age, gender, ethnicity, sexual orientation, religion, etc.
2. A variety of work-based questions (104 in all) based on a five-point Likert scale
3. A small number of open questions about working at Nationwide, with a free-form response box to allow comments to be made by employees.

In 2005, 91 per cent of employees (approx 14 000) completed the survey.

The 104 work-based questions are grouped into a number of different themes or indices, including employee satisfaction, pay and benefits, leadership and group image, training and development, and employee and customer commitment.

The results are collated by ORCI and reports are produced at Group, divisional, departmental and team levels for distribution to managers across the business. To retain anonymity and confidentiality, no reports are issued with less than six responses. The reports include peer and external benchmarking data, and a comparison to the previous year's results.

On receipt of the reports, local managers will normally organize team meetings to disseminate the results and form action plans to look into poor scoring themes or themes showing a decline in results.

At a company level, the results are made available through different media, including an intranet site and an in-house magazine.

Some of the 2005 results were as follows.

Factor	Favourable response
Employee satisfaction	77%
Employee commitment	83%
Employer of integrity	87%
Satisfaction with work–life balance	78%

Continued

Case study 16.1   Satisfaction surveys at Nationwide Building Society—cont'd

Using ORCI enables external benchmarking on a number of questions with other financial services providers and other industries. Generally, Nationwide benchmarks very favourably. When compared with other financial services organizations, out of the 41 benchmarked questions Nationwide came top – 11 question scores were the highest, 13 were second, and six were third.

The survey itself has changed very little over the last 3 years, and there are a large number of questions that have been there from the beginning. This gives the survey great power as over time trends can be established in the data that allow progress or regression to be seen. Similarly, it enables the impact of certain initiatives to be seen.

Nationwide take the results of the survey one step further than most and links the data to their customer and business performance data. This research (Project Genome) has led to the model shown in Figure 16.1.

The links between committed employees, committed customers and better business performance have been established. The data for satisfaction with pay, coaching, values and committed people all come from ViewPoint.

Through the model we can say that a 3 per cent shift in employees 'values' results in customer commitment increasing by 1 per cent, bringing in an increased net present value of £6.5 million in mortgage sales. The model allows line-of-sight from employee behaviours through customer behaviours to the bottom line. Consequently, the employee opinion survey can be used as an early warning system to future business performance.

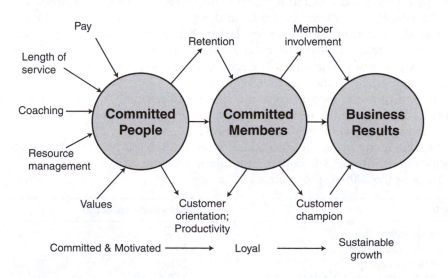

Figure 16.1 Nationwide's Genome model.

> ### Case study 16.1   Satisfaction surveys at Nationwide Building Society—cont'd
>
> It is valuable to exercise a degree of caution regarding employee opinion surveys as they measure employee's perceptions. These perceptions may be well-rooted or transient, and may depend on what side of the bed the employee got out of that morning. The timing of the survey is also very important, as conducting one during a redundancy period, for example, is highly likely to skew results. One other point to consider is the 'say–do' paradox. Employees will not necessarily take the course of action they say they will in the survey. A high response rate and data over time will overcome most of these potential problem areas.
>
> To have been named as the *Sunday Times* 'Best Big Company to Work For' in 2005, voted for by employees, is a pretty good indication that Nationwide has come a long way since the unease of the early 1990s. Listening to and acting on employees' feedback has been critical to that success.
>
> *Source: Stuart Bernau, Commercial & Communications Director,*
> *Nationwide Building Society.*

16.5   Treating customers fairly

Central to the concept of satisfaction is that customers feel that they have been treated fairly. Indeed, there is a close connection between the notion of fairness and trust, in that people display a willingness to trust individuals and organizations that they consider to act in ways that are fair. The corollary to this is that resentment and mistrust are the consequences of customers being exposed to what they consider to be unfair practices. Set within the context of managing ongoing customer relationships, it is imperative that organizations endeavour to build trust through being seen to act fairly. To quote from Berry and Parasuraman (1991):

> trust requires fair play. Few customers wish to build and continue a relationship with a firm they perceive to be unfair.

The concept of fairness is assuming growing significance in a range of contexts throughout the world. For example, fair-trade products have become a feature of the market for fruit and vegetables and packaged food and drink products on a global basis. In essence, fairness has to do more with adherence to the *spirit* of what is the right thing to do rather than conformance with the letter of the law. In an environment characterized by fairness, organizations must increasingly strive to avoid hiding behind punitive and unfair contractual terms. The Office of Fair Trading in the UK was established with the goal of making markets work well for consumers. It sets out to make sure that consumers have as much choice as possible across all the different sectors of the marketplace. According to the OFT, when consumers have choice they have genuine and enduring power. To quote from its website:

> As an independent professional organization, the OFT plays a leading role in promoting and protecting consumer interests throughout the UK, while ensuring that businesses are fair and competitive. Our tools to carry out this work are the powers granted to the OFT under consumer and competition legislation.

It carries out the following activities in pursuit of its goal:

- enforcement of competition and consumer protection rules
- market studies into how markets are working
- communication to explain and improve awareness and understanding.

Fairness has also established itself firmly as part of the agenda of the Financial Services Authority (FSA). Indeed this is nothing new, as the requirement to treat customers fairly is clearly laid out in Principle 6 of its Principles for Business, which states:

> A firm must pay due regard to the interests of its customers and treat them fairly.

It began to address the issue of fairness in earnest in 2001, with the publication of *Treating Customers Fairly After the Point of Sale* and its reinforcement through a series of presentations, along with various formal dialogues and consultations with the industry. Lying behind this initiative are the FSA's concerns that rules-focused regulation and market forces have so far failed to safeguard consumers from being treated unfairly. Writing in its commentary on the FSA's TCF initiative, Kirk and Middleton (2004) point out that:

> Due to low levels of financial capability and the complexity of financial services products, customers are often unable to assess effectively where they are being treated unfairly, and cannot exercise sufficient power to penalize firms who treat their customers unfairly.

In common with the OFT, the FSA does not propose a definition of what constitutes fairness, nor does it set out to present a firm set of rules. Rather, it chooses to address the issue of fairness through its promulgation via a principles-based approach. Senior management are expected to define and interpret what fairness means within the context of their own organization. It is for senior management to decide how fairness should manifest itself in terms of strategy, culture and operations. Moreover, mere compliance with the requirements of the FSA's rulebook will not be sufficient to demonstrate that an organization is treating its customers fairly.

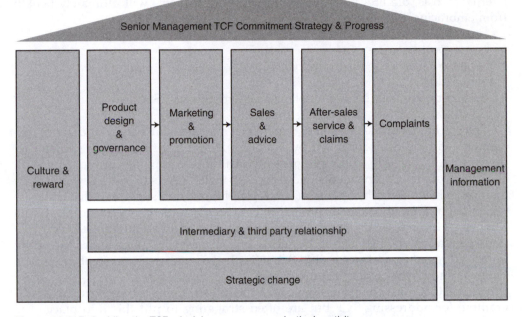

Figure 16.2 Embedding the TCF principle across an organization's activity.

The FSA has advised the organizations it authorizes that the TCF principle should be embedded in all parts of the organization and at all levels. As an aid to appreciating fully the scope and extent of TCF, the FSA has devised the conceptual scheme shown in Figure 16.2.

In practical terms, TCF should be considered in situations such as:

1. *Product design*. Many firms make use of consumer research in designing new products, but they need to ensure that this is used in the correct way.
2. *Remuneration*. There are areas where salespeople may create risks to TCF, if not appropriately managed or incentivized.
3. *Complaints management*. The quality of work to investigate and assess complaints varies widely from firm to firm.

As part of its TCF programme, the FSA has conducted consumer research which has elicited the following definitions of fairness:

- Give customers what they paid for
- Do not take advantage of customers
- Offer customers the best product you can
- Exhibit clarity in all customer dealings
- Do your best to resolve mistakes as quickly as possible
- Show flexibility, empathy and consideration in customer dealings.

Rather than viewing this as yet another imposition that will add to the burden of overhead costs, the FSA is of the opinion that the industry will ultimately benefit from embracing TCF, in the form of:

- more repeat business
- greater confidence in the industry
- fewer rules
- fewer complaints upheld by the Financial Ombudsman Service.

A recent life insurance customer experience management survey and set of discussions with 50 companies, led by Mulberry House Consulting, has shown that there is wide disparity in the progress life insurance companies are making with TCF. In most areas, respondents had recognized what needs to be achieved in their own organization and had plans in place, but the research suggested that progress was often at an early stage or limited in consistency and scope. According to the Mulberry House research, the majority of companies that had progressed with TCF implementation claimed also to be seeing business benefits (sometimes including improved retention and cross-selling), but few had formal measures in place to track progress and target process improvements.

It seems that most companies have identified the need for a more structured programme for addressing TCF but are often struggling to put this into place. The Mulberry House survey showed clearly that, as the FSA would expect, in most companies the CEO is the major sponsor of TCF. However, the internal champions are often next-level directors, which immediately separates efforts by business silo. Separation of internal structures and customer management processes typically work against the provision of a seamless and consistent customer experience. Although plans are usually in place, the Mulberry House study suggests there is much still to be achieved to ensure TCF is deployed consistently across all aspects of participating organizations.

As at the time of writing, Ernst & Young are exhorting companies to respond to the requirements of TCF most appropriately by:

- conducting a systematic review of strategy and operations
- identifying possible areas of vulnerability
- providing detailed documentation of policies and procedures supporting TCF
- having plans to build TCF into business-as-usual.

This is wise advice given that the FSA intends to incorporate an assessment of firms' effectiveness and ability to show that they treat customers fairly in their member appraisal process, called ARROW. It will issue further guidance on the subject in 2006, and continue to publish examples of good and bad practice. Again, Ernst & Young has proposed a useful battery of questions that senior management would do well to consider when determining their approach to TCF, and these are presented in Box 16.1.

Whichever country the reader resides in, it is likely that some form of TCF initiative will arise, if indeed it has not already done so. Regulators aside, it is axiomatic of good marketing strategy and execution that fairness is firmly embedded as a core principle.

Box 16.1 'From board room to boiler room'

From our experience, many firms are likely to be surprised by the wide range of interventions that may be required to ensure they can satisfy the FSA's expectations; from business strategy and high-level decision-making through to training of frontline staff and revision of remuneration and incentive systems.

Senior management should be able to answer key questions demonstrating how they meet their TCF obligations. There is no right or wrong answer to any question, and the responses should be driven from consideration of the impact TCF may have on the overall business strategy and how it operates. Without boundaries and guidance set at a strategic level, *ad hoc* decision-making at an operational level risks not treating customers fairly (or, conversely, in trying to treat customers fairly, ending up treating shareholders unfairly).

Some questions management may want to consider include:

- What does fairness mean in terms of your target customers, products and service promise, and what are the key fairness principles that will guide action within your business?
- How do you balance the objective of increasing sales and profit with the requirement to treat customers fairly?
- How do you ensure you have a full understanding of your target market, considering customers' financial needs and capability?
- What steps do you take to assess the risks to customers in a product during the product development process and throughout a product's lifecycle?
- What steps do you take to ensure marketing materials are understandable and understood, and that they provide a clear and balanced assessment of the risks, charges and penalties of the product, as well as the benefits?
- How do remuneration strategies encourage sales and marketing people to treat customers fairly?
- What steps do you take to check the customer understands and can afford the product being offered?
- How do you ensure charges are always transparent and understood?
- What steps do you take to keep customers informed about changes in the wider environment that may affect their product after the point of sale?
- What barriers do you have that may make it difficult or expensive for customers to exit or switch their products or suppliers?
- What steps have you taken to ensure your complaints handling process is easy for customers to follow and that it ensures each complaint is treated fairly?
- What is your process for ensuring you identify and tackle the root causes of complaints to prevent them re-occurring?
- What management information is available to senior management to track how fairly customers are treated, and how is this information used?

Source: Kirk and Middleton (2004).

16.6   Summary and conclusions

Central to the marketing concept is the idea that an organization can enhance its overall performance by taking a customer-orientated view of its business and focusing on the delivery of customer satisfaction. This general idea is encapsulated in the concept of the service profit chain. Satisfaction and value are both seen as being important evaluations of the service experience and as determinants of customer retention and loyalty. Satisfaction is concerned with the extent to which a service is able to deliver against customer expectations, while value is concerned with the range of benefits offered by the service relative to its associated costs. As with service quality, consumer evaluations of satisfaction and value play a major role in the development of relationships with financial services providers. Customer dissatisfaction and/or poor value are potential reasons for terminating any financial services relationship.

Careful measurement of satisfaction is an important element of any relationship marketing/CRM programme. Indeed, in some of the best examples, the measurement of customer satisfaction will be accompanied by the measurement of employee satisfaction, as the latter can serve as an important determinant of the former. While there is a variety of approaches available to measuring satisfaction, there are many benefits to be gained by the use of an external and independent agency for data collection and analysis. However, the value of such exercises is crucially dependent on the organization's willingness to use the information that is generated. Simply undertaking customer and employee satisfaction surveys without a serious commitment to act upon their results will be of little value in managing customer relationships.

In financial services in particular, the management of customer relationships is increasingly focusing attention on the concept of fairness and the need to treat customers fairly. Although such initiatives have been prompted by regulatory bodies and are probably most developed in the UK, it seems likely that the fairness agenda will increasingly become part of good relationship management across the financial services sector world-wide.

Review questions

1. Why should financial services organizations be concerned about delivering customer satisfaction?
2. What is customer satisfaction, and how does it differ from service quality and value?
3. What role do expectations play in relation to customer satisfaction? How should organizations seek to manage customer expectations?
4. What are the key steps in developing an effective consumer satisfaction survey?
5. Why is fairness so important in the marketing of financial services? In which areas of marketing is treating customers fairly of greatest significance?

Customer relationship management in practice

Learning objectives

By the end of this chapter you will be able to:
- appreciate how elements of the marketing mix need to be modified when used as part of a customer development strategy
- appreciate the importance of integrating the marketing mix associated with customer acquisition and development
- understand how to evaluate the contribution made by marketing to an organization
- understand marketing's wider contribution within the contexts of corporate social responsibility and sustainability.

17.1   Introduction

The appreciation of marketing's role in managing continuing customer relationships requires a quantitatively different approach to the use of the marketing mix than applies where customer acquisition is the primary purpose of marketing. It is interesting to note how much of the language used in connection with acquiring customers appears somewhat militaristic. Terms such as strategies, campaigns, targets, tactics and marketing armoury all seem to somehow resonate with a notion that marketing is concerned with a heroic battle to *win* customers. As commented upon earlier, objection-handling forms an important element of sales training and is symptomatic of an adversarial, if not confrontational, mind set. Hopefully, it has been firmly established that to see marketing just in terms of the single-minded pursuit of new customers deserves to be consigned to the history of the marketing of financial services.

By way of contrast, the discourse regarding marketing's role in customer development has attached itself to the language of social science and anthropology. Words such as relationships, communities, dialogue, intimacy and advocate are commonly encountered in the context of the use of marketing to retain and develop customers following the point of acquisition. This change of emphasis has implications for the ways in which individual components of the marketing mix are used. Importantly, it has implications for the cultural context within which marketing activities reside. The coercive customer-acquisition based model of marketing often seemed to coincide with organizational cultures that were typified as being macho, male-orientated and somewhat cynical. In such cultures, the rewards and recognition systems were overly biased in favour of new business key performance indicators, such as number of new policies (not customers) issued, value of new premiums, new loan cases proposed, and value of loans approved.

The existence of the customer funnel has meant that a numbers game based upon new customer acquisition was the dominant business model for many organizations.

Such a cultural backdrop resulted in practices that over-rewarded elements within the distribution channels, under-rewarded staff involved in serving the day-to-day needs of customers, and delivered poor value to customers. Sales organizations often wielded undue power and influence, and this rendered organizations vulnerable to a range of risks and dangers. Poor-quality business, bad debts, mis-sold products and a number of often unforeseen risks have resulted from organizations where cultures were too acquisition-based.

With the emphasis firmly placed upon the maintenance of long-term customer relationships and the engendering of advocacy, the culture and the marketing mix must interact to reinforce each other. The remainder of this chapter considers the implications of marketing's role in keeping customers in terms of the use of the individual elements of the marketing mix. Additionally, it devotes some attention to matters concerning the implementation of marketing principles and practices and how their success might be evaluated. Finally, it considers marketing's role in the discharging of an organization's corporate social responsibility and how marketing can contribute to the sustainability agenda which is assuming ever more significance.

17.2   People and culture

When the emphasis of marketing becomes orientated more toward the retention and development of customer relationships, the culture must adapt accordingly. For example, there has to be a recognition that responsibility for determining the experience of customers belongs to almost the entire organization. It is no longer appropriate for sales organizations to wield undue power. In the past this has led to abuses which have caused detriment to those involved in administering customer services. However, in the customer-orientated culture of the present and future, administration staff see themselves as shouldering major responsibility for delivering customer satisfaction. Through their interactions with customers they can provide valuable feedback to improve elements of service procedures and systems, and even product design. Those involved in the IT function must perceive that they are empowered to use their knowledge, skills and resources to improve customer satisfaction. Similarly, people involved in, say, procurement can play a valuable role in improving the quality of bought-in products and services such that the organization operates more efficiently for the benefit of customers. Such benefits may arise because of improved functionality for customers or, possibly, by reducing costs and thereby making price reductions possible.

What is indicated is the necessity for all staff to appreciate the ways in which what they do, and how they do it, impacts upon customer perceptions. In the ideal world, all members of staff will see themselves as being, to some extent, customer-facing. Businesses that are based upon the maintenance of long-term customer relationships, as opposed to essentially the one-off sale, see the *people* element of the mix as representing a primary, if not *the* primary, determinant of customer satisfaction and advocacy. It is interesting to note evidence that the Yorkshire Building Society has identified regarding the importance of experienced staff in enhancing levels of customer satisfaction. The Society has conducted extensive research into the factors that appear to be causally and independently associated with high levels of customer satisfaction and hard-nosed commercial performance. The analysis suggests that such a causal relationship is in evidence in branches that have relatively low staff turnover and a high average length of services. Staff in such branches display relatively high levels of commitment to the organization, and this is reflected in relatively superior business results across a balanced scorecard of key performance indicators. Although not independently verified, such a finding is indicative of the importance of continuity of staff/customer interaction in the maintenance of mutually beneficial long-term relationships.

17.3   Product considerations

Of paramount importance is that a product should be fit for purpose. This means that care should be taken to ensure that the features that comprise, and functionality that applies, to a product should be clearly identified at the point of purchase and be well-evidenced for the lifetime of the product.

Owing to the particular characteristics of financial services products as outlined in Chapter 3, care has to be taken to ensure that products are presented in as transparent a way as possible. In the absence of sufficient transparency, customers may unwittingly buy a product that is suitable for their needs or personal circumstances. Regulators often lay down quite prescriptive requirements with regard to the disclosure of product features at the point-of-sale. However, responsible marketing should not depend solely on the regulator; it is up to the individual product provider to ensure that products are presented in a suitably transparent manner. It is relatively straightforward to carry out a study to establish the degree to which consumers understand the product features as presented in promotional and point-of-sale material. Such basic research could obviate costly administration queries, complaints handling and, potentially, compensation for mis-sold or misrepresented products. Leading on from transparency at the point of initial sale is the requirement to ensure that the provider is able to deliver the features and functionality that it promises. In the past, it was commonplace for new products to be launched even though the systems and administrative infrastructure to deal with a range of customer requirements during the lifetime of the product had not been put in place. The euphemism for these unresolved processes is 'deferred features', and their prevalence was the price that had to be paid for launching new products within an unrealistically short timescale. There have been examples in which around 50 per cent of total IT development resource has been devoted to resolving deferred features. An example of such a deferred feature could be the ability to handle, say, a switch from one fund into another fund in the case of a unit-linked whole-of-life policy or a personal pension. Deferred features create a range of difficulties for an organization, and can be a major contributory factor in the lessening of respect for and credibility of a marketing department. The IT systems development staff find involvement in deferred features a source of frustration. Administration staff find themselves having to devise various manual work-arounds while they wait for the outstanding systems support to be made available. Such a scenario can typically occur in organizations that are overly orientated in favour of new business to the detriment of the long-term interest of customers. Indeed, in the long term the interest of customers aligns with the commercial interest of the company itself. Again, there are cultural implications that can be readily imagined.

Thus, product development should be organized such that what is promised at the time of initial purchase can be fully supported from the launch date of the product.

A further consideration regarding *product* is that product design should seek to provide sufficient flexibility to cope with reasonable changes in a customer's circumstances during the anticipated lifetime of the product. There are certain changes which might reasonably be expected to occur with regard to most financial services. Therefore, the ability to respond appropriately to changing circumstances is an important aspect of most financial products, certainly those with a duration of more than 12 months. The lack of sufficient product flexibility results in poor persistency and poor product profitability. It can act greatly against the customer's interests where penalty charges are applied to products that lapse in their early stages. Clearly, a judgement has to be made regarding the costs associated with proving flexibility for the duration of a long-term product. However, the failure to do so, within reason, may result in much higher costs to the organization.

17.4   Pricing and value

Care must be taken to ensure that *price* is managed in such a way as to safeguard a long-term, mutually beneficial relationship. There is little point in attracting new customers with a price that is so low as to be commercially unsustainable. Equally, the practice of acquiring customers with an attractive price tag only subsequently to introduce a substantial price rise is a cynical practice that can endanger long-term relationships. Nationwide Building Society has a policy of behaving in an even-handed fashion in respect of its pricing policy to new and existing members. In Case study 12.1 we saw how Nationwide approaches what is a significant philosophical issue regarding this somewhat controversial matter, and readers are advised to refer back to it.

A pricing policy that is geared towards customer retention and development has to address the respective merits of long-term customer value over short-term product profitability. This emphasizes the need to model long-term customer value and evolve a pricing policy that achieves a balance between such value and the short-term profit requirements of the company. This makes it all the more important that a company's systems architecture is able to provide a holistic view of an individual customer's relationship with the company. By joining up all of the customer's product holdings, the company can identify opportunities to add value to the customer through special pricing arrangements. This is consistent with the model for retention proposed by Bittner and Zeithaml regarding what they term 'financial bonds', discussed in Chapter 14.

Such a finely-tuned, customer-based (as opposed to a policy-or account-based) system also permits effective new product pricing initiatives to take place. For example, Fidelity was promoting a reduction in the initial charge on three of its funds from 3.25 per cent to 0.5 per cent for existing customers in January 2006 who choose to transact their business on-line. By way of contrast, at the same time M&G Securities Ltd announced the introduction of what it terms the 'X' Share Class on its PEP and ISA products. The 'X' Share Class allows the customer to invest at no initial charge, but with a diminishing exit fee, during the first 5 years. M&G points out that such a pricing policy is consistent with its belief that equity investment should be for the medium to long term, and typically for a minimum of 5 years. However, the company additionally offers the choice of investing in the 'A' Share Class, whereby there is no exit fee payable but, depending upon the fund chosen, there is usually an initial charge. CRM-based marketing places heavy emphasis upon cross-selling and up-selling to existing customers, and well-designed use of pricing policies can play a key role in its success.

17.5   Advertising and promotion

A particular feature of marketing in the context of existing customer development has been the usage of promotional campaigns and programmes aimed specifically at such individuals. At a very basic level it is obviously important that consistency is achieved between what is said and presented during the acquisition process, and that which is said and presented during the lifetime of the customer lifecycle. This is, at least in part, to do with the issue of expectations, discussed in Chapter 15. Advertising and promotional devices have a major role to play in activities such as customer retention, up-selling, cross-selling and advocacy development. Much of what was presented in Chapter 11 regarding communication and promotion applies in the context of marketing to existing customers. However, once an individual becomes a customer there is a presumption that the provider company really does have in-depth, detailed knowledge about that customer, and that the customer's needs can be addressed on a highly personalized basis. To refer back to the concept of zones of tolerance (see Chapter 15), customers exhibit a relatively narrow zone of tolerance with regard to the communications they receive. They expect a high degree of relevance, customer knowledge and accuracy. Crucially, there is a presumption that their custom is valued and that the relationship is appreciated and respected.

In contrast to the acquisition of new customers, direct-response type forms of communication are significantly more important when marketing to existing customers.

Largely, this is because of the availability of detailed customer data that allows messages and propositions to be targeted on an individual basis with great precision. Therefore, competencies in direct mail, telemarketing and the Internet are especially important when using the marketing mix for existing customers. We saw in the previous section how companies such as M&G and Fidelity make extensive use of direct mail as a means of promoting special offers to existing customers.

One of the most significant developments in recent years has been that of loyalty programmes. Unlike one-off *ad hoc* mail-shots and campaigns, the loyalty programme aims to engender the achievement of long-term customer base goals through the use of the marketing mix. Such goals are typically based upon providing long-term value for money to the customer. Amongst the goals that apply to such programmes are:

- customer retention
- customer advocacy
- increased share of customer wallet
- competitive advantage.

In the context of current customers, communication has an important role to play in providing reassurance that the relationship is in the customer's best interests. This relates to the concept of cognitive dissonance. Cognitive dissonance concerns the feelings of anxiety that are frequently associated with important decisions. Well-chosen and carefully executed messages can aim to reassure customers that they are exercising sound judgement in maintaining a relationship with the provider company. This has become especially significant in the field of financial services in marketplaces that are close to (or at) saturation point. Such marketplaces result in customer acquisition strategies that blatantly seek to achieve defections from competitors. Clear evidence of this is to be seen in sectors such as the gas and electricity market and telecommunication arenas, where defection-based strategies are commonplace. The use of marketing communications programmes to reassure customers of the wisdom of declining the overtures of competitors and maintaining an existing relationship can work effectively in conjunction with the customer retention model of Bitner and Zeithaml referred to in Chapter 14. Again, the availability of a great deal of information about individual customers lends itself to highly focused, well-targeted customer communication. This may involve media such as direct mail, the Internet or call-centres. Financial services have to give careful consideration to this aspect of the use of communication, given the long-term nature of many of its products and the significance of life-time customer value in determining the profitability of individual companies.

17.6 Distribution and access

In the context of customer development, there are many linkages between *people* and *place*. Take the case of the bank branch; its role is far more significant as a distribution point for existing customers than as a means of securing new customers. Indeed, it is interesting to note the case of Barclays, whereby its process of opening current accounts for new customers requires the customer to arrange an appointment with what it terms a *personal banker*. Cashiers are not empowered to open new accounts, unlike at NatWest, HSBC and Lloyds TSB, where counter staff are permitted to open new customer accounts.

The branch is the most visible and potent manifestation of the bank for most of its personal customers. Thus, the way in which it transacts the requirements of customers has a profound influence upon customer perceptions. Indeed, the branch is, arguably, the most powerful means a bank or building society has for increasing customer value by soliciting for product cross-sell and up-sell. In this way, branch-based distribution has a powerful selling resource that is not available to its non-branch-based, remote rivals. Of course, this capability comes at a cost, and such organizations are continually evaluating the value-added of individual branches and adjusting their portfolios of branch outlets.

The role played by branch staff is crucial in satisfying the needs of customers whilst reconciling this with the needs of the bank itself. This calls for skill and diplomacy in striking the right balance between providing services associated with a product currently held and endeavouring to introduce the possibility of the customer buying an additional product. For example, a customer may call in at her branch to pay a bill and the cashier notice that the customer maintains a significant credit balance. This might indicate an opportunity to sell, say, an investment product of some kind. Skill and sensitivity are needed to introduce this possible cross-sell opportunity, such that the customer does not feel that she is somehow being taken advantage of. To a considerable extent, the answer lies in adopting an approach that is customer-centric and will demonstrably provide value for her. It is also important to ensure that such branch staff are skilled and trained in interpersonal skills of a high order. It is fair to say that few things are as likely to cause customers irritation, dissatisfaction and defection than the perception of being coercively sold to every time they enter a branch.

The use of the branch as a means of distributing additional products to current customers relies squarely upon the *people* element of the marketing mix. Other scenarios that also facilitate the role of people are those involving direct face-to-face sales and service, such as an insurance company's direct salesforce, or the call agent in a telephone call-centre.

Direct sales-forces are of immense importance as a means of reinforcing customer relationships. Insurance agents of all forms, brokers, direct sales advisers and independent financial advisers can all be instrumental in reinforcing the relationship between product provider and customer. The expressions *hunters* and *farmers* are sometimes used in the context of direct sales-forces. *Hunters* are advisers that perform the role of acquiring new customers, whereas *farmers*, as the name implies, are responsible for looking after the servicing needs and new product requirements of existing customers. Sometimes companies have a *hunting* sales team that is distinct from a separate *farming* sales team. Such a division of responsibilities, so it is argued, permits a high degree of focus on the respective goals of acquiring, and developing customer relationships. There is much to commend such an argument; however, in practice, customers often build a positive, trusting relationship with the adviser who initially sold the product to them and resent being handed off to the *farming* adviser. For this reason, companies that experiment with the hunting/farming-focused approach tend to revert to the hybrid model whereby all advisers are responsible for both hunting and farming. This latter approach is more in keeping with the relationship marketing philosophy in that, by having the responsibility for an ongoing customer relationship, the adviser is more likely to provide only what he or she knows can be delivered. A well trained, properly resourced, conscientious direct sales-force is a powerful vehicle for generating both shareholder value and customer benefits.

The clear separation of hunting and farming roles is more prevalent in the business-to-business environment, where the need for complex, costly and time-consuming new business pitching can make such an arrangement practically and economically viable. For example, a finance company selling leasing facilities to used-car dealers may need considerable effort to prospect for business and secure such a sale. However, the setting-up of the new processes and procedures, and their continuing review, can be even more complex and time-consuming, and call for a different skill set requiring a dedicated organizational structure. Thus, the complexity of many aspects of large-scale B2B product service provision frequently calls for a degree of specialization that makes the separation of sales and client management roles a necessity.

In Case study 17.1, we see how National Savings & Investments has successfully integrated elements of the marketing mix concerning both customer acquisition and development. A particular feature of the NS&I case is that the company has outsourced all of its administration functions to Siemens Business Services.

Case study 17.1   National Savings & Investments

Background

National Savings & Investments is the UK's third largest retail savings and investment provider, with an 8 per cent market share and accounting for some £70bn of invested assets. It has more than 26 million customers who between them generate something like 60 million transactions each year via the telephone, Internet, post office and mail. In 1999, NS&I outsourced 90 per cent of its functions (operations, processing and infrastructure development) in the UK's largest Public Private Partnership (PPP). The relationship has evolved through several stages, beyond that of client/supplier to one of co-dependent partnership.

People and processes

The outsourced call-centre and NS&I's client management teams enjoy close relationships. Most call-centre staff are recruited from back-office roles, so new staff have a working knowledge of the business which helps to smooth the process when customers are changing channels. The Training Team assesses telephony aptitudes, customer orientation, communication and attention to detail, and an interview process focuses on business awareness, cooperation and commitment. Sales and Service Delivery Managers share personal objectives to maximize effectiveness. This approach to partnership development is summarized in Figure 17.1.

Case study 17.1   National savings & investments—cont'd

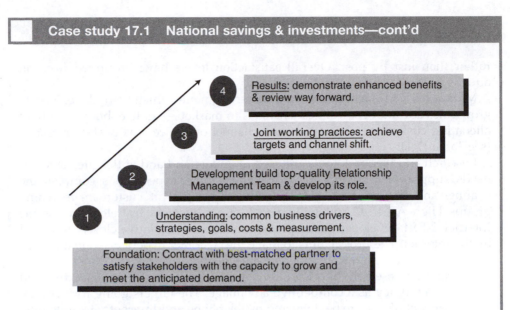

Figure 17.1 Partnership development.

The partnership's commitment to staff is evidenced by upper quartile employment terms, including Employee Bonus and Recognizing Excellence Schemes; Defined Benefit Pensions; and opportunities to influence working environment and processes. Training is co-ordinated and delivered in-house by a specialist team. Customer Service Representatives (CSRs) complete a 30-week modular programme covering 9 key call elements. Employee Opinion Survey outputs are analysed, and plans put in place to address improvements.

Distribution
The rapid expansion and development of NS&I's telephony channel has been a key business aim with achieved growth as follows:

- Capacity has increased from 160 to 285 seats (120 to 250 FTEs) in the last year
- From a standing start annual telephone sales have risen over eight-fold, from £188m in 2000/2001 to £1399m in 2004/2005
- Call volumes have increased from 811 000 to 2 993 000 over the same period, all handled by a person – not by IVR (interactive voice recognition)
- Telephone and Internet sales now make up 30 per cent of all sales but, as the overall target has also increased significantly, we still receive the same value of sales from the post office.

Customer management and research
The drive for direct sales growth to support the modernization of the business was not at the expense of the loyal existing customer base. These results were achieved by a combination of building awareness of the telephone service plus building capability by making NS&I's products available for sale by telephone

Continued

Case study 17.1   National savings & investments—cont'd

rather than just by post. Overall satisfaction levels have improved from an already high 90 per cent to 93 per cent.

Market research identified key customer segments which were developed to grow sales and move lower-cost channels to market – e.g. telephony – without alienating customers whose preferred channel of choice was postal or branch (see Table 17.1).

Research and feedback tools are used to understand and anticipate customer needs, support NS&I's strategies to exceed customer expectations, complete the channel and become best-in-class. With 51 per cent of customers matching groups High AB to C and willing to transact business by telephone or the Internet, NS&I developed its telephony mobilization initiative closely followed by the Internet. The project aims to make the customer experience one that they would wish to repeat, with further enhancements.

Building on research, NS&I will enhance its customer experience to build customer advocacy as a competitive advantage. The targets going forward are for 50 per cent of sales to be delivered by telephone and Internet. The following feedback tools are employed: *focus groups and customer panels, frequently asked questions*, whereby customer views are assessed for recurring themes, issues and

Table 17.1 Segmentation at NS&I

Key telephone focus	Age profile	Social group profile	Telephone propensity	Likelihood of telephone use for segment
Mature mainstream	62	A and low DE	Not a key segment for telephone but an opportunity to wean some off traditional channels	Low
Prosperous retirees	61	High AB	A key segment with a higher than average propensity to buy by phone and then transact by phone	Medium
Savvy mature	62	B	A key segment with the highest propensity to buy by phone and then transact by phone	Medium
Planners	40	B	A key segment with a high propensity to buy by phone and then transact by phone	High
Career builders	26	B	A target segment with a propensity to buy by phone and electronic means	High
Established professionals	40	C	A target segment and would be willing to buy by phone	High

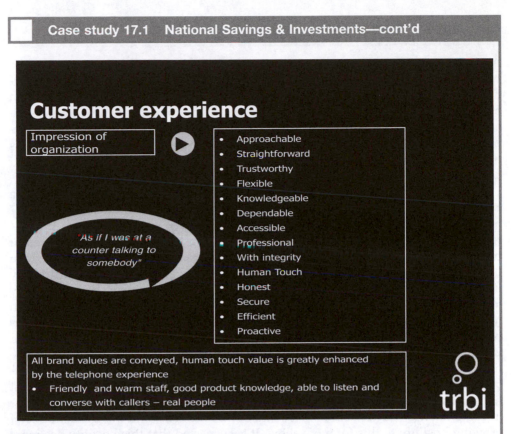

Case study 17.1   National Savings & Investments—cont'd

Figure 17.2 The customer experience.

improvement areas, and *mystery shopper surveys*. Additionally, a monthly *customer telephone survey* is conducted by MORI in which recent service users are interviewed for comments on what they consider important, their experience, and how NS&I compares with other financial service providers.

The customer experience

Independent research is used to evaluate the customer experience (see Figure 17.2). Some headline facts are as follows:

- 97 per cent of our calls are answered within 20 seconds
- 99.5 per cent of sales calls and 98 per cent of all calls are answered first time
- Low staff churn (*c.* 11 per cent) ensures that call-centre staff are experienced; understand products, culture and objectives; and excel at providing customers with high-quality service
- Success in delivering brand values is measured.

Source: Jill Waters, Head Of Direct Sales, National Savings & Investments.

17.7   Processes

As an element of the financial services marketing mix for customer development, *process* plays a role in facilitating the delivery of both service and administrative routines as well as the purchasing of additional products. Although the *people* element of the mix has a role to play in providing the sales administrative functions associated with customer development, processes are closely allied. For example, the telephone call-centre and Internet have made an enormous contribution to the progress of customer development in view of their capacity to perform selling, buying and administrative roles.

The Internet has empowered customers to satisfy their needs in respect of data availability and the performance of a range of administrative functions on a 24/7 basis, at minimal cost. As such, it complements the much more costly branch-based resources of banks and building societies. However, it is important to note that it performs a complementary rather than a substitutional role, at least at this stage in the development of the market. The telephone call-centre has been particularly important as part of the marketing mix for customer development. It is a relatively low-cost means of providing a range of purchasing and administrative routines. In recent years, the offshore outsourcing of call-centres, most notably to India, has played an increasing role for companies such as Fidelity, Norwich Union and GE Capital. They offer a low-cost means of transacting inbound customer administration and buying requests. However, more controversial is their role in proactive outbound selling to the existing customer bases of a range of industries, not just financial services. The mobile phone and telecomm sector has been especially active in using offshore call-centres to make outbound sales calls, and there is evidence of growing hostility to this form of selling. It is suspected that this hostility has more to do with its intrusiveness than with the origin of the actual call itself. Nevertheless, the cost-effectiveness of the use of unsolicited outbound sales calling must be balanced against its negative impact upon overall customer satisfaction levels.

In the case of the use of the Internet and call-centre, aspects of design and process often serve to frustrate customers and reduce their satisfaction rather then heighten it. Websites can be difficult to navigate and make presumptions about the nature of enquiries that may not best reflect the needs of customer or indeed prospective customers. For example, it is commonplace for such sites to be product-based, rendering it impossible to make enquiries of a general nature. Complaints handling is often poorly dealt with, and a number that have been reviewed request purely written requests for service and resolution. The absence of appropriate telephone numbers to assist the customer or a failure to respond to calls is a frequent source of irritation.

Call-centres can result in similar frustrations, as automatic call-handling procedures (IVR) fail to deliver the required degree of service responsiveness. What is indicated is far greater use of what is termed the *customer journey*. By this term we mean that executives should thoroughly test the responsiveness, functionality and effectiveness of both Internet- and telephone-based processes at first hand. This is somewhat analogous to the practice of supermarket CEOs devoting considerable personal time to their customers' experiences as users of their stores. Such an approach has yielded enormous benefits, not only to shoppers but also to the shareholders of those retail companies.

No matter what elements of the marketing mix are used to develop customer relationships over the long term, it is vital that effort be expended in assessing their impact. It is relatively straightforward to measure the impact of the customer acquisition process – a prospect either buys, and thus becomes a customer, or declines the invitation. Both types of individual can be invited to take part in some form of feedback aimed at informing future policies and practices. However, once a prospect has become a customer, there is a wide continuum of ways in which the customer interacts with and is exposed to the provider company. All of the customer's interactions with the marketing mix have an impact, at both the subconscious as well as the conscious level, in forming perceptions – negative and positive.

ResponseTek is a company that has evolved a methodology for capturing the experience of customers as a means of identifying business improvements. It uses the precepts of gap analysis as a means of identifying areas for improvement. The goal of engendering higher levels of advocacy also plays a key role in ResponseTek's approach. It emphasizes that the voice of today's customer is a powerful one, made all the more so by the Internet and via blogs and online chat. In ResponseTek's view, companies can choose to maintain their traditional push/pull marketing efforts and deliver what they think customers need and want. Alternatively, they can adopt ResponseTek's Customer Experience Management (CEM) framework that has been designed to enable them to listen better to their customers and act upon the insights that arise. Case study 17.2 explains ResponseTek's approach in more detail.

Case study 17.2   Customer experience management at ResponseTek

By means of CEM, a company can incorporate the voice of its customers into its business strategies and operations. The aim is the development of trust and loyalty that will lead to the ultimate goal of advocacy. According to ResponseTek, it is not sufficient simply to monitor the impact of advocacy and satisfaction of one's customers. Instead, it is necessary to take customer advocacy and satisfaction to a higher level of understanding by enabling a company to understand the root cause of customer satisfaction and advocacy. Once such root causes are identified, effective, well-focused actions can be implemented to increase satisfaction, advocacy and profitability. ResponseTek claims that its core suite is the only software platform that delivers a complete set of Customer Experience Management capabilities, comprising:

- Multi-channel experience collection
- Analysis
- Reporting
- Workflow management
- Closed-loop feedback.

Continued

Case study 17.2   Customer experience management at ResponseTek—cont'd

The CEM methodology is based upon three core elements, namely:

1. *Involve*: capture the customer's experience whenever and wherever it occurs. This means continuously gathering customer insights – whether customer, company or event-initiated – from any channel, such as the call-centre, web or in-store point of sale, when they want, and when their opinions are formed at the moment of delight or disappointment.

2. *Integrate*: integrate the customer's voice into processes and employee activities. Staff, partners and executives need to be able to make informed decisions based on real-time customer-experience information. The right information needs to be filtered to the right person at the right time, from the executive level down to frontline employees. Users should be able to communicate improvements or comments back to the customer.

3. *Improve*: continuously turn customer experience insight into actionable improvements. The ability to facilitate enterprise-wide communication and change based on customer experience information is another critical aspect in achieving the greatest customer experience management benefits. Actionable, closed-loop communication capabilities enable companies to align business strategies with customer insights, and in the process create customer advocates.

Figure 17.3 shows how ResponseTek seeks to integrate all aspects of CEM into a unified conceptual framework described as the customer-driven enterprise.

Aon Reed Stenhouse (ARS) is one of a number of financial services organizations using ResponseTek's system. ARS is the Canadian division of AON, a global provider of risk management and insurance broking services. Faced with increasing competition and limited understanding of its customers, ASR was looking for an efficient solution to improve retention, improve understanding of customers and, through that better understanding, improve the customer experience, this allowing ASR to set itself aside from the competition. ResponseTek implemented a system of ASR which provided regular monitoring of real-time customer experiences, a 'dashboard' system to provide senior management with daily summaries of the customer experience by segment and by region, and an early warning system for 'at risk' customers (potential defectors) on a daily basis.

David Cliche, marketing manager for ASR summarized the benefits of implementing CEM:

We had to respond to the changing competitive landscape of the Insurance industry and look for alternative ways to make better informed business decisions. ResponseTek helped us to accomplish this by integrating the voice of the customer into our business processes ... We now know a lot more about

> **Case study 17.2   Customer experience management at ResponseTek—cont'd**

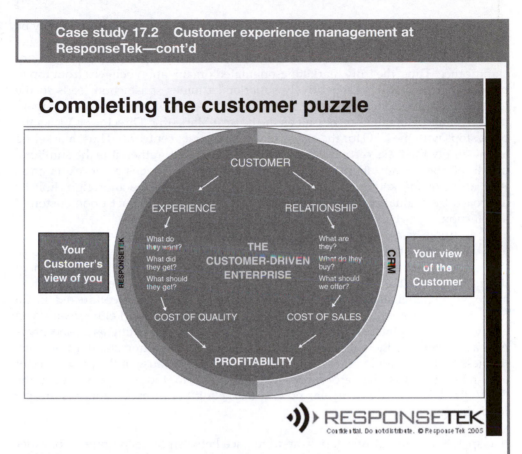

Figure 17.3 ResponseTek's customer-driven enterprise framework.

our customers than we did before. Rather than one touchpoint, we are now able to understand our interactions with customers throughout their lifecycle. Knowing what our customers want and the complementary products and services they need is invaluable information.

Source: Yalman Khan and Richard Sharp, ResponseTek.

17.8   Evaluating marketing performance

In this section we will consider issues concerning the implementation of marketing concepts and practices and how their contributions might be evaluated. By now it has been firmly established that marketing is less about the practical activities engaged in by departments bearing that name but, rather, constitutes a business philosophy or orientation. Central to this orientation is understanding the customers' problems, needs and wants, and then providing the means by which these may be satisfied. Quite simply, marketing is about getting and keeping customers, and success in this endeavour demands that the customers' interests are given paramount significance. Thus, the truly marketing-orientated organization believes from top to bottom that delivering competitively superior customer satisfaction leads to the long-term optimization of all stakeholder interests. Arguably, the CEO of an organization should view him- or herself as the *de facto* Marketing Director or VP, as the buck stops with the CEO for the organization's customer centricity. Thus, marketing is not simply the tasks carried out by the marketing team; rather, it is the sum total of all of the organization's activities that impact upon customer experience. Any audit of marketing performance should therefore take a thorough, holistic approach by evaluating the outcomes of all functions that impact upon customer satisfaction.

In addition to assessing the degree of marketing orientation organizationally, and the impact of all departments that have an influence upon customer perceptions, there remains the need to assess the contribution of the marketing department itself. It falls to the marketing team to ensure that the activities of marketing strategy, customer acquisition and customer development are conducted in an appropriate, effective, efficient and professional manner. Marketing teams can easily become responsible for undermining credibility in marketing as a concept, as well as that of its adherents, by failing to operate to the required standard of effectiveness, efficiency and professionalism. This can arise because of the prevalence of a number of gaps that are somewhat analogous to those that occur in the SERVQUAL model. Of particular note in marketing performance analysis are the following gaps:

- Gap 1: The external role gap – the difference between the expectations of other functional management and staff regarding the role of marketing and its actual role and responsibilities.
- Gap 2: The internal role gap – the difference in expectations between marketing management and staff regarding their roles.
- Gap 3: The external delivery gap – the difference between what external management and staff expect marketing to deliver and what they perceive it to deliver.
- Gap 4: The internal delivery gap – the difference between what the marketing team set out to deliver and what they believe they actually do deliver.

It may be readily appreciated that all four of the above gaps involve a combination of what is perceived and what can be objectively evidenced. The two constructs may well not be in alignment if senior marketing management fails to devote sufficient attention to the management of perception. There are many examples of hardworking, productive marketing teams that do a great job of influencing customer perceptions of their company whilst failing to manage their department's internal perception. Too often the assessment of performance by senior marketing management is biased in favour of Gap 4, followed by Gap 2. Scant attention is devoted to addressing Gaps 1 and 3, and this oversight serves to undermine marketing's credibility. Therefore, senior marketing staff must ensure that they identify the dangers inherent in all four gaps and formulate strategies to close them.

Marketing executives need to be acutely aware of the risks that may be associated with any given activity or course of action. Indeed, it is probably fair to say that there are more risks facing the unwary in the field of financial services than in most other commercial sectors. Financial and regulatory risks present particular challenges, and failure to exercise due prudence and diligence can in extreme cases lead to the collapse of an enterprise.

Chief Executives and Marketing Directors frequently struggle to evaluate the value they gain from their marketing resources. The Canford Centre for Customer Development has set out to assess marketing's contribution to corporate goals by means of the Marketing Mentor®. Through the use of Marketing Mentor®, CEOs and Marketing Directors have the means to identify which marketing activities they should:

- maintain, as they make a valid and worthwhile contribution to corporate goals and should be continued
- improve, as they are performing at a level below that expected of them and should be the focus for an improvement programme
- initiate, as they are not currently in evidence and should be introduced to marketing's programme of activities
- delete, as they add little value to the organization's goals and should be abandoned.

Central to its methodology is the assertion that marketing performance rests upon seven core moments of truth, namely:

1. Marketing strategy
2. Customer acquisition
3. Customer development
4. Product and service management
5. Communication and perception management
6. Planning and implementation
7. People management and development.

Finally, rigour, flair and judgement will come to nought unless the individual marketing executive is able to make things happen. In spite of the commonplace mantra of 'empowerment', an array of forces acts to prevent marketing-related change taking place. Numbered among such inhibiting forces are:

- Risk aversion
- Fear of failure
- Individual and group cynicism
- Inertia and lack of corporate ambition
- Senior management control-freaking
- Blame-orientated cultures.

The above list is neither comprehensive nor are the points fully mutually exclusive; however, each captures the essence of the kind of organizational backdrop that makes it difficult to become a truly marketing-orientated organization.

17.9   Corporate social responsibility (CSR)

Alferoff *et al.* (2005) have commented that during the course of the last 20 years a range of factors have been responsible for profound changes in the operating climate for contemporary financial service organizations, including the following:

● globalization and/or regionalization
● marketization and/or public private partnerships
● the speed and transparency of communications
● the shift to a service economy
● the retreat from, or constraint of, public welfare in favour of private provision.

At the same time, there has been an increased demand from various stakeholders, including national governments, international bodies and regulators, for a greater focus on corporate ethics and social responsibility.

Governments worldwide are now looking to create greater transparency, openness and responsiveness in the business sector by introducing both 'hard' and 'soft' legislation to improve standards of corporate governance in the boardroom and social responsibility towards internal and external stakeholders. Despite these demands, made more urgent by several high-profile scandals, major problems surround the very definition of corporate social responsibility, added to which is a lack of any consensus as to whether it should be a central part of business policy and practice.

As already mentioned, CSR is assuming ever more importance on the world stage, and the American life assurer Mutual of America has been furthering its own CSR agenda for many years through the medium of the Mutual of America Foundation. In Case study 17.3 we can see how the Foundation has used the Community Partnership Award as an important element of its contribution to fulfilling its responsibilities to CSR.

Case study 17.3   Mutual of America and corporate social responsibility

Mutual of America is one of a handful of mutual life insurance companies of scale still operating in the United States. Mutual of America was originally named the National Health and Welfare Retirement Association (NHWRA), and began business on 1 October 1945 offering retirement plans and insurance coverage.

NHWRA was unique in setting up a retirement system for not-for-profit health and welfare organizations. Such groups had been generally unable to obtain coverage from insurance carriers, at the time, due to the small numbers of people employed. Furthermore, their employees were not eligible to participate in Social Security, which excluded workers in most not-for-profit organizations. Thus an obvious need existed for a new type of retirement organization.

> **Case study 17.3   Mutual of America and corporate social responsibility—cont'd**

The Company was originally capitalized in 1945 with a loan from the Community Chest (now the United Way), and in 1984 became Mutual of America Life Insurance Company and soon was licensed to do business in all 50 states. At the end of 2005, Mutual of America's assets totalled more than US$11bn dollars.

Mutual of America is known today as a company that offers products and services of the highest quality backed by the financial strength of a first-class organization. It is a direct writing company in that it does not employ independent or commission-based producers. All of its products are marketed and serviced by its own full-time salaried professional staff. Another important indication of its approach to mutual ethics is that the company does not sell any product that incorporates a surrender penalty. Unlike many of its competitors, Mutual of America encourages its customers to be direct users of its web-based systems instead of having to gain access to such facilities via the sales agent.

The company has a long history of community-based activities and charitable giving, and in 1996 established the Community Partnership Award (CPA). Underpinning the CPA is the desire to encourage not-for-profit organizations, such as charities and community support organizations, to become more professional in their approach and enjoy a greater degree of financial security. Now in its eleventh year, the CPA is firmly established as an annual national competition for not-for-profit organizations. The CPA scheme aims to encourage greater partnership between public, private and social sector organizations devoted to the public good. Such partnerships have addressed issues such as child abuse, teenage unemployment, homelessness, the mentally ill and a range of other social and community issues. The CPA's mission:

> recognizes outstanding non-profit organizations in the United States that have shown exemplary leadership by facilitating partnerships with public, private or social sector leaders who are working together as equal partners, not as donors and recipients, to build a cohesive community that serves as a model for collaborating with others for the greater good.

An example of this is the Boys' and Girls' Club of Hartford, Connecticut. The club was experiencing difficulties in raising funds and securing suitable facilities for its recreational activities. It identified a small plot of land that adjoined a local college (Trinity College), and successfully negotiated with the college's Board of Directors for it to share the college's own sports facilities. This allowed the club to offer a wide range of facilities to neighbourhood young people, with a minimal capital investment. In addition to the provision of sporting facilities, Trinity College students acted as both sporting and academic mentors to the young people who were members of the club. In addition to the club's own sports, art and computer facilities, its young people have access to Trinity

Continued

> **Case study 17.3   Mutual of America and corporate social responsibility—cont'd**

events and facilities: concerts and plays, playing fields, a swimming pool, library and technology rooms. From Monday through to Friday after 3 pm, and on Saturday mornings, Trinity students engage in work-study programmes, internships and volunteer activities at the club. Working alongside Boys' and Girls' Club staff, they help with homework, coach sports, teach art and computer skills, and run programmes in character development, leadership and life skills for the young people. In this way a vibrant community resource has been developed which has achieved real synergies for the various stakeholder groups involved.

The CPA has grown to the point where it receives several hundred applications each year for the competition. An independent assessment panel reduces this number to a shortlist, and these applications are subject to a more rigorous appraisal before the winners are finally chosen. An important aspect of the CPA is that considerable resources are devoted to promoting the ideas and best practices that are identified through the judging process. In this way, knowledge is shared and added to for the benefit of the wider not-for-profit sector in the United States.

Source: Thomas Gilliam, Chairman, Mutual of America Foundation.

17.10   Towards a sustainable future

In many respects, marketing and consideration of the future are inextricably linked. This relationship is in evidence in marketing's role in seeking to understand the forces that will shape the marketplace of the future. Strategic marketing planning describes the processes that formally assess environmental trends, and presents scenarios for responding to those trends in order to sustain an organization's future survival and success. Customer relationship marketing is based upon the notion of continuity and responding to the changing needs of the individual customer over an extended period of time. Thus, the term sustainability has particular resonance in the context of marketing. Its significance extends beyond marketing and strikes at the very core of the organization's future survival.

It is the authors' view that marketing can contribute to the issue of sustainability in two particular ways. First, it has a crucial role to play in ensuring the survival and future success of the organization itself through the role it plays strategically and tactically. Secondly, it can play a role in contributing to wider issues regarding social and environmental sustainability. Let's call the former *internal sustainability* and the latter *external sustainability*.

As far as internal sustainability is concerned, marketing plays a vital role in maintaining the strategic triangle referred to at various points in the book. Of particular note is the importance of marketing's role in environmental scanning. It is only by continually refreshing one's knowledge of the forces that will shape future demand and supply that organizational survival can be safeguarded. For this reason it is vital that environmental scanning is suitably wide-ranging to provide the necessary degree of helicopter vision. This is particularly important in the case of multinational players. For example, if we consider the demographic profile of the world's major groupings, we observe that the population of North America, Europe and Japan (what we might call the old economies) amount to the order of 800 million people. The population of China is some 1.33 billion, and the combined populations of the Muslim world stretching from the Atlantic coast of Africa eastwards to the Indonesian archipelago is greater than 2 billion. Major cultural differences apply between these three basic groupings, and, clearly, multinational organizations have to be especially well-tuned to their respective drivers of change. Scenario planning is a technique that is particularly useful as a means of endeavouring to identify possible opportunities and threats in the macro-environment of the multinational organization. Such an approach can serve as a means of stimulating new insights that challenge received wisdom and the *status quo*. A world view based purely upon the conventional mindset of the G8 capitalist democracies may be woefully inadequate as a basis for shaping strategies in future.

Additionally, marketing has an obligation to discharge its responsibilities in respect of its use of the marketing mix such that it does not endanger the future prospects of the organization it seeks to serve. This involves an acute awareness of the risks associated with marketing activities on the one hand, and the need to exercise sound commercial judgement on the other. As far as the former is concerned, it calls for a thoroughgoing appreciation of regulatory and legal requirements as well as sound husbandry of corporate resources. Some years ago, an ill-conceived sales promotion for Hoover involving free transatlantic flights almost brought about the collapse of the company. The lack of effective controls concerning the use of the promotion and the qualification rules cost the company dearly – both financially and in terms of its reputation.

Sound commercial judgement is vital, and innovation in the fields of market and product development needs to be able to withstand robust challenges to its commercial probity before progressing too far.

In March 2006, analysis conducted by Cazalet Consulting (www.cazalet-consulting.com) demonstrated that hardly any net new pensions saving had taken place in the UK during the previous 4 years. The analysis pointed to the declared new business results of the industry being based almost entirely upon churning existing pension investments. Whilst the intermediaries responsible for transacting such transfers have benefited in terms of the fees and commissions they have generated, this has not served the long-term interests of providers or consumers. The analysis of single-premium pension sales reveals that it can take some 8 or 9 years simply to recoup the commission paid from the charges levied on the customer. If the life company's own initial costs are added, it can take 10–12 years for the policy to break even. Curiously, though, the commission clawback period is typically just three years. It might well be concluded that this acts as an encouragement to churn business, with all the detriment to consumers and providers that this implies. Cazalet shows that a £40 000 single-premium pension does not reach profitability until year 13. Even worse is the example they give of a £150-per-month regular premium pension. Even making no allowances for discontinuations, such a product, using Cazalet's model of charges, does not become profitable until year 18 of its life. After allowing for discontinuances (lapses of 7.5 per cent and transfers of 2.5 per cent of in-force business each year – better than actual industry experience), the product is still loss-making in year 25.

If Cazalet's analysis is accepted, it casts a shadow over business models that are in evidence in the contemporary UK life and pensions industry. Marketing has a duty to devote its energies to products, pricing, promotional and distribution practices that best serve the long-term interests of customers and providers, such that they both enjoy the benefits of a positive-sum game.

Finally, let us turn our attention to the issue of external sustainability. Again, it should fall to marketing to appreciate the interrelationships between the organization and variables at play in the external environment beyond the micro-environment referred to in Part I. There is gathering evidence of an appreciation of how marketing can contribute to broader issues concerning the social and physical environment. The avoidance of practices that involve polluting the atmosphere and the efficient use of natural resources, for example, have a role to play in contributing to environmental sustainability. A number of companies throughout the world have become role models for the adoption of environmental policies. A particularly compelling example is the Swedish insurance company Folksam. Folksam was one of 19 insurance companies in the world to become the initial signatories of the UNEP Statement of Environmental Commitment. The Statement now has in excess of 180 signatories from the insurance industry, and the number is growing steadily. Case study 17.4 provides some interesting insights into Folksam's approach to environmental well-being and sustainability.

Case study 17.4   Folksam and sustainability

Folksam is a mutual company whose vision states: 'We work for a long-term sustainable society in which the individual feels secure'. With over four million customers, and managing over SEK 130 billion of assets on their behalf, Folksam has been one of the 10 best workplaces in the Fortune ranking of European companies.

Reducing carbon emissions

Folksam has been in the vanguard in introducing policies aimed at contributing to environmental sustainability. To ensure that Folksam's environmental objectives are made fully clear to all those concerned, parts of the business are now environmentally certified to ISO 14001. Some years ago, Folksam introduced a staff travel policy to encourage efficient car use in connection with claims inspections by ensuring that driving schedules are full and by having special 'inspection days'. The policy also prescribes the means of transport to be used on different routes. Additionally, staff are expected to avoid air and car travel between the company's main sites in Stockholm and Gotenburg, and to travel by rail whenever possible. It has calculated how much carbon dioxide emissions this saves.

Case study 17.4   Folksam and sustainability—cont'd

For the seventh successive year, in 2004 the Folksam Climate Index measured Swedish enterprises' carbon dioxide emissions and the steps they were taking to reduce them, and the results are published in the public domain.

Ridding the countryside of car wrecks
Up to 350 000 abandoned car wrecks used to litter the Swedish countryside at any time. Folksam has been working with the Keep Sweden Tidy Foundation to create greater awareness of the fact that it is an environmental offence in Sweden to abandon vehicles and leave them in a manner that may harm the environment.

Over 100 000 car wrecks have been recovered so far. Since the campaign began, the countryside has been cleared of almost one tonne of mercury, 650 tonnes of lead and 140 cubic metres of battery acid, all of which could have damaged the environment. Another 60 000 tonnes of metal has been recycled.

Folksam benefits commercially from its environmental policies and makes big savings by setting high environmental standards. In the period 2000–2004, it has saved as much as SEK 200 million on car repairs by reusing original parts and by repairing plastic parts and windscreens. The amount saved through these practices in 2004 was SEK 62 million – money which is passed on to Folksam's customers in the form of lower premiums.

A guide to environmentally conscious house renovation
Each year Folksam spends SEK 800 million on building repairs, which makes it one of Sweden's biggest buyers of building materials. As a big client, Folksam is in a position to make demands on price and on environmental performance. Another way in which it makes a difference is through an annual publication called *Byggmiljoguiden*, a comprehensive guide to building products and materials that spare the environment and safeguard the nation's health. *Bygmiloguiden* has become a unique source of information for builders, property managers, local councils, architects and home owners. There is no other collection of data that gives such a comprehensive picture of the environmental impact of building materials, and 100 000 copies of the guide had been distributed by 2005.

Making demands on contractors
Folksam has agreements with 300 building contractors and 1200 car repair shops and scrapyards. Given that it has 25 per cent of the Swedish home and car insurance market, many contractors in these industries are anxious to make agreements with the company. This enables Folksam to impose exacting environmental and quality demands on those selected. Any firm wishing to be considered as a potential contractor must complete a detailed environmental specification. There are specifications for builders, car repair shops and scrapyards. Thanks to this approach, Folksam has been the first insurance company in the world to introduce green policy conditions. These represent a promise to the customer that the company will always pay attention to environmental considerations when settling claims.

Source: Kjell Wirén, Folksam.

▋ 17.11   Summary and conclusions

Strategies to initiate, maintain and develop customer relationships must be supported by appropriate marketing practice and, particularly through the use of the marketing mix, by developing relationships with existing customers as well as acquiring new ones. Effective marketing to an existing customer base requires a thorough understanding of customer needs and expectations, and a willingness to respond to those needs. This in turn requires a market- or customer-orientated organizational culture which ensures commitment to meet customer needs at all levels of the organization. However, relationship marketing does not just imply an unconditional imperative to cross- and up-sell to an existing customer base. Requirements of corporate social responsibility and sustainability imply that marketing managers must be aware of and responsive to the broader social consequences of the products and services they provide, and the ways in which they are marketed.

More generally, successful marketing exponents display a heightened appreciation of the fact that good practice represents a combination of a number of factors, notably:

1. The rigorous application of relevant concepts and tools
2. Creative insight and flair
3. Sound commercial judgement
4. Drive and can-do attitude
5. Social responsibility.

It is to be hoped that this book has made a contribution to at least the first of the above five factors. Important as that factor is, of itself it is insufficient to ensure the successful application of marketing to the commercial needs of a financial services enterprise. The rigorous application of good marketing processes has to be complemented by creative flair that resonates with the predilections of staff, distributors and customers. Given two very similar options, as humans we will typically make a choice in favour of that which is the more interesting, attractive and appealing. Again, rigour and flair will fail to guarantee success unless the proposals and outputs of marketing executives display sound commercial judgement. There is no place for naivety in those involved in marketing, and credibility is earned by the demonstration of well-justified and well-argued cases that can convince even the most sceptical of colleagues of marketing's value. Yet, notwithstanding the commercial imperative, marketing must be conditioned by and responsive to its social context. Finally, focus must never be lost regarding the simple fact that marketing is about getting and keeping customers. Ultimately, its success can only be judged on that basis.

Review questions

1. What are the characteristics of the cultures of companies that seem to be dominated by customer acquisition? Compare and contrast these with those that seem to be advocates for a relationship-based approach to marketing.

2. What principles do you think should underpin the pricing policies of financial services companies to ensure equitable treatment of new and existing customers?
3. Discuss the role that marketing can play in furthering the goal of environmental sustainability. Do you believe that it is a legitimate use of marketing resources?
4. Identify which banks and insurance companies operating in your country you believe are the best exemplars of CRM. What in particular impresses you about their CRM policies and practices?

Bibliography

Albrecht, K. and Zemke, R. (1985). *Service America: Doing Business in the New Economy*. Dow Jones-Irwin.

Alferoff, C., Knights, D. and Starkey, K. (2005). *Corporate Social Responsibility and Financial Service Organisations*. Financial Services Research Forum, October.

Ansoff, I (1965). *Corporate Strategy*, McGraw Hill, New York.

Armitage, S. and Kirk, P. (1994). The performance of proprietary compared with mutual life offices. *Service Industries Journal*, **14(2)**, 238–261.

Arora, R., Tamer Cavusgil, S. and Nevin, J. R. (1985). Evaluation of financial institutions by bank versus savings & loan customers: an analysis of factor congruency. *International Journal of Bank Marketing*, **3(3)**, 47–55.

Athanassopoulos, A. and Labroukos, N. (1999). Corporate customer behaviour towards financial services: empirical results from the emerging market of Greece. *International Journal of Bank Marketing*, **17(6/7)**, 274.

Athanassopoulou, P. and Johne, A. (2004). Effective communication with lead customers in developing new banking products. *International Journal of Bank Marketing*, **22(2)**, 100–125.

Atkinson, A., McKay, S., Kempson, E. and Collard, S. (2006*). Levels of Financial Literacy in the UK: A Baseline Study*. Financial Services Authority (available at http://www.fsa.gov.uk/pubs/consumer-research/crpr47.pdf).

Babakus, E. and Boller, G. W. (1991). An empirical assessment of the SERVQUAL scale. *Journal of Business Research*, **24**, 253–268.

Baker, M. J. (1993). Bank marketing – myth or reality? *International Journal of Bank Marketing*, **11(6)**, 5–11.

Bank of England (2006). *Economic Indicators*. Research Paper 06/12, 1 March, House of Commons Library.

Bateson, J. E. G. (1977). Do we need service marketing? In: P. Eiglier, E. Langeard, C. H. Lovelock *et al.* (eds), *Marketing Consumer Services: New Insights*. Marketing Science Institute Report No 77–115.

Bell, C. R. and Zemke, R. (1987). Service breakdown: the road to recovery. *Management Review*, **October,** 32–35.

Belton, E. F. (1989). The distribution war. *Canadian Insurance*, **94(11)**, 16, 24.

Berman, B. (2005). How to delight your customers. *California Management Review*, **48(1)**, 129–151.

Berry, L. L. (1980). Services marketing is different. *Business*, **30(3)**, 24–29.

Berry, L. L. (1981). The employee as customer. *Journal of Retail Banking*, **3(1)**, 33–40.

Berry, L. L. and Parasuraman, A. (1991). *Marketing Services, Competing Through Quality*. Free Press.

Berry, L. L., Zeithaml, V. A. and Parasuraman, A. (1985). Quality counts in services too. *Business Horizons*, **28(3)**, 44–52.

Berry, L. L., Parasuraman, A. and Zeithaml, V. A. (1988). The service-quality puzzle. *Business Horizons*, **July–August**, 35–43.

Berry, L. L., Zeithaml, V. A. and Parasuraman, A. (1990). Five imperatives for improving service quality. *Sloan Management Review*, **31(4)**, 29–38.

Best, R. J. (2005). *Market Focused Management*. Pearson.

Bitner, M. J. (1990). Evaluating service encounters: the effects of physical surroundings and employee responses. *Journal of Marketing*, **54(2)**, 69–82.

Bitner, M. J. (1992). Servicescapes: the impact of physical surroundings on customers and employees. *Journal of Marketing*, **56**, 57–71.

Bitner, M. J., Booms, B. H. and Tetreault, M. S. (1990). The service encounter: diagnosing favorable and unfavorable incidents. *Journal of Marketing*, **54**, 71–84.

Black, N., Lockett, A. D., Ennew, C. T. *et al.* (2002). Modelling consumer choice of distribution channels: an illustration from financial services. *International Journal of Bank Marketing*, **19(4)**, Ch. 4.

Blodgett, J. G., Hill, D. J. and Tax, S. S. (1997). The effects of distributive, procedural, and inter-actional justice on post-complaint behaviour. *Journal of Retailing*, **2**, 185–210.

Booms, B. H. and Bitner, M. J. (1981). Marketing strategies and organisation structures for service firms. In: J. Donnelly and W. R. George (eds), *Marketing of Services*, pp. 47–51. American Marketing Association.

Bowen, D. E. and Schneider, B. (1988). Services marketing & management: implications for organizational behaviour, *Research in Organizational Behaviour*, **10**, 43–80.

Bowles, T. (1985). Does classifying people by lifestyle really help the advertiser? *Admap*, **May**, 36–40.

Boyd, W. L., Leonard, M. and White, C. (1994). Customer preferences for financial services: an analysis. *International Journal of Bank Marketing*, **12(1)**, 9–15.

Brady, M. K. and Cronin, J. J. (2001). Some new thoughts on conceptualising perceived service quality: a hierarchical approach. *Journal of Marketing*, **65**, 34.

Brady, M. K., Cronin, J. J. and Brand, R. (2002). Performance-only measurement of service quality: a replication and extension. *Journal of Business Research*, **55(1)**, 17.

Brown, T. J., Churchill, G. A. and Peter, J. P. (1993). Improving the measurement of service quality. *Journal of Retailing*, **69(1)**, 127–139.

Brynner, A. J. and Despotidou, S. (2000). *Effect of Assets on Life Chances*. Centre for Longitudinal Studies, Institute of Education.

Buch, J., Rhoda, K. and Talaga, J. (2002). The usefulness of the APR for mortgage marketing in the USA and the UK. *International Journal of Bank Marketing*, **20(2)**, 76.

Building Societies Association (2001). *The History of Building Societies*. BSA.

Burton, D. (1994). *Financial Services and the Consumer*. Routledge.

Burton, D. (1996). Ethnicity and consumer financial behaviour: a case study of British Asians in the pensions market. *International Journal of Bank Marketing*, **14(7)**, 21–31.

Buttle, F. (1996). SERVQUAL: review, critique, research agenda. *European Journal of Marketing*, **30(1)**, 8.

Caine, N. (2005). Bond is too good to be true. *Sunday Times*, 15 May, 5, 6.

Cardone-Riportella, C. and Cazorla-Papis, L. (2001). The internationalisation process of Spanish banks: a tale of two times. *International Journal of Bank Marketing*, **19(2)**, 53–67.

Carmen, J. M. (1990). Consumer perceptions of service quality: an assessment of the SERVQUAL dimensions. *Journal of Retailing*, **66(1)**, 33–56.

Caron, J. K. (1987). Upgrading delivery systems for success in a changing market. *Bottomline*, **4(3)**, 27–28.

Chan, A. K. K and Ma, V. S. M. (1990). Corporate banking behaviour: a survey in Hong Kong. *International Journal of Bank Marketing*, **8(2)**, 25–31.

Chan, R.Y.-K. (1993). Banking services for young intellectuals. *International Journal of Bank Marketing*, **11(5)**, 33–40.

Cheron, E. J., McTavish, R. and Perrien, J. (1989). Segmentation of bank commercial markets. *International Journal of Bank Marketing*, **7(6)**, 25–30.

Christopher, M., Payne, A. F. T. and Ballantyne, D. (1991). *Relationship Marketing: Bring Quality, Customer Service and Marketing Together*. Butterworth Heinemann.

CIA (2006). *CIA World Fact Book* (available at http://www.cia.gov/cia/publications/factbook/).

Council on Financial Competition (1995). http://www.councilonfinancialcompetition.com.

Coyne, K. P., Hall, S. J. D. and Clifford, P. G. (1997). Is your core competence a mirage? *McKinsey Quarterly*, **1**, 40.

Crosby, L. and Stephens, N. (1987). Effects of relationship marketing on satisfaction, retention, and prices in the life insurance industry. *Journal of Marketing Research*, **24(4)**, 404–411.

Czepiel, J. A., Solomon, M. R. and Surprenant, C. F. (eds) (1985). *The Service Encounter: Managing Employee/Customer Interaction in Service Businesses*. Lexington Books.

Dall'Olmo Riley, F. and de Chernatony, L. (2000). The service brand as relationship builder. *British Journal of Management*, **11(2)**, 137–151.

Darton, D., Hirsch, D. and Strelitz, J. (2003). *Tackling Disadvantages: A 20-year Enterprise*. Joseph Rowntree Foundation.

Devlin, J. F. (2003). Brand architecture in services: the example of retail financial services. *Journal of Marketing Management*, **19**, 1043–1065.

Devlin, J. F. and Azhar, S. (2004). Life would be a lot easier if we were a Kit Kat: practitioners' views on the challenges of branding financial services successfully. *Journal of Brand Management*, **12(1)**, 12.

Devlin, J. and and Ennew, C. T. (1997). Understanding competitive advantage in retail financial services. *International Journal of Bank Marketing*, **15(3)**, 77–82.

Devlin, J., Ennew, C. T. and Mirza, M. (1995). Organisational positioning in financial services retailing. *Journal of Marketing Management*, **11(1–3)**, 119–132.

Diacon, S. (2006). Framing effects and risk perceptions: the effect of prior performance presentation format on investment fund choice, *Journal of Economic Psychology* (forthcoming).

Diacon, S. R. and Ennew, C. T. (1996). Ethical issues in insurance marketing in the UK. *European Journal of Marketing*, **30(5)**, 67–80.

Dick, A. S. and Basu, K. (1994). Customer loyalty: toward an integrated conceptual framework. *Academy of Marketing Science Journal*, **22(2)**, 99.

Doole, I. (1998). Benchmarking the competencies and capabilities of SMEs successfully competing in international markets. PhD working papers, cited by I. Doole and R. Lowe, in *International Marketing Strategy: Analysis, Development and Implementation*, 2nd edn. International Thomson Business Press.

Doyle, P. (2000). Value-based marketing. *Journal of Strategic Marketing*, **8(4)**, 299–311.

Drake, L. and Llewellyn, D. T. (1995). The price of bank payment services. *International Journal of Bank Marketing*, **13(5)**, 3–11.

Draper, P. and MacKenzie, E. (1996). The returns to policyholders from alternative organisational structures: evidence from the UK life assurance industry. Working Paper 98.6, Centre for Financial Markets, Research Management School, University of Edinburgh.

Edwards, P. and Turnbull, P. W. (1994). Finance for small and medium-sized enterprises: information and the income gearing challenge. *International Journal of Bank Marketing*, **12(6)**. Research paper.

Eigler, P. and Langeard, E. (1977). A new approach to service marketing. In: P. Eigler, E. Langeard, C. H. Lovelock *et al.*, *Marketing Consumer Services Report No. 77-115*, pp. 31–58. Marketing Science Institute.

Engel, J. F., Blackwell, R. D. and Miniard, P. W. (1991). *Consumer Behaviour*, 6th edn. Dryden Press.

Ennew, C. T. (1992). Consumer attitudes to independent financial advice. *International Journal of Bank Marketing*, **10(5)**, 13–18.

Ennew, C. T. (1993). *The Marketing Blueprint*. Blackwell.

Ennew, C. T. and Binks, M. R. (1996a). Good and bad customers: the benefits of participating in the banking relationship. *International Journal of Bank Marketing*, **14(2)**, 5–13.

Ennew, C. T. and Binks, M. (1996b). The impact of service quality and service characteristics on customer retention: small businesses and their banks in the UK. *British Journal of Management*, **7(3)**, 219–230.

Ennew, C. T. and Binks, M. R. (1999). Impact of participative service relationships on quality, satisfaction and retention: an exploratory study. *Journal of Business Research*, **46(2)**, 121.

Ennew, C. T. and McKechnie, S. (1992). Green marketing: can the banks respond? *International Journal of Bank Marketing, Marketing Intelligence & Planning*, **10(7)**, 8.

Ennew, C. T. and Sekhon, H. (2003). *The Financial Services Trust Index: A Pilot Study*. Financial Services Research Forum.

Ennew, C. T. and Sekhon, H. (2004). *The Role of Trust in the Financial Services Sector: a marketing perspective*. Financial Services Research Forum.

Euromonitor (2004). *Financial Cards in South Africa* (available at http://www.euromonitor.com/Financial_Cards_in_South_Africa).

European Commission (2006). *The Internal Market*. EC.

File, K. M. and Prince, R. A. (1991). Sociographic segmentation: the SME market and financial services. *International Journal of Bank Marketing*, **9(3)**, 3.

Foster, M. (2000). *Trends and Driving Factors in Income Inequality and Poverty in the OECD Area*. OECD Labour Market and Social Policy, Occasional Paper No. 42.

Gabbott, M. and Hogg, G. (1994). Consumer behaviour and services: a review. *Journal of Marketing Management*, **10**, 311–324.

Garvin, D. A. (1988). Managing quality. *McKinsey Quarterly*, **3**, 61–70.

Genetay, N. (1999). Ownership structure and performance in UK life offices. *European Management Journal*, **17(1)**, 107–115.

Ghoshal, S. and Bartlett, C. A. (1998). *Managing Across Borders*. Random House.

Goode, M., Moutinho, L. A. and Chien, C. (1996). Structural equation modelling of overall satisfaction and full use of services for ATMs. *International Journal of Bank Marketing*, **14(7)**, 4–12.

Grant Thornton UK LLP (2006). An analysis of the suitability of advertising and financial promotions in the UK's financial services sector (available at www.grant.thornton.co.uk).

Grönroos, C. (1984). A service quality model and its marketing implications. *European Journal of Marketing*, **18(4)**, 36–44.

Grönroos, C. (1988). Service quality; the six criteria of good perceived service quality. *Review of Business*, **9(3)**, 10–13.

Grönroos, C. (1990). Relationship approach to marketing in services contexts: the marketing & organizational behaviour interface. *Journal of Business Research*, **20**, 3–11.

Grönroos, C. (1998). Marketing services: the case of a missing product. *Journal of Business & Industrial Marketing*, **13(4/5)**, 322.

Gummesson, E. (1987). The new marketing – developing long-term interactive relationships. *Long Range Planning*, **20(1)**, 10.

Hamel, G. and Prahalad, C. K. (1991). Corporate imagination and expeditionary marketing. *Harvard Business Review*, **July–August**, 81–92.

Hardwick, P. and Letza, S. (2000). The relative performance of mutual and proprietary life insurance companies in the UK. *Insurance Research and Practice*, **15(2)**, 40–46.

Harness, D. and Marr, N. (2001). Strategies for eliminating a financial services product. *Journal of Product and Brand Management*, **10(6/7)**, 423.

Harrison, T. S. (1994). Mapping customer segments for personal financial services. *International Journal of Bank Marketing*, **12(8)**, 17–25.

Hart, C. W. L., Heskett, J. L. and Sasser, W. E. (1990). The profitable art of service recovery. *Harvard Business Review*, **July–August**, 148–156.

Henson, S. W. and Wilson, J. C. (2002). Case study: Strategic challenges in the financial services industry. *Journal of Business and Industrial Marketing*, **17(5)**, 407–418.

Heskett, J. L., Jones, G. W., Loveman, W. E. Jr and Schlesinger, L. A. (1994). Putting the service-profit chain to work. *Harvard Business Review*, **72(2)**, 164–174.

Hooley, G. J. (1995). The lifecycle concept revisited: aid or albatross? *Journal of Strategic Marketing*, **3(1)**, 23.

Hume, J. (2004). Islamic finance: provenance and prospects. *International Financial Law Review*, **23(5)**, 48–50.

International Co-operative and Mutual Insurers Federation (2003). *Valuing Our Mutuality II*, October. ICMIF.

Jain, A. K., Pinson, C. and Malhotra, N. K. (1987). Customer loyalty as a construct in the marketing of bank services. *International Journal of Bank Marketing*, **5(3)**, 49–72.

Jenkins, D. and Yoneyama, T. (2000). *The History of Insurance, Volume 1*. Pickering and Chatto.

Jensen, M. (1991). The politics of corporate finance. *Journal of Applied Corporate Finance*, **4**, 13–33.

Jobber, D. (2004). *Principles & Practice of Marketing*, 4th edn. McGraw Hill.

Johne, A. and Harborne, P. (2003). One leader is not enough for major new service development: results for a consumer banking study. *Service Industries Journal*, **23(3)**, 22–39.

Kamakura, W. A., Ramaswami, S. N. and Srivastava, R. K. (1991). Applying latent trait analysis in the evaluation of prospects for cross-selling of financial services. *International Journal of Research in Marketing*, **8**, 329–349.

Kaspar, H., van Helsdingen, P. and de Vries, W. Jr (1999). *Services Marketing Management: An International Perspective*, p. 404. John Wiley & Son.

Kaynak, E. and Yucelt, U. (1984). A cross-cultural study of credit card usage behaviours: Canadian and American credit card users contrasted. *International Journal of Bank Marketing*, **2(2)**, 45–57.

Kennington, C., Hill, J. and Rakowska, A. (1996). Consumer selection criteria for banks in Poland. *International Journal of Bank Marketing*, **14(4)**, 12–21.

Kirk, T. and Middleton, P. (2004). *'Is it Fair?': responding to regulatory, consumer and social pressure to provide fair treatment to financial services customers*. Ernst & Young.

Knights, D., Sturdy, A. and Morgan, G. (1994). The consumer rules: an examination of rhetoric and 'reality' of marketing in financial services. *European Journal of Marketing*, **28(3)**, 42–54.

Knights, D., Leyshon, A., Alferoff, C. and Signoretta, P. (2004). *Delivering Financial Services in the Home*. Financial Services Research Forum Report, University of Nottingham.

Kohli, A. K. and Jaworksi, B. J. (1990). Market orientation: the construct, research propositions, and managerial implications. *Journal of Marketing*, **54(2)**, 1–18.

Kotler, P. (1994). *Marketing Management: Analysis, Planning, Implementation and Control*, 8th edn. Prentice-Hall.

Lam, R. and Burton, S. (2005). Bank selection and share of wallet among SMEs: apparent differences between Hong Kong and Australia. *Journal of Financial Services Marketing*, **9(3)**, 204.

Laroche, M., Rosenblatt, J. A. and Manning, T. (1986). Services used and factors considered important in selecting a bank: an investigation across diverse demographic segments. *International Journal of Bank Marketing*, **4(1)**, 35.

LeBlanc, G. and Nguyen, N. (1988). Customers' perceptions of service quality in financial institutions. *International Journal of Bank Marketing*, **6(4)**, 7–18.

Lehtinen, U. and Lehtinen, J. R. (1991). Two approaches to service quality dimensions. *Service Industries Journal*, **11(3)**, 287–303.

Leonard, M. and Spencer, A. (1991). The importance of image as a competitive strategy: an exploratory study in commercial banks. *International Journal of Bank Marketing*, **9(4)**, 25–29.

Levesque, T. and McDougall, G. (1996). Determinants of customer satisfaction in retail banking. *International Journal of Bank Marketing*, **14(7),** 12–20.

Levitt, T. (1960). Marketing myopia. *Harvard Business Review*, **July–August,** 26.

Levitt, T. (1980). Marketing success through differentiation – of anything. *Harvard Business Review*, **January–February**.

Lewis, B. R., Orledge, J. and Mitchell, V. (1994). Service quality: students' assessments of banks and building societies. *International Journal of Bank Marketing*, **12(4),** 3–12.

Lewis, B. R. and Spyrakopoulos, S. (2001). Service failures and recovery in retail banking: the customers' perspective. *International Journal of Bank Marketing*, **19(1),** 37–48.

Leyshon, A., Signoretta, P. and French, S. (2006). *The Changing Geography of British Bank and Building Society Branch Networks, 1995–2003*. School of Geography, University of Nottingham.

Lovelock, C. H. (1981). Why marketing management needs to be different for services. In: J. H. Donnelly and W. R. George (eds), *The Marketing of Services*, pp. 5–9. AMA Proceedings.

Lovelock, C. H. (1983). Classifying services to gain strategic marketing insights. *Journal of Marketing*, **47(3),** 9.

Lovelock, C. H. and Gummesson, E. (2004). Whither services marketing? In search of a new paradigm and fresh perspectives. *Journal of Service Research*, **7(1),** 20.

Lovelock, C. H. and Yip, G. S. (1996). Developing global strategies for service businesses. *California Management Review*, **38(2),** 64.

Loveman, G. W. (1998). Employee satisfaction, customer loyalty and financial performance. *Journal of Service Research*, **1(1),** 18–31.

McKechnie, S. (1992). Consumer buying behaviour in financial services: an overview. *International Journal of Bank Marketing*, **10(5),** 4–12.

McLaughlin, C. P. and Fitzsimmons, J. A. (1996). Strategies for globalizing service operations. *International Journal of Service Industry Management*, **7(4),** 43–57.

Mills, P. S. (1999). *Islamic Finance*. Palgrave.

Mols, N. P.., Bukh, P. N. D. and Blenker, P. (1997). European corporate customers' choice of domestic cash management banks. *International Journal of Bank Marketing*, **15(7),** 255.

Murray, K. B. (1991). A test of services marketing theory: consumer information acquisition activities. *Journal of Marketing*, **55,** 10–25.

Murphy, J. A. (1996). Retail banking. In: F. Buttle (ed.), *Relationship Marketing Theory and Practice*, pp. 74–90. Paul Chapman Publishing.

Myners, P. (2004). *Myners Review of the Governance of Life Mutuals: final report*. HM Treasury.

Narver, J. C. and Slater, S. F. (1990). The effect of a market orientation on business profitability. *Journal of Marketing*, **54(4),** 20.

Office of Fair Trading (1999). *Financial Exclusion of Vulnerable Consumers*. PN02/99, 13 January (available at www.oft.gov.uk).

O'Lauglin, D., Szymigin, I. and Turnbull, P. (2004). From relationships to experiences in retail financial services. *International Journal of Bank Marketing*, **22(6/7),** 522.

Oliver, R. L. (1997). *Satisfaction: a behavioural perspective on the consumer*. McGraw Hill.

Page-Adams, D. and Sherraden, M. (1996). *What We Know About Effects of Asset Holding: Implications for Research of Asset-Based Anti-Poverty Initiatives*. Centre for Social Development, No 96(1).

Panigyrakis, G. G., Theodoridis, P. K. and Veloutsou, C. A. (2003). All customers are not treated equally: financial exclusion in isolated Greek islands. *Journal of Financial Services Marketing*, **7(1),** 54–66.

Parasuraman, A., Zeithaml, V. A. and Berry, L. L. (1985). A conceptual model of service quality and its implications for future research. *Journal of Marketing*, **49,** 41–50.

Parasuraman, A., Zeithaml, V. A. and Berry, L. L. (1988). SERVQUAL: a multiple item scale for measuring consumer perceptions of service quality. *Journal of Retailing*, **64(1),** 14–40.

Parasuraman, A., Berry, L. L. and Zeithaml, V. A. (1991). Refinement and reassessment of the SERVQUAL scale. *Journal of Retailing*, **67(4),** 420.

Paulin, M., Perrien, J. and Ferguson, R. (1997). Relational contract norms and the effectiveness of commercial banking relationships. *International Journal of Service Industry Management*, **8(5)**, 435.

Payne, A. (2000). *Marketing Management: a relationship marketing perspective*. MacMillan Business.

Pilbeam, K. (2005). *Finance and Financial Markets*. Palgrave Macmillan.

Pont, M. and McQuilken, L. (2005). An empirical investigation of customer satisfaction and loyalty across two divergent bank segments. *Journal of Financial Services Marketing*, **9(4)**, 344.

Porter, M. E. (2002). What is strategy? In: H. Mintzberg, J. Lampel, J. B. Quinn and S. Ghoshal (eds), *The Strategy Process: Concepts, Contexts, Cases*, 4th edn. Prentice-Hall.

Porter, M. E. (1980). *Competitive Strategy*. Free Press.

Porter, M. E. (1985). *Competitive Advantage*. Free Press.

Prahalad, C. K. and Hamel, G. (1990). The core competence of the corporation. *Harvard Business Review*, **May–June,** 79.

Rajatanavin, R. and Speece, M. (2004). The sales force as an information transfer mechanism for new service development in the Thai insurance industry. *Journal of Financial Services Marketing*, **8(3)**, 244.

Rathmell, J. M. (1966). What is meant by services? *Journal of Marketing*, **30(4)**, 32.

Reichheld, F. A. (1993). Loyalty-based management. *Harvard Business Review*, **March–April,** 64–73.

Reichheld, F. A. (1994). Loyalty and the renaissance of marketing. *Marketing Management*, **2(2)**, 10–21.

Reichheld, F. F. and Sasser, W. E. (1990). Zero defections: quality comes to services. *Harvard Business Review*, **September–October,** 105–111.

Reinartz, W. and Kumar, V. (2002). The mismanagement of customer loyalty. *Harvard Business Review*, **80(7)**, 86.

Ries, A. and Trout, J. (1986). *Positioning: The Battle for Your Mind*. McGraw Hill.

Rucci, J. A., Kirn, S. P. and Quinn, R. T. (1998). The employee–customer–profit chain at Sears. *Harvard Business Review*, **76(1)**, 83–97.

Rust, R. T. and Oliver, R. W. (1994). Video dial tone. *Journal of Services Marketing*, **8(3)**, 5.

Saxena, M. (2000). Interview with Ajay Kelkar (available at http://www.exchange4media.com/Brandspeak/brandspeak.asp?brand_id=811, HDFC Bank – www.HDFCBank.com).

Saxena, M. (2006). Tech it or leave it: banker's choice. Economic Times (available at http://www.etstrategicmarketing.com/smJan-Feb1/per_bank.htm).

SEC (undated). Website for US Securities and Exchange Commission (available at http://www.sec.gov/about/whatwedo.shtml).

Shapiro, B. P. and Jackson, B. B. (1978). Industrial pricing to meet customer needs. *Harvard Business Review*, **November–December,** 119–127.

Sharma, N. and Patterson, P. G. (2001). Switching costs, alternative attractiveness and experience as moderators of relationship commitment in professional, consumer services. *International Journal of Service Industry Management*, **11(5)**, 470.

Shostack, G. L. (1982). How to design a service. *European Journal of Marketing*, **16(1)**, 49.

Silvestro, R. and Cross, S. (2000). Applying the service profit chain in a retail environment: challenging the 'satisfaction mirror'. *International Journal of Service Industry Management*, **11(3)**, 244.

Stewart, D. M. (1998). An exploration of customer exit in retail banking. *International Journal of Bank Marketing*, **16(1)**, 6–14.

Storbacka, K. (1994). *A relationship marketing perspective on the link between service quality and customer profitability in retail banking. International Quality in Services Conference*. Norwalk.

Storbacka, K. and Lehtinen, J. (2001). *Customer Relationship Management: Creating Competitive Advantage through Win–Win Relationship Strategies*. McGraw Hill.

Storbacka, K., Strandvik, T. and Grönroos, C. (1994). Managing customer relationships for profit: the dynamics of relationship quality. *International Journal of Service Industry Management*, **5(5)**, 21.

Swift, R. S. (2001). *Accelerating Customer Relationships: Using CRM and Relationship Technologies*. Prentice Hall.

Tax, S. S., Brown, S. W. and Chandrashekaran, M. (1998). Customer evaluations of service complaint experiences. *Journal of Marketing*, **62**, 60–76.

Teas, R. K., Dorsch, M. J. and McAlexander, J. H. (1988). Measuring commercial bank customers' attitudes towards the quality of the bank services marketing relationship. *Journal of Professional Services Marketing*, **4(1)**, 75–95.

Treacy, M. and Wiersema, F. (1996). *The Discipline of Market Leaders*. Addison-Wesley.

Turnbull, P. W. (1982a). The purchasing of international financial services by medium- and large-sized UK companies with European subsidiaries. *European Journal of Marketing*, **16(3)**, 111–121.

Turnbull, P. W. (1982b). The role of the branch bank manager in the marketing of bank services. *European Journal of Marketing*, **16(3)**, 31–36.

Turnbull, P. W. (1982c). The use of foreign banks by British companies. *European Journal of Marketing*, **16(3)**, 133–145.

Turnbull, P. W. (1983). Corporate attitudes towards bank services. *International Journal of Bank Marketing*, **1(1)**, 53–66.

Turnbull, P. W. and Gibbs, M. L. (1987). Marketing bank services to corporate customers: the importance of relationships. *International Journal of Bank Marketing*, **5(1)**, 19–26.

Turnbull, P. W. and Gibbs, M. L. (1989). The selection of banks & banking services among corporate customers in South Africa. *International Journal of Bank Marketing*, **7(5)**, 36–39.

Turnbull, P. W. and Moustakatos, T. (1995). Marketing and investment banking: practical and theoretical challenges. *International Journal of Bank Marketing*, **14(2)**, 26–37.

Vargo, S. L. and Lusch, R. F. (2004). The four service marketing myths: remnants of a goods-based, manufacturing model. *Journal of Service Research*, **6(4)**, 324.

Veloutsou, C., Daskou, S. and Daskou, A. (2004). Are the determinants of bank loyalty, brand specific? *Journal of Financial Services Marketing*, **9(2)**, 113.

Verma, R., Zafar, I. and Plaschka, G. (2004). Understanding customer choices in e-financial services. *California Management Review*, **46(4)**, 43.

Waite, N. (2001). *Welfare and the Consumer Society: New Opportunities for the Third Way*. The Canford Centre for Customer Development, on behalf of The Association of Friendly Societies.

WARC (2003). *The Financial Marketing Pocket Book* (available at www.warc.com).

Ward, D. (2002). The costs of distribution in the UK life insurance market. *Applied Economics*, **34**, 1959–1968.

Whitelock, J. (2002). Theories of internationalisation and their impact on market entry. *International Marketing Review*, **19(4)**, 342–347.

Whitelock, J. and Jobber, D. (2004). An evaluation of external factors in the decision of UK industrial firms to enter a new non-domestic market: an exploratory study. *European Journal of Marketing*, **38(11/12)**, 1437.

Willetts, D. (2003). *Old Europe? Demographic Change and Pension Reform*. Centre for European Reform (available at http://www.cert.org.uk/).

World Trade Organisation (2001). WTO successfully concludes negotiations on China's entry. Press release 243, 17 September (available at http://www.wto.org/english/news_e/pres01_e/pr243_e.htm).

World Trade Organisation (2004). *International Trade Statistics*. WTO.

Yeung, M. C. H. and Ennew, C. T. (2001). Measuring the impact of customer satisfaction on profitability: a sectoral analysis. *Journal of Targeting, Analysis and Measurement for Marketing*, **10(2)**, 106–116.

Yip, G. S. (1994) Industry drivers of global strategy and organization. *The International Executive (1986–1998)*, **36(5)**, 529.

Zeithaml, V. (1981). How consumer evaluation processes differ between goods and services. In: J. H. Donnelly and W. R. George (eds), *The Marketing of Services*, pp. 186–190. AMA Proceedings.

Zeithaml, A. V. (1988). Customer perceptions of price quality and value: a means-end model and synthesis evidence. *Journal of Marketing*, **52**, 2–22.

Zeithaml, V. and Bitner, M. J. (2003). *Services Marketing: integrating customer focus across the firm*. McGraw Hill/Irwin.

Zeithaml, V. A., Parasuraman, A. and Berry, L. L. (1985). Problems and strategies in services marketing. *Journal of Marketing*, **49**, 33–46.

Zeithaml, V. A., Berry, L. L. and Parasuraman, A. (1988). Communication and control processes in the delivery of service quality. *Journal of Marketing*, **52**, 35–48.

Zeithaml, V., Berry, L. and Parasuraman, A. (1996). The behavioural consequences of service quality. *Journal of Marketing*, **60(2)**, 31.

Zineldin, M. (1995). Bank-company interactions and relationships: some empirical evidence. *International Journal of Bank Marketing*, **13(2)**, 30–40.

Index

WHERE THERE'S A WILL

John Mortimer

WINDSOR
PARAGON

First published 2003
by
Viking
an imprint of Penguin Books Ltd
This Large Print edition published 2003
by
BBC Audiobooks Ltd
by arrangement with
Penguin Books Ltd

ISBN 0 7540 8686 0 (Windsor Hardcover)
ISBN 0 7540 9374 3 (Paragon Softcover)

Grateful acknowledgement is made for permission
to reproduce extracts from the following:
'The Tower' by W. B. Yeats. Reprinted by
permission of A. P. Watt Ltd on behalf of
Michael B. Yeats.
'A Slice of Wedding Cake' by Robert Graves.
Reprinted from *The Complete Poems* published by
Carcanet Press.

British Library Cataloguing in Publication Data available

Printed and bound in Great Britain by
Antony Rowe Ltd., Chippenham, Wiltshire

For Gus, Joe, Felix,
Dora and Beatrix

It is time that I wrote my will . . .
I have prepared my peace
With learned Italian things
And the proud stones of Greece,
Poet's imaginings
And memories of love,
Memories of the words of women,
All those things whereof
Man makes a superhuman
Mirror-resembling dream.
W.B. Yeats, 'The Tower'

Let's choose executors, and talk of wills.
William Shakespeare, 'Richard II'

CONTENTS

ix

CHAPTER ONE

WHERE THERE'S A WILL

'All advice is perfectly useless,' my father told me when he sent me away to school. 'Particularly advice on the subject of life. You may, at a pinch, take your schoolteacher's word on the subject of equilateral triangles, or the Latin-1 word for "parsley"; but remember that life's a closed book to schoolteachers, if you want my honest opinion.'

And yet the temptation to give advice is almost irresistible. From the book of Leviticus, which forbade homosexuality and the eating of prawns, through Lord Chesterfield's letters informing his son how to act like a gentleman, through Victorian doctors who advised the young that masturbation leads to blindness ('Can I just do it until I'm short-sighted?' some bright child is alleged to have asked), to present-day classes on citizenship, endless varying diets, or calls to save the universe by the segregation of rubbish, we have always been bombarded with advice. The state of the world doesn't offer much evidence of each generation having benefited from the wise words of their elders. All that could be said of a book that told the author's grandchildren how to live their lives is that it would be singularly ineffective.

'If you'll take my advice,' said the late Sir Patrick Hastings, cross-examining an habitual offender in his threatening Irish brogue, 'you'll answer the question truthfully.'

'The last time I took your advice, Sir Patrick,'

1

the witness said, 'I got four years.'

I can think of only one piece of advice which has effectively influenced my life. When I was about seven years old I locked myself into the lavatory at the Negresco Hotel in Nice. A carpenter was called to release me. When I was extricated the hotel manager, in perfect English, said he had a word of warning for me which I should take extremely seriously. 'Let this be a lesson to you, my boy,' he said. 'Never lock a lavatory door for the rest of your life!' I never have, but this course of conduct has led to no strange encounters or indeed affected my conduct in any other way.

However, at the end of a life, there may be a natural desire to take stock of your possessions and decide what, if anything, can be dusted off and usefully passed on. Such bequests can be easily rejected as, perhaps, too familiar articles of furniture.

'Let's choose executors, and talk of wills.' So said Richard II at the time of his defeat and approaching death. And my father chose Shakespeare's line as the epigraph of his single book, *Mortimer on Probate*, still a standard work on the law governing testamentary dispositions. The cases he did in court included arguments about last wills written on a blown duck egg, or on the tail of a kite, but not, as Rider Haggard once wrote, on the naked back of a woman who had to be filed at Somerset House.

Death, in the probate cases we used to do, was the preliminary to endless family feuds, bitter recriminations and lengthy contested claims to the bedroom furniture, the elderly Bentley or the set of golf clubs. It has to be said that the deceased often

2

encouraged this infighting by making contradictory promises to friends and relatives in order to ensure their visits and a kindly interest in a lonely old age. All the same, after twenty years spent knocking around the criminal courts, it's hard to remember cases which showed human nature as more selfish, more predatory, redder in tooth and claw, than those probate actions which concerned the remnants of a finished life and the property of the dead.

What can we leave behind that will be of any use to our relatives, apart from the second-best bed, the deflated pension fund, the bundle of letters carelessly left undestroyed, the cupboard full of old suits or vintage evening dresses, the sporting prints and the doubtful Chippendale?

Having decided to make his will, W. B. Yeats announced from his tower that he had 'prepared my peace / With learned Italian things / And the proud stones of Greece, / Poet's imaginings / And memories of love, / Memories of the words of women, / All those things whereof / Man makes a superhuman / Mirror-resembling dream'. These were, no doubt, wise choices. No one is likely to start an embittered and fiercely fought legal action over the possession of a poet's imaginings, memories of the words of women or even all the things whereof man makes a superhuman, mirror-resembling dream.

And yet such bequests may be of far greater value than the seaside bungalow, the tarnished silver or the four-seater sofa. Apart from his intimate knowledge of the law of probate, my father left me his memories of Shakespeare, Browning and the Sherlock Holmes stories,

3

together with his laughter, which I can hear quite often echoing in my children's mouths, and his sudden rages at trivial inconveniences such as cold plates, waiting for things and soft eggs. He left me, I also have to admit, his house and garden; but it's for an approach to life, a view of our brief existence suspended between two vast eternities, that I am just as grateful.

Wills are not usually places to find comments on life as it has been lived. If they are subject to prolonged and expensive interpretation, it's only to discover what items of property fall into residue or the precise effect of an act of revocation. Nor are the old, near to death, necessarily wise. Many of the greatest crimes, much of the most bigoted behaviour leading to widespread suffering and mass slaughter, have been committed by angry old people stuck, like trucks in the soft sands of the desert, in the errors of their ways. King Lear, until moments of madness brought him some illumination, had far less understanding of the human condition than the clear-sighted young Cordelia. Indeed, old age can lead to panic and irresponsibility. Old men may contract near-fatal marriages or old women may fall victims to drink and cosmetic surgery. The account of accumulated wisdom may, at the end, be seriously overdrawn and an intelligent teenager may be a far more reliable guide to life than an old person with a plastic hip or a face-lift.

So where should we look, outside ourselves, for an awareness of the human condition, a country which can never be entirely explored but glimpsed, more or less widely, and penetrated in varying degrees of depth?

4

What can be said is that the passage of time, the addition of this or that invention, even of many scientific discoveries, has not necessarily helped towards this essential understanding. It can be argued that no writer had a clearer insight than Shakespeare, and he managed to achieve this in a world without refrigeration, Darwin, Freud, Bill Gates, e-mails, television or the mobile phone. The characters in the plays of Euripides are no less capable of revealing universal truths than those created by Eugene O'Neill or Harold Pinter. All great literature, so far as our understanding of the essential facts about ourselves goes, is modern literature.

And what is true of literature may be true of history also. The contemporary holy wars of Islam are as wrong-headed but, so far at least, less deep in blood than the Crusades. Ireland is endlessly re-enacting the days of Oliver Cromwell and William of Orange. Yugoslavs were murdering each other as a result of divisions in the Roman Empire. And yet we are busily closing our eyes to all these valuable clues. Shakespeare is dying out in schools, no one learns poetry by heart and literature seems to have begun with *Animal Farm*, *Lord of the Flies* and, perhaps, *The Hobbit*. History begins, in our schools, with the Russian Revolution or, at its most remote, the origins of the 1914 war.

So the Delphic instructions to know ourselves, Shakespeare's advice, put into the mouth of Polonius in one of the rare moments when he was being sensible, 'to thine own self be true', and Montaigne's announcement that living 'is my trade and my art' are made harder by severing relations with the past. Perhaps Yeats's bequests are, in fact, the most valuable assets we can leave, the 'learned Italian things . . . the proud stones of Greece' and, above all, 'Poet's imaginings'. These may give us wider, clearer views, but the whole truth is still unknowable. The definitive map of our universe doesn't exist. Those who think they know it all usually know the least; those who think they have all the answers have always lost the plot.

CHAPTER TWO

CHANGING YOUR LIFE—AND 'THE MAN IN SNEAKERS'

I live surrounded by ageing rockers. Joe Brown of The Bruvvers is in the next village, Jim Capaldi of Traffic is in a nearby town, George Harrison, until his untimely death, lived in Henley, and our great friends are a beautiful pair of twins, known to us as the Heavenlies, who are married to members of the group Deep Purple. Jon Lord, the keyboard player and one of the founders of the group, has changed his life and now successfully composes classical music. One of my own changes of life is more rapid and fundamental.

I am at my first rock concert, admittedly late in life. Deep Purple, having toured the world and played to many thousands of enthusiasts in Bengal, where they were greeted with headlines like 'The Rock Heroes are in Town', are giving a concert in Oxford. The theatre is packed with an almost all-male audience, many of them playing air guitar or standing with their arms raised, swaying to the music.

I am standing in the wings, drinking champagne out of a paper cup as the band crashes triumphantly through the sound barrier. Ian Paice completes a miraculous drum solo and throws his sticks into the applauding audience with the elegance of Marie Antoinette chucking out a few cakes to the hungry mob below her windows. As I clap enthusiastically, a man standing beside me

7

asks, 'Are you Ian Paice's dad?'

'Yes,' I say modestly. 'I'm Ian's dad and we're terrifically proud of the boy.' It was a moment of relief, a sudden escape from too many other problems. I could give up being myself and concentrate on being the delighted father of a brilliant drummer, if only for half an hour. Occasionally, meeting other rock bands and talking to drummers, I become Ian's dad again. All this only points to something else I should mention in a will, the importance, in a long life, of changing it whenever possible.

If you feel stuck in any kind of a rut you might contemplate the chameleon life of Lorenzo Da Ponte, the Jew who became a Catholic priest, the librettist of the three greatest operas ever written, the friend of Casanova, Mozzart (as he always spelled the composer's name) and two successive Austrian emperors, who married an English wife and ended up living in New York, owning an opera house and teaching Americans about Italian poetry.

In that great period of history which included the Age of Reason and the French Revolution, the world of Rousseau and Napoleon, Byron, Wellington, Shelley and Goethe, Mozart and Beethoven, Da Ponte appears in flashes of light, enjoying extraordinarily different lives in various disguises. Even his name wasn't his. The child of a Jewish family which had converted to Catholicism because, in the province of Venice, Jews were not allowed to marry, the future librettist was given the name of the bishop who baptized him.

We get a glimpse of Da Ponte in the priests' seminary at Cenada, where, in six months, he learned most of Dante's *Inferno* by heart, as well as the best sonnets and songs of Petrarch and 'the most beautiful works of Tasso'. He was fluent in Latin and became a brilliant teacher. Now we see him taking holy orders, followed by a succession of unpriestly love affairs. An anonymous denunciation accused him of an 'evil life'. Someone had seen a woman put her hand in his breeches. He fled from Venice to avoid his trial by the Inquisition and was sentenced, in his absence, to seven years in a prison cell without light.

After a tender love affair with the wife of an innkeeper, and having renamed himself for a short while with the eccentric pseudonym of 'Lesbonico Pegasio', he appears again in Vienna as 'poet' to the Burg theatre, and the favourite of Emperor Joseph II. So we find him writing libretti for three operas, one by Mozart, one by Salieri and one by Martini, feeling as he writes that 'I am reading the *Inferno* for Mozart, Tasso for Salieri and Petrarch for Martini.' He is working for twelve hours at a stretch, assisted by a bottle of Tokay on his right, his inkwell in front of him and a box of Seville snuff on his left, with a beautiful young girl, the housekeeper's daughter, to bring him a biscuit, a cup of coffee or merely her smiling face.

Da Ponte's lasting fame rests on his writing the words for *Don Giovanni*, *The Marriage of Figaro* and *Così fan tutte*. He was convinced, in these works, as in his life, that quick and complete changes of mood are essential. So, in *Don Giovanni*, scenes of farce (the changing of clothes between the Don and Leporello) are followed by moments of high comedy, tragedy and, finally, the refusal to repent, which has made Don Giovanni into an existentialist hero as he is dragged down to hell.

In *Così fan tutte* Da Ponte makes changes of identity more significant than changes of mood. The silly bet, which has caused the pair of male lovers to return in disguise to test the fidelity of their mistresses, becomes stranger and more bewildering when each mistress falls for the charms of the other's lover. Those who dismiss *Così* as a ridiculous story with deathless music seem unaware of this disturbing development. Does it, can it, mean that we are creatures without any personality, one lover, in the moment of temptation, being as good as another? In Da Ponte's libretto the possibility remains that, in the inevitable 'happy' ending, the girls actually marry the wrong partners, although this is not the way we can bear to see it performed nowadays. The pride we take in being consistent and individual souls would be far too deeply disturbed.

We can't resist a look at Da Ponte in a country house party just before the first night of *Don Giovanni*. The house was on the outskirts of Prague and the October weather was still warm and beautiful. 'People lingered happily in the open air, with the feeling that days like this were a blessing,' one of the guests wrote. It was at this party that Mozart was lured into an upstairs room and the door was locked until he finished the yet unwritten overture. Da Ponte appears at this party with an aged librarian from the Castle of Dux. This was a man who may have been a model for the sensual Don, and who also had a rascally servant. 'Signor Casanova seems to be a really worthy old man,' one of the guests is reported to have said to Da Ponte,

10

who replied, 'There you are making a terrible mistake. He's an adventurer who has spent his days playing cards, brewing elixirs and telling fortunes.'

After the party Da Ponte hurried back to Vienna. And the elderly Casanova, who wrote, 'the first business of my life has been to indulge my senses. I felt myself born for the fair sex', may have sat in the theatre to hear the Don tell Leporello, 'Women are more necessary to me than the bread I eat or the air I breathe.' The old man must have felt himself living again as the seducer on the stage.

Da Ponte had gone, having business to do, fresh love affairs to attend to and other opera libretti to write. He travelled to England and then turned up unexpectedly in Boston, after a terrible crossing of the Atlantic without a mattress or regular meals, to teach and sell Italian books. And then he was in New York, opening his new opera house. Some Americans objected to watching music drama sung in Italian. Da Ponte invited them to dinner, where delicious garlic-scented, succulent Italian dishes were set before them. Before they could start eating, all these delights were cleared away and replaced by bowls of American corn. The dinner also had changed identity.

Finally the opera house burnt down, but Da Ponte lived on until his ninetieth year, respected, grey-haired, still handsome and smiling through all life's changes. When he died, he had an elaborately theatrical funeral at the Roman Catholic Cathedral on 11th Street. His grave was, like Mozart's, unmarked, the cemetery has been built over and no trace of this extraordinary consumer of life exists except on the stage.

Changing the life that's been allocated to you, throwing in your hand and asking for a redeal, may require courage and determination. Our friend Derek has both. He was born the only child of two poor, totally underprivileged Jamaican immigrants in Battersea. He is now a rich and successful businessman and financial adviser, and perhaps the only black master of foxhounds in England.

Once again it's the story of a remarkable teacher, a woman at Derek's state school who liked this obviously bright little boy and invited him for weekends to her cottage in Norfolk, where he learned how to ride. When he left school, he got a job in the Attorney-General's office, made contacts and entered the world of big business. So, quick-witted and ready with an apt phrase, Derek was able to change the unpromising hand he had been dealt.

He was sailing over a fence in his full master of foxhounds regalia when a hunt saboteur shouted up at him, 'Two hundred years ago they would've been hunting you.'

'Oh yes, my dear,' Derek shouted back, 'and five hundred years ago, I would've been eating you!'

Derek is a Tory. His reason for this must be a constant accusation to those of us who are on the left, and should be a weight on the conscience of a new generation of politicians. 'When I was a poor boy in Battersea,' he said, 'and saw the way Labour treated its own people, I decided to become a Conservative.'

*   *   *

Hitchcock's movie *North by Northwest* has an early scene in a crowded hotel lounge. A bellboy is walking among the guests calling out that he's got a message for Mr George Caplan. Cary Grant, who isn't Caplan, raises his hand because he wants to make a telephone call to his mother. The villains, who have been looking for Caplan in order to kill him, assume that Cary Grant has answered the bellboy's call and that he is, therefore, the man they're after. For the rest of the film Grant has to live the life of a stranger who turns out not to exist, avoid his assassins and share the non-existent stranger's troubles; so easy is it to slide from one identity to another.

The best of times, so far as I was concerned, was when I was both a writer and a defence barrister. The lawyer was able to learn many secrets, to meet a huge variety of people, to bear their misfortunes with great heroism and see the solutions to their problems quite clearly. Talking to juries and judges in court, I was always telling them things I thought they'd like to hear. What I thought, what I felt, was immaterial. I was someone else's voice doing my best to persuade tribunals of other people's innocence. But early, very early in the morning, before the judges, the jury members or those under arrest were awake, I was a writer trying to be entirely myself, saying exactly what I thought in a voice I hoped was no one else's.

This led to an enjoyably varied way of life. I used to spend breakfast time with a suspected murderer in an interview room in the cells under the Old Bailey, I would have lunch with the judges, who ate and drank with their wigs on at the City of

13

London's expense, and in the evening I would have dinner with an actress. I could go, when court ended, to a rehearsal room. In doing so, I seemed to step from the world of make-believe and 'let's pretend' to the harsh reality of the theatre, where an attempt, at any rate, is being made to say something truthful about the human condition.

Most lives are long enough to play at least two parts; but the problems of identity raised by *Così fan tutte* remain. I'm writing this in Italy, and back in England a week ago Leo McKern died. He was an actor who magnificently portrayed a character I'd written, Rumpole, the claret-swigging, small-cigar-smoking, fearless upholder of our great legal principles, trial by your peers, the presumption of innocence and the rule that the police shouldn't invent more of the evidence than is strictly necessary. At a restaurant I go to near our home in England, the owner saw a newspaper headline, 'Rumpole Dies', and for days she spoke in hushed and, I'm relieved to say, regretful tones about my unfortunate death. Rumpole doesn't exist except in books and television plays. I, who wrote him, am still, unaccountably, alive. The actor who pretended to be him is dead. No wonder the newspaper headline was confusing.

*   *   *

And what about 'The Man in Sneakers'? I do wear trainers, gym shoes, whatever you call them, because of the state of my feet. Dressed otherwise respectably, I am in the bar of the Essex House in New York with my actress daughter, Emily, and her newly wed actor husband, Alessandro. We are with

14

our respective families and are about to go to the opening of a film he is in. Emily moves a little away from our group to take a photograph of us all.

She is now close to a man sitting at a bar table who takes her hand and, looking at her lovingly, says, 'Sit down with me! I'll buy you drinks all the evening and liberate you from the man in sneakers.'

She disillusioned him, perhaps too soon, and told him that the man in the sneakers was her father. My change of life was short and I was no longer the well-known menace padding round New York in worn white trainers for the purpose of seducing young women.

CHAPTER THREE

GETTING DRUNK

I am in a broadcasting studio with a number of guests including a boy band. One of them, or one of their controllers, has just emerged from detox and everyone, including the chat-show host, is listening with the greatest respect to his account of kicking a habit. Then they turn to me. 'Have you got any addictions?' they ask. Their faces show how tolerant and understanding they are prepared to be.

'Not really,' I say. 'Except I do have my first glass of champagne around six o'clock in the morning.'

There is an awed, deeply sympathetic silence, and then the host says, 'Are you having counselling for that?'

'No,' I have to confess, 'I'm not having counselling.'

'Well, how long has this been going on?'

'Ever since I could afford to have a glass of champagne at six o'clock in the morning,' was what I had to admit.

It seems that, in classical times, drunkenness was considered a sort of higher ecstasy, such as the elevated states enjoyed by mystics, poets and lovers, in which the soul becomes separated from the body. The ecstatic behaviour of the disciples at Pentecost caused them to be accused, according to the commentaries of Erasmus, of being pissed out of their minds.

Montaigne is harder on drunkenness and more

17

suspicious of ecstasy, but then he lived in a time when a great lord, famous for his success in several wars, never drank less than two gallons of wine at every 'ordinary meal'. Montaigne has a cautionary story of a lady with a chaste reputation who, while provocatively asleep at her fireside after drinking a great deal of wine at dinner, was impregnated by a young farm labourer without her having any idea of what was going on. So he welcomes the fact that, in his day, heavy drinking was declining, 'because we threw ourselves into lechery much more than our fathers did'.

No doubt Montaigne drank in a reasonable manner; but learning to drink can be a painful, although a necessary experience. The art master at Harrow bicycled with us to sketch the suburban countryside—a few patches of agricultural land which then existed around Ruislip reservoir—and, on the way home, we used to knock back an extraordinary number of gin and limes in the local pubs—a sickening experience. In my first term at Oxford my friend Henry Winter and I managed to drink several bowls of sherry and then boil blue Bols and crème de menthe in an electric kettle and drink the horrible result. I have to say I felt none of the higher ecstasies, nothing to compare with the out-of-body and soulful pleasure of mystics and lovers, and nothing to approach the joy of the disciples at Pentecost, nothing in fact but the nauseating sensation of a room spinning out of control. Coming back to reality, I found a theology student from next door kneeling beside me in silent prayer.

Since then no gin, lime, Bols, sherry or crème de menthe have passed my lips. I'd go so far, with

Montaigne, as to say that being really drunk is not a pleasant experience, and being cornered by a drunken person who repeats every sentence at least six times is as bad as being drunk yourself, and that drunk scenes in plays or films are never funny. It's also true to say that, although crimes are committed to pay for drugs, very few crimes are committed under their influence, whereas drink, particularly a mad mixture of snowballs, vodka and pints of lager, leads to bloodstained quarrels between friends, assault and often murder.

On the other hand, a world without wine would be an extremely depressing place, and no equally enjoyable drink has ever been invented. My grandfather, a Methodist who signed the pledge and thereafter drank nothing but a temperance beverage of his own invention, which apparently produced in him all the outward and visible signs of mild intoxication, might as well have stayed with the wine. There is something strangely depressing about lunch with people who drink nothing but water. W. C. Fields said it should be avoided because fish fuck in it. What is needed is some sort of lesson in schools for intelligent drinking. Nowadays schoolchildren spend a great deal of time watching films about the evil consequences of drugs, dire warnings which seem to have little or no effect, or learning how to use the computer, which can be picked up quite simply at any age. Basic truths about how to know when to refuse another glass could be included in the GCSE syllabus.

The study of champagne might be reserved for A-levels. The French and the Italians are in dispute about its origins. According to the French, it was invented by a little monk, Dom Perignon. Italians trace this life-enhancing drink back to ancient Rome, when it was kept in urns buried in the earth. It was dark in colour and drunk qualified with water, except at orgies.

It's greeted as the 'King of all the wines' in *Die Fledermaus*, and a glass of it was taken at midday by Charles Ryder at Oxford to shock his puritanical cousin in *Brideshead Revisited*. It can cure aching legs and dispel colds, and a glass drunk to the overture of *The Marriage of Figaro* can banish depression. It's by no means a drink reserved for right-wing toffs. Trotsky was devoted to it, Chekhov called for a glass of it before his brief life ended and Nye Bevan invented the National Health Service aided by frequent bottles of it. I have been called a 'champagne socialist' (or even a 'Bollinger Bolshevik') because I think this cure-all should be made readily available on the NHS.

The study of drinking would take in a great deal of English literature, from Chaucer to Kingsley Amis, and should conclude with Byron's answer to hangovers, printed in the verses that precede *Don Juan*:

> I would to heaven that I were so much clay,
> As I am blood, bone, marrow, passion, feeling—
> Because at least the past were pass'd away—
> And for the future—(but I write this reeling,
> Having got drunk exceedingly today,
> So that I seem to stand upon the ceiling)
> I say—the future is a serious matter—
> And so—for God's sake—hock and soda water!

20

CHAPTER FOUR

THE GRAND PERHAPS

It's notable that the list of bequests Yeats prepared in his tower didn't, in any clear way, leave his descendants any particular faith in God. He does say, 'That, being dead, we rise, / Dream and so create / Translunar Paradise.' But he has already made his view of 'Death and life' clear. 'Till man made up the whole, / Made lock, stock and barrel / Out of his bitter soul'. So, is the translunar paradise beyond the grave a creation merely of the dreams of a bitter soul? Such dreams would not have been particularly attractive to my father. 'The immortality of the soul?' he used to say. 'Isn't that rather a boring conception, like living for all eternity in some vast hotel with absolutely nothing to do in the evenings?'

I suppose we hand on what we have ourselves inherited. I received from early childhood the opinions of a Darwinian evolutionist father ('Huxley was to Darwin,' he used to say, 'as St Paul was to Christ') and a mother who was, from her early days as an art student, a Shavian 'New Woman', a painter who had exhibited in the Paris Salon, with a head full of Clive Bell and Roger Fry and the paintings of Cézanne, and who never seemed troubled by the possible existence of any God. My father was more openly dismissive, at least of the Creation story. 'You couldn't possibly make a horse in seven days,' he told me in childhood. 'You couldn't even evolve one over

21

seven centuries.' Accordingly I lived through my school life, and many Church of England services, unbaptized, unconfirmed and more or less quietly unbelieving. Being an only child, I had every opportunity of observing my mother and father closely and I have to say that the absence in their lives of the 'Grand Perhaps' didn't cause any deterioration in their behaviour. They didn't, so far as I could see, take to drink or lovers; they didn't, when invited out to dinner, pocket the spoons; nor did they defraud the Inland Revenue.

Far from abusing me, they trusted me with continual kindness. My mother forsook her art and devoted her life to helping my father in his blindness with as much devotion as any saint. My father, as a barrister, fought hard for his clients and carried on his practice, fixing witnesses with his clear blue, sightless eyes and remembering every date and every page in the bundle of correspondence when his world went dark. He also kept on gardening, pricking out seedlings and getting news of them, when they burst into flower, from my mother and me. Neither the loss of sight nor the approach of death caused him to turn to God.

George Eliot, who stopped going to church on principle, walked in the Fellows' Garden of Trinity College, Cambridge, solemnly speaking three words: 'God', 'Immortality' and 'Duty'. She then announced that the first was inconceivable, the second unbelievable but the third 'absolute and peremptory'. The early atheists thought good behaviour was more important, and of greater value, because it wasn't inspired by the hope of supernatural favours or the fear of any eternal punishment. I believe my mother and father had a similar sense of duty, perhaps more cheerfully expressed because my father was a great one for jokes. I suppose it was their example that made it possible for me to separate good behaviour from religious belief. It has seemed to me since that the worst crimes and cruelties can be committed by people who think they are carrying out God's will. It's hard to imagine that anyone who didn't believe they were obeying some sort of divine command could bring themselves to bury a young mother up to her neck in the sand and stone her to death for having committed adultery.

Yet no one can deny that the Christian belief in the supreme importance of each individual soul was a great advance on faiths which thought of slaves as soulless. The King James Bible is of extraordinary power and beauty, and subsequent cack-handed translations now used in churches have reduced a work of inspired poetry, said P. D. James, a woman with strong religious beliefs, to mere improbability. Much of the literature I've valued, the art I've most enjoyed, has been produced by unquestioning Christians. Whether I'm a believer or not, I'm a part of a Christian civilization.

The difficulty, as George Eliot and many others before and since her have found, is how to reconcile the existence of a loving and omnipotent God with, to give only one instance, the Holocaust. The argument that God has given us free will so we can choose to behave with ghastly cruelty and pay the bill for it in the hereafter can be applied to the Nazis who built the gas chambers and the guards who drove men, women and children into them. It falls down completely when you try to apply it to the children who were pushed down the steps to their deaths. They had no chance to exercise free will. They hadn't behaved badly. So what are they, then? To say they are simply the victims of an experiment the Almighty made when he allowed the Gestapo to do as it liked seems morally repulsive. And what about children stricken with leukaemia, teenagers dying of cancer, those who have lived impeccable and selfless lives strangled slowly to death by motor neurone disease? Free will doesn't enter this equation, the debate is about the inexplicable and apparently reckless use of omnipotence.

If this still puzzles you, I have to report that I have consulted some impressive authorities and received no very clear guidance. Cardinal Hume told me it was one of the great mysteries and it was not granted to us, nor should we ask, to know everything. This is probably the easiest way out of the difficulty. Archbishop Runcie said that every hill has a way down as well as a way up, which didn't seem to me a very helpful observation. The best reply I had came from the writer Malcolm Muggeridge, who cast God as a sort of supernatural Shakespeare, a great dramatist of the skies. 'As you know,' Muggeridge told me, 'a good play has to have heroes as well as villains, tragic as well as comic moments, piles of corpses at the final curtain instead of a happy ending.' So are good and evil merely the tools of an Almighty Playwright, eternally at his desk and thinking up new plots? Are we all, so far as God is concerned, like the 'poor player / That struts and frets his hour upon the stage'? It is, I suppose, possible, but it's not

24

exactly a comforting explanation.

Macbeth, the creation of a mortal dramatist, takes advantage of the absence of his enemy Macduff in England to send men to his castle to murder his wife and children. All his 'pretty chickens and their dam, / At one fell swoop'. When Macduff gets this news he calls out, 'Did heaven look on, / And would not take their part?' It's a question that has, as yet, received no satisfactory reply.

* * *

It's almost dark. There's still a pale, yellowish light over the tops of black trees at the end of the border. The garden is full of children, all girls. They've been swimming in the pool and they're now eating burgers in buns, sausages in more buns, and warming their hands at the barbecue. They come from Blackbird Lees, an Oxford housing estate full of crack cocaine and crashed cars. Although their homes are quite near the countryside, they come on their holidays not knowing the difference between a cow and a lamb, and are surprised that either animal should produce the food on sale in Tesco. The girls are playing with a football which looks, in the shadows, as white as a skull. Wherever they kick it, it is retrieved and laid back at their feet by our dogs.

I have brought up the subject of George Eliot in my conversations with Paul, the ex-vicar. He is a bald, perpetually smiling, slightly deaf, former champagne salesman who has spent the afternoon taking the girls from Blackbird Lees to Legoland. He has little patience with the idea of unbelievers behaving well and doing their duty more thoroughly because it's their responsibility and not imposed by an omnipotent creator.

'Whoa!' Paul utters a cry, when in disagreement, like a man pulling at the reins of a runaway horse. 'That's altogether out of order! If atheists behave well it's because God gets behind them and makes them do it.'

So God is kind to atheists? You might have thought he would let them go to Hell in their own way, instead of which he causes them to act as an example to many of the faithful. This was, I suggested, out of character, and I remembered that Randolph Churchill, having read through the Old Testament, told Evelyn Waugh that he hadn't realized quite what a shit God was. 'Well,' I was saying to Paul, 'he was always smiting people. Of course you remember how angry he was with King Saul? He'd specifically instructed Saul to destroy the people of Amalek 'and spare them not; but slay both man and woman, infant and suckling, ox and sheep, camel and ass'. Saul, contrary to orders, spared the life of Agag the king and kept the best of the sheep, and of the oxen, 'and of the fatlings, and the lambs, and all that was good, and would not utterly destroy them'. As a result of this God repented of having made Saul king, news which caused the prophet Samuel to weep all night.

'Whoa!' Paul called out more loudly, again reining in the galloping horse. It was a cry to which the girls from Blackbird Lees paid no attention at all. 'That's completely out of order. The Old Testament's full of mistakes, and then Jesus came and put it all right.'

'But the people who did all that smiting . . .'

26

'God gives us free will to make a complete bog-up of our lives. It was their choice what they did. Their choice entirely.'

'So you believe in free will?'

'Of course. God allows us that.'

'But if he's an all-powerful God, doesn't everything turn out as he's decided?'

Paul called out 'Whoa' again, understandably as this question has caused great difficulty among religious thinkers. Aquinas, who pondered these matters deeply, was sure that as every operation results from some power, the cause for every operation must be God. So if God didn't produce the Nazi murderers, at least he took no steps to stop them. This is unthinkable and yet the idea of a helpless God permitting evil is equally difficult. Is he merely, as F. H. Bradley wrote, 'not a "Creator" at all, but somehow a limited struggling sort of chap like ourselves, only bigger and better, and loves us and tries to help us, and we ought to stick to him'?

The pale yellow sky has faded over the trees. There is only light shining from the house and from guttering candles on the tables. The children are hunting in the darkness for shoes, T-shirts or a lost towel. The Reverend Paul smiles at them benevolently. The confusions through which Aquinas tried to find a way, wanting to separate the responsibility of man (the proximate agent) from that of God (the first agent), worry him not at all. The girls who are taking last swigs of Coke, last bites of beef in a bun, have had no choice but to be born, brought up, schooled in the Blackbird Lees estate, where a cow or a sheep might seem like a creature from outer space. I had done nothing to

27

acquire the dark garden except to be born into it. So what about free will? There was a rhyme in my childhood:

> There was a young man who said, 'Damn!
> It's born in me that I am
> A creature who moves
> In predestinate grooves,
> I'm not even a bus, I'm a tram!'

Down at the Old Bailey I had, day in and day out, seen sons and daughters of judges, or top barristers, punishing the sons and daughters of burglars, fraudsters and street-fighters for what must have seemed to them a natural, even a preordained, way of life. Were the elements so mixed in the Reverend Paul, the circumstances of his life so strong, that he had no option but to give up the champagne trade and devote his life to helping the poor escape conviction for debt and to taking children from violent council estates to Legoland? Is marriage a real choice? How many attractive and available people do we meet who fancy us? We don't choose our sexual preferences or cheerful or gloomy dispositions, our illnesses or, in most cases, our deaths.

One thing can be said about free will: those, like the Calvinists, who deny its existence are a depressing and disagreeable lot. Unless we can assume we are capable of making choices and controlling our destiny, laws can't function, politicians can't be held to account, great artists can't be praised or bad painters and indifferent poets justly criticized. Shakespeare was in two minds about the matter. 'As flies to wanton boys, /

28

are we to the gods; They kill us for their sport,' said Lear. But Hamlet speaks of the first time when his dear soul was 'mistress of her choice'. It's not vanity but practical necessity that compels us to see ourselves as free spirits, capable of taking charge of our own destiny. Although our freedom in that regard may be far narrower than we often like to think.

The garden is empty now. The girls have gone and Paul has offered me his arm to help me back into the warmth and light of the house. If the atheist George Eliot was behaving more like a Christian than many Christians, if the gloomiest determinist still holds criminals responsible for their actions, how much do these age-old questions matter? Can there be a natural instinct for good behaviour, like a belief in natural justice, and if so does it matter if it shines from a divine light or has evolved from the human instinct of mutual aid? The point at which beliefs meet may be more significant, more useful to contemplate, than their sources.

I used to meet the ageing but still mischievous Graham Greene often over lunch at Felix au Port, the restaurant not far from his home in Antibes. He was persuaded of the truth of the Christian story by a passage in St John's Gospel which describes two men, St Peter and 'that other disciple', running to the sepulchre after Mary had, in the dawn, seen that the stones at its opening had disappeared. Peter and 'that other disciple' ran together but 'that other disciple' outran Peter and arrived first. This was a detail, Graham Greene assured me, that couldn't possibly have been invented and had the very stamp of reliable

29

evidence about it. So the story must be true.

I found this a convincing argument, and my atheism was subject to a moment of doubt, as was, at many times, Graham's belief in the 'Grand Perhaps', which is how Bishop Blougram described God in Browning's poem. As we agreed about so many things, Graham Greene quoted other lines from the same poem which seemed to sum up his religion and my atheism.

> All we have gained then by our unbelief
> Is a life of doubt diversified by faith,
> For one of faith diversified by doubt:
> We called the chess-board white,—we call
>   it black.

It's good to know that both the faithful and the faithless can still be playing from the same chessboard.

CHAPTER FIVE

AN OLD WOMAN COOKING EGGS

To the proud stones of Greece and poet's imaginings other bequests must be added to make up the superhuman, mirror-resembling dream. I have a gallery of pictures in my head so that, if I went blind, I could still enjoy them. I would direct you to the National Gallery of Scotland, one of the least exhausting, most rewarding collections in the world that, in a few comfortably intimate rooms, contains more masterpieces to the square foot than you have the right to expect. Among the saints and great ladies, the naked beauties and the suffering martyrs, taking her rightful and honourable place is an old woman cooking eggs.

Velázquez went to Madrid in his twenties and very soon became a court painter, truthfully observing pale-lipped kings, overdressed infantas and the sad faces of the palace dwarfs. Before that he served five years' apprenticeship to a Sevillian painter whose daughter he married and, taking time off from his religious paintings, looked hard and clearly into the kitchen.

The everyday scene in the Edinburgh gallery is lit in the sort of way the painter learned from Caravaggio, so that the objects in the kitchen achieve an extraordinary significance. The old woman has an aquiline, Sevillian nose, sharp eyes, a firm mouth and grey hair. The white cloth on her head and shoulders falls in soft folds on the coarse material of her dress. She has the suntanned, loose-

31

skinned hands of her age but one of them holds an egg carefully and the other delicately points a small wooden spoon, ready to drip a little oil in which we can see eggs setting, their yolks and whites clear in the pan. An unsmiling peasant boy is carefully dripping in more oil and the old woman watches him anxiously. The miracle of the painting is the exact and loving re-creation of oil, eggs and earthenware, the shine on the brass pots, the shadow of a knife on a china dish, the feeling of flesh and cloth. Forget all concerns about blessings or terrifying events occurring beyond the grave, this picture celebrates the significant moment when the eggs start cooking and another spoonful of oil has to be dribbled in.

The old woman, or someone very like her, turns up again in another of Velázquez's kitchen scenes, this time in London's National Gallery. Her head is again covered with a white cloth and she is instructing a sulky and unwilling Martha on how to pound garlic and cook some fresh fish and more eggs. In a mirror we can see that Jesus has arrived at the door and is about to engage the no-doubt-eager Mary in a conversation about life, death and the miracle of salvation. Far more interesting to the old woman is seeing that the fish is cooked properly, dinner is on the table in time and the garlic is well pounded.

Velázquez went on to paint grander scenes. Venus, the Goddess of Love, lies naked, admiring herself in a mirror held up by Cupid, presenting to us her splendid bottom. He painted kings on prancing horses and military triumphs such as the surrender of Breda and royal persons hunting wild boar. He became famous in Italy for his portrait of

Pope Innocent X, a merciless military commander. His final act was to decorate the Spanish Pavilion on the Isle of Pheasants for the marriage of the Infanta Maria Theresa.

Through all these great events, wars and festivals, the lives of kings and Popes, the old woman remained busy in the kitchen, dealing with the important things in life, such as the exact amount of olive oil needed to fry eggs.

CHAPTER SIX

THE DOMINO THEORY AND THE TYRANNY OF MAJORITIES

Avoid those whose views on every subject can be confidently predicted after you have discovered what they think about one. You know, with some people who utter dire threats about global warming, for instance, that they are going to be hostile to smokers, motor cars, jokes about mothers-in-law, school nativity plays, strip shows and the swallowing of live oysters. Equally tedious are those who complain about high taxes and are bound to be in favour of the death penalty, take a tough line on asylum seekers and are hostile to gay weddings, homeopathic medicines, Muslims and conceptual art.

'Our interests,' Browning wrote, 'are on the dangerous edge of things / The honest thief, the tender murderer / The superstitious atheist'. Characters without contradictions are like eggs without salt. They have failed to work out what they really think about all these great or trivial matters and meekly accept the rule that pushing over one domino will lead to the collapse of a whole line of others. Surprising beliefs are the most precious. Enoch Powell, for instance, at least had a mind that went beyond dominoes. Thought of as a racist because he made his 'rivers of blood' speech, warning of violence as a result of mass immigration, he was, surprisingly, passionately opposed to the death penalty. In his somewhat

35

strangled voice, he said that there was no evidence that hanging had any effect on the murder rate and that it was an 'avoidable brutality' in a world in which we have quite enough unavoidable brutalities to contend with. He was also against listening to music. 'I don't like things,' he explained, 'that interfere with one's heartstrings. It doesn't do to awaken longings that can't be fulfilled.' He also resented Harold Wilson for having given up power voluntarily. He had always admired Diocletian for doing this very thing, but Harold Wilson, for Enoch Powell, had somehow spoiled or cheapened the great Emperor's gesture. Although no admirer of trade unions, he said he would willingly raise his hat to any union leader who had been promoted to the House of Lords, 'if I happened to recognize him and was wearing a hat at the time'. This eccentric collection of opinions was too much for party politicians, who like a straightforward game of dominoes, and Enoch Powell, the only politician since the war who could write Greek verse while sitting on the front bench, had a career which ended in deep disappointment.

We now have a New Labour government that not only has the whole range of politically correct opinions, but is tempted to enforce them by law against those with contrary views. Beliefs about how you live your life, matters of private decision, views best kept for private enjoyment, prejudice or entertainment, can't be imposed by the operation of the criminal law. Attempts to enforce such views can only make a government the subject of ridicule.

The sort of conduct that should be subject to the law was well defined by John Stuart Mill. Mill was an extraordinary character. His father, the son of a shoemaker, was a Scottish philosopher. Thanks to him, John Stuart learned Greek at the age of three but had to wait until his eighth year before he conquered Latin. By the time he was thirteen, he had more than a working knowledge of logic and political economy. Grown to manhood, he always started his day's work at the offices of the East India Company with tea, bread and butter, and a lightly boiled egg. He wrote incessantly on political economy, on poetry, history and religion. He was a botanist who played the piano and was greatly afflicted by melancholy. He was also deeply in love with his wife, the former Mrs Taylor, whom he regarded as a superior being. When he published his essay *On Liberty*, he wrote:

The sole end for which mankind are warranted, individually or collectively, in interfering with the liberty of action of any of their number, is self-protection. The only purpose for which power can be rightfully exercised over any member of a civilized community against his will is to prevent harm to others. His own good, either physical or moral, is not sufficient warrant. He cannot rightfully be compelled to do or to forbear because it will be better for him to do so, because it will make him happier, because in the opinions of others to do so would be wise or even right. These are good reasons for remonstrating with him, or reasoning with him, or persuading him, or entreating him, but not for compelling him, or visiting him with any evil in case he do otherwise. To justify that, the conduct from which it is desired to deter him must be calculated to produce evil to someone else.

Another sentence from Mill seems to me of the greatest importance: 'Over himself, over his own body and mind, the individual is sovereign.' So what we do to ourselves, what we smoke, eat or drink or say, is entirely our own affair. We can spend our lives risking our necks mountain climbing or skiing, wolf down chocolates and read trashy novels, pursue great love affairs or sit staring contentedly into space, work out in the gym or forswear all exercise, and it's absolutely nothing to do with the government.

When governments say that they have a majority on their side when attempting to enforce a particular view of life upon those who don't happen to agree with them, they should remember Mill on the tyranny of majorities. A democracy isn't judged by the number of times a majority gets its own way but by the freedom allowed, and the respect paid, to the rights of minorities. But society too can try to impose some deadening uniformity by the despotism of the opinion of the majority. 'It presumes to tell men what to think or read, it discourages spontaneity and originality, strong character and unconventional ideas,' Mill wrote. 'Society . . . practises a tyranny more formidable than many kinds of political oppression, since . . . it leaves fewer means of escape, penetrating much more deeply into the details of life, and enslaving the soul itself. Protection, therefore, against the tyranny of the magistrate is not enough; there needs protection also against the tyranny of the prevailing opinion and feeling.'

When he was almost sixty John Stuart Mill, apparently to his surprise, was elected to Parliament as a 'working man's candidate' for Westminster. He made himself unpopular by campaigning for women's suffrage and writing an essay on *The Subjugation of Women*. He also became a secular godfather to the Earl of Amberley's second son, whose name was Bertrand Russell. Eight years later he followed his beloved wife to their grave in Avignon. The memory of Mill, and what he wrote, should be handed on in the wills of every generation.

Leave Country Sports Alone, an organization of Labour supporters in favour of foxhunting, is a cause which has the great advantage of flouting the domino theory and defying the social and legal diktats of New Labour thinking. The many decent and reasonable people who enjoy foxhunting—and the many more who dislike the idea of it intensely—will never agree. What is important is that one side shouldn't enforce its views by the use of the criminal law. Dragging the many middle-aged women and pony-club girls who hunt off to our overcrowded prisons would be an absurdity. Hunting would seem to fall within Mill's definition of an area in which the law should not interfere with the way in which you or I wish to lead our lives. It does no harm to other persons—unless you wish to count a fox as a person, which leads you into anthropomorphic arguments or the world according to Disney.

Mainly, it seems, to placate its backbenchers, denied any power and restless at its conservative behaviour, the government is threatening to introduce a bill to ban hunting. Four hundred thousand assorted country dwellers marched through London to protest at this, and what they feel is a general neglect of farming and the countryside. Not much good at marching, I was invited to lead the wheelchair battalion.

I was given an electric wheelchair, a sort of battery-operated scooter with a seat, in which I was supposed to lead the small army of the handicapped. They were lined up on the Embankment and we were found a space to join the long column of marchers.

I suppose I shouldn't have been surprised to find that the occupants of motorized wheelchairs are intensely competitive. As soon as we got going, they speeded up and challenged me for the lead. A very large lady in a bright red and powerful wheelchair drew up alongside. She was driving a Rambler, she said, which could cross country and in which she had ascended Mount Snowdon. There was room for eight bottles of wine under the bonnet of this remarkable vehicle and during the Jubilee celebrations the police had attempted to arrest her on the suspicion that she was drunk in charge of her wheelchair. They invited her to get out of it and join them in the station, but when she told them that it would take at least eight strong officers to lift her out of the Rambler they decided, wisely, to let her go on her way.

So we sped along the Embankment, under the bridges where the crowds waved at us and the police clapped; and the mounted police, who are often seen on the hunting field, were also approving. There have been left-wing hunters, Trotsky and Engels and, in my youth, Reggie Paget, a well-known Labour MP who rode to hounds.

Trollope and Siegfried Sassoon, no right-wing bigots, wrote glowingly of the sport. But the large woman in the Rambler, who could never clear a fence or draw a covert, once cheerfully tipsy in charge of her wheelchair, turning out to protest against a ban on hunting, seemed to me an excellent example of someone who refuses to be submerged in the values of the majority. Whatever you might think of her, you could never have predicted her views like a row of dominoes.

CHAPTER SEVEN

OUTDOOR SEX

'She crawled with a rustle of grass towards me, quick and superbly assured. Her hand in mine was like a small wet flame which I could neither hold nor throw away. Then Rosie, with remorseless, reedy strength, pulled me . . . down, down into her wide green smile and into the deep subaqueous grass.'

I should include in my will a strong recommendation of the joys of alfresco sex, as described by Laurie Lee when he tasted kisses and cider. Recently our New Labour government introduced a comical bill into Parliament which would ensure that in future Laurie and his Rosie would end up in the nick for making love in a public place.

'The first of May, the first of May, outdoor fucking starts today,' went an old American rhyme. Not if the New Puritans in power had their way it wouldn't, not on the first of May or any other time this spring. The lovers and their lasses were about to be cracked down on.

Mr Blunkett, the Home Secretary, is not a man unfamiliar with poetry. He must surely have read *Cider with Rosie*, Laurie Lee's sun-filled bucolic memoir. He even took part in Laurie's memorial service and spoke highly of that poet and great celebrator of love in the cornfields. He must remember, too, Shakespeare's lover and his lass

43

That o'er the green corn-field did pass,
In the spring time, the only pretty ring time,
When birds do sing, hey ding a ding, ding;
Sweet lovers love the spring.

Why on earth should Mr Blunkett, or Hilary Benn, son of Tony Benn, the great firebrand of the left, who is the Home Secretary's junior minister, seek to confine the sweet lovers to Wormwood Scrubs, where very few birds can be heard singing?

There can be few people who, looking back on happy moments of their lives, can't remember love in the open air. It wasn't a cornfield perhaps, but the edge of a wood, or a warm beach at night with the gentle sound of waves retreating.

My own, long-ago introduction to sex was late at night, in the bracken on the common, after we had collected glow-worms in our handkerchiefs. After all these years I find myself waiting the arrival of the police.

The countryside in summer has always been the place for love:

Someone stole my heart away,
Riding in a load of hay . . .
Heather beds are soft—
And silken sheets are bonny,
But I would give it all
To go with my man Johnny.

Hearts were broken 'coming through the rye'. Hayricks and long grass were thought of as just as romantic and far more suited to the occasion than silken sheets and soft mattresses, and were no doubt a great deal healthier than dubious

44

lunchtime hotels, places which were not available to most country lovers and their lasses.

Now it has been suggested that not only cornfields and commons should be out of bounds. You wouldn't even have been able to make love in your own garden if the Sexual Offences Bill had become law. Frustrated couples would have had to confine themselves to weeding in a sexy way, or mowing the lawn with smothered eroticism. Love on the lawn was to be made a criminal offence. 'Come into the garden, Maud', even if the 'black bat, night, has flown', could only be an invitation to admire the dahlias. Not only had the government decided to tell us how to behave in our own gardens, but love in cars, the subject of many happy teenage memories, was to be added to the ever-growing list of New Labour crimes.

I remember my father, a prominent and successful divorce lawyer, coming home to me in my nursery and telling me that he had had a great success in proving adultery when 'really the only evidence we had was a pair of footprints upside down on the dashboard of an Austin Seven motor car parked in Hampstead Garden Suburb'. Such adultery, no doubt calling for a good deal of athletic skill, was not only to be grounds for divorce but the subject of a criminal conviction. Sex in any place that could possibly be described as 'public' was to be banned outright.

A difficult question arose with regard to the mile-high club. There is something about air travel, a rush of adrenalin caused by a mixture of fear, business-class champagne and the excitement of foreign travel, which so turns people on that they are tempted, once they have struck up an

45

acquaintance with a person of the opposite sex in the next seat, to suggest a joint visit to the lavatory not too long after the safety belt sign has been switched off.

This might, after long legal argument, be held to be a private act. What about the couple in a well-known London club whose eyes met across the dining room so lovingly that the man suggested they repair to the facilities downstairs? When the lady replied, 'Your place or mine?' and he went for hers, they would have been committing no crime, because the newly suggested law, according to the young Benn, would have determined that sex in lavatories might be all right if the door is kept closed. What is there left to say about a government bill which suggests that love in the loo is OK, but do it in a cornfield and you've committed a serious crime?

So the car parks and the lay-bys in which some vehicles may be gently rocking would have been subject to police raids. I remember when our car broke down, late at night, on our way home to our house in the country. Knocking politely on the window of a Volvo parked on the edge of a wood where a couple were preparing to make love, I asked them for a lift. With extraordinary kindness they drove us home. When they had done so I offered them the hospitality of a spare bedroom. They said no, they preferred their own car and the dark corner of the wood. They were, of course, hardened criminals.

The thinking behind these proposals, if they could be dignified with such a word, was that the great British public must be spared the sight of anyone making love. It's true that, while making

46

love is extremely enjoyable, watching other people doing it is not such a great treat. But are we to assume that the public is incapable of averting its eyes or passing quickly by? Are we bound to peer into every parked car or gaze into every garden, hoping for a shock?

When we won the last war, when VE Day was declared, Hyde Park was covered with ecstatic couples having sex. It would have been a night of celebration for New Labour's police. But now you would have to take a good deal of trouble, and perhaps a detour, to see an act of love. In a long life, I can't say I remember many occasions when I have stumbled on a couple locked in an intimate embrace. If I had, I don't see why it should have caused me any particular distress.

The vast majority of films and a great deal of television today portray acts of simulated sex, so the British public must, by now, at least know what it looks like. It wouldn't come as a great shock to anyone even if they happened upon it in the cornfields or noticed it, as I believe you sometimes can, in the showers attached to the Houses of Parliament.

We live, as I'm writing this, in the most extraordinary times. Our prisons are so overcrowded that there is no room in them, apparently, for burglars. The courts are overworked, the Crown Prosecution Service is near to breakdown and yet the lover and his lass, arrested in the cornfield, might have been sent to jail.

So I leave you the memories and possibilities of woods and fields, the corners of churchyards or the back seats of Toyotas. In his wise and beautiful book, Laurie Lee writes of country life when he got to know Rosie: 'It is not crime that has increased, but its definition. The modern city, for youth, is a police-trap. Our village was clearly no pagan paradise, neither were we conscious of showing tolerance . . . The village neither approved nor disapproved, but neither did it complain to authority.'

The government's proposals to ban outdoor sex provoked such hostility and derision among the saner members of the House of Lords, where the bill was introduced, that they will have to be dropped. Other strange provisions of the Sexual Offences Bill, however, remain. It will, from now on, be a serious crime to have sex with anyone with learning difficulties. You should therefore prepare a short examination paper for your partner as part of the foreplay. If he or she fails to pass, the gig will have to be off. Even if your girlfriend can find her way easily through Proust in French, you will have to satisfy the court that she hadn't a speech defect which might prevent her from saying, 'No.' It will also be a sad day for those with learning difficulties, who won't be allowed to have sex with anyone else, including other people with learning difficulties.

Finally, the bill contains a new offence of oral rape. This led one peeress, during the debate, to ask plaintively, 'Have women no longer teeth?'

Enough of sexual offences. Let's all go out into the garden.

CHAPTER EIGHT

SHAKESPEARE'S FAVOURITES

Shakespeare, like Richard II, talked of wills and famously left his second-best bed to his wife. He left no advice, however, rightly believing that it's a dramatist's business to ask questions and not provide answers. His characters speak their own thoughts and not his, but perhaps we get closest to him when we hear the voices of those that he loved the most. They were not the kings and queens or even the princes, the great heroes and heroines, the giants with a fatal flaw or the star-crossed lovers, who had, he said, a great deal in common with poets and lunatics. No, the characters he loved were the men and women of common sense, clear heads, loyal, stoical, able to see through the mists of self-delusion and deceit out of which great tragedies come.

They don't have starring roles, but they are the best friends of the heroes or heroines and if only they were listened to much trouble might be avoided. One such character, clearly loved by the author, is Kent, true to King Lear as he lives through his master's reign from arrogance to madness and gentle resignation. 'I do profess to be no less than I seem;' says Kent in his creed. To 'serve him truly that will put me in trust; to love him that is honest; to converse with him that is wise, and says little; to fear judgement; to fight when I cannot choose; and to eat no fish.'

Another embodiment of the loyal and truthful

49

man of common sense is, of course, Horatio, of whom Hamlet said:

> . . . thou hast been
> As one, in suffering all, that suffers nothing,
> A man that fortune's buffets and rewards
> Hast ta'en with equal thanks . . .
> Give me that man
> That is not passion's slave, and I will wear him
> In my heart's core, ay, in my heart of heart,
> As I do thee.

After which Hamlet, thinking he has expressed himself too emotionally to be the stoical character he so much admires, says, 'Something too much of this . . .' Perhaps our problem today is that we have too many Hamlets and not enough Horatios.

Kent, Horatio, the favoured character turns up again and again in more complex forms as, for instance, Enobarbus in *Antony and Cleopatra* or the more cynical Lennox in *Macbeth*. When Owen Glendower, the Welsh wizard, says 'I can call spirits from the vasty deep' and Hotspur replies 'Why, so can I, or so can any man; / But will they come when you do call for them?' the dashing young hero becomes one with the common-sensible enemy of pomposity and pretension. Emilia, Iago's clear-sighted wife, can berate the murderously jealous Othello, 'O gull! O dolt! As ignorant as dirt!' and express the common sense of the audience, cutting the heroic, poetic, easily deceived Moor of Venice down to size so that we can be allowed to feel some sympathy for him at the end of the play. There is a great deal of this straight-talking spirit in Rosalind, and Juliet's loquacious and boring old nurse has more good sense in her little finger than the Franciscan confessor Friar Laurence has, with his dotty plans calculated to cause a tragedy, in his entire body.

This stoical character, who can survey the vagaries of the world with a smile of tolerant amusement, until some mindless horror makes him or her call out, 'O dolt! As ignorant as dirt!', comes close to that adopted by Michel, Lord of Montaigne, another writer with a tower, his shelves crammed with books and his walls covered with quotations from Greek and Roman philosophers. He did his best to incorporate the stoical attributes of the great past civilizations into the Christianity of the Renaissance and to discover 'a sane and decent manner of life'. John Florio, who translated Montaigne, was undoubtedly a friend of Shakespeare and there is, in the British Museum, a copy of Florio's Montaigne with Shakespeare's name, some say in his handwriting, written in it. Whether *The Essays* influenced the later plays, or confirmed Shakespeare's feeling for his favourite characters, the views of the glovemaker's son from Stratford and the heir to the country round the vineyards of Château Eyquem echo each other, and add their valuable bequests to succeeding generations.

Montaigne wrote little about the afterlife but he was concerned to reconcile the humanist to the process of dying. 'I want death to find me,' he wrote, 'planting my cabbages—caring little for it and even less about the imperfections of my garden.'

51

CHAPTER NINE

LISTENING

The world's full of talkers, with not nearly enough listeners. This leads to many lonely people wandering from room to room in their quiet empty houses, asking and answering questions from and to themselves. Too many of us rabbit on about ourselves, repeating what we know already, and fail to discover anything about the curious lives and the unopened histories of the passenger in the corner seat, the sad-eyed, lonely drinker at the end of the bar or the apparently ill-assorted couples in the holiday hotel.

The art of listening is one that has to be learned by lawyers. You may think of Rumpole's life as one of incessant chatter, forever up on his hind legs making speeches or asking questions. Yet a good half of a barrister's life is spent listening in silence in his chambers room or during a prison visit.

It was as a divorce barrister that I learned of the hotelier husband who fixed up a lengthy trough from his bedroom window to the vegetable garden, so that he could urinate in comfort and water the runner beans at the same time. This device caused embarrassment to the hotel's visitors who were taking tea in the garden. His wife, not unnaturally, wanted to end the marriage. At the trial the husband asked if he might give evidence standing on his head. This request was curtly refused. I heard from the lady who joined a wife-swapping club in Croydon, 'mainly to give my husband some sort of interest in life', and fell deeply in love with her swap. I learned more than perhaps I needed to know about the husband who armed his children with lavatory brushes and put them through small-arms drill with these implements every morning before sending them off to school. I also heard much of the husband who would write letters to his wife's furniture which he then pinned to it, such as, 'You are a cheap and vulgar little sideboard. Please return to whatever bargain basement you came from! You are certainly not wanted in this establishment.'

I listened carefully to the elderly man who carried out a number of alleged 'mercy killings' who told me his evidence would be given by his 'puppet master', who would speak through a hole in my client's head. I defended a certain Anthony Sorely Cramm, of whom the judge said, 'Best name for a bugger I ever heard', and, being in a merciful mood, said he might go instead of prison to a Salvation Army hostel, at which Mr Cramm called out in desperation from the dock, 'For God's sake, send me to prison!' I learned how a talented artist came to invent a non-existent Victorian photographer and forged a large number of photographs of the slum children of Victorian London which completely fooled the National Portrait Gallery. I also heard the story of a rich young man who, when asked what he had done when he stabbed his mother, said, 'I have either murdered a prostitute or killed a peacock in paradise.'

But strange, almost unbelievable stories are not available only to lawyers. They are all around you if you are prepared to listen. After a brief

54

acquaintance a friend told me that, when he was a youngish boy, his mother left his father. The father, a correct and presumably sane army officer, told his son that his mother was dead. This is what he believed until he was in his late twenties, and was staying in a house in Scotland. There was a grey-haired woman there who was married to an air vice-marshal. After dinner she took my friend aside and told him she was his mother but it would embarrass her husband if he found this out, so would he please call her 'auntie'. Another casual friend told me that when he was a small boy his father came to his bedroom and said, 'I found this chap had been making love to your mother, so I shot him. I hope that's all right.' He then switched off the light and left the room.

It's not only friends, however casual, but total strangers who, in the first chance encounter, have told me about their unhappy marriages, their request to God for advice on divorce and even about the size, often a disappointment to them, of their virile members. All that is needed to open the floodgates is a look of rapt attention and an opening request which can be as unsubtle as, 'Do please tell me the story of your life.' Ten to one, no one has ever asked them this and they've been longing to tell it.

All this will be of great assistance to you if you're thinking of going in for the business of writing; at least it will convince you that there is no such thing as an ordinary life. Such encounters may be of even more direct assistance. I found myself sitting at lunch next to a grey-bearded, energetic-looking man who started the conversation by asking me a question. 'What do you do,' he said, 'when your

55

boat meets a force eight gale in the Channel—what do you do with your female crew?'

I confessed that I had no experience of yachting and asked him what *he* would do.

'Double my fist, punch her on the chin and stun her.' He spoke as though it was the most obvious course to take. 'If she's unconscious she's far less likely to slip overboard.'

'And what do you do when she wakes up?'

'Get her to make a cup of tea.'

It was time to ask if his sport of yachting wasn't extremely dangerous.

'It's not dangerous at all if you can't swim,' he told me. 'If you can swim you try to swim to the shore and invariably drown. If you can't swim, you cling to the wreckage and they'll send out a helicopter for you.' So he gave me the title of a book called *Clinging to the Wreckage*. It was at the same lunch table that an elderly man, who had remained silent throughout the meal, suddenly asked me, in a loud voice, if I could get my gamekeeper to eat rooks.

So there's no better occupation than listening, only interrupting to ask for further and better particulars. An acquaintance came up to me with a friend and asked if I knew 'Baghdad Price'.

'No, I don't know Mr Price,' I had to confess, and was lucky enough to ask why he was called 'Baghdad'. Did he perhaps come from Iraq?

'No. It's just that he's a most terrible shot. And when out shooting once he shot his father by mistake. So they call him Bag Dad.'

There aren't many Iraqi jokes around at the moment, so this was one worth listening for.

CHAPTER TEN

BELIEVING IN SOMETHING

We used to have them—once we had them quite seriously—passionately held political beliefs. In England, at least; perhaps in Europe and America, they disappeared long ago. You could, I suppose, say that a cure has been found and, like tuberculosis and scurvy, we no longer suffer so badly from them. Or you might take the view that they have just gone out of fashion, like waistcoats and long johns. For whatever reason, they are certainly not around much any more. It's difficult to know, in these grey days, when the left has become the right, what sort of political beliefs, if any, I could hand on to another generation which has shown, so far, an almost passionate lack of interest in the subject.

We certainly had political beliefs when I was young, and got them as inevitably as measles and chickenpox and other long-lasting infectious diseases. The world seemed so simple then. The right, in the shape of Nazis, Fascists and those Conservatives who tolerated them, was indisputably evil. The noble left was for liberty, socialism and the rights of man. An added attraction, for those of us who were growing up in public schools, was that the left was, on the whole, in favour of the abolition of these uncomfortable and, we believed, class-ridden institutions.

But my political beliefs began before I arrived at Harrow. I was at a preparatory school at the time

57

of the war in Spain, which seemed a clear conflict of the goods versus the bads. It was also an age when a great part of the map was coloured pink, and I wrote poems expressing my contempt for the British Empire and the works of Kipling, both of which attitudes I have now lived to regret. I read Orwell and Auden and Hemingway, and I saw myself in Spain, bumping in a bullet-holed car across a dusty orange grove with a gun in one hand and a guitar in the other, prepared to die fighting the Fascists.

When I got to Harrow I did become, encouraged by a circular from Esmond Romilly, Jessica Mitford's husband, who was anxious to stir up a spirit of rebellion in public schools, a one-boy Communist cell, and I got puzzling and contradictory instructions from party headquarters in King Street when Stalin and Hitler were, for a short time, allies, until Germany invaded Russia. I first saw London burning from Harrow churchyard and, although the prospect of reaching a respected old age seemed dicey, we never doubted, even when France fell, that Fascism would eventually be defeated.

I spent the war in a government film unit writing scripts and joining the union. So at meetings I got called 'Comrade' and 'Brother', which was a great improvement on school, when I was 'Mortimer' or 'Boy' when they wanted me to clean their shoes. We added to our simple belief that the Nazi hordes would be defeated the hope that, when peace returned, there would be a new classless society, with free dentistry, free milk for schoolchildren and jobs for all. In short, we longed for the return of a Labour government. Much to our amazement, our wishes were granted.

Looking back down the long corridor of the years, I can't remember England ever being so united as it was during the war, or so hopeful as during the Attlee government. It was the world dreamed of by those who took part in army education schemes and who read *Penguin New Writing* and the *New Statesman*. It introduced the welfare state and dented, although it couldn't destroy, the class system. It did sensible deals with various unions. Nye Bevan became our favourite politician, a silver-tongued, champagne-drinking reformer who loved the arts and enjoyed parties. Politics had changed, to conform to some of our dearly held beliefs.

Many of these achievements survived during subsequent Conservative governments. The welfare state continued, the Health Service appeared to work and trade union leaders were invited in for beer and sandwiches, not treated like dangerous revolutionaries who undermined the state. Then came the Sixties, and the flower power children, offered new exotic delights, not unnaturally lost interest in domestic politics and found Harold Wilson and James Callaghan unexciting figures compared with Mick Jagger, Dr Timothy Leary and the Bhagwan.

Some sort of consistency remained, however, until the advent of Mrs Thatcher, when beliefs, strong and strident, re-entered the world of politics. She believed totally in the ethics of the corner shop, the values of the marketplace, the dribbling down of prosperity from the seriously rich to the less fortunate classes and the unreliability of foreigners.

In these circumstances, of course, those of us on the leftish side of politics had our beliefs strengthened and our faith increased. No doubt there could be, there undoubtedly had to be, a better way, liberal, humane, concerned with justice, equality and the pursuit of happiness, with perhaps still a little socialism in it. All this would come about with another Labour government.

And then the politicians of the left, both in England and in America, performed a surprising somersault. They became Conservatives. This, they no doubt thought, was rather a clever thing to do. It meant they could appeal to a basically Conservative electorate and leave right-wing politicians gasping for breath, lost for words and with absolutely nothing to complain about. It also had the effect of leaving the left's longtime supporters disenfranchised, disappointed and understandably confused. No doubt the new leadership thought that such party faithfuls would vote for them anyway, so their old-fashioned principles could be safely ignored.

Now we have watched a Labour government with a huge majority behave as though the word 'liberal' were a term of abuse and 'human rights' an easy way out for criminals. It has sought to diminish trial by jury, chip away at the presumption of innocence by introducing evidence of previous convictions and has abolished the principle of double jeopardy. It proposes to imprison suspected terrorists and the mentally sick without trial. It contemplates returning refugees to countries where they may face torture, in contravention of our obligations under the Convention of Human Rights. I was recently talking to Michael Heseltine,

60

once the Tarzan of the right-wing jungle. I asked him if he was still active in any way in politics. 'Not really,' he said. 'We've got a Conservative government in power, so why should I worry?' Politicians do make it very hard to have deeply held political beliefs.

There are certain principles, however, which have to be clung to in spite of party loyalty or the contortions of politicians. The rights of man, fair trials and justice for the poor and oppressed have to be maintained, regardless of the discouragement and disillusion which go with the fight for all liberal causes. These are attacked, as we have seen, by those who advertise their left-wing credentials. Such concerns may not be the whole of a life and may be an unexpected part of it. In this context, it might be interesting to consider the often-ignored political conscience and concerns of Lord Byron.

*   *   *

I first got to know Byron because we went to the same school, not at the same moment of history, but his dagger and his Turkish slippers were still in the library and I tried to lie on that grave in Harrow churchyard where he lay to write poetry. An iron grille made the stone hard to lie on, and the suburban view is not as inspiring as it no doubt was in his day.

In the business of leaving, to my heirs and assigns, poet's imaginings, I couldn't leave out the poet whose great acts of imagination undoubtedly included himself. The wonder and lovable quality of Byron is that, having cast himself as a beautiful but damned romantic poet, limping towards some

61

inevitable doom, he felt an irresistible urge to take the piss out of this carefully invented character.

Byron's *Don Juan* is one of the great masterpieces of European literature, but he called his work 'poeshy' and said he didn't rank poetry high in the scale of intelligence. Speaking of religion, he said, 'I deny nothing, but doubt everything.' Everything, of course, included himself. No one's set of beliefs was further removed from the domino theory. You could, if you chose, call him inconsistent; but when his wife, Annabella, accused herself of inconsistency, Byron regretted he had found her guilty of no such offence and added, 'Your consistency is the most Formidable Apparition I have ever encountered.' In his own life, he was careful to avoid the Formidable Apparition, managing to combine his innate conservatism with a true love of liberty and revolutionary fervour, his romanticism with downright common sense and his puritanism with sensuality. Such potent mixtures, and contradictions, produced a more interesting character than his wife's mathematical certainties.

I once went to speak to the boys at Eton. I was in a long room which used to contain many classes in which the boys were beaten, bullied and bored by the slow, laborious recitation and translation of Virgil and Horace. The walls are decorated with the names of hundreds of dead Etonians, carved by their owners, and all in capital letters. There is, however, one name in cursive or italic script—and that is 'Shelley'. At Harrow there is an identical room, and there also all the names are in capital letters, with one exception—'Byron'. There is no reason to think that they had ever met during their schooldays. In later life Byron found 'poor Shelley, the <u>least</u> selfish and mildest of men—a man who had made more sacrifices of his fortune and feelings for others than any I have heard of'. A remarkable testimonial, although the puritan in Byron thought it necessary to add, 'with his speculative opinions I have nothing in common, nor desire to have'. One thing they did have in common, however: they were two boys determined to be different from everyone else.

There are writers, like Oscar Wilde, whose lives are so colourful, exotic and apparently doomed that the stories they lived overshadowed the stories they invented. Byron is one of these. It's enthralling to read about his finding fame and infamy in England, his shrugging off the exhibitionist Caroline Lamb, who stalked him dressed as a pageboy, speculating about whether or not his love for his half-sister was ever consummated, following him into exile as he rattles across Europe in his coach with his doctor and his silver dinner service, to his loves and adventures in Italy.

We can picture the damp, dark ground floor of the Palazzo Mocenigo, where Byron stored his carriages and his menagerie of dogs, birds and monkeys, which included the alarming Swiss mastiff Mutz, who once turned tail and ran to avoid the attack of a pig in the Apennines. We can see him among the 'gloomy gaiety of the gondolas on the silent canals'. Following the accounts of this exotic life, we may easily forget Byron's strong belief in freedom and social justice.

The jobs of the stocking weavers of Nottingham, in Byron's home county, were threatened by the introduction of new frames, that would increase production and reduce the number of workers needed. In fact the new frames produced shoddier and less marketable stockings. Their introduction was welcomed by the employers and cursed by the workers, who, facing unemployment, responded by breaking the new machinery in a Luddite rage and occasionally rioting. A Tory government introduced a bill which would punish such irresponsible behaviour with the sentence of death.

On 27 February 1812, before he awoke to find himself famous and when *Childe Harold* was still in the press, Byron rose in the House of Lords to oppose this measure in a speech that achieved Dickensian heights of irony and anger. The frame breakers, he said, were men convicted 'on the clearest evidence, of the capital crime of Poverty; men, who had been nefariously guilty of lawfully begetting several children, whom, thanks to the times, they were unable to maintain. Considerable injury has been done to the proprietors of the improved Frames. These machines were to them an advantage, inasmuch as they superseded the necessity of employing a number of workmen, who were left in consequence to starve.'

Dealing with this horrific imposition of the death penalty, he said, 'Is there not blood enough upon your penal code, that more must be poured forth to ascend to Heaven and testify against you? How will you carry the Bill into effect? Can you commit a whole country to their own prisons? Will you erect a gibbet in every field . . . Place the country under martial law? Depopulate and lay waste all around you? And restore Sherwood Forest as . . . an asylum for outlaws?'

At the end of his speech, he described the only

64

sort of court likely to hang a frame breaker: 'there are two things wanting to convict and condemn him; and these are, in my opinion,—Twelve Butchers for a Jury, and a Jeffries for a Judge!'

This superb speech has been criticized as an 'overwrought vision of a nation reduced to political anarchy'. Lord Holland thought it 'too full of fancy', although Byron, 'having put the Lord Chancellor very much out of humour' (still a worthwhile thing to do), was glowing with success. His critics seem to have regarded the Tory bill as some more or less harmless addition to the criminal law. The outrageous nature of the proposal called for all the rhetorical weapons available in a great poet's armoury.

A week after this speech *Childe Harold* was published and on 21 April in the same year he was on his feet again, speaking in favour of Catholic emancipation in Ireland. Catholics were not allowed to become sheriffs who appointed jurors, with the result that an all-Protestant jury acquitted a Protestant when three 'reliable and respectable witnesses saw him load, take aim, fire at, and kill' a Catholic. He also pointed out that had the Irish Duke of Wellington been a Catholic, he would never have been allowed to command an army or even rise from the ranks.

He also spoke in favour of a petition to reform the ludicrous and corrupt electoral system presented by a certain Major Cartwright. Typically, the Whigs, alleged to be the more liberal party, had, in the manner of politicians, failed to support these sensible proposals and Byron was a lonely and brave voice, encouraged only by an elderly earl who was unpopularly in favour of the French

Revolution. When Byron told his friend Moore about it he said, 'in a mock heroic voice', that he had been delivering a speech that was a 'most flagrant violation of the Constitution'. When Moore asked him what it was about, he seemed to have forgotten. As his most recent biographer, Fiona MacCarthy, here fairly says, the things he cared most about (poetry, love and liberal causes) he spoke of with 'a throwaway response', or even the greatest frivolity.

His short life ended dramatically in the battle to free 'the Isles of Greece' from Turkish tyranny. This grand gesture had its moments of absurdity, as when Achilles-style helmets were ordered from a hatters in Piccadilly, but there's no reason to doubt the genuineness of his attachment to the cause, which bore some resemblance to the Spanish Civil War of my childhood. This struggle was romantic and seemed, from a distance, to be morally clear: the good against the bad, the noble Greeks, inheritors of an ancient democracy, against the Fascist equivalent, cruel and authoritarian Turks. There was even an International Brigade composed of idealistic European liberals, paid for by Byron.

He arrived with high hopes, having spent £4,000 on a Greek fleet to sail to Missolonghi. He took with him Pietro Gamba, the brother of his mistress, Teresa Guiccioli, who was 'hot for revolution'. He was much taken with the warlike appearance of the Greek soldiers, the Suliotes, of whom he expected great things. As with any war fought for an ideal, it was not long before disillusion set in.

Missolonghi was a wretched place, waterlogged, evil-smelling, a breeding ground for mosquitoes and disease. There were misunderstandings with the London Committee, money was short and Byron spent a fortune of his own. The forces of freedom in Greece were divided into rival groups, each plotting against the other. In too many instances, the freedom fighters behaved no better than their oppressors, raping women, dashing Turkish brains out against brick walls and massacring prisoners. Even Pietro Gamba spent a huge amount of money on a sky-blue uniform with expensive accessories. 'This comes of letting boys play the man,' Byron wrote; 'all his patriotism diminishes into the desert for a sky blue uniform.'

Worst of all, the fine Suliote soldiers, on whom he had pinned such high hopes, proved totally unreliable. They quarrelled endlessly, refused to attack Lepanto, as Byron had planned, and fought with the International Brigade so violently that a Swedish officer was stabbed and killed by a Suliote soldier. As a result of this, a number of British artificers threatened to return to England.

'Having tried in vain at every expense and considerable trouble and some danger to unite the Suliotes,' Byron wrote, 'for the good of Greece and their own—I have come to the following conclusion—I will have nothing more to do with the Suliotes. They may go to the Turks, or the Devil,—they may cut me into more pieces than they have dissensions among themselves,—sooner than change my resolution.' He had found, like many of those who have struggled for great liberal and liberating causes and beliefs, that the difficulty isn't so much fighting the enemy as stopping your friends murdering each other.

In the foul-smelling, muddy swamps of

Missolonghi, Byron took a fever, had a stroke and lay, at times, unconscious. The doctors, who recommended merciless bleeding and fastened a leech to his forehead, hastened his death. His heroism lay in his ceaseless attempts to heal differences, to prevent atrocities so far as he could, to keep his temper and to retain his belief in the justice of the cause.

He was not entirely disillusioned. Freedom would still be a glorious thing, even if the heroes of the resistance turned out to be dubious and self-seeking. 'Whoever goes into Greece at present,' he wrote in his journal, 'should do it as Mrs Fry went into Newgate [Prison]—not in the expectation of meeting with any special indication of existing probity, but in the hope that time and better treatment will reclaim the burglarious and larcenous tendencies which have followed this General Gaol delivery.'

This is excellent advice to all those anxious to join liberal, freedom-seeking, left-wing movements. Go among your fellow protesters in the merciful spirit of a prison visitor, because you are likely to meet some extremely doubtful fish.

CHAPTER ELEVEN

LYING

Michel, Lord of Montaigne, was always a reasonable and tolerant man, but he was particularly hard on liars. 'An accursed vice,' he wrote. 'It is only our words which bind us together and make us human. If we realized the weight and horror of lying, we would see that it is more worthy of the stake than other crimes.'

A kindlier but anonymous commentator coupled two biblical pronouncements to describe lying as 'an abomination unto the Lord, but a very present help in time of trouble'. Like many other things, a lie can be a serious crime, a source of evil, a forgivable vanity or an act of mercy. Lies can be used to brighten an otherwise bleak and underpopulated life. They often reveal more about the liar than what emerges when he or she is telling the truth.

A writer of fiction must have a confused view of the truth. To a novelist the whole world is potential fiction. But leaving the peculiar question of a writer's attitude aside for a moment, what can I say that will be of any use to my inheritors about telling the truth and the occasional use of kindly deception?

In my childhood I lied very early to make my life sound more interesting. I was really the son of Russian aristocrats, smuggled out of the country after the revolution and hidden in a trunk on the Trans-Siberian Railway. The barrister and his wife who took me in were not my parents, but a kindly couple who cared for me after my true mother and father had been shot in Siberia. Whenever I began to lose faith in the likelihood of this story I dropped hints about my mother's infidelity, my parents' forthcoming divorce and the fact, which I thought would be more interesting than the dull reality, that I was about to become the child of a broken home. This invention was soon detected by those friends I took home for lunch on Sundays, who saw my parents still irritatingly devoted. I suppose I thought these and other lies about myself were necessary to brighten the dull plod through school and lonely holidays. At least they led to a determination to make life more interesting than my childhood inventions.

There may be something curiously creative about those who cling to childhood fantasies in adult life, and invent wartime adventures, perilous escapes or legendary love affairs to keep boredom at bay. One such was certainly Jeffrey Archer, Lord Archer of Weston-super-Mare, of whom my friend Ned Sherrin said, 'He was the only seaside pier [peer] not to have been performed on by the transvestite comedian Danny La Rue.' He wrote novels and took up politics, becoming the Chairman of the Conservative Party, but his greatest work of fiction may have been his life. He invented his education, his sporting achievements and much else about himself, and, I'm sure, enjoyed the results. When I was connected with the Howard League for Penal Reform, we held a drinks party on the terrace of the House of Lords for the purpose of raising money from the great and the good. Jeffrey Archer kindly came down to say a few words to the assembled company. 'Thirty years ago,' he began, 'I was having lunch with John Mortimer in a London club and John told me to join the Howard League, which I did and I have never regretted it.' This was kindly intended and produced a few cheques. The only trouble with it was that I have never had lunch with Jeffrey Archer in a London club or anywhere else. It was a small and no doubt irrelevant lie, but the truth didn't come naturally to him.

Unfortunately, Jeffrey Archer applied his talent for invention to a libel case he was involved in. I saw him last in the Old Bailey, a small, still cheerful figure peering over the edge of the dock. 'It's an honour to see you at my trial,' he said and added, 'What are you doing for lunch?' Sadly I never joined him at 'the little Italian place where they do a very quick meal' and he went off to serve what I thought was an unnecessarily long sentence in a prison from which he still managed to emerge for lunch.

Even Montaigne, safe in his tower from having to rely on anything as 'a present help in time of trouble', might have forgiven the small lies merely intended to cheer up or smooth the lives of close friends and casual acquaintances such as, 'You are looking well', or, 'I did think your poem was brilliant' or even, 'How beautiful you are today!' Even if they are true, you should use these compliments carefully. My wife was, as always, looking beautiful, but I made the mistake of telling her this when telephoning from America, which made even a truthful statement sound like an invention. But even if not strictly accurate, scattering these consoling words like confetti could hardly be a major crime, calling for burning at the stake.

To be convicted of being a serious liar you have to make a statement that you don't believe in or you know to be untrue. So members of the Flat Earth Society or those who, like the great Sir Arthur Conan Doyle, assure us that the dead are readily available to speak at seances and that there are fairies at the bottom of the garden, are not liars. The statements they make may be untrue but they are convinced that they are telling the truth. In fact, they are in the same position, I think, as many unreliable witnesses. Such witnesses go through details of the car crash, the course of the quarrel in the pub that led to the stabbing with the broken glass, the row at home that ended with a head coming into fatal contact with the stone around the hearth. They are convinced of the version of events most favourable to themselves and become sure that it must be the truth.

It's for this reason that false witnesses in court can sound so convincing. Appeal courts often defer to trial judges, who, they say, 'have seen the witnesses and can form a view as to their credibility'. Often seeing a witness is a poor, even a misleading guide. The worst liars may remember to wear ties and suits, speak considerately in time with the judge's pencil, call him 'My Lord' and survive a scorching cross-examination. Those who stammer, contradict themselves, take offence at hostile questions and come to court looking like an unmade bed can often be telling nothing but the truth.

So what of the advocate who has to stand up in court and repeat a quite possibly untrue account of

72

events? Is he saying something he doesn't believe to be true? Quite possibly; but the advocate has gone through a process well known to those struggling for religious faith, the suspension of disbelief. My own disbelief was kept hanging up in the robing room of the Old Bailey for years. A barrister's job is to put the case for the defence as effectively and clearly as would his client if he had an advocate's skills. The barrister's belief or disbelief in the truth of this story is irrelevant: it's for the jury to decide this often difficult question. Would this explanation of a barrister's role defend him from the strict judgement of Montaigne? I know that most non-lawyers find it hard to understand and their most frequent question is, 'How can you defend a man you know to be guilty?' The answer is that if he tells you he's guilty, you can't call him to tell a story you know to be untrue. But if he says he didn't do it, you must put his case. You are a mouthpiece, a spokesman in an argument which is directed not at uncovering the truth, but at deciding whether or not the prosecution has proved guilt beyond reasonable doubt.

Life as a mouthpiece for more or less convincing stories can, in the end, prove unsatisfactory. For the writer the situation is entirely different. For him, falsehood is not a thing which has to be decided by other people. He is no longer a stand-in for anyone else. He must look into himself and find the particular truth which is his alone and be faithful to it in all that he writes. He must express a view of the world which seems truthful to him, regardless of what anybody else may think about it. So although it may seem odd, the person whose

73

trade has least to do with lying is not the lawyer or the businessman or, most certainly, the politician. It's the writer of fiction.

CHAPTER TWELVE

THE COMPANIONSHIP OF WOMEN

This section is intended for those of my heirs and assigns as happen to be men. Men are undoubtedly going through a hard time nowadays. It's not such a hard time as women went through when they couldn't own property or divorce their husbands for adultery and felt compelled to publish their novels under assumed masculine names. In divorce cases they could be valued in cash terms, as though they were so much real estate, and if they found their husbands no longer sexually attractive they could be met with a legal proceeding known as a Petition for Restitution of Conjugal Rights (Restitution of Convivial Nights, the old hands in the Probate, Divorce and Admiralty Division used to call it). If the conjugal rights were not forthcoming a hard-up and estranged husband could claim maintenance from his rich, lawfully wedded wife on the grounds of her 'wilful refusal' of sex.

Men may never be the victims of such absurd acts of subjugation. Their difficulties are more subtle but, none the less, real. Boys at school are easily outdistanced by girls, who take their lessons more seriously and are not, on the whole, proud of failure. Women are more realistic and open-minded than men, who tend to live in a world of wishful thinking, fantasy and make-believe. For that reason I always welcomed women on juries, although the old-fashioned criminals I defended

75

thought that a woman's place was in the kitchen, or looking after the children, and not out robbing banks or sitting in judgement on hard-working safe breakers and those accused of long-firm fraud.

I'm conscious of the fact that all that I have just written is sexist, politically incorrect, oversimplified and grossly unfair to the male sex. Male and female characteristics are not evenly distributed to men and women. Quite apart from homosexual preferences, there are men with strong female perceptions and women with a masculine tendency to self-delusion. But I suppose the reasons for most women's realistic attitude to life lie in the physical changes she has to suffer. Bleeding and stopping bleeding and coping with the agony of childbirth are traumas such as no man has to suffer. His only certain suffering is death, thoughts of which can, even in old age, be postponed indefinitely. Forcing a living, breathing human being out of your body is an encounter with reality from which men find themselves thankfully absolved. It's hard enough for us to pluck up the courage to be in the room when this alarming process is taking place.

Perhaps it's having gone to an all-boys school that made me for the rest of my life prefer the company of women. Homosexuality seemed to be the only choice on offer in my schooldays. We scarcely saw a woman, there were no female teachers and our meals were served by two footmen in blue coats with gold buttons (they frequently cut themselves shaving and would bleed in the cabbage) and a butler in tails. The boys, when not involved in sexual approaches to each other, seemed greatly interested in sport, which included a strange version of football played with a ball shaped like a cheese and, from time to time, the throwing of a stick on to the ground with a strange cry of 'Yards!'

Sometimes games and sex became curiously involved. One of the butlers was said to conceal himself behind a bush on the way to the games fields. He would then covertly change his tailcoat for football clothing and trot down to join in the rugby scrum. This gave him ample opportunity to interfere with the boys. Brought up in this atmosphere, I rapidly became allergic to any game which involved chasing a ball up and down a muddy field in a fine drizzle. I have to confess that this reluctance to participate has spread to all games, even those such as contract bridge and backgammon, during which there is little danger from partially disguised butlers out for sex.

It has also confirmed my belief that hell would be an eternal masculine public-school reunion, or a black-tie dinner of all-male chartered accountants. When Yeats wrote his poem, and made his will, he included 'Memories of the words of women' as part of the recipe for a 'superhuman, mirror-resembling dream'. The words of men in the locker room or down the pub during a boys' night out are not of such a superhuman dream-like quality.

And, in spite of David and Jonathan, Hamlet and Horatio, Caesar and Antony, Bush and Blair, women have a greater gift, I think, for friendship. It's true that girls in school can be extraordinarily bitchy to each other; but both at school and in afterlife they are capable of forming great networks of friends to spread news and gossip and cheerfully discover the inadequacies of their husbands. The air between mobile phones is heavy with the words of women confiding in each other—and of men failing to communicate.

So it is always better to sit in a restaurant with a woman. Fantasies can wander freely over the creamed spinach and Dover sole. There are always vague possibilities hovering over the table, however young or old the couple. Perhaps it's more restful if they have been lovers in the past, if that is over and done with and perhaps seems, in retrospect, even better than it was at the time. If they are very old and not quite sure whether it happened or not, it's better to assume that it did and speak with the appropriate nostalgic yearning for the past. Whatever the relationship was, is or might have been, you can be sure that women will drink as much and smoke more vehemently between courses than men; but they will be more full of shared secrets, astute observations, anecdotes to be treasured and opinions to be expounded than men at a restaurant table. You are soon lulled into the belief that you are the only person in the world they would ever say half of these things to.

Looking back down the long corridor of the years, you will be able to remember so many glorious women and wonder why it is that so many of them have married such appalling husbands. Robert Graves wrote a poem on this subject and ended with a thought I share:

> Or do I always over-value woman
>   At the expense of man?
>   Do I?
>   It might be so.

CHAPTER THIRTEEN

CAUSING OFFENCE

Causing offence, together with smoking, fox-hunting and the enjoyment of a motor-car, is now considered criminal conduct by the politically correct. This is a serious mistake. A life during which you're caused no offence would be as blandly uneventful as death itself. Being caused offence stirs up the spirits, summons up the blood and starts the adrenalin flowing. A parliamentary system that includes an official opposition and an adversarial method of trial proves the effectiveness of going on the offensive to reach the truth. A state in which everyone tiptoed around whispering for fear of hurting somebody's feelings would be dull beyond human endurance. A political or religious belief which can't stand up to insult, mockery and abuse is not worth having.

The sad signs are, however, that anxiety about causing offence has reached the point of insanity. A town council was censured recently for advertising a job for candidates with 'pleasing personalities'. This was objected to as it might cause offence to people with displeasing personalities. The three towering geniuses of European culture, Shakespeare, Mozart and Leonardo da Vinci, were not allowed to appear on the euro note as they might, in their separate ways, cause offence: Mozart because he was a 'womanizer', Shakespeare because he wrote *The Merchant of Venice*, a play judged to be anti-

Semitic, and Leonardo because he was reported to fancy boys. Now the euro note carries a picture of a rather dull bridge.

The urge to ban words which might possibly cause offence has now become surreal. The sublime works of P. G. Wodehouse describe many decent and dependable characters, some being members of the Drones Club, as 'good eggs'. You would think this would be praise everyone would value. I remember doing an interview with Raquel Welch, whom I found, rather to my surprise, to be an 'excellent egg'. When I wrote that, there were no cries of protest, the beautiful actress in question appeared to regard it as a compliment, and I was not aware of having caused offence to anyone.

Now, however, it appears that a police officer calling anyone a good or indeed any sort of egg would be strictly reprimanded. Why on earth should that be? You may well ask. Of course, the answer is extremely simple. 'Egg and spoon' is cockney rhyming slang for 'coon' and so 'egg' is a word of racial abuse, isn't it? Or is it? Partridge's dictionary of slang gives no authority for the egg and spoon theory, and there must be many to whom this involved connection would never occur. However, in the world we live in, this is no doubt an excellent reason for keeping P. G. Wodehouse's face off the euro note.

Sensitive police officers were also deeply concerned when a Home Office minister urged them to get down to the 'nitty-gritty' of a certain problem. You will have realized at once why this is a term of racist abuse and likely to give terrible offence. The Home Office minister, it seems, was ignorant of what every trainee constable knows: the bilges at the bottom of slave ships were where the dirty water sloshed around the grit from the ballast. Any reference to this area, where slaves were once kept in chains, would naturally be deeply offensive to a law student from Ghana or a young doctor from Sierra Leone. Or would it? Referring once more to the great Partridge, you will find that the expression 'nitty-gritty' has its origins among the black musicians in New York in the 1930s, a time when very few slave ships were crossing the Atlantic. And even if it did have to do with the ghastly trade in human beings, what's wrong with using the words to describe the unpleasant basic reality of a problem?

But the desperate need to find words which might, just possibly, offend someone requires no logic or even a working knowledge of the language. The university teacher in America who used the word 'niggardly' knew that it had absolutely nothing to do with the colour of anyone's skin, but apparently his audience and the university authorities didn't. So he lost his job.

If you are English and say you don't mind at all being called a 'whingeing Pom' in Australia, if you are Scots and are not in the least offended by jokes about your being careful with your money, you are told that it's perfectly all right for those who are so secure, so complacent, so self-satisfied that they can even take a bit of offence without serious danger. But the idea that there are other, weaker, more easily offended people who may go into a decline if told that they are, after all, good eggs seems to me intolerably patronizing.

The fact that words are held in such awe is no doubt flattering to writers. We are dealing in goods which are thought of as being as deadly as bullets, as destructive as Exocet missiles. In the beginning was the word. This is one of the comparatively rare moments when I find myself in complete agreement with God. In fact the word, in the Old Testament, *is* God. Words can be used for some of His most terrible purposes, for starting wars, for pronouncing death sentences on criminals and cancer sufferers, for inciting rebellions and ordering hideous reprisals, for announcing great and poetic truths and for lying and deceit. No one can deny their power and, with all respect to Dr Dolittle, they are what separate us from the animals. But how far should the use of words be a criminal offence? Threats to kill, conspiracies to murder or to rob, incitements to violence, even, under more sensible libel laws than those we have in England at present, perhaps untrue or unjustified accusations of bad behaviour that cause financial loss must be against the law. But, for heaven's sake, words that give offence, as indeed the word of God has down the ages to many people, are an essential part of life.

'Have you heard the argument? Is there no offence in't?' the guilty King asks Hamlet as the Players start to re-enact his crime. 'No offence i' the world,' Hamlet lies, and it's as well that he does. A play with no offence in it would make a dull evening in any theatre. Indeed, it might be said that the arts advanced on a tide of offence. The Puritans in the times of Cromwell, true ancestors of the politically correct, found the glory of the Elizabethan and Jacobean dramatists so offensive that they closed the theatres and acting was made a criminal offence punishable by flogging. Satirists from Juvenal to Pope and onwards handed out strong doses of offence, often in exquisite couplets. Shelley's *Queen Mab* was considered so offensive that its printer was put on trial for blasphemy. Byron, writing 'God Save the King / It is a small economy' on the death of George III, was as offensive about the monarch, and such popular heroes as the Duke of Wellington, as *Private Eye* manages to be today. *Madame Bovary* was thought so offensive that Flaubert was put on trial for it, as was Baudelaire for *Les Fleurs du Mal*. Ibsen's *Ghosts* offended by dealing with hereditary syphilis, and in my lifetime *Ulysses*, *Lady Chatterley's Lover* and *The Well of Loneliness* were all banned. Arthur Miller's *A View from the Bridge*, in which men kissed, and John Osborne's *A Patriot for Me* couldn't be played unless the theatres were, for some archaic legal reason, turned into clubs. It was feared that they might offend the public at large. In painting, Whistler's river views deeply offended Ruskin. Practically everyone was hugely offended by the first Impressionist exhibition and the Surrealists caused even more offence than pickled cows or Tracey Emin's bed.

It is true to say that Mrs Radclyffe Hall's story of lesbian love, *The Well of Loneliness*, having been clearly found unfit for human consumption by a London Police Court magistrate in the 1930s, was a few years ago read aloud on BBC Radio as the 'Book at Bedtime'. Fashions in what is or is not offensive change over the years and it might even be said that the present standards of sensitivity are sillier than ever. You can understand, even if you don't agree with, public discomfort about an open discussion of hereditary syphilis or lesbian love. It's harder to believe that any sane person could be seriously concerned about good eggs or getting down to the nitty-gritty.

The most serious offence, it once was thought, would be caused if free speech were to be allowed on the subject of religious beliefs. Living in a country where we assumed speech to be free, it was something of a shock to discover that we still had a blasphemy law that, in true medieval fashion, made offensive remarks about religion a crime. In the 1930s a Mr Gough was sent to prison for suggesting that Christ looked like a clown when he rode into Jerusalem on a donkey. In the 1970s James Kirkup wrote a poem describing the Roman centurion's physical desire for the dead body of Christ when He was taken down from the cross. This poem was published in the magazine *Gay News*. The editor of that paper was convicted of blasphemy and sentenced to a term of imprisonment. Although the prison sentence was quashed on appeal, the surprising fact remained that we had a blasphemy law which protects only the Church of England (you can say what you like about the Pope) and no other religion. The inevitable result of this was that other religious groups wanted one too and a Labour Home Secretary, who is to civil liberties what terriers are to rats, was on the point of making it a crime to cause offence to anyone's religious belief, until good sense and the House of Lords spared us, for the moment, any such legislation. Another result was that those who defended the fatwah, the death sentence passed in Iran against Salman Rushdie because of what he had written about the prophet Mohammed, were able to tell us that we have a law against blasphemy so how could we criticize Islamic fundamentalists?

It is surely absurd to believe that Christians, who have survived persecution, martyrdom and generations of religious wars, would crumble at a few words of mockery, criticism or even abuse. It seems to me to be an insult to the religious beliefs, as well as to those who hold them, to say that they need the special protection of a law which makes it a criminal offence to hurt people's feelings.

When the jury was out in the *Gay News* trial, Mrs Whitehouse, the litigious leader of the National Viewers' and Listeners' Association, prayed with her supporters in the corridors of the Old Bailey for a guilty verdict. In his autobiography the judge revealed that he felt the hand of God writing his summing-up. If this were so, God has defined our blasphemy law as one having no requirement of intent (you needn't *mean* to upset any one) and one without any defence of literary merit. The Almighty has clearly changed his mind since the more liberal days when *On the Origin of Species* was published and 'intent' was said to be a vital part of the offence. No one wanted to put Darwin in the nick.

Writers and artists must learn to withstand mockery, abuse and misunderstanding as an essential part of their careers. Men and women of various political beliefs, however sincerely held, must expect derision. It seems very strange that the Church of England, often seen as among the gentler religions, should wish to be protected by a censor or find it necessary to combine its beliefs with the threat of imprisonment.

In fact being caused offence not only stimulates debate but confirms belief and strengthens it.

Milton, no enemy of religion, had it right when he wrote 'if we have free speech truth will look after itself'. And if we have a censorship which stops us offending anyone, the truth may be concealed in the surrounding blur.

CHAPTER FOURTEEN

LIVING WITH CHILDREN

When I think of my childhood it smells of bracken. The common near which we lived was covered with the stuff—crisp, brown and crackling in the winter, green and sticky with sap in the summer. In this bracken Sam Rockall, Iris and I would build houses, rescue broken plates and cups from the nearest rubbish dump, drink Tizer the Appetizer and consume jam sandwiches, gob-stoppers and bags of crisps that always contained, in those days, a little blue bag of salt. Sam Rockall's father was a bodger, a person who cut down the beech trees, turned them into chair legs on a foot lathe and then sold them, for a few pounds a gross, to the furniture makers in High Wycombe.

So every day during my school holidays, we played together, often staying out until the sun went down and the glow-worms shone on the common. Then we went home to what Sam and Iris called tea and my parents called dinner. Although, from time to time, Iris would volunteer to show me her knickers and I occasionally presented her with a Woolworth's necklace, our activities were entirely innocent.

Often I bicycled seven miles to the river at Henley and swam in the dark, brackish waters where your feet tangled in the rushes or sank into the riverbed so that the mud oozed between your toes. No one swims in the river now—a pity, because in spite of its being the receptacle into which the lavatories of pleasure boats are emptied, it had a good deal more interest than a chlorinated swimming pool.

So I bicycled, and talked to strangers—a slightly mad monk and an artist I found doing a painting of Henley Bridge. I don't think my parents worried very much, or wondered where I was. Perhaps they were relieved at my absence. When I was at home, I would perform scenes from my favourite musical films and, having no brother or sister, I had to be both Fred Astaire and Ginger Rogers. Having a child in those days didn't seem to be a matter of perpetual anxiety.

Even at my prep school we were allowed to bicycle round Oxford to buy fruit and materials to assemble model aeroplanes or, in my case, copies of *Theatre World*. My parents used to treat me with mild amusement and I don't remember being put under any pressure to pass exams. The freedom, some people nowadays might even call it the neglect, of a 1930s childhood was a good preparation for an uncertain future. When I was sixteen war broke out and from the heights of Harrow churchyard we could see the sky coloured red as London burned. There could be no further guarantee of safety.

Childhood now seems a far more sheltered, even claustrophobic, period of life. Television and the Internet are mechanical devices that have taken the place of imaginary adventures, when you could be a captain in the French Foreign Legion galloping to relieve a fortress in the desert, or an outlaw desperate to reach his hideout in the woods.

There was no television in my childhood, of course, but we had radio, with *ITMA*, *In Town*

Tonight and *Dick Barton, Special Agent*. But radio is a form that does call for an act of the imagination; the world is not presented to you in small, bright pictures or in flickering letters on a screen.

All these mechanical aids mean staying indoors. You can lie in the long grass or on a beach with a book but the telly has to be plugged in, in a room. And children today get driven to school (if middle class and living in London in large and inappropriate four-wheel drives) and back. If the children were out leading imaginary charges, or hiding in the bracken for fear of arrest by the King's officers, today's parents would be consumed with anxiety.

To some extent this is understandable. We live, it seems, in the age of paedophilia. The onset of this undoubted danger is a mystery to me. At boarding school we had the odd errant butler and some over-affectionate masters, but no one thought of the danger of being dragged into a strange car and ending up, perhaps dead, in the bracken.

In the 1950s and 1960s I did a large number of divorce cases. Warring wives would make the most terrible allegations against their husbands, but I can't remember any charge of paedophilia. Now practically every case in the Family Division contains such accusations. They are, of course, easy to make and are apparently included as a matter of course in American matrimonial cases. Should we believe that this horror emerged, like sex, at the time of the Beatles' first LP and grew with the encouragement of the Internet? Whatever the answer to these questions, parents have the right to be nervous. But we can't let the worst cases, however horrible, overshadow our children's lives.

Childhood, after all, has to be an age of discovery. These are days you'll remember vividly all your life, even when you're old and forget why you came into a room. It must never be allowed to become the age of anxiety.

The anxiety has been greatly increased by this government's multiplication of exams and emphasis on starting training as a middle manager in a computer company from the age of six. Parents have made things worse by worrying unduly about exam results and seeing that their children work a great deal harder than most middle managers in computer companies. During a career as a barrister, and as a writer in a number of different forms, I have to say that no one has ever asked me how I did in any school exams, or what kind of degree I got.

Our present Minister of Education has said, in a phrase that proclaims his total unsuitability for the post, that no one should study classics or medieval history and that education unconnected with qualifications for a job is 'dodgy'. This is dangerous rubbish. Childhood is the time when you should enrich your life, learn poetry, be thrilled by history, do plays, go to the cinema and look at pictures. The qualifications for a job, such as, for example, Minister of Education, can be picked up quite easily later in life.

Childhood, you should remember, is a pretty tough time to be alive. You reach, at first, only as high as grown-up people's knees and then to their crotches. For this reason, you are not often referred to or included in the conversation. Sometimes you are spoken of as though you weren't there, or, if there, incapable of speaking for yourself. Strange, hairy people with patronizing smiles and penetrating voices will ask each other, 'Does he like his school?' or 'Is he enjoying his cricket? All boys like cricket.' Down at crotch level you know it's not worth saying you hate your bloody school and cricket is about as interesting an occupation as watching paint dry. You were a boy and although you were only truly excited by the plays of Noël Coward, the lyrics of Cole Porter and Jerome Kern, the seemingly casual, elegant, incredibly skilled tap-dancing of Fred Astaire, cricket is what boys like.

This, anyway, was my experience of childhood. But my parents, although they may have laughed gently at my eccentricities, didn't patronize me. When they went out to dinner or to the theatre they took me with them and there was very little talk of cricket. All the same, I was sent away to schools ruled, as much as anything, by fear. Some of the masters treated us with undisguised contempt. 'Revolting boy,' a pallid and supercilious French teacher would snort. 'Convey my sympathy to your unfortunate parents.' The masters we loved were Mr Retty (Rats), who taught us to foxtrot and, taking the woman's position on the parquet, would issue such gentle commands as, 'Chassé, boy! Please do chassé.' And Mr Jacques, who would sing to us, accompanying himself on a banjo, such songs as 'The Captain's name was Captain Brown and he played his ukulele as the ship went down' and 'Your baby has gone down the plughole'.

Children are extremely resilient and can somehow brave the fear-ridden schools of the past and the overprotection, overtesting exam mania and paedophilia obsession of today (Mr Rats would

91

be instantly dismissed for taking the woman's part when fox-trotting with us, his arm around our waists). The only advice I can give to my heirs and assigns is to beseech them to treat children as equals: don't patronize them or ignore them or behave as though they were in some way disabled and not entirely sane.

It is also advisable to arrange your life so that you always have a young child living with you. If this, as the years go by, becomes increasingly difficult, borrow as many children as possible from the neighbours and try as hard as you can not to earn their contempt. Children can spot pomposity, insincerity and self-regard a mile off and are the best possible antidote to such diseases. They should always be heard, but they may not be seen. Let's hope they are up a tree somewhere, reading a book that has nothing to do with getting a job.

CHAPTER FIFTEEN

INTERESTING TIMES

According to a Chinese proverb, you should avoid 'interesting times', a piece of advice I would endorse. The trouble is that the world is never at peace, and interesting times interrupt most lives more or less disastrously.

I was born only five years after the 1914–18 war ended and at my prep school we drew pictures of soldiers with tin hats and bloodstained bandages, graves in fields of poppies with Camel and Fokker aeroplanes machine-gunning each other in the sky. At the Armistice Day services on the football field we sang 'Lest we forget' and an ex-army padre would urge us to go 'over the top' to our common entrance exams and school certificates. Our masters still suffered from shell shock and battle fatigue and some had pieces of shrapnel lodged in their bodies, a fact which didn't improve their tempers.

By the time I was sixteen another war had started, an event that we had long been expecting. We had heard the hysterical speeches of Hitler on the wireless and discovered that he was making yet another final demand. At one moment a senior master came into the classroom and told us that our Prime Minister had met Hitler in Munich and 'peace in our time was assured'. After that, watching the news reels that tempered my delight in the latest Fred Astaire-Ginger Rogers musical film, I felt sure of war in my time. I still believed that the odds on my survival were better than those against soldiers in the first war, who had a one-in-four chance only of lasting beyond the first months in the trenches.

When I discussed my future with my father and I was finding it hard to choose between becoming a conscientious objector or a fighter pilot, he told me to 'avoid the temptation to do anything heroic'. This was advice I took and, after bombs started falling in London, I became, as a result of various shadows about the lungs, a scriptwriter in uniform, writing propaganda (we called them documentary) films about the progress of the war for the Ministry of Information. It's true that I was doing nothing much more heroic than fire-watching on the roof of Pinewood Studios. In the morning the streets were full of broken glass. In spite of all this the time of war contains some of the happiest years I can remember. This may seem a shameful thing to admit to in a period of unparalleled horror, genocide and the destruction of entire cities, but it's true. I'm sure that during the great disasters of history, the Hundred Years War, the Black Death, the Reign of Terror or the Battle of the Somme, there were people, somewhere, quite enjoying themselves. It's not a thing to be particularly proud of.

So, drinking with Dylan Thomas and the Scottish painters Colquhoun and MacBryde in the Swiss Pub in Soho, going without bananas, eating strange food—whale steak ('Moby Dick and Chips')—and being so hard pressed for alcohol that communion wine, sometimes qualified with spirits (gin and altars), occasionally appeared at parties. I was falling in and out of love and living in the

94

house of the owner of a contraceptive shop who blew up her wares and painted them jolly colours to serve as balloons at Christmas. All this seemed part of a normal and normally happy youth.

Our situation then cannot be compared to the wantonly cruel attack on the twin towers in New York. No comparisons can possibly diminish the horror of that event. Although the Blitz may have scored as many deaths in a week as the American tragedy in a day, we were in a war and death from the air was, in those years, an everyday occurrence. New York, unlike London and Berlin, has never been the object of bombardment or occupied by an enemy, like Paris or Rome. All the same, it's worth thinking for a moment about morality in times of war and the reality of a projected 'war against terrorism'.

The Second World War seemed undoubtedly just. If we had lost it millions more innocent people would have been murdered in gas chambers, freedom would have become a criminal offence and there would have been a triumph of evil. The good were our allies: the Russians, who suffered huge casualties in the war against Hitler; the Americans, who for the second time came to the rescue of Europe; and, of course, the freedom fighters. All over Europe the defeated countries were heroically and secretly carrying on the fight. These rebels would, I suppose, have been called 'terrorists' by their occupying masters, who would torture and kill them, together with many innocent civilians, after every act of subversion. To us they were not just 'freedom fighters' but heroes, or in many cases heroines, of the resistance. Some time ago I was talking to an elderly woman in the South of France. When she was no more than a schoolgirl in the occupied zone, she wanted to join the local resistance group. In order to qualify for entry, she had to have shot at least one German officer. So she pedalled around with a loaded revolver in the basket on her handlebars. The first officer she saw had grey hair and looked rather like her uncle, so she couldn't shoot him. The next was sitting on a fallen tree reading a book, an attitude she found appealing, so he was spared. The third, wearing a moustache and out for a run, had nothing particularly attractive about him, so she shot and killed him and was able to join the group.

She didn't tell me more about her underground activities, but had she lobbed a bomb into a café which contained a handful of enemy officers and their girlfriends, together with a number of innocent customers, and blown up the lot of them, she would still have been greeted as a heroine of the resistance, which, to us, she undoubtedly was.

Most people in the West, certainly everyone in Israel, would agree that the Palestinian suicide bombers, who kill women and children, are terrorists. Not many people remember when Palestine, as the land of Israel was once called, was in that obscure state, a British Protectorate. Were the Jewish members of the Stern Gang, those who hanged a British sergeant with piano wire or organized the bomb in the King David Hotel with murderous results (the organization in which Prime Minister Begin started his political career), 'freedom fighters' or 'terrorists'? What, looking at the matter from an entirely neutral standpoint, would we call them now?

A terrorist, the dictionary tells us, is 'one who favours or uses terror-inspiring methods of governing or of coercing government or community'. This would certainly cover Russian activities in Chechnya and Israeli invasions into Palestinian territory, killing innocent men, women and children and even employees of the United Nations, in a prolonged attempt to fight ruthless terrorism with ruthless terrorism. The word 'terrorist' could certainly have been applied to Nelson Mandela before his trial. If it means the calculated mass killing of civilians to obtain an end, it must be applied to the destruction of Hamburg and Düsseldorf and, of course, to the dropping of H-bombs. So all these activities can be defined as 'terrorism' if they are committed by an enemy or 'freedom-fighting' if by a friend. If so, the conception of a 'war' against it calls for the most careful thought.

Of the old, violent anarchist groups it was said that they always contained one pathological killer, one selfless idealist and one police spy. It was difficult, at first glance, to tell which was which, but the idealist was always the most dangerous. A 'war against terrorism' is an impracticable conception if it means fighting terrorism with terrorism. The feelings on both sides are not that they are taking part in some evil and criminal act but risking their lives heroically for what they consider to be a just cause. You could understandably reduce terrorism by improving security and increasing the number of police spies, but it can only finally be reduced by removing the number of just causes. ANC terrorism was pointless after the end of apartheid. Terrorism in Israel will stop only when a just solution has been agreed to and the occupied territories handed back. Terrorism has existed in Ireland since Elizabeth I sent the Earl of Essex out in an unsatisfactory attempt to quell the rebels. However, since former terrorists have become government ministers in Northern Ireland, some progress has been made and sometimes the signs are hopeful. Long ago I defended a Protestant terrorist, we'll call him Ian, who was charged with gun-running under the cover of a chemist shop in Hammersmith. I remember the case vividly because of the remarkable dialogue with the police superintendent.

SUPERINTENDENT: Well, Ian, where's the gun?
IAN: Sure the only gun I've got is between my legs and it gets me into constant trouble with my wife, Noreen.

The case proceeded and Ian was given a fairly lenient term of imprisonment by an Old Bailey judge who probably favoured the Protestant cause.

Dissolve to Waterstone's bookshop in Belfast many years later. I am signing books and an extremely respectable-looking middle-aged lady in a twin set and pearls comes up and asks me to sign a book for her two sons, who are both now practising as lawyers in Northern Ireland. She also tells me that they have a very nice home near the Mountains of Mourne. Then she says suddenly and to my considerable surprise, 'Ian died ten years ago.'

'Ian?'

'Yes. Surely you remember him? You defended him about the guns run through the chemist shop

98

in Hammersmith.'

So she was Noreen, who once gave Ian trouble about the gun between his legs.

It was only a small light at the end of one dark tunnel and it would be ridiculous to suppose that all the terrorists or the freedom fighters, whatever you call them, will end up with sons who are respectable barristers with lovely homes in the Mountains of Mourne.

Now that we have been involved in another war, causing the deaths of many innocent civilians, you may wonder if there is any such thing as a civilized way of conducting warfare. I can think only of the far-off days when Federico da Montefeltro was born, perhaps an illegitimate child, in the year Henry V of England died. Up to the age of fifteen he got an excellent education in Mantua, learning not only Latin and Greek but horsemanship, fencing, painting, music and dancing. When he inherited his dukedom, his study in the palace was lined with portraits of his heroes, including Dante and Petrarch, Homer and Virgil, Plato, Aristotle and St Augustine. He became the patron of the greatest artists of his day, Raphael and Piero della Francesca among them. When he marched out to war, musicians played and poets read their latest works aloud. All of this makes him sound entirely different from the sort of guns for hire who appear in the novels of Freddy Forsyth, though Duke Federico of Urbino was, to put it bluntly, a mercenary.

The city states of a disunited Italy were constantly at war. Florence fought Siena, Venice and Naples, and the Papal territories were either forging uneasy alliances or fighting each other.

Duke Federico sold his military services to the highest bidder, but once bought he was a loyal and effective commander. No doubt his price went up when, in contemporary lists of the leaders whom young princes should try to emulate, Federico's name was mentioned along with those of Philip of Macedon, Alexander the Great and Julius Caesar. Sometimes his engagements were hard-fought battles, sometimes they seem to have been more civilized occasions. At the Battle of La Molinella, at which Federico commanded the forces of Florence and Milan against the Venetians, as neither side appeared to be winning he and the other mercenary leader decided to call the whole thing off. Machiavelli wrote of it with some contempt: 'Neither side wavered, no one fell, a few prisoners and a wounded horse being the only casualty of the encounter!'

The positive outcome of these battles, sometimes bloody, occasionally polite, was that Federico built 'on a rugged site of Urbino a palace which many believe to be the most beautiful in all Italy', according to Castiglione, the author of *The Courtier*. In an upstairs gallery hangs the most enigmatic and chilling of all small paintings, Piero della Francesca's *Flagellation*.

Piero was a great mathematician, a student of Euclid with such a perfect sense of perspective that he could draw a vase seen from four different angles at the same time. The lines of the buildings, the geometrically perfect placing of events, are mathematically satisfying—it's the subject of the picture that freezes the blood. In the distance something terrible is going on: the whipping of the near-naked Christ bound to a pillar. The men in the foreground are taking absolutely no notice of this scene. They are talking quietly together, engrossed in some plot or political machination remote from human suffering.

Piero certainly came to Urbino and his geometry may well have had its effect on the deeply satisfying architecture at the Ducal Palace. You can stand in its courtyard and feel what a building of perfect proportions, conceived with mathematical precision on the scale of humanity, can do to banish anxiety and calm the spirit. It's undoubtedly the greatest legacy of a civilized soldier who had participated in other people's wars.

Federico died of a fever contracted on the damp and marshy banks of the Po in a battle against the Venetians and the Pope. Although he lived by selling war like takeaway pizzas, he was said to be 'known for his clemency' and entitled to be called 'the father of the miserable and protector of the afflicted'.

*   *   *

I was writing this in January, a refugee from an English winter, in a garden where red, yellow and white roses were in bloom and the call to prayer from the mosque in the village echoed across the orange groves. We were in the south of Morocco, where the people are gentle, smiling, anxious to please and many of them speak French. They might be regarded by the American and European tourists who are staying away as part of the Islamic hordes who threaten the very existence of our Western civilization.

We were almost alone in this hotel ten years ago

during the Gulf War, and now it was once again a place of peace. Early in the morning an icy wind blew from the desert but by ten o'clock the sun had risen high over the trees and we were sitting by the pool with Roland. He was a Swiss dealer and collector of ancient coins who once had in his hands the first known money, pieces of gold stamped with the sign of King Croesus. Naturally the talk turned to Baghdad—in a country that was once called Mesopotamia, Roland remembered, the birthplace of our civilization, which spread to Egypt, Greece and Rome before being washed up on the shores of our small and distant island.

It was part of the Persian Empire, conquered by Alexander the Great, said Roland, who can track the course of history from the coins that may have changed hands in Babylon. I could remember only that the Hanging Gardens were one of the Seven Wonders of the World and a childhood nursery rhyme which gave the city a feeling of magic.

> How many miles to Babylon?
> Threescore miles and ten.
> Can I get there by candle-light?
> Yes, and back again.

'The Persian empire was conquered by Alexander the Great,' said Roland, who had seen coins to prove it. 'Then Alexander married a Persian wife and divided his empire among his generals. Much later, in the time of Charlemagne, the biggest city in the world was in Mesopotamia, called Medina al Salaam, the city of peace, later known as Baghdad. It was once so glitzy and exotic that New York was known as Baghdad on the subway.'

'Roland knows everything,' I told his wife.

'Not quite everything,' she said. She was calm and beautiful—a grandmother whose banker parents were turned out of Yugoslavia by Tito and arrived, penniless, in Geneva. 'Everything about coins and history perhaps. But not quite everything.' She slid into the pool and swam away, as expertly as a young girl, blowing out air under water.

At lunch by the flowering bougainvillea, with a view of the snowline on the Atlas Mountains, the waiters in long white djellabas moved quietly out of the shadows. We drank cold, pink Moroccan wine and Roland was on to his special subject, crusader coins, many of which had their crosses changed to crescents for use by the Arabs.

'When a crusader lost a leg,' he told us, 'his followers would put a red-hot sword on the stump and rely on God to do the rest. The Arabs already had skilled surgeons who cauterized and sewed up the wounds.

'Mesopotamia became part of the Ottoman Empire,' said Roland, continuing with history as told by the money clinking in the purses and pockets of long-lost generations. 'It was owned by the Turks. When Turkey was defeated in the 1914–18 war, the Allies carved up its possessions with quite arbitrary boundaries and placed an arbitrary king, Feisal, on the throne of Iraq. These kings ruled until a revolution led by the Baath party finally produced Saddam Hussein who was, of course, backed by America. Now politicians think we are about to fight barbaric Muslim hordes. In fact Arabs are at the centre of civilization. They invented algebra [an Arabic word], conquered

103

almost the whole of Spain and managed to live there perfectly happily with the Sephardic Jews.'

*   *   *

Rashid, the young waiter who helps me to my seat by the pool and settles me down to write until lunchtime, has just got married. By a pure coincidence, his wife is Rashida, so *Rashid and Rashida* sounds like a happy opera, perhaps a little-known work by Rossini. He brought us his wedding photographs. Rashida is very young and pretty, wearing a tiara and a glittering robe for the occasion. She and Rashid gave each other ceremonial dates and sips of milk. Rashida had her hands and feet stained with henna. They knew each other in their schooldays. Rashida's mother died giving birth to her and her father left home to live in Fez with another wife. She lived with an uncle she called 'papa' and was clearly delighted to have a family of her own. Rashid, putting the wedding photographs away in a plastic bag, was also delighted. 'Goodbye, celibacy,' is what he said.

We drove through the camels and donkey carts in the back streets of Taroudannt and climbed a perilous staircase to Rashid and Rashida's spotless apartment. The biscuits and pancakes, the tea and the coffee were laid out and the television was alight with soundless cartoons. Rashid had changed out of his white djellaba and was wearing black jeans, a black zipper jacket and very dark glasses, so that he looked like a young film director of the Jean-Luc Godard era.

After tea we sat with Rashid (but without Rashida) and Mustapha the driver in the bar of the

104

Hotel Taroudannt. This was a narrow courtyard with a long flowerbed in its centre, from which trees grew and numberless small tortoises stirred in perpetual motion. Rashid and Mustapha knew almost everyone who passed, most of them seemed to be their relations and all got a kiss, including a policeman. I was drinking pastis and feeling, for the moment, entirely happy. Then someone asked me to explain why the Americans and the British should wish to kill Arab women and children. It was a question I found difficult to answer.

* * *

Rita, the hotel's Moroccan owner, was the granddaughter of a grand vizier to the king, a man able to sit down to dinner with a different wife every day of the week. She is married to an Italian and she is one of the few Muslims to have gone through a Catholic wedding ceremony. She talked about the Sunnis and the Shias in Iraq who, sharing almost exactly the same religion, hate each other more bitterly than they hate Christians or Jews. There seems to be no greater cause for mutual loathing than sharing similar religious beliefs, so Catholic and Protestant have slaughtered each other throughout history. The end of Saddam, Rita said, will mean civil strife, anarchy and chaos.

We thought we were going to war because Saddam Hussein refused to reveal the existence, or non-existence, of 'weapons of mass destruction'. Had he done so, it seemed, he would have been allowed to go on tyrannizing in peace. Then the story changed and we were going to fight him anyway, and for the more persuasive reason that

105

Iraq was ruled by terror, torture and mass executions. Perhaps wars don't happen for logical or even readily understandable reasons. Who remembers in what war, for what just or unjust cause, the charge of the Light Brigade was blunderingly launched? Who can disinter, with any accuracy, the causes of the 1914–18 war, in which millions marched cheerfully to their deaths? What exactly were the decimated regiment of the Gloucesters up to in Korea? What was the point of the long-drawn-out death, destruction and demoralization of the unsuccessful American war in Vietnam? Do world leaders provoke wars because they are thought to unite the electorate and make loyalty to the government a patriotic duty? Or is it that societies feel, like the doctors who applied the leeches to Lord Byron's temples, that an occasional bloodletting is essential to our health?

Whatever the reason, it seemed a good idea to sit in a garden where the roses bloom in winter and enjoy the moment of safety in a peaceful Arab country. All this was before the war which would end quite suddenly, when Saddam Hussein took my father's advice and avoided the temptation of doing anything heroic.

No weapons of mass destruction would be found and the Al Qaeda terrorists would turn up, alive and unharmed, in Saudi Arabia. The blasted ruins of Mesopotamia are to be repaired by companies close to President Bush's government, and the discovery of mass graves has persuaded us, if we need persuading, of the horrors of Saddam's regime. The Shias, the Sunnis and the Kurds are now free to quarrel with each other, and there is

106

nothing, unhappily, to suggest that the times are likely to become less interesting.

CHAPTER SIXTEEN

TIMING AND THE ART OF ADVOCACY

The art of advocacy is not used only in courtrooms. Lovers pursuing their claims, parents persuading their children, businessmen after a bargain, salesmen trying to sell double glazing, husbands making excuses for absences and neglect, all have to find persuasive arguments, presenting their cases with as much charm as possible and hoping for a verdict of 'not guilty'. Pleas in mitigation have to be made to aggrieved partners. Arguments have to be won by searching questions. In all these situations tact is necessary and appropriate timing is essential.

My father once appeared in court for a comedian who told him, after the case had been won, that he greatly admired his timing. Rightly realizing that pauses, moments of, if possible, pregnant silence that keep the audience waiting eagerly were extremely effective, he adopted the practice of silently counting up to ten before he asked the first question in cross-examination. When I tried this, totally lacking his authority, the judge told me, quite crossly, to get 'on with it', and added, 'We can't all sit here watching you standing in silent prayer, you know.'

I admired another smoothly accomplished advocate, Cyril Salmon, who used to stroll negligently up and down the front bench, toying with a gold watch chain or cigar cutter, as he lobbed questions deftly over his shoulder at the witness box. When I tried this, another judge said, 'Do keep still! It's like watching ping-pong.'

Taking time requires a certain amount of courage. The vital words in the theatre and the law courts are 'slow down'. The most accomplished timer of jokes I ever encountered is the actor Leslie Phillips. Born into a poor family with a father who died young, he started his stage career at the age of eleven and has hardly been out of work since. He grew from a child actor into a juvenile lead in the 'Doctor' films and radio comedy. His way of saying 'Hellow!' in a drawn-out and lecherous manner made him famous. I met him first when he fell in love with my stepdaughter and there was a serious danger that he might end up calling me 'Dad' or, worse still, 'the Guvnor'. No marriage, however, took place. Leslie went on to play Falstaff and Gayev in *The Cherry Orchard* and, to my great delight, consented to be in a play of mine. His slow, amused, sardonic delivery delighted the audience but what I found most remarkable was his ability to get two laughs out of one joke.

The Leslie Phillips technique is to receive the feed line in silence but to act the response so that the audience is almost sure of what the answer's going to be. They feel safe to laugh for the first time. After a suitable wait, Phillips delivers the punch line and the audience laughs louder and again, because their guess has proved correct. Unhappily I had by this time left the bar and couldn't give his technique a try-out in court.

I'm also grateful to Leslie for a story he told me about a time when he was a young assistant stage manager in a West End theatre. The star was a well-known actor, famous for his infallible comic timing. At one point in the play he had to leave the stage with the leading lady and return immediately to answer the telephone. Accordingly they both left, but the male star didn't return. The audience was left to enjoy the spectacle of an empty stage and listen to an unanswered telephone. When the actor's absence was further prolonged the young Leslie Phillips was sent to find him. He discovered him without difficulty making passionate love to the leading lady up against the ropes at the back of the stage. A tug on the back of the star's jacket merely got a command of, 'Go away, boy.' The audience had to endure another ten minutes of watching an empty stage. This is an example of very poor timing indeed.

*   *   *

Nothing delights an audience more than to have their suspicion of a joke, or the mystery which conceals a crime, confirmed. Much has been written about similarities between the law courts and the theatre—usually missing the point. However, talking to a jury has this in common with writing a story or unfolding the plot of a play. The first rule is not to be boring. This is hard in long cases about such matters as the evasion of value added tax and I remember, at the end of one such trial, congratulating the jury on having sat through what was undoubtedly one of the most tedious cases ever heard at the Old Bailey. The judge countered this by starting his summing-up, 'It may surprise you to know, members of the jury, that it is not the sole purpose of the criminal law of England to entertain Mr Mortimer.'

The rebuke was no doubt well phrased and entirely just. But awakening the imagination of a jury, making your listeners see themselves in strange circumstances, understanding the motives of a different, no doubt alien cast of characters—all this is necessary if a jury, or even a judge, is to arrive at the truth. Criminal responsibilities can't be judged by statistics, or social surveys, or even by referring to similar cases. It's necessary to imagine just what it would be like to be the man in the pub quarrel, the wife in the violent domestic dispute, the abused Asian student on the night in question in Kensington, Bradford or Birmingham Perry Bar.

Overacting in the theatre and law courts is finished. Gone and forgotten are the arrivals in court of such advocates as Sir Edward Marshall Hall. He was always preceded by a clerk carrying a pile of clean handkerchiefs, a second followed with a carafe of water and the third brought the air cushion. If the prosecution evidence got nasty, Marshall Hall would blow his nose, a sad and terrible trumpet, on each of the handkerchiefs. If it got worse, he would knock over the carafe of water. If it became really dangerous, he would slowly and deliberately blow up the air cushion until the jury could pay attention to nothing else.

John Maude, son of the actor Cyril Maude, who became an Old Bailey judge, used to announce that his client was going to give evidence in a criminal trial (always a dangerous proceeding) by saying, 'You can imagine what a nerve-racking experience it must be for anyone to go into that witness box, members of the jury. It must be terrible for the *innocent*. I will now call William Sykes' (or

112

whatever his client's name might have been). So he conferred an aura of innocence on however shifty a character he was defending.

As in the world outside the courtroom, you can soon tell your friends from your enemies. The jury members who laugh at your jokes and those who greet them with expressions of stern disapproval, those who lean forward to be sure of catching every word of your cross-examination and those who put down their pencils and stare vaguely up to the ceiling. You have to decide between strengthening the resolve of your friends and trying to convert your enemies. By the time it comes to your final speech you'll hope to have done as much as possible of both. At the conclusion of the speech we all have our favourite peroration.

Marshall Hall had his great 'scales of justice' act. 'If you are in doubt, members of the jury,' he used to say, 'if you find the case for the defence and the prosecution evenly balanced—' here he would stretch his arms out like a pair of scales '—then you must put into the defence side that little featherweight—the presumption of innocence.' And now one outstretched arm would sink. 'And the answer should be, must be, a verdict of not guilty!' One cynical judge told the jury he was always thankful when Sir Edward started his 'scales of justice' act because it meant that his speech would soon be coming to an end.

I worked out a slightly different conclusion. 'Members of the jury,' I used to say, 'tomorrow you will go back to your jobs and your homes. You will forget all about the Black Spot pub, the missing diary pages, the broken salad knife and the uneaten dog food at Number 12A Mafeking Avenue' (or whatever the particular facts of the case might have been). 'To you this has been only a short interruption. A minute part of your life. But to the man / woman sitting there in the dock, it means the whole of his / her life. And we leave that life, with confidence, in your hands.' I thought this good enough to give to Rumpole, my fictional barrister, who was successful with it in a number of cases.

Things don't always run smoothly, however. A friend of mine had just embarked on the peroration of his final speech for the defence to an attentive jury when he saw that the judge was busily engaged in writing a note. When it was finished, it was folded and given to the usher, who brought it to my learned friend just as he had reached the most moving and dramatic moment. He paused and looked down at the note, which said, 'Dear Jim. I thought you'd like to know that your flies are open and I can see your cock.'

An advocate's life is not an easy one, and dangers and pitfalls should always be expected.

CHAPTER SEVENTEEN

MALE CLOTHING

Montaigne found it incredible that

men alone should have been brought forth in a difficult and necessitous state which can only be sustained by borrowing from other creatures . . . if we had been endowed at birth with under garments and trousers there can be no doubt that Nature would have groomed those parts of us which remained exposed to the violence of the seasons with a thicker skin, as she has done for our finger tips and the soles of our feet.

As the process of evolution hasn't led to our being born with trousers, men have to choose an appearance in which to dress themselves for life as an actor chooses clothes for a part. It's a good and perhaps the easiest thing to stick to the clothing of the best part of your life, probably the fashions of your youth.

My father wore spats to his work in the Probate, Divorce and Admiralty Division. Spats have now gone totally out of existence and the word is now used only for an argument or the past ejection of saliva. My father's spats were made of cloth that fastened under his feet and crossed his ankles and the top half of his shiny black boots. In summer his linen spats were white and he also wore a white waistcoat. In winter the waistcoat was black and the spats dark grey. He also wore a stiff winged collar with a bow tie, as Winston Churchill did, a gold watch chain across his stomach, a black jacket and dark striped trousers. He was uncomfortably aware of the words of one of the judges of the Probate, Divorce and Admiralty Division who had said to a less carefully dressed barrister, 'It gives me little pleasure to listen to a legal argument from a member of the bar wearing light grey trousers.'

When I was very young I collected cigarette cards portraying the great dandies. My favourite was Beau Brummell, who would cheerfully spend two hours attempting to tie the perfect cravat and who asked a fellow snappy dresser, out walking with the Prince Regent, 'Who's your fat friend?' I wrote up for a small walking stick (then known as a 'whangee') and a monocle, as I hoped to look like Bertie Wooster, a member of the Drones Club and the employer of the incomparable Jeeves, who enforced strict codes of clothing on his master.

I also wore a dinner jacket with a soft turned-down collar to my shirt (instead of the conventional stiff and upstanding variety). In this I was imitating King Edward VIII, who had fallen in love with an American divorcée and was about to abdicate. My father and I always wore dinner jackets when dining in hotels and restaurants or going to the theatre. When we turned up in evening dress at a cinema in Torquay the whole audience burst into spontaneous applause. At Harrow we wore top hats and tails on Sundays and for attending the annual cricket match against Eton. On this occasion a silver-topped cane with a dark blue tassel was also carried. The whole outfit caused considerable mirth on the Underground when you travelled on your way to Lord's.

At university I took, for a while, to purple corduroy trousers, bow ties and a large-brimmed sombrero. I would wear this outfit whilst smoking black Balkan Sobranie cigarettes. I must have looked ridiculous. Luckily I started to go to the tailor in Oxford who has made my clothes ever since and who has a long record of my unfortunately expanding body. In this shop men are judged by their clothes. When a Mr Varney was in charge he said he couldn't bear to see Robin Day, a famous political commentator and interviewer on television. 'That Mr Day,' he said, 'is a national disgrace, an object of scorn and derision who should never be allowed to appear on television as the mere sight of him must cause universal pain and distress.' When I asked him what exactly was so appalling about Robin Day, he spoke as though naming the most unforgivable sin. 'I don't know who cuts his jackets,' he said, 'but when that Mr Day points his sleeve almost rides up to his elbow.'

I grew up in the days of 'sports jackets' made of tweed and preferably so well worn that they had leather round the cuffs and leather patches on the elbows. They were worn with cavalry-twill trousers and chukka boots to visit the saloon bar before Sunday lunch. Those were the days of three-piece suits and trousers with braces, although sock suspenders were already on the way out. A friend of mine laughed so loudly at Frank Sinatra's sock suspenders (she called them braces on his socks) when he prepared himself for an act of love that the great singer was deeply hurt and sex was taken off the menu. I survived, at least young at heart, into the era of Afghan waistcoats, velvet trousers,

117

bangles, beads and Nehru jackets.

Since then I have reverted to the sort of clothing I wore when I emerged into life, became a barrister, published a first novel and took on a wife with four children and, in the years immediately following, would have two more. Costume designers, in period plays and films, seldom realize that men hope to preserve the appearance of their youth and may be as much as forty years behind the fashion. In *A Christmas Carol*, written in 1843, old Mr Fezziwig is still wearing a Welsh wig. So the fashions of today, unstructured suits, fleeces and baseball caps worn back to front, may still be decking out very old men in the year 2050.

Defence barristers down at the Old Bailey had to avoid looking too rich or too inexperienced. Gowns should be elderly, perhaps torn and inexpertly mended. Waistcoats were probably egg-stained. The wigs, obstinately retained since they were the height of fashion, should be yellowing with age and, if possible, disintegrating. If one had to be bought new, an alarmingly expensive purchase, it should be kicked round the room and left out in the rain, a white wig being a sure sign of a far too recent call to the bar. This is Rumpole's courtroom appearance and was mine also. To it I added large cuff links which twinkled at the jury and, I hoped, retained their interest when all else failed.

Writers have been less anxious to conceal signs of success. Dickens appeared all decked out in gorgeous waistcoats with gold chains and rings, as did Disraeli. Oscar Wilde progressed from velvet knee breeches and carnations dyed green to curly brimmed bowler hats and coats with astrakhan

118

collars. Nowadays any collection of writers is deliberately 'dressed down' like workers in city offices, determined to bond with each other by wearing only casual clothes on Fridays.

Finally, a few words of warning. T-shirts are unflattering to aged and scrawny necks, shoulder-length hair seems unsuitable when it's grey and ponytails trapped in an elastic band are always a danger. An exception to this rule is the shortish, neat, impeccably clean, grey to white ponytail of my friend Jon Lord, late of Deep Purple, now the composer of classical music. He also wears his ponytail with impressively dark clothing. Someone described Baudelaire's 'fine sombre clothing' and that always seemed to me a desirable way to dress. But then Baudelaire's hair was cropped very short, like, as they also said, *une vraie toilette de la guillotine*', so perhaps that's not such a good idea either.

CHAPTER EIGHTEEN

BEING VULGAR

Speaking of Byron, George Eliot called him 'the most vulgar-minded genius that ever produced a great effect on literature'. It's questionable if Byron's mind was notably vulgar. His sense of irony never deserted him, and when at his most tender, even sentimental, moments he couldn't resist laughing at himself:

> And Julia sate with Juan, half embraced
> And half retiring from the glowing arm,
> Which trembled like the bosom where 'twas
>   placed
> Yet still she must have thought there was no
>   harm,
> Or else 'twere easy to withdraw her waist;
> But then the situation had its charm,
> And then—God knows what next—I can't go
>   on;
> I'm almost sorry that I e'er begun.

However, to deny all vulgarity to Byron would be grossly unfair. Vulgarity is not, as George Eliot would have it, something to be avoided at all costs. And you should not, in life or in literature, be afraid of sentimentality either. Some of the best things in life, works that are a pleasure to be handed on to the generations to come, have vulgarity and sentimentality in spades. And I don't mean seaside postcards or old music hall songs, but the greatest works of Dickens, Chaucer, Sterne, James Joyce and Rabelais. Indeed it's impossible to read through, say, the novels of Virginia Woolf without longing for a touch, a mere hint of vulgarity or sentimentality, a tear-jerking scene perhaps, or even a joke about a fart. Benjamin Britten and his circle of friends used to say that Puccini's operas 'are all right, it's just the music that's so terrible'. And yet you can be tearful at the end of *La Bohème* or be swept away by the shameless melodrama of *Tosca* more easily than by Britten's cold and more tasteful music.

And if Byron was vulgar-minded, how about Shakespeare? In the purely literary sense it's hard to criticize his poetry and infallible sense of drama. There are only very occasional over-ornate moments of showing off and sentimentality, as in:

> And pity, like a naked new-born babe,
> Striding the blast, or heaven's cherubim hors'd
> Upon the sightless couriers of the air,
> Shall blow the horrid deed in every eye,
> That tears shall drown the wind . . .

The more showy paintings of Rubens, the falling clouds of female flesh, might be described as vulgar, as might Toulouse-Lautrec's lesbians and prostitutes or the satirical drawings of George Grosz. Picasso could be vulgar but not, strangely enough, Matisse; and there is a tender vulgarity in Kurt Weill. Critics might say that the poetry of Rudyard Kipling, with its easy rhythms and populist appeal, is vulgar but this was the source of his confident mastery of verse. Vulgarity is, at least, energetic.

122

The actor Donald Wolfit, playing Shylock, sharpened his knife during the trial scene and then dropped it point downwards until it stood quivering, stabbing the stage. 'Terribly vulgar effect,' said Gielgud with a sniff of disapproval. And yet great acting, as practised by Laurence Olivier, had its elements of vulgar showing-off. He entered as Othello, blacked up and with a rose in his mouth. He died hanging upside down, his ankles grasped by terrified spear-carriers, as Coriolanus. He swooped down from a high ramp as Hamlet, holding the sword that killed Claudius like an avenging angel. He imagined the scream of pain a small animal might emit if it found its tongue frozen to the ice and gave it to the blinded Oedipus. He slid down the length of a stage curtain as Mr Puff in *The Critic*. Terribly vulgar indeed, but all wonderful moments in the theatre.

The Russian writer Nabokov thought Dostoevsky vulgar and said that reading his books was like enjoying the more lurid crime stories in some sensational newspaper, which is perhaps why *Crime and Punishment* and *The Brothers Karamazov* exercise their compulsive fascination.

Oscar Wilde mocked Dickens for his vulgar sentimentality in writing the death of Little Nell. Perhaps Dickens didn't feel as strongly about Nell, for all her slightly embarrassing sweetness, as he did for Jo, the little crossing sweeper in *Bleak House*. And when Jo died of poverty and neglect he comes straight out of the book and steps down to the footlights:

Dead, your Majesty. Dead, my lords and gentlemen. Dead, Right Reverends and Wrong

Reverends of every order. Dead, men and women, born with Heavenly compassion in your hearts. And dying thus around us every day.

You could say this is sentimental, which it is. You might find the effect vulgar. I know it to be magnificent.

*   *   *

In another sense Shakespeare has a healthy sense of vulgarity. Even his most serious texts are dotted with sexual innuendoes, and he didn't rule out fart jokes. Launce in *Two Gentlemen of Verona* takes personal responsibility for the indiscretion of his dog, Crab: 'he had not been there—bless the mark!—a pissing while, but all the chamber smelt him'. Shakespeare was also certain of a laugh from the groundlings when Pompey, in *Measure for Measure*, announces that his surname is Bum. 'Troth, and your bum is the greatest thing about you,' says Escalus, 'so that in the beastliest sense you are Pompey the Great.'

'Vulgar' was a term of abuse much used in my youth. It could be applied to furniture ('what a vulgar little chair'), seaside resorts (Brighton and Blackpool) and even after-dinner drinks (crème de menthe frappé). It was vulgar to say 'serviettes' instead of 'table napkins' or 'lounge' instead of 'sitting room'. Wearing a ready-made bow tie, or eating asparagus with a fork or peas on a knife, all such things were thought of as unforgivably vulgar. It was horribly vulgar to pour your tea into your saucer to cool it (once a common practice) or wear brown shoes with a blue suit or have a gnome in your front garden. There was a whole world of things which non-vulgar people, including, of course, the Bloomsbury group, would never permit. Harrow, among the English public schools, was thought of as 'vulgar', producing unreliable characters wearing scuffed suede shoes who drove battered sports cars and frequented gin palaces on the Great West Road. The alleged vulgarity of old Harrovians attracted John Betjeman so much that, although he had been to Marlborough, he used to put on a Harrovian boater and sit at the piano playing Harrow school songs. Nothing excited him more than carefully observed vulgarity.

Such definitions of vulgarity belong to an arcane snobbery and a vanished standard of good taste. Now political correctness has tried to enforce an artificial code of polite conduct on our basic instinct to laugh at most things, including, sex, death and going to the lavatory. In life and in literature there may still be opportunities to show off, exaggerate, embellish and startle. The only advice I would give to those who come after me is, 'If you can find a streak of vulgarity in yourself, nurture it.'

CHAPTER NINETEEN

THE MARKETPLACE

My uncle Harold was rich. I think that in the 1930s, when such things were more rare, he was a millionaire. His father had owned a furniture shop in Tottenham Court Road and a patented bed spring. He left the shop to his other son, Ambrose Heal, and the bed spring to my uncle Harold. Out of this device, by the time he married my aunt Marjorie, Harold owned a factory at Staples Corner, on the outskirts of London, making mattresses which were so comfortable that King George V, having hurt his back during the 1914–18 war, chose to sleep on one.

My rich uncle was mildly eccentric. He had his waistcoats made with flannel flaps behind to keep his bottom warm. He designed his own wide-brimmed hats and drove a Lagonda. He was also superstitious, refusing to walk under ladders or have lilies in the house, and feared the thirteenth of each month. In the taste of the 1930s he designed some good furniture, including the desk I am writing on now. Towards the end of his life, he flew into a terrible temper with my aunt because she wrote a shopping list out on a clean envelope. In spite of his wealth, he considered this a terrible waste.

I don't think we ever envied my uncle's wealth, the Lagonda and the country estate with the cottages in which the workers would be given boxes of biscuits and pounds of tea at Christmas. All this took place in the days when doctors, lawyers, schoolteachers, even architects were thought to follow useful, valuable callings, with rules against professional misconduct. Millionaires seemed to us, on the whole, to be something of a joke.

We scarcely ever heard the word 'entrepreneur' and if we did it was used to describe the middleman who produced nothing. He intervened between the manufacturer and the consumer and made easy money out of both of them. Now entrepreneurs are thought to follow the most worthwhile of all professions and every child, in the market-oriented way of New Labour education, should be taught the art of becoming one. Indeed, this calling has been judged to rank so high in the field of human endeavour that President Bush, in one of his wilder flights of verbal confusion, was heard to say, 'The trouble with the French is that they haven't got a word for "entrepreneur".'

The change became complete in the Thatcher years. As the factory gates closed there were no jobs for manufacturers any more and we became a nation of shopkeepers and hairdressers. It was then that politicians, 'entrepreneurs' and practically everyone else began to speak, in tones of religious awe, about the 'marketplace'. Ignore the fact that Jesus made some uncalled-for remarks about the poor being blessed, forget the sometimes uncommercial nature of art or literature that reveals the truth about our lives, and instead take everything down to the marketplace to discover how it sells and how much it's worth.

All this comes as something of a surprise to those of us who know marketplaces. From Portobello and the Caledonian Road to the great souk of Marrakech, they are places for the quick disposal of stolen property, where you will be offered sham antiques and quack medicines, where you can have your wallet and your bottom pinched, where you may be sold a dead bat as a sovereign cure for sciatica, or tickets for a non-existent lottery, and where some seemingly helpful and committed guide will lead you, infallibly, to the shop owned by his relatives in order that you may be deceived over the price of carpets. And if it's said that the great, established businesses or the world's global corporations have little in common with the back streets of Marrakech, you have only to remember Enron and its accountants and directors to appreciate that marketplaces are where no sucker ever gets an even break.

The other mantra of the Thatcher era was 'consumer choice' and this conception lingers on as the great opportunity of our times. The heavenly marketplace, if it is to do its job properly, must be furnished with at least fifty-seven varieties of everything. Anyone who has fewer than this number of varieties of yoghurt to choose from is not living life to the full. And to see this blessing working at its best you must 'shop around', which means, I suppose, trudging wearily from one supermarket to another, comparing the price of cornflakes.

The idea that a wide choice is always a desirable, or even a useful, part of life can be tested in the cases of restaurants and television. You know that when you are handed a heavy menu, bound in vellum with a dangling gold tassel, offering you fifteen choices of everything, you can be sure none of it will be any good. Eat somewhere where the whole offering is chalked up on a short board and it's likely to be profoundly satisfactory.

In the best period of television there were only two choices, so that a play or a film commanded a huge and united audience. As the choices multiplied the programmes, reduced to a desperate grab for ratings, noticeably deteriorated. But the remorseless process goes on until the viewer can enjoy the luxury of flicking through fifty channels of identical rubbish. With not enough money, or advertising, to provide for all these outlets, what the audience is offered is what Proverbs called 'a small choice of rotten apples'.

The doctor who makes a friend of his patients, the lawyer who defends death penalty cases in distant countries for no fee, the schoolteacher who opens a child's eyes to a new world of books and poetry—such people do nothing that can be measured in marketplaces. The greatest painters, composers and writers don't offer you choices, they present you with what only they can do, and you must take it or leave it. So when such subjects as the values of the marketplace are discussed, you will probably not have much to contribute. You can repeat a poem in your head and wait until the conversation is over. But if anyone starts talking about 'level playing fields', get up and steal quietly from the room.

CHAPTER TWENTY

LAW OR JUSTICE

As I have said, my first encounter with the law was in the Probate, Divorce and Admiralty Division. Probate cases were the ones in which ruthless relatives fought tooth and nail for the furniture. Admiralty cases, where the judge sat in front of a large anchor and seafaring men arrived unrolling charts, were closed books to us and called for specialist lawyers with a knowledge of salvage and chartering vessels. Divorce was sexier, more dramatic and supplied our daily bread, so that in my childhood I was housed, fed, watered, clothed and educated almost entirely on the proceeds of adultery, cruelty and wilful neglect to provide reasonable maintenance.

The divorce laws at the time I started life as a barrister, in the late 1940s, dramatically illustrated the gulf between the law and reality, the law and morality or, in many cases, the law and justice.

Today, of course, ending a marriage is a matter of filling out a form, dividing up the property and saying, 'Cheerio!' When I started practice you had to prove something extremely serious like cruelty or adultery. One of my first clients was a husband, longing to end his marriage, who was finding it extremely hard to discover anyone prepared to commit adultery with his wife. He was reduced to the horrifying expedient of disguising himself in a false beard, a false moustache and a pair of dark glasses and creeping into his own bungalow, in full

131

view of the neighbours, pretending to be his own co-respondent. The plot was discovered and the unfortunate husband was sent to prison for 'perverting the course of justice'. I thought this was extremely hard. If you can't sleep with your own wife wearing a false beard, what can you do? His case showed, however, in an extreme form, an unbridgeable gap between the law, justice, morality or even common sense.

Matrimonial law had come down from the ecclesiastical courts, through the years when women couldn't own property or divorce their husbands for adultery, unless it was coupled with cruelty. It had been humanized to some extent by the writer and independent MP A. P. Herbert in the 1930s, but when I started just after the war a husband could still get damages from his wife's lover. This entailed an argument in court about her value in hard cash. In these unseemly proceedings, a husband had to argue that his wife was a fabulous cook, mother and lover and therefore worth a great deal. The ungallant lover, however, swore she was a cold fish in bed and never did the washing-up. There was no such thing as a divorce by consent; in fact consent was called 'connivance' and was a bar to freedom from an unhappy marriage.

In these circumstances lawyers, and very often judges, had to achieve fair and reasonable solutions for their unhappy clients, not only with no assistance from the law but very often in spite of it. This raises the question, do laws have to be respected and obeyed simply because they're there?

Once again it's a poet's imaginings which provide the most helpful debate and throw the

132

brightest light on this question. *Measure for Measure* tells of an old, rarely used Viennese law making fornication punishable by death. The Duke, like God taking a sabbatical, leaves the city and appoints as his regent the puritanical, rigorous, painfully virtuous Angelo. The normal and perfectly harmless young Claudio is guilty of what the brothel keeper's servant, Pompey, calls 'Groping for trouts in a peculiar river'. Mistress Overdone, with a duller use of language, says Claudio is to have 'his head . . . chopped off . . . for getting Madam Julietta with child'. Angelo is dedicated to the belief that the letter of the law has to be obeyed and to hell with natural justice.

The debate starts when Escalus, 'an ancient Lord' and servant of the Duke who, full of humanity and common sense, is another of Shakespeare's favourite characters, tries to plead Claudio's case, asking Angelo to think:

Whether you had not sometime in your life
Err'd in this point which now you censure him,
And pull'd the law upon you.

Angelo's answer is simple. 'We must not make a scarecrow of the law' so it becomes a 'perch' and not a 'terror' for ravens and lawless birds. Furthermore, our own possible weaknesses are no excuse for not strictly enforcing the legal code. ' 'Tis one thing to be tempted, Escalus,' he says. 'Another thing to fall.' A jury condemning a thief to death, he agrees, may contain a 'thief or two / Guiltier than him they try,' but that makes no difference to the laws we all have to obey. Don't tell me about my guilty thoughts, Angelo is saying,

133

but 'When I, that censure him, do so offend / Let mine own judgement pattern out my death'.

The theoretical debates become drama when Claudio's beautiful sister, Isabella, on the point of becoming a nun, comes to plead for her brother's life. Angelo lusts after her and feels himself sorely tempted to go groping for trouts just like the criminal he despises. Before the breakdown of Angelo the seagreen incorruptible, in his scenes with Isabella, the conflict between the strict upholder of the letter of the law and natural justice is played out.

At first Angelo is obdurate: 'Your brother is a forfeit of the law, / And you but waste your words.' 'Why, all the souls that were were forfeit once,' Isabella reminds him. 'And He that might the vantage best have took / Found out the remedy.' So there is a power greater than the law, that of Christ who redeemed all our sins, who broke the strict laws of the Pharisees and died a convicted criminal. 'How would you be,' she asks Angelo, 'if He, which is the top of judgement, should / But judge you as you are?' This is Escalus's argument returning. What we regard as the just process of criminal trials is not much more than sinful human beings punishing each other. True religion points the way to a more merciful process.

But not always. The law is never more cruel, or more oblivious to the arguments of Escalus and Isabella, than when it claims to have God on its side. The proceedings of the Inquisition and the Shia laws, if enforced in Islamic states, can outdo the ancient criminal code of Vienna in wanton ferocity. A modern Angelo might be a regent in the Middle East prepared to order an errant wife to be stoned to death. And, in Europe, who would Isabella have to call on in this faithless age? No God, perhaps; but is there, in the bravest hearts, some system of natural justice better than current laws can provide? Can there be?

The answer must depend on the view you take of the human condition. Are people naturally destructive, immoral, predatory and self-seeking, only to be kept in order by harsh laws and fiercely deterrent mandatory sentences? Or are men and women naturally orderly, merciful, humane and bred with a need for justice and mutual aid? Of course these qualities, or defects, are not evenly distributed, and undoubtedly there is much of each in all of us, but when it comes to the law some sort of distinction can be drawn. Are you a Shylock or a Bassanio?

Shylock pinned his faith on the words in the contract, the nature of his bond and the duty of the state to uphold the letter of the law regardless of human suffering. Bassanio put another point of view. More important than the sanctity of the law was the plight of the individual parties in the particular case. If the enforcement of contracts were all-important, a man would die with a pound of flesh carved off near to his heart. Therefore Bassanio pleads to Portia, who has come to judge the case: 'And I beseech you / Wrest once the law to your authority: / To do a great right, do a little wrong, / And curb this cruel devil of his will.' So forget the wording of the statute, ignore the terms of the contract, and, in the name of natural justice, do what you think is right.

The late Lord Denning, a man full of charm who passed judgement in short, workman-like sentences spoken in a carefully preserved Hampshire accent, always said he was a 'Bassanio man'. What was important to him was justice in the individual case and not the omnipotence of the law. His decisions, on this basis, led to frequent appeals to the House of Lords, where the judges, apparently more sympathetic to Shylock's line of legal argument, frequently reversed his decisions. The gulf will still exist and Isabellas will be appealing to Angelos to show a little humanity far into the future.

Perhaps she could have a word with the judges in the new, politically correct divorce courts, which have swung round to a different absurdity. In one of the last cases I was concerned with, a husband returning unexpectedly one afternoon to his home in Golders Green found his wife enjoying sex with three members of a pop group. To pay for her entertainment he found, after the divorce, that he had to sell his house and his business to give her half of all he possessed as well as half of his future earnings. I hasten to say that the law is not sexist in this respect. A famously successful woman writer, finding her husband in bed with her secretary, had to reward him equally and was faced with a similar financial disaster.

A judge who also had medical qualifications once told me the following story. He was trying, long ago, a perfectly friendly action between a woman's husband and her lover to determine which of them, and they were both well off, should pay for her child's education and future support. The parties agreed to a blood test and when the judge got the report it was perfectly clear that neither of the two men before him, but some third, possibly penniless, stranger must be the father of the child. He tore up the report, threw it into the wastepaper basket and invited the two men to his room. There he told them that the blood test had established nothing with any clarity and that they should agree to share the cost of bringing up the child. What he did was certainly against the law and, just as certainly, right.

CHAPTER TWENTY-ONE

FAMILY VALUES

When you hear a politician lecturing the nation on the subject of family values you know that he (it's almost always a he) has probably left a weeping wife at home, has quarrelled with his children and is having it off with his 'work experience' researcher. No doubt there are many happy families, and they're not all the same, but close families, like the quiet country cottages Sherlock Holmes observed from the train, can be torture chambers for those imprisoned in them. Murder has this in common with Christmas, most of it goes on in the family circle.

Family values, down the centuries, have not had a particularly good press in literature—unless you count the works of Dickens, who, in real life, nailed up the door which led to his wife's bedroom. The domestic murder in a bath and the subsequent curse upon the house of Atreus, the unhappy state of the Danish royal family when a prince's father was poisoned by his uncle, the ghastly dinner parties hosted by the Macbeths when ghosts were on the guest list don't make encouraging reading for newlyweds. The home lives of Henry VIII, the Crippens or Mary Queen of Scots don't encourage family values.

Violence, betrayal, lingering curses and sudden death aren't the only drawbacks to family life. Even as politicians are parading its virtues you can hear across the country the sound of stifled yawns. Mrs

Patrick Campbell, in some ways an unlikely propagandist for marriage, spoke of it as 'the deep, deep peace of the double bed after the hurly-burly of the chaise-longue'. The trouble with double beds is that people tend to go to sleep in them. When I did divorce cases I found that couples, married to other partners, had enthusiastic and apparently deeply satisfactory love affairs until a divorce set them free to marry. When they did so the excitement evaporated. There were no more furtive telephone calls, no element of danger when they listened for a creaking stair or an unexpected key in the front door, no hours snatched in the back of a Ford Cortina parked in a dark wood. It all became legal, respectable and above board and, in many sad cases, they went off it.

Even the most happily married have a certain admiration for illicit lovers, who were always the heroes and heroines of ancient literature. Lancelot is a more attractive figure than King Arthur, Cleopatra than Octavia. We were once delayed for three hours at Heathrow Airport while an aged engineer with a beard did something to the pipes. The captain, a handsome middle-aged man with greying sideboards, carried his cap under his arm and walked among us from time to time, sympathizing with our frustration and promising that all would be well. When we finally rose into the air his gently reassuring voice came over the Tannoy. 'This is your captain, Johnny Montague-Smith. We are now on our way and I can assure you that this aircraft is completely safe. If it weren't I wouldn't be in it because I have no intention at all of dying in a plane crash. My dear old father told me that the only decent way for an English gentleman to die is shot through the heart in the bed of his best friend's wife.'

From there on we all, even the most respectably married, had every faith in Captain Johnny Montague-Smith and believed him when he said he wouldn't die in an aeroplane crash.

With out chained friend, perhaps a jealous foe,
The dreariest and the longest journey go.

So wrote Shelley, whom Byron found the 'least selfish' and 'mildest of men', denouncing marriage as though he were a fugitive from a chain gang. Such dire warnings as this, and the American who said that marriage is very like a Florida hurricane, 'it starts off with all that sucking and blowing and you end up by losing your house', do more for family life than the hard sell of unreliable politicians. Because it's not as grim as all that. You may well find a true friend and not a deadly foe and the journey shouldn't be entirely dreary. Children who like their parents to be married are our only tenuous claim to immortality.

In the future, when it's taken over by my heirs, there may be changes in the business of childbirth, when science becomes involved, with far-reaching results. Last week we were in New York to see the opening of a film starring my attractive actor son-in-law Alessandro. He also has a handsome, charming brother. They are members of an Italian-American family and have the fine looks of their Sardinian artist grandfather, who arrived penniless in New York in 1942 and was lucky not to be met with our present 'crackdown' on asylum seekers. After the opening of a film he starred in,

141

Alessandro had a meeting with one of the film's executives, who inquired if he'd mind asking his father to donate his sperm to her lesbian girlfriend. Surprisingly enough, Alessandro's father, an adviser to the government in Washington, was reluctant to do so.

Family life is going to take a battering from a new law suggested by politicians who proclaim its values; and this also concerns sperm donors. Those actors who have rested too long, or men of other professions down on their luck, who wank for a few pounds and provide a supply for would-be parents in difficulty must now make their names and identities known to the families they help to create. You can see horrendous scenes following. The resting actor might win the lottery and be sued for the maintenance of all the children his part-time occupation produced. Or, perhaps worse, the wanker for money might want to claim 'his' children and take over the family.

Worse still, parents are to be compelled to tell their children whom their natural, or sperm-giving, father was. As a considerable percentage of children born in marriage are not in fact fathered by their mother's husband, secrets will be suddenly revealed to everyone's embarrassment and a sudden rise in the divorce rate will follow. Jewish custom, which traces descent solely from the mother, is more sensible and more discreet. Our own lawgivers can't accept the fact that there are many things in family life that are best kept shrouded in mystery.

Family life, in my experience, far from being dull and secure, is a constantly unfolding drama. One Saturday evening, at our home in the country, my youngest daughter had brought home a boyfriend with whom her relationship was over. He was naturally depressed, possibly suicidal. Alessandro's mother was staying with us and preparations for his and my daughter Emily's wedding were gripping the household like the production of a major film. In the kitchen where we assembled, the cat, who lives a secret life in and out of the upstairs windows, entered in pursuit of a mouse. The cat was pursued by a liberated Jack Russell, who showed every sign of wanting to eat it. With her nerves already at breaking point, my fox-hunting wife grabbed the mouse and prepared to kill it with a single blow from the wooden hammer more often used to flatten steaks. This led to a general uproar of protest from my daughters, the ex-boyfriend and Alessandro's mother. Raising the hammer, my wife was resolute. 'If this mouse lives,' she said, 'there'll be eight more mice in the world before you've had time to count.' As the argument increased there was a gentle knock on the kitchen door and Elizabeth, our neighbour from a mile down the hill, entered holding a cup. 'Can any of you spare a little of that liquid you use for cleaning contact lenses?' was what she asked.

In her surprise, my wife relaxed her grip on the mouse, which made a dash for freedom. The cat was gathered up, the Jack Russell expelled and the now ex-boyfriend cheered up. Family values were seen at their best.

CHAPTER TWENTY-TWO

MISSED OPPORTUNITIES

'I'm not very good at sex, Jane. But with you I'll really *try*,' is a pretty hopeless sort of approach to any woman, but I'm assured it was said to a friendly publicist by one of her more serious and not entirely successful authors. Equally hopeless are such gambits as 'My wife doesn't understand me,' or, even worse, 'Sex with you would do wonders for my prose style.' If you want to improve your prose style, read Gibbon, Lytton Strachey, Evelyn Waugh and Hemingway. If you want to make love it is better to say so plainly, without claiming any literary reward for your trouble.

My wife overheard a different, more sporting approach on the hunting field. A would-be lover rode up to a handsome, lively middle-aged woman and said, 'I say, Daphne, how about a gun in your shoot?' The reply was, I'm afraid, disappointing. 'No thanks,' she said, 'I'm fully syndicated at the moment.'

It's well known that John Betjeman, summing up his regrets on his deathbed, said, 'Not enough sex,' and it is the missed opportunities of your youth that will haunt your old age. I shall never forget the friendly girl who, long ago, said, 'Let's go down to Soho and do something sordid.' I, in my stupidity, thought she was suggesting some rather dirty restaurant and turned down the offer. There will be a long future of kicking yourself for not understanding such simple approaches as, 'Where

145

will you be spending the night?' and you answered, 'I'd better be going home. I've got a lot to do in the morning.' A lot to do! Whatever it was has long been forgotten; what will always be remembered is the night that didn't happen.

It's often said that men desire women for their looks but women fancy men for some less reliable quality, like their characters or their supposed position in the world. We, the vast majority of non-beautiful people, can only hope this is true.

If it is, it puts men at an unfair advantage. If you work hard at it, you might be able to improve your character, or even your position in the world. Beauty is something you can do absolutely nothing about. It is distributed in the most unfair, politically incorrect and anti-democratic manner. It is bestowed on the least deserving and often denied to the best, unselfish and kindly intentioned people. Quite often the unfair nature of this gift causes resentment, not only from jealous women. I have known beautiful girls who have been badly treated and slighted by men who feel eclipsed by such spanking looks.

I have a beautiful wife and beautiful daughters and I would never say they don't deserve such luck. The fact is mildly surprising, however, as I look, as some newspaper put it kindly, 'like a bag of spanners'. The great majority of male spanner lookalikes must work out a careful approach and avoid anything as hopeless as promising to try hard. Stendhal, no oil painting but a man who notched up his conquests on his braces, relied on laughter and boasted, perhaps truthfully, that he could beat the record of the best-looking men. There is much to be said for this approach. My experience as a counsel for the defence down at the Old Bailey was that if you could get the jury laughing you were likely to win the case. The more solemn the proceedings became, the less happy the verdict was likely to be.

If it's not true that men are loved only for their characters, or their positions of power, it's equally mistaken to believe that all women are called upon to be reproductions of Miss Dynamite or Catherine Zeta-Jones. One of the miracles of life is that few people pass through it without finding someone to love them. Awkward, even impossible people find love and it's a great convenience if they find it with each other. As someone said, it was very kind of God to arrange for Thomas Carlyle to marry Jane Carlyle, because 'it meant that only two people were unhappy instead of four'.

The mysterious forces which compel the most unlikely to dedicate their lives to each other can't be explained. I can only repeat that missed opportunities, in life and love, may haunt you for ever. Opportunities should be taken gratefully, even if the results may be somewhat bizarre. Long ago, in the distant days of Angus Steak Houses and Mateus Rosé and Frankie Vaughan singing 'Give Me the Moonlight', I took a new-found friend out to dinner. Later I drove her back to her flat in a London square in which the front doors were flanked by rows of bells for different apartments. She suggested I come up to hers after I'd parked the car. Before she left me she touched her hair and said, 'I'd better warn you. All this comes off.'

Left alone in the car, I came to the conclusion that what she had told me meant that she was bald. Did I want to get into bed with a bald-headed woman? No, I did not. Should I not then turn the car around and drive straight home without any further explanation? Perhaps. But wouldn't that be a cowardly, even a mean and unkind thing to do? It wasn't, after all, her fault that she was bald and it would be dreadful to remind her of the fact in such a dramatic fashion. I hit on another solution. I'd take my glasses off. My sight is so short that I wouldn't be able to see how bald she was.

After I'd parked the car I rang the top bell, as I had seen her do beside the front door, and was rewarded by a deeply sexy voice saying, 'Come upstairs.' I obeyed, with my glasses off, and found the top flat's door opened by a blurred but distinctly bald figure wearing a dressing gown. I threw my arms round it, only to discover it was a bald-headed, quite elderly man and I was in the wrong house.

Having beaten a hasty and apologetic retreat, I finally got to the right flat and found that my companion had perfectly acceptable hair which had been covered with a wig. It was, as I say, a bizarre evening but not one I've lived to regret.

CHAPTER TWENTY-THREE

MAKING A FUSS

At one time, again it was in the time of my youth, the hotels, the restaurants, the railway stations of England rang to the sound of middle-aged, middle-class men making a fuss. Cold plates, warm drinks, late trains, slow waiters would set them off in a roar. Their voices, raised in anger, could be heard in Europe as they progressed from Calais to the Promenade des Anglais in Cannes, complaining about the state of the lavatories or the inadequacy of the breakfasts.

They had, no doubt some of them had, been unhinged by the 1914–18 war. We had a prep school master who used to shout, 'Strafe and shell you, boy!' as he hurled books at our heads and then, wretchedly apologetic, compensated us with small gifts of money. Our young ears were blasted by middle-aged rage. For the children of such men, life was a perpetual embarrassment; you had to pretend that the red-faced aggrieved adult seated at your table was no sort of relation.

The law courts, in these early days, echoed with ill-temper. There was a judge who used to throw his pencil down in a pet and call out in a loud voice, 'We are not a stable!' if he thought his court wasn't receiving the respect it deserved. Another would greet a nervous barrister by saying, 'If you want to practise I suggest you practise at home.' Offended advocates would bang out of courts; clerks would have to be sent to reconcile them to judges who

149

had gone too far. Even without such interruptions, proceedings were often unfriendly. 'Your argument, Mr Smith,' said one judge to the future Lord Birkenhead, 'is simply going into one of my ears and out of the other.'

'Perhaps, my Lord,' was the advocate's reply, 'that's because there's nothing in between.'

When the judge, further goaded, said, 'Why do you think I'm sitting here, Mr Smith?' the answer was, 'It's not for me to inquire into the inscrutable ways of providence.'

Birkenhead was highly skilled at turning a fuss to his advantage. Having failed to be elected as a member of the Reform Club, he habitually, when passing its doors, called in to use its lavatory. After many anxious meetings, the committee decided it was time to make a fuss and a fuss, of a surprisingly gentle sort, was made by the secretary. He met the peer on his way out of the Gents. 'Lord Birkenhead,' he fussed politely, 'I've been asked to remind you that this *is* a members' club.'

'Oh, really?' His Lordship did his best to sound interested. 'Is it that *as well*?'

Unless you have Birkenhead's gift for repartee it's unwise to lose your temper in court. You may, of course, make a considerable fuss, and even pretend extreme anger, but to lose it in reality would be extremely dangerous. In real life the ability to make a fuss has been secretly curtailed by the intolerance of children. In my childhood we listened patiently when our fathers bellowed protests against waiters who invariably interrupted their best stories just before the punch line by asking, 'Who's having the fish?'

Now if you go into a shop and interrupt the

conversation behind the counter by asking for a little help in choosing the lingerie, your children will flee from you, hide behind the coats, pretend you're not related or even set off for home. It's a battle you can't win, so it's better to keep quiet, or reserve your fussing for worthier issues, such as the destruction of the presumption of innocence or other matters in which the children may allow you to fuss.

Dickens—not, as I have said, perfect in his attention to family values—could make a magnificent and effective fuss when the occasion demanded it. He wrote *Nicholas Nickleby* and put an end to ghastly Yorkshire schools. He derided and scorned the law's unbearable delays, the Poor Law and the hopeless inefficiency of government bureaucracy. He discovered that there were more than 100,000 London children who had no education, even at a 'ragged school'. And the ragged schools he visited were very ragged indeed, filled with children living by thieving and prostitution, filthy, illiterate and 'with all the deadly sins let loose'. He was moved to give a lecture, or write a pamphlet, on the desperate plight of children who slept in doorways, under bridges and in saw-pits. Happily he didn't write a pamphlet but produced *A Christmas Carol*, in which what he called the 'doomed children' appear as Ignorance and Want, sheltering under the cloak of the Spirit of Christmas Present.

So fuss as much as you like about poverty, overcrowded prisons, locked-up children and social injustice, or even the abolition of outdoor sex, but lay off the waiter.

151

It's not that young people can't make fusses for themselves. In fact they have taken the place of the middle-aged, middle-class man in protesting at the unfairness of life, the disgusting ostentation of their parents' car or their mother's consumption of cigarettes. Sometimes their fusses can be well phrased and effective.

We were travelling to Australia for a family Christmas in the sun when Emily's then boyfriend, a talented actor, joined the plane at Singapore and, although booked in steerage, joined my daughter in club class, sharing her seat and starting to snog her enthusiastically. Sitting next to them, it was my turn to pretend that I was no relation, until the steward arrived and told the lover that he was embarrassing those seated in club class and would he kindly return to the tourists.

At this he stood up and, projecting in a way that might have been heard throughout the plane, declaimed, 'Very well. But, everyone, look at this! This is what they did to Romeo and Juliet.'

CHAPTER TWENTY-FOUR

GIVING MONEY TO BEGGARS

You should, I think, provided you have any of it at all, give money to beggars.

Begging is, after all, an ancient and honourable profession. Indian priests depended entirely on the contents of their begging bowls, monks and wandering friars begged for Jesus. Giving money to beggars produces a minor sense of generosity and well-being in the giver and some immediate satisfaction in the recipient. Such pleasant transactions are anathemas to those New Puritans who now rule us, and may survive to rule over you, the heirs to this testament. As in the grim reign of Oliver Cromwell, begging is to be made a criminal offence (in the days of the Great Protector, actors were subject to the same law). So the street sleepers, the unhappy children who have left home after a domestic row, the confused ageing women sleeping under newspapers, all of whom put their hands out to you as you pass from the theatre to the restaurant, will be given criminal convictions and moved, at huge public expense, from the nests they have made in doorways and under arches to Her Majesty's Prisons.

I spent some time talking to the street sleepers in an area of London between Lincoln's Inn Fields and the Embankment. They included middle-aged men who couldn't cope with filling in forms, paying rent and taxes, applying for jobs they didn't get or queuing up for public assistance. There was also a man who had been the manager of a supermarket with a car, holidays on the Costa Brava and a wife he loved very much who left him to go off with a soldier. After a period of misery he met an Italian girl at evening classes. They got married but she and their baby were run down and killed on a pedestrian crossing. This was too much for him. He locked up his house, posted his key back through the letter box and went to live on the streets.

The dedicated street sleepers, the respectable beggars who are no longer young, don't want to move into hostels where they might be attacked by young tearaways and have the few possessions they wander around with all day stolen. They don't go entirely without food. Four-wheel drives from the Home Counties come, often accompanied by a vicar intent on good works, and soup is ladled out. Late at night they get the leftover sandwiches from Marks & Spencer in bin liners. By this time they have become quite choosy, throwing out the BLTs in a search for the prawn and mayo. Except on the coldest nights, street-sleeping suits them so well that an elderly lady who had been taken into hospital begged to be rescued by her friends. They called at the hospital and managed, looking, I suppose, like porters, to trundle her out of the building in her bed and push her down to her preferred sleeping place—under the arches of an office block not far from the river.

These arches provide the four-star accommodation. Underneath them it's dry and out of the wind, and the regulars have their places reserved with their trannies and paperbacks, their blankets and old newspapers, all ready for the night. Do they beg? Well, of course they do. If you

154

can get a place at the end of Hungerford Bridge you can make thirty pounds on a good day. Not many of them get this prime spot. It may go to the younger generation, who sleep where the heat comes up from the kitchens behind the Strand Palace Hotel.

Are they aggressive? I have to say that I haven't met an aggressive beggar in London. In New York, crossing 58th Street from the Plaza Oyster Bar to the Wyndham Hotel, I came up against a huge black man in a long, dark overcoat who said, in deep and threatening tones, 'Give me fifty dollars!' I managed to ask him if he would be content with thirty-five and, rather to my surprise, he said, 'All right, give me thirty-five dollars!' And so the deal was done.

Before we dismiss all those asking for our loose change as criminals, we should consider whether we're not all beggars. Every morning a shoal of letters and faxes arrives at my home begging for money for dozens of different causes, from the provision of deaf aids in African villages to funding a Conceptual Arts Centre in East Anglia. Many of the requests are persuasive and the causes worthy and they come with shiny brochures, well-designed graphics and forms asking for sums of money beyond the wildest dreams of anyone sitting in front of a saucer on the end of Hungerford Bridge.

The great and the good give lunches, or evenings with champagne and canapés, on the terrace of the House of Lords, at which they can beg from each other and solicit money for each other's favourite charities. I have gone begging for the Royal Court Theatre, the Howard League for Penal Reform, various other theatres and institutions, with my hand shamelessly held out to tycoons, managers of trust funds and government representatives. Like the street sleepers on the Embankment, I have tried to shame total strangers into parting with their loose change.

We don't beg only for money. We beg for love, doing our best to look needy and anxious to please. The world of advertising is devoted to begging people to spend money on things they may not really need. Politicians, those who seek to imprison far more honest and straightforward beggars, beg shamelessly for votes in exchange for promises they are never going to keep.

So what should be done about beggars? The confused and, perhaps, abused young who have left home after a quarrel clearly need looking after. But the older practitioners who have mismanaged their lives, or even prefer the freedom of the streets, should be left to exercise a profession more honourable than that of many bankers, share pushers or sellers of pension schemes. They will need your help from time to time in their efforts, which should be warmly welcomed by the New Labour government, to transfer the business of welfare to the private sector.

CHAPTER TWENTY-FIVE

EATING OUT

I have already advised you to avoid restaurants which offer multiple choices, twelve starters, fifteen main courses, all sorts of puddings, described on shiny paper in a menu bound in scarlet with gold tassels. As with the choices offered nowadays on television, these are likely to provide no more than a wide selection of rubbish.

There are other basic rules, such as avoiding any restaurant where the name of the chef is known to the public; still worse if he—it always seems to be a 'he'—appears on television. Also run a mile from any eatery where the waiter starts to lecture you on the food. Conversation, in some highly expensive joints I have visited, has ground to a halt during the cheese course while Damon or Jasper, our waiter for the evening, gives a lengthy talk on the history of the Caerphilly, or describes the exact amount of fermentation undergone by the *chèvre* from the valley of the Loire. All you need to do while you're eating cheese is to get on with the argument, or the reconciliation, the friendship or the remotely possible consummation you came out for.

Worse even than lectures about the cheese are instructions on how to eat. I have been in a Florida restaurant where we were fitted up with bibs like so many middle-aged babies and talked down through the crab. The language was that used to land aeroplanes in distress and the same calm, reassuring voice was adopted by the waiter: 'Grasp

157

the claw firmly in the left hand and crack the hard shell of the claw with the instrument provided. A sharp pressure should produce a crack which will enable you to scoop out the crab flesh. This you can dip into either the French mayonnaise or the Thousand Island Sauce.'

Food in France, Italy or China is based on peasant cooking and has been handed down from grandmothers to mothers and daughters, who stick to traditional dishes. Supermarkets, fast-food outlets and the American cultural invasion have diminished our home cooking and most of our restaurants have lost all contact with the food we used to think of as traditionally English. Boiled mutton and caper sauce, baked jam roll, even steak and kidney pudding seem as remote as bowler hats or cherrywood pipes. Dominating star chefs have broken with the past and we are no longer the land of roast duck and apple sauce, roast lamb and mint sauce (a delicacy which always puzzled the French), but the country of rocket and sun-dried tomatoes, monkfish artfully arranged with pink sauce, a single peeled prawn and a sprig of dill, or a little castle made of venison doused in redcurrant coulis, which has also been used to draw patterns on the side of the plate.

Traditional English cooking could also be found in pubs but with one or two notable exceptions they, too, have surrendered to Caesar salad, pesto risotto and New Zealand Sauvignon. So, to find cooking which is still hanging on to its roots, you'd better go to France or, if you take my advice, to Italy.

'I have prepared my peace,' Yeats wrote, 'with learned Italian things'. Italian things, not necessarily learned, must be part of any sensible last will and testament. The English need Italy as gardens need the sun. It can teach us how to live with our history, to find drama in everyday life and lighten our national tendency to gloom. It was always so. From the nineteenth century our greatest writers, from Byron to Browning to D. H. Lawrence, fled to Italy, and all tourists there were known as 'Inglese', regardless of their country of origin. So a Florentine hotelier was heard to say, 'I've got ten Inglese in tonight, four are French, four German and two Russian.' Harold Acton, wholly dedicated to Italy, told me that Pen Browning, the Brownings' son, was 'extremely interested in fornication' and so the bars and restaurants around Florence are peopled by direct descendants of the Barretts of Wimpole Street.

Every Italian city had not only its own history but also its own masterpiece in the cathedral, its own food, its own wine and often its own language. The Neapolitan dialect is incomprehensible to the pure-speaking Florentine. You wouldn't expect to eat spaghetti with clams in Bologna or wild boar pâté in Naples. If you want a town where the present and the past are still vividly alive, go to Siena. It's divided into parishes, which compete in the extraordinary horse-race round the scallop-shell-shaped piazza twice a year. The Palio, which celebrates a victory over rival Florence, takes only a few minutes but the preparations and the processions are unforgettable. The horses spend the previous night in local churches, to which they are led by men singing, and if they manure the marble floors it's a sign of luck. The long procession before the race, with parishioners in

159

medieval costume throwing twirling flags into the air as high as the houses, unwinds slowly. Knights in armour, with their visors down, ride by to celebrate the parishes that no longer exist. Finally the Palio itself, a huge silver dish, is driven round on a cart drawn by white oxen. The secret ambition of all the parishes is not to win (winning entails a great deal of expense) but to have their enemy come second—a true humiliation.

The Palio has more importance than even the beauty of the event in Europe's most perfect city centre. Loyalty to your parish is so great that women giving birth in a hospital outside their home area take a little tray of earth from their home parish to put under the bed. And the parishes organize events, football matches, parties and dinners for young and old, rich and poor, all the year round. The system works so well that there is little juvenile crime in Siena. It should certainly be tried in Birmingham, preferably with a colourful horse-race round the Bull Ring.

Italian communists, who are about as far to the left as English Liberals, have done well in the preservation of Siena; but I must warn you about a deterioration in the Communist Party. One of the greatest pleasures you can look forward to in the summer is the outdoor opera in front of the cathedral in San Gimignano, the city of tall towers and Ghirlandaio. The former communist mayor wore Armani suits, drove a Mercedes, had a most elegant wife and always got us front-row seats at the opera, and occasional champagne. Sadly he has retired, and the present communist mayor wears trousers that might have come from Marks & Spencer and drives something like a Fiat Uno. He

160

failed to provide us with champagne or front-row seats, so we detected a decline in the standards of Italian communism. Nothing has deteriorated, however, in the joy of watching the dusk turn to darkness and the moon rising as Rigoletto's tragedy unfolds, or hearing *Tosca* sung to an accompaniment of wailing car alarms in the neighbouring streets.

There is no deterioration either in the restaurant I'll leave to you. You must cross the Piazza del Campo in Siena and find a narrow street at the side of the Palazzo Pubblico. A little way up this street is Le Logge. You can sit outside it next to the façade of a Renaissance church, opposite the houses where the young are shouting down from bedroom windows and the old are sitting in chairs outside the front doors to enjoy the endless drama of the streets. As the motor bicycles whip by, a music student on holiday plays the flute and wandering refugees try to sell you erotic cigarette lighters. Or you can eat inside in an elegant nineteenth-century room which looks like the Café Momus in *La Bohème*. You can eat malfatti, a sort of pasta rarely met elsewhere, and drink the wine Gianni and Laura, who own the place, produce on their vineyards near Montalcino.

We are often in Italy with Ann Mallalieu and her husband, Tim Cassell, both lawyers but, whereas she is a Labour member of the House of Lords, he is full of charm and way to the right, not only of Genghis Khan but of Tony Blair and Margaret Thatcher. Some years ago Ann was defending a number of gay sadomasochists who, although harmless to others, found pleasure in nailing each other's genitalia to wooden boards in the privacy of

161

an airport hotel. It was Tim asking his wife, as barristers will, 'When's your penis torture beginning, darling?' that caused a great many heads to turn as we sat having our pre-dinner drinks in the Piazza del Campo.

Gianni invited us all to lunch in a house near to their vineyard. We sat down at a long table under the vines with all their friends, relations and waiters. After a good many bottles of wine, our hosts began to sing, quietly at first and then with growing fervour, *'Ciao, bella, oh! Ciao, bella, oh ciao bella, oh ciao, ciao, ciao.'* Our friend Tim joined in lustily, smiling and happy until I told him that what he was singing was a song of the communist resistance, at which point he stopped singing with an expression almost as pained as though he had been nailed up in some airport hotel.

CHAPTER TWENTY-SIX

THE PURSUIT OF HAPPINESS

It's as hard for a writer to describe happiness as it is to create a totally good character. Most of Shakespeare's comedies and many of his tragedies end with the re-establishment of a normal, peaceful and happy existence. But that's a state he carefully avoids writing about because it wouldn't be particularly good theatre. When happiness breaks out on the stage it is time to ring down the curtain. Henry James spoke for many writers when he referred to the 'bread sauce of the happy ending'. If happiness doesn't make good theatre, is it something to be actively pursued in life?

On the whole politicians don't think so. They have achieved greater fame by offering us blood, tears and sweat, saying grimly, 'Today the struggle,' and recommending death on the barricades or the battlefield as a more exciting option. Religions have also, by and large, taken a pretty grim view of existence.

The Greek gods, it's true, seemed capable of enjoying a good time. They may have been wilful, jealous, temperamental and frequently uncaring, but they were at least interested in sex and would take the trouble to transform themselves into various animals in the pursuit of love. For mere mortals, moments of sun-soaked delight, and the excitement of the Dionysian revels, were forever overshadowed by darker fears and terrors. On account of some, perhaps unconscious, crime or inherited shortcoming, the Furies would pursue you relentlessly and to the ends of the earth.

Christianity offered happiness beyond the grave, but it has been less encouraging during what Noël Coward said he believed in, 'life before death'. The way to heaven is often portrayed as hard and stony, demanding self-sacrifice, confession of sins, begging forgiveness, even martyrdom before receiving the final reward. Religions have prescribed penitence, pilgrimages or holy wars. There has been, among the faithful, very little talk of enjoying a thoroughly good time.

I suppose that the idea of humanity's right to happiness started at the time of the American Declaration of Independence, which as far as I can discover was the first document which held the truth to be self-evident that all men are endowed with certain inalienable rights, among which were 'life, and liberty, and the pursuit of happiness'. In spite of worries about wealth, diet, terrorism, eating too much salt, taking exercise and failing to conform to the company's image, most Americans do feel, I'm sure, that happiness is worth pursuing. The English are resigned to its being as incalculable, and perhaps as disappointing, as the weather.

Is the idea of happiness an entirely human invention? Animals are contented when they are feeding or asleep, a condition dogs enjoy most of the time. When they're awake and going about their business, they seem usually nervous, peering about them for signs of danger and taking sudden fright. Horses shy at a blown newspaper, a footstep in the woods sends rooks clattering up to the sky, rabbits panicking and deer cantering into the darkness of closer trees, deeper undergrowth. As Shelley knew, human beings also find moments of contentment suddenly filled with anxiety, which sends us scurrying away into the shadows:

> We look before and after;
> We pine for what is not;
> Our sincerest laughter
> With some pain is fraught.

At high moments of love, how many men are looking furtively at their watches behind some tousled head and thinking, It's time I was back in the office? How many women are wondering how on earth they got involved with a person who keeps his socks on? At the liveliest restaurant dinner, someone is worrying about the bill. On the most idyllic beaches there is a general concern about flies, mosquitoes, where the children have got to now or how to make conversation for a whole week with a partner who's usually at work all day and sleeps in front of the television at night. Like nervous animals, our natural state is one of anxiety.

We worry about most things, and then worry about worrying, or worry if we suddenly find there's nothing much to worry about. And if you've got nothing to worry about, the government will oblige by starting a war, for instance, or telling you that the streets are about to be taken over by violent and abusive beggars. Politicians are in desperate need of fear and anxiety in order that they may appear to be the only persons who can steer us safely through these dangers.

I can only suggest you do your best to banish anxiety, possibly with a glass of champagne, and lay yourself open to the moment when happiness becomes irresistible. I'm writing this at a good time of the year. The beech trees are covered with fresh, green leaves—we are going to have a birthday lunch in the garden. My grandchildren will play in the mysterious sunken copses, disused flint pits now filled with tall and ancient trees, where I also played as a child. The daffodils will be in flower and the dogs will be jumping over them. There is every possible reason for happiness; but it's also a moment of sadness too. How many more such birthdays will there be? It's sad my mother never saw Rosie and Emily, my daughters, grow up. Although Shelley was right about our sincerest laughter being fraught with sadness, it's the sadness, in a way, which makes happiness complete.

There is a story about a devoted fisherman, in love with the sport, who went to sleep and found himself, on a perfect day, fishing in a clear stream. Every time he cast he hooked a fine salmon. After this had happened a dozen times in succession he asked the gillie where he was. Was it, perhaps, heaven? No, he was told, it's hell. Happiness too often or too regularly repeated becomes misery. And here perhaps we're getting near to what happiness is for me. Happiness is a by-product. If it's sought for deliberately, desperately, it's elusive and often deceptive, like the distant sight of an oasis. If you aim to live a life that is eventful, interesting, exciting, even though it's bound to be also disappointing, frustrating and with inevitable moments of despair, happiness may, from time to time, unexpectedly turn up.

When I was a child I was stage-struck. Now I

only have to go into an empty auditorium to see a rehearsal, or even those draughty, dusty, church halls where the seats are indicated with marker tape on the floor and the actors are drinking instant coffee out of paper cups, to find excitement, a flow of adrenalin, a happiness and an expectation that I suppose some people get from robbing banks. That's the moment of happiness which usually gets to its high point in the final rehearsal. From then on it's downhill, the piece is done and then shown, and alas the public are let in. Anxiety mounts, worries take over—will they, won't they, like it? The gloom lifts gradually, normal life returns and you prepare for another moment of happiness and another exposure to disaster.

And for writers, certainly for barristers after they have won cases, and, I imagine, for surgeons after a successful operation and architects after the building has gone up, there is greater happiness in finishing things. This happiness is also of course combined with some feeling of loss. I think it has been best described by Edward Gibbon, who speaks of the moment of triumph when he laid down his pen, having completed *The Decline and Fall of the Roman Empire*: 'But my pride was soon humbled, and a sober melancholy spread over my mind, by the idea that I had taken an everlasting leave of an old and agreeable companion.'

And happiness can take you over completely and without regret at the most unexpected and apparently inappropriate moments. Basingstoke was once a pleasant country town, but soulless new buildings and gigantic office blocks have made it drearily unattractive. I was performing in the theatre there and, because the dressing room was

167

down a long flight of stairs, they fixed me up with somewhere to change in a small paint shop at the side of the stage. The sink was full of paintbrushes, paint-stained newspapers littered the floor, the walls were decorated with old saws and various tools, and there was, of course, no loo. One of the actresses I was performing with found me a bucket.

So there was I on a wet Sunday evening, peeing into a bucket in a small paint shop beside a stage in Basingstoke. It suddenly occurred to me, much to my surprise, that I was completely happy.

CHAPTER TWENTY-SEVEN

LOOKING AFTER YOUR HEALTH

I have to confess that when a doctor asked me if I found myself out of breath when taking exercise, I had to say, 'How would I know? I've never taken exercise.'

Exercise has become, in my lifetime, the modern form of prayer. When religious belief faltered, and faith in immortality and an afterlife free of any kind of physical disability faded, it became essential to prolong a healthy life on earth by all available means. Gyms, saunas and swimming pools took the place of churches and chapels. A little sports bag slung over the shoulder took the place of hymn books and missals as the faithful passed to their devotions. The father confessor was replaced by the personal trainer; voices once raised in hymns are now united in the muted drone of the yoga class and the muttered counting of swimming-pool lengths.

It's hard to say if these new religious rituals bring as much joy to the congregations as older forms of religion and it's difficult to know exactly how effective they are. You seldom see a happy, even a cheerful-looking, jogger and it's often said that the only people who lose weight from massage are the masseurs, who sweat away, kneading bulging stomachs or inflated bottoms. However that may be, and as with the older religious observances, it's not the immediately obvious results that matter but the assertion of faith in a better life to come.

I don't particularly want to hand my atheistical prejudices on to those who will come after me. It's true that the word 'gym' has always been associated in my mind with smelly plimsolls, cold showers, daunting vaulting horses, ropes I couldn't climb and unnecessary dashes to the top of the wall bars. 'Taking exercise' at school always meant for me changing into shorts and then hiding in the loo behind the squash court with a good book. I don't mean to recommend a total disbelief in the worship of health, but to inspire, perhaps, a little agnosticism.

No one could ever wish you a painful illness, a shortened life or a serious disability. The complaints I inherited, asthma and glaucoma, are enough of an inconvenience. And yet you may find some minor ailment, a disability you can learn to live with, could have its advantages. If one of your legs gives up the struggle against old age, you can experience the pleasure and privilege of a wheelchair at airports and be drawn, like an emperor on his chariot, through the struggling crowds to be taken first on to the plane. At JFK you will be driven in a further triumph past the half-a-mile-long queue of travellers waiting to have their passports stamped, to be whisked through with the minimum amount of fuss.

Failing eyesight has also proved useful and there are moments when it's a help to reduce the world around you to a comforting blur. When I was briefed in obscenity cases, it was part of our duty to watch the blue movies we were defending put on by the sergeant in charge of the projector at Scotland Yard. To actually see these entertainments was likely to put you off sex, at least until next Thursday. To protect myself against this affliction I used to take off my glasses and the picture was then reduced to a formless pink blur. I was spared the pain of one defendant who, at his trial, begged the judge to send him down to the cells so that he might not have to watch the stuff he sold. 'No,' said the merciless and hard-hearted judge, 'you'll sit in the dock and watch every second of it!'

Moderate deafness can also have its advantages. If you are known to be hard of hearing you obviously haven't heard inconvenient remarks or instructions. Evelyn Waugh derived great pleasure and assistance from his ear trumpet. When a conversation at dinner bored him he would merely lower it and retreat into merciful silence and contemplation.

Another advantage of the minor disability is that it provides fresh conversational openings as an alternative to the weather or the war. People can say, 'How's the leg?' and feel they have done you a kindness, which you needn't repay by telling them. Long ago I knew an elderly barrister, healthy and quite free from pain, who had an imaginary complaint which he called 'my old trouble'. 'How are you, Hugh?' people used to say to him, and he'd answer, 'Perfectly all right, apart from my "old trouble", of course.' 'Well, how is the old trouble?' 'Much as always, I'm afraid.' This 'old trouble' saved him from dinner parties ('I'd love to of course, but the old trouble's been playing me up in the evenings lately'), holidays he didn't want to go on, or cases he felt sure he'd lose. I merely mention it in passing, but an 'old trouble' is something you may find extremely useful as the years go by.

CHAPTER TWENTY-EIGHT

INVENTIONS AND THE DECLINE
OF LANGUAGE

During my lifetime inventions have fallen upon us as thick and fast as cluster bombs in some war against terrorism, with the intention of destabilizing the civilian population. Life, let us say between the publication of *David Copperfield* and *Mrs Dalloway*, didn't change enormously. But since then it has altered greatly due to a proliferation of inventions. It's as hard to think of Virginia Woolf surfing the Internet, or walking with a mobile phone clamped to her ear, riding an exercise bicycle, watching a DVD or sending a text message as it is to think of the Duke of Wellington in a Jeep or Shakespeare with a word processor.

It's tempting to wonder how many of the inventions of the past century we might have been better off without. Take the aeroplane, for instance. It has transformed warfare from an event in which trained soldiers kill each other on distant battlefields to occasions when death is rained down indiscriminately on innocent civilians, while the professional fighters fly at a great height in comparative safety.

I can remember the train journeys to the South of France in my childhood, asleep in a dark mahogany compartment, dinner under the pink-shaded lights of the restaurant car, waking up at three in the morning to the clatter of newspaper trolleys on Lyons station and going back to sleep, until you woke up again to bright sunlight on the olive groves. Perhaps it's only the memories of childhood which make it seem a better experience than sitting, vaguely terrified, as a tubular machine bumps and rattles its way through the clouds offering you plastic food and no view of the countryside.

All right, it's no doubt far too late to do without the aeroplane, but did we ever need the mobile phone? Watch the crowds go by, one hand pressed to the side of their heads as though they are all suffering from a powerful earache, muttering incessantly to other marchers in other crowds clasping their hands to the side of their faces. The climax to the widespread use of the new technology came when a man was seen relieving himself in the Gents of a London hotel. One hand held his member and directed his stream, with the other he was expertly sending a text message on his mobile phone. Once people sat still to make phone calls. Now the summons of some particularly maddening little tune is the cue for a walk round the garden or a heaven-sent opportunity to start making a cheese soufflé with the free hand. It's doubtful if this invention has added much to the sum total of human happiness.

Then there is computer technology, an invention that throws off such a strong atmosphere of sexual allure that it makes our leaders feel young, up to date, thrusting and in touch, and in schools learning to manipulate these devices seems to have crowded out lessons in history, literature and music. My first thought about computers was that they slowed down communication considerably. Take getting into a hotel room, for instance. In my youth you arrived and the receptionist looked in a book, ticked something with a pen, unhooked a key and you were in. Now you're met with a puzzled girl whose name is on a little plaque pinned to her lapel. She starts to play the computer like a bewildered and uncertain composer in search of a tune—a considerable time passes and various chords are struck and discord often follows. Once I was allocated a room in a part of the hotel that hadn't yet been built.

No doubt you can get reams of information from computers, and find out all about Einstein, Gérard de Nerval and cheap air tickets, and you can work from home. There lies the greatest danger. Soon office life will be a thing of the past, everyone will stay at home all day, peering at screens and communicating by e-mail, often irritating their husbands and wives or partners, who long for the days when they were out of the way by seven thirty in the morning. There will be an end to office romances, kisses snatched in the postroom and the fascinating plots and counter-plots of office politics. Lonely workers at home will remember with nostalgia the happy days of catching the eight fifteen to Waterloo.

We might ask the scientists of our time to give it a rest, take a long holiday and stop inventing things for at least another half a century. It's important to remember that all these ingenious ways of sending messages have no importance in themselves. The 'medium is the message' is one of the world's silliest remarks. The message is the message, and it doesn't matter whether you send it by e-mail, a note in a bottle or on a picture postcard. The book, or the poem, or the play is what counts and it doesn't matter if it's written with a pen on a long sheet of ruled paper, as I am writing now, or on the most highly developed word processor. No machine can help with the rhythms of your prose, even if it can spell better than you can.

Whether or not it's the fault of information technology, there has been an extraordinary deterioration in our language, at least as it's spoken by the governing classes. Words have been reduced to letters so they can fit on to a text message, and such invitations as CU4T are moderately entertaining; but in general the technological age has resulted in our language becoming divorced from grammar, growing curiously inflated and getting lost in the sort of meaningless haze that affects the directions for assembling furniture bought in parts.

Nouns like 'access', 'source' and 'task' now reappear as verbs. You can 'access' almost anything, from the refrigerator to directory inquiries. The jargon has even spread to the theatre, where new dramas get regularly 'workshopped' before audiences 'access' them. So I might 'source' a play and 'task' someone to 'workshop' it. Among the more ludicrous titles invented for government officials we are now to have an 'access regulator' who will see who gets into university. The phrase could be equally applied to a lift attendant.

This is Beverley Hughes, a government minister, as quoted by Matthew Parris in *The Times*. She is talking, although you might not notice the fact, about identity cards:

'I think an entitlement card could offer some

important contributions both to the challenges we face and also to some important new concepts that we're trying to introduce to this issue around entitlement and also around citizenship, but the most important thing is that we actually stimulate debate, a widespread debate, among ordinary people, and I think, I *hope* that because we have actually, genuinely tried to bring a really fresh look and some creative thinking to the debate, that I hope people will be, I hope, pleasantly surprised by the document; it's very comprehensive, it looks at all the issues for and against, and the important thing, as I say, is that we want to hear the voices of ordinary people.'

This has every misuse of language to which politicians are prone, including avoiding the words 'identity card', which sounds like the engine of a fascist dictatorship, and calling the same thing an 'entitlement card', which sounds as though you've won something. This is the hope behind changing the word 'refugees', which makes us feel sorry for fugitives from some tyranny, to 'asylum seekers', which seems to describe awkward people who are always trying to get something for nothing. We can no longer use the word 'unemployed' because unemployment has, of course, been abolished, so we have to talk about 'job seekers'. To call the unfriendly act of shooting your own side 'friendly fire' or the death of innocent civilians 'collateral damage' is equally cowardly and inane.

It is, of course, totally unfair but nevertheless instructive to compare Beverely Hughes to Queen Elizabeth I. You might say that they are both politicians, but Elizabeth lived at a time when you didn't seem to be able to open your mouth without speaking beautifully, whereas Beverley is of a generation that has seen our language reach the point of collapse. I don't know how long it took Elizabeth to work out what she was going to say to the fleet at Tilbury. Perhaps she did it off the cuff. I'm quite sure she didn't read her speech off a piece of paper with her head down. 'I know I have the body of a weak and feeble woman,' she said, 'but I have the heart and stomach of a king, and of a king of England too; and I think foul scorn that Parma or Spain, or any prince of Europe, should dare to invade the borders of my realm.'

It isn't only the highly educated monarch in the distant past who can still teach us how our language can be clearly and beautifully used. The 'Notable British Trials' series is full of memorable phrases used by those convicted of serious crimes. Armstrong, a Welsh solicitor, handing a poisoned scone to an intended victim, politely said, 'Excuse fingers'. Edith Thompson, an incurable romantic, a sort of Madame Bovary of Wanstead Park, was in love with a young seaman called Frederick Bywaters, whom, so it was said, she induced to stab her husband to death. One of her love letters to Bywaters is, I think, a fine example of the plain, simple but moving use of our language:

It was rather fun on Thursday at the Garden Party. They had swings and roundabouts and flipflaps, coconut shies, Aunt Sallies, Hoopla and all that sort of thing. I went in for them all and shocked a lot of people, I think. I didn't care though. I'd got a rather posh frock on, a white georgette with rows and rows of jade ribbon and white fur and large white hat, but all that didn't deter me from going into a fried fish shop in Snaresbrook and buying fish and chips. Getting it home was the worst part—it absolutely smelt the bus out. I didn't mind—it was rather fun—only I wished you had been with me. I think two halves would have enjoyed themselves, better than one half by herself.

Goodbye, for now, darlingest pal.

Edith Thompson and her lover were both hanged in 1923. The Court of Appeal said it was 'rather an ordinary sort of case'. Perhaps she died because she was too much in love, and expressed it too well.

CHAPTER TWENTY-NINE

AVOIDING UTOPIA

A map of the world which doesn't contain Utopia, Oscar Wilde said, is not worth looking at. While I think it's admirable to have Utopia on your map and that you can keep it in mind, even set off in what you imagine to be its direction, there must be no serious danger of your ever reaching it. Utopia, should it exist, might be like the common view of heaven, with absolutely nothing to complain about. Boredom in Utopia might soon set in because there would be no more to try for.

All the same, many people have described Utopia, from Thomas More to William Morris. In Samuel Butler's *Erewhon* (an anagram of nowhere), criminals are sent to hospital and the sick to prisons, an idea which has a superficial attraction but one which might not be entirely practical. In the real world attempts to produce Utopian societies have had, on the whole, disastrous results.

Russia during the Stalin era was no doubt more like hell than heaven, a place of terror rather than a just city. But Russia in the time of glasnost, the early Gorbachov years and the end of the Afghan war seemed to many people a refuge from the shallow and monetarist West. It was a country with a blessed absence of advertisements, where everyone on the Underground had their heads stuck in *War and Peace* or the translations of Dickens and J. B. Priestley, where the workers went to the ballet, where Chekhov and Gogol were seen as gods and the population spent its leisure hours cultivating the deep resources of the Russian soul.

I first met Gorbachov's Russia when I went to Moscow with our National Theatre. It was a tour of Shakespeare's three great last plays of reconciliation and forgiveness. There were minor inconveniences of course. I was shown into a hotel bedroom only to find two men in crumpled blue suits lying on the bed, watching television and eating pickled cucumbers out of a plastic bag. They were extremely reluctant to move, and I had to unpack and even start to undress before they finally left. One of the actors was less lucky. He came back late from the theatre to find a man asleep in his bed. When he complained to the stern-faced woman at the end of the corridor, she only gave an uncaring laugh and put up a small camp bed beside his unknown companion. Breakfast might take a couple of hours to come, but Muscovite friends would invite you to their houses and set out every piece of ham and cheese, every drop of vodka they still had in their cupboard, for your entertainment. Caviare and champanski were cheap at the National Hotel if you could pay by Barclaycard.

Emily was learning Russian at school and she became fluent in the language on her first visit, when she fell in love with a Russian poet. It was he who led her across Red Square in the moonlight, with the red lights twinkling over the Kremlin, and told her it was an extraordinary honour to be walking across Red Square hand in hand 'with a girl whose father defended the Sex Pistols . . .' I found it to be a general rule that the children of reasonably well-off, middle-class homes fell in love with the soulfulness of Russia. Those with more working-class backgrounds found that it stood for everything they were determined to get away from and hated it. Peter Hall, the theatre's multi-talented director, left suddenly by train for England after the oppressive Moscow reminded him too painfully of his childhood before he got into Cambridge and became a star.

But even then, in Moscow, where the ideal Utopian city was still only a distant shape on the map, I remember talking to the chain-smoking director of the Moscow Art Theatre, who was lamenting the lack of any new writers to replace not only Chekhov and Turgenev but the lesser-known authors who managed, in subtle ways, to ridicule the Party tyranny. 'They used to shake the bars of the cage,' he said, 'and that gave them their strength. Now the cage no longer has bars, they can walk about freely and they don't know where to go.' This was an unusual argument for censorship, and another warning against the discovery of Utopia.

So we moved on to Tbilisi, which is less like Utopia and more like Naples, and the Georgians, who gave birth to Stalin, think less about their souls than drinking endless toasts and persuading girls to make love at first sight. One of the actresses, wandering through the town, was accosted by a man who said, 'You have very nice breasts and I know a quiet square where we can make love immediately.'

The lorries containing the scenery and costumes broke down on the road from Moscow so that the three last plays had to be performed by actors in jeans and T-shirts, using rulers for swords. This made them look even more wonderful, but we wondered why we ever thought there was, during the Cold War, any serious danger of Russia conquering the world when they couldn't deliver the scenery for *The Tempest*.

I next visited the country some thought of as Utopia when Emily was spending a year in Moscow as part of her course at university. The soul was not, by then, the only concern of the Russians, nor did its study provide their main occupation. A big and beautiful art deco hotel near Red Square had been restored to become one of the most expensive in Europe. Having booked a table there with some difficulty, I had to feign a sudden heart attack when I saw the prices on the menu and take refuge back in the old National Hotel.

Life, however, had become easier. Great jars of caviare, duck, pork chops and Georgian wine were available for a few dollars in the market. We didn't have to take taxis (the statue of Lenin with his hand raised is said to have caught him in a vain attempt to stop a Moscow taxi). Emily walked into the middle of the road to stop any passing car which would postpone its original journey and take us to wherever we wanted to go for a few more dollars. I have seen, to my horror, Muscovites divert ambulances and even fire engines in this way.

Emily's first love, her Russian poet, still seemed to stand for the old soulful days although their romance was over. He took us to the Writers' Union, beautifully housed in the building Tolstoy used as the Rostov mansion in *War and Peace*.

When we'd first gone there it had, in fact, contained many writers. Now there were as many businessmen talking on their mobile phones. Our poet fetched bottles of variously flavoured vodka from the cellar, read us his published poem for Emily and lamented the break-up of the Soviet Union. We got seriously drunk, remembering lost times.

But there were still great moments. Emily took a course at the Moscow Art Theatre, and I watched her teacher recite Pushkin with a cigarette dangling from his lower lip. We stocked up with food from the market and had a party in Emily's flat. The place was filled with actors, some sang and one mimed the dilemma of a hunter who, with a fat bird in the sights of his gun, had an irresistible urge to visit the lavatory. There was something of soul left.

More recently Emily went back to Russia, wanting to find Stanislavsky's house and undertake further research for a book about Olga Knipper, Chekhov's wife. Her poet met her at the airport and suggested they retire to the lavatory to smoke dope and then have lunch at the Pizza Hut. Moscow, where the streets and subways were once the safest in the world, is now a city of rapes and muggings, and automatic rifles can be bargained for and bought in the kiosks which once sold sweets and magazines or, occasionally, a single shoe.

Emily went to find Stanislavsky's house, where Chekhov, writing in the garden, heard the distant sound of a little train that was reproduced in *The Cherry Orchard*. All she found was an empty field with a small notice telling visitors that Stanislavsky's house was once there. Travelling further, she found, still standing, the home of Nemirovich-Danchenko, Stanislavsky's and Chekhov's great inspirer at the Moscow Art Theatre. The house was full of workmen who had been sent to repair it but, never having been paid, couldn't get back to Moscow. Utopia was finally off the map, or it had been converted to the everyday world of crime, poverty and the doubtful values of the marketplace.

Communism and Christianity, it's been said, are the two great Utopian ideals, and we don't really know if they'd work because they've never been tried. Much the same thing can be said about democracy, which Western states, believing they have come nearer to Utopia than the darker tyrannies of the Third World, claim as their great glory and the solution to all political problems.

I suppose democracy was most nearly achieved in ancient Greece, when everyone except women and slaves took part in the government. The result was usually disastrous and led to the death of Socrates, just as the introduction of democracy in England would lead to the restoration of hanging, which the majority of the population favour. Far from having government by the people and for the people, in England we hand over what amounts to absolute power to the leader of the party with the majority of seats in Parliament. Far from the people having a say in government, the present Prime Minister has involved us in a war that most people didn't want when it started. France and Germany, whose governments obeyed their people's wish to have no part in the war, are abused as traitors to the cause of peace and democratic rule.

186

You should be wary of Members of Parliament who claim special wisdom and the right to power because they are 'democratically elected'. At periodic elections we vote for the party we have always supported and the leader who most appeals to us. Nowadays, when the hustings have fallen silent and barracking has gone out of style, few people can remember, or perhaps have ever heard, the name of their local MP unless he's a member of the government or appears on television. It's noticeable that the House of Lords, where, at the moment, no one is elected by the public, has on the whole more interesting and better-informed debates and is far more active in protecting civil rights against the brutal assaults perpetrated by Labour home secretaries who represent the party that won the election. Perhaps the House of Lords, as it is at present constituted, is attractive because, as Lord Melbourne said of the Order of the Garter, 'There's no damned merit about it.'

Our system, which we call democracy, at least leaves us the right from time to time to get rid of those who wish to govern us. And, if it's nowhere near Utopia, it is probably the best of all imperfect systems. All I can do is to advise you to be very cautious of those who claim to represent you and order you about for your own good.

*   *   *

Oscar Wilde, who knew Bernard Shaw and went to meetings of the Fabian Society, had socialism on his Utopian map. The great advantage of such a system, he thought, was that you would no longer have to endure the pain of feeling pity for the poor

187

and the oppressed and could happily devote yourself to life and art with a clear conscience. It's an attractive argument and might be more persuasive if socialist governments had been more successful in putting an end to poverty and oppression.

It was in his life, in spite of all its imperfections and misfortunes, rather than in his political beliefs, that Wilde showed the true sweetness of his nature. His friend Oswald Sickert had died and his widow had shut herself away in her room, inconsolable, and refused to see anyone. Wilde called at the house but Nellie Sickert, her daughter, told him her mother wouldn't see him. When the mother repeatedly called out, 'Send him away,' from behind a locked door, Wilde said he'd stay in the house until she opened it to him. Finally she did and he was admitted to her room. Nellie Sickert waited downstairs for the inevitable inconsolable tears.

There was a long silence and then, incredibly, she heard a strange and unexpected sound. It was her mother laughing. Wilde had charmed her, cheered her, amused her and brought her back to life. Perhaps in that moment he got nearer to Utopia than all the political systems ever thought of or looked for on maps.

CHAPTER THIRTY

FIRES WERE STARTED

One of my heroes has always been Prometheus, chained to a rock, his liver pecked out by the birds every day and restored for further torture each night—and all for conferring one of the greatest benefits on mankind. He gave back fire to us after the king of the gods, an unreliable character with dubious morals, had withdrawn it. Prometheus tricked the Olympians into eating merely the bones and fat of the beasts sacrificed to them. He also described that yawning gap which still exists between us and our gods.

Thanks to Prometheus, fire played a great part in my childhood. We had a daily ceremony, during school holidays, of burning the rubbish to the accompaniment of 'You're the cream in my coffee' played on a wind-up gramophone. We would light fires in one of the two copses in the garden and cook sausages, or bake potatoes in the dying embers, pulling them out with sticks, blowing off the grey ash and eating them with butter.

One of the few advantages of my public-school education was the fireplace in our rooms. You could not only make toast but start a self-taught cooking course with, say, an occasional mushroom omelette. In those extraordinary days the butler, whose name was George, would appear in your room and, Zeus-like, rake out the fire with a poker, say, 'Good night, sir,' and shut us down for the night. It was my difficult room-mate Tainton who

189

heated the poker handle until it was just red hot and left it out in the hope that George would seize it and burn off several fingers. George knew exactly what was going on. He used Tainton's best Sunday trousers as a readily available poker holder and burned a large hole in the seat.

Forget Proust's little cake, for me there is no smell more reminiscent of childhood than leaves burning in the autumn, and the place of the fire in the garden, behind the frames and the small greenhouse, has always been a source of great pleasure. Christmas and birthdays are especially welcome because of the vast amounts of wrapping paper to be burned. At other times you have to make do with the 'Business', 'Money' and 'Sports' sections of the heavyweight newspapers. Add to these the usual household rubbish, the mass of uninvited faxes and half of each morning's post and you can get a blaze which sends sparks into the trees and lights up the cabbages.

Of course I have had accidents. For some reason I put a pair of tailor-made trousers, my braces and a short-wave radio into a cardboard box in order to carry them downstairs. At the end of my session with the bonfire, I heard a faint murmuring, a voice, possibly speaking in a foreign language, uttering a vague complaint among the ashes. It was what remained of the short-wave radio. Further investigation revealed the metal parts of the braces. It was a misfortune, but slight and bearable when you compare it to what happened to Prometheus.

Am I, then, a closet pyromaniac? Possibly. There was one unpleasant judge down at the Old Bailey who, when sentencing arsonists, always alleged that setting fire to things caused such offenders to experience an orgasm. I can honestly say that lighting a fire has never had this result so far as I'm concerned. To me a satisfactory fireplace is a sign of peace, happiness and good will, as it was for Dickens when the fires lit up and warmed the Christmases at Dingly Dell. Scrooge's miserliness was proved by the fact that he allowed only one coal on his clerk's fire, and kept the coal box locked in his own room. A roaring fire is the Dickensian sign of generosity.

One of the many advantages of the hotel we stay in in Morocco is the fire in the bedrooms. The logs are dry, dead wood from the orange groves and cork trees. On the whole they burn easily but there is some degree of skill required in building them into a little pyramid which you can light with a single sheet of the *Daily Telegraph* someone has brought over on the plane. With its help, and a few twigs from the lemon tree outside the window, you can start what the French-speaking Moroccans call *'une bonne cheminée'*. Arabs who live in hot countries are always fearful of the cold, wearing sweaters and thick socks under their djellabahs and being expert on keeping log fires going. There are few pleasures to beat going to bed with big logs in the *'cheminée'*, reading a little and then switching off the lamp to go to sleep by flickering firelight.

Back in England there are too many empty grates, although there are still unexpected delights. I did a week of performances at the King's Head, a pub theatre in Islington. To my delight there was a coal fire in my dressing room and there were two young assistant directors, who had majored in theatre studies, to keep it going throughout the evening.

At home I can stop work around six o'clock and find happiness in the sitting room with a packet of firelighters and a box of matches. There's a little anxiety before our logs, heavy with rain and sap, unlike the quick-burning wood of Morocco, start to burn; but then there's a lot to watch. 'Pictures in the fire' they used to call it in my childhood; the pictures are what you choose to make of them, but in any event, it's far more interesting than sitting looking at a radiator.

Don Giovanni, who, like Prometheus, refused to repent and so became a hero in the Romantic age, was dragged down to the fires of hell. At least, I have always thought, they must be warmer than the cold and marmoreal corridors of heaven. Even if neither of these places are found to exist, you can guess what I want done with my body when the time comes to read out my will. At least the grave needn't be cold.

CHAPTER THIRTY-ONE

A WRITER'S LIFE

'You speak of fame, of happiness, of a glorious, interesting life and to me all these nice words, pardon me, are just like Turkish delight which I never eat.'

So says Trigorin, the moderately successful writer in Chekhov's play *The Seagull*, and he goes on to describe the writer's perpetual guilt: 'Day and night I am overwhelmed by one besetting idea: I must write, I must write, I must write. I have scarcely finished one long story when I must somehow start another, then a third, after that a fourth . . .'

It's true that guilt follows a writer wherever he goes, an unnecessarily faithful dog, always yapping at his heels. When bank managers, surgeons, garage mechanics or head waiters go on holiday to Minorca or the Amalfi coast, their work stays at home; the bank, the operating theatre, the garage or the restaurant doesn't accompany them in their hand baggage. Work would be impossible for them, at least for a carefree fortnight. But for a writer work is never impossible; the pen and the notebook, or, I suppose, even the laptop, are always with him, and can be brought out in any hotel lounge, café, train or aeroplane. A writer never has an excuse for not working. If any of you think of taking up the business, you will have to remember that the world is full of blank sheets of paper waiting to be filled, and endless hours in which you should have completed your daily thousand words. 'I write ceaselessly, as though travelling post haste, and I can't do otherwise,' Trigorin goes on. 'Where's the splendour and glory in that, I ask you?'

With this burden of guilt to dispose of, I've found it best to start as early in the day as possible. 'Before I bath, shave or shit or anything like that,' was Graham Greene's programme for his daily routine number of words, which, inexorably, built up to a brilliant lifetime's work. However you time it, and starting at six a.m. seems to get harder as the years go by, it's best to get it done by lunchtime, before the first drink and the heavy-lidded afternoon; although you can pull yourself together at around five o'clock to correct what you wrote in the morning and feel, of course, dissatisfied with it.

All of this might seem a simple, even routine business, if a writer's only job were to write. I assume that you were born with an ear for prose or poetry, a gift for constructing sentences which catch the reader's attention, the ability to describe a scene or advance an argument which will seem truthful and surprising—but this is only half of it. A writer not only has to write, he has to live in order to have something to write about. And of the two occupations, living is much the hardest.

'I see a cloud resembling a piano—' Trigorin again—'and I think I must mention [that] in a story . . . I catch a whiff of heliotrope. Immediately I register it in my mind: a cloying odour, a widow's flower, to be mentioned in a description of a summer evening. I catch you and myself up at every phrase . . . to lock up at once in my literary warehouse, it may come in useful.'

194

You can rely on childhood, a period when every endless afternoon, every corner of the garden, every night fear, moment of loneliness or rare triumph, seems brilliantly lit and clear in your memory. This part of life is every writer's free gift to start with; further experiences have to be worked at and, perhaps, suffered for.

Love, hope, disappointment, exultation and despair will no doubt come, even if uninvited. What you'll need is some knowledge of how other people behave at moments of crisis, how they talk, what avenues of retreat and concealment they discover, or with what unexpected bravery they deal with apparently impossible lives. For this purpose it's a great help to get a job which has nothing to do with writing but one in which as many people as possible are likely to confide in you. You might be a priest or a doctor or a social worker, a hairdresser or an agony aunt, or seek employment with a dating agency.

I count myself extremely lucky to have been called to the bar in my twenties and to have immediately found middle-aged women, businessmen and suburban housewives ready to pour out all the secrets of their lives. I was fortunate enough to meet murderers, con men, contract killers, politicians with unrevealed scandals and, on one horrible occasion, an assistant hangman. All of this was a great privilege and seems to me to have been more useful than moving, with the publication of my first novel—an event which happened shortly before I got called to the bar—into the world of editors, publishers and other writers. The bar exams are pretty dull, as is learning law academically when it's not connected with real human beings in trouble, but it's well worth it for the help you may get as a writer.

You will also have to face the fact that, as a writer, you will be a difficult if not a maddening person to live with. The writer is seldom entirely involved in any situation. Some part of him is standing aside, the detached observer, taking notes to store in his 'literary warehouse'. This is deeply frustrating to those in need of a fully committed love affair, or even a completely meaningful quarrel. On the rare occasions when I am in dispute with my wife, a partner in what is an unusually happy marriage, I am memorizing her dialogue so that I may give extracts from it to Hilda Rumpole in one of her many disagreements with her fictional husband.

The fact that writers are hard to live with is another good reason for getting a job where you'll meet real people and learn something of their secrets. 'You may become a writer,' my father told me when I had confessed my secret ambition. 'You might even become a moderately successful writer. But consider the horrible life your wife would lead if you were such a thing. Writers are at home all day, wearing a dressing gown, brewing tea, stumped for words. Choose a job which will get you out of the house, if only for the sake of your poor wife. Why don't you divorce a few people? It's not very difficult.' So, wisely he guided me towards the bar.

Getting to know people, living an eventful life with useful experiences, such tasks have to be faced, and can be performed by the writer. But there still remains a daunting question for the author of fiction. What on earth is the story?

Story-telling, it has to be admitted, has gone somewhat out of style. A plot has come to be considered a mechanical thing, unimportant compared to fine writing, startling but unconnected situations or a novel attitude to life. And yet a plot, a story, is what induced weary audiences to stay awake listening to Homer, or what still makes us turn the page or watch the unfolding of a play. Unless the reader, or the listener, wants to know what happens next, he or she quickly loses interest. Stories are therefore essential to the writer of fiction; but where they come from is often a mystery, and the great worry is that they may not come at all.

There is general agreement that the characters should create the plot, and that the plot shouldn't be there to create the characters. However, in his *Aspects of the Novel* E. M. Forster contemplated the embarrassing situation when wonderfully created characters refuse to bestir themselves to act out any scene of a story:

In vain it (the plot) points out to those unwieldy creatures (the characters) the advantages of the triple process, complication, crisis, and solution so persuasively expounded by Aristotle. A few of them rise and comply . . . but there is no general response. They want to sit and brood or something. And the plot (which I here visualize as a sort of higher government official) is concerned at their lack of public spirit.

Every writer in search of a story must recognize this agony but I can't agree with Forster's dismissal of the plot as a sort of busybody bureaucrat. Hamlet, Lear and Othello have their characters revealed through the plots and counter-plots that concern them and we wouldn't have learned much about them if nothing had ever happened.

In a time when plots are considered to be of minor importance, it's still recognized that crime stories, tales of detection, can't do without them. For this reason crime writing is regarded, in some quarters, as a sort of inferior occupation, the popular musical compared to the grand opera of the serious novel. And yet much of the greatest literature could, in one sense, be described as crime writing. Aeschylus's *Agamemnon* and *Hamlet* are certainly crime stories. *Othello* is a story about the theft of a handkerchief. *Macbeth* deals with the unpleasant murder of a house guest, and the effect or non-effect of remorse after that crime has been committed. The works of Dickens, which are regarded as mainstream literature, depend greatly on crime. *Bleak House* produced a detective and *Great Expectations* depends on the introduction of a criminal very early in the proceedings. It has been suggested that the slow unfolding of a mystery that is known to the author but isn't exposed to the reader is the mark of a crime story. But again, *Great Expectations* is founded on a mystery that is not revealed until the conclusion of the book. All writers in all fields use mystery, suspense, the withholding of information, the puzzlement and the final enlightenment of the reader.

So when you have learned that a workable plot is

not something confined to detective fiction, you have to look for a story and wonder, and this is certainly the hardest part of a writer's life, where on earth it might be discovered. Shakespeare got most of his plots from his comparatively small library of books and transformed them, but we are not Shakespeare. It has also been said that there are only a few basic stories in the world, *Cinderella* and *Blue Beard* both having given birth to numerous descendants, but even this thought may not comfort you. How can you make a fully developed, credible and yet surprising, revealing and mysterious story enter your head when it is needed? The answer is that you can't. You have to wait for a miracle to happen, and such periods of waiting can be extremely painful.

There are certain things you shouldn't do. Film producers want writers to provide a 'treatment', or a sort of synopsis of events, before they settle down to produce a script. Such treatments are a waste of time, impossible to write and a pain to read. No story can exist until the characters come to life, start to think, feel, talk and play their part in its creation, and don't sit silently sulking in the way Forster described.

I don't think you need to have a whole story in your head before you start writing. You should know, I believe, what you want to say about the human condition. You should have a theme. You should know the place and the characters and probably have an idea of the final destination. And then start to write, because writing pulls down writing in a way that plans and treatments and synopses can never manage. So you can begin anywhere, probably by writing a speech for one or more of the characters, bringing them to life and setting them to work on the plot. If you get them right, they may start to tell a story for you. With any luck you may have the surprising pleasure of writing something which seemed unimportant at the time but turns out to be the very point, the axle on which the story turns. If you get a character right, he or she may tell you what their problem is of their own accord.

If you are very lucky, you may reach that miraculous moment when a character does something that is totally unexpected. You will look at your piece of paper in amazement and think, I never dreamt that you, of all people, would do a thing like that. And then you know that you are on to a thoroughly good thing.

Given the right characters in a situation full of possibilities, the story may begin to tell itself. Of course, it will be up to you to write it, in the voice you will have found which is now, I hope, yours and no one else's. If you're looking for advice on how you should feel when writing, you need look no further than to Muriel Spark, who, in her novel *It's a Far Cry from Kensington*, gave her most precious secrets away.

You are writing a letter to a friend . . . Write privately, not publicly, without fear or timidity . . . So that your true friend will read it over and over and want more enchanting letters from you. Before starting the letter rehearse in your mind what you are going to tell . . . But don't do too much, the story will develop as you go along, especially if you write to a special friend, man or woman, to make them smile or laugh or cry . . . Remember not to think of the reading public, it will put you off.

Writing like this may give you great pleasure. Even Trigorin in *The Seagull* found it 'pleasant'. But then he had to admit that the worse moment comes when the public reads it: 'Yes, charming and clever, but a long way off Tolstoy.' Or: 'It's a fine thing but Turgenev's *Fathers and Children* did it better.' 'And so,' he says, 'until I drop into my grave it will always be "charming and clever", "charming and clever", nothing more—and after I am dead, acquaintances passing my tomb will say . . . ' "A fine writer, but he didn't write as well as Turgenev".'

CHAPTER THIRTY-TWO

THE ATTESTATION CLAUSE

Yeats, having made his will on the top of his tower, resolved to compel his soul to study 'in a learned school', until

> Testy delirium
> Or dull decrepitude,
> Or what worse evil come—
> The death of friends, or death
> Of every brilliant eye
> That made a catch in the breath—
> Seem but the clouds of the sky
> When the horizon fades:
> Or a bird's sleepy cry
> Among the deepening shades.

It may not be necessary to go through the stage of testy delirium, or even dull decrepitude. Death comes as unexpectedly to the young as it does to the old and our continued existence, Montaigne pointed out, is something of a favour. Both Jesus Christ and Alexander the Great died at the age of thirty-three. Montaigne then went on to list the many surprising or comical ways in which death can suddenly overtake you. One of the ancestors of the Duke of Brittany, it seems, was killed 'by a bump from a pig'. Another choked to death on a pip from a grape. An emperor died from a scratch when combing his hair. Aeschylus was warned against a falling house and he was always on the alert, but in vain: he was killed by the shell of a tortoise which slipped from the talons of an eagle in flight.

The Lord of Montaigne then lists those who died 'between a woman's thighs'. Among them were a captain of the Roman Guard, the son of Guy di Gonzaga, the Duke of Mantua, a Platonic philosopher and Pope Clement V. Such a death, although no doubt delightful for the man concerned, most have been deeply embarrassing for the woman whose thighs were on offer.

We were in the South of France one year when there was a serious outbreak of forest fires. Small aeroplanes were used to scoop up water from the sea, fly over the burning trees and douse the flames. An innocent and harmless man was happily snorkelling, observing the clouds of bright little fish, when he was scooped up by an aeroplane, carried off and dropped on to a blazing inferno. After writing her death scene, Hardy said that the 'President of the Immortals had ended his sport with Tess'. At least the sport in that case was of a serious, even tragic nature. In the other cases outlined above, the President of the Immortals would seem to be an unprincipled practical joker with a warped sense of humour.

Conscious as he was of falling tortoiseshells and fatal hair combs, and would be now of scooping aeroplanes, Montaigne said he was always prepared for the sudden arrival of death, which might visit him at any hour: 'Being a man who broods over his thoughts and stores them up inside him, I am always just about as ready as I can be when death does suddenly appear.' And he had this advice to give: 'If you have profited from life, and you have had your fill, go away satisfied.' And he ended his message on the subject: 'We must rip the masks off things as well as off people. Once we have done that we shall find underneath only the same death which a valet and a chambermaid got through without being afraid. Blessed the death which gives no time for preparing gatherings of mourners.'

*　　　*　　　*

I seem to have completed my will. I can sign it off and there will be the usual attestation clause, in which the witnesses certify that they have seen me sign in their presence and in the presence of each other.

I have relied on many witnesses, far more than the usual two, to endorse my will. I have placed particular reliance on Shakespeare, Byron, Montaigne, Oscar Wilde, Yeats, Da Ponte and a number of barristers, judges, assorted criminals and companionable women. None of the advice I've offered needs to be taken, none of the likes and dislikes I've displayed have to be shared. There is only one paragraph I'd underline, one truth I hold to be self-evident.

The meaningful and rewarding moments aren't waiting for us beyond the grave, or to be found on distant battlefields where history's made. They can happen quite unexpectedly, in a garden perhaps, or walking through a beech wood in the middle of the afternoon. If we are to have a religion, it should be one that recognizes the true importance of a single moment in time, the instant when you are fully and completely alive.

The rain had fallen steadily out of a grey,

gunmetal sky. On 4 January, the day of Emily's wedding, the sun appeared and shone brightly over the cold countryside. We rode to the village church in a karma car, a somewhat ornate vehicle lined with mirrors, smelling of flowers and incense, a small fleet of which had arrived from Notting Hill Gate. Turville Church has long been part of our lives. My mother and father are buried in the churchyard, which fades into the surrounding fields, as is Lucy, a close childhood friend of Emily's who was tragically killed by a car when she was no more than nine years old. The church was filled to bursting and I managed to walk my daughter reasonably quickly up the aisle as Jon Lord played the music he had written for her on the organ. At the end of the service, Sam Brown, daughter of Joe Brown of The Bruvvers, and her friends sang 'I'm putting all my eggs in one basket'. Emily emerged, married, into the sunlight and, in a shower of confetti, arranged her bouquet on Lucy's grave.

Then we had a party. A tent enveloped the terrace of the house. There was dinner and dancing to a Mexican punk band, friends of Alessandro's who had travelled from Los Angeles to the Chilterns. A small boy, commercially minded, collected autographs from Emily's film-star friends and sold them round the room, insisting on 'hard cash'.

After the fireworks I sat looking at the circular brick platform at the end of the terrace where the Mexican punks were playing and singing. It was where, as an only child, I had done my one-boy shows, having to be both Fred and Ginger or, in my savagely cut version of *Hamlet*, duelling with myself, quarrelling with myself as my own mother, or drinking my own poisoned chalice. It was where Emily had acted plays with her friends from school and here, sometime in the future, another person whose sex was, as yet, unascertained, might be showing off, performing or inventing a story on the same small, circular, open-air stage.

So, at that moment, and what a moment, I could look round at my children and grandchildren, whose ages range from fifty-three to twelve. I could still trace my father's voice in their jokes, their laughter and their way with language. Their words will echo out into the future, with their children and their children's children. It's my father's claim to immortality—and mine also.

It was a day worth passing on in any last will and testament.